AUST'S MODERN TREATY LAW AND PRACTICE

FOURTH EDITION

This new edition of a textbook first published in 2000 provides a comprehensive account of the law of treaties from the viewpoint of two experienced practitioners. It draws on the combined experience of Anthony Aust, the original author, and Jeremy Hill, until recently Legal Counsellor in the Foreign, Commonwealth and Development Office, London. The book provides a wealth of examples of the problems experienced with treaties on a daily basis. The authors explore numerous precedents from treaties and other related documents, such as non-legally binding instruments. Using clear and accessible language, the authors cover the full extent of treaty law, with both practitioners and students in mind. *Aust's Modern Treaty Law and Practice* is essential reading for officials in governments and international organisations, lawyers practising in international law, and teachers and students of law, political science, international relations and diplomacy who have an interest in treaties.

JEREMY HILL joined the Foreign Office (now FCDO) in 1982. His posts have included Assistant Legal Adviser and subsequently Legal Counsellor advising on treaties; Legal Adviser in the British Embassy, Bonn, during German Unification; Legal Counsellor in the Attorney General's Office; Legal Adviser to the UK Representation to the EU in Brussels; Ambassador to Lithuania; and Ambassador to Bulgaria. From 2017 to 2021 he was head of the FCDO legal team dealing with treaties in the context of the UK's exit from the EU. In 2019 he was awarded a C.M.G. for services to British foreign policy.

'This fourth edition of *Aust's Modern Treaty Law and Practice* is thoroughly updated and revised in light of developments over the last ten years, including Brexit. It has much that is new and illuminating, including on "non-binding instruments", reservations, provisional application and *jus cogens*. The new author, Jeremy Hill, has retained the "Aust-spirit"; the book remains as accessible as ever.'

Sir Michael Wood, KCMG, KC

'Jeremy Hill's deep expertise and safe hands guide us through a much needed refresh to an essential desk guide for anyone involved or interested in the treaty drafting and making process. At a time of growing nationalism, this book is a timely reminder of how interconnected and interdependent our world is, and the role of treaties to help address global challenges that transcend boundaries.'

Rashmin Sagoo, Director of the International Law Programme, Chatham House

AUST'S MODERN TREATY LAW AND PRACTICE

FOURTH EDITION

JEREMY HILL

Formerly Legal Counsellor, Foreign, Commonwealth and Development Office, London

CAMBRIDGE
UNIVERSITY PRESS

CAMBRIDGE
UNIVERSITY PRESS

Shaftesbury Road, Cambridge CB2 8EA, United Kingdom

One Liberty Plaza, 20th Floor, New York, NY 10006, USA

477 Williamstown Road, Port Melbourne, VIC 3207, Australia

314–321, 3rd Floor, Plot 3, Splendor Forum, Jasola District Centre, New Delhi – 110025, India

103 Penang Road, #05-06/07, Visioncrest Commercial, Singapore 238467

Cambridge University Press is part of Cambridge University Press & Assessment, a department of the University of Cambridge.

We share the University's mission to contribute to society through the pursuit of education, learning and research at the highest international levels of excellence.

www.cambridge.org
Information on this title: www.cambridge.org/highereducation/isbn/9781009186940
DOI: 10.1017/9781009186933

First published 2000
Second edition 2007
Third edition 2013
4th printing 2016
Fourth edition 2023

A catalogue record for this publication is available from the British Library

A Cataloging-in-Publication data record for this book is available from the Library of Congress

ISBN 978-1-009-18694-0 Hardback
ISBN 978-1-009-18692-6 Paperback

For colleagues past and present, in the Foreign, Commonwealth and Development Office, and in other government departments

CONTENTS

Appendices

FOREWORD TO THE FIRST EDITION

The law of treaties is one of the branches of international law whose roots go back furthest in time. With the emergence of political communities came the need for them to deal with each other, to settle questions in dispute without having to go to war, to arrange the consequences of success or failure after a war had been fought, to strike alliances, organise matters of trade, settle territorial limits to their power, and so on. For such matters they needed from early times some accepted rules covering two matters: the sending of envoys and the making of agreements. Both have remained central to the conduct of what we now call international relations.

Over centuries, the rules and practices governing those agreements have evolved into the modern law of treaties. The evolutionary process is a continuing one. A book on the law of treaties written at the end of the nineteenth century is recognisably about the same subject as its equivalent written today. Yet, while the general body of the law remains broadly stable, times change and bring with them changes in the law. International organisations have emerged as significant actors in the treaty-making process; multilateral treaties are nowadays concluded more frequently, and have more parties, than used to be the case – a reflection of the enormous increase in the number of states during the course of the present century – and there have been great technological changes, especially in communications, which have noticeably affected the process by which treaties are negotiated and concluded.

The modern law is now authoritatively set out in the Vienna Convention on the Law of Treaties 1969, and in its parallel Convention of 1986 on treaties made by international organisations. They are, however, not only far from a complete code on the subject, they are also not free from continuing controversy even in respect of matters which they do deal with (such as the vexed topic of reservations, which the International Law Commission is presently studying once again, having previously reported on the matter in 1951); moreover, as is so often the way, new issues have arisen which were not envisaged when the principal Vienna Convention of 1969 was concluded. A new book on the law of treaties, surveying the subject some thirty years after the Vienna Convention was concluded, is timely.

What, however, makes the present volume particularly welcome is its manifest concern with the practical aspects of the law of treaties. Undoubtedly the law of treaties exercises a great intellectual fascination. Many issues directly or indirectly raise large questions of legal theory. Furthermore, some treaties are of enormous historical significance, like the Peace of Westphalia of 1648 and the Treaty of Rome of 1957. But it must always be recalled that treaties are essentially instruments for regulating by agreement the myriad day-to-day affairs of states. International travel and broadcasting, international posts and telecommunications, international trade – these and many other matters, which are usually taken for granted, are dependent upon a network of often very detailed treaties, both bilateral and multilateral.

For this array of treaties – essential for the conduct of international relations, but seldom eye-catching – the negotiating process is well established. So too are most of the relevant legal rules. But however well-developed international rules and processes may be, they have a practical dimension to which much less attention is usually paid. This is doubly unfortunate. The true significance of many rules is illuminated by being seen in the perspective of their application in practice, while the steps which need to be taken in applying the rules can be as important as the rules themselves, going far to explain why many things are as they are.

It is the great virtue of this volume that in looking at the law *and* its practical context, it grounds the treatment of the law of treaties firmly in the real world of international relations, foreign ministries and diplomacy. That is the world about which Anthony Aust is exceptionally well qualified to write. As one of the former senior legal advisers in the Foreign and Commonwealth Office,[1] who has served not only in London but also in diplomatic posts abroad (including as Legal Adviser to the United Kingdom Mission to the United Nations in New York from 1988 to 1991), he brings to this book a wealth of experience on all aspects of treaty law and practice. That experience, and the insights which flow from it, pervade every chapter.

Everyone concerned with treaties and the law relating to them, whether on a day-to-day basis, occasional practitioners in the field or as outside observers of the treaty process, will benefit greatly from Anthony Aust's up-to-date and practical treatment of the subject. I warmly commend this volume, which is a welcome addition to the literature in this field.

Sir Arthur Watts KCMG QC

[1] He retired as Deputy Legal Adviser in 2002.

PREFACE TO THE FOURTH EDITION

The last six years has seen an unprecedented level of treaty-making by the United Kingdom in the context of its withdrawal from the European Union. This has brought with it all sorts of challenging questions about treaty law and practice. The first port of call, not only for the legal teams in the Foreign, Commonwealth and Development Office (FCDO) but across the British government, has always been the Third Edition of 'Aust', as we refer to it. 'Aust' has always had something interesting and relevant to say.

Sadly, Anthony (Tony) Aust himself passed away during this period, in December 2017. All of us in the FCDO treaty team felt, however, that the book should be continued and updated. Cambridge University Press were at the same time looking to produce a new edition, and the completion of the UK's exit from the EU created for me an opportunity to do this.

I had the privilege to work closely with Tony, particularly for the first five years of my Foreign Office career, from 1982 onwards, when I first advised on treaty law. Our rooms were opposite each other. Tony was always warm, helpful and practical and it is no surprise that these qualities come through in the text of this book. I have tried to preserve this warmth and accessibility, though I have inevitably had to amend the text, sometimes significantly, to bring it up to date. By popular demand, I have kept his quotations at the start of the various chapters.

Since we all know the book simply as 'Aust', I thought it best to reflect this in the title, in the hope that the book will continue to be known as such, and Tony's original authorship appropriately recognised.

I am aware that the book has universal appeal and lies on practitioners', teachers' and students' desks all over the world. Although many examples are drawn from UK practice, I have sought to make the analysis universally applicable.

I am grateful to a large number of former colleagues, scholars and practitioners (some in other Foreign Ministries) who have helped me either by looking over a particular section or chapter, or by giving more general help and advice. I would like to thank particularly Sir Michael Wood, as well as Angus Ackroyd, Catherine Adams, Wojciech Baginski, Paul Bentall, Sir Franklin Berman, Paul Berman, Rieks Boekholt, Michael Boon, Michael Boulton, Daniel Breger, William Butler, Debbie Burgin, Gavin Burtenshaw, David Chambers, Georgina Clarke, Philip Day, Kulwant Dulai, Stephen Durrant, Victoria Fowler, Anissa Gardam, Richard Gardiner, Tal Geron, Debra

Gerstein, David Goddard, Anna Joanna Gralak, Kate Hamilton, Dale Harrison, Arancha Hinojal, Nita Humphreys, Fraser Janeczko, Alice Lacourt, Susan Laffey, Samuel Linehan, Vyaj Lovejoy, Caroline Mack, Sarah Macrory, Michael Mattler, Stephan Michel, David Nanopoulos, Babu Rahman, Laura Rees-Evans, Gerry Regan, Greg Reisman, Justine Rodier, Paul Scullion, Sarah Smith, Adam Slawson, Lucinda Stallard, Alice Vickers, Chanaka Wickremasinghe and Jonathan Worboys. I worry that even this list is incomplete.

Needless to say, all views expressed are my own and I bear responsibility for all errors. Nothing in it should be taken as an expression of official government policy. The writing of this book has not been subsidised by any public or private source.

I would also like to thank Sir Iain Macleod, until recently the FCDO Legal Adviser, and Sally Langrish, his successor, for giving me the opportunity to work again on treaty law in recent years, and the many other FCDO and government colleagues who have worked with me on treaties during my career. I owe them all an enormous debt, and this edition of the book is dedicated to them.

I would finally like to thank Cambridge University Press, particularly Rachel Norridge and Lorraine Slipper, for all their hard work in bringing this to publication.

I express my appreciation to the British Ministry of Defence for permission to reproduce Appendix C and the FCDO for permission to reproduce Appendices I, J, K, L, M, N and O.

ARTICLES OF THE CONVENTION CITED IN THE TEXT

TABLE OF TREATIES

The date given in respect of a treaty is the date of signature, or the date of adoption, or the date on which the treaty was open for signature, as the case may be, except where otherwise stated.

AJIL	*American Journal of International Law*
ATS	*Australian Treaty Series*
CoE	Council of Europe
CTS	*Consolidated Treaty Series*
EHRR	European Human Rights Reports
ETS	*European Treaty Series*
Hertslet	*Hertslet's Commercial Treaties*
ILM	*International Legal Materials*
ILR	*International Law Reports*
LNTS	*League of Nations Treaty Series*
OJ	*Official Journal of the European Community/Union*
TIAS	*Treaties and Other International Acts Series* (United States)
UKTS	*United Kingdom Treaty Series*
UNTS	*United Nations Treaty Series*

Multilateral Treaties

Bilateral and Trilateral Treaties

TABLE OF NON-LEGALLY BINDING INSTRUMENTS

Although the Tables make a division into treaties and non-legally binding instruments, this is done purely to help locate the reference to the appropriate instrument in the text and does not purport to take a definitive view on an instrument's status, which may be contested.

The date given is the date of signature or adoption, except where otherwise stated.

Multilateral Non-Binding Instruments

Bilateral Non-Binding Instruments

TABLE OF CASES

AC	Appeal Court Reports (Court of Appeal (EW) and HL (UK))
AD	Annual Digest of Public International Law Cases (now incorporated into the International Law Reports)
AER	All England Law Reports
CLR	Law Reports of the Commonwealth
ECHR	European Court of Human Rights
ECR	European Court Reports
EHRR	European Human Rights Reports
EW	England and Wales
EWCA (Civ.)	Court of Appeal (Civil) (EW)
EWHC (Admin)	High Court (Administrative) (EW)
HCA	High Court of Australia
ICJ	International Court of Justice
ICTY	International Criminal Tribunal for the former Yugoslavia
ILM	International Legal Materials
ILR	International Law Reports
PCIJ	Permanent Court of International Justice
QB	Queen's Bench Reports (EW)
RIAA	Reports of International Arbitral Awards
SCLR	Scottish Civil Law Reports
UKHL	House of Lords (i.e., as UK 'Supreme Court')
UKSC	Supreme Court of the United Kingdom
WLR	Weekly Law Reports (EW)

GLOSSARY OF LEGAL TERMS

acceptance, approval	Same effect as ratification.
accession	Same effect as ratification, but not preceded by signature.
adherence	General term for consent to be bound.
consent to be bound	To ratify, accept, approve or accede to a treaty.
contracting state	A state which has consented to be bound by a treaty, *whether or not the treaty has entered into force* (Article 2(1)(f)).
customary international law	Rules derived from general practice among states and accompanied by *opinio juris* (see pp. 13–15).
domestic law	Internal law of a state (sometimes called municipal or national law).
erga omnes	Valid for all, even without their consent (see pp. 268–269).
estoppel	The principle that a state cannot act inconsistently if it has acquiesced in a particular situation or taken a particular position with respect to it (see pp. 65–66).
exchange of notes	Two or more instruments which constitute either a treaty or a non-legally binding instrument (see p. 36).
ex gratia	As a matter of discretion.
final act	Formal document recording the results of a diplomatic conference, especially one to adopt a multilateral treaty (see p. 105).
full powers	Formal document authorising a person to sign a treaty or do other acts with respect to a treaty (Article 2(1)(c)) (see pp. 92–93).
international law	The body of rules legally binding on states and other subjects of international law in their relations with each other.
international legal personality	Being a person or legal entity to which international law attributes rights and obligations (mostly states and international organisations).
jurisdiction	The right in international law for a state to exercise authority over its nationals and persons and things in its territory, and sometimes abroad (extraterritorial jurisdiction).
jus cogens	Peremptory rule of international law (see p. 328).
lex ferenda	A rule one would like to be international law.
lex lata	An existing rule of international law.

Memorandum of Understanding	Name given to certain non-legally binding instruments and (occasionally) treaties (see pp. 34–35).
MFN	most-favoured nation (the principle of not discriminating between one's trading partners).
MOU	Memorandum of Understanding: usually a form of non-legally binding instrument (see pp. 34–35).
negotiating state	A state which took part in the drawing up and adoption of the text of a treaty (Article 2(1)(e)).
NBI	Non-binding instrument.
non-binding instrument	An instrument which is not binding under international law, meaning the same, therefore, as non-legally binding instrument (see Chapter 3).
non-legally binding instrument	An instrument which is not binding under international law.
opinio juris	General belief by states that a non-treaty rule is legally binding on them (see pp. 13–15).
party	A state which has consented to be bound by a treaty *and* for which the treaty is in force (Article 2(1)(g)).
primary legislation	Law made by a legislature (cf. secondary legislation).
private international law	The domestic law dealing with cases with a foreign element (also known as conflict of laws).
ratification	Following signature, the expression of a state's consent to be bound by a treaty.
reservation	A unilateral statement, however phrased or named, made by a state when consenting to be bound by a treaty by which it purports to exclude or to modify the legal effect of certain provisions of the treaty in their application to that state (Article 2(1)(d)) (see Chapter 8).
secondary legislation	Legislation by the executive under a power given by primary legislation.
signatory	Not a precise term. Should be used only to describe a state which has signed, but not yet ratified, a treaty; but best avoided (see p. 125 *et seq.*).
sovereignty	The right of a state to act independently of other states, subject only to such restrictions as international law imposes.
state	A defined territory with a permanent population and a government.
subject of international law	Possessor of rights and obligations in international law, mainly states and international organisations.
subordinate or subsidiary legislation	Secondary legislation.
third state	A state which is not a party to a treaty (Article 2(1)(h)) (see Chapter 14).
travaux préparatoires (or *travaux*)	Preparatory work of a treaty (see pp. 255–258).
treaty	See Chapter 2.
ultra vires	Without legal authority.

ABBREVIATIONS

the Convention / the 1969 Convention / VCLT	Vienna Convention on the Law of Treaties 1969
1978 Convention	Vienna Convention on Succession of States in respect of Treaties 1978
1986 Convention	Vienna Convention on the Law of Treaties between States and International Organizations or between International Organizations 1986
AFDI	*Annuaire français de droit international*
ARIO	Responsibility of International Organisations, Report of the ILC on the Work of its 63rd session, 2011
Article	An article of the Vienna Convention on the Law of Treaties 1969 (unless otherwise indicated)
ASIL	American Society of International Law
ATCM	Antarctic Treaty Consultative Meeting
Aust Handbook	A. Aust, *Handbook of International Law* (2nd ed., Cambridge University Press, Cambridge 2010)
BIICL	British Institute of International and Comparative Law
BIT	Bilateral investment treaty
BFSP	British and Foreign State Papers
Blix and Emerson	H. Blix and J. Emerson (eds.), *The Treaty Maker's Handbook* (Oceana Publications, Dobbs Ferry, NY 1973)
BYIL	*British Yearbook of International Law*
CAA	Civil Aviation Authority
Can YBIL	*Canadian Yearbook of International Law*
CAHDI	Council of Europe Committee of Legal Advisers on Public International Law
CCAMLR	Convention on the Conservation of Antarctic Marine Living Resources 1980
CEDAW	Convention on the Elimination of All Forms of Discrimination against Women 1979
CERD	Convention on the Elimination of All Forms of Racial Discrimination 1965
CFR	US Code of Federal Regulations
CITES	Convention on International Trade in Endangered Species of Wild Flora and Fauna 1973
CJEU	Court of Justice of the European Union

Cmd.	Command Papers (UK) (official publication)
CoE	Council of Europe
Corten and Klein	O. Corten and P. Klein (eds.), *The Vienna Conventions on the Law of Treaties: A Commentary* (Oxford University Press, Oxford 2011)
CPG	Central People's Government (China)
CPTPP	Comprehensive and Progressive Agreement for Trans-Pacific Partnership 2018
CRC	Convention on the Rights of the Child 1990
CSCE	Conference on Security and Co-operation in Europe
Crawford	J. Crawford, *The Creation of States in International Law* (2nd ed., Cambridge University Press, Cambridge 2006)
Crawford/Brownlie	J. Crawford (ed.), *Brownlie's Principles of Public International Law* (9th ed., Oxford University Press, Oxford 2019)
CRPD	Convention on the Rights of Persons with Disabilities 2008
CSCE	Conference on Security and Co-operation in Europe
CTBT	Comprehensive Nuclear-Test-Ban Treaty 1996
CWC	Chemical Weapons Convention 1993
Dörr and Schmalenbach	O. Dörr and K. Schmalenbach, *Vienna Convention on the Law of Treaties: A Commentary* (2nd ed., Springer Verlag, Berlin, Heidelberg 2018)
DPRK	Democratic People's Republic of Korea (North Korea)
DTAs	Double Taxation Agreements
EC	European Communities
ECHR	European Convention on Human Rights
ECtHR	European Court of Human Rights
ECJ	European Court of Justice
EEAS	European External Action Service
EJIL	*European Journal of International Law*
EMEP	Convention on Long-Range Transboundary Air Pollution 1979
ENMOD Convention	Convention on the Prohibition of Military or Any Other Hostile Use of Environmental Modification Techniques 1976
ESA	European Space Agency
EU	European Union
Euratom	European Atomic Energy Community
Evans	M.D. Evans (ed.), *International Law* (5th ed., Oxford University Press, Oxford 2018)
FAO	Food and Agriculture Organization
FCDO	Foreign, Commonwealth and Development Office, London
FCO	Foreign and Commonwealth Office, London (as it was called until September 2020)
Finnish YBIL	*Finnish Yearbook of International Law*
FRY	Federal Republic of Yugoslavia (1992–2003)
Gardiner	R. Gardiner, *Treaty Interpretation* (2nd ed., Oxford University Press, Oxford 2015)
GATT	General Agreement on Tariffs and Trade 1947

Ger YBIL	*German Yearbook of International Law*
Hague Recueil	*Recueil des cours de l'Académie de droit international*
Hansard	Record of UK parliamentary debates (House of Lords or House of Commons)
HKSAR	Hong Kong Special Administrative Region
Hollis, Oxford Guide	D.B. Hollis (ed.), *The Oxford Guide to Treaties* (2nd ed., Oxford University Press, Oxford 2020)
IAEA	International Atomic Energy Authority
IAJC	Inter-American Juridical Committee
ICAO	International Civil Aviation Organization
ICC	International Criminal Court
ICCPR	International Covenant on Civil and Political Rights 1966
ICESCR	International Covenant on Economic, Social and Cultural Rights 1966
ICJ	International Court of Justice
ICLQ	*International and Comparative Law Quarterly*
ICRC	International Committee of the Red Cross
ICSID	International Centre for Settlement of Investment Disputes
IFC	International Finance Corporation
IFIs	international financial institutions
ILA	International Law Association
ILC	International Law Commission
ILC Commentary	Commentary of the ILC on its final draft articles on the Law of Treaties (YBILC (1966) vol. II, 173–274)
ILC Conclusions	Draft Conclusions on subsequent agreements and subsequent practice in relation to the interpretation of treaties, Report of the ILC on the Work of its 68th session, 2016, UNGA 71st Session, Supplement No. 10, A71/10. 13
ILC Guide to Practice	Guide to Practice on Reservations to Treaties, Report of the ILC on the Work of its 63rd session, 2011, UNGA 66th Session, Supplement No. 10, Addendum 1, Doc. A/66/10/Add. 1. 8
ILIB	International Law in Brief
ILM	International Legal Materials (published by the ASIL)
ILO	International Labour Organization
IMF	International Monetary Fund
IMO	International Maritime Organization
IPPA	Investment Promotion and Protection Agreement
ITLOS	International Tribunal for the Law of the Sea
ITU	International Telecommunication Union
JCPOA	Joint Comprehensive Plan of Action 2015
JLG	Joint Liaison Group
Kolb	R. Kolb, *The Law of Treaties: An Introduction* (Edward Elgar, Cheltenham UK, Northampton MA USA 2016)
LGDJ	Librairie générale de droit et de jurisprudence (main French publishing house in law)

McNair	A.D. McNair, *The Law of Treaties* (2nd ed., Clarendon Press, Oxford 1961)
MFN	most-favoured nation
MOU	Memorandum of Understanding
MPEPIL	*The Max Planck Encyclopedia of Public International Law* (Oxford University Press online), at https://opil.ouplaw.com/home/mpil
NATO	North Atlantic Treaty Organization
NBI	Non-binding instrument
NILR	*Netherlands International Law Review*
NPT	Nuclear Non-Proliferation Treaty 1968
OAS	Organization of American States
OAS Guidelines	Guidelines of the Inter-American Juridical Committee of the Organization of American States on Binding and Non-Binding Agreements (2020)
O'Connell	D.P. O'Connell, *International Law* (2nd ed., Stevens, London 1970)
OECD	Organisation for Economic Co-operation and Development
OPCW	Organisation for the Prohibition of Chemical Weapons
Oppenheim	*Oppenheim's International Law*, R. Jennings and A. Watts (eds.) (9th ed., Longmans, London 1992)
OSCE	Organization for Security and Co-operation in Europe
PCA	Permanent Court of Arbitration
PCIJ	Permanent Court of International Justice
PLO	Palestine Liberation Organization
POWs	prisoners of war
PTBT	Partial Test Ban Treaty 1963
RCADI	*Recueil des Cours de l'Academie de Droit International de la Haye*
Reuter	P. Reuter, *Introduction to the Law of Treaties* (2nd English ed., Kegan Paul, London 1995)
RGDIP	*Revue générale de droit international public*
Rome Statute	Statute of the International Criminal Court
SAR	Special Administrative Region
Shaw	M.N. Shaw, *International Law* (9th ed., Cambridge University Press, Cambridge 2021)
SFRY	Socialist Federal Republic of Yugoslavia
SI	Statutory Instrument (UK secondary legislation)
Sinclair	I. Sinclair, *The Vienna Convention on the Law of Treaties* (2nd ed., Manchester University Press, Manchester, UK and Dover, NH, USA 1984)
SOFA	Status of Forces Agreement
TCA	EU–UK Trade and Cooperation Agreement 2020
TEU	Treaty on European Union 1992
TFEU	Treaty on the Functioning of the European Union 2008
TIEAs	Tax Information Exchange Agreements
UNCED	United Nations Conference on Environment and Development
UNCITRAL	UN Commission on International Trade Law

UNCLOS	United Nations Convention on the Law of the Sea 1982
UN Depositary Practice	Summary of Practice of the Secretary-General of the United Nations as Depositary of Multilateral Treaties
UN Doc.	United Nations official document
UNEP	United Nations Environment Programme
UNESCO	United Nations Educational, Scientific and Cultural Organization
UNGA	United Nations General Assembly
UNHCR	UN High Commissioner for Refugees
UNICAT	UN Convention against Torture 1984
UNIDROIT	Institute for the Unification of Private Law
UNJurYbk	*United Nations Juridical Yearbook*
UN Multilateral Treaties	Multilateral Treaties Deposited with the Secretary-General of the United Nations
UNSC	United Nations Security Council
UN Treaty Handbook	*United Nations Treaty Handbook*, Revised Edition of 2012
UST	*United States Treaties and Other International Agreements*
VCCR	Vienna Convention on Consular Relations 1963
VCDR	Vienna Convention on Diplomatic Relations 1961
VCLT	Vienna Convention on the Law of Treaties 1969
Villiger	M.E. Villiger, *Commentary on the 1969 Vienna Convention on the Law of Treaties* (Martinus Nijhoff Publishers, Leiden, Boston, MA 2009)
WA	EU–UK Withdrawal Agreement 2020
Whiteman	M. Whiteman, *Digest of International Law* (Government Printing Office, Washington, DC 1963–73) 15 vols.
WHO	World Health Organization
WIPO	World Intellectual Property Organization
WMO	World Meteorological Organization
WTO	World Trade Organization
YBIL	*Yearbook of International Law*
YBILC	*Yearbook of the International Law Commission*

Introduction

Experience is the name everyone gives to their mistakes.[1]

Like contracts in ordinary life, treaties have always been an indispensable tool of diplomacy. They date from even before the classical period of Greece, the Egyptian and Hittite kings having concluded a treaty in about 1259 BCE.[2] After 1815, so many treaties were adopted that Canute-like words of caution were voiced. By 1914, there were already perhaps over 8,000 treaties in force. With the establishment of the League of Nations, the rate of treaty making increased dramatically.[3] Up to July 1944, the League registered another 4,822 treaties, to which should be added those concluded between non-members of the League. Since 1945, over 158,000 treaties have been registered with the United Nations, though this is perhaps only about 70 per cent of all treaties that have entered into force.

So, anyone whose work or interest involves international law needs to know about the law of treaties. And the purpose of this book is to deal with the subject in a comprehensive, up-to-date and practical way. Unlike other aspects of international law, the making and operation of treaties happens every day, and so understanding treaty practice enhances knowledge of the law of treaties.

The law of treaties is generally not about the substance of treaties (the rights and obligations they create), but about the law governing how treaties are made and operated. In the same way, in domestic law the law of contract deals with the nuts

[1] Oscar Wilde, *Lady Windermere's Fan*, Act I.

[2] For the treaty of Ramses II of Egypt and Ḫattušili III of Ḫatti, see G. Beckman, *Hittite Diplomatic Texts* (Scholars, Atlanta 1999) and G. Beckman, 'Hittite Treaties and the Development of the Cuneiform Treaty Tradition', in M. Witte and others (eds.), *Die deuteronomistischen Geschichtswerke: Redaktions- und religionsgeschichtliche Perspektiven zur 'Deuteronomismus'-Diskussion in Tora und Vorderen Propheten* (Walter de Gruyter, Berlin, New York 2006), 279–301. For treaties of the ancient Near East, see G. Sulyok, 'Treaties, Origin', *MPEPIL* (2014).

[3] For a short history of treaties since c.250 BCE, including an account of their growth in the nineteenth century, see C. Tietje, 'The Changing Legal Structure of International Treaties as an Aspect of an Emerging Global Governance Architecture', Ger YBIL 42 (1999) 26–55, 30–35; for a survey of treaties in the formation of international law and the historic functions of treaties, see R. Lesaffer, 'Treaties within the History of International Law', in M. J. Bowman and D. Kritsiotis (eds.), *Conceptual and Contextual Perspectives on the Modern Law of Treaties* (Cambridge University Press, Cambridge 2018), 43–75; and for an assessment of treaty law in the 1930s, see 'Introductory Comment' in AJIL Supp. (1935) 666–671.

and bolts of contracts, not their substance. The substance is a matter for those who negotiate and conclude the treaty, and is often known as 'treaty law'.

I am very fortunate to have been able to practise international law in a leading foreign ministry. My perspective (and that of Anthony Aust before me) is therefore that of a practitioner; and this book is very much a distillation of our many years' experience. My aim, like the previous author's, is to inform the reader about all aspects of the law and practice by collecting the information in one convenient place. Although I have tried to avoid using too many British precedents, many examples are necessarily drawn from our personal knowledge or that of our colleagues.

Whenever possible, I have used primary sources. I have also tried to present the material in a way that will help to answer questions such as: what *is* a non-binding instrument? Where can I find the text of a treaty? Can part of a state make a treaty? When are full powers needed? What is consensus? What does Article 18 really mean? How does 'dualism' work? Can a state withdraw an instrument of ratification? What does a depositary do? How do I set about drafting a treaty?

But this is not just a book by a legal practitioner for legal practitioners. Although, hopefully, legal advisers in foreign ministries and international organisations will find it helpful, it has been written with a particular eye to the needs of officials generally. All of them have to deal with treaties. Some will have had legal training; many have not. There are few foreign ministries that have a legal department staffed by professionally qualified, full-time lawyers. Many will have diplomats with varying degrees of legal training, but who will during their career do other jobs with little legal content; and a lot of legal work has to be done by officials with no legal training at all. Inevitably, their work will include treaties.

Although the concepts of sovereignty and jurisdiction are basic to a proper understanding of international law, problems involving them do not arise constantly. But every day a treaty is being drafted, negotiated, concluded, signed, ratified, interpreted and – sometimes – breached. Many ordinary human activities are governed by treaties, although usually without those affected being aware of it. Some activities are possible only because they are authorised by treaties. For example, a vast and complex network of multilateral and bilateral treaties regulates the operation of civil aircraft engaged in international transport.

Although this book does not presume to be an academic work, I hope it will also be useful to writers on, and teachers and students of, international law. Those who deal in specialised international subjects, such as economic law, environmental law and human rights law, should also find things to interest them. They, as well as students of politics and international relations, need to have an understanding of the international legal framework within which their field of study operates, of which treaties are an essential part.

I believe this book still offers a special insight into treaty law and practice from both a practical and academic perspective, even though in recent years the literature on treaties has multiplied. *The Law of Treaties: An Introduction*[4] by Robert Kolb offers a clear and succinct overview of the law. *The Oxford Guide to Treaties*,[5] edited by Duncan Hollis, now in its Second Edition, provides an impressive and comprehensive array of essays not only on legal and practical issues but also on more conceptual aspects. The *Research Handbook on the Law of Treaties*,[6] edited by Christian Tams, Antonios Tzanakopoulos and Andreas Zimmermann, explores particular developments and new thinking, as does *Conceptual and Contextual Perspectives on the Modern Law of Treaties*,[7] edited by Michael Bowman and Dino Kritsiotis. The latter half of that book gives an insight into the ways in which treaties are handled in different areas of international law and different international organisations. Valuable articles on particular topics are also to be found in *40 Years of the Vienna Convention on the Law of Treaties*, edited by Alexander Orakhelashvili and Sarah Williams,[8] and *The Law of Treaties beyond the Vienna Convention*, edited by Enzo Cannizzaro.[9]

The *Handbook on Good Treaty Practice*[10] by Jill Barrett and Robert Beckman, like this book, focuses on practical aspects but goes deeper into matters such as running a treaty office or concluding a treaty. Commentaries on the Vienna Convention on the Law of Treaties, which include those edited by Olivier Corten and Pierre Klein[11] and by Oliver Dörr and Kirsten Schmalenbach,[12] and that written by Mark E. Villiger,[13] are an important source of analysis of each Vienna Convention article, and between them contain full bibliographies. I have found all three commentaries hugely valuable.

The scholarship and lucid style of McNair's *Law of Treaties*[14] can still be read for its brilliant insights, but relies heavily on precedents from the distant past, which are drawn mainly from the United Kingdom. McNair also published just five years before the draft of what was to become the Vienna Convention emerged from the International Law Commission (ILC). O'Connell's *International Law*[15] suffered the disadvantage of being published just after the adoption of the Vienna Convention; his chapters on treaties rely heavily on judicial decisions rather than the practice of states. Nevertheless, it is a masterly summary of the essentials of the law of treaties, and of problems that are still with us today. A number of other general books on

[4] Edward Elgar, Cheltenham UK, Northampton MA USA 2016 (*Kolb*).

[5] 2nd ed., Oxford University Press, Oxford 2020 (*Hollis, Oxford Guide*).

[6] Edward Elgar, Cheltenham UK, Northampton MA USA 2014.

[7] Cambridge University Press, Cambridge 2018.

[8] BIICL, London 2010.

[9] Oxford University Press, Oxford 2011.

[10] Cambridge University Press, Cambridge 2020.

[11] O. Corten and P. Klein (eds.), *The Vienna Conventions on the Law of Treaties: A Commentary* (Oxford University Press, Oxford 2011) (*Corten and Klein*).

[12] O. Dörr and K. Schmalenbach, *Vienna Convention on the Law of Treaties: A Commentary* (2nd ed., Springer Verlag, Berlin, Heidelberg 2018) (*Dörr and Schmalenbach*).

[13] M. E. Villiger, *Commentary on the 1969 Vienna Convention on the Law of Treaties* (Martinus Nijhoff Publishers, Leiden, Boston MA USA 2009) (*Villiger*).

[14] A. D. McNair, *The Law of Treaties* (2nd ed., Clarendon Press, Oxford 1961) (*McNair*).

[15] D. P. O'Connell, *International Law* (2nd ed., Stevens, London 1970) (*O'Connell*).

international law,[16] which are more up to date, contain excellent summaries of the law of treaties.

Blix's and Emerson's *The Treaty Maker's Handbook*[17] is limited to precedents of treaty forms and clauses, and is now rather dated. Sinclair's *The Vienna Convention on the Law of Treaties*[18] is an essential guide to the negotiation of the Convention, and explains with characteristic clarity the difficult issues that faced the negotiators and how they were dealt with, if not always satisfactorily resolved. But it is not, and does not purport to be, a comprehensive guide. Reuter's *Introduction to the Law of Treaties*[19] is good to read and thought-provoking, but idiosyncratic. Jennings' and Watts' 9th edition of *Oppenheim's International Law*[20] contains a concise summary of the law, and the incomparable footnotes remain a valuable source of material, but it is now slightly dated.[21] There are many good books on particular aspects of treaty law, such as Richard Gardiner's *Treaty Interpretation*,[22] to which I have referred in the related chapters.

As far as possible, this book illustrates law and practice by reference to precedents drawn from about 1975 onwards, but I have sought to supplement many of the older precedents by newer ones. Precedents before 1975 are cited only if they are still clearly relevant or instructive.

Because of the central role played by the Vienna Convention, a good deal of the book is a commentary on it. I know only too well the frustration of trying to find out – especially under pressure – precisely what an article of the Convention means and how it has been applied. So I have included a table, 'Articles of the Convention Cited in the Text', at pages xxv–xxix, which lists where each article is cited.

How to Use This Book

Unless the context indicates otherwise, references to 'the Convention', 'the Vienna Convention' or 'the 1969 Convention' are to the Vienna Convention on the Law of Treaties 1969; and, unless otherwise indicated, a reference simply to, for example,

16 For example, M. N. Shaw, *International Law* (9th ed., Cambridge University Press, Cambridge 2021) (*Shaw*), chapter 15, 787–833; M. Forteau, A. Miron and A. Pellet, *Droit International Public* (9th ed., LGDI, Paris, 2022); J. Crawford (ed.), *Brownlie's Principles of Public International Law* (9th ed., Oxford University Press, Oxford 2019) (*Crawford/Brownlie*), chapter 16, 353–380; and M. Fitzmaurice, 'The Practical Working of the Law of Treaties', in M. D. Evans (ed.), *International Law* (5th ed., Oxford University Press, Oxford 2018) (*Evans*), chapter 6, 138–171. The *Max Planck Encyclopedia of Public International Law* (Oxford University Press, Oxford online) (*MPEPIL*), at: https://opil.ouplaw.com/home/mpil, also contains valuable articles on various aspects of the law of treaties, including M. Fitzmaurice, 'Treaties', *MPEPIL* (2021).

17 Oceana Publications, Dobbs Ferry, NY 1973 (*Blix and Emerson*).

18 2nd ed., Manchester University Press, Manchester UK, Dover NH USA 1984 (*Sinclair*).

19 2nd English ed., Kegan Paul, London 1995 (*Reuter*).

20 R. Jennings and A. Watts (eds.), *Oppenheim's International Law* (9th ed., Longmans, London 1992) (*Oppenheim*).

21 A new edition (the 10th edition) is due to be published in 2023.

22 2nd ed., Oxford University Press, Oxford 2015 (*Gardiner*).

'Article 18' is to an article of the Convention. Whereas in previous editions the term 'MOU' (Memorandum of Understanding) was used to refer generally to a non-legally binding instrument, unilateral or multilateral, I have in this edition abandoned that practice and preferred instead to say 'non-binding instrument' or 'non-legally binding instrument'.[23] I have reserved the abbreviation 'MOU' specifically for instruments entitled 'Memorandum of Understanding', which in many cases will be non-legally binding, but in a few cases not. There is a complete list of abbreviations at pages lxv–lxix.

The Footnotes and References

The footnotes are overall more substantive than in the previous editions. When as a practitioner you reach for a book, you first and foremost want the answer, but if you don't find the answer or the answer is not sufficiently detailed, you want to know where to look next. And you need to be able to go straight to it – the exact page reference or the exact treaty. I have therefore tried to include fuller citations where possible, and to indicate where the reader might follow up points which cannot be developed fully in this book. The footnotes have numerous cross-references, especially to other articles of the Convention. The Convention must be seen as a whole; its articles do not stand alone – there is much interconnection. Whenever possible, for the text of treaties I have given the *United Nations Treaty Series* (UNTS) reference (in particular the UNTS registration number, which is essential for accessing the text of a treaty easily online) or, in the case of UK treaties, the *UK Treaty Series* (UKTS) reference. A glossary of legal terms has been included at pages lxiii–lxiv to help those who are not familiar with this area of law.

Emphasis

When words in a quotation are emphasised, the emphasis is mine unless otherwise indicated.

Errors, Omissions, Comments and Material

Inevitably, you will find the occasional error or omission, and will no doubt disagree with some of the views expressed. As with previous editions, your suggestions and comments, and new material, would be much appreciated, and can be sent by post to Jeremy Hill c/o Academic Law, Cambridge University Press and Assessment, University Printing House, Shaftesbury Road, Cambridge CB2 8EA, United Kingdom, or by email to jeremyhill.treaties@gmail.com.

[23] See Chapter 3.

1

Vienna Convention on the Law of Treaties 1969

The Convention clearly marked the beginning of a new era in the law of treaties.[1]

This book is necessarily devoted largely to the Vienna Convention on the Law of Treaties of 1969 ('the Convention'), which contains the body of rules that determine whether an instrument (document) is a treaty, how it is made, brought into force, amended, terminated and operates generally. It is not so concerned with the *substance* of a treaty (the rights and obligations created by it), which is sometimes referred to as 'treaty law'. That is a matter for the negotiating states. For good reason, the Convention has been called 'the treaty on treaties'.[2] Although the Convention does not occupy the whole ground, it covers the most important areas, and is the starting point for any description of the modern law and practice of treaties. Thus, it merits its own chapter. This chapter's other purpose is to define the scope of this book by mentioning briefly those aspects of the law of treaties that the Convention does not deal with.[3]

The Convention also does not expressly cover non-legally binding 'agreements' between two or more states or other subjects of international law, since the participants normally intend that such instruments should not be governed by international law, or, for that matter, any law. But there are some similarities between treaties and non-legally binding instruments, and some instruments drafted as non-legally binding may, albeit infrequently, depending on the context, have some legal effect. These issues are discussed in more depth in Chapter 3.

The UN General Assembly established the International Law Commission (ILC) in 1947 with the object of promoting the progressive development of international law and its codification.[4] The law of treaties was one of the topics selected by the ILC at its first session in 1949 as being suitable for codification. A series of eminent British international legal scholars (Brierly, Hersch Lauterpacht, Fitzmaurice and Waldock) were appointed as (successive) Special Rapporteurs. Their task (which took them some

1 *Reuter*, 15, para. 32.

2 See R. D. Kearney and R. E. Dalton, 'The Treaty on Treaties', AJIL 64 (1970) 495–561, for an account of the Conference.

3 This book does not deal, for example, with 'international agreements' between a state and a company that is wholly or partly governed by the law of a state: see Article 3 of the Convention.

4 For more about the ILC, see P. S. Rao, 'International Law Commission', *MPEPIL* (2017).

fifteen years) was to draw up a coherent account of the already well-developed customary international law on treaties. In 1966, the ILC adopted a final set of draft articles. The UN Conference on the Law of Treaties considered them in 1968 and 1969. It adopted the Vienna Convention on the Law of Treaties on 23 May 1969, and the Convention entered into force on 27 January 1980. As at May 2022, it had only 116 parties out of the 193 states that are members of the United Nations today. Some of the reasons for this will be discussed below.

The full text of the Convention is at Appendix A. A comparative table that relates the Convention articles to the ILC's final draft articles and its commentary on them is in 8 ILM (1969) 714–727.

Flexibility of the Convention

The Convention is the prime achievement of the ILC. Although now over fifty years old, the Convention is likely to remain unchanged for many decades to come. It codified, and to some degree developed, the law on treaties as it had evolved through the practice of states. Like the UN Charter,[5] the intelligent drafting of the Convention has enabled states to continue or to modify their practice without distorting or departing from the rules of the Convention. This is important, since practice has not stood still since 1969.

Nevertheless, the Convention's rules provide a framework that is sufficiently flexible to accommodate such developments. In fact, many of the provisions expressly envisage states departing from the rules of the Convention. For example, Article 7(1) requires the representative of a state to produce full powers in order to adopt the text of a treaty, but then makes an exception that recognises that states often agree to dispense with full powers. This is just one, small, example; in many other places the Convention also acknowledges that states will want to depart from the Convention's rules.[6] The rules are thus largely residual, leaving treaty practice very much in the hands of states – as it should be.

The Convention is by no means incapable of coping with the demands of the twenty-first century. For practitioners, for whom the Convention is their 'bible', the Convention does not need mending or, rather, amending. It has proved itself to be a most adaptable tool, well able to deal with the challenges to treaty making presented by the many important developments in international life since 1969. However, although the law of treaties is flexible, it is not always wise to depart from established practice unless it is really necessary.

[5] Charter of the United Nations, 26 June 1945: UKTS (1946) No. 67.

[6] See also Articles 9(2), 10(a), 11, 12(1)(b), 13, 14(1)(b), 15, 16, 17(1), 20(1), (3) and (4)(b), 22, 24, 25, 28, 29, 33(1) and (2), 36(1), 37(1), 39, 40, 41, 44(1), 55–60, 70(1), 72(1), 76–78 and 79(1).

Scope of the Convention

The Convention does not cover all matters to do with treaties. In particular, it applies only to treaties between states (Article 1).

Treaties with or between Other Subjects of International Law

States do not enter into treaties only with other states; they enter into treaties with other subjects of international law, in particular international organisations; and international organisations enter into treaties with each other. The Convention does not apply to such treaties, which are the subject of the Vienna Convention on the Law of Treaties between States and International Organisations or between International Organisations 1986,[7] which, in effect, applies to those treaties the provisions of the 1969 Convention suitably adapted. Where states that are parties to the 1969 Convention are parties to a treaty to which other subjects of international law, in particular international organisations, are also parties, *as between the states parties* to the treaty, it is the 1969 Convention that applies, not customary international law (Article 3(c)). As we will see later in this chapter, there is a strong convergence between the rules of the Convention and customary international law, but some differences remain. These may at first sight appear to concern nuances or detail, but sometimes they are of practical importance.

International Organisations

Where the treaty constituting an international organisation (i.e., its constitution) and a treaty adopted *within* the organisation are concluded by states parties to the 1969 Convention, the Convention will apply to such instruments, but this is without prejudice to any relevant rules of the organisation (Article 5). Those rules may, for example, govern the procedure by which treaties are adopted within the organisation, how they are to be amended and the making of reservations.[8]

Oral Agreements

For reasons of clarity and simplicity, the definition of treaty in Article 2(1)(a) includes only an international agreement that is 'in written form',[9] thus excluding oral

[7] 25 ILM (1986) 543–592. The Vienna Convention on the Law of Treaties between States and International Organizations or between International Organizations of 1986 is, however, not yet in force. This field is therefore still governed by customary international law. See Chapter 22, pp. 400–402.

[8] See, for example, the procedures relating to International Labour Organization (ILO) Conventions in the *Handbook relating to international labour Conventions and Recommendations*, Centenary Edition 2019, International Labour Standards Department, at: www.ilo.org/wcmsp5/groups/public/—ed_norm/—normes/documents/publication/wcms_697949.pdf.

[9] See Chapter 2 on the definition of 'treaty'.

agreements. But this does not affect their legal force, or the application to them of any of the rules of customary international law to which they would be subject independently of the Convention (Article 3(a)). Even today, oral agreements between states are not unknown, though they are extremely rare.[10]

Two often quoted examples are, first, the *Eastern Greenland* case, where the Permanent Court of International Justice found that an oral declaration by Nils Claus Ihlen, the Norwegian Minister for Foreign Affairs, in response to a request from the Danish Minister with regard to sovereignty over Greenland, a 'question falling within his province', was 'binding upon the country to which the Minister belongs';[11] and second, the dispute between Denmark and Finland about the construction by Denmark of a bridge across the Storebælt (Great Belt), which was settled in 1992 in a telephone conversation between the Danish and Finnish Prime Ministers, in which Finland agreed to discontinue its case against Denmark before the International Court of Justice (ICJ) in return for a payment by Denmark.[12] There was no joint record of the substance of the agreement.[13]

Other examples cited in the literature[14] include a commitment made in 1971 by the Prime Minister of Turkey, Nihat Erim, to prohibit the production of poppy (opium) in return for a promise by President Nixon to deliver weapons to Turkey,[15] and an oral agreement reached in negotiations at Beijing Airport in September 1969 between Chinese Premier Zhou Enlai and Soviet Premier Alexei Kosygin to settle a border clash.[16]

While some states are open to the existence of oral agreements, though rarely using them in practice,[17] others are not.[18] US law requires an oral agreement to be

[10] Another possible view is that oral agreements between Ministers of the sort described in the next paragraph are more common than is generally thought, but are simply rarely subject to legal dispute or as 'unconditional and definitive in form' as the Ihlen Declaration; or else they are given legal effect (if that is intended) in other ways.

[11] *Legal Status of Eastern Greenland (Denmark* v. *Norway)* (1933), PCIJ Reports, Series A/B, No. 53, 71, and 91 (dissenting opinion of Judge Anzilotti); see R. Higgins, *The Development of International Law through the Political Organs of the United Nations* (Oxford University Press, Oxford 1963), 254.

[12] See 'International Court of Justice: Order Discontinuing the Proceedings in Case concerning Passage through the Great Belt (Finland v. Denmark), Introductory Note by M. Koskenniemi', 32 ILM (1993) 101, particularly para. 9, at 103. For the text of the ICJ Order, see 32 ILM (1993) 104–105.

[13] The fact of the settlement was, however, communicated to the ICJ in a letter from the Agent of Finland to the Registrar dated 3 September 1992, which was confirmed in a letter from the Agent of Denmark dated 4 September 1992: *Passage through the Great Belt (Finland* v. *Denmark)*, ICJ, Correspondence, at www.icj-cij.org/en/case/86/correspondence.

[14] See *Oppenheim*, 1045–1046, para. 459 and n. 4; *Corten and Klein*, 70–71.

[15] RGDIP, vol. 79 (1975) 542 *et seq.*; *Kolb*, 17.

[16] Qin X., 'Oral Agreements and Chinese Relevant Practice', *Chinese Journal of International Law* 4(2) (2005) 465–479, 474–475.

[17] D. B. Hollis, 'A Comparative Approach to Treaty Law and Practice', in D. B. Hollis, M. R. Blakeslee and L. B. Ederington (eds.), *National Treaty Law and Practice* (Martinus Nijhoff, Leiden 2005), 12–13.

[18] D. B. Hollis, 'Defining Treaties', in *Hollis, Oxford Guide*, 11, 24, n. 94; *Guidelines of the Inter-American Juridical Committee on Binding and Non-Binding Agreements* (2020) , adopted by Resolution CJI/RES. 259

reduced to writing by the US government.[19] In the absence of some record, it will be difficult to establish an oral treaty's existence and content.[20] Oral agreements, in the strict sense, are also impossible to register with the UN Secretariat in accordance with Article 102 of the UN Charter.[21] But many oral agreements will in fact be recorded in minutes or *procès-verbaux*, and thus in effect become written agreements.[22]

No Retrospective Effect

The Convention applies only to those treaties that are concluded by states after the date the Convention enters into force for them (Article 4).[23] There is no definition in the Convention of the word 'concluded',[24] and 'conclusion' can be variously applied,[25] depending on the context, to (1) the adoption (and opening for signature, if applicable) of a text; or (2) the signature of a text, subject to a further step indicating consent to be bound, such as ratification or acceptance; or (3) the point in time when there is a definite engagement by the parties to be bound by the instrument under international law (which may be signature if the treaty is not subject to ratification or acceptance); or (4) the process extending from adoption of the text to ratification. 'Conclusion' is a distinct concept from 'entry into force': hence Part II of the Convention is entitled 'Conclusion and entry into force of treaties', although a treaty may enter into force, for example, upon signature or ratification.

There is no problem in applying the rule in Article 4 to bilateral treaties. The VCLT will apply only to treaties concluded between States A and B after the entry into force of the VCLT for and in respect of States A and B.[26] In the case of a multilateral treaty, the VCLT will apply to those states that participated in the conclusion of the treaty after the VCLT entered into force for them, but not to other states.[27] The VCLT entered into force on 27 January 1980. The Law of the Sea Convention 1982

(XCVII-O/20), published by the Secretariat for Judicial Affairs of the Organization of American States (OAS), 1 November 2020, OEA/Ser.Q/VII.3, OEA/Ser.Q/CJI/doc.614/20 Rev.1 Corr.1 (*OAS Guidelines*), Annex II with Commentary, 45 and n. 32, at: www.oas.org/en/sla/iajc/docs/Guidelines_on_Binding_and_Non-Binding_Agreements_publication.pdf.

19 1 U.S.C. §112b. 20 Hollis (n. 18), 24. 21 *Corten and Klein*, 71.

22 *Dörr and Schmalenbach*, 57–58.

23 For an account of the negotiation of Article 4, see *Sinclair*, 230. See also P. McDade, 'The Effect of Article 4 of the Vienna Convention on the Law of Treaties 1969', ICLQ 35 (1986) 499–511; E. Vierdag, 'The Time of the "Conclusion" of a Multilateral Treaty', BYIL 59 (1988) 75–111.

24 The words 'conclude', 'concluded' or 'conclusion' are used in various provisions of the Convention, including in the definition of a 'treaty' in Article 2(1)(a).

25 See also Chapter 6, p. 106. For discussion of the various views, taking account of the *travaux préparatoires* and a textual analysis of the provisions of the Convention, see *Gardiner*, 232–235; *Villiger*, 78–79; and Hollis (n. 18), 21–22.

26 *Sinclair*, 8. 27 *Sinclair*, 8–9; *Corten and Klein*, 82–83; *Villiger*, 112–113.

(UNCLOS) was concluded on 10 December 1982.[28] Thus, for those states that were parties to the VCLT on that date, its rules will apply as between them with regard to UNCLOS. Article 4 of the VCLT provides, however, that the rule against retrospection is without prejudice to the application of any rules of the VCLT to which treaties would be subject under international law independently of the VCLT. So, those rules of the VCLT that reflect customary international law apply (but as customary law) to treaties concluded before the entry into force of the VCLT, or concluded afterwards but before the VCLT entered into force for parties to those treaties.[29]

State Succession, State Responsibility and the Outbreak of Hostilities

For the avoidance of doubt, Article 73 confirms that the Convention does not prejudge any question that may arise concerning a treaty from succession of states,[30] from the international responsibility of a state[31] or from the outbreak of hostilities between states.[32] Since the Convention does not deal with these matters, they are largely governed by customary international law, and are discussed in later chapters of this book.

Bilateral, Multilateral and Plurilateral Treaties

The term 'bilateral' describes a treaty between two states (or between a state and another subject of international law, such as an international organisation), and 'multilateral' refers to a treaty between three or more states (or subjects of international law). It is also possible, however, to classify as bilateral treaties those where two or more states (and/or international organisations) form one party, and another state or states (and/or international organisations) the other party.[33]

The term 'plurilateral' treaty is mostly used to describe a treaty to which three or more states are parties but where overall participation is limited to three states or a

[28] Here, 'concluded' is used in the context that UNCLOS was adopted by the Third UN Conference on the Law of the Sea and opened for signature, together with the Final Act of the Conference, at Montego Bay, Jamaica, on 10 December 1982.

[29] On the application by the ICJ in the case concerning *Kasikili/Sedudu Island (Botswana* v. *Namibia)* of Article 31 of the VCLT to a treaty of 1890, see the note by M. Shaw in ICLQ 49 (2000) 967–968. The case itself is reported in ICJ Reports (1999) 1045; 39 ILM (2000) 310; 119 ILR 467. As to the *Gabčíkovo* case and the Convention, see pp. 14–15 and 301–308.

[30] See Chapter 21.

[31] See Chapter 20, pp. 365–370. See also *Gabčíkovo-Nagymaros Project (Hungary* v. *Slovakia)*, ICJ Reports (1997) 3, at 38–39, para. 47; 37 ILM (1998) 162; 116 ILR 1.

[32] See Chapter 16, pp. 318–320.

[33] The same would apply to a treaty between an international organisation and its member states of the one part, and a non-member state of the other part, e.g., treaties concluded by the European Union (or previously the European Communities) and its member states with a third country (often termed 'mixed agreements'). The multiplicity of named subjects on the EU side simply reflects divisions of competence. Such treaties are still essentially bilateral agreements. See also Chapter 22, pp. 412–413.

relatively small number. 'Plurilateral' is not defined in the Convention (nor is 'bilateral' or 'multilateral') but the concept of a treaty with a limited number of parties is reflected, for example, in Article 20(2).[34] Plurilateral agreements are normally concluded between a limited number of parties due to their specific subject matter or geography.[35] Care is, however, needed in identifying the precise relationship between the parties. In the case of a genuinely plurilateral agreement, the parties will be acting individually on an equal footing, for example, the Comprehensive and Progressive Agreement for Trans-Pacific Partnership (CPTPP)[36] or the United States–Mexico–Canada Trade Agreement,[37] as distinct from an agreement where, despite the multiplicity of parties, there are essentially two sides, even if there is a mix of collective and individual activity.[38] And, in the case of entry into force, it may sometimes be necessary for all the negotiating states to ratify, or provisionally apply, the treaty for it to become operational,[39] or it may be possible for the treaty to become operational once a certain number of states have ratified (or provisionally applied) it,[40] and for the treaty to be operational (pending further ratifications) only as between those states.

A plurilateral agreement may still sometimes be referred to as a multilateral agreement (since 'multilateral' literally means 'many sides', without specifying how many); and a multilateral agreement which has been opened for signature to a large number of states, if it has been ratified and entered into force only for a few, may sometimes de facto become 'plurilateral'.[41] The term 'plurilateral agreement' has a distinct technical meaning in the World Trade Organization (WTO) Agreement,[42] where agreements described in Annexes 1 to 3 of the Agreement are referred to as 'Multilateral Trade Agreements' and are binding on all WTO members, while Annex 4 contains two agreements, referred to as 'Plurilateral Trade Agreements', which are binding only on those WTO members that are party to these agreements.[43]

[34] See p. 149.

[35] For example, the Agreement between Finland, Estonia and Sweden regarding the M/S *Estonia* 1995: 1890 UNTS 176 No. 32189; with Additional Protocol 1996: 1947 UNTS 404 No. 32189; UKTS (1999) No. 74.

[36] [2018] ATS 23; incorporating, by reference, provisions of the original Trans-Pacific Partnership (TPP): see New Zealand Foreign Affairs and Trade website: https://www.mfat.govt.nz/.

[37] At US Trade Representative website.

[38] For example, the EU–Central America Association Agreement: OJ L 346, 15.12.2012.

[39] As in the case of the US–Mexico–Canada Trade Agreement 2018 (n. 37).

[40] As in the case of the CPTPP (n. 36).

[41] *Dörr and Schmalenbach*, 34.

[42] 1867 UNTS 4 No. 31874; 33 ILM (1994) 1144. See specifically Article II.2 and II.3.

[43] When the WTO Agreement entered into force on 1 January 1995, Annex 4 included four plurilateral agreements. However, two of those agreements – the International Dairy Agreement and the International Bovine Meat Agreement – were terminated at the end of 1997. See P. Van den Bossche and W. Zdouc, *The Law and Policy of the World Trade Organization* (4th ed., Cambridge University Press, Cambridge 2017), 53; and *Dörr and Schmalenbach*, 34. The position in practice is more complex again. Plurilateral agreements in the WTO can be divided into: (1) open plurilaterals, which are concluded amongst a group of Members but where the commitments or obligations are offered to the whole Membership on a most-favoured nation (MFN) basis; and (2) closed plurilaterals, where the commitment and obligations are binding only amongst

Generally, the Convention does not distinguish between bilateral and multilateral treaties, and Article 60(1) is the only provision limited to bilateral treaties. Articles 40, 41, 58 and 60 refer expressly to multilateral treaties, and the provisions on reservations and on depositaries are relevant only to multilateral treaties.

The Convention and Customary International Law

The various provisions mentioned above, and the preamble to the Convention, confirm that insofar as questions are not regulated by the Convention, the rules of customary international law continue to apply.[44] Treaties and custom are the main sources of international law.[45] The ILC has stated: 'To determine the existence and content of a rule of customary international law, it is necessary to ascertain whether there is a general practice that is accepted as law (*opinio juris*).'[46] Customary law is thus made up of two elements: (1) evidence of a substantial uniformity of practice by a substantial number of states; and (2) *opinio juris* – a general recognition by states that the practice is settled enough to amount to a binding obligation in international law.[47]

Some multilateral treaties largely codify customary law. But if a new rule of international law created by a treaty is followed in the practice of non-parties, it can lead to the evolution of a customary rule which will be applicable as between such non-parties, and between them and the parties.[48] This can happen even before the treaty has entered into force.[49] Although many provisions of UNCLOS went beyond mere codification of customary rules, the negotiations proceeded on the basis of consensus, even though the final text was put to the vote. It was therefore that much easier during the twelve years before UNCLOS entered into force in 1994 for most of its provisions to become accepted as representing customary law.[50] This was

the participants. This latter category of closed plurilaterals is that referred to in Article II:3 of the WTO Agreement as 'Plurilateral Trade Agreements'.

[44] See generally, A. Watts, 'The International Court and the Continuing Customary International Law of Treaties', in N. Ando, E. McWhinney and R. Wolfrum (eds.), *Liber Amicorum Judge Shigeru Oda* (Kluwer Law, The Hague 2002), 251–266.

[45] Article 38(1) ICJ Statute contains the most authoritative and complete statement of the sources of international law, which the ICJ shall apply.

[46] Draft Conclusion 2, *Draft conclusions on identification of customary international law with commentaries*, adopted by the ILC in 2018: Report of the ILC on the Work of its 70th session, 2018, UNGA 73rd Session, Supplement No. 10, Doc. A/73/10, 117–156.

[47] See further *Shaw*, 58–78; R. Churchill, V. Lowe and A. Sander, *The Law of the Sea* (4th ed., Manchester University Press, Manchester 2022), 12–18.

[48] See the *North Sea Continental Shelf cases*, ICJ Reports (1969) 3, at 41–47, paras. 70–85; 41 ILR 70–77.

[49] See H. Thirlway, 'The Law and Procedure of the International Court of Justice', BYIL 61 (1990) 1–133, 87.

[50] See T. Treves, 'Codification du droit international et pratique des Etats', Hague Recueil, IV, 223 (1990) 25–60; H. Caminos and M. R. Molitor, 'Progressive Development of International Law and the Package Deal', AJIL 79 (1985) 871–890.

important since, even by July 2022, UNCLOS still had only 168 parties, which did not include Iran or the United States.

An accumulation of bilateral treaties on the same subject, such as investment, may in certain circumstances be evidence of a customary rule.[51]

To What Extent Does the Convention Reflect Rules of Customary International Law?

A detailed consideration of this question[52] is beyond the scope of this book. It is not usually of great concern to lawyers in their day-to-day work but can become important in the close examination of some issues, for example, the termination of a treaty.[53] When questions on the law of treaties arise during negotiations, whether for a new treaty or about one concluded before the entry into force of the Convention, the rules set forth in the Convention are invariably relied upon, even when the states are not parties to it.

The question whether a particular rule in the Convention represents customary international law is likely to arise if the matter is litigated, and often the court or tribunal will take the Convention as its starting - and normally also its finishing - point. This is certainly the approach taken by the ICJ, as well as other courts and tribunals, international and national.[54] In *Kasikili/Sedudu Island (Botswana* v. *Namibia)*,[55] in 1999, the ICJ interpreted and applied an 1890 treaty between Germany and the United Kingdom in accordance with Articles 31 and 32 of the Convention, even though the Convention clearly does not apply retrospectively.[56]

Earlier, in its 1971 opinion in *Namibia (South West Africa)*,[57] the ICJ held that the rules of the Convention concerning termination of a treaty for breach 'may in many respects be considered as codification of existing customary law', and applied Article 60 (termination of a treaty for breach). In 1973, the Court held that Article 52 recognised that treaties concluded by the threat or use of force were void, and that Article 62 (fundamental change of circumstances) reflected, or was in many respects a codification of, customary international law.[58] In 1997, in its *Gabčíkovo* Judgment,

[51] See Thirlway (n. 49), 86.

[52] See *Villiger*, 1–27; *Dörr and Schmalenbach*, 90–94, with particular attention to the list of articles reflecting customary international law at 92 and the bibliography at 97; and *Corten and Klein*, 85. *Corten and Klein* also includes a separate short analysis of the customary status of each article, where relevant, under the article heading; *Sinclair*, 10–24; *Case Concerning Armed Activities on the Territory of the Congo* (New Application: 2002) *(Democratic Republic of the Congo* v. *Rwanda)* (Jurisdiction and Admissibility), Judgment, ICJ Reports (2006) 3, at 51–52, para. 125; *Racke* (1998), Case C-162/96; 1998 ECR-I-3688; 37 ILM (1998) 1128; 117 ILR 399, esp. paras. 20 and 25–29.

[53] See p. 308. [54] See pp. 240–241.

[55] ICJ Reports (1999) 1045, at 1059, para. 18; 39 ILM (2000) 310, 320; 119 ILR 467.

[56] See the note on the case by M. Shaw, ICLQ 49 (2000) 967–968; see also the section 'No Retrospective Effect', pp. 10–11.

[57] ICJ Reports (1971) 3, at 46–47, para. 94; 49 ILR 2.

[58] *Fisheries Jurisdiction (United Kingdom* v. *Iceland)* (Jurisdiction), ICJ Reports (1973) 3, at 14 and 18, paras. 24 and 36, respectively; 55 ILR 183.

the principal treaty at issue predated the entry into force of the Convention for the parties to the case. Nevertheless, the Court brushed aside the question of the possible non-applicability of the Convention's rules to questions of termination and suspension of treaties, and applied its Articles 60–62 as generally reflecting customary law.[59]

Given previous similar pronouncements by the Court, and the references in *Gabčíkovo* and subsequent judgments, it is fair to assume that the Court will take the same approach in respect of virtually all of the provisions of the Convention.[60] This is not surprising. Despite what some critics of the Convention may assert, any codification of the law will inevitably reduce the scope for judicial law making. For most practical purposes, treaty questions are resolved by applying the rules of the Convention.[61]

Effect of Emerging Customary Law on Prior Treaty Rights and Obligations

Most treaties are bilateral, and so contractual in nature. Most multilateral treaties are also like contracts, in that they do not purport to lay down rules of general application. But, since 1945, so-called law-making multilateral treaties have become so numerous that a sizeable number of topics have come to be regulated by both customary law and treaty law. Since international law has no hierarchy of sources of law, custom and treaty being autonomous, it has been argued that, even when custom has been codified, it retains its separate existence. This is a controversial theory,[62] and may not reflect the approach to legal problems taken by foreign ministry legal advisers. When dealing with an actual problem, naturally they give more weight to a treaty rule than to a different customary rule.

Nevertheless, new customary rules which emerge from economic changes or dissatisfaction with a treaty rule can sometimes result in a modification in the operation of a treaty rule. In *Fisheries Jurisdiction (United Kingdom* v. *Iceland)*

[59] ICJ Reports (1997) 3, at 36–38 and 62, paras. 42–46 and 99; 37 ILM (1998) 162; 116 ILR 1. See Chapter 16, pp. 301–308. For a more cautious approach to the procedural provisions of the Convention, specifically Article 66 (Procedures for judicial settlement, conciliation and arbitration), see *Democratic Republic of the Congo* v. *Rwanda* (Jurisdiction and Admissibility) (n. 52), 51–52, para. 125. *Kolb* (at 23) also distinguishes the status of certain procedural provisions.

[60] M. Mendelson, 'The International Court of Justice and the Sources of International Law', in V. Lowe and M. Fitzmaurice (eds.), *Fifty Years of the International Court of Justice* (Cambridge University Press, Cambridge 1996), 63–89, 66; Thirlway (n. 49), 3; A. Aust, 'Limping Treaties: Lessons from Multilateral Treaty-Making', NILR 50(3) (2003), 243–266, 248–251. But see also *Case Concerning Armed Activities on the Territory of the Congo* (n. 52).

[61] 'The [CJEU] has observed that the customary international law of treaties forms part of the European legal order, and it generally follows the VCLT (implicitly or explicitly); the World Trade Organization (WTO) Dispute Settlement Body and the International Tribunal for the Law of the Sea (ITLOS) have also emphasized the customary status of the VCLT rules of treaty interpretation.' *Crawford/Brownlie*, 354. See also pp. 240–241.

[62] See *Military and Paramilitary Activities in and against Nicaragua (Nicaragua* v. *United States of America)*, Merits, ICJ Reports (1986) 14, at 92–97, paras. 172–182; Thirlway (n. 49), 43–44.

(Merits)[63] in 1974, the ICJ decided that, since the adoption in 1958 of the High Seas Convention,[64] the right of states to establish 12-mile fishing zones had crystallised as customary law, despite the provisions in that convention regarding freedom of fishing on the high seas.

International law does *not* contain any principle of *acte contraire*, by which a rule can be altered only by a rule of the same legal nature. Article 68(c) in the ILC's 1964 draft articles provided that the operation of a treaty may be modified by the 'subsequent emergence of a new rule of customary international law relating to matters dealt with in the treaty and binding upon all the parties'.[65] Although the article was not included in the ILC's final draft articles, this was only because the ILC did not see its mandate as extending to the general relationship between customary law and treaty law.

Reference Material on the Convention

The single most valuable source of material on the meaning and effect of the articles of the Convention remains the Commentary of the ILC on its final draft articles and contained in its final report on the topic.[66] A comparative table, which relates the Convention articles to the ILC's final draft articles and its Commentary, is in 8 ILM (1969) 714. The history of the drafting of the articles can be found in the *ILC Yearbooks*, beginning in 1950. However, since the Vienna Conference naturally made changes to the draft articles, one needs to refer also to the summary records of the Conference.[67] Rosenne produced a comprehensive guide to the negotiating history (*travaux*).[68] This should be used in conjunction with Wetzel's and Rauschning's book, which has (in English) the text of all the most important *travaux*.[69] There are useful accounts of the negotiations in *Sinclair* and by Kearney and Dalton,[70] all of whom took part in the Vienna Conference.

[63] ICJ Reports (1974) 3, at 22, paras. 49 *et seq.*; 55 ILR 238.

[64] 450 UNTS 11 No. 6465; UKTS (1963) No. 5.

[65] YBILC (1964) vol. II, 198.

[66] YBILC II (1966) 173–274, at: www.un.org/law/ilc, or A. Watts, *The International Law Commission, 1949–1998*, vol. II (Oxford University Press, Oxford 1999), chapter 8.

[67] UN Doc. A/Conf. 39/11 and Add. 1. The *documents* produced at the Conference are in A/Conf. 39/11/ Add. 2.

[68] S. Rosenne, *The Law of Treaties* (Oceana Publications, Dobbs Ferry, NY 1970).

[69] R. G. Wetzel and D. Rauschning, *The Vienna Convention on the Law of Treaties: Travaux Préparatoires* (Alfred Metzer Verlag, Frankfurt am Main 1978).

[70] 64 AJIL (1970) 495–561.

2

What Is a Treaty?

> the intolerable wrestle with words and meanings.[1]

Like the 1969 Vienna Convention, this book is concerned primarily with treaties between states. Article 2(1)(a) defines a 'treaty' as:

> an international agreement concluded between States in written form and governed by international law, whether embodied in a single instrument or in two or more related instruments and whatever its particular designation.[2]

As with most of the Convention, although the definition is expressed to be for the purposes of that Convention, and is limited to treaties between states, its elements now represent customary international law.[3] The definition itself in most aspects is quite straightforward, but the main challenge is to establish whether a particular instrument falls within it.[4]

Definition of 'Treaty'

'An International Agreement'

To be a treaty, an agreement has to have an international character. When we examine the other elements of the definition, we will see what that means. The Convention uses 'treaty' as a generic term. The constitution, law or practice of some states divides treaties variously into categories such as inter-state, intergovernmental, inter-

[1] T. S. Eliot, *East Coker*, Pt 2.

[2] Compare the definition offered in the *OAS Guidelines* 1.2: 'A binding international agreement concluded between States, State institutions, or other appropriate subjects that is recorded in writing and governed by international law, regardless of its designation, registration, or the domestic legal procedures States employ to consent to be bound by it.' Guidelines of the Inter-American Juridical Committee on Binding and Non-Binding Agreements, adopted by Resolution CJI/RES. 259 (XCVII-O/20), published by the Secretariat for Judicial Affairs of the Organization of American States (OAS), 1 November 2020, OEA/Ser.Q/VII.3, OEA/Ser.Q/CJI/doc.614/20 Rev.1 Corr.1 (in this chapter *OAS Guidelines* or, simply, *Guidelines*).

[3] See Chapter 1, pp. 13–16.

[4] H. Thirlway, 'The Law and Procedure of the International Court of Justice', BYIL 62 (1991) 1–75, 4–5.

ministerial, executive or administrative agreements.[5] The Convention does not recognise such distinctions, although 'the provisions of paragraph 1 [of Article 2] regarding the use of terms in the present Convention are without prejudice to the use of those terms or to the meanings which may be given to them in the internal law of any State'.[6]

Treaties can also be described as 'universal' or 'regional', but the name 'treaty', in itself, has no legal significance.[7] It is similar with the somewhat tautological term '*international* treaty', which is often used by the media and politicians. Although it might perhaps be used to distinguish a treaty (properly so called) from historical agreements with indigenous peoples,[8] it is better to avoid it completely. A 'constituent treaty' is one establishing an international *organisation.*

Treaties can be bilateral or multilateral (between three or more parties). Most of the Convention applies to both types. A '*plurilateral* treaty' is a treaty made between a limited number of states for reasons relating to the specific subject matter or geography and is, in effect, a form of multilateral treaty.[9]

The ILC's Commentary makes clear that the definition of treaty includes those international agreements drafted in a less formal manner ('in simplified form'), which by the 1960s were being increasingly used.[10] There is, for example, no difference in legal effect between a treaty contained in a *formal*, single instrument and a treaty constituted by the more *informal* method of an exchange of notes, provided it satisfies the other elements of the definition (see the examples in Appendices B, E and F). In 1945, there was still some uncertainty whether international agreements drafted in a less formal way could properly be called treaties, and this was reflected in Article 102 of the UN Charter, which requires the registration of 'every treaty and every international agreement'. But by the 1960s there was no longer any doubt on the matter. The question whether an instrument is 'informal' or in 'simplified form' does not in itself determine whether it is a treaty, or whether it falls into the category of 'non-legally binding instruments', where there is no intention to create obligations in international law.[11] An instrument entitled 'memorandum of understanding' or 'exchange of letters', for example, may be binding or non-binding (and thus a treaty, or not) depending on factors other than its name or structure.[12] From the legal point of view, 'agreements may be concluded in whatever form, solemn, express or tacit'.[13]

The lack of requirements in respect of form or formalism[14] can, however, create uncertainty whether a document or related documents constitute a treaty, or some

[5] There is no difference, as a matter of international law, between a treaty framed between states themselves or between the governments of those states. In some cases, however, the constitutions or domestic legal systems draw a distinction, which determines which procedures are to be followed internally.

[6] Article 2(2) VCLT. See YBILC (1962) vol. II, 163; *Corten and Klein*, 55–56.

[7] But see *McNair*, 739–754, on the differing character of treaties.

[8] On treaties with indigenous peoples, see Chapter 4, pp. 78–79.

[9] See Chapter 1, pp. 11–12.

[10] See commentary on draft Article 2 in YBILC (1966) vol. II, 173, 188–189.

[11] See Chapter 3.

[12] See pp. 21–26, 34–36 and 41–49.

[13] *Kolb*, 25.

[14] This includes, for example, lack of formal procedures relating to its conclusion. See *Kolb*, 27.

other form of binding obligation, or a non-binding instrument.[15] This is not the case where the intentions of the parties to create a treaty are clear and they follow standard forms and procedures for conclusion of a treaty. The instrument will then be a treaty. But uncertainty can arise where standard procedures are not followed, or where the intentions of the parties and the language used are ambiguous, and the document at issue forms part of a more complex picture.

This is likely to be so particularly where a document (especially one which becomes relevant to a dispute) falls within one of the following categories:

(1) records of meetings, protocols (in the sense of records), agreed minutes, *procès-verbaux*;
(2) joint memorandums, memorandums of understanding, memorandums of consultations, instruments with ambiguous titles, instruments with ambiguous form or terminology;
(3) communiqués or statements by heads of state or government, or foreign ministers;
(4) unilateral, bilateral or joint declarations.

All of the instruments listed above are commonly used in the diplomatic process. In the vast majority of cases, states use them with the specific intent that they should be *non-legally binding* under international law, and therefore *not* a treaty. Most of the time, therefore, care is taken to ensure that this is clear from the drafting and the context and, as a result, *normally there is no doubt as to their non-binding status.*[16] But the case law shows that such instruments can still, in particular circumstances, be evidence of a binding agreement.

What then are the determining factors? The cases provide a guide, but they can be divergent or even contradictory[17] and often turn on their own particular facts. It has been suggested that there are two broad approaches: an 'intent' test and an 'objective' test. The first emphasises the subjective intention of two (or more) sides to create legal rights and obligations; the second favours a more objective analysis based on the subject matter and terms of an instrument. In practice, the distinction between the two may be more apparent than real, since establishing an intention usually requires also an objective analysis of the text and the context.[18]

[15] This theme runs throughout the analysis in this chapter of the VCLT definition of a treaty, and Chapter 3, which looks more thoroughly at non-binding instruments.

[16] See Chapter 3, pp. 41–49. Some regional initiatives have made an important contribution in analysing the criteria for non-legally binding instruments, for example the *OAS Guidelines* (n. 2) and the discussion in the Council of Europe Committee of Legal Advisers on Public International Law (CAHDI): see the statement of the Chair of CAHDI, 3 November 2021, p. 6, at: 1680a4669e (coe.int).

[17] M. Fitzmaurice, 'Treaties', *MPEPIL* (2021), para. 12.

[18] See the quotation in point (c), p. 23, from the case *Obligation to Negotiate Access to the Pacific Ocean (Bolivia* v. *Chile)*, ICJ Reports (2018) 507, at 539, para. 91; the Commentary on *OAS Guideline* 3.2, 77, and more fully, 47 and 77–83; D. B. Hollis, 'Defining Treaties', in *Hollis, Oxford Guide*, 24–27.

In this vein, the Tribunal in the *South China Sea Arbitration* stated:[19]

> To constitute a binding agreement, an instrument must evince a clear intention to establish rights and obligations between the parties. Such clear intention is determined by reference to the instrument's actual terms and the particular circumstances of its adoption. The subsequent conduct of the parties to an instrument may also assist in determining its nature. This test is accepted by both Parties and has been articulated in a number of international cases, including *Aegean Continental Shelf*, *Maritime Delimitation and Territorial Questions between Qatar and Bahrain (Qatar* v. *Bahrain)*, and *Land and Maritime Boundary (Cameroon* v. *Nigeria)*.[20]

The case of *Qatar* v. *Bahrain*,[21] however, is an example where the stated intention of one side was not determinative. The parties agreed that an exchange of letters of December 1987 constituted an international agreement but Bahrain disputed whether the Minutes of a meeting in December 1990 could likewise be regarded as legally binding. The ICJ rejected this contention, saying that:

> The Minutes are not a simple record of a meeting [...]; they do not merely give an account of discussions and summarize points of agreement and disagreement. They enumerate the commitments to which the Parties have consented. They thus create rights and obligations in international law for the Parties. They constitute an international agreement.[22]

The Court brushed aside the objection that the Foreign Minister of Bahrain had not intended the Minutes to be a binding agreement:

> The Court does not find it necessary to consider what might have been the intentions of the Foreign Minister of Bahrain or, for that matter, those of the Foreign Minister of Qatar. The two Ministers signed a text recording commitments accepted by their Governments, some of which were to be given immediate application. Having signed such a text, the Foreign Minister of Bahrain is not in a position subsequently to say that he intended to subscribe only to a 'statement recording a political understanding', and not to an international agreement.[23]

[19] *An Arbitral Tribunal constituted under Annex VII to the 1982 United Nations Convention on the Law of the Sea (The Republic of the Philippines* v. *The People's Republic of China)*, Award on Jurisdiction and Admissibility, PCA Case No 2013-19 (29 October 2015), para. 213.

[20] The references for the cases cited: *Aegean Sea Continental Shelf (Greece* v. *Turkey)*, Judgment, ICJ Reports (1978) 3, at 39, para. 96; *Maritime Delimitation and Territorial Questions (Qatar* v. *Bahrain)*, Jurisdiction and Admissibility, ICJ Reports (1994) 112, at 120–122, paras. 23–29; *Land and Maritime Boundary (Cameroon* v. *Nigeria; Equatorial Guinea intervening)*, Judgment, ICJ Reports (2002) 303, at 427, 429, paras. 258, 262–263.

[21] *Qatar* v. *Bahrain*, Jurisdiction and Admissibility (n. 20).

[22] *Qatar* v. *Bahrain*, Jurisdiction and Admissibility (n. 20), 121, para. 25.

[23] *Qatar* v. *Bahrain*, Jurisdiction and Admissibility (n. 20), 121–122, para. 27.

Any attempt to summarise the jurisprudence is somewhat hazardous but the following aspects have been considered in international judicial decisions: (a) form and designation; (b) terminology; (c) subject matter, terms and context; (d) intent; (e) level of negotiator or signatory of instrument; whether agreement is subject to ratification (or not); (f) definitive or conditional terms, and clarity; (g) subsequent practice and lack of objections; and (h) registration (or non-registration) with the Secretary-General of the United Nations. These will be examined briefly in turn.

(a) Form and designation

As the Tribunal stated in the *South China Sea Arbitration (Jurisdiction)*, 'the form or designation of an instrument is . . . not decisive of its status as an agreement establishing legal obligations between the parties'.[24] Similar statements are to be found in the separate opinion of Judge Ruda in the *WHO Regional Office Advisory Opinion*,[25] the *Newfoundland/Nova Scotia Arbitration* (First Phase)[26] and the *Temple of Preah Vihear* case.[27] Article 2(1)(a) of the Convention affirms that designation is not determinative ('whatever its particular designation').[28] In the *South West Africa* cases, the ICJ noted that there is a great variety in the usage of names to which the character of treaty stipulations has been attached.[29] In the *Aegean Sea Continental Shelf* case, the ICJ said that 'it knows of no rule of international law which might preclude a joint communiqué from constituting an international agreement to submit a dispute to arbitration or judicial settlement . . .', although in that case the Court concluded that it did not.[30]

[24] *South China Sea Arbitration* (n. 19), para. 214.

[25] *Interpretation of the Agreement of 25 March 1951 between the WHO and Egypt*, Advisory Opinion, ICJ Reports (1980) 73, at 123.

[26] 'The Parties also agreed that no specific requirements of form exist under international law for a treaty. There is no requirement under international law that a treaty be subject to ratification. Nor is there any requirement as to the designation of the instrument in question or as to the form in which it is signed or approved. What matters, ultimately, is the intention of the Parties to be bound by the agreement under international law. The International Court of Justice has confirmed this approach in a succession of cases.' Award of the Tribunal in the *Arbitration Between Newfoundland and Labrador and Nova Scotia concerning Portions of the Limits of Their Offshore Areas, First Phase*, 17 May 2001, 128 ILR 425, at 450, para. 3.15.

[27] *Temple of Preah Vihear (Cambodia* v. *Thailand)*, Preliminary Objections, ICJ Reports (1961) 17, at 31; 33 ILR 418. Although supportive of the general point about *treaty* form, the document in question raised a narrower point, whether a particular form was necessary for a declaration of acceptance of compulsory jurisdiction of the ICJ. See comment in Hollis (n. 18), n. 121.

[28] See further pp. 30–31.

[29] 'The fact that the Mandate is described in its last paragraph as a Declaration [*exemplaire* in the French text] is of no legal significance.' *South West Africa Cases (Ethiopia* v. *South Africa; Liberia* v. *South Africa)*, Preliminary Objections, Judgment, ICJ Reports (1962) 319, at 331. See also Judge Ruda in the *WHO Regional Office Advisory Opinion* (n. 25), 122: 'I do not attach legal importance to the description by some of the 1951 Agreement as a "host" or "headquarters" agreement . . . What is important is the content of the treaty and what rights and obligations were assumed by virtue of that instrument.'

[30] *Aegean Sea Continental Shelf* (n. 20), 39, para. 96. The Court goes on to say: 'Accordingly, whether the Brussels Communiqué of 31 May 1975 does or does not constitute such an agreement essentially depends on the nature of the act or transaction to which the Communiqué gives expression; and it does not settle the question simply to refer to the form – a communiqué – in which that act or transaction is embodied.'

In the *Hoshinmaru* case, the International Tribunal for the Law of the Sea (ITLOS) stated that 'the Protocol or minutes of a joint commission such as the Russian-Japanese Commission on Fisheries may well be the source of rights and obligations between Parties', although again in that case the Tribunal decided that they were not.[31] But even if form is not decisive, it may be relevant.[32] In the *Bolivia* v. *Chile* case, the ICJ held that an exchange of notes was not an international agreement partly on the basis that it did not reflect the standard form for such exchanges.[33]

(b) Terminology

Some aspects of terminology, for example the title (as explained above), may not be determinative and indeed may sometimes be discounted. But, more generally, the terminology used in an instrument will be an important, if not decisive, indication as to its binding or non-binding character, or at least of the parties' intentions. The question of what terminology should be used by practitioners to reflect the non-binding nature of an instrument (if that is intended) is discussed further in Chapter 3.[34] The Tribunal in the *South China Sea Arbitration (Jurisdiction)* made a detailed analysis of the terms of the *Declaration on the Conduct of Parties in South China Sea (DOC)*, including the preamble, the signature block, and the use of terms such as 'commitment', 'undertake' and 'agree'.[35] In the *Indian Ocean (Somalia* v. *Kenya)* case, the ICJ noted that 'the inclusion of a provision addressing the entry into force of the MOU is indicative of the instrument's binding character'.[36] In examining the status of various instruments in the *Bolivia* v. *Chile* case, the Court took a close look at the language used in them.[37]

31 *'Hoshinmaru' (Japan* v. *Russian Federation)*, Prompt Release, Judgment, ITLOS Reports 2005–2007, 18, at 46, para. 86.

32 *Newfoundland/Nova Scotia Arbitration* (n. 26), 451, para. 3.18: 'But if questions of form are not decisive they are nonetheless relevant. The absence of a signed document, especially on a matter of importance such as the determination of an international boundary; the use of language which is vague or which does not appear to embody any immediate commitment; a shared understanding between the parties to negotiations that their in principle agreement is to be embodied in some later formal document or is to be subject to some subsequent process of implementation in order to become binding – such factors may together or separately lead to the conclusion that a statement does not constitute a binding agreement under international law.'

33 *Bolivia* v. *Chile* (n. 18), 546, para. 117: 'However, the Notes exchanged between Bolivia and Chile in June 1950 do not contain the same wording nor do they reflect an identical position, in particular with regard to the crucial issue of negotiations concerning Bolivia's sovereign access to the Pacific Ocean. The exchange of Notes cannot therefore be considered an international agreement.'

34 See pp. 46–48.

35 *South China Sea Arbitration* (n. 19), paras. 214–218. The Tribunal concluded, having regard to a range of factors, that the Declaration of Conduct was not a legally binding instrument.

36 *Maritime Delimitation in the Indian Ocean (Somalia* v. *Kenya)*, Preliminary Objections, Judgment, ICJ Reports (2017) 3, at 21, para. 42.

37 For example, *Bolivia* v. *Chile* (n. 18), 550–551, paras. 135 and 138.

(c) Subject matter, terms and context

In the *Bolivia* v. *Chile* case, the ICJ stated:

> for there to be an obligation to negotiate on the basis of an agreement, the terms used by the parties, the subject-matter and the conditions of the negotiations must demonstrate an intention of the parties to be legally bound. This intention, in the absence of express terms indicating the existence of a legal commitment, may be established on the basis of an objective examination of all the evidence.[38]

As has already been noted, the Court in *Qatar* v. *Bahrain*, quoting its judgment in the *Aegean Continental Shelf* case, and the Tribunal in the *South China Sea Arbitration (Jurisdiction)*, said that, above all, one should have regard to the instrument's 'actual terms and to the particular circumstances in which it was drawn up'.[39] In the *Aegean Continental Shelf* case itself, the context was important in determining whether a joint communiqué constituted a binding agreement.[40] The *OAS Guidelines* include 'the circumstances surrounding the agreement's conclusion' as evidence indicative of its status.[41] In the *Bay of Bengal (Bangladesh/Myanmar)* case, the ITLOS emphasised that 'the circumstances' in which the Agreed Minutes were adopted 'do not suggest that they were intended to create legal obligations'.[42]

(d) Intent

The quotation from the *Bolivia* v. *Chile* case in (c) above[43] supports this point, too. And the comments made earlier in respect of the 'intent' test and the 'objective' test apply equally here.[44] The Tribunal in the *Newfoundland/Nova Scotia Arbitration* placed particular emphasis on intention,[45] although this must be read in the context of the Tribunal's reasoning overall, which considered a range of factors. Intention to create legal obligations may, in particular, be regarded as a criterion for determining whether an instrument is 'governed by international law' in accordance with the definition of a treaty in Article 2(1)(a) of the Convention.[46]

(e) Level of negotiator or signatory of instrument; whether agreement is subject to ratification (or not)

The status and authority of the negotiators, or of the signatory of a particular instrument or communication, may be indicative of an intention to create legal

[38] *Bolivia* v. *Chile* (n. 18), 539, para. 91.
[39] *Qatar* v. *Bahrain* (n. 20), 121, para. 23; *Aegean Continental Shelf* (n. 20), 39, para. 96.
[40] *Aegean Continental Shelf* (n. 20), 43, para. 105.
[41] *OAS Guideline* 3.4 (n. 2). See also the Commentary (*Surrounding Circumstances*) on *Guideline* 3.4.
[42] *Delimitation of the Maritime Boundary in the Bay of Bengal (Bangladesh/Myanmar)*, Judgment, ITLOS Reports 2012, 4, at 35, para. 93.
[43] See n. 18. [44] See pp. 19–21. [45] See n. 26. [46] This is discussed further at pp. 28–29.

relations.[47] In the context of deciding whether a state is bound by a particular instrument, courts and tribunals have been influenced by Article 7 of the Vienna Convention (which codifies customary international law), to the effect that:

> by virtue of their functions and without having to produce full powers, Heads of State, Heads of Government and Ministers for Foreign Affairs are considered as representing their State for the purpose of performing all acts relating to the conclusion of a treaty. These State representatives, under international law, may also duly authorize other officials to adopt, on behalf of a State, the text of a treaty or to express the consent of the State to be bound by a treaty.

The fact that the senior representatives mentioned in Article 7[48] do not have to produce full powers does not necessarily mean that they are competent to create binding obligations in each particular case. An agreement, even an informal agreement, may still be subject to some further procedure such as ratification. This will turn on the facts.[49] But a two-step procedure (signature, followed by ratification) will not necessarily be inferred. It is possible for treaties to enter into force upon signature, and the ICJ has been willing to apply that principle to instruments at issue before it, if justified by the evidence.[50] In *Cameroon* v. *Nigeria*, the ICJ rejected Nigeria's argument that its Head of State was not constitutionally competent to bind the government in the particular circumstances of the case.[51] In contrast, in the *Bay of Bengal (Bangladesh/Myanmar)* case, the ITLOS decided that, where the head of the Myanmar delegation was not of the level described in Article 7, there was no evidence of such authority.[52]

(f) Definitive or conditional terms, and clarity

If an instrument lacks definition, or is conditional, or if a party's behaviour lacks clarity or consistency, that might point to an absence of binding obligations. In the *Aegean Continental Shelf* case:

> the information before the Court concerning the negotiations between the experts and the diplomatic exchanges subsequent to the Brussels Communiqué appears to confirm that the two Prime Ministers did not by their 'decision' undertake an unconditional commitment to submit the continental shelf dispute to the Court.[53]

[47] *Newfoundland/Nova Scotia Arbitration* (n. 26), 449, para. 3.19.
[48] On full powers, see pp. 94–95.
[49] *Newfoundland/Nova Scotia Arbitration* (n. 26), 449, para. 3.19.
[50] For a statement of the principle, see *Cameroon* v. *Nigeria* (n. 20), 429, para. 264; *Somalia* v. *Kenya*, Preliminary Objections (n. 36), 22, para. 45.
[51] *Cameroon* v. *Nigeria* (n. 20), 430–431, paras. 265–268.
[52] *Bay of Bengal (Bangladesh/Myanmar)* (n. 42), 36, para. 96.
[53] *Aegean Continental Shelf* (n. 20), 43, para. 106.

In the *Bay of Bengal (Bangladesh/Myanmar)* case, the Tribunal considered that the instrument before it (Agreed Minutes) was a 'conditional understanding' and did not constitute an agreement.[54] The Tribunal in the *Newfoundland/Nova Scotia Arbitration* emphasised the need to establish a 'definitive' agreement, which (inter alia) was 'sufficiently clear, so as to allow the boundary to be determined by a process of legal interpretation of the agreement'.[55] If the language used is vague or broad, or overtly diplomatic rather than legal in character, that will point towards an expression of political will rather than a binding agreement.[56]

(g) Subsequent practice and lack of objections

The subsequent actions of a party, including evidence of acquiescence or the absence of objections, may indicate tacit agreement. In some cases, for example, where the matter concerns the delimitation of a maritime boundary, the threshold will be high. In *Nicaragua* v. *Honduras*, the ICJ stated:

> Evidence of a tacit legal agreement must be compelling. The establishment of a permanent maritime boundary is a matter of grave importance and agreement is not easily to be presumed.[57]

When weighing evidence in favour of a claim of tacit agreement, clarity and consistency are also relevant. In *Somalia* v. *Kenya, Merits*, the ICJ rejected Kenya's claim that Somalia had acquiesced, stating that 'the conduct of Somalia between 1979 and 2014 in relation to its maritime boundary with Kenya, as examined above, in particular its alleged absence of protest against Kenya's claim, does not establish Somalia's clear and consistent acceptance of a maritime boundary'.[58] In *Kasikili/Sedudu Island (Botswana* v. *Namibia)*, subsequent practice was again insufficient to establish evidence of an agreement.[59]

(h) Registration (or non-registration) with the Secretary-General of the United Nations

Article 102 of the UN Charter[60] requires 'every treaty and every international agreement' to be registered with the UN Secretariat and provides in paragraph 2:

[54] *Bay of Bengal (Bangladesh/Myanmar)* (n. 42), 35, para. 92.
[55] *Newfoundland/Nova Scotia Arbitration* (n. 26), 457, para. 3.30.
[56] *Bolivia* v. *Chile* (n. 18), 544–552, paras. 108–139.
[57] *Territorial and Maritime Dispute between Nicaragua and Honduras in the Caribbean Sea (Nicaragua* v. *Honduras)*, Judgment, ICJ Reports (2007) 659, at 735, para. 253. See also *Bay of Bengal (Bangladesh/Myanmar)* (n. 42), 36, para. 95. See also *Delimitation of the Maritime Boundary in the Atlantic Ocean (Ghana/Côte d'Ivoire)*, Judgment, ITLOS Reports 2017, 4, at 70, para. 212.
[58] *Maritime Delimitation in the Indian Ocean (Somalia* v. *Kenya)*, Judgment, 12 October 2021, at para. 80. See also para. 88.
[59] *Kasikili/Sedudu Island (Botswana* v. *Namibia)*, ICJ Reports (1999) 1045, at 1087, para. 63, and 1091, para. 68.
[60] At https://treaties.un.org/doc/publication/ctc/uncharter.pdf; UKTS (1946) No. 67.

> No party to any such treaty or international agreement which has not been registered in accordance with the provisions of paragraph 1 of this Article may invoke that treaty or agreement before any organ of the United Nations.

Article 80 of the Vienna Convention similarly requires that treaties shall, after their entry into force, be transmitted to the Secretariat of the United Nations for registration.[61] Is, therefore, failure to register an instrument determinative of its status as a treaty? The weight of scholarly opinion suggests not.[62] In *Qatar* v. *Bahrain*, the Court considered that 'non-registration or late registration ... does not have any consequence for the actual validity of the agreement, which remains no less binding upon the parties'.[63] Registration or non-registration may, however, be evidence of the parties' intentions towards a particular instrument. In *Somalia* v. *Kenya, Preliminary Objections*, the fact that Kenya had registered an MOU with the UN, and that Somalia had not objected over a five-year period, reinforced the ICJ's view that the MOU was a binding agreement.[64] From the perspective of the UN Secretariat, registration of an instrument submitted by a member state does not imply a judgment by the Secretariat on the nature of the instrument, the status of a party or any similar question. Nor does acceptance by the Secretariat for registration confer on the instrument the status of a treaty or an international agreement if it does not already have that status.[65]

'Concluded between States'

A treaty can be concluded between a state and another subject of international law, in particular an international organisation, or between international organisations.[66] But an agreement between so-called international or multinational companies, or even between a state and such a company, is not a treaty. In 1952, the International Court of Justice in *Anglo-Iranian Oil Company (United Kingdom* v. *Iran)* (Preliminary Objections)[67] held that an oil concession granted by a state to a foreign company was

[61] Article 80(1) VCLT: 'Treaties shall, after their entry into force, be transmitted to the Secretariat of the United Nations for registration or filing and recording, as the case may be, and for publication.'

[62] See Hollis (n. 18), 31–32, particularly references in n. 153; D. N. Hutchinson, 'The Significance of the Registration or Non-Registration of an International Agreement in Determining Whether or Not It Is a Treaty', *Current Legal Problems* 46(2) (1993) 257–290, particularly 265–276.

[63] *Qatar* v. *Bahrain*, Jurisdiction and Admissibility (n. 20), 122, para. 29. The Court added: 'The Court therefore cannot infer from the fact that Qatar did not apply for registration of the 1990 Minutes until six months after they were signed that Qatar considered, in December 1990, that those Minutes did not constitute an international agreement.'

[64] *Somalia* v. *Kenya*, Preliminary Objections (n. 36), 21–23, paras. 42–46.

[65] Note of the Secretariat, 2486 UNTS, p. XXXV.

[66] See Chapter 22.

[67] ICJ Reports (1952) 89, at 112; 19 ILR 507.

not a treaty, because the state of nationality of the company was not party to the concession. Even when, as sometimes happens, an agreement between a state and a company provides that it shall be interpreted in whole or in part by reference to rules of international law, that does *not* make it a treaty.[68] There are, however, a small number of treaties between states to which certain non-state entities can also be parties, but this does not affect their status as treaties.

A treaty does *not* have to be expressed to be between states as such. Since a state is a legal concept, not a natural person, its head of state, its government or some other organ or agency of the state has to act on its behalf. A treaty may, therefore, be expressed to be concluded by heads of state, governments, ministries or other state organs or agencies.[69]

'In Written Form'

The Convention does not apply to oral agreements.[70] But, even though the modern practice is for the original text of a treaty to be typed or printed, there is no reason why a treaty should not be contained in an email or, in practice, be constituted by an exchange of such communications. Provided the text can be reduced to a permanent, readable form (even if this is done by downloading and printing out from a computer), it can be regarded as in written form.[71] The absence of original, signed copies is not a problem, provided there is a means of authenticating the 'signature'.

In September 1998, US President Clinton and Irish Prime Minister Ahern issued, by electronic means, a Communiqué on Electronic Commerce. They did so by each operating a separate computer terminal and using electronic signatures, that is, data in electronic form which is attached to or logically associated with other electronic data and serves as a method of authentication. The 'signature' must therefore be uniquely linked to the signatory, identify them, be created by means under their sole control, and be linked to the data in a way that would reveal if it were to be subsequently changed.[72]

But apart from the Ahern–Clinton example, there is still sparse evidence of state practice of electronic signature of treaties. The Australian Department of Foreign Affairs and Trade website notes that the Australia–Singapore Digital Economy

[68] See C. Greenwood, 'The Libyan Oil Arbitrations', BYIL 53 (1982) 27–81. See pp. 28–29 concerning agreements between states that are governed by domestic law, and treaties that refer to domestic law. See also, on the issue of state contracts, *Dörr and Schmalenbach*, 81–84.

[69] See also n. 5; and pp. 17–18, and p. 51 (inter-institutional agreements).

[70] On oral agreements, see pp. 8–10.

[71] See s. 5(6) of the (UK) Arbitration Act 1996: 36 ILM (1997) 165.

[72] See the Directive on a Community Framework for Electronic Signatures (1999/93/EC), from which the technical details have been taken; s. 7 (UK) Electronic Communications Act 2000 and the Electronic Signatures Regulations 2002 (SI 2002 No. 318). See also pp. 31–32 (unsigned treaties).

Agreement was signed digitally on 6 August 2020.[73] In the periods of COVID-19 restrictions, the United Kingdom modified its practice of requiring authentic texts of bilateral treaties to be signed simultaneously by both parties in the presence of each other. For example, the UK–Australia Free Trade Agreement was signed at a virtual ceremony by the Australian Trade Minister, Dan Tehan, in Adelaide and the UK Secretary of State for International Trade, Anne-Marie Trevelyan, in London.[74] The UK also agreed with a few bilateral partners, where tight deadlines were involved in its exit from the European Union, to exchange, by electronic means, notes notifying completion of procedures (allowing entry into force of the agreement), with hard copies to follow.

'Governed by International Law'

This phrase can be considered as embracing two elements: first, that there should be an *intention to create obligations under international law*; and second, that a treaty should be governed by *international* law as opposed to *domestic* law.

The importance of an intention to create obligations under international law has already been discussed above. By defining a treaty as an agreement governed by international law, the ILC excluded non-legally binding instruments from its draft articles.[75] A non-binding instrument may still often be loosely referred to as an 'agreement' (although this is not advised) if it represents a deal between states or other subjects of international law, even if there is no intention that it should be legally binding.

The use of non-binding instruments has grown in recent years and they are now a significant vehicle for the conduct of business between states. They cover a wide range of subjects and issues of political significance. Conversely, the fact that some treaties, bilateral or multilateral, have little substance, 'hard' obligations or enforcement mechanisms, does not affect their treaty status.[76] Non-binding instruments are, however, not normally subject to a parliamentary process or publication, which means that often they operate in the discreet world of diplomacy rather than in the public eye.[77] They are discussed more fully in Chapter 3.

[73] [2020] ATS 13. See: www.dfat.gov.au/trade/services-and-digital-trade/australia-and-singapore-digital-economy-agreement.

[74] A separate exchange of notes specified that the date of signature of the Agreement in the United Kingdom would be deemed to be 16 December 2021 and in Australia would be deemed to be 17 December 2021. Each side undertook to sign the other participant's original copy of the treaty as soon as possible after these dates.

[75] See S. Rosenne, *Developments in the Law of Treaties 1945–1986* (Cambridge University Press, Cambridge 1989), 104–107.

[76] See K. Raustiala, 'Form and Substance in International Agreements', AJIL 99 (2005) 581–614. Examples would include the International Covenant on Economic, Social and Cultural Rights 1966: 993 UNTS 3 No. 14531; UKTS (1977) No. 6; and the brief treaty at Appendix B.

[77] See H. Hillgenberg, 'A Fresh Look at Soft Law', EJIL 10 (1999) 499–515.

The requirement for a treaty to be 'governed by international law' also distinguishes treaties from agreements between states governed by domestic law.[78] States can contract with each other under domestic law, under which the agreement is more likely to be a contract than a treaty. They may do so if the subject matter is exclusively commercial, such as the purchase of commodities in bulk. The contract may specify that the law of the contract is the law of one of the parties or the law of a third state.

It is possible, however, for an agreement to be principally governed by international law, but for some provisions to be regulated by domestic law,[79] in which case it may be concluded that the agreement is a treaty 'which refers – as a form of *renvoi* – to a national law to regulate some of its provisions'.[80] On the other hand, if, say, a state agrees to take (or grant) a lease of land from another state for an embassy, there will usually be an instrument under domestic law, which in some cases might implement an umbrella undertaking provided for in a treaty.[81] There are examples of loan agreements between states being subject to international law (without any reference to national law)[82] or being subject to a specified national law.[83] A treaty may also be used as an umbrella agreement, governed by international law, for the subsequent award of contracts which would be governed by domestic law.[84]

'Whether Embodied in a Single Instrument or in Two or More Related Instruments'

This phrase recognises that the classic form of a treaty – a single instrument (Appendix B) – has for a long time been joined by treaties drawn in less formal ways, such as exchanges of notes. These play an increasingly important role. An exchange of notes usually consists of an initiating note and a reply note (Appendices E and F). But in 1994, in *Qatar* v. *Bahrain*, the ICJ had to consider the legal effect of a *double* exchange of letters between (1) Qatar and Saudi Arabia, and (2) Bahrain and Saudi Arabia.[85] Having agreed to use its good offices to help to resolve territorial disputes between the other two states, Saudi Arabia sent each of them letters in identical terms proposing certain settlement procedures. Each wrote to Saudi Arabia

78 On the interaction between investment treaties and contractual rights, see C. McLachlan, L. Shore and M. Weiniger, *International Investment Arbitration: Substantive Principles* (2nd ed., Oxford University Press, Oxford 2017), 117–140.

79 See Article 19 Elixir Consortium Agreement 2013: UKTS (2015) No. 23.

80 *Corten and Klein*, 42.

81 See the UK–USSR Agreement concerning the Mutual Provision of Sites 1987: 1655 UNTS 413 No. 28490; UKTS (1987) No. 42; and the UK–Russia Exchange of Notes concerning the Commercialisation of Sites 2004: 2309 UNTS 239 No. 41169; UKTS (2005) No. 3.

82 See the Denmark-India Agreement on a Danish Government Loan to India 1986: 1456 UNTS 195 No. 24633.

83 See the examples cited in *Dörr and Schmalenbach*, 38.

84 See the UK–Ukraine Framework Agreement on Official Credit Support 2021: UK Country Series, Ukraine (2021) No. 1, where, according to the Explanatory Memorandum presented to the UK Parliament, Ukraine required such an international law agreement in order to meet the requirements of its procurement law (Command Paper No. CP 553).

85 *Qatar* v. *Bahrain* (n. 20) 112, para. 17.

accepting the proposal. Saudi Arabia then announced that the two states had agreed to go to the ICJ. This complicated scheme was necessary because of political sensitivities, and the text of each letter and of the announcement had been agreed in advance with Saudi Arabia by Qatar and Bahrain; and, thus, although three states were involved, there were in fact only two parties: Qatar and Bahrain.

Although the form of a double exchange was unusual, there are examples of treaties being constituted by two or more principal instruments (important treaties may have several subsidiary instruments). The so-called Algiers Accords 1981[86] constituted treaty arrangements for dealing with claims between Iran and the United States, including the Iran-US Claims Tribunal, and were established by: (1) two Declarations by Algeria – a General Declaration and a Declaration concerning the Settlement of Claims – setting out the formal commitments that had been made to it (as a go-between) by Iran and the United States, and Undertakings by the two states, which together constituted a treaty; and (2) an Escrow Agreement between the United States, the Federal Reserve Bank of New York, Bank Markazi, Iran and the Central Bank of Algeria, acting as escrow agent.

A treaty that is part bilateral and part multilateral can be constituted by a series of parallel exchanges of notes, all identical in substance, between one state and a number of states (A–B; A–C; A–D, etc.).[87] In such a case, it is important to make clear in the notes who are the parties. In an exchange between, say, four states there could be *four* parties (A, B, C and D), or *two* parties (A and B + C and D).[88] When there are only two parties it may also be necessary to make clear whether the treaty can be terminated by one of the parties only, or whether one of the states constituting the (collective) party can, by withdrawing from the treaty, bring about its termination.

An exchange of notes on the interpretation of a treaty may be subsidiary to it and concluded at the same time. It does not itself have to be a treaty, though sometimes it is.[89]

The drafting of (normal) exchanges of notes is discussed in Chapter 23.

'Whatever Its Particular Designation'

As noted above,[90] the designation (title) of an instrument is not determinative of its status either as a treaty or as a non-legally binding instrument, although it is often indicative of what the parties or participants intend.

86 20 ILM (1981) 223; 75 AJIL (1981) 418; 62 ILR 595.

87 See the six parallel Exchanges of Notes between Germany and Belgium, Canada, France and others concerning (1) the Status of their Forces and (2) the Convention on the Presence of Foreign Forces 1990: 30 ILM (1991) 415 and 417; *McNair*, 29–30.

88 See the two Memorandums of Understanding on the Avoidance of Overlaps etc. relating to Deep Seabed Areas of 1991: UKTS (1991) No. 52, and UKTS (1995) No. 4.

89 See, e.g., the Australia–UK Exchange of Notes concerning the Double Taxation Convention 2003: 2258 UNTS 119 No. 40224; UKTS (2004) No. 5.

90 See pp. 21–22.

One of the most mystifying aspects of treaty practice is the unsystematic way in which treaties are designated (named). Writers have sought to explain – sometimes at great length and unconvincingly – why certain names are given to particular categories of treaty. That task has become even more difficult today, the names chosen being even more confusing, inconsistent and changeable than in the past. It is often more a matter of the practice of international organisations or groups of states, or political preference, which determines how a treaty is named.

Sometimes a multilateral treaty is called an 'international convention', though that is tautological. In fact, many other names are also problematic. Both the UN Charter 1945[91] and the Charter of the Commonwealth of Independent States 1993[92] are treaties, but the Organization for Security and Co-operation in Europe (OSCE) Charter of Paris 1990,[93] the Russia–United States Charter of Partnership and Friendship 1992[94] and the OSCE Charter for European Security 1999[95] are, despite their grand-sounding names, all non-binding instruments.

A Treaty Does *Not* Have to Be Signed

There are other matters which the Convention does not deal with, at least explicitly. For example, the Convention's definition of treaty is notable in that it makes no mention of signature; and it is apparent from other provisions, such as Articles 12 and 13, that signature is *not* a necessary requirement for a treaty. For example, a treaty can be constituted by an exchange of *third-person* diplomatic notes, which, according to long-standing diplomatic practice, are initialled but not signed, and which are usually expressed to be between, say, the foreign ministry (or one of its departments) and a foreign embassy, not between individuals.[96]

Indeed, there can be circumstances when the use of an unsigned (or even an uninitialled) instrument is preferable for political reasons. The Decision of the Heads of State and Government, adopted at a meeting of the European Council at the Edinburgh Summit on 12 December 1992, concerning certain problems raised by Denmark about the Treaty on European Union (Maastricht Treaty) is not in customary treaty form, but is regarded by the member states as a treaty, and has been registered and published as such.[97] Given the particular circumstances, some of the less confident leaders were reluctant to be seen signing it. They were skilfully advised that signature was not necessary.

[91] At https://treaties.un.org/doc/publication/ctc/uncharter.pdf; UKTS (1946) No. 67.

[92] 34 ILM (1995) 1279. [93] Charter of Paris for a New Europe: 30 ILM (1991) 193.

[94] 31 ILM (1992) 782. [95] 39 ILM (2000) 255.

[96] See the UK–China Exchange of Notes concerning the Establishment of a Consulate-General at Guangzhou and Edinburgh 1996: 1957 UNTS 234 No. 33507; UKTS (1996) No. 100. See p. 36, and Appendix F.

[97] 1765 UNTS 98 No. 30685; UKTS (1994) No. 2. It might also be seen as an agreement made in connection with the conclusion of a treaty: Article 31(2)(a).

A more routine example is to be found in the – rather unusual – practice of the Food and Agriculture Organization (FAO). Treaties adopted by the FAO Conference are not signed, but are subject to *acceptance* by member states, which is equivalent to ratification.[98] Similarly, the Refugees Protocol 1967[99] could not be signed, only acceded (or succeeded) to, even though the Refugees Convention 1951,[100] which it supplements, could be signed. There are also examples of states concluding treaties by means of resolutions. The treaty establishing the Preparatory Commission of the Comprehensive Nuclear Test-Ban Treaty 1996 (CTBT)[101] was effected by a resolution of states that had signed the CTBT.[102]

Unilateral Declarations

Although unilateral declarations are not considered to be treaties as a matter of theoretical analysis,[103] they can be a source of binding obligations upon states, and their underlying principles are sufficiently similar to some aspects of treaty law to make further explanation of them here worthwhile. The analysis in this section relates to unilateral declarations as a separate source of binding obligation rather than as a declaration (such as an interpretative declaration or form of reservation) made in the context of conclusion of a treaty. The latter is discussed further in Chapter 8.[104]

The *Guiding Principles* adopted by the ILC in 2006[105] probably represents the best summary of the law relating to unilateral declarations.[106] Discussion of the legal effects of unilateral declarations is not, however, a recent phenomenon. In Brierly's *First Report on the Law of Treaties* in 1950, he noted that there was a 'considerable division of opinion as to the extent to which international legal rights arising other than *ex delicto* can be created by a truly unilateral act'. He commented that, if the rationale for unilateral acts being binding rested on the presumed consent of the beneficiary, they might fall within the definition of a treaty. But if not, the 'confinement in the present draft of "treaties" to "agreements" [served] sufficiently to exclude unilateral declarations'.[107]

The most influential cases concerning unilateral declarations in the former sense are the *Nuclear Tests* cases – *Australia* v. *France* and *New Zealand* v. *France* – before

[98] See, e.g., the so-called Compliance Agreement 1993, Article X: 2221 UNTS 120 No. 39486; 33 ILM (1994) 968. See also the General Convention on Privileges and Immunities of the UN, Final Article, s. 31 (1 UNTS 15 No. 4; UKTS (1950) No. 10). On acceptance, see pp. 120–121.

[99] 606 UNTS 267 No. 8791; UKTS (1969) No. 15.

[100] 189 UNTS 137 No. 2545; UKTS (1954) No. 39.

[101] UKTS (1999) No. 46.

[102] 35 ILM (1996) 1439.

[103] See the passage from the *Nuclear Tests* cases quoted in the following paragraph.

[104] See pp. 134–141.

[105] *Guiding Principles applicable to unilateral declarations of States capable of creating legal obligations, with commentaries thereto* (2006) 58th Session, UN Doc. A/61/10 (in this chapter referred to as the *Guiding Principles*).

[106] See also *Oppenheim*, 1188–1193, para. 577, which has many good examples.

[107] J. L. Brierly, First Report on the Law of Treaties, YBILC II (1950) 222–248, 227, para. 20.

the ICJ in 1974.[108] It is worth quoting in full a key paragraph in each of the judgments:[109]

> It is well recognized that declarations made by way of unilateral acts, concerning legal or factual situations, may have the effect of creating legal obligations. Declarations of this kind may be, and often are, very specific. When it is the intention of the State making the declaration that it should become bound according to its terms, that intention confers on the declaration the character of a legal undertaking, the State being thenceforth legally required to follow a course of conduct consistent with the declaration. An undertaking of this kind, if given publicly, and with an intent to be bound, even though not made within the context of international negotiations, is binding. In these circumstances, nothing in the nature of a *quid pro quo*, nor any subsequent acceptance of the declaration, nor even any reply or reaction from other States, is required for the declaration to take effect, since such a requirement would be inconsistent with the strictly unilateral nature of the juridical act by which the pronouncement by the State was made.

The Court went on to say that not all unilateral acts imply obligation; but a state may choose to take up a certain position in relation to a particular matter with the intention of being bound – the intention is to be ascertained by interpretation of the act.[110] As to the question of form, there were no strict or special requirements. It made no essential difference whether a statement was made orally or in writing.[111] Good faith and the principle of *pacta sunt servanda* applied equally to unilateral declarations as they did to treaties.[112]

The *Guiding Principles*, in their preamble, acknowledge that:

> it is often difficult to establish whether the legal effects stemming from the unilateral behaviour of a State are the consequence of the intent that it has expressed or depend on the expectations that its conduct has raised among other subjects of international law.

In other words, it is not always clear how much the legal effect of a unilateral declaration depends on the intention of the formulating state, or arises more from the principle of estoppel.[113] The passage quoted above from the *Nuclear Tests* cases emphasises intention. In the *Bolivia* v. *Chile* case, the Court observed that 'there is no evidence of an intention on the part of Chile to assume an obligation to negotiate'. It therefore concluded that an obligation to negotiate Bolivia's sovereign

[108] *Nuclear Tests (Australia* v. *France)*, Judgment, ICJ Reports (1974) 253; *Nuclear Tests (New Zealand* v. *France)*, Judgment, ICJ Reports (1974) 457.

[109] Para. 43 of *Australia* v. *France*, and para. 46 of *New Zealand* v. *France*.

[110] Para. 44 of *Australia* v. *France*, and para. 47 of *New Zealand* v. *France*.

[111] Para. 45 of *Australia* v. *France*, and para. 48 of *New Zealand* v. *France*.

[112] Para. 46 of *Australia* v. *France*, and para. 49 of *New Zealand* v. *France*.

[113] *OAS Guidelines*, 39 (n. 2).

access to the sea could not rest on any of Chile's unilateral acts referred to by Bolivia.[114]

To determine the legal effects of such declarations, it is necessary to take account of their content, all the factual circumstances in which they were made and the reactions to which they gave rise.[115] A unilateral declaration binds the state internationally only if it is made by an authority vested with the power to do so.[116] It may be addressed to the international community as a whole, to one or several states or to other entities.[117] It entails obligations for the formulating state only if this is stated in clear and specific terms. In the case of doubt as to the scope of the obligations resulting from such a declaration, such obligations must be interpreted in a restrictive manner.[118]

Memorandum of Understanding

One must be extremely careful in assessing the status of any instrument called a 'Memorandum of Understanding' (often referred to as an 'MOU'). In the past, the term has been used generically to describe a non-legally binding instrument. But there are now a number of instances of 'Memorandum of Understanding' being used by states as a title of binding treaties, or of instruments which appear to have binding intent,[119] even if their status is not entirely clear. Only by studying carefully all the terms of such an instrument can one – usually – determine its status. This edition of the book, therefore, uses 'non-legally binding instrument' or 'non-binding instrument' as the generic terms for such instruments and reserves 'memorandum of understanding' for a specific instrument bearing that title.[120]

The practice of designating a treaty as a memorandum of understanding appears to have started in a small way after the Second World War, three being concluded in the 1950s in connection with the Treaty of Peace with Italy.[121] The reason may have been

[114] *Bolivia* v. *Chile* (n. 18), 554–555, paras. 145–148, at para. 148.

[115] *Guiding Principle* 3. See also *Bolivia* v. *Chile* (n. 18), at para. 147, after citing the *Nuclear Tests* cases: 'The Court also asserted that, in order to determine the legal effect of a statement by a person representing the State, one must "examine its actual content as well as the circumstances in which it was made"' (*Armed Activities on the Territory of the Congo (New Application: 2002) (Democratic Republic of the Congo* v. *Rwanda)* (Jurisdiction and Admissibility), Judgment, ICJ Reports 2006, 28, para. 49).

[116] See *Guiding Principle* 4. [117] *Guiding Principle* 6.

[118] *Guiding Principle* 7. It goes on to say: 'In interpreting the content of such obligations, weight shall be given first and foremost to the text of the declaration, together with the context and the circumstances in which it was formulated.'

[119] For examples of MOUs which have been registered with the UN Secretariat and published in the UN Treaty Series, and which appear to have binding intent, see the Turkey–Korea MOU on Cooperation in the Fields of Cultural Heritage 2013: 3000 UNTS 107 No. 52162; and the South Africa–Singapore MOU 2005: 2520 UNTS 131 No. 45033.

[120] This section, therefore, gives a short résumé only of the use of the title 'Memorandum of Understanding' in specific instruments. For a discussion of non-binding instruments more generally, see Chapter 3.

[121] MOU Regarding German Assets in Italy 1947: 138 UNTS 111 (No. 1863); UKTS (1947) No. 75; for other related agreements, see: 258 UNTS 372 No. 3679; UKTS (1956) No. 52; and 283 UNTS 138 No. 4113; UKTS (1957) No. 51. See also the MOU relating to the Western Sectors of Berlin 1949: 42 UNTS 356 No. 296.

a desire, perhaps for political reasons, for a less formal appearance. More recent examples of treaties designated as memorandums of understanding are the MOU relating to the Implementation of the Guidelines for Transfers of Nuclear-Related Dual-Use Equipment 1992;[122] the (two) MOUs of 1991 on the Avoidance of Overlaps and Conflicts relating to Deep Sea-Bed Areas;[123] the MOU concerning the establishment of the Inter-Organisation Programme for the Sound Management of Chemicals 1995;[124] and the Memorandum concerning Conservation Measures for Marine Turtles off the Atlantic Coast of Africa 1999.[125] An even more misleading name for a treaty is the Provisional Understanding regarding Deep Seabed Matters of 1984.[126] On the other hand, the MOU on Port State Control of 1982 is unquestionably a non-binding instrument.[127]

The United States has concluded many bilateral treaties called memorandums of understanding,[128] as have the European Union and United Nations; for example, in the case of the latter, the (ill-fated) UN–Iraq Memorandum of Understanding 1998 concerning weapons inspections.[129]

The reasons why states (or international organisations) choose to adopt non-legally binding instruments in certain cases is explored further in Chapter 3. As for why states (or international organisations) choose to designate a treaty as a 'Memorandum of Understanding', this is more likely to happen when the subject matter concerns practical cooperation between specific government departments, technical matters, a specific project, or a framework for further cooperation. Occasionally, a state (or an international organisation) will be asked by another state (and may even agree) to call a treaty a 'Memorandum of Understanding', so that the requesting state can avoid the heavier constitutional requirements which other agreements might require before entry into force. Many states, however, like the United Kingdom, avoid using 'Memorandum of Understanding' for any binding instrument, so as not to confuse their practice of using that title for non-binding instruments.

Since an instrument called a Memorandum of Understanding may be a treaty or a non-binding instrument, occasionally it will make its status clear by a specific provision, for example that it shall be legally binding on the parties or (more usually) non-legally binding for the participants, as the case may be.[130]

122 31 ILM (1992) 1094. 123 See n. 88. 124 34 ILM (1995) 1311.

125 39 ILM (2000) 1. It should also be noted that it is expressed to be 'an agreement' under Article IV(4) Bonn Convention on the Conservation of Migratory Species of Wild Animals 1979: 19 ILM (1980) 15; UKTS (1990) No. 87.

126 1409 UNTS 464 No. 23601; 23 ILM (1984) 1354; UKTS (1985) No. 24. 127 21 ILM (1982) 1.

128 See, e.g., the US–Korea MOU on Communications Security Equipment 1993: 1751 UNTS 201 No. 30579; and the Brazil-US Embassy MOU 1993: 1905 UNTS 95 No. 32475.

129 2005 UNTS 209 No. 34375; 37 ILM (1998) 501. See also the UN–Iraq Memorandum of Understanding on implementation of Security Council resolution 986 (1995), 20 May 1996 (1926 UNTS 9 No. 32851; 35 ILM (1996) 1097).

130 See Article 8(6) MOU between the EC and the National Tourism Administration of China 2004 (OJ L 83/14, 20.03.2004).

Exchange of Notes

The name 'exchanges of notes' poses the same issue as the name 'Memorandum of Understanding': these exchanges may constitute either a treaty or a non-binding instrument. Many such exchanges are concluded each year. If the exchange is intended to be a treaty, it is customary to provide expressly that it '*shall constitute an agreement* between our two Governments' (see Appendix E). If intended to be a non-binding instrument, it is usual to specify that the exchange '*records the understanding* of our two Governments', or to use a similar formula (see Appendix G). Although exchanges of notes tend not to be on matters of major political importance, or only supplementary to a treaty, a few have been substantial. The United Kingdom–United States Lend-Lease Agreements 1940–1941, under which the former was lent sixty badly needed destroyers in return for leases of bases, were constituted by exchanges of notes.[131]

An exchange of *notes* can either be (a) in the form of a first person note from a Foreign Minister (or other relevant Minister) to an Ambassador, or from an Ambassador to a Minister, on behalf of their government, to which the other replies (see Appendix E);[132] or more usually (b) in the form of a third person note issued from the Foreign Ministry to the Embassy of another state in the relevant capital, or from the Embassy to the Foreign Ministry, on behalf of their government, to which the other replies (see Appendix F).[133] An exchange of *letters* would issue in the first person from a Foreign Minister (or other relevant Minister) to an Ambassador, or from an Ambassador to a Minister, on behalf of their government, to which the other replies.[134] There are variations in practice, particularly in respect of an exchange of notes. There are, for example, cases of notes being drafted in the third person in the name of the Embassy or Foreign Ministry but signed by a named individual (normally a Minister or Ambassador).[135]

Guidance on drafting both types of exchange of notes (and exchange of letters) can be found in Chapter 23.[136] In UK practice, exchanges of notes are far more common than exchanges of letters, but both types of exchange, if drafted in proper legally binding form, would have the same legal effect.

Protocol

Although some stand-alone treaties have been called protocols, nowadays that name is generally used for (a) supplementary treaties (such as an optional protocol on dispute settlement – see below); or (b) amending treaties; or (c) legally binding

[131] 203 LNTS 201; 204 LNTS 15; UKTS (1940) No. 21 and (1941) No. 2.

[132] See the UK–Uruguay Exchange of Notes concerning the transfer of the Hut Located in Hope Bay 1997: at Appendix E or 2038 UNTS 263 No. 35251; UKTS (1998) No. 16; UK–Morocco Exchange of Notes in respect of Protocol 4 of the Association Agreement 2019: UK Country Series, Morocco (2020) No. 1.

[133] See the UK–Denmark Exchange of Notes concerning the UK's Exclusive Economic Zone 2009: at Appendix F or UKTS (2010) No. 1.

[134] See the UK–Ireland Exchange of Letters concerning Common Exemptions 2011: UKTS (2011) No. 40.

[135] See the Spain–Panama Exchange of Notes on mutual recognition etc. of national driving licenses, 2012 and 2014: 2995 UNTS 175 No. 52024.

[136] See pp. 440–444.

instruments on a discrete (but often important) subject that are annexed to a treaty and are an integral part of it.[137] However, the word 'Protocol' is also used in the practice of some states to record the outcome of a particular meeting or round of negotiations, where its precise legal effect may be unclear.[138] The word should therefore be used (and read) with care.

Optional Protocol

This name is used for a treaty that is closely associated with another principal treaty, sometimes (though not necessarily) adopted at the same time. The term 'optional' is used to indicate that a party to the main treaty does not have to become a party to the Protocol. In the case of older treaties, issues covered include, for example, nationality or settlement of disputes under the main treaty.[139] More recent examples relate to fields such as human rights, where an Optional Protocol may deal with either procedural or substantive issues.[140]

Less Usual Treaty Names

Treaties have always been given a variety of names, including less usual ones like covenant,[141] administrative agreement,[142] concordat,[143] agreed minute,[144] terms of reference,[145] declaration,[146] and our old friend, memorandum of understanding.

[137] See Article I.3 Treaty on Conventional Armed Forces in Europe (CFE) 1990: 30 ILM (1991) 1; UKTS (1993) No. 44.

[138] The so-called 'Minsk-1 Agreement', whereby a ceasefire in Ukraine was agreed on 5 September 2014 by a Trilateral Contact Group, was entitled 'Protocol on the results of consultations of the Trilateral Contact Group', at: www.osce.org/ru/home/123258.

[139] See the Optional Protocol to the Vienna Convention on Diplomatic Relations (VCDR), concerning Acquisition of Nationality 1961 (500 UNTS 223 No. 7311) and the Optional Protocol to the VCDR, concerning the Compulsory Settlement of Disputes 1961 (500 UNTS 241 No. 7312; UKTS (1965) No. 19).

[140] See the First Optional Protocol to the International Covenant on Civil and Political Rights (ICCPR) 1966 (999 UNTS 302 No. 14668; 6 ILM (1967) 368; UKTS (1977) No. 6), establishing an individual complaint mechanism; the Second Optional Protocol to the ICCPR 1989 (1642 UNTS 414 No. 14668), aiming at the abolition of the death penalty; and the Optional Protocol to the Torture Convention 2002 (2375 UNTS 237 No. 24841), establishing the Subcommittee on Prevention of Torture and other Cruel, Inhuman or Degrading Treatment or Punishment.

[141] See the ICCPR 1966 (999 UNTS 171 No. 14668).

[142] See the Administrative Agreement to Supplement the NATO Status of Forces Agreement 1993: UKTS (1999) No. 5.

[143] This appears to be reserved for agreements concluded by the Holy See, e.g., the Concordat between Spain and the Holy See 1953 (1219 UNTS 49 No. 19671). See J. Klabbers, *The Concept of Treaty in International Law* (Kluwer Law International Law, The Hague 1996), 42–44.

[144] See the Canada–EC Agreed Minute concerning International Humane Trapping Standards 1997 (2761 UNTS 33 No. 48681).

[145] See the Terms of Reference of the International Nickel Study Group 1985 (1566 UNTS 29 No. 27296).

[146] See the Maroua Declaration between Cameroon and Nigeria, 1 June 1975 (1237 UNTS 320 No. 19976) and *Cameroon* v. *Nigeria* (n. 20), 429–431, paras. 262–268. For Political Declarations, see pp. 138–139.

A 1992 treaty between Lithuania and Russia on the withdrawal of Russian forces from Lithuania was concluded with the name 'timetable', its substance consisting only of detailed tables of military assets. The document was originally annexed to a treaty on the same subject. There was a political problem over signature of the treaty, but, since it was important that the withdrawal should proceed on a proper basis, the Lithuania–Russia Timetable alone was signed, and later registered as a treaty with the United Nations.[147] A supplementary treaty to the CTBT, adopted by a resolution of the signatory states, is called simply 'text'.[148]

If one encounters an instrument with a less usual name, for example a 'solemn declaration',[149] 'compact'[150] or 'platform',[151] all the relevant aspects should be examined carefully before drawing conclusions about its status. The China–United Kingdom Joint Declaration on the question of Hong Kong of 1984 is clearly a treaty, and was registered as such with the United Nations by both parties.[152] The title was chosen for political reasons.

In the distant past, a 'Final Act' occasionally constituted a treaty,[153] but this is no longer so.

Colloquial Names

The Chicago Convention 1944 is more correctly called the Convention on International Civil Aviation, but, since it was adopted in Chicago, it is usually referred

147 1690 UNTS 395 No. 29146. Sadly, the name was changed on registration to 'Agreement between the Republic of Lithuania and the Russian Federation on the Rules of Conduct and Functioning of Units, Subunits and Servicemen of the Armed Forces of the Russian Federation being withdrawn from the Republic of Lithuania'.

148 The full title is Text on the Establishment of a Preparatory Commission for the Comprehensive Nuclear Test-Ban Treaty Organization 1996: UKTS (1999) No. 46. For an argument that it is not a treaty, see M. Asada, 'CTBT: Legal Questions Arising From its Non-Entry-Into-Force', *Journal of Conflict and Security Law* 1 (2002) 85–122, 105–113.

149 Normally made by Heads of State or Government at a summit meeting. See the Solemn Declaration on European Union signed by EC Heads of State etc. at Stuttgart on 19 June 1983 (European Bulletin 6/1983, 24); and the Solemn Declarations made by the Sovereigns/Heads of State or Government of OPEC Member Countries at Algiers, 4–6 March 1975, at Caracas, 27–28 September 2000 and at Riyadh, 17–18 November 2007: www.opec.org/opec_web/static_files_project/media/downloads/publications/Solemn_Declaration_I-III.pdf.

150 See the Global Compact for Safe, Orderly and Regular Migration, adopted by Resolution of the General Assembly on 19 December 2018: UN Doc. A/RES/73/195; and the Global Compact on Refugees, Report of the UN High Commissioner for Refugees (13 September 2018), UN Doc. A/RES/73/12 (Part II), adopted by the General Assembly on 17 December 2018: UN Doc. A/RES/73/151.

151 See what is often called the 'Durban Platform for Enhanced Action', or more fully, UNFCCC Decision 1/CP.17, Establishment of an Ad Hoc Working Group on the Durban Platform for Enhanced Action, 11 December 2011, UN Doc. FCCC/CP/2011/9/Add.1; and the analysis (including discussion of legal form) in L. Rajamani, 'The Durban Platform for Enhanced Action and the Future of the Climate Regime', ICLQ 61 (2012) 501–518.

152 1399 UNTS 33 No. 23391; 23 ILM (1984) 1366; UKTS (1985) No. 26.

153 See AJIL Supp. 29 (1935) 719–720. On present usage of 'Final Act', see p. 105.

to as the Chicago Convention.[154] Sometimes a treaty that is adopted in one state but signed in another will be known – at least colloquially – by the name of the place where it was adopted. The Dayton Agreement 1995 (the General Framework Agreement for Peace in Bosnia and Herzegovina) is generally, and most conveniently, referred to after the place where it was adopted, though it was signed in Paris.[155] The Landmines Convention 1997 is sometimes also known as the Ottawa Convention, since it was conceived and opened for signature there, although adopted in Oslo.[156] The Locarno Pact 1925[157] was negotiated at Locarno, but signed in a room in the Foreign Office in London, which has been known ever since as the Locarno Room.

There are other examples.[158] And the media has much to answer for. A treaty is now very rarely called a 'pact',[159] but sub-editors regularly use this word as convenient shorthand, especially in headlines. The 'Locarno Pact' was a series of treaties. The famous 'Kellogg–Briand Pact' 1928 was, in fact, the General Treaty for the Renunciation of War.[160]

Unless it is clear from the context which treaty is being referred to, one should avoid shorthand terms such as the 'Hague', 'Geneva' or 'Vienna' Convention, since many treaties adopted in those cities have titles starting with the name of the city.

Pactum de contrahendo

Latin phrases should always be approached with caution: they can conceal more than they reveal. This is especially so with *pactum de contrahendo*, the exact meaning of which is uncertain.[161] The most usual meaning of the term is an agreement between parties creating a binding obligation to conclude a future agreement on a particular subject.[162] But it has also been used to refer to an agreement to include certain clauses in future agreements between the same parties; and an agreement to become party to a treaty that has already been concluded, such as the celebrated undertaking by Poland in the Treaty of Versailles to accede to the Berne Convention on Railway Transport.[163] Even if the parties to a *pactum de contrahendo* are left to work out the concrete details of the final agreement, they are under an obligation to pursue that agreement in good faith. If a party should subsequently refuse to make an agreement

[154] Convention on International Civil Aviation (Chicago Convention 1944: 15 UNTS 295 No. 102; UKTS (1953) No. 8.

[155] 35 ILM (1996) 75. [156] 2056 UNTS 241 No. 35597; 36 ILM (1997) 1509; UKTS (1999) No. 18.

[157] The main instrument was the Treaty of Mutual Guarantee between Belgium, France, Germany, Great Britain and Italy: 54 LNTS 305. This, together with the other treaties, was initialled at Locarno on 16 October 1925 and signed at London on 1 December 1925.

[158] See the letters page of *The Times*, 14 December 1995.

[159] For past use of the term, see AJIL Supp. 29 (1935) 721. [160] 94 LNTS 57; UKTS (1929) No. 29.

[161] *McNair*, 27–29; *Oppenheim*, 1224–1225, para. 599; *O'Connell*, 202; A. Lester, 'Bizerta and the Unequal Treaty Theory', ICLQ 11 (1962) 847–855, 849.

[162] See H. Owada, 'Pactum de contrahendo, pactum de negotiando', *MPEPIL* (2008), para. 3.

[163] *McNair*, 29, n. 1.

or unreasonably delay its conclusion, this could violate the *pactum* and constitute a breach of international law.[164]

The *pactum de contrahendo* can be distinguished from an agreement to negotiate a treaty (*pactum de negotiando*), which does not go as far as to commit the parties to concluding a final agreement,[165] although the parties must still act in good faith.[166] Under Article VI of the Nuclear Non-Proliferation Treaty (NPT) 1968[167] each party:

> undertakes to pursue negotiations in good faith on effective measures relating to cessation of the nuclear arms race at an early date and to nuclear disarmament, and on a treaty on general and complete disarmament under strict and effective international control.

The extent of the legal obligation arising from a *pactum de contrahendo* or *pactum de negotiando* depends largely on the intention of the parties as determined by the specificity of their commitment and the interpretation to be placed on the language used.[168]

Modus vivendi

This term was used mostly in relation to agreements concerning fisheries, maritime boundaries or commercial relations at the end of the nineteenth and the first half of the twentieth century.[169] The term has fallen out of use as a title to a treaty and is now used more to describe a treaty that is intended to be temporary, or for non-binding arrangements, particularly on fisheries matters. More common titles for instruments determining fisheries arrangements of short duration are now, for example, interim agreement,[170] subsidiary agreement[171] or agreed record of consultations.[172]

[164] Owada (n. 162), para. 4.

[165] See H. Thirlway, 'The Law and Procedure of the International Court of Justice', BYIL 63 (1992) 1–96, 3–10, and *Railway Traffic between Lithuania and Poland*, PCIJ Reports (1931), Series A/B. No. 42, 109; 6 AD 403.

[166] See also the commitment to negotiate a future relationship in the Political Declaration made by the European Union and the United Kingdom in parallel to the Withdrawal Agreement: see p. 139.

[167] 729 UNTS 161 No. 10485; 7 ILM (1968) 809; UKTS (1970) No. 88; TIAS 6839. See also Part I(1) of the Quadripartite Agreement 1971 (880 UNTS 124 No. 12621; 10 ILM (1971) 895; UKTS (1972) No. 111); and R. R. Churchill and A. V. Lowe, *The Law of the Sea* (3rd ed., Manchester University Press, Manchester 1999), 442.

[168] Owada (n. 162), para. 7. See also the cases cited within this article.

[169] See W. Burek, 'Modus Vivendi', *MPEPIL* (2019). One of the more recent examples, concerning commercial relations, is the Modus Vivendi relating to the Application of Most-Favoured-Nation Treatment between the Belgo-Luxembourg Economic Union and Turkey 1947 (37 UNTS 223 No. 579).

[170] See the Iceland–UK Exchange of Notes constituting an Interim Agreement regarding the Fisheries Dispute 1973 (900 UNTS 94 No. 12886; UKTS (1973) No. 122), and *Fisheries Jurisdiction (United Kingdom v. Iceland)* (Merits), ICJ Reports (1974) 3, at 17–20, paras. 35–41; 55 ILR 238. See also AJIL Supp. 29 (1935) 717.

[171] See the Australia-Japan Subsidiary Agreement concerning Japanese Tuna Long-Line Fishing 1997 (2007 UNTS 43 No. 34448).

[172] See the Agreed Record of Fisheries Consultations between UK and Norway for 2022, 21 December 2021: https://assets.publishing.service.gov.uk/government/uploads/system/uploads/attachment_data/file/1043183/uk-norway-bilateral-fisheries-agreed-record-21122021.pdf.

3

Non-legally Binding Instruments

> Open covenants of peace, openly arrived at, after that there shall be no private international understandings of any kind, but diplomacy shall proceed always frankly and in the public view.[1]

Since 1919, when US President Woodrow Wilson issued this sincere but rather unworldly appeal, diplomacy has continued to develop many new ways of doing business. Even when the subject matter is proper and lawful, diplomats know that it is not possible for all international deals to be embodied in treaties, whether they are on trivial or important matters. Yet the deal needs to be formalised on paper in some way. Hence, the relentless rise of what might be termed 'non-binding instruments' which, although concluded between states, are *not* legally binding.

Such non-legally binding instruments have been variously described as 'political agreements', 'political commitments', 'gentlemen's agreements', 'non-legally binding agreements', 'non-binding agreements', 'de facto agreements', 'non-legal agreements', and so on. Diplomats – who are well aware of such instruments – often refer to them, and not only in English, simply as 'memorandums of understanding' or 'MOUs'. But calling an instrument a memorandum of understanding does not, in itself, determine its status, since – most confusingly – some treaties are also called 'memorandum of understanding'.[2] To avoid confusion, this edition has adopted 'non-binding instrument' as the generic term for such instruments in preference to 'Memorandum of Understanding' or 'MOU'.

Non-binding instruments operate as *political* commitments, and are to be distinguished from treaties because they are *not* agreements governed by international law. A non-binding instrument may, however, still loosely be referred to as an 'agreement' (though this is not advised), as it represents a deal between states, albeit one not legally binding in international law. And sometimes (as with 'memorandum of understanding') it may feature in its title words such as 'declaration', 'protocol', 'agreed minute' or 'side letter', which could equally be used for a binding instrument and which do not make its intended status entirely clear.[3]

1 G. A. Finch, 'The Peace Conference of Paris, 1919', quoting Woodrow Wilson, AJIL 13(2) (1919) 159–186, 161.

2 See Chapter 2, pp. 34–35.

3 See Chapter 2, pp. 19–21 on the definition of a treaty.

The extent to which non-binding instruments are a significant vehicle for the conduct of business between states (or between states and international organisations) has until relatively recently not been well known outside government circles.[4] In fact, a large number of such instruments are concluded every year covering a wide range of subjects, though many are never published.[5] It is fair to say that, as the usage of non-binding instruments has grown, so also has concern about divergent practice and the potential for misunderstanding between participants about their status or effect. This has led to helpful initiatives, for example, in the Organization of American States (OAS) and in the Council of Europe[6] to discuss current practice and agree a common approach. The Guidelines of the Inter-American Juridical Committee on Binding and Non-Binding Agreements, together with the Final Report and Commentary,[7] drawn up under the auspices of the OAS, with Dr Duncan B. Hollis as rapporteur, are a particularly valuable resource.

In addition, concern has grown about the political and procedural aspects of the use of non-binding instruments. In the United States, it has been asserted that 'almost all of the most consequential (and often controversial) international agreements made by the last three presidential administrations were nonbinding'.[8]

This chapter therefore discusses what type of instruments are at issue, how non-binding instruments might be drafted, what their legal status might be, who can conclude them, why states conclude them as against a treaty, what are the advantages, what are the risks, what legal effects they might have, what their relationship is with soft law, and what state practice is. The question how to distinguish between a treaty and a non-binding instrument has already been analysed in Chapter 2.

But, first, a word of warning: because the use of non-binding instruments is now so widespread, some officials may see them as the norm, with a treaty being used only when it cannot be avoided. The very word 'treaty' may conjure up some of the apparent fearsome formalities of diplomacy or lengthy parliamentary procedures. One of the tasks of international lawyers is to explain the legal differences between a treaty and a non-binding instrument. This includes, most importantly, the

[4] See H. Hillgenberg, 'A Fresh Look at Soft Law', EJIL 10 (1999) 499–515.

[5] A published example of a non-binding (plurilateral) MOU is the MOU on Port State Control in the Caribbean Region 1996: 36 ILM (1997) 237.

[6] An Expert Workshop on 'Non-Legally Binding Agreements in International Law', organised by the German Federal Foreign Office and the University of Potsdam in the framework of the German Chairmanship of the Committee of Ministers of the Council of Europe, was held on 26 March 2021, on the occasion of the 60th CAHDI meeting. See the Chair's summary at https://rm.coe.int/chair-summary-cahdi-workshop-2021-non-bind-agreemts/1680a25782. On the OAS, see the following footnote.

[7] Guidelines of the Inter-American Juridical Committee on Binding and Non-Binding Agreements, adopted by Resolution CJI/RES. 259 (XCVII-O/20), published by the Department of International Law of the Secretariat for Judicial Affairs of the Organization of American States (OAS), 1 November 2020, OEA/Ser. Q/VII.3, OEA/Ser.Q/CJI/doc.614/20 Rev.1 Corr.1 (hereafter referred to as *OAS Guidelines*).

[8] C. A. Bradley, J. Goldsmith and O. A. Hathaway, 'The Rise of Nonbinding International Agreements: An Empirical, Comparative, and Normative Analysis', *University of Chicago Law Review* 90 (2023), forthcoming, Research Paper, at 4.

advantages and disadvantages of a treaty and a non-binding instrument, and why, in the particular circumstances, the latter might be preferable to a treaty. In general, unless there is a particular advantage in having a non-binding instrument – such as confidentiality – there should be no reason to avoid having a treaty. On the other hand, there is no reason, in principle, to prefer a treaty over a non-binding instrument unless there is a need to create legally binding rights and obligations in international law or there are real constitutional or other domestic legal requirements for a treaty.

Types of Non-legally Binding Instrument

The category of non-binding instruments embraces not only bilateral (or plurilateral) instruments of a transactional nature (many bearing the title of Memorandum of Understanding) but also multilateral instruments which, amongst other things, implement frameworks established by treaties or set non-binding norms (and thereby constitute what can be described as 'soft law').

Chapter 2 has already given examples of where the title 'Memorandum of Understanding' is accorded to a treaty.[9] Published examples of non-binding bilateral (or plurilateral) MOUs concluded by states are relatively rare because, by definition, they are not published in countries' treaty series or registered with the UN Secretariat, nor (generally) are they submitted to parliaments. But, in practice, MOUs (that is, in this context, documents with the title MOU drafted in non-binding form) are employed in most areas of international relations, including defence, trade, aid, transport, culture, and all aspects of diplomacy. In fact, they may be found in any area. In many cases, all things being equal, a treaty could be used instead.

A particularly common use of a non-binding instrument is for arrangements between agencies and institutions of one state with their counterparts in another (or with an international organisation or institution thereof).[10] Such instruments may, for example, cover practical cooperation between financial, aviation or other agencies, or between national or sub-national authorities.[11] Different states may take different approaches to these inter-institutional 'arrangements' or 'agreements', both in terms of their use of legally binding or non-binding form, and in their view as to whether they engage the responsibility of the state itself (as distinct from the

[9] See pp. 34–35.

[10] *OAS Guideline* 1.5 (n. 7) defines an inter-institutional agreement as: 'An agreement concluded between State institutions, including national ministries or sub-national territorial units, of two or more States. Depending on its terms, the surrounding circumstances, and subsequent practice, an inter-institutional agreement may qualify as a treaty, a political commitment, or a contract.'

[11] See the MOU between the UK Civil Aviation Authority (CAA) and the Singapore CAA 2020: https://publicapps.caa.co.uk/docs/33/UKCAA%20CAAS%20MOU%2018%20DEC%20%202020.pdf; and the list of over forty MOUs concluded by the UK Financial Conduct Authority with overseas regulators at www.fca.org.uk/about/agreements-overseas-regulators.

institution alone).[12] There are many examples where it is clear from the form and terminology used that both sides regard them as non-binding. But care needs to be taken to ensure that this is indeed the result (if that is desired). As *OAS Guideline* 5.4 specifies, 'States should expect the legal effects of an inter-institutional agreement to track to whatever category of agreement—a treaty, a political commitment, or a contract—it belongs'.[13]

While 'Memorandum of Understanding' may be the most common title and form of a bilateral non-binding instrument, there are many other titles and forms which can be used, as noted already in Chapter 2, including record of meeting, protocol (in the sense of record), agreed minutes, *procès-verbal*, joint memorandum, memorandum of consultations, (joint) communiqué, (joint) declaration, (joint) statement or programme. An example of a high-profile plurilateral (though essentially bilateral) agreement called 'plan of action', which was non-binding at least in the view of the United States, is the Joint Comprehensive Plan Of Action (JCPOA), concluded between Iran and China, France, Russia, United Kingdom, the United States, Germany and the European Union in 2015.[14]

Non-binding instruments in the multilateral context are now used generally for standard setting in all areas and particularly for negotiated norms in fields such as human rights, the environment, trade and financial cooperation. They are often adopted to advance on, or implement, previous obligations under an umbrella or framework agreement, or as the outcome of a particular conference, or of a particular initiative within an international organisation. They may take the form of a code of conduct,[15] guidelines,[16] plan of action,[17] programme of action,[18] final act,[19] declaration,[20] or goals and principles.[21] But there is no limit to the breadth and ingenuity of form and title.

[12] D. B. Hollis, *Second Report on Binding and Non-Binding Agreements*, Inter-American Juridical Committee, 92nd Regular Session, OEA/Ser. Q, CJI/doc.553/18 (6 February 2018), paras. 12–14, 23–33.

[13] *OAS Guidelines* 5.4.1–5.4.4 (n. 7) expand on the legal effects of an inter-institutional agreement. See further in this chapter, in the section 'Legal effects' on pp. 62–66.

[14] The JCPOA was concluded at Vienna on 14 July 2015 and incorporated in Annex A to Security Council Resolution 2231 (2015), adopted on 20 July 2015, S/RES/2231 (2015). US President Trump gave notice of withdrawal from the JCPOA on 8 May 2018.

[15] See the Code of Conduct for Responsible Fisheries 1995: www.fao.org/3/v9878e/v9878e00.htm.

[16] See OECD (2011), OECD Guidelines for Multinational Enterprises: http://dx.doi.org/10.1787/9789264115415-en.

[17] See the International Plan of Action to Prevent, Deter and Eliminate Illegal, Unreported and Unregulated Fishing, Rome, FAO, 2001: www.wto.org/english/tratop_e/rulesneg_e/fish_e/2001_ipoa_iuu.pdf.

[18] See the UN Programme of Action to Prevent etc. the Illicit Trade in Small Arms, adopted 20 July 2011: https://digitallibrary.un.org/record/477974?ln=en.

[19] See Final Act of the Conference on Security and Co-operation in Europe (CSCE) (Helsinki Final Act)1975: 14 ILM (1975) 1293.

[20] See the Rio Declaration on Environment and Development, 14 June 1992: UN Doc. A/CONF.151/26 (vol. I), 31 ILM (1992) 874.

[21] See the UN Environment Programme (UNEP) Goals and Principles of Environmental Impact Assessment: Decision 14/25 of the Governing Council of UNEP, Nairobi, 17 June 1987, UNEP(092)/E5.

Practical Steps towards Creating a Non-legally Binding Instrument

How can states who wish to conclude a non-binding instrument achieve that? We have already discussed in Chapter 2, in the context of the definition of a treaty, the factors which may lead a court or tribunal to determine that an instrument is a treaty. The factors which determine that an instrument is non-binding are the converse of that. It is important to note that different states may use different tests as to whether they consider a text to be binding or non-binding, and the negotiation of each instrument has to be treated on a case-by-case basis, in light of its own special factors.[22] But those intending to draft a non-binding instrument can help their cause by evidencing a clear intention to conclude a non-binding instrument; by using the right terminology; by choosing the right form for the subject-matter in question; and by considering whether to include express provisions as to the instrument's non-binding status.

Evidencing an Intention to Conclude a Non-legally Binding Instrument

As explained in Chapter 2, if states conclude an instrument that they do *not intend to be governed by international law*, that will be a strong indicator that the instrument is not binding in international law, and will not therefore be a treaty. How best to evidence that intention will depend on the circumstances. But the *OAS Guidelines* recommend certain best practices:

3.1.1 States should rely on the actual terms used and the surrounding circumstances to discern whether or not an agreement will arise (or has already come into existence).

3.1.2 When in doubt, a State should confer with any potential partner(s) to confirm whether a statement or instrument will—or will not—constitute an agreement (and, ideally, what type of agreement it will be).

3.1.3 A State should refrain from affiliating itself with a statement or instrument if its own views as to its status as an agreement diverge from those of any potential partner(s) until such time as they may reconcile their differences.[23]

In the case of bilateral instruments, there were, in the experience of the previous author, Anthony Aust, at least two instances of a disagreement between the participants about their status coming to light when the instrument was on the point of being signed, and four after it had become effective. In two of the latter cases, the disagreement became apparent only once a dispute had arisen, and this may well have been a factor. In both cases, the instrument was supplementary to a treaty. One

[22] See para. 6.iii (Methods of Identification), Final Report on the *OAS Guidelines* (n. 7).
[23] *OAS Guidelines* (n. 7).

solution to the problem is for the state that intended to conclude no more than a non-binding instrument to send – and well in advance – a diplomatic note to the other state on the following lines: 'the instrument will come into operation on the understanding that it does not constitute a treaty and neither side will publish it as a treaty or seek to register it as a treaty with the United Nations'. Hopefully, the other side will either reply agreeing with this, or not reply. Either may be enough. A reference to the point should, of course, also be made at the outset of the negotiation of the instrument.

Although the problem of differing views as to an instrument's status appears to occur chiefly in the case of bilateral instruments, occasionally there can be controversy too about the status of multilateral instruments. Critics of the Global Compact for Safe, Orderly and Regular Migration[24] alleged that, even though it was expressed to be non-legally binding, it would give rise to binding commitments.[25]

Using the Right Terminology

Although the law of treaties does not require a treaty to be in any particular form or to use special wording,[26] lawyers practising in foreign or other ministries normally draft instruments using carefully chosen terminology. Most states now follow a practice of manifesting their intention to conclude a treaty by consciously employing a fairly standard form, and by using mandatory terminology such as (in English) 'shall', 'agree', 'undertake', 'rights', 'obligations' and 'enter into force'.

In contrast, when they do *not* intend to conclude a treaty, but rather a non-binding instrument, instead of 'shall' they use a less mandatory term, such as 'will'; such terms as 'agree' or 'undertake' are avoided; the instrument is expressed to 'come into operation' or 'come into effect'; and most of the final clauses usually found in treaties, and the *testimonium*, are omitted or simplified.

[24] Global Compact for Safe, Orderly and Regular Migration, adopted 19 December 2018: UN Doc. A/RES/73/195.

[25] The UN Secretary-General António Guterres stressed that the Compact was not legally binding, would not give migrants rights to go anywhere and reaffirmed 'only the fundamental human rights'. See the House of Commons Library Briefing Paper, 'The United Nations Global Compact for Migration', No. 8459, 29 August 2019, p. 27. The preamble to the Compact affirmed: 'This Global Compact presents a non-legally binding, cooperative framework that builds on the commitments agreed upon by Member States in the New York Declaration for Refugees and Migrants.' See also discussion of legal aspects of the Compact in A. Desmond, 'A New Dawn for the Human Rights of International Migrants? Protection of Migrants' Rights in Light of the UN's SDGs and Global Compact for Migration', *International Journal of Law in Context* 16(3) (2020) 222–238; and V. Chetail, 'The Global Compact for Safe, Orderly and Regular Migration: A Kaleidoscope of International Law', *International Journal of Law in Context* 16(3) (2020) 253–268.

[26] *Temple of Preah Vihear* (Preliminary Objections), ICJ Reports (1961) 17, at 27, 31–32.

Table 3.1 *Comparison of treaty and NBI terminology*

Treaty	*Non-binding instrument*
article	paragraph
agree	decide, accept, approve
agreement	arrangement, understanding
authentic	equally valid
continue in force	continue to have effect
done	signed
enter into force	come into effect, come into operation
obligations	commitments[27]
parties	participants, governments
rights	benefits
shall	will
undertake	carry out
undertakings	understandings

Table 3.1 illustrates some of the words most commonly used in a treaty and a non-binding instrument, respectively.[28] But it should be stressed that the terminology used for non-binding instruments is not analogous to the practice (at least in common law countries) with *domestic law contracts*, where the use of 'will', as opposed to 'shall', should *not* necessarily be read as denying the intent to create a legally binding obligation.

Although the designation of the instrument is not dispositive, the person drafting an instrument should choose a title which indicates as clearly as possible whether the intention is to create a binding or non-binding instrument. Titles such as treaty, convention, agreement, covenant and protocol tend to be used with binding instruments (treaties), while those such as understanding, statement of intent, memorandum of understanding (*memorandum d'entente* or *memorandum de entendimiento*), arrangement(s) and declaration tend to be used with non-binding instruments.[29]

Choosing the Right Form for the Subject Matter

The subject matter in itself does not determine the choice of treaty or non-treaty form, since the same subjects can be found in both treaties and non-binding

[27] Some states may, depending on the overall context and other language used, regard 'commit' and 'commitment' as binding language.

[28] A larger table comparing treaty and non-binding instrument (NBI) terminology is at Appendix H of this book (p. 486). The treaty at Appendix B and the MOUs at Appendices C and D illustrate the main differences. Further guidance on treaty and NBI drafting is given below.

[29] Para. 3, Table 2, *OAS Guidelines* (n. 7).

instruments. But the *significance* of the subject matter may play a role in determining whether a government wants an instrument that is definitive and binding,[30] or whether a state's parliament expects the matter to be dealt with by procedures in which it has a say. That said, a treaty can be pretty insubstantial (see the UK–Albania Agreement on Co-operation in the Field of Tourism 1994),[31] and a non-binding instrument can be extremely important *politically* (see the Helsinki Final Act 1975).[32]

Express Provisions as to Non-legally Binding Status

In many cases, negotiating states will clearly evince an intention to conclude a non-binding instrument by inserting appropriate language in the text itself or in another document relating to its adoption. The states that adopted the Helsinki Final Act 1975 made clear their intention not to enter into a treaty by stating at the end of the instrument that it was 'not eligible for registration [i.e., as a treaty] under Article 102 of the [UN] Charter'.[33] When the OSCE adopts important instruments that are not treaties, it continues to make this clear. So, the OSCE Document of the Stockholm Conference on Confidence- and Security-Building Measures and Disarmament in Europe 1986 provides that: 'the measures adopted in this document are politically binding'.[34] The OSCE Charter of Paris 1990 provides that it is not eligible for registration.[35] In the OSCE Code of Conduct on Politico-Military Aspects of Security 1994, paragraph 39 provides that it is 'politically binding', and, accordingly, 'this Code is not eligible for registration under Article 102'.[36] An instrument adopted by the UN Conference on Environment and Development (UNCED) is engagingly entitled 'Non-legally Binding Authoritative Statement of Principles regarding Forests 1992'.[37] The NATO–Russia Founding Act 1997 refers in its preamble to 'political' commitments.[38] When transmitting a copy of it to the UN Secretary-General, the NATO Secretary-General stated explicitly that it was not eligible for registration under Article 102 of the UN Charter.

30 There is still a debate whether certain subjects require treaty form, the parties' views notwithstanding: see Commentary on *OAS Guideline* 3.3 (n. 7), recalling (in n. 138) that Roberto Ago suggested that commitments on certain subjects (e.g., territorial boundaries) must be treaties whatever the parties' intentions (YBILC I (1962), 52, para. 19).

31 1883 UNTS 214 No. 32030; UKTS (1994) No. 42.

32 See n. 19; see also the Amended London Guidelines for the Exchange of Information on Chemicals in International Trade, UN Doc. UNEP/GC.15/9/Add.2/Supp. 3 (1989) (available from UNEP).

33 Helsinki Final Act (n. 19). Only treaties can be registered under UN Charter Article 102: 'Every treaty and every international agreement entered into by any member of the United Nations ... shall as soon as possible be registered with the Secretariat'.

34 Stockholm, 19 September 1986: 26 ILM (1987) 191, 195, para. 101.

35 Adopted at Paris, 21 November 1990: 30 ILM (1991) 193.

36 OSCE, Code of Conduct on Politico-Military Aspects of Security, 3 December 1994: Doc. FSC/1/95, www.osce.org.

37 Adopted at Rio de Janeiro, 13 June 1992: A/CONF.151/6/Rev.1; 31 ILM (1992) 882.

38 36 ILM (1997) 1007, 1008.

Sometimes a bilateral instrument includes a statement that it represents a political commitment and does not constitute a legally binding agreement. Any doubt as to the status of the Israel–United States Declaration on Trade in Services 1985 is dispelled by the preamble, which declares that 'the principles set forth below shall not be legally binding'.[39] Such express statements feature in a number of other instruments concluded by the United States.[40] They, and similar categorical statements, should be conclusive as to the intended status of the instrument. But the use of such formulas is not yet common, and omitting them certainly does *not* indicate that the instrument was intended to be a treaty.

The Practice of States and International Organisations

States have long used political commitments. In their early form, they were conceived as personal commitments among officials, but later came to accommodate national commitments. In 1907, for example, Japan and the United States promised to constrain emigration to the United States via a commitment, described as a non-binding agreement by its drafter, Secretary of State Robert Lansing.[41] In recent decades, state practice has resulted in widespread use of non-binding instruments. As the practice emerged, foreign government negotiators may have been rather bemused by requests, usually from Commonwealth states, to change the title of a draft from 'agreement' to 'memorandum of understanding' or 'arrangement', and every 'shall' to 'will'. But what some may have previously seen as a slightly tiresome - even quaint - obsession is now a firmly established practice in international relations.

Commonwealth States

The over fifty states that are members of the Commonwealth will often use non-binding instruments, bilateral or multilateral, among themselves, even in those cases where other states might employ a treaty, though there is a growing number of exceptions, particularly in fields where legally binding obligations are more or less

[39] 24 ILM (1985) 679.

[40] See the MOU between Environment Canada and US Department of the Interior for the Conservation and Management of Shared Polar Bear Populations, 8 May 2008, at: www. asil.org. At the end is the unequivocal statement that: 'This Memorandum of Understanding is not legally-binding and creates no legally-binding obligations on the Participants.' See also ASIL ILIB, 11 September 2012 for a Russia–US MOU for Cooperation in Antarctica, 8 September 2012.

[41] Memorandum by the Division of Far Eastern Affairs, 11 January 1924, *Papers Relating to the Foreign Relations of the United States 1924*, vol. 2, US Department of State (1939), 339–374.

unavoidable.[42] The Commonwealth Secretariat itself was established in 1965 by an MOU entitled 'Agreed Memorandum'.[43]

European Union

In the EU's external relations with third states and international organisations, the EU Treaties provide for the use of international agreements (treaties), which are subject to the procedures in Article 218 of the Treaty on the Functioning of the European Union (TFEU).[44] But the EU, like national governments, has made increasing use of non-binding instruments, such as memoranda of understanding, letters of intent, joint declarations, arrangements and exchanges of letters.[45] A number of EU institutions and bodies have concluded such arrangements, notably the European Commission and the European External Action Service (EEAS), either on behalf of the Union as a whole or limited to their own administrative responsibilities. The EEAS has, for example, concluded arrangements for practical cooperation with regional groupings such as the League of Arab States and the African Union.[46] The European Commission has concluded instruments for cooperation with other international organisations,[47] strategic cooperation with particular countries,[48] joint declarations for particular initiatives,[49] and implementation of action plans or financial programmes.[50] Not all the non-binding instruments are publicly available, although many are on the transparency register.

In drafting these instruments, the EU appears to follow accepted practice in terms of form and language. For as long as the EU institutions have used non-binding instruments, there have been questions about the proper procedure for their internal

[42] There are examples of bilateral treaties between Commonwealth countries in the fields of trade, health, social security, bilateral investment, air services, double taxation, status of forces, maritime boundaries and extradition. On the last of these, see the India–UK Extradition Agreement 1992 (1824 UNTS 190 No. 31237).

[43] 4 ILM (1965) 1108. See pp. 410–411 for more on the Commonwealth.

[44] See consolidated version, [2008] OJ C115/47.

[45] See the very full account in A. Ott, 'Informalization of EU Bilateral Instruments: Categorization, Contestation, and Challenges', *Yearbook of European Law* 39 (2020) 569–601.

[46] The MOU with the League of Arab States 2015 is not published. The EU–African Union MOU on Peace, Security and Governance 2018 is at: https://eeas.europa.eu/sites/default/files/medghme_2018.05.23_16.31.36_5c4n7108_1_0.pdf.

[47] With the Council of the EU, the Council of Europe–EU MOU 2007: https://eeas.europa.eu/sites/default/files/mou_2007_en.pdf; the European Commission and UN–ECLAC MOU 2006: https://eeas.europa.eu/archives/docs/la/docs/mou_eclac_071106_en.pdf.

[48] For example, the Colombia–EU MOU 2021: https://eeas.europa.eu/sites/default/files/memorandum_of_understanding_colombia-eu_en_0.pdf.

[49] Joint Declaration on the Central African Forest Initiative: Commission Decision 4 December 2015, C(2015) 8742/F1; on EU–Belarus Joint Declaration establishing a Mobility Partnership: Commission Decision 15 June 2015, C(2015) 3955 final.

[50] EU–Ukraine MOU 2020: https://ec.europa.eu/info/sites/default/files/economy-finance/ukraine_memorandum_of_understanding_eu_version.pdf.

authorisation within the Union. The inter-institutional procedures for adoption of the instruments are amenable to the jurisdiction of the Court of Justice of the European Union (CJEU) and have to respect the division of competences and institutional balance.[51] Following a challenge from the Council to the Commission's conclusion of an MOU with Switzerland, the Secretaries General of the Council, Commission and EEAS drew up arrangements setting out the administrative procedures to be followed before signature or agreement of an non-binding instrument.[52]

Organization of American States

The Second Report for the Inter-American Juridical Committee (IAJC) study of Binding and Non-Binding Agreements[53] provides an extensive summary of the practice of a number of the OAS member states.[54] In their responses to the Rapporteur's questionnaire, the member states acknowledged a separate category of non-binding agreements or what might be termed political commitments, and defined this category in terms of commitments that lack any legal force. OAS states used a variety of different titles, including 'memorandum of understanding', statements or letters of intent, 'political declaration'[55] and joint declarations and communiqués.[56] Peru, Ecuador, Uruguay and Colombia placed inter-institutional commitments within the category of non-binding agreements, whereas Mexico suggested that an inter-institutional agreement might be governed by international law. Uruguay suggested that that inter-institutional agreements could be either binding or non-binding.[57]

In differentiating between treaties and political commitments, five of the member states – Brazil, Colombia, Mexico, Peru and the United States – specifically invoked 'intent' as the deciding criterion. For the Dominican Republic, Jamaica and Uruguay, the agreement's structure and the language used were determinative. But even those who supported the 'intent' test would look to the structure and language of the text as the best evidence of 'intent'.[58]

[51] Case C-233/02 *France* v. *Commission*, ECLI:EU:C:2004:173, para. 40; Case C-660/13 *Council* v. *Commission*, ECLI:EU:C:2016:616.

[52] Follow-up to Judgment in Case C-660/13 – Arrangements between Secretaries General on non-binding instruments, 4 December 2017, 15367/17.

[53] D. B. Hollis, *Second Report on Binding and Non-Binding Agreements*, Inter-American Juridical Committee, 92nd Regular Session, OEA/Ser. Q, CJI/doc.553/18 (6 February 2018). See especially paras. 11–20.

[54] Argentina, Brazil, Colombia, the Dominican Republic, Ecuador, Jamaica, Mexico, Peru, Uruguay and the United States. Responses were subsequently received from Canada, Panama and Paraguay. See p. 14 and notes 6 and 7 of the Final Report: Guidelines of the Inter-American Juridical Committee on Binding and Non-Binding Agreements, adopted by Resolution CJI/RES. 259 (XCVII-O/20), Department of International Law, OAS Secretariat for Judicial Affairs, 1 November 2020, OEA/Ser.Q/VII.3, OEA/Ser.Q/CJI/doc.614/20 Rev.1 Corr.1

[55] See further on 'political declarations' at pp. 138–139.

[56] Hollis (n. 53), para. 12.

[57] Hollis (n. 53), para. 14.

[58] Hollis (n. 53), para. 16.

On the use of language, the OAS member states' practice is largely consistent with those of other states. Words like 'agree', 'must', and 'shall', and references to 'parties', are more appropriate for treaties, whereas verbs like 'should', 'promote', 'seek', together with words like 'best efforts', 'intentions' and 'understandings', are indicative of a non-binding arrangement. A clause providing for 'entry into force' would be more appropriate for a treaty, as would describing provisions as 'articles', whereas providing for an instrument to have 'effect', and the use of 'paragraphs', would indicate non-binding character.[59] Several member states recommended the inclusion of an express clause in non-binding agreements to the effect that they did not establish legal obligations.[60]

Canada

Canada uses non-legally binding instruments in international relations to express political and moral commitments as opposed to undertakings governed by public international law.[61] These instruments can be in single documents usually entitled 'Memorandum of Understanding' or 'Arrangements', or can be constituted by Exchanges of Notes or Letters. There is a preference for a non-binding instrument if a matter is of a routine or technical nature, or appears to fall entirely within the existing mandate and responsibility of a department or agency, and if it does not contain substantive matter which should be legally binding. While recent Canadian practice dictates that Memorandums of Understanding or Arrangements are not legally binding, Canada recognises that not all states view these instruments as such, and that simply labelling a document as a 'Memorandum of Understanding' or 'Arrangement' is not enough to ensure that it will not be considered as an agreement governed by international law by some of the participants to the instrument.

Canada advises its departments and agencies to take care to ascertain before negotiating a non-binding arrangement that the other participants agree that the arrangement is not binding under international law. Non-binding instruments can be negotiated between Canada and another sovereign state, but much more commonly are constituted between a Canadian government department, an agency, or a province or other sub-national government or parastatal organisation, and a similar body in another country. Although considered non-binding by Canada, such instruments

[59] Hollis (n. 53), paras. 17–18.

[60] Brazil, Peru and Uruguay. Peru, for example, often includes a clause stating: 'The present memorandum of understanding does not give rise to any rights or legal obligations between the participants' or '... is not legally binding'. Uruguay suggested a clause that reads: 'This Instrument shall not create obligations or international responsibility for the Parties'. Hollis (n. 53), para. 19.

[61] This section on Canadian practice draws heavily on Global Affairs Canada, *Policy on Tabling of Treaties in Parliament*, Annex C, *International Instruments That Are Not Binding under Public International Law (Memoranda of Understanding)*, https://treaty-accord.gc.ca/procedures.aspx?lang=eng.

follow a particular form and must respect Canadian policies and practices. The terminology used must clearly indicate that these are not legally binding instruments. Their provisions should be cast as expressions of intent rather than as obligations.

Germany

Germany signs each month around fifteen non-legally binding agreements with a range of international partners, including states, subordinated state entities or international organisations. The actors concluding such declarations can differ widely. Non-legally binding agreements can be signed, for example, by the German Federal Government, by single ministries, the subordinate authorities or the German *Länder*.[62]

German practice acknowledges that there is no uniform state practice on the title to be given to non-legally binding instruments: while the term MOU for some states clearly indicates a non-legally binding instrument, other states conclude MOUs containing binding obligations under international law. For this reason, Germany avoids usage of this term, preferring to call non-legally binding instruments 'Joint Declaration of Intent',[63] although, since some states regard this title as too weak, the title 'MOU' cannot always be avoided. In the case of an MOU signed in 2017 by the Federal Minister for Economic Affairs and Energy, together with colleagues from six other countries,[64] the text of the document expressly stated at the end:

> This Memorandum of Understanding does not create any rights or obligations under national or international law and does not intend to replace or modify any existing legal obligations between the signatories.

Germany subjects the entire document to comprehensive scrutiny in order to determine its legal character. The wording as well as its structure is carefully checked to ensure that it contains not a single sentence suggesting a legally binding instrument. A glossary of terms to use and to avoid is attached to the internal Guidelines.[65] Germany also distinguishes non-binding instruments in terms of the formal paper which it uses for the relevant document, the type of signature ceremony and the way in which such instruments are archived.[66]

[62] This account is drawn from S. Talmon, 'Germany directs attention to questions surrounding non-legally binding international agreements', German Practice in International Law (GPIL), 21 May 2021, at: https://gpil.jura.uni-bonn.de/2021/05/germany-directs-attention-to-questions-surrounding-non-legally-binding-international-agreements/.

[63] *Richtlinien für die Behandlung völkerrechtlicher Verträge* (the German Federal Government's internal Guidelines for dealing with international treaties), 133: www.auswaertiges-amt.de/blob/2481616/31364feaa9019e4a9281796ceda6362d/rvv-data.pdf.

[64] MOU of the Pentalateral Energy Forum on Emergency Planning 2017: www.benelux.int/files/8814/9846/9643/Penta_MoU_emergency_planning.pdf.

[65] *Richtlinien* (n. 63), 141. [66] Talmon (n. 62).

Japan

Article 73 of the Constitution of Japan provides for the Cabinet to conclude treaties, although it needs to obtain the prior or, depending on the circumstances, subsequent approval of the Diet.[67] The Ministry of Foreign Affairs is the only entity in Japan responsible for the interpretation and implementation of treaties and other international agreements, as well as the modalities relating to their conclusion. International agreements are treated as falling into two categories: those that require Diet approval and those concluded under the auspices of the executive. The latter are termed administrative arrangements. Broadly speaking, agreements which require Diet approval are those which raise legislative or budgetary issues, or which are otherwise considered politically important.[68] As with other states, the making of legally binding treaties is carefully scrutinised in Japan so as to avoid any misunderstanding as to the legal nature of an instrument.

Japan recognises that agreements may adopt different titles such as protocol, agreement, charter, exchange of notes, agreed minutes or memoranda. It appears that, in distinguishing between treaties and other agreements, Japanese practice places emphasis on the intention of the parties, while recognising that this must be evidenced, for example, by the objective and the language used by the parties. The procedural aspects may also indicate whether there is intention on the part of a state for an instrument to be legally binding.[69]

United States

A more detailed account of US procedures in respect of treaties is given in Chapter 10.[70] This section summarises US practice only with respect to non-binding instruments.[71]

Article II of the Constitution states that the president 'shall have Power, by and with the Advice and Consent of the Senate, to make Treaties, provided two thirds of the Senators present concur'. The Executive has, however, concluded large numbers of 'executive agreements', which are not subject to the Article II process. These are subject to requirements that (a) they be published and (b) they be submitted to Congress within sixty days of entry into force, in accordance with the Case Act.[72]

[67] See Y. Nakanishi, 'Defining the Boundaries of Legally Binding Treaties – Some Aspects of Japan's Practice in Treaty-Making in Light of State Practice', *International Community Law Review* 20(2) (April 2018), 169–191, particularly 185–188, on which this account is based.

[68] Nakanishi (n. 67), 186 and footnote 67. [69] Nakanishi (n. 67), 187. [70] See pp. 202–206.

[71] For a full analysis of US practice on non-binding instruments, see Bradley *et al.* (n. 8).

[72] United States International Agreements 1 USC §112b, which was amended in 1994 and 2004. For the original text, see 18 ILM (1979) 82. For an amended text, see www.govinfo.gov/app/details/USCODE-2011-title1/USCODE-2011-title1-chap2-sec112b.

The provisions in the Case Act have been implemented by Federal Regulations,[73] which give guidance to departments and agencies of the US government as to the type of instruments that the Act requires to be notified to Congress. The Regulations thus cover those instruments that fall within the definition of treaty (as that term is understood by international law), and lay down criteria by which to judge whether a particular instrument is a treaty.[74] The following extracts are particularly relevant:

(1) *Identity and intention of the parties* ... The parties must intend their undertakings to be legally binding, and *not merely of political or personal effect. Documents intended to have political or moral weight, but not intended to be legally binding, are not international agreements* [i.e., treaties] ...

(5) *Form.* Form as such is not normally an important factor, but it does deserve consideration. Documents that do not follow the customary form for international agreements, as to matters such as style, final clauses, signatures, or entry into force dates, may or may not be international agreements. Failure to use the customary form may constitute evidence of a lack of intent to be legally bound by the arrangement. If, however, the general content and context reveal an intention to enter into a legally binding relationship, a departure from customary form will not preclude the arrangement from being an international agreement. Moreover, the title of the agreement will not be determinative.

Decisions will be made on the basis of the substance of the arrangement, rather than on its denomination as an international agreement, a memorandum of understanding, exchange of notes, exchange of letters, technical arrangement, protocol, note verbale, aide-memoire, agreed minute, or any other name.

These extracts adopt a not dissimilar approach to that of other states: there must be an intention to enter into legally binding obligations, and use of non-customary treaty form may indicate that the parties did *not* intend to enter into legally binding obligations. But it is also clear that, in US practice, use of non-treaty language does not necessarily preclude the instrument from being an international agreement if 'the general content and context reveal an intention to enter into a legally binding relationship'.

Whereas the practice of other states seems to be fairly consistent as to the use of particular terminology to distinguish MOUs from treaties, US practice is (or was) less so. This practice resulted in some instruments having uncertain status in international law. The China–US MOU on the Protection of Intellectual Property 1992 states that the two governments 'reached a mutual understanding', but includes some treaty language.[75] The MOU between the same two states on Prohibiting Import and Export Trade of Prison Labor Products 1992 says in the preamble that

[73] 22 Code of Federal Regulations (CFR) §181, at: www.govinfo.gov/content/pkg/CFR-2011-title22-vol1/pdf/CFR-2011-title22-vol1-part181.pdf.

[74] See CFR § 181.1–2.

[75] 2249 UNTS 314 No. 40079; 34 ILM (1995) 677.

they 'have reached the following understanding', but then says that 'The Parties agree'.[76] The operative provisions use MOU terminology, but the final clauses and *testimonium*[77] are in treaty form.

More recent guidance[78] shows that, on questions of terminology, US practice is closely in line with that of other states. They advise negotiators to avoid using the term 'Parties' in non-binding documents, and encourage the use of other terms such as 'Participants'. With respect to the actions to be taken, US negotiators should avoid terms such as 'shall', 'agree' or 'undertake', and terms such as 'should' or 'intend to' or 'expect to' should be used instead. In place of the term 'entry into force', the document might express that the arrangement 'is to come into operation' or that 'activities are to commence' for the 'participants'. Similarly, negotiators should avoid final clauses that state 'Done at' or 'Concluded at'.

As to the effect of political commitments (as against treaties) from the US perspective, the statement made by the US State Department in respect of the commitments made in parallel to the START treaty in 1991 is still apposite:

> An undertaking or commitment that is understood to be legally binding carries with it both the obligation of each Party to comply with the undertaking and the right of each Party to enforce the obligation under international law. A 'political' undertaking is not governed by international law .... Until and unless a party extricates itself from its 'political undertaking', which it may do without legal penalty, it has given a promise to honor that commitment, and the other Party has every reason to be concerned about compliance with such undertakings. If a Party contravenes a political commitment, it will be subject to an appropriate political response.[79]

How and Why States Use Non-legally Binding Instruments Rather Than Treaties

Non-legally binding instruments like the Helsinki Final Act 1975[80] and the NATO–Russia Founding Act 1997[81] were, of course, disseminated widely because of their high political importance. Although such documents are most often cited as examples of non-binding instruments (NBIs), they are not typical of the numerous NBIs concluded each year, which are usually concerned with more mundane matters and are of little interest outside the narrow circle of those who have to negotiate and implement them.

[76] 31 ILM (1992) 1071, 1072. [77] For an explanation of these two terms, see pp. 429–438.

[78] US Department of State, *Guidance on Non-Binding Documents*, Archive, Documents 2009–2017, https://2009-2017.state.gov/s/l/treaty/guidance/index.htm.

[79] Department of State, Article-by-Article Analysis of START Documents 352 (1991), reprinted in S. Treaty Doc. No. 20, 102nd Congress, 1st Session 1086 (1991), and in Section III.E of the Study by the Congressional Research Service 'Treaties and Other International Agreements: The Role of the United States Senate', S. Report 106-71 (2001), 106th Congress, 2d Session.

[80] See n. 19. [81] See n. 38.

But all who wish to know more about treaties should be aware of the thousands of such NBIs and the important role that they play.[82]

The main reasons for using NBIs in preference to treaties are confidentiality and convenience, of which there are various aspects.[83]

Confidentiality

An obvious reason for preferring an NBI to a treaty is confidentiality. Since an NBI is not a treaty, there is generally no national or international requirement, or indeed need, to publish it. In the United Kingdom, even an unclassified NBI is not published unless there is a special reason, such as the political importance of the subject or because it is closely associated with a treaty. If the NBI is confidential, it will not be published. Being neither a 'treaty' nor an 'international agreement', an NBI is not required by Article 102 of the UN Charter to be registered with the UN.[84] If NBIs are registered in error, the mere act of registration does *not* make them treaties.

Many arrangements, especially in the defence field and other sensitive areas, are naturally kept confidential for reasons of national security and should therefore be found only in NBIs.[85] All states do this, and no one would suggest that they should be publicly available, although it is sometimes necessary for national parliaments to be informed of their contents on a selective or confidential basis.[86] Often, a defence treaty will have numerous NBIs supplementing it. Given the importance of the subject matter, the UK–US Polaris Sales Agreement 1963 might seem surprisingly short, comprising just sixteen articles.[87] But a careful reading will show that it is an 'umbrella' treaty. Article II(2) provides that each party's representatives are authorised 'to enter into such *technical arrangements*, consistent with this Agreement, as may be necessary'. This is a reference to the immensely detailed (and very highly classified) technical and financial NBIs that were necessary during the life of the Agreement. The UK–US Agreement on the use of Ascension Island 1985 is even more explicit on the question of the instrument to be used for recording the detailed

[82] See Appendix C, 'Memorandum of Understanding on Defence Contacts and Cooperation Between the Government of the Republic of Austria and the Government of the United Kingdom of Great Britain and Northern Ireland 1997'.

[83] See also the account in Bradley *et al.* (n. 8), 29–36.

[84] About US practice, see pp. 54–56.

[85] For example, US Secretary of State Henry Kissinger gave confidential security assurances to Israel in the context of negotiating the Sinai Peace Accords. Some of these he clearly regarded as non-legally binding (although at least one of the MOUs *was* a treaty). See US–Israel Early Warning System Agreement 1975 (26 UST 2271); US–Israel Memorandum of Understanding 1975 (32 UST 2150); M. Medzini (ed.), *Israeli Ministry of Foreign Affairs, vol. 3: Israel's Foreign Relations: Selected Documents 1974–77* (Ministry of Foreign Affairs, Jerusalem 1982), 281–290 (reproducing the texts of the Sinai Peace Accords).

[86] See pp. 54–55 concerning the Case Act.

[87] 474 UNTS 49 No. 6871; UKTS (1963) No. 59. Polaris was a submarine-launched ballistic missile with a nuclear warhead. It has now been replaced by Trident.

arrangements. The treaty has only one substantive paragraph, which provides that the arrangements

> shall be established in a *memorandum of understanding* to be concluded between the Ministry of Defence representing the Government of the United Kingdom and the Department for Defense representing the Government of the United States.[88]

Although most implementing NBIs are made under bilateral treaties, they are also used for certain multilateral treaties, especially in the defence field.

Lack of Formality

With an NBI, there is no need for elaborate final clauses or the formalities (international or national) that surround treaty making. More often than is the case with a treaty, an NBI will become effective on signature. Thus, an NBI can generally be negotiated, signed and come into effect more quickly than a treaty. Even when a treaty enters into force on signature, the internal procedures required before it can do so may be lengthy. In some cases, these problems may be such that the only practicable way of proceeding is by way of an NBI. Not being a treaty, an NBI is generally not subject to any constitutional procedures, such as presentation to the legislature, though that will depend on the constitution, laws and practice of each state. In the context of the United Kingdom's exit from the European Union, NBIs were in a few cases used as 'bridging mechanisms' to enable the terms of agreements with certain countries to apply informally before the newly negotiated treaties could come into force.[89]

Like treaties, NBIs are signed by ministers or senior officials, though probably more often by senior officials than is the case for treaties.[90] This is, however, more a reflection of the generally lower importance of the subject matter. There are significant exceptions when the NBI is a statement of high political intent, such as the Helsinki Final Act 1975[91] and the NATO–Russia Founding Act 1997,[92] both of which were signed by heads of state and government.

[88] Exchange of Notes concerning military facilities on Ascension Island 1985: 1443 UNTS 25 No. 24571, UKTS (1985) No. 39. See also the reference to 'implementing arrangements' in Article 7 UK–US Agreement for Co-operation in Research and Development of Weapons Detection 2002: UKTS (2005) No. 23.

[89] See, e.g., the Diplomatic Note from UK to Colombia, 18 October 2019, at: www.gov.uk/government/publications/exchange-of-notes-between-the-uk-and-andean-countries. The 'bridging mechanism' with Colombia was extended by a further (non-binding) exchange of notes, September 2021, available at the same link.

[90] Signature, however, may not always be required to create an NBI. Neither the Rio Declaration nor the Shanghai Communiqué was signed by the participants: Rio Declaration (n. 20); US–China Joint Communiqué, 28 February 1972 (Shanghai Communiqué): Foreign Relations of the United States, 1969–1976, vol. XVII, China, 1969–1972, Document 203.

[91] See n. 19. [92] See n. 38.

Amendment

A distinct advantage of an NBI is the ease with which it can be amended. Since it is not a treaty, any amendment can be effected with the same ease and speed with which the NBI itself was concluded. Even when a treaty has a built-in simplified procedure for amendment, this will still involve certain formalities.[93] In the case of arrangements, such as collaborative defence projects or development aid, which involve complicated technical or financial provisions, there is often a need to make frequent (and sometimes major) modifications. When the arrangements are multilateral, the need for a method of amendment with the least possible formality and delay is often essential for their effectiveness.[94]

Termination

The termination provisions of many NBIs can be quite similar to those found in treaties. A period of notice is usually provided for, although this may be less than the six to twelve months commonly found in treaties, at least in multilateral treaties. Sometimes there is no provision for termination, especially when the NBI is supplementary to a treaty. Difficult questions can then arise. A free-standing NBI can probably be terminated by giving reasonable notice, although, since it is not a legally binding instrument, failure to give due notice may, at least as a matter of law, have no consequences. On the other hand, if the NBI is supplementary to a treaty and the NBI has no termination clause, can it be terminated before the treaty itself is terminated? Much may depend on its purpose. If it is essential for the implementation of the treaty, the arguments against termination of the NBI only are stronger. But again, since it is not legally binding, there should be no *legal* obstacle to giving immediate notice, although it could be damaging *politically*.

Dispute Settlement

An NBI will usually have some provision regarding the settlement of disputes about its interpretation or application, and typically will provide that they be settled by negotiation and *not* be referred to any third party, court or tribunal. Such a provision is sometimes inserted as a further indication that the instrument is not intended to be legally binding.

93 For further discussion of traditional and tacit forms of treaty amendment, see Chapter 15.

94 The NBIs that accompanied the Basel Banking Accords and the work of the Financial Action Task Force (FATF) are two examples of this phenomenon. Basel Committee on Banking Supervision, 'Basel II Accords: International Convergence of Capital Measurement and Capital Standards: A Revised Framework 2006': www.bis.org/publ/bcbs128.htm; FATF 'Recommendations of the Financial Action Task Force 2003': www.fatf-gafi.org/media/fatf/documents/recommendations/pdfs/FATF%20Recommendations%202003.pdf.

Although Article 102(2) of the UN Charter provides that unregistered treaties cannot be invoked before organs of the UN, including the ICJ, in practice they can be invoked before that Court.[95] It therefore follows that an NBI could also be invoked, though whether this would help the legal argument may depend on whether, in the particular circumstances, the NBI has any legal consequences.

Interpretation

For the interpretation and application of NBIs, it is convenient and reasonable to apply, by analogy, the rules for the interpretation of treaties insofar as they are not at variance with the non-legally binding nature of NBIs. The *travaux* of an NBI may be as important as those of a treaty, though they may be even more difficult to find. In certain cases, an NBI might constitute a subsidiary or subsequent agreement for the purposes of Article 31(2)(a) or (3)(a).

Agreements with Non-states

When a state wishes to enter into an agreement with a non-state, or part of a federal state that has not been given delegated treaty-making power, this can often best be done by using an NBI. To the extent that NBIs rest on political and moral bases rather than international law, there is no reason to limit their creation to the actors who can make treaties.

Risks in Using Non-legally Binding Instruments

A too-ready recourse to NBIs can carry risks. We have already mentioned the potential risk of disagreement as to status, but there are other issues.

Respect for Non-binding Instruments May Be Less Than for Treaties

Because an NBI is not legally binding, sometimes there may be a temptation not to take the commitments in it as seriously as those in a treaty. This would be to ignore the fact that political commitments engage the *good faith* of states. Even though failure to carry out an NBI does not usually have legal consequences, that certainly does not mean that a state is free, politically or morally, to disregard it. Not only would it be dishonourable to disregard an NBI, but it could also provoke a damaging political response.[96] For example, when North Korea failed to follow through on a

[95] See the discussion in *Maritime Delimitation and Territorial Questions (Qatar* v. *Bahrain)*, Jurisdiction and Admissibility, ICJ Reports (1994) 112, at 121–122, paras. 26–29.

[96] See also P. Kooijmans, 'The International Court of Justice and the Law of the Sea: Some Reflections', in J. Makarczyk (ed.), *The Theory of International Law at the Threshold of the 21st Century* (Brill Academic, Dordrecht 1995), 425–430.

political commitment to suspend uranium enrichment, the US suspended aid it had promised to provide and sought international sanctions.[97]

Possible Lack of Care in Drafting

Some government officials might regard the drafting of an NBI as not requiring the same close attention as the drafting of a treaty. But, in many cases, the content of an NBI could equally well be put into a treaty, and an error in the drafting of an NBI could give rise to the same friction in relations as an error in a treaty. Even though the commitments in an NBI are political rather than legal, that is no reason for them to be expressed with less precision than they would be in a treaty.

Depending on the constitution and internal procedures of each state, it will not usually be essential for the foreign ministry to draft all NBIs. However, when another ministry drafts an NBI, it should consult its own foreign ministry before sending the draft to another government, and at all key stages thereafter. It is the task of the foreign ministry to explain the differences between a treaty and an NBI – why one rather than the other may be advantageous (or not) in the particular case – and to ensure that the form and wording is appropriate for whatever instrument is chosen. Unfortunately, too often another ministry may produce a draft that is a mixture of treaty and NBI language, or a draft that uses mostly treaty language but is headed 'memorandum of understanding' (or similar) in the mistaken belief that this is the magic phrase that makes it not legally binding. The foreign ministry must then try to put matters right.

Lack of Implementing Legislation

Although an NBI is not legally binding, that does not mean that it may not need to be implemented in domestic law. The United States, for example, implemented the multilateral Kimberley Process NBI on eliminating trade in 'blood diamonds' via statute.[98] NBIs are also often used for matters concerning the status of armed forces sent to another state. Sometimes the law needed to implement such an NBI will already be in place, but if not, care must be taken to ensure that the NBI will not come into effect until any necessary primary or secondary implementing legislation has been made.

Difficulty in Finding Non-legally Binding Instruments

One important practical advantage of a treaty is that being published (usually in a special series) and, hopefully, also registered with the United Nations, it is much

97 See S. Harrison, 'Time to Leave Korea', *Foreign Affairs* 80(2) (2001) 62–78, at 67.

98 Clean Diamond Trade Act, 19 USC §§ 3901–3913 (2003); Interlaken Declaration on the Kimberley Process Certification Scheme for Rough Diamonds, 5 November 2002.

easier to find, not only for members of the public but also for officials. NBIs are very easily 'mislaid'. Those officials responsible for implementing an NBI should keep a copy of it (the signed text, *not what seems to be* the final draft) somewhere easily accessible and, perhaps even more important, where their successors will be able to find it (i.e., not only in the archives). As a fail-safe measure, the Treaty Section of a Ministry of Foreign Affairs might keep a copy of each NBI concluded either by the Foreign Ministry or by other ministries. This would also help to monitor developing practice in respect of NBIs.

Non-legally Binding Instruments and 'Soft Law'

The question whether non-binding instruments constitute 'soft law' has been, and is still, widely debated, not least because of the growth of 'soft law' instruments in the multilateral sphere. The following analysis presents only one perspective. It is helpful in this context to distinguish between bilateral instruments and multilateral instruments.

Bilateral non-binding instruments, with few exceptions, do not set out to create norms which apply to the wider international community. For the most part, they deal with a specific area of cooperation between two states (or between states and international organisations) or between their Ministries or agencies. Nevertheless, bilateral non-binding instruments might be described as 'soft law' in the sense that:

(1) the commitments are not 'hard law', that is, they do not create legal obligations but instead constitute a political or moral type of commitment;[99]
(2) the commitments are sometimes broadly drawn, for example in terms of mutual cooperation;[100]
(3) if they relate to a treaty or to another set of obligations they may have a legal effect on these, for example as an aid to interpretation;[101]
(4) despite their non-binding nature, they nevertheless may be considered relevant in legal proceedings as evidence of the parties' intention, behaviour or subsequent practice;[102]

[99] Political commitments in NBIs should still be taken as seriously as legal commitments. See also n. 78.

[100] See, for example, the MOU between the IMO and the OSPAR Commission 2018, at: www.ospar.org/documents?v=39043.

[101] See *Gardiner*, 245, discussing 'subsequent agreements' in the context of Article 31(3)(a) of the Convention; and, concerning the practice of investment tribunals, see S. W. Schill, 'Sources of International Investment Law: Multilateralization, Arbitral Precedent, Comparativism, Soft Law', in S. Besson and J. d'Aspremont (eds.), *The Oxford Handbook on the Sources of International Law* (Oxford University Press, Oxford 2017), 1095–1115.

[102] See, for example, the exchanges of notes and letters between the UK and US authorities referred to in the case of *R. (Charles & Dunn)* v. *Secretary of State for Foreign and Commonwealth Affairs* [2020] EWHC 3185 (Admin), at paras. 21–36.

(5) again, despite being non-binding, they may contain some kind of enforcement mechanism;[103]

(6) they may anticipate the entry into force of more or less the same provisions in treaty form, thus acting as a 'bridging mechanism' towards a future treaty or a form of non-binding provisional application of a future treaty;[104] or

(7) they may constitute commitments of a type which the same state might equally put (or has put, in other cases) in binding treaty form, for example concerning status of forces.[105]

While each of (1) to (7) above may be true in their own way, they do not, however, necessarily justify the description of a non-binding bilateral instrument as 'soft *law*'. If the commitments in an instrument are non-legally binding, and the parties knowingly and carefully enter into them on that basis, the starting point is that they do not constitute law at all.[106] That does not mean that they sit in a world without law. Because they are concluded within the sphere of international relations, of which so much is governed by international law, they will always have the potential to interact with the international legal order. Hence, such an instrument might have legal effects in a subsequent dispute, as per (3) and (4) above, or as described further below. But, if the instrument does not have binding structure and language, and is not accompanied by legal intent, the possibility that it might have some legal effect does not convert *ab initio* non-binding commitments into binding obligations, or make a non-binding instrument a treaty.

In the case of multilateral non-binding instruments, the arguments are similar, but the case for at least some such instruments being considered 'soft law' is stronger. This is not so much because they intend to influence states' behaviour in a particular direction, or might lead to countermeasures in the event of a breach, since those are also characteristics of political commitments. But many such instruments have a clear normative aspect. Where that is the case, there are two different approaches towards its effect, which have been described as the 'bright line' school and the 'grey zone' school.[107] For the bright line school, informal international law making is 'either law or it is not'. For the grey zone school, informal international law making 'could be clearly law, but it could also fall somewhere in between, that is, in the grey zone separating law from non-law'.[108] Whereas the bright line school probably draws too

[103] The JCPOA (n. 14) had a dispute settlement mechanism linked to the lifting or imposition of sanctions, and action in the Security Council: paras. 36–37.

[104] In the context of the UK's exit from the EU, NBIs were used as 'bridging mechanisms' to enable the terms of trade agreements with certain countries to apply before the newly negotiated treaties could come into force.

[105] So, for example, Article 26.1 UK–Kenya Agreement concerning Defence Cooperation 2015 (UKTS (2016) No. 34), which states that it superseded the MOU between the two parties on Visiting Forces 2010.

[106] See K. Raustiala, 'Form and Substance in International Agreements', AJIL 99 (2005) 581–614, at 586.

[107] J. Pauwelyn, 'Is It International Law or Not, and Does It Even Matter?', in J. Pauwelyn, R. A. Wessel and J. Wouters (eds.), *Informal International Lawmaking* (Oxford University Press, Oxford 2012), 125, at 127–129.

[108] Pauwelyn (n. 107), 129.

stark a distinction between law and non-law, the grey zone school may not distinguish sufficiently between 'being law' and 'having legal effect'.

In practice, there are a number of ways in which multilateral non-binding instruments may interact with the international legal order.[109] They may:

(1) be a form of implementation of prior binding obligations, for example under an umbrella agreement;[110]
(2) be an aid to interpretation of binding obligations, either because there is a specific link (by providing clarification or context) or as 'general principles';[111]
(3) expect the participating states to adopt domestic legislation in line with the instrument;[112]
(4) become, even as they are, a basis for state practice and *opinio juris*, and thus, over time, customary international law;[113] or alternatively,
(5) constitute precursors for conclusion of a future treaty, thus possessing a 'pre-law' function.[114]

Such features do not of themselves turn the commitments of a non-binding instrument into 'hard law' or engage the legal responsibility of the participating states, even if the commitments are concrete and precise. It is, however, possible for a treaty to contain both legally binding and non-legally binding provisions, though one should examine rigorously whether the relevant provisions are still obligations, just vaguely drawn, or whether they are genuinely non-legally binding. One could describe vaguely drawn obligations of 'hard law' (that is, in a treaty) as 'soft law',[115] but that it is not what is meant in (1) to (5) above. These are intended to describe aspects of a multilateral non-treaty (that is, non-binding) instrument.

Legal Effects of Non-legally Binding Instruments: Estoppel

Some of the possible legal effects of non-binding instruments have been described above. However, two further questions arise: first, whether non-binding instruments are

109 See also D. Thürer, 'Soft Law', *MPEPIL* (2009), paras. 18–34.
110 The FAO has used both binding and non-binding instruments to promote implementation of the fisheries provisions of UNCLOS 1982: A. Boyle, 'Soft Law in International Law-Making', in *Evans*, 119, at 127. Boyle also gives other examples.
111 See, for example, the Universal Declaration of Human Rights 1948 (GA Res. 217 A III, UN GAOR 3d Session, UN Doc. A/810, 1948), and Boyle (n. 110), 133–134.
112 For example, the Kimberley Process (n. 98).
113 Boyle (n. 110), 128; *Military and Paramilitary Activities in and against Nicaragua (Nicaragua* v. *United States of America)*, Merits, Judgment. ICJ Reports (1986) 14, at 100, para. 189; *Legality of the Threat or Use of Nuclear Weapons*, Advisory Opinion, ICJ Reports (1996) 226, at 241–243, paras. 28–33.
114 Final Declaration of the Conference of States Parties to the 1925 Geneva Protocol on the Prohibition of Chemical Weapons, 11 January 1989, which paved the way for the Chemical Weapons Convention 1993: 1974 UNTS 45 No. 33757.
115 See, for example, the Framework Convention on Climate Change 1992 (1771 UNTS 107 No. 30822; UKTS (1995) No. 28), cited in Boyle (n. 110), 131–132.

subject to the principles of good faith and *pacta sunt servanda*; and second, whether legal consequences can arise for such instruments through estoppel.

Treaties are subject to the principle of *pacta sunt servanda* as embodied in Article 26 VCLT: 'Every treaty in force is binding upon the parties to it and must be performed by them in good faith.'[116] However, this principle attaches to a prior binding obligation. There must first be a binding 'pact' which has to be observed. Similarly, the principle of 'good faith' does not of itself create or impose a free-standing obligation under international law.[117] The principles do not therefore apply to non-binding instruments. Even if there is an expectation of compliance with a non-binding instrument, that is a political or moral expectation, not a legal expectation, subject to a possible exception in relation to estoppel below.

In general terms, estoppel may be invoked where:

> (a) a State has made clear and consistent representations, by word, conduct, or silence; (b) such representations were made through an agent authorised to speak for the State with respect to the matter in question; (c) the State invoking estoppel was induced by such representations to act to its detriment, to suffer a prejudice, or to convey a benefit upon the representing State; and (d) such reliance was legitimate, as the representation was one on which that State was entitled to rely.[118]

If in the case of a non-binding instrument the representations are constituted by the undertakings in the instrument, there would appear to be a high threshold to cross to establish estoppel, since the participants have normally entered into such arrangements knowing that they are non-binding and taking care to ensure that this outcome is achieved. It is somewhat illogical, therefore, in the absence of other circumstances, to consider that the representations themselves, simply by virtue of the fact that the participants have relied on them, even to the detriment of one of them, are converted from non-binding into binding commitments.

This is in line with the position of the Tribunal in the *Chagos Arbitration*:

> Not all reliance, even to the clear detriment of a State, suffices to create grounds for estoppel. A State that elects to rely to its detriment upon an expressly non-

[116] See further on *pacta sunt servanda*, pp. 188–189.

[117] A. Zimmermann, *Possible Indirect Legal Effects of Non-legally Binding Instruments*, Paper for CAHDI Expert Workshop, 26 March 2021, Strasbourg, 14–16: https://rm.coe.int/1-2-zimmermann-indirect-legal-effects-of-mous-statement/1680a23584. See also *Border and Transborder Armed Actions (Nicaragua* v. *Honduras)*, Jurisdiction and Admissibility, ICJ Reports (1988) 69, at 105, para. 94: 'The principle of good faith is, as the Court has observed, "one of the basic principles governing the creation and performance of legal obligations" (*Nuclear Tests*, ICJ Reports (1974) 253, at 268, para. 46; 457, at 473, para. 49); it is not in itself a source of obligation where none would otherwise exist.' See also the Commentary on *OAS Guideline* 5.3 (n. 7) (The Effects of Political Commitments), 61.

[118] The Arbitral Tribunal in *Chagos Marine Protected Area Arbitration (Mauritius* v. *United Kingdom) (Award of 18 March 2015)*, PCA Case No 2011-03 (2018), 31 RIAA 359, at 544, para. 438. See also *Land, Island and Maritime Frontier (El Salvador/Honduras)*, ICJ Reports (1990) 92, at 118–119, para. 63; *Oppenheim*, 527, para. 154, n. 6.

> binding agreement does not, by so doing, achieve a binding commitment by way of estoppel. Such reliance is not legitimate.[119]

In the absence of special provision, it is inherent in non-binding arrangements that any disputes arising are resolved by diplomatic means rather than binding enforcement mechanisms. There are cases where non-binding instruments have such mechanisms, but this must call into question whether the instrument itself is truly non-binding. By the same reasoning, it would in principle be inconsistent with a non-binding instrument for a participant to seek a legal remedy, even via estoppel, to enforce it.

It is, however, possible to conceive of circumstances where estoppel could arise in respect of a non-binding instrument. This could be, for example, (a) where there was not, in fact, agreement between the participants about the status of the instrument, and one of the participants has subsequently held out the agreement to be legally binding; or (b) where the subsequent practice or subsequent behaviour of one of the parties has otherwise appeared to convert a non-binding commitment into a binding obligation;[120] or (c) where both parties have used non-binding form for convenience and not as a statement of their real intent, although here it is difficult to see how an intent different to the form and language could be established.

One might take the case of an MOU between State A and State B, under which State A expresses its 'intention' to pay State B €4 billion over a period of ten years to pay half the cost of building a dam. State B then starts building the dam. After five years, the dam is half built and State A has paid out €2 billion. It then has a change of government, and the new government decides to stop the funding. It is possible that a legal remedy based on estoppel could arise here, although it would depend upon all the circumstances and upon what representations (and qualifications) had been made. As noted already, there is a high threshold to cross.

Are Non-legally Binding Instruments Simply Treaties in Disguise?

State practice shows that governments see a practical need for non-binding instruments, and are prepared to take measures to ensure a genuine distinction between binding and non-binding commitments. All the evidence suggests that the use of such instruments has grown in recent years, both in the bilateral and multilateral spheres, and that states see advantage in this. If states want to use such instruments, if they draft

[119] *Chagos Marine Protected Area Arbitration* (n. 118), 547, para. 445.

[120] Possibilities (a) and (b) are along the lines of what Judge Fitzmaurice said in *Temple of Preah Vihear (Cambodia* v. *Thailand)*, Judgment of 15 June 1962, Separate Opinion of Sir Gerald Fitzmaurice, ICJ Reports (1962) 52, at 63: 'The real field of operation, therefore, of the rule of preclusion or estoppel, *stricto sensu*, in the present context, is where it is possible that the party concerned did not give the undertaking or accept the obligation in question (or there is room for doubt whether it did), but where that party's subsequent conduct has been such, and has had such consequences, that it cannot be allowed to deny the existence of an undertaking, or that it is bound.'

and conclude them in a particular form, and act subsequently on the basis that they are non-binding, it is hard to argue that the status (or more correctly, the non-legally binding status) of such instruments is different from what the states intend.

The prevalence of such practice, and the widespread awareness of this in the international community, means that there is no need for a presumption as to whether a hypothetical agreement does or does not have treaty status. In most cases, agreements are now drafted consciously with the question of binding or non-binding status in mind. So the real question is not so much what should one *presume to be the status*, but more as to what one *considers the status to be*, having regard to the form and language of the instrument, and the evidence of the parties' intent. In some cases, of course, there will still be ambiguity, but it is still best to resolve this by an assessment of the form, language and intent (and other factors relating to the definition of a treaty or non-binding instrument), rather than by a presumption either way.

Critics of non-binding agreements raise two further practical arguments against their use. The first is that the growth of 'soft law' through multilateral non-binding instruments inhibits the growth of 'hard law' either in the form of treaties or in the form of customary international law. But, as already suggested above, non-binding instruments may act as the only way a prior binding treaty, or indeed a particular area of law, can be implemented or progressed. And since customary international law is established by state practice and *opinio juris*, this can be equally achieved on the basis of non-binding instruments which gradually obtain universal approval.

The second argument is that, in some systems, because of the lack of parliamentary oversight, non-binding instruments defeat democratic accountability. This is not, however, a legal question but one which has to be addressed politically within the context of each country's constitutional system.

Non-legally Binding Instruments in Domestic Courts

A final question is: to what extent will domestic courts apply an MOU or other non-binding instrument?[121] Not all MOUs will be treated in the same way. There is a difference, for example, between a non-binding instrument which is material evidence of the position or actions of the parties (for example, a bilateral instrument made between two states to cover a particular matter) and a non-binding instrument such as a recommendation, report or guideline (or an MOU), which may be relevant to the interpretation of obligations arising from a treaty.

[121] See A. Aust, 'Domestic Consequences of Non-treaty (Non-conventional) Treaty-Making', in R. Wolfrum and V. Roben (eds.), *Developments of International Law in Treaty Making* (Springer, Berlin 2005), 487–496.

Examples of the former category are MOUs concluded with another state concerning the deportation of a person with assurances,[122] the treatment of refugees,[123] the transfer of prisoners,[124] extradition of a person in difficult or special circumstances,[125] or privileges and immunities to be accorded to foreign diplomatic staff.[126] In each of these cases, the MOU has been relevant not so much as an aid to interpretation but as a document indicative of the position or action of a party (normally the UK government in the case of the UK courts) which is the subject of judicial review. The non-binding status of the instrument has not, in such cases, detracted from its potential significance. Hence, in *Rahmatullah* Lord Kerr stated:

> It is common case that the 2003 MoU is not legally binding. It was, said Mr Eadie QC, who appeared for the Secretaries of State, merely a 'political' arrangement. But its significance in legal terms should not be underestimated. That significance does not depend on whether the agreement that it embodies was legally binding as between the parties to it. As Lord Neuberger of Abbotsbury MR said [2012] 1 WLR 1462, para 37, the 2003 MoU was needed by the UK in order to meet its legal obligations under article 12 of [Geneva Convention] 3 and article 45 of [Geneva Convention] 4 . . . Put plainly, the UK needed to have in place an agreement which it could point to as showing that it had effectively ensured that the Geneva Conventions would be complied with in relation to those prisoners that it had handed over to the US. The 2003 MoU was the means of meeting those obligations.[127]

In terms of the weight to be accorded to an MOU, Lord Kerr added:

> Memoranda of understanding or their equivalent, diplomatic notes, are therefore a means by which courts have been invited to accept that the assurances

[122] *Othman* v. *United Kingdom* (2012) EHRR 1, European Court of Human Rights (ECtHR); *Othman (aka Abu Qatada)* v. *Secretary of State for the Home Department* [2013] EWCA Civ 277, UK Court of Appeal; *J1* v. *Secretary of State for the Home Department* [2013] EWCA Civ 27, UK Court of Appeal.

[123] See *AG and Others* v. *Secretary of State for Justice* [2014] 1 LRC 189, [2013] NRSC 10, Supreme Court of Nauru; *R. (Bashir and others)* v. *Secretary of State for the Home Department (AIRE Centre intervening)* [2018] 3 WLR 573, [2017] EWCA Civ 397, UK Supreme Court.

[124] *Rahmatullah* v. *Secretary of State for Defence and another (JUSTICE intervening)* [2012] 3 WLR 1087, UK Supreme Court.

[125] *R. (B and others)* v. *Westminster Magistrates' Court and others* [2015] AC 1195, UK Supreme Court; *Zain Taj Dean* v. *The Lord Advocate and the Scottish Ministers*, 2019 Scot (D) 6/6, [2019] HCJAC 31, Appeal Court, High Court of Justiciary.

[126] *R. (Charles & Dunn)* (n. 102).

[127] *Rahmatullah* (n. 124), para. 11. At para. 13, Lord Kerr also referred to the UK Government's submission in the case of *Othman* v. *United Kingdom* (2012) EHRR 1, at para. 164. 'The Government reiterated that the assurances contained in the MoU had been given in good faith and approved at the highest levels of the Jordanian Government. They were intended to reflect international standards. There was no lack of clarity in them, especially when the MoU was interpreted in its diplomatic and political context. . . . To criticise the MoU because it was not legally binding (as the applicant had) was to betray a lack of an appreciation as to how MoUs worked in practice between states; they were a well-established and much used tool of international relations.'

> which they contain will be honoured. And indeed courts have responded to that invitation by giving the assurances the weight that one would expect to be accorded to solemn undertakings formally committed to by responsible governments.[128]

That is not to imply that the courts will regard a government's undertakings in an MOU as decisive: it will depend on all the circumstances of the case and a factual evaluation.[129]

As for the use of non-binding instruments as an aid to interpretation, courts across a variety of legal systems appear open to arguments that draw on less traditional sources but will proceed with caution.[130] One can find examples of states where instruments of soft law are considered, but at the low end of persuasive authority: much less than unimplemented treaty norms, and less than implemented treaty norms (e.g., in Canada).[131] But there are also examples of cases where a court, when interpreting a particular human rights treaty provision, has had regard to a body of principles in the human rights field or the comments of the Human Rights Committee (e.g., in Japan).[132] In a case concerning a South African tax debt owed by a British Virgin Islands company, the UK Court of Appeal considered an MOU relevant to the interpretation of a tax treaty between the UK and South Africa.[133] In cases where the 'soft law' instrument has been incorporated into domestic law, courts (e.g., in Kenya and Israel) have had no difficulty in applying the instrument, as one would expect.[134]

[128] *Rahmatullah* (n. 124), para. 15.

[129] *RB (Algeria)* v. *Secretary of State for the Home Department; U (Algeria)* v. *Secretary of State for the Home Department; Othman* v. *Secretary of State for the Home Department* [2009] 4 All ER 1045, [2009] UKHL 10, House of Lords (now replaced by UK Supreme Court), Lord Hope at 235–236.

[130] M. Kanetake and A. Nollkaemper, 'The Application of Informal International Instruments before Domestic Courts', *George Washington International Law Review* 46(4) (2014) 765–807, at 774–779.

[131] S. Beaulac and J. H. Currie, 'Canada', in D. Shelton (ed.), *International Law and Domestic Legal Systems* (Oxford University Press, Oxford 2011), 116–157, at 156.

[132] S. H. Bong, 'Japan', in D. Shelton (ed.) (n. 131), 360–384, at 382–383.

[133] *Ben Nevis (Holdings) Ltd and another* v. *Revenue and Customs Commissioners* [2013] STC 1579, [2013] EWCA Civ 578, UK Court of Appeal, at paras. 39–40.

[134] Kanetake and Nollkaemper (n. 130), 772.

4

Capacity to Conclude Treaties

> The making of treaties is one of the oldest and most characteristic exercises of independence or sovereignty on the part of States.[1]

Treaties are made between subjects of international law, in particular, between states,[2] between states and international organisations, and between international organisations. This book deals primarily with treaties between states. Chapter 22 deals with treaties between states and international organisations, and between international organisations.

Every state possesses the capacity to conclude treaties (Article 6). This chapter is concerned with how the treaty-making power is exercised by a state; by parts of the state, such as the constituent units of a federal state; or by, or on behalf of, the overseas territories of a state. It also deals with some special cases: the Cook Islands and Niue, Vatican City (the Holy See), Taiwan, Palestine, Turkish Republic of Northern Cyprus, Somaliland, Western Sahara, and indigenous peoples.[3]

A treaty made between states may be expressed to be made by heads of state, or on behalf of the states, their governments or, less often, their ministries or state agencies. A head of state treaty is used when the subject matter is of exceptional political importance, such as the various constituent treaties of the European Union, though it is not necessary for heads of state to sign in person, and constitutional monarchs do not usually sign anyway.[4] There is no difference in international law between a treaty concluded on behalf of states and one concluded on behalf of governments, ministries or state agencies,[5] since a treaty entered into by a government, ministry or state agency binds the state, and a change of government will, in itself, *not* affect its binding force. For this purpose, the term 'state' generally does not include public bodies that have legal personality separate from that of the state.[6] However, under some constitutions it may be necessary or desirable to use the inter-state form when the provisions of the treaty need to be given full effect in domestic law.

1 *McNair*, 35.

2 Generally on the legal concept of the state, see J. Crawford, *The Creation of States in International Law* (2nd ed., Cambridge University Press, Cambridge 2006) (*Crawford*).

3 See pp. 71–79. 4 See *McNair*, 18–19. 5 See *Oppenheim*, 346–348, para. 109.

6 See the definition of 'party' in Article 2(1)(g): 'a State which has consented to be bound by the treaty and for which the treaty is in force'. See also *McNair*, 668–670.

A treaty expressed to be concluded on behalf of ministries or state agencies may be chosen in order to avoid constitutional procedures. In principle, however, ministries should not conclude treaties when they include matters for which other ministries are responsible in domestic law. A treaty on, say, the status of armed forces will normally include provisions on, among other things, jurisdiction and tax exemption. Since these are not matters for which a defence ministry would normally have domestic responsibility, the treaty should be expressed to be between the governments or states. Although this should make no difference to the respective rights and obligations of the state parties, it may also be a useful reminder of the need to consult other ministries before concluding the treaty.

Similar considerations apply to the conclusion of MOUs and other non-binding instruments (NBIs).[7] It is more common, however, for an NBI to be expressed as being between governments or departments of government rather than between states.

By 'state' is meant a sovereign independent state. This requires territory with a settled population, a sovereign government and independence from any other state. Applying such generally accepted criteria is not always easy. All 193 members of the United Nations can now be regarded as states, though in the past this was not so. Even when they were still republics of the Soviet Union, the Byelorussian SSR (now Belarus) and the Ukrainian SSR (now Ukraine) were able to become parties to at least UN treaties, though their UN membership was only as a result of a political deal under which they were members from the beginning of the United Nations.[8] There are still certain special cases where there is doubt whether a particular entity is a state or, where it is clearly not a state, whether it may still be allowed to participate in a treaty, though not always as a state party.

Special Cases

The Cook Islands and Niue

The legal status of the Cook Islands (population about 14,000) and Niue (population about 1,500) are both self-governing states in free association with New Zealand, with their citizens retaining New Zealand nationality.[9] Both are considered by New Zealand, and the UN Secretary-General in his capacity as depositary of treaties, as

[7] See Chapter 3.

[8] L. M. Goodrich, E. Hambro and A. P. Simons, *The Charter of the United Nations* (3rd ed., Columbia University Press, New York 1969), 81–83.

[9] For the New Zealand Ministry of Foreign Affairs and Trade website defining the relationship with the Cook Islands, including the 4 Year Plan agreed in October 2021, see www.mfat.govt.nz/en/countries-and-regions/australia-and-pacific/cook-islands/. For relevant constitutional provisions of the Cook Islands and statements, see www.ck/govt.htm#mis.

having treaty-making capacity, and this has been accepted, expressly or tacitly, by many states.[10] The Guidance on International Treaty Making issued by the New Zealand Ministry of Foreign Affairs and Trade states:

> While not fully independent, the Cook Islands and Niue are recognised as 'states' at international law. Since the mid-1980s they have generally conducted their own treaty making. In 1988 the New Zealand Government declared to the Secretary-General of the United Nations that from that point onwards, New Zealand treaty actions would not extend to the Cook Islands or Niue unless expressly done on their behalf. New Zealand treaties that were extended to the Cook Islands and Niue prior to 1988 (and, in a few cases, since 1988) continue to apply to the Cook Islands and Niue.[11]

In the last thirty years, the Cook Islands (and to a lesser extent Niue) have become parties to many multilateral treaties under their 'all states' clauses, and full members of some UN specialised agencies (but *not* the United Nations, to which neither has applied for membership).[12] In 2019, it became party to four WIPO copyright treaties.[13] Although it has not yet been recognised generally as a sovereign state, the Cook Islands has established diplomatic relations with over twenty states (including Australia, France, Germany and New Zealand) and international organisations.

Following a referendum in 2006, held under the auspices of the UN Special Committee on Decolonisation, Tokelau remains an overseas territory of New Zealand without the rather special status of the Cook Islands or Niue.

Vatican City (the Holy See)

The main purpose of the Vatican City is to support the religious functions of the Holy See.[14] But, as a result of the so-called Lateran Pacts 1929 between the Holy See and

[10] Available at: http://treaties.un.org/Pages/HistoricalInfo.aspx. See the entries for the Cook Islands and Niue. See also the Cook Islands–US Peace Corps Agreement 1981 (1285 UNTS 114 No. 21171) in which New Zealand is not mentioned. On the special status of the Cook Islands and Niue, see *Crawford*, 629–633.

[11] International Treaty Making, Guidance for government agencies, New Zealand Ministry of Foreign Affairs and Trade, September 2021, at www.mfat.govt.nz/assets/About-us-Corporate/Treaties-Model-instruments/International-Treaty-Making-Guide-2021.pdf.

[12] In 1995, the Cook Islands became a party to UNCLOS under Art. 305(1)(c) as a self-governing associated state with competence to enter into treaties in respect of the subject matter of that Convention. This would seem to have been because the provision had been drafted deliberately to cover countries like the Cook Islands. But the Cook Islands became a party in its own right to the UN Convention on the Rights of Persons with Disabilities 2006 (2515 UNTS 3 No. 44910).

[13] See Cook Islands Accedes to Four Key WIPO Copyright Treaties, at: www.wipo.int/portal/en/news/2019/article 0013.html.

[14] For a thorough discussion of the status of the Vatican City and the Holy See respectively, see *Crawford*, 222–233.

(Mussolini's) Italy,[15] and recognition or acquiescence by states, the Vatican City (albeit tiny in area and with a resident population of papal functionaries) is nevertheless a subject of international law, a full member of some international organisations, and a party to several bilateral and multilateral treaties.[16]

The Holy See is a distinct legal entity from the Vatican City and a separate subject of international law. Like the Vatican City, its exact legal status is not clear. It has joined various intergovernmental organisations, is party to a substantial number of bilateral and multilateral treaties, sends and receives diplomatic representatives, and has been granted permanent observer status at the United Nations.[17] The sovereign of both the Vatican State and the Holy See is the Pope. The Vatican State constitutes the territorial basis for the Holy See, which has unimpeded sovereign powers and jurisdiction over the Vatican State.[18] There appears to be no clear systematic reason determining when it is the Holy See or the Vatican City which will become party to a treaty or convention.[19]

Taiwan

Following the civil war in China, which left the mainland under the control of the communist forces, the (nationalist) government of the Republic of China fled to the island of Taiwan (Formosa). In 1949, the victorious communists proclaimed the People's Republic of China (PRC), which soon became generally recognised. Yet the government on Taiwan still claims to be the government of all China, and has therefore *not* claimed *separate* statehood for Taiwan.[20] The trade deal between China and Taiwan, which ended tariffs on hundreds of products traded between China and Taiwan, was therefore not embodied in a treaty. Nor is the Cross-Straits Economic Cooperation Framework Agreement of 19 June 2010 a treaty.[21] Although drawn up as one, and having the provisions one expects to find in a treaty, it is expressed to be between the Straits Foundation and the Association for Relations Across the Taiwan Straits, that is, 'front organisations' for China and Taiwan.

As the purported government of China, Taiwan has diplomatic relations and treaties only with some small and developing states. In January 2002, Taiwan (under the name 'Chinese Taipei') became a member of the World Trade Organization, on

[15] They consisted of the Treaty of Conciliation, with an annexed Financial Convention (amended in 1985) and the Concordat: AJIL Supp. (1929) 187; 130 BFSP 791.

[16] *Oppenheim*, 325–329, paras. 99–102; *Shaw*, 224–225. See also AJIL Supp. 29 (1935) 701–703.

[17] C. Ryngaert, 'The Legal Status of the Holy See', *Goettingen Journal of International Law* 3 (2011) 829–859.

[18] See G. Westdickenberg, 'Holy See', *MPEPIL* (2006), paras. 2–5. For a viewpoint arguing against statehood, see J. R. Morss, 'The International Legal Status of the Vatican/Holy See Complex', *European Journal of International Law* 26(4) (November 2015) 927–946.

[19] Westdickenberg (n. 18), para. 11.

[20] See *Crawford*, 198–221; and B. Ahl, 'Taiwan', *MPEPIL* (2020).

[21] See the ASIL ILIB for 1 November 2010.

the basis that it is a separate customs territory, in the same way as Hong Kong, China and Macao, China and the European Union previously.

The liaison offices (not diplomatic missions) in Taipei of over a dozen states, including Australia, the Netherlands, New Zealand, Sweden and the United Kingdom, have concluded 'agreements' with the Taiwan authorities on matters such as double taxation.[22] As such states do not recognise Taiwan as a state, the agreements, though containing some treaty-type language, are not treaties. China is aware of the agreements, but is not known to have objected.

Other ways have been found by which Taiwan can effectively participate, though not as a party, in certain other treaties. For example, on 5 September 2000 Taiwan entered into a non-binding arrangement:[23] the Arrangement for the Participation of Fishing Entities in the Convention on the Conservation and Management of Highly Migratory Fish Stocks in the Western and Central Pacific Ocean 2000.[24]

Palestine

During the armed conflict with Arab States in 1967, Israeli forces occupied all the territories that had constituted Palestine under the Mandate, including the West Bank and East Jerusalem (from Jordan); as well as the Gaza Strip (from Egypt – the *land* territory of which was relinquished by Israel to the Palestinian Authority in 2005); and the Golan Heights (from Syria). The territories so occupied are generally considered to be under military occupation subject to the limitations of the Hague Regulations 1907 (Section III) and the Fourth Geneva Convention.

In November 1988, the Palestine National Council and the Parliamentary Assembly of the Palestine Liberation Organization (PLO) declared a State of Palestine, which claims the occupied territories. Since 1993, a number of bilateral instruments between Israel and the PLO have been concluded that cannot be regarded as treaties, the terminology 'the two sides' being used.[25] In 1994, a nascent Palestinian government was established, the Palestinian Authority.[26] Because of the threat of US veto in the UN Security Council, in 2011 Palestine was not admitted as a member of the United Nations[27] but, pursuant to UN General Assembly resolution

[22] For example, the Agreement between the British Cultural Office, Taipei and the Taipei Representative Office in the United Kingdom for the Avoidance of Double Taxation 2002, at https://assets.publishing.service.gov.uk/government/uploads/system/uploads/attachment_data/file/507421/taiwan-dta_-_in_force.pdf. The agreement is not published in the UK Treaty Series. A Protocol to the Agreement was signed at London on 11 August 2021.

[23] For non-binding instruments and arrangements, see Chapter 3.

[24] See Arrangement for the Participation of Fishing Entities at www.oceanlaw.net/texts.

[25] See the Declaration of Principles on Interim Self-Government Arrangements 1993 (32 ILM (1993) 1525) and the Sharm el-Sheikh Memorandum 1999 (38 ILM (1999) 1465).

[26] For details, see *Shaw*, 215–218.

[27] See UNGA Resolution 52/250 (1998). However, Palestine became a member of UN Educational, Scientific and Cultural Organization (UNESCO) in 2011 by 102 votes for, 14 against and 52 abstentions *and* had also

67/19 adopted on 29 November 2012,[28] Palestine assumed the status of a UN 'non-member observer State'.

Given that the Palestinian Authority lacks control over much of the territory it claims, Palestine has not yet succeeded in being generally recognised as a state, although a large number of states have done so.[29] 'The State of Palestine' has in recent years acceded to a number of multilateral treaties, though this has met with objections from some parties.[30] The question of its acceptance of the jurisdiction of the International Criminal Court (ICC), and its subsequent accession to the Rome Statute, has been subject to extensive consideration in the context of proceedings concerning the ICC's territorial jurisdiction in Palestine.[31] The European Union's bilateral Interim Association Agreement was concluded in 1997[32] on the Palestinian side by the 'Palestinian Liberation Organization (PLO) for the benefit of the Palestinian Authority of the West Bank and the Gaza Strip',[33] and a subsequent agreement in the form of an Exchange of Letters was concluded in 2011 by 'the Palestinian Authority of the West Bank and the Gaza Strip'.[34]

Turkish Republic of Northern Cyprus

The so-called Turkish Republic of Northern Cyprus (TRNC) is recognised by, and has treaties with, only one state: Turkey.[35] Following the decision of representatives of the Turkish Cypriot community in 1963 to cease participating in organs of the Republic of Cyprus, and refusing to recognise its laws, there were extensive population movements resulting in the majority of the Turkish Cypriots moving to the north of the island. In 1974, following a coup d'état in the Republic of Cyprus, inspired by the then military regime in Greece, the Turkish army invaded the north,

to sign and ratify the UNESCO Constitution (though the latter was merely a formality): Palestine Admitted to UNESCO | UNESCO History - UNESCO Multimedia Archives. Despite its name, UNESCO is *not* a part of the United Nations, and has no body, similar to the UN Security Council, which gives a permanent member a veto over an application for membership.

28 A/Res/67/19. 29 At the time of writing, some 139 states recognise Palestine.

30 See, for example, the objections in respect of the Rome Statute referred to in the 'Prosecution request pursuant to article 19(3) for a ruling on the Court's territorial jurisdiction in Palestine', ICC-01/18, 22 January 2020, para. 131.

31 See the Prosecution request (n. 30), and the Decision of Pre-Trial Chamber I on the 'Prosecution request pursuant to article 19(3) for a ruling on the Court's territorial jurisdiction in Palestine', ICC-01/18, 5 February 2021. See also *Shaw*, 217.

32 OJ L 187, 16 July 1997, 3–135.

33 A similar Interim Political, Trade and Partnership Agreement, signed at Ramallah, 18 February 2019, was concluded by the UK also with 'the Palestine Liberation Organization (PLO) for the benefit of the Palestinian Authority of the West Bank and the Gaza Strip': UK Misc. Series (2019) No. 14. In its Explanatory Memorandum submitted to Parliament in February 2019, the UK Government stated: 'Nothing in the UK–Palestinian Authority Interim Agreement should be interpreted as recognition by the UK of Palestine as a State. Accordingly, the Agreement is not formally a treaty falling within the scope of section 25(1) of the Constitutional Reform and Governance Act 2010.'

34 See *Crawford*, 144–145; *Shaw*, 212–213. 35 See *Shaw*, 235–236.

and continues to occupy it.[36] A buffer zone (the Green Line) separates the occupied north from the south. The Republic of Cyprus became a member of the European Union on 1 May 2004, but, for the time being, not in respect of those areas in which the government of the Republic of Cyprus does not exercise effective control (i.e., the occupied north).

Somaliland

Somaliland is part of the State of Somalia.[37] Somaliland was until 1960 a UK protectorate (in practice a colony). For a few days in 1960, it was independent. Then it became part of Somalia, though *in practice* Somaliland seceded from Somalia in 1991 after the fall of the communist dictator of that state, Siad Barre. But, so far, Somaliland has not been recognised by any state.[38] It can, therefore, at most enter into non-binding instruments.

Western Sahara

In 1963 the UN added Western Sahara to its list of non-self-governing territories. In 1975, the International Court of Justice (ICJ), in an Advisory Opinion, recognised the right of the people of Western Sahara to self-determination.[39] In 1976, following the withdrawal of Spain from the territory (population about 300,000), it was partitioned between Mauritania and Morocco. When Mauritania withdrew in 1979, Morocco took control of the whole territory. Today, Morocco continues to govern most of the territory, save for a small part in the east which is controlled by the Polisario Front.[40] The Polisario Front has disputed Morocco's sovereignty over the territory and fought a guerrilla war with Morocco. That ended in 1991 with a UN-brokered ceasefire. A UN-organised referendum on the final status of the territory has been repeatedly postponed.[41]

In 2012, the Polisario Front brought a challenge against the Council of the European Union in respect of the application to Western Sahara of an Agreement between the EU and Morocco concerning liberalisation measures on agricultural

[36] See *Oppenheim*, 189–190, para. 55; *Crawford*, 143–147.

[37] Somalia was described by many as a 'failed state' because its government controlled only a small part of the capital, Mogadishu, thanks to soldiers from a neighbouring state, but Somalia was throughout this time still a member of the United Nations.

[38] See *Crawford*, Index.

[39] *Western Sahara*, Advisory Opinion, ICJ Reports (1975) 12, at 68, para. 162. And see C. Feinäugle, 'Western Sahara (Advisory Opinion)' *MPEPIL* (2007).

[40] See A. Whelan, 'Council v. Front Polisario Case', *MPEPIL* (2019), para. 7; Case T-512/12, *Front Polisario* v. *Council of the European Union* (10 December 2015), ECLI:EU:T:2015:953, para. 16.

[41] See Whelan (n. 40), para. 7. See also *Crawford*, 606–647 (Non-Self-Governing Territories).

products,[42] which amended the EU–Morocco Association Agreement. While the General Court in its 2015 judgment rejected the Polisario Front's arguments, it found that the territorial scope of the Association Agreement encompassed Western Sahara (as part of 'the territory of the Kingdom of Morocco'), and that the Council had an obligation:

> . . .where it intended to approve an agreement which was applicable to a 'disputed territory' such as Western Sahara and sought to facilitate the export to the European Union of products originating in that territory, to examine in advance all the relevant facts of the individual case, and in particular to ensure that the production of those products was not carried out in a manner detrimental to the population of that territory and did not entail infringements of fundamental rights of the persons concerned.[43]

The CJEU, however, upheld an appeal by the Council against that decision on the grounds that the separate status of Western Sahara as a non-self-governing territory, which followed from the principle of self-determination, meant that the Agreement could not be interpreted so as to include Western Sahara within its territorial scope.[44] It also found, based on the principle that a treaty does not create third party obligations or rights without consent, that the people of Western Sahara would need to consent to any application of trade preferences to products originating in Western Sahara. The same reasoning was followed by the CJEU in a subsequent case concerning the application of the EU–Morocco Fishing Partnership Agreement[45] to the waters adjacent to Western Sahara.[46]

The EU and Morocco amended the previous agreements in the light of the two CJEU judgments. The EU consulted the people of Western Sahara and then expressly extended trade preferences under the EU–Morocco Association Agreement to certain products originating in Western Sahara (without the territorial scope of the Agreement

[42] Agreement in the form of an Exchange of Letters between the EU and Morocco concerning reciprocal liberalisation measures on agricultural products etc. 2010: OJ L 241, 7.09.2012, 4–47; 3002 UNTS 180 No. 37068.

[43] Judgment of the General Court in Case T-512/12 (n. 40), paras. 223–247, summarised by the CJEU in Case C-104/16 P, *Council of the European Union* v. *Front Polisario* (21 December 2016), ECLI:EU:C:2016:973, para. 47.

[44] Case C-104/16 P (n. 45), paras. 84–127.

[45] EC–Morocco Fisheries Partnership Agreement, initialled 28 July 2005: OJ L 141, 29.05.2006, 4–37; amending Protocol 2013: OJ L 328, 7.12.2013, 2–39.

[46] Case C-266/16 *Western Sahara Campaign UK* v. *Commissioner for Her Majesty's Revenue and Customs and Secretary of State for Environment, Food and Rural Affairs* (27 February 2018) ECLI:EU:C:2018:118. In the UK litigation following the CJEU decision, with the agreement of the parties the judge made declarations which stated that 'These state that neither the Association Agreement nor the Fisheries Partnership Agreement encompass either the territory of Western Sahara or the waters adjacent to it [and] . . . that HMRC erred in law in not exercising its power to investigate and query the stated place of origin of products originating in Western Sahara and imported into the UK under the country code "MA" in EUR.1 certificates': [2019] EWHC 684 (Admin), para. 12, Queen's Bench Division, Administrative Court (London).

covering Western Sahara), while the amended Fisheries Agreement expressly included within its scope the waters adjacent to the territory of Western Sahara. In a further challenge brought by the Polisario Front, the General Court in its 2021 judgment held that the Polisario Front had the necessary legal capacity to bring a case before the Court, and upheld the applicant's argument that the requirement relating to the consent of the people of Western Sahara, as a third party to the agreements at issue, had not been respected by the previous EU consultation.[47] As at May 2022, these judgments are the subject of appeal. In parallel to this, the Western Sahara Campaign UK has brought a challenge against the UK government[48] in respect of trade preferences to certain products originating in Western Sahara under the UK–Morocco Association Agreement concluded in 2019 in the context of the UK's withdrawal from the European Union.[49]

Indigenous Peoples[50]

During the period of colonisation, the colonial states concluded treaties with indigenous peoples for the cession of territory, the most notable being probably the Treaty of Waitangi between the United Kingdom and certain Māori chiefs in 1840.[51] Though the status of these treaties was uncertain, influential voices regarded them as international treaties.[52] Through the nineteenth century, however, the growing practice was for such agreements to be considered within the framework of national law. By the first half of the twentieth century, the general view was that agreements with indigenous peoples were not treaties in the sense then prevailing under international law.[53] But, in recent decades, this has been reassessed, and 'agreements with local rulers' have been considered as derivative roots of title, and not original titles obtained by occupation of *terrae nullius*.[54] The international community has been concerned to ensure that rights under the original treaties are respected.[55] While

[47] Judgments in Case T-279/19 and in Joined Cases T-344/19 and T-356/19, *Front Polisario* v. *Council* (29 September 2021), ECLI:EU:T:2021:639, ECLI:EU:T:2021:640.

[48] *Western Sahara Campaign UK* v. *Secretary of State for International Trade and others*, QBD, Administrative Court, pending hearing at the time of writing.

[49] UK–Morocco Association Agreement 2019: UK Country Series, Morocco (2019) No. 2. The application of trade preferences under it to Western Sahara follow the approach in the amended EU–Morocco Association Agreement.

[50] See *Crawford*, 260–274; T. Grant, 'Who Can Make Treaties? Other Subjects', in *Hollis, Oxford Guide*, 150–172, at 157–158; *Dörr and Schmalenbach*, 77–79, paras. 56–58; A. Peters, 'Treaty Making Power', *MPEPIL* (2009), paras. 66–71; G. Alfredsson, 'Treaties with Indigenous Peoples', *MPEPIL* (2011); *Oppenheim*, 1217, para. 595, n. 2.

[51] 1840: 6 Hertslet 579; 29 BFSP 1111.

[52] See Peters (n. 50), para. 67.

[53] See Max Huber in the *Island of Palmas Case [Netherlands* v. *United States of America]* (1928) 2 RIAA 829, 858: 'As regards contracts between a State ... and native princes or chiefs of peoples not recognized as members of the community of nations, they are not, in the international law sense, treaties or conventions.'

[54] *Western Sahara*, Advisory Opinion (n. 39), at 39, para. 80.

[55] See Article 37, UN Declaration on the Rights of Indigenous Peoples, UNGA Res 61/295, 13 September 2007, Annex.

stopping short of attributing to indigenous peoples treaty-making capacity, the right of indigenous communities to enter private and public agreements has been recognised.[56] New Zealand has included specific provisions relation to the interests of Māori in free trade agreements.[57]

Federations (and Analogous Entities)

Some states have constitutions under which the state is divided into political subdivisions.[58] The constituent units of a federation are the typical case, though this and other terms used to describe the constitution of a state must be treated with caution; no two constitutions, and especially *federal* constitutions, are the same, although certain patterns can be discerned.[59] The constituent units of a federation do not have territorial sovereignty, but, as a matter of constitutional law, they have exclusive competence over certain matters, share competence with the federation on some matters, and have no competence on all other matters.

Federal constitutions vary on the question of whether the constituent units have the power to enter into *treaties*.[60] The Australian states and Canadian provinces have no such power.[61] But, in order to exercise more control over *non-treaty arrangements*, at the end of 2020 Australia enacted legislation that gives the Federal Minister for Foreign Affairs powers to prevent a prospective foreign arrangement being concluded by a constituent state from proceeding, and to cancel an existing arrangement, where the arrangement is not consistent with Australia's foreign policy or adversely affects Australia's foreign relations.[62] With respect to Canada, Quebec has

[56] See *Dörr and Schmalenbach*, 79, para. 58; Grant, (n. 50), 158; and Article 36(1) UN Declaration on the Rights of Indigenous Peoples (n. 55).

[57] See chapter 26, UK–New Zealand Free Trade Agreement: UK Country Series, New Zealand (2022) No. 1.

[58] See the ILC Commentary on Article 4 of the Draft Articles on the Responsibility of States for Internationally Wrongful Acts, YBILC 11 (2001), Part Two, 40–42 (https://legal.un.org/ilc/); or J. Crawford, *The International Law Commission's Articles on State Responsibility* (Cambridge University Press, Cambridge 2002), 94–99.

[59] *McNair*, 36.

[60] See Grant (n. 50), 151–156; Peters (n. 50), paras. 19–32; W. Rudolf, 'Federal States', *MPEPIL* (2011), paras. 18–27.

[61] B. Opeskin, 'Federal States in the International Legal Order', NILR (1996) 353–386 (n. 45 and generally). See also G. van Ert, 'The Legal Character of Provincial Agreements with Foreign Governments', *Les Cahiers de Droit* (2001) 1093–1124; D. Hollis, M. R. Blakeslee and L. B. Ederington (eds.), *National Treaty Law and Practice* (Martinus Nijhoff, Leiden 2005), 91.

[62] Australia's Foreign Relations (State and Territory Arrangements) Act 2020 (Cth), and the associated Australia's Foreign Relations (State and Territory Arrangements) Rules 2020. The Act covers 'foreign arrangements', which are arrangements between state and territory governments (and their entities) and foreign entities. The term 'arrangement' is defined very broadly to mean a written arrangement, agreement, contract, understanding or undertaking, whether or not it is legally binding, made in Australia or elsewhere and whether entered into before or after the Act commences.

concluded over 700 agreements with foreign states, institutions or subnational units,[63] many of which are called '*ententes*', which have less than treaty status.[64]

Although the US Constitution prohibits the states of the Union from entering into 'agreements' with foreign states, they have in fact entered into them, particularly in recent decades, though most appear to have been only with the constituent units of other federations or not to have been in legally binding form. The subjects have been largely in the fields of trade, development, finance and culture.[65] Thus, it is doubtful if any are treaties, as that term is defined in the Convention.[66]

On the other hand, some federal constitutions authorise their constituent units to enter into agreements (that may, or may not, be treaties) on matters within their legislative competence or if they have the specific approval of the federation, though it is generally in respect of a limited range of subjects.[67] Under the German Constitution (Basic Law), the *Länder* have limited power to conclude 'agreements' in their own name on matters relating to *Land* legislation.[68] Nevertheless, the prior consent of the federal government is needed for each agreement. Since 1949, the *Länder* have concluded many such agreements, mostly with neighbouring states, concerning technical matters such as border arrangements. Under the Swiss Constitution, the Confederation has comprehensive treaty-making power, but the cantons may conclude 'agreements' (which again may, or may not, be treaties) within the area of their competence. They can be negotiated by a canton, but must be approved by the Federal Council before they can be signed.[69] Since 2000, some 30 new agreements have been concluded.

Neither of these examples suggests that such agreements are binding only on the constituent unit. Given the need for federal consent, they *may* be properly regarded, at least in international law, as ultimately the responsibility of the federal state.[70] This

[63] C.-E. Côté, 'Federalism and Foreign Affairs in Canada', in C. A. Bradley (ed.), *The Oxford Handbook of Comparative Foreign Relations Law* (Oxford University Press, Oxford 2019), 277–296, 284–286.

[64] See *OAS Guidelines*, 62–63, Commentary on *Guideline* 2.2, n. 81: 'See Canada Response ... indicating that "only the Canadian federal government can bind Canada" to treaties rather than government ministries or provinces; "provinces and territories can only conclude non-binding instruments".' See also Grant (n. 50), 155.

[65] H. J. Michelmann and P. Soldatos (eds.), *Federalism and International Relations* (Clarendon Press, Oxford 1990), 283–287.

[66] See also the MOU on Economic and Trade Relations between the State of Indiana (USA) and the Government of the UK, signed at Indianapolis, 27 May 2022: available on UK Department for International Trade website. The MOU states expressly that it is not legally binding (Section 10).

[67] *Oppenheim*, 248–255, paras. 75–76.

[68] Article 32(3) *Grundgesetz* (Basic Law). See, generally, Hollis *et al.* (n. 61), 317–347; Rudolf (n. 60), paras. 19–27.

[69] See R. Portmann, 'Foreign Affairs Federalism in Switzerland', in C. A. Bradley (ed.), *The Oxford Handbook of Comparative Foreign Relations Law* (Oxford University Press, Oxford 2019), 297–314, 307–308.

[70] There may be exceptions where the other state (contracting party) has agreed to limit itself to recourse against the constituent unit in event of a breach, or the responsibility of the federal state under a treaty may be limited by the terms of a federal clause in the treaty: see ILC Commentary (n. 58), 42, para. (10).

is not so surprising. Most states are unitary, with one government and one legislature. They do not look with favour on federations that seek special treatment for their constituent units. It is not enough for a federal constitution to purport to confer on the constituent units the power to conclude an agreement or a treaty, or for the federation to assert it. When another state concludes an agreement with a constituent unit of a federation, it is not that state's responsibility to acquaint itself with the – inevitably complex – rules governing the relationship between the federation and its constituent units. The main concern of a state dealing with a constituent unit is the problem of implementation and, if necessary, enforcement. It is, therefore, right to be cautious about entering into an agreement with a constituent unit without an assurance that the unit is acting on behalf, or with the authority, of the federation. There will then be less doubt that it is a treaty, and that the federation will be ultimately responsible for it in international law. If a constituent unit has not been duly authorised by the federal government, the legal status of the instrument could well be more problematic. Unless it is governed by, say, domestic law – in which case it may be a contract – it may be no more than a non-binding instrument. The same would apply to agreements between governments and municipalities of other states.

Such sharing of power, and particularly legislative power, between a federation and its constituent units can cause huge problems for the federal state when it wishes to become party to a treaty that requires implementation also in the law of the constituent units. This can be dealt with to some extent by the use of territorial and federal clauses, and federal reservations and declarations. Alternatively, a state can always conclude a non-binding instrument with a constituent unit of a federation. The Canada–United Kingdom Social Security Convention 1997 provides for the United Kingdom to conclude 'understandings' *(ententes* in the French text) with a Canadian province on matters within the latter's jurisdiction and consistent with the Convention.[71]

Belgium

Although a small country by land area, since 1993 Belgium has had a particularly complex federal structure. It is composed of three regions and three 'communities' (Flemish, French and German). Each region has exclusive competence for a wide range of matters in its area, including water resources and the environment, and is empowered by the Belgian Constitution to enter into *treaties* on such matters.[72] In 1994, the Walloon Region, Flemish Region and Brussels-Capital Region

[71] UK–Canada Convention on Social Security 1997: 2038 UNTS 344 No. 35254; UKTS (1998) No. 43 (Article 13). See also the UK–State of Indiana MOU (n. 66).

[72] See A. Alen and P. Peeters, 'Federal Belgium within the International Legal Order', in K. Wellens (ed.), *International Law: Theory and Practice, Essays in Honour of Eric Suy* (Kluwer Law, The Hague 1998), 123–143; *Revue Belge de Droit International* 1 (1997) 337–338.

entered into two treaties with the Netherlands and France regarding the rivers Meuse and Scheldt.[73]

However, the provisions of the Belgian Constitution do not mean that Belgium is not responsible in international law for the carrying out of treaties entered into by its regions. On signing the 1994 Treaty of Accession of Austria, Finland and Sweden to the European Union, Belgium made a declaration that it *and* the communities and regions had 'entered into an undertaking at the international level'. The other member states made a counter-declaration (which Belgium confirmed was correct) that the Belgium declaration was an explanation of Belgian constitutional law, and that Belgium alone was responsible for discharging the obligations of the treaty.[74] When signing the Amsterdam Treaty 1997, Belgium stated that its signature also bound the communities and the regions, but confirmed that Belgium alone 'would bear full responsibility for compliance with the obligations entered into in the Treaty'.[75] Belgium also made a similar statement in respect of treaties concluded both by the European Community and its member states ('mixed agreements').[76]

Scotland, Wales and Northern Ireland

The United Kingdom is still essentially a unitary state, but constitutional changes that have come into force from 1999 onwards have devolved certain legislative and executive powers to Scotland, Wales and Northern Ireland. Although the Scotland Act 1998 reserves to the United Kingdom the power to make treaties, their observation and implementation is not reserved and the Scottish Parliament enjoys legislative competence to implement treaty obligations in some contexts.[77] Nevertheless, the United Kingdom remains solely responsible under international law for *all* treaty obligations. Similar arrangements pertain to Wales[78] and Northern Ireland. The Northern Ireland Act 1998 has similar provisions, and permits ministers of the Northern Ireland government to enter into certain informal arrangements (i.e., non-binding instruments) with the government of Ireland.[79] Administrative procedures on the conduct of international relations, insofar as they affect the Scottish, Welsh and Northern Ireland administrations, are set out in separate 'concordats'

[73] Agreements on the Protection of the Rivers Meuse and Scheldt 1994: 34 ILM (1995) 851.

[74] OJ 1994 No. C 241/402, 29.08.1994. [75] OJ 1997 No. C 340/307, 10.11.1997.

[76] OJ 1995 No. C 157/1, 23.06.1995. For mixed agreements, see p. 412. After the Treaty of Lisbon, such agreements have been concluded by the EU and its member states.

[77] Scotland Act 1998, section 30 and Schedule 5, para. 7. On the legislative competence of the Scottish Parliament in respect of international agreements, see *Reference by the Attorney General and the Advocate General for Scotland – United Nations Convention on the Rights of the Child (Incorporation) (Scotland) Bill; and Reference – European Charter of Local Self-Government (Incorporation) (Scotland) Bill*, [2021] UKSC 42, UK Supreme Court.

[78] See Section 108A and Schedule 7A, Government of Wales Act 2006.

[79] Northern Ireland Act 1998, sections 4(1) and 53, and Schedule 2, para. 3.

agreed between the Foreign, Commonwealth and Development Office and the administrations.[80]

Bosnia and Herzegovina, Republika Srpska and the Federal Republic of Yugoslavia

The parties to the Dayton Agreement 1995[81] were Bosnia and Herzegovina, Croatia and the Federal Republic of Yugoslavia (FRY). The preamble notes an agreement of 29 August 1995, 'which authorised the delegation of the FRY to sign, on behalf of the Republika Srpska, the parts of the peace plan concerning it, with the obligation to implement the agreement that is reached strictly and consequently [sic]'. Annexed to the Dayton Agreement were several detailed agreements to which Republika Srpska and the Federation of Bosnia and Herzegovina are expressed to be parties, even though they are constituent parts of Bosnia and Herzegovina, and agreements between Bosnia and Herzegovina, Republika Srpska and the Federation. The FRY 'endorsed' the agreements and, in the case of two of them, the FRY Foreign Minister gave a written assurance that the FRY would 'take all necessary steps, consistent with the sovereignty, territorial integrity and political independence of Bosnia and Herzegovina, to ensure that the Republika Srpska fully respects and complies with' them. Thus, one state gave, in effect, undertakings to another state for the performance of an agreement by a constituent part of that other state. In respect of other agreements, the two self-governing entities of Bosnia and Herzegovina (Republika Srpska and the Federation) may enter into agreements with states and international organisations with the approval of the parliamentary assembly.[82]

Kosovo

Kosovo unilaterally declared independence from Serbia on 17 February 2008. This was coordinated with other states in the international community, although Serbia contested Kosovo's statehood, and continues to do so. In October 2008, the ICJ was asked the following question by the UN General Assembly: is the unilateral declaration of independence by the Provisional Institutions of Self-government of Kosovo in accordance with international law? On 22 July 2010, the ICJ concluded, by ten votes to four, that the adoption of the declaration of independence did not violate general international law, Security Council Resolution 1244 (1999) or the

80 See D: Concordat on International Relations (under Memorandum of Understanding and Supplementary Agreements), October 2013, at: https://assets.publishing.service.gov.uk/government/uploads/system/uploads/attachment_data/file/316157/MoU_between_the_UK_and_the_Devolved_Administrations.pdf.

81 35 ILM (1996) 75. See also *Crawford*, 528–530; P. Gaeta, 'The Dayton Agreements and International Law', EJIL 7(2) (1996) 147–163. Signature of the Dayton Agreement in Paris on 14 December 1995 was witnessed by the Spanish, UK and Russian Prime Ministers, the German Chancellor, and the French and US presidents.

82 Article III.2.d Constitution of Bosnia and Herzegovina.

constitutional framework.[83] As at May 2022, over 100 states that are members of the United Nations have recognised Kosovo as a state.

Hong Kong and Macao Special Administrative Regions

The Special Administrative Regions (SARs) of Hong Kong and Macao are both part of China, but a special treaty regime – based on the principle of 'one country, two systems' – has been established for each of them. (The regime for the Macao SAR is similar to that of the Hong Kong SAR.)[84]

The circumstances of the handover of Hong Kong to China at midnight on 1 July 1997 were unique and do not provide much in the way of insight into more usual treaty problems. But because the arrangements made for the continuation of Hong Kong's treaty relations are of interest beyond China and the United Kingdom, some detail might be helpful.

The future status of Hong Kong was agreed by a treaty, the China–United Kingdom Joint Declaration on the Question of Hong Kong 1984.[85] After the handover on 1 July 1997, Hong Kong was to have the status of a Special Administrative Region of China and be known as the 'Hong Kong Special Administrative Region' (HKSAR). Under the treaty, it is entitled to a high degree of autonomy, except for foreign and defence affairs, which are the responsibility of the Central People's Government (CPG).[86] Matters with respect to the conclusion of treaties are governed by the following principles.[87]

Section XI of Annex I to the Joint Declaration provides, in part, that:

> The application to the [HKSAR] of international agreements to which the People's Republic of China is or becomes a party shall be decided by the Central People's Government, in accordance with the circumstances and needs of the [HKSAR], and after seeking the views of the [HKSAR] Government. International agreements to which the People's Republic of China is not a party but which are implemented in Hong Kong may remain implemented in the [HKSAR].[88]

[83] *Accordance with International Law of the Unilateral Declaration of Independence in Respect of Kosovo*, Advisory Opinion, ICJ Reports (2010) 403 (Advisory Opinion on Kosovo).

[84] See at: http://treaties.un.org/pages/HistoricalInfo.aspx under 'China', see Note 1, Note 2 (Hong Kong) and Note 3 (Macao).

[85] 1399 UNTS 33 No. 23391; 23 ILM (1984) 1366; UKTS (1985) No. 26. The Joint Declaration entered into force on 28 May 1985. As to its treaty status, see p. 38. For the legal and political background to the negotiation, see BYIL 60 (1989) 593–598; for the UK Government paper of April 1996 on the application of international agreements after 30 June/1 July 1997, see BYIL 68 (1997) 529–535.

[86] See also Articles 12 and 13 Basic Law – the Hong Kong Constitution, at: www.basiclaw.gov.hk/en/index/.

[87] On the continued application of treaties to the Hong Kong SAR after 1 July 1997, see pp. 387–391.

[88] See also Article 153 Basic Law.

Section 3(9) and (10) of the Joint Declaration authorises the HKSAR to establish economic relations with the United Kingdom and other countries, and provides that the HKSAR may on its own maintain and develop economic and cultural relations and conclude relevant agreements. The details are elaborated in Annex I to the Joint Declaration, in particular, in section XI on foreign affairs, which provides, in part, that:

> The [HKSAR] may, using the name 'Hong Kong, China', maintain and develop relations and conclude and implement agreements with States, regions and relevant international organisations in the appropriate fields, including the economic, trade, financial and monetary, shipping, communications, tourist, cultural and sporting fields.[89]

Thus, the HKSAR may conclude treaties in these fields, which, because of the generality of the wording, include matters such as free trade, double taxation,[90] social security, intellectual property and customs cooperation.[91] It may do so without seeking authority from the CPG, general authority having been conferred by China in the Joint Declaration and reiterated in the Basic Law. Such treaties can be bilateral or multilateral, though many multilateral treaties will not be open to full participation by a non-state entity like the HKSAR. Naturally, there cannot be bilateral treaties between China and the HKSAR, though there are several *arrangements* between them on matters of obvious mutual concern, such as mutual legal assistance in civil and commercial matters.[92]

Annex I to the Joint Declaration makes specific provision for treaties in certain areas that involve particular aspects of sovereignty, and where it is therefore desirable that there should be no uncertainty as to the powers of the HKSAR. In the case of bilateral treaties for *reciprocal juridical assistance*, section III (and Article 96 of the Basic Law) provides that the CPG shall 'assist or authorise' the HKSAR to make appropriate arrangements. This means that the CPG must either take part in the negotiations or authorise the HKSAR to negotiate and conclude treaties on matters such as mutual legal assistance, reciprocal enforcement of judgments, surrender of fugitive offenders and transfer of prisoners. Authorisation may be given either generally or specifically. In practice, the CPG has given authorisations and not sought to

[89] See also Article 151 Basic Law.

[90] See the UK–HKSAR Double Taxation Agreements, the first in 2000 (2169 UNTS 4 No. 38015; UKTS (2001) No. 36), and the second in 2010 (2961 UNTS 135 No. 51470; UKTS (2011) No. 35).

[91] For a list and the full text of the major bilateral agreements concluded by the HKSAR, see the website of the Department of Justice, Government of the HKSAR, at: www.doj.gov.hk/en/external/international_agreements.html.

[92] For a list of such *arrangements* in the legal, administrative and economic spheres, see the Department of Justice, Government of the HKSAR website, at: www.doj.gov.hk/en/mainland_and_macao/arrangements_with_the_mainland.html. For arrangements in other areas, for example environment, aviation and shipping, consult the website of the responsible Department.

participate in the negotiations: the HKSAR thus enters into bilateral treaties in these fields in its own right.[93]

Section VI of Annex I to the Joint Declaration provides that the HKSAR shall be a separate customs territory, and may participate in relevant *international trade agreements and organisations* (including preferential trade arrangements), and arrangements regarding international trade in textiles.[94] For this purpose, the HKSAR does not need authorisation from the CPG. In 1995 Hong Kong became a founding member of the World Trade Organization; China becoming a member in 2001. Both China and the HKSAR are members of the International Textiles and Clothing Bureau and the World Meteorological Organization. As a member in its own right of those organisations, the HKSAR has a vote. The HKSAR is also an Associate Member of the World Tourist Organisation and the International Maritime Organization, so it is entitled to participate in the activities of the organisations, but not to vote in their assemblies.

Detailed provisions for *air services* are made in section IX of Annex I.[95] These provide, in particular, that 'acting under specific authorisations from the CPG', the HKSAR may:

(1) renew or amend air services agreements previously in force (note that, in fact, air services agreements between the United Kingdom and third states that had been extended to Hong Kong by the United Kingdom were replaced before handover by new agreements between Hong Kong and the third states); and
(2) negotiate and conclude, after handover, new air services agreements providing routes for HKSAR-based airlines. (Note: all scheduled air services to and from the HKSAR which do not operate to, from or through so-called mainland China are regulated by such agreements.)

Since the handover, several new air services agreements have been concluded, most entering into force on signature.[96] Section IX also contains standing authority for the HKSAR to negotiate and conclude all arrangements implementing air services agreements, that is, non-binding arrangements. These provisions enabled the HKSAR to continue to develop as a major centre for international air services, and to promote the interests of HKSAR-based airlines.

[93] See the UK–HKSAR Mutual Assistance in Criminal Matters Agreement 1998 (2188 UNTS 198 No. 38569; UKTS (2002) No. 18); and the Belgium–HKSAR Mutual Legal Assistance in Criminal Matters Agreement 2004 (2469 UNTS 261 No. 44342).

[94] See also Article 116 Basic Law. [95] See also Articles 133 and 134 Basic Law.

[96] See, e.g., the HKSAR–Ukraine Agreement concerning Air Services Transit 2002: 2183 UNTS 429 No. 38473. For a list of air services agreements (as at 9 September 2018), see the Department of Justice, Government of the HKSAR, website, at: www.doj.gov.hk/en/external/table1ti.html.

Section XIV of Annex I to the Joint Declaration contains the undertaking of the CPG to 'assist or authorise' the HKSAR to conclude *visa abolition agreements*.[97] Again, in practice the CPG has authorised the HKSAR to negotiate agreements on its own.

Up to the present day, the HKSAR has signed a large number of bilateral treaties[98] on a wide range of subjects, including investment promotion and protection, mutual legal assistance in criminal matters, surrender of fugitive offenders, transfer of prisoners, visa abolition and air services. The treaties usually specify in the preamble that the government of the HKSAR has been 'duly authorised to conclude this Agreement by the Central People's Government of the People's Republic of China'.[99]

In practice, these agreements have been signed either 'For the Government of the Hong Kong Special Administrative Region of the People's Republic of China' (i.e., in the name of the HKSAR government), or 'For the Hong Kong Special Administrative Region of the People's Republic of China' (i.e., in the name of the HKSAR).

The HKSAR not being a sovereign state, there are no ratification procedures in the HKSAR as such. For bilateral treaties, which require the completion of internal procedures before they can enter into force, the usual practice in the HKSAR is to enact implementing legislation if this is needed, and then for the HKSAR government to notify the other party to the treaty that the HKSAR has completed its internal procedures necessary for the entry into force of the treaty.

Overseas Territories

Most overseas (i.e., non-metropolitan) territories were, and still are, in constitutional law, colonies, over which the parent state (colonial power) exercises control. The parent state can determine the extent (if any) to which the territory has control of its internal affairs and, even for the most advanced territories, the parent state will usually retain responsibility for defence and foreign affairs. A territory cannot conclude treaties without the authority of the parent state. Nor can it enter into diplomatic relations, though consular posts may be established in the territory with the permission of the parent state. But some territories have been given such extensive responsibility in foreign affairs that some states have failed to appreciate that they are not sovereign and independent.

Overseas territories do not have an inherent power to conclude treaties, but may be authorised by the parent state to negotiate, or even conclude and enter into them, in certain specific subject areas, either generally or ad hoc. The United Kingdom has

[97] See also Article 155 Basic Law. [98] See n. 91.

[99] See, e.g., the UK–HKSAR Transfer of Sentenced Persons Agreement 1997 (2068 UNTS 41 No. 35810; UKTS (1998) No. 51). More recent agreements on this subject include those with the Czech Republic (2013) and India (2015), at: www.doj.gov.hk/en/external/table5ti.html.

conferred a limited general power on Bermuda by means of a general 'instrument of entrustment' (i.e., an authority issued by the parent state) to conclude agreements of, inter alia, 'purely local concern' with Commonwealth states, the United Nations or other approved states. Under this, Bermuda has concluded several treaties with Canada and the United States, with which it has close ties. But the United Kingdom remains ultimately responsible for the performance of such treaties. (In the past similar entrustments were given to Hong Kong.) States do not, of course, have to enter into treaties with an overseas territory rather than the parent state, but, if they do, they will look to the parent state for redress if the territory does not carry out the treaty, since the territory acts in effect as agent for the parent state.

Normally, the treaty should be signed by the governor or other officer administering the government of the territory, not by a minister of the territory. Whether full powers[100] will be needed depends on the practice of the parent state, but evidence of the territory's authority to sign, or indeed ratify, may be required by the other state, or by the state or international organisation hosting the negotiation of a multilateral treaty. Any full powers are, therefore, likely to be signed by the parent state or possibly by the governor of, or other officer administering, the territory on instructions from the parent state, provided that is acceptable to the other state or, in the case of a multilateral treaty, the host of the relevant conference. However, it would seem that, in practice, an instrument of entrustment is generally accepted in place of full powers if the governor, other officer administering the government of the territory or the premier/chief minister or another minister of the territory, signs the treaty. Instruments of ratification are now normally deposited by the government of the territory, having been signed by the premier/chief minister. It is important that the procedure is acceptable to the other state or international organisation; otherwise there might be some doubt as to whether the treaty is valid. In short, everything depends on the attitude of the other state or international organisation.

Another procedure may be for the parent state to enter into a treaty with another state expressly for the territory. The New Zealand–United Kingdom Social Security Agreement 1994[101] applies only to the (British) Channel Islands.[102] The procedure is particularly suitable when the subject concerns territorial sovereignty or foreign policy. The France–UK Maritime Delimitation of Montserrat and Guadeloupe Agreement 1996[103] is in respect only of the French metropolitan *département* of

[100] See Chapter 5.

[101] Agreement on Social Security between the UK (on behalf of the States of Jersey and the States of Guernsey) and New Zealand 1994: 1913 UNTS 258 No. 32649; UKTS (1995) No. 92.

[102] See p. 215–216 on the status of the Channel Islands and the Isle of Man.

[103] UNTS 66 No. 36143; UKTS (1997) No. 28. See also a similar treaty, the UK–Honduras Treaty concerning the Delimitation of the Maritime Areas between the Cayman Islands and the Republic of Honduras 2001: 2207 UNTS 498 No. 39224; UKTS (2002) No. 25.

Guadeloupe and the British territory of Montserrat. The UK–Spain Agreement on Taxation and the Protection of Financial Interests regarding Gibraltar 2019 applies only to Gibraltar.[104]

Where a multilateral treaty provides that 'any state' may become a party to it, whether a state can become a party only in respect of an overseas territory will depend on the nature and geographical scope of the treaty. The United Kingdom became party to the Agreement establishing the South Pacific Commission 1947,[105] the territorial scope of which is limited to the non-self-governing territories in the South Pacific administered by the parties. (The Commission has now been renamed the Pacific Community.) The Agreement for the Establishment of the Indian Ocean Tuna Commission 1993[106] was ratified initially by the United Kingdom *only* in respect of the British Indian Ocean Territory.[107]

Some multilateral treaties permit territorial entities that are not independent to be parties. Article 305 of UNCLOS 1982[108] permits certain self-governing associated states and internally self-governing territories to become parties, provided they have competence over matters governed by the Convention, including competence to enter into treaties on such matters. The HKSAR is party in its own right to several such treaties. Some treaties allow overseas territories to participate in an organisation established by the treaties when they have a particular interest in the subject matter. Article 43 of the Convention on the Conservation etc. of Highly Migratory Fish Stocks in the Western and Central Pacific Ocean 2000[109] permits seven named overseas territories to take part in the work of the Commission, but without the right to vote.

Agreements with the Parent State or between Its Overseas Territories

As between a parent state and one of its territories, or between its overseas territories, there can be no international relations, since only the parent is sovereign;[110] and any

[104] See Article 9, UK–Spain Agreement on Taxation and Protection of Financial Interests regarding Gibraltar 2019: UK Country Series, Spain (2019) No. 1.

[105] 97 UNTS 227 No. 1352; UKTS (1952) No. 21.

[106] 1927 UNTS 330 No. 32888; UK Misc. Series (1994) No. 41.

[107] The UK ratified initially on 31 March 1995. On 22 December 2020, the UK deposited an instrument of acceptance of the Agreement in its own right.

[108] 1833 UNTS 397 No. 31363; 21 ILM (1982) 1261; UKTS (1999) No. 81. The Cook Islands and Niue are both parties.

[109] 2275 UNTS 43 No. 40532.

[110] In relation to the particular circumstances of the UK, Mauritius and the Chagos Archipelago in 1965, see *Legal Consequences of the Separation of the Chagos Archipelago from Mauritius in 1965*, Advisory Opinion, ICJ Reports (2019) 95, at 137 para. 172: 'In the Court's view, it is not possible to talk of an international agreement, when one of the parties to it, Mauritius, which is said to have ceded the territory to the United Kingdom, was under the authority of the latter.'

agreement between them will not be legally binding in law. When there is need for an agreement, it may be convenient – and will avoid any mistaken implication that it is legally binding – to draft it as if it were an MOU or 'administrative agreement'. An agreement between an overseas territory and a company or individual will be binding under the law of the territory, or of the parent state or another state, whatever is agreed.

5

Full Powers

> We have judged it expedient to invest a fit person with Full Power to conduct negotiations on Our part in respect of Our United Kingdom of Great Britain and Northern Ireland: Know, therefore, that We, reposing especial Trust and Confidence in the Wisdom, Loyalty, Diligence and Circumspection of our Trusty and Well-beloved Sir Patrick Henry Dean, Knight Commander of Our Most Distinguished Order of Saint Michael and Saint George . . .[1]

The quotation is just a small extract from old-style full powers that was still being used by the United Kingdom not so long ago. Some states may still use similar antiquated language. It is therefore not so surprising that an air of mystery still surrounds the topic. Admittedly, it is not the most thrilling aspect of the law of treaties, but failure to follow the complex, but clear, rules on full powers can lead to much needless extra work, vexation and, indeed, even embarrassment. So, please read on.[2]

Full powers is no more than a document produced as evidence that the person named in it is authorised to represent their state in performing certain acts in relation to the conclusion of a treaty, in particular its signature. The production of full powers is a fundamental safeguard for the representatives of other states that they are also dealing with a person with the necessary authority. This is equally important for the depositary of a treaty in view of the heavy responsibilities that person has to discharge. But given the important, yet limited, purpose of full powers, *before doing any act covered by them, the holder must still obtain specific instructions from their government before they exercise those powers.*

In the past, full powers were invariably required. The growth of treaties in simplified form (for example, an exchange of notes), and the general trend towards informality in treaty making, might lead one to think that the need for full powers is no longer so great today. That is not so. With the substantial increase in the number of states and the enormous growth in treaty making, especially multilateral treaties, full powers have assumed a renewed importance. Whether a treaty is bilateral or multilateral, it is

[1] For the whole text, see *Blix and Emerson*, 40–41.

[2] For the origin of modern full powers, see D. O'Connell, 'A Cause Célèbre in the History of Treaty-Making', BYIL 38 (1967) 71–90.

essential to know in every case whether or not full powers will be needed and, if so, to ensure that they are provided *in good time.*

Credentials

Credentials are *not* full powers. A delegate attending an international conference at which a multilateral treaty is to be negotiated needs to submit to the government or international organisation hosting the conference a document, known as 'credentials', issued by their state, authorising them to represent it.[3] Credentials will be issued, in accordance with the rules applicable to the conference, by or on behalf of the head of state or government or, more usually, by the foreign minister or a person authorised by them (see Appendix I). But the representative, by virtue of their credentials, does *not* have the authority to do more than adopt the text of a treaty and sign the final act. This is so even if the treaty is subject to ratification. So, the representative always needs specific instructions from their government before they can *sign* a treaty, and full powers if these are required. The same applies to a duly accredited representative to an international organisation, and even with respect to a treaty adopted within the organisation, unless the representative has *general full powers* (see below). Full powers and credentials can, however, be combined in one document.

Meaning of Full Powers

Article 2(1)(c) defines 'full powers' as:

> a document emanating from the competent authority of a State designating a person or persons to represent the State for negotiating, adopting or authenticating the text of a treaty, for expressing the consent of the State to be bound by a treaty, or for accomplishing any other act with respect to a treaty.

Although the definition refers to several different acts, *it is only those acts that are actually specified in the document that will be authorised.* The phrase 'any other act with respect to a treaty' includes:

(1) acts with respect to treaty status, such as acts declaring invalid, terminating or withdrawing from, or suspending the operation of, a treaty (see Article 67);
(2) declarations or notifications in the nature of binding instruments which extend or modify the obligations of the state, such as territorial extension or a notification of provisional application; and
(3) declarations under Article 36(2) of the Statute of the International Court of Justice.[4]

[3] On credentials, see R. Sabel, *Rules of Procedure at the UN and at Inter-Governmental Conferences* (3rd ed., Cambridge University Press, Cambridge 2018), 61–70.

[4] UN Depositary Practice, para. 105.

More to the point, the phrase 'any other act with respect to a treaty' also includes signatures *ad referendum* or signatures subject to ratification.

General Rule

A person is considered as representing a state for the purpose of adopting or authenticating the text of a treaty, or for the purpose of expressing the consent of the state to be bound by it, *if* (a) the person produces appropriate full powers, *or* (b) it appears from the practice of the states concerned, or from other circumstances, that their intention is that this person should be considered as representing the state for such purposes and thus to *dispense* with full powers (Article 7(1)(b)).

Unless withdrawn, full powers remain valid for as long as there is outstanding any act which they cover.

Bilateral Treaties

The ability to dispense with the production of full powers is important for bilateral treaties. Today, states may agree to dispense with full powers provided the other state has not requested them, though it is only prudent to seek confirmation (preferably in writing) that the other state is willing to dispense with them. This is especially so if the treaty is to be signed at a level below that of foreign minister. If the treaty is to enter into force on signature, it may also be prudent to obtain a formal assurance in advance that the person signing for the other state has authority to do so. In principle, full powers could be required even for a note that is to form part of an exchange of notes constituting a treaty, but, in practice, this is not done.[5] If states are content to enter into treaty relations by using simplified forms, it would be rather inconsistent (but not legally wrong) to require such a formal document as full powers. Where a bilateral treaty is subject to ratification or similar procedure, states may be more ready to agree to dispense with full powers.

Multilateral Treaties

Today, credentials are usually sufficient authority for all acts connected with the conclusion of a multilateral treaty, including signing the final act,[6] but *not* for signature of the treaty and subsequent acts with respect to it. Even if it is subject to ratification, full powers are required to sign a multilateral treaty unless the negotiating states agree otherwise. This may happen if the number of states involved is small, but the UN Secretary-General, or the chief administrative officer of other international organisations, will usually insist on full powers being produced for the signature of treaties for

[5] UK treaty practice is not to provide full powers to conclude an agreement in the form of an Exchange of Notes or Letters unless the other party requires this.

[6] See p. 105 with reference to the relative insignificance of signing a final act.

which they are to be the depositary. When full powers are required, the state or international organisation convening the conference must verify that they are valid and consistent with accepted depositary practice, even if such convenor is not to be the depositary of the treaty.[7] The host state or international organisation, and later the depositary, must also check that each state is entitled to become a party to the treaty. Even if a representative has valid full powers, it does *not* follow that their state is entitled to become a party, in which case it should not, of course, be invited to sign the treaty.

When Full Powers Are Never Required

Article 7(2) contains exceptions to the general rule that full powers are required. Because of their functions, the following are considered as representing their state and do *not* have to produce full powers:

(a) Heads of state, heads of government and foreign ministers, for the purpose of performing all acts relating to the conclusion of a treaty. Because of their ostensible authority, such persons ('qualified authorities')[8] are not required to produce full powers for the purpose of adopting, authenticating or signing the text of a treaty or of expressing consent to be bound by it.

(b) Heads of diplomatic missions, for the purpose of adopting the text of a treaty between their state and the state to which they are accredited. Article 3(1)(c) of the Vienna Convention on Diplomatic Relations (VCDR) 1961[9] provides that the functions of a diplomatic mission include negotiating with the government of the receiving state. Thus, the head of mission may adopt the text of a treaty between the two states. Although Article 7(2)(b) of the 1969 Convention does not refer to authenticating the text, it is unlikely that a state would require production of full powers for this purpose. However, unless full powers have been dispensed with, they are required for the purpose of signing a treaty, even if signature will not constitute consent to be bound.

(c) Representatives accredited by states to an international conference or to an international organisation or one of its organs, for the purpose of adopting the text of a treaty within that conference, organisation or organ. For a long time most multilateral treaties have been drawn up and adopted at international conferences or within international organisations and, provided a representative has been duly accredited, there is no need for them to have full powers for the

[7] Norway convened the conference which adopted the Landmines Convention 1997 (2056 UNTS 241, No. 35597; 36 ILM (1997) 1509; UKTS (1999) No. 18), but it was opened for signature in Ottawa (sometimes it is called the 'Ottawa Convention'), and the depositary is the UN Secretary-General.

[8] This is the term used by UN Depositary Practice, para. 101.

[9] 500 UNTS 95 No. 7310; UKTS (1965) No. 19.

adoption of the treaty. Permanent representatives to international organisations may have general full powers anyway.

General Full Powers

In order to avoid having to produce full powers on each occasion that a treaty is to be signed within an international organisation, a state may issue its permanent representative to the organisation with general full powers. This is common for permanent representatives to the United Nations and, sometimes, their deputies. General full powers can be issued either separately or combined with credentials. The general full powers for a previous permanent representative to the United Nations is at Appendix K.[10] Unless specifically provided for, general full powers will not authorise acts in relation to a treaty adopted at a *conference convened by the organisation*, rather than a treaty adopted *within the organisation* (e.g., by an annual or special assembly).

Granting a person general full powers does not, of course, empower that person to do as they like; as with special (i.e., ordinary) full powers, that person will still need to seek specific instructions from their government before doing any act in relation to a treaty. The way these are given depends on the constitution and practice of that state, and is of no concern to other states or the depositary.

General full powers should be deposited with the secretariat of the organisation as soon as possible, and a copy (preferably certified by the secretariat as a true copy of the deposited original) retained by the permanent mission in case there is any question in future as to whether general full powers were deposited or as to their precise terms. (Bitter experience teaches that the copy should be kept by the permanent mission on a special file for easy retrieval at short notice.)

Procedure

Although the form and content of full powers, and the issuing of them, will depend on the constitution and practice of each state, they must, in the words of the definition in Article 2(1)(c), issue from the competent authority of the representative's state. In accordance with recognised international practice, this means one of the qualified authorities, though it is generally the foreign minister.

If the treaty is between heads of state, the competent authority to issue the full powers will be the head of state, unless they are to act in person. Although these days presidents often sign politically important treaties (and occasionally even non-binding instruments), monarchs (or at least the constitutional variety) seldom sign treaties, even those expressed to be between heads of state.

[10] See also UN Depositary Practice, para. 102.

The wording of full powers does not have to be elaborate, but it must confer, in an unambiguous manner, authority for the person named to do the act in question, such as sign the treaty, and must include the following:

(1) Full names of the person authorised. An authority issued simply to 'the Ambassador of Ruritania' is not sufficient.
(2) Full title of the treaty. If it is not yet clear what that will be, the treaty should be identified by reference to its subject matter and the name of the conference or international organisation where the negotiations are taking place. There is *no need* to specify the expected date or place of signature of the treaty.
(3) Signature of one of the qualified authorities. A facsimile signature is *not* acceptable. Nor is it sufficient for full powers to be signed 'on behalf' of one of the qualified authorities. Full powers may *not* be issued by, say, a deputy foreign minister, *unless* they are in charge of the foreign ministry *ad interim* or is acting foreign minister. Nor will they be acceptable if issued by another, albeit cabinet, minister, apart, that is, from the prime minister.[11]
(4) Date and place of signature of the full powers.
(5) Official seal. This is optional, but usual.

A simple formula is at Appendix J.[12]

If signature of a multilateral treaty is to be definitive (i.e., will in itself amount to consent to be bound by the treaty), the (future) depositary may require that the full powers state explicitly that the power to sign is without reservation as to ratification, acceptance or approval.

Full powers cannot be used by a deputy, or person acting for the person named in the full powers, unless they are also named expressly in the full powers. It is, therefore, prudent to name at least two persons, especially if the leader of a delegation is a minister who may be called home at short notice. This can be done within the same instrument.

Full powers are *not* needed when a representative deposits an instrument signed by any of the qualified authorities, such as an instrument of ratification.

The provision of full powers may take some time. Since today foreign ministers are increasingly, and annoyingly for treaty departments, abroad, those responsible for the negotiation of a treaty should keep in mind the possible need for full powers. Today, negotiations are often not led by the foreign ministry. It is then the responsibility of the

[11] UN Depositary Practice, paras. 105 and 123. The latter paragraph is worth quoting in full: 'However, an instrument signed for example by the "Vice-Minister for Foreign Affairs" is not acceptable unless it clearly appears that he is in charge of the Ministry ad interim or otherwise. By the same token, instruments signed by a minister other than the Minister for Foreign Affairs, for example an instrument signed by the Minister for Foreign Trade, will not be accepted, even if the subject-matters of the treaty would internally fall within the competence of that Minister. The Secretary-General would, however, accept such an instrument if it was accompanied by a declaration by one of the three qualified authorities witnessing that under the legislation of his State the Minister in question is authorized to bind the State in respect of the treaty concerned.'

[12] See also *Blix and Emerson*, 38–39.

senior foreign ministry representative on the delegation to ensure that matters such as full powers are dealt with in good time. Advice should be sought from the foreign ministry treaty experts on whether full powers will be required. If the foreign ministry is content to dispense with them for a *bilateral* treaty, this should be proposed to the other side. But the request of one side for full powers should not be seen as in any way casting doubt on the status or authority of the persons on the other side: it may well be either a domestic requirement of the other state or just the state's normal practice. In the case of *multilateral* treaties concluded at international conferences or within international organisations, the rules of procedure of the conference or organisation generally do not make provision for full powers. Therefore, unless there has been an express agreement to dispense with them, the *general* rule applies and full powers will be needed for signature. Certainly, the UN Secretary-General will always insist on them if they are to be the depositary of the treaty.

In all cases, full powers should be submitted to the future depositary for verification in good time before the intended date of signature. In difficult cases, it may be prudent to clear the text of the full powers in draft with the future depositary.

For when an *overseas territory* signs a treaty, see page 88.

Sending Full Powers by Scanned Copy

Should the need for full powers have been overlooked, or if there has been a delay in obtaining them, some secretariats may accept full powers conveyed in a scanned electronic copy attached to an email sent in the name of the person who granted the full powers, provided that the depositing state undertakes to proceed with the deposit of the signed copy and does so immediately the original instrument arrives at the state's mission or embassy. The depositary has a duty to the other negotiating states to do their best to ensure that only duly appointed representatives sign. With the rapid expansion of the international community to nearly 200 states, and with it a significant increase in the number of diplomats and other officials attending international meetings and conferences, it is that much more difficult to verify whether each representative is duly authorised.

Proxy Signature

Although it is exceptional, a state may authorise a minister or official of another state to sign a treaty on its behalf. Unless the negotiating states agree otherwise, the principal state must provide the proxy with full powers.

Invalid Acts

Article 8 provides that an act relating to the conclusion of a treaty that is performed by someone who cannot be considered under Article 7 as authorised to represent a state for that purpose is without legal effect unless it is confirmed by that state. Ratification of the treaty will constitute confirmation, as will conduct by the state that evidences the acceptance by it of the act, such as publication by it of the treaty or its implementation. However, if the authority of a representative to express the consent of their state to be bound (e.g., by signature alone) has been made subject to a specific restriction, the representative's failure to observe that restriction cannot be invoked as invalidating the consent of the state, unless the restriction was notified to the other negotiating states before the representative expressed consent (Article 47).

Similarly, a state cannot invoke Article 46 by claiming that its consent to be bound by a treaty has been expressed in violation of its internal law regarding competence to conclude treaties if the consent has been expressed by one of the qualified authorities (since under Article 7(2)(a) each of them has authority to express consent by virtue of their office), unless the violation is manifest and has 'at least been properly publicized'.[13]

[13] See *Land and Maritime Boundary between Cameroon and Nigeria (Cameroon* v. *Nigeria: Equatorial Guinea intervening)*, Judgment, ICJ Reports (2002) 303, at 430, para. 265; cited in *Maritime Delimitation in the Indian Ocean (Somalia* v. *Kenya)* (Preliminary Objections), Judgment, ICJ Reports (2017) 3, at 23, para. 48. See further at pp. 321–324.

6

Adoption and Authentication

And where, though all things differ, all agree.[1]

Adoption

Once negotiations are complete, it is necessary for the states that have taken part in drawing up the treaty to adopt the text. This is the first decisive stage in the conclusion of a treaty.[2] Then the text has to be authenticated. Thereafter, states can express their consent to be bound by the treaty (see Chapter 7).

The term adoption is not defined in the Convention, but is the formal act by which the form and content of the treaty are settled; and a state that takes part in the drawing up and adoption of the text is known as a 'negotiating state' (Article 2(1)(e)).[3] Unless the circumstances suggest otherwise, the act of adoption does *not* amount to authentication of, or consent to be bound by, the treaty, *or* mean that the treaty has entered into force. However, as will be explained, in the case of *bilateral* treaties these various stages are sometimes run together.

The rules on adoption in Article 9 embody the classic principle that, unless otherwise agreed, adoption needs the consent of all the states that participated in drawing up the text. Until recent times, this was the norm. The article, however, recognises that, since the Second World War, in drawing up treaties in large international conferences or within international organisations, the practice has been for adoption by the affirmative vote of a specified majority of the states. The pre-war unanimity rule is now restricted to the adoption of bilateral treaties or treaties drawn up by only a few states (so-called plurilateral treaties). However, consensus is now frequently sought for multilateral treaties even though it is not always attainable.

[1] Alexander Pope (1688–1744), *Windsor Forest*, 13.
[2] Part II, Section 1 of the Convention is headed 'Conclusion of Treaties', and covers not only capacity and full powers, but also adoption, authentication and consent to be bound, in that order.
[3] The term is also found in Articles 10, 12(1)(b), (2)(a), 14(1)(b), 15(b), 25 and 76(1).

Bilateral Treaties

Adoption of the text of a bilateral treaty is often done by initialling, though even then it may not always be easy to establish the precise time at which the text can be said to have been adopted, since the text is often not finally settled until shortly before the treaty is to be signed. In that case, adoption is, in effect, by signature, which will often also express consent to be bound. This telescoping of the stages of treaty making is normal for bilateral treaties, but rare for multilateral treaties.

Treaties Adopted at International Conferences

The adoption of the text of a treaty at an international conference requires the vote of two-thirds of the states 'present and voting' (that excludes abstentions) unless, by the same majority, they decide to apply a different rule (Article 9(2)). These rules were formulated by the ILC and based on general practice in the 1960s. But for many years since then, treaties have been adopted by conferences convened under a UN General Assembly resolution, for example UNCLOS 1982 or, for that matter, the Vienna Convention on the Law of Treaties 1969 itself. The UN Secretariat will prepare, in consultation with the states concerned, draft rules of procedure, including a rule for voting. One of the first tasks of the conference will be to adopt the rules. Some argue that to adopt the rules a simple majority is sufficient, while others say a two-thirds majority is necessary; in practice, the rules are almost invariably adopted by consensus.[4]

The term 'international conference' is not defined in the Convention and is not a term of art, but it is probably safe to say that, at least for present purposes, any meeting of three or more states to negotiate a treaty is a conference. The smaller the number of negotiating states, the less likely it is that they will agree to accept less than unanimity. In addition, the subject matter may be such as to require unanimity, either for political reasons or because, without unanimity, the treaty might be ineffective because a key state or states that might be outvoted would decide not to become a party. Given the nature of disarmament treaties, the negotiation of them in the UN Disarmament Commission is done on the basis of unanimity.

Consensus

Since the text of the Convention was adopted in 1969, the wheel has come almost full circle. The two-thirds majority rule, or similar rules, was felt at the time to be necessary to protect the interests of states that might be in a minority at the conference. But with the rapid rise in the number of states, the rule became

[4] R. Sabel, *Rules of Procedure at the UN and at Inter-Governmental Conferences* (3rd ed., Cambridge University Press, Cambridge 2018), 26–30.

insufficient to protect the interests of a small minority of important and influential states, which usually represent less than one-third of the membership of the United Nations. Unless their interests were properly taken into account, the treaty might be ineffective. For example, in the 1970s the developed countries were regularly outvoted when multilateral treaties were adopted at conferences convened by the United Nations. The conference that drew up the Vienna Convention on the Representation of States in their Relations with International Organisations of a Universal Character 1975[5] was a failure from the start because it was unacceptable to most states that host international organisations and conferences,[6] which then (and since) happened to be mostly developed countries. The contentious parts having been voted through against their objections, the Convention has not been adhered to by any major host state. If it were to enter into force, it is therefore unlikely to have much practical effect.[7]

This, and other examples, eventually led to the realisation that for a multilateral treaty to be truly effective the substance has to be generally acceptable to all the negotiating states. This is especially so for law-making treaties, such as those prescribing rules regarding human rights and treaties establishing international organisations. Thus, the concept of consensus (sometimes called 'general agreement') began to gain ground in the 1970s, and is now often incorporated in rules of procedure. There is no agreed definition of this (albeit) important procedural innovation; the formulation of the concept has differed according to the circumstances, but the three main features of consensus are:

(1) it is not the same as unanimity;
(2) a state can join a consensus even if it could not vote in favour; and
(3) it is not incompatible with 'indicative voting' (a straw poll).[8]

For the purposes of decision making in the Council of the International Seabed Authority, consensus is defined in Article 161(8)(e) of UNCLOS 1982[9] as 'the absence of any formal objection'. The Rules of Procedure of the Organisation for Security and Co-operation in Europe define consensus as 'the absence of any objection expressed by a participating State to the adoption of the decision in question'.[10]

Some regimes, such as that of the Antarctic Treaty System, always proceed by unanimity or consensus in treaty making. And even when rules of procedure provide for adoption by a specified majority, it is normal for there to be attempts to reach consensus. Voting is used only as a last resort.

[5] UN Doc. A/CONF.67/16 (1975).

[6] AJIL (1975) 730–758; *Digest of US Practice in International Law* (1975), 40.

[7] See A. Aust, 'Limping Treaties: Lessons from Multilateral Law-making', NILR 243 (2003) 256–268.

[8] J. Evensen, 'Working Methods and Procedures in the Third United Nations Conference on the Law of the Sea', *Hague Recueil IV* 199 (1986) 483–486.

[9] 1833 UNTS 397 No. 31363; 21 ILM (1982) 1261; UKTS (1999) No. 81.

[10] Rule II(A)2.

Retaining majority voting as a fall-back can, at least in the final stages of negotiations, help to promote consensus, since a state that might otherwise be considering blocking consensus will know that it could be outvoted. The rules of most conferences therefore still provide for voting. The Third United Nations Conference on the Law of the Sea 1973–1982 proceeded on the basis that:

> The Conference should make every effort to reach agreement on substantive matters by way of consensus and there should be no voting on such matters until all efforts at consensus have been exhausted.[11]

This was not written into the rules of procedure, but contained in a declaration that was itself adopted by consensus. In the event, the Conference proceeded by way of consensus right up to its final substantive session, when there was voting on a number of amendments and on the adoption of UNCLOS as a whole. Rule 33 of the UN Conference on Straddling Stocks 1993–1995 provided that:

> The Conference should conduct its work on the basis of general agreement.[12] It may proceed to vote in accordance with Rule 35 only after all efforts at achieving general agreement have been exhausted. Before doing so, the Chairman shall inform the Conference that all efforts at achieving general agreement have been exhausted.[13]

The use of consensus does, however, mean that, because some – perhaps many – states will still be unhappy with the result, they are more likely to try to modify the application of the treaty to them by means of reservations or interpretative statements. It also means that the quality of the text may suffer. The lengthy process of seeking consensus can result in texts of considerable complexity or obscurity. The negotiation of only one new article for the Chicago Convention 1944, Article 3 *bis*, took up the whole three weeks of a conference.[14] But this is the price one has to pay for achieving a text that will have a better chance of securing wide adherence.

If the support of a state that is blocking consensus is critical for the success of the treaty, voting the text through may prove to be a pyrrhic victory. India blocked adoption of the CTBT[15] in the Committee on Disarmament, which operates by consensus. The matter was then taken to the UN General Assembly, where the treaty was adopted by a vote of 158 to 3 (Bhutan, India and Libya), with five abstentions. The treaty cannot enter into force until 44 (named) states have all ratified it; they include India, North Korea, Pakistan and the United States.

The Landmines Convention 1997[16] was negotiated under considerable pressure, and produced a text that was not entirely satisfactory. The basic proposal had been developed by a relatively small group of states, which did not include the United

[11] A/CONF.62/30/Rev.3 and A/CONF.62/121, para. 21. [12] Yet another term for 'consensus'.
[13] UN Doc. A/CONF.164/6 (1993). [14] 23 ILM (1984) 705; UKTS (1999) No. 68.
[15] 35 ILM (1996) 1439. [16] 2056 UNTS 241 No. 35597; 36 ILM (1997) 1509; UKTS (1999) No. 18.

States, China or Russia. Because it became clear to the United States that it could not obtain consensus for its amendments, or even a two-thirds majority, it did not call for a vote, but announced that it would be difficult for it to become a party. The Landmines Convention entered into force on 1 March 1999, but without the United States, China or Russia as a party. Some of its effectiveness may well therefore be lost.

These remarks might also be made about the Rome Statute of the International Criminal Court (ICC) 1998,[17] which was adopted by a vote, with the United States voting against. China, Russia and many Arab states are not parties to the Rome Statute. The outcomes in such cases are partly due to (largely domestic) political factors and partly to pressure to complete negotiations by a fixed deadline. In contrast to other important treaty negotiations, most of the participants in the ICC conference were opposed to having a second session (as happened in the case of the VCLT) or prolonging the session ('stopping the clock').

Authentication

Before a negotiating state can decide whether to consent to be bound by a treaty, it needs to know precisely what the final text is. This will be especially important when a state has to seek the approval of its legislature before it can consent to be bound. The process of establishing the final text is known as authentication, and consists of a formal indication that a document contains the 'authentic and definitive' text (Article 10). Although, at least in theory, the text could still be changed at any time before signature, for multilateral treaties it is important that, in practice, there should be a point of no return as far as the text is concerned.

Authentication is done by an act or a procedure.

Bilateral Treaties

Initialling the text of a bilateral treaty is normally regarded as amounting both to adoption *and* authentication, at least if the treaty is to be in only one authentic language. However, in practice each state is free to suggest technical, or even substantive, changes at any time before signature.

Multilateral Treaties

For a multilateral treaty, a formal procedure of adoption followed by authentication is important. In the past, authentication was usually done by signing the text. This was possible when the number of states involved was quite small and the authentic text was in only one language; in those far-off days usually French. But today multilateral treaties normally have several authentic languages, and so other methods are needed.

[17] 2187 UNTS 91 No. 38544; 37 ILM (1998) 998; UKTS (2002) No. 35.

The business of negotiating a multilateral treaty is often a confused affair, as demonstrated in the case of the Rome Statute 1998. Even when one has the services of a highly experienced secretariat, the final stages of what is usually a lengthy negotiating process are hectic, and errors and inconsistencies invariably creep into the text due to the pressure to adopt it by a certain date. It is not unusual for the basic negotiating text to be solely in English, and for some of the other language texts to be available only at the end of the conference, if then. There is a need not only to check the adopted text for typographical inconsistencies and errors (i.e., copy-edit), but also to translate it, or complete its translation, into any other authentic languages.[18]

Article 10 therefore provides that the text of a treaty is established as authentic and definitive by such procedure as may be provided for in the text or agreed upon by the states participating in its drawing up. In the absence of such procedure, authentication is by signature, signature *ad referendum*, or initialling of the text or the Final Act incorporating the text. Initialling is probably the most usual way of authenticating the text of a multilateral treaty that is to be between only a few states. For other multilateral treaties, initialling is usually replaced by a more formal procedure, as discussed below.

Treaties Adopted within an International Organisation

Article 10 does not govern the authentication of treaties adopted within an international organisation as such, because Article 5 preserves the applicability of the rules of the organisation. It is common practice for a treaty adopted within an international organisation to be authenticated by the adoption of a resolution by an organ of the organisation, such as an assembly of the member states, or by an act of authentication performed by a duly authorised authority of the organisation, such as the president of the assembly or the chief executive officer. The FAO Constitution provides that the text of a treaty adopted by the FAO Conference is authenticated by the certification of two copies of the treaty in all the FAO languages by the Chairman of the FAO Conference and the FAO Director-General. One certified copy is deposited in the FAO archives once the treaty has entered into force; the other is sent to the UN Secretary-General for registration. Authentic copies, certified by the Director-General only, are sent to the FAO members.

The text of a treaty negotiated at a conference convened by the United Nations has usually been in English. The UN Secretariat will then normally prepare the text in the remaining authentic languages (with inputs from the UN membership) *before* the treaty is adopted. Similarly, once the negotiation of a treaty within a subsidiary body of the General Assembly (such as one of the main committees) is finished, a cleaned-up text in all the authentic languages will be prepared by the UN Secretariat. A draft

[18] See UN Depositary Practice, paras. 38–47.

resolution with the text annexed will then be presented to the General Assembly for formal adoption by a resolution.

But in either case, there may still be need for corrections to be made to the text.[19] So a preferable procedure, not yet consistently applied, is to submit the draft text in all authentic languages to the designated depositary as soon as its drafting is finalised and *before* its adoption. This helps to ensure that typographical errors have been corrected, the numbering and cross-references adjusted, the accuracy of document citations ensured and any other errors in the text corrected. The depositary then sends the changes to the negotiating states for any comments. Such an approach, hopefully, avoids cumbersome correction procedures. In recent years, a number of important treaties were, for understandable political reasons, signed immediately on adoption before the text could be properly checked. Also some treaties, although not signed immediately after adoption, have been adopted without being fully checked, with the result that numerous errors then had to be corrected. Sometimes the errors raised points of substance.

Final Act

The Convention mentions final acts only in Article 10(b). A final act is a formal statement or summary of the proceedings of a diplomatic conference. It will include basic facts about the conference, such as its purpose; which states attended; who presided; who chaired the various committees, and their composition. Treaties adopted by the conference and other related documents, such as resolutions and agreed or national interpretative statements, will be attached. An example is the Final Act of the Vienna Conference on the Law of Treaties.[20] It is usual for each negotiating state to sign the final act although this is optional. If a state does sign it, that does *not* commit the state to sign or ratify any treaty attached to it. Nevertheless, and depending on what is decided at the conference, signing the final act may have certain consequences, some of which may be important, such as entitlement to membership of a preparatory committee. Full powers are not needed to sign a final act, the credentials of the representative being enough.

The Helsinki Final Act of the Conference on Co-operation and Security in Europe 1975 had no treaty attached to it. But, unlike most final acts, because it contained lengthy, substantive (though *not* legally binding) provisions of great *political* importance, and thus might have been mistaken for a treaty, that Final Act contains a statement that it 'is not eligible for registration under Article 102 of the Charter of the United Nations'.[21] It is therefore a non-binding instrument.

[19] See pp. 342–345 on correction of errors; and 40 ILM (2001) 532.

[20] See also the Final Act of the 1996 Special Meeting of Contracting Parties to Consider and Adopt a Protocol to the London Convention 1972 (36 ILM (1997) 4).

[21] 14 ILM (1975) 1293.

When Is a Treaty 'Concluded'?

Although the Convention refers to the 'conclusion' of a treaty no less than twenty-three times, unfortunately it does not define the term[22] (treaties may also be said to have been 'made' or 'entered into', but these are equally imprecise words). But the absence of a definition does not cause problems in the day-to-day work of a foreign ministry. For most purposes, a bilateral treaty is regarded as having been concluded when it is signed by both states. Depending on the circumstances, a multilateral treaty is generally regarded as having been concluded on signature of the final act (or other means by which it is adopted) or, if applicable, on the date the treaty is opened for signature, whichever is the later. For example, the Convention on the Elimination of All Forms of Racial Discrimination (CERD) 1966[23] was adopted in 1965 before its text had been authenticated. It was then opened for signature on 7 March 1966, and it is this *latter* date by which it is known. Although it has been suggested that 'concluded' refers to the entry into force of the treaty, this cannot be sustained as a general proposition, except when a treaty is brought into force by signature. The date of conclusion may be of some importance in the application of the rules in Article 4 (non-retrospection), Article 30 (successive treaties) and Article 59 (termination of a treaty by conclusion of a later treaty).[24]

[22] See Chapter 1, p. 10. See also E. Vierdag, 'The Time of the "Conclusion" of a Multilateral Treaty', BYIL 59 (1988) 75–111.

[23] 669 UNTS 195 No. 9464; UKTS (1967) No. 77.

[24] For discussion of Article 30, see pp. 235–237, and for Article 59, see pp. 299–300.

7

Consent to Be Bound

and here is the paper that bears his name upon it as well as mine.[1]

The term 'contracting state' describes a state that has consented to be bound by a treaty, even though it may not yet have entered into force (Article 2(1)(f)). A 'party' is a state that has consented to be bound by a treaty *and* for which the treaty is in force (Article 2(1)(g)). At that point – and only then – is the state fully bound by the treaty (Article 26), although certain procedural-type provisions will be operative even before.[2] To consent to be bound is, therefore, the most significant, positive act that a state can take in relation to any treaty. This chapter explains the various means by which consent can be expressed. Chapter 8 deals with entry into force. However, as will be explained, although two quite distinct steps are necessary to become a party – express consent to be bound by the treaty *and* its entry into force – they can sometimes take place at the same time.

Participation in a Treaty

In Chapter 4 we saw that entities can be parties to treaties, but this does *not* mean that the main entity, a state, can be a party to any treaty. This should be clear in the case of bilateral treaties. But whether a state (or another subject of international law, such as an international organisation) can participate in a multilateral treaty depends entirely on the terms of the treaty. So, if the treaty specifies that 'UN members' only can become parties, a state such as the Vatican City or the Cook Islands cannot be a party to that treaty.

The practice of the Council of Europe (CoE) is especially illuminating. The conditions for participation are not prescribed by the constitution of that international organisation, but by the practice of its Committee of Ministers that represents all the member states. Since the CoE is a regional organisation, it does not normally conclude treaties open to all states; that is more for international organisations of a universal

[1] British Prime Minister Neville Chamberlain on returning from his meeting with Hitler at Munich, September 1938.

[2] See in particular Article 18.

nature, such as the United Nations or the UN specialised agencies (which, despite the name by which they are called, are *not* part of the United Nations). Nevertheless, the practice of the CoE has evolved such that one can identify six general categories of participation:[3]

(1) treaties open only to members of the CoE, such as the European Convention on Human Rights (ECHR) 1950;[4]
(2) 'partial agreements' that are open to only some CoE members. The (CoE) Pharmacopoeia Convention 1964[5] is open to the original signatories and such other CoE members as the Council of Ministers may invite;
(3) treaties open to all CoE members, plus members of other international organisations that are of importance for the treaty,[6] and to member states of the European Union;
(4) treaties open to all (states and international organisations) that took part in its elaboration;[7]
(5) increasingly, treaties where the European Union, or its predecessors, is entitled to be an original signatory; and
(6) by an invitation from the Council of Ministers to accede to a particular treaty, usually after it has entered into force. This is still the main means by which a non-member of the Council of Europe, and sometimes other international organisations, can participate in its treaties.[8]

A state can consent to be bound by a treaty in various ways. It does not usually do so by adopting[9] or authenticating the text of a treaty, or by signing a final act; it must do something further. Article 11 lists the ways in which a state can express its consent to be bound:

- signature;
- exchange of instruments constituting a treaty;
- ratification, acceptance or approval;
- accession; or
- any other agreed means.

[3] See S. Akermark, 'Reservation Clauses in Treaties Concluded Within the Council of Europe', ICLQ 48 (1999) 479–514, 480–481.
[4] Convention for the Protection of Human Rights and Fundamental Freedoms, 1950: 213 UNTS 221 No. 2889; UKTS (1953) No. 71; ETS No. 5, amended by subsequent Protocols.
[5] 1286 UNTS 69 No. 21200; UKTS (1974) No. 32; ETS No. 50.
[6] The CoE Convention on Mutual Administrative Assistance in Tax Matters 1988 (1966 UNTS 215 No. 33610; UKTS (2010) No. 14); ETS No. 127), is also open to all Organisation for Economic Co-operation and Development (OECD) members.
[7] See the CoE Convention on Human Rights and Biomedicine 1997: 2137 UNTS 171 No. 37266; ETS No. 164.
[8] See the CoE Convention on Insider Trading 1989: 1704 UNTS 133 No. 29471; UKTS (1992) No. 7; ETS No. 130. See also below on preconditions for accession.
[9] But see also p. 124 on Article 11 VCLT.

Signature

It is quite common for consent to be expressed by signature, that is *definitive* signature, as opposed to *simple* signature, which is signature that is subject to ratification. So definitive signature[10] is more likely for a bilateral treaty or one between only a few states. In that case, the treaty will often provide also for entry into force on signature by *all* the participating states. This will probably be possible only if there is no need for new legislation.

Article 12 provides that *signature alone* expresses consent to be bound when:

(a) the treaty so provides;
(b) it is otherwise established that the negotiating states were so agreed; or
(c) the intention of a state that signature should express its consent is apparent from the full powers of its representative or was expressed during the negotiations.

These days a treaty will normally either specify how consent is to be expressed or this will be implicit from its terms. Therefore, when it is intended that signature is all that is necessary, this will be reflected in the entry-into-force clause. Typically, if the treaty is to be between two states, it may provide only that the treaty 'shall enter into force on the date of signature'. This formula has the advantage that it also effectively prevents a party from later claiming that the treaty is not in force because it has not been ratified.

In 1990, Iraq claimed this in respect of the Iraq–Kuwait Agreed Minutes 1963,[11] in which the two states recognised their joint boundary, even though the treaty did not provide for ratification and had been registered by Kuwait with the United Nations soon after it had been signed. The Security Council did not agree with Iraq.[12]

In the past, when a treaty provided for signature but was silent as to how consent to be bound was to be expressed, there was sometimes doubt as to whether ratification was necessary. The Convention does not resolve the matter, but it is of little practical importance today. It has long been the practice of states, whenever they intend a treaty to enter into force by a procedure involving more than just signature, to provide evidence of that intention, usually by an express provision in the treaty. Furthermore, when a treaty provides for ratification, it is presumed that a state has not become bound by its conduct unless that is clearly its intention.[13] If there is no indication, express or implied, of the need for ratification, the treaty will be presumed to enter into force on signature.[14]

Unless the treaty provides otherwise, a state is free to express its consent to be bound by signature even if other states require that their signature be ratified, but this is

[10] See pp. 91–95 on full powers for definitive signature. [11] 485 UNTS 321 No. 7063.

[12] Resolution 687 (1991), adopted on 3 April 1991: see the sixth preambular paragraph, and operative paragraph 2.

[13] *North Sea Continental Shelf cases*, ICJ Reports (1969) 3, at 25–26, para. 28; 41 ILR 29.

[14] *Sinclair*, 39–41.

exceptional. However, some states may sign a multilateral treaty that is subject to ratification with no intention of *ever* ratifying, but stating nevertheless that they are a 'signatory'. Since there are many who do not understand treaty procedures or terms that well, or at all, they may well believe, wrongly, that their state is a party.

Two, or even more, persons can sign for the same state, but this should not be encouraged. One signature for each state is all that is usually needed. More is only asking for trouble, since those who are not members of the qualified authorities will require full powers.[15] But if they insist, one solution is for such persons to sign as, so-called, distinguished witnesses, for whom no full powers are needed.

Sometimes not all the papers are ready, translations in particular. It is possible, in certain circumstances, to add a translation at a later stage. This is more easily done in the case of a treaty subject to ratification, as it can occur between signature and ratification.[16]

An unusual procedure was adopted for the ceasefire agreement of 4 October 1995 between Bosnia and Herzegovina, Croatia and the Federal Republic of Yugoslavia. Because Karadžić and other Bosnian Serb leaders had already signed it, President Izetbegović of Bosnia and Herzegovina refused to do so. Instead, he signed a photocopy of it with the Bosnian Serb names covered up.[17]

'Open for Signature'

Although some multilateral treaties concluded in the aftermath of the Second World War are 'open to signature' indefinitely,[18] for many years now multilateral treaties, especially those concluded within the United Nations or at a conference convened by the United Nations, will provide that they will be open for signature until a specified date, after which signature will no longer be possible. Thereafter a state may only accede (see, e.g., Articles 81 and 83 of the Convention).[19]

Signature ad referendum

It can happen that a state that had been willing for *signature alone* to bring a treaty into force discovers at a late stage before signature that it is not yet ready for entry into force. Inserting a provision postponing entry into force can solve this problem. But this may not be possible in all cases, since it might be difficult to amend the signature copies of the treaty, particularly if this has to be done at short notice and they are in more than one language. One solution is for the representative of the state

[15] See Chapter 5. [16] See also pp. 262–266.

[17] See R. Holbrooke, *To End a War* (Random House, New York 1998), 196–198.

[18] See the four Geneva Conventions 1949: 75 UNTS 3 Nos. 970–973; UKTS (1958) No. 39, and the Constitution of the UN Educational, Scientific and Cultural Organization (UNESCO): 4 UNTS 275 No. 52; UKTS (1946) No. 50.

[19] On accession, see pp. 121–123.

concerned to sign, but add after his signature '*ad referendum*' or words to that effect. If later confirmed, the signature will constitute full signature of the treaty (Article 12(2)(b)).

Confirmation can take any form, but is best done by diplomatic note or letter, *never* orally. Some states sign *ad referendum* to indicate that the treaty has to be referred for parliamentary approval before it can be ratified. But if the treaty provides that signature is subject to ratification, it is unnecessary to sign *ad referendum*.

The Convention leaves open the question of the effective date of a signature *ad referendum*. In principle, the signature should be effective from the date of signature, not confirmation: unlike ratification, confirmation is of the signature, *not* of the treaty. But it is open to the negotiating states to agree to a later date. Whether determining the exact date is of any importance will depend on the nature and content of the treaty.

Place of Signature

Whether in the form of a single instrument or an exchange of instruments, a treaty is usually signed in the same place and at the same time. But, exceptionally, a bilateral treaty can be signed in a third state. This does not necessarily need that state's consent, but, as a matter of courtesy, it should be informed. However, a treaty can be signed in different places and at different times if this is necessary for reasons of convenience, protocol or simply politics. A multilateral treaty between only a handful of states will sometimes be signed by one of them and then circulated to the others for their signature.

On 13 December 2001 the Swedish Foreign Ministry, acting for the host state, Sweden, sent a note to the fourteen other states and two international organisations that had negotiated the Global Water Partnership Organisation Memorandum of Understanding (a treaty or an NBI, it is not clear). The note suggested that either (1) the document could be signed in Stockholm by each state or international organisation or (2) a signed original could be signed by each of them and then returned to the depositary (who would be the Executive Secretary of the Organisation). (It was not clear if this meant that one original copy would be passed around the seventeen signatories or if they would each sign their 'own' original.) The note also said that course (2) would constitute 'adherence' to the document, though this suggestion did not reflect what appears to have been agreed, which provided for a two-stage process. Course (2) was not necessary and could have led to problems. Sometimes there can be very special circumstances requiring a document to be signed in an unusual way. None existed in this case.[20] Trying to cut corners on well-established procedures is normally ill-advised.

[20] Retained from the Third Edition, p. 91, based on Anthony Aust's materials. Aust retained a copy of this document.

Some notes (constituting an exchange of notes) are exchanged like normal correspondence, but most are exchanged simultaneously in the same place. For political reasons, separate original copies of a treaty between India and Pakistan were signed in their respective capitals but at the same time.[21] A defence MOU was once signed in the following way. Each minister signed one original in his capital and sent it to the other minister. They then telephoned each other to say that they were ready to sign the original each had received from the other. Each then did so, dating and retaining that original. There is no reason in principle why separate original copies of a treaty should not be signed simultaneously in different places (with each side undertaking to sign the other participant's original copy of the treaty as soon as possible after these dates);[22] or why both original copies should not be signed sequentially in different places on the same day,[23] or exceptionally in different places within a period of a few days.[24] But this should be done only if there are special circumstances, with all the implications carefully thought through. The scope for mistakes is great.

Doubt about Signature

When a treaty is signed, but if then or later there is doubt about the authority of the signatory to sign, the matter can be cured by ratification by the signatory state even if the treaty does not provide for it.

Initialling

Initialling is commonly used as the means by which a text is *adopted or authenticated.* Initialling the text of a treaty will constitute *signature* only if the negotiating states have so agreed (Article 12(2)(a)). However, where a treaty is constituted by an exchange of third-person diplomatic notes, these are usually initialled, though occasionally signed.[25] Initialling so as to constitute signature is to be discouraged for other forms of treaty.[26]

In order to avoid misunderstandings, consent to be bound should therefore *not* be expressed by initialling unless the negotiating states are clearly agreed that this will be the legal effect (see the discussion below of the rather exceptional Dayton

21 M. Tabory, 'Registration of the Egypt-Israel Peace Treaty', ICLQ 32 (1983) 981–1003, 996.

22 For example, the UK–Australia Free Trade Agreement, see Chapter 2, p. 28.

23 The EU–UK Withdrawal Agreement (WA) and the EU–UK Trade and Cooperation Agreement (TCA) were signed in Brussels and London on 24 January 2020 (WA) and 30 December 2020 (TCA).

24 See the signature of the UK–US Air Transport Agreement, UKTS (2021) No. 12, signed in Washington on 10 November 2020 and in London on 17 November 2020.

25 See the UK–China Exchange of Notes concerning the Establishment of a Consulate-General at Guangzhou and Edinburgh 1996: 1957 UNTS 234 No. 33507; UKTS (1996) No. 100; and Appendix F.

26 See Chapter 6.

Agreement). But if initialling is acceptable, it is obviously preferable for each state to initial; a mixture of initials and signatures could easily lead to confusion as to the effect of initialling. When initialling is for the purposes of adoption or authentication of the text only, it is important that the initials are *not* placed in the signature block (the place under the *testimonium* where the representatives sign), but rather in a lower corner of each page.

The Dayton Agreement

Like so much about the Dayton Agreement 1995,[27] the arrangements for expressing consent to be bound and entry into force were unique. The text of the Dayton Agreement was adopted on 21 November 1995 near Dayton, Ohio in the United States. Adoption was effected by the *signature* by the three states: Bosnia and Herzegovina, Croatia and the Federal Republic of Yugoslavia (i.e., Serbia and Montenegro) of an Agreement on Initialling. This provided that: (1) by *initialling* each signature block of the Dayton Agreement and its annexed agreements the parties *expressed their consent to be bound* by them; (2) that the parties committed themselves to *signature* in Paris of the Dayton Agreement and its annexed agreements, 'in their present form ... thus establishing their *entry into force*'; and (3) that the Agreement on Initialling would enter into force *on signature.* Thus, the *initialling* of the Dayton Agreement and *signature* of the Agreement on Initialling together amounted to consent to be bound by the Dayton Agreement. Signature in Paris on 14 December 1995 was, apart from political considerations, only for the purpose of bringing the Dayton Agreement into force.

Witnessing

Sometimes the signature of a treaty between two or only a few states will, because of its political importance, also be signed by the heads of state or government, or foreign ministers of third states or by individuals as witnesses. The practice is not new. There are examples from as long ago as the Middle Ages, and no doubt before, of senior officials witnessing the signatures of heads of state. The signature of a witness, however distinguished or powerful, has no legal significance; in itself, it will not make the state of the witness a guarantor of the performance of the treaty. It is no more than a reflection of the involvement of those states or individuals in the negotiations, or in promoting them, and an expression of their wish that the treaty should be a success. The Camp David Accords 1979[28] and the Dayton Agreement are perhaps the prime examples. Signature of the latter was witnessed in Paris by the

[27] General Framework Agreement for Peace in Bosnia and Herzegovina (Dayton Agreement), initialled at Dayton, Ohio, 12 November 1995, and signed at Paris, 14 December 1995: 35 ILM (1996) 75.

[28] 1136 UNTS 116 No. 17813 and 1138 UNTS 72 No. 17855; 18 ILM (1979) 362–389 and 530–536. See Tabory (n. 21), 997.

presidents of France and the United States, the heads of government of Germany, Russia and the United Kingdom, and the representative of the EU, each adding their signatures after those of the parties. The Israel–Jordan Treaty of Peace 1994 was witnessed by the US president.[29] The Sharm el-Sheikh Memorandum 1999 between Israel and the Palestine Liberation Organization (PLO) was necessarily in the form of a Memorandum, but because of its political importance was witnessed on behalf of Egypt, the United States and Jordan.[30] The Agreement on Succession Issues 2001[31] between all the former Yugoslavia republics was initialled by the neutral chairman of the lengthy negotiations, Sir Arthur Watts.

Exchange of Instruments Constituting a Treaty

It is common for treaties to be constituted by an exchange of instruments. The exchange usually takes the form of an exchange of diplomatic notes (or sometimes of letters; the terminology is not legally significant). About one-third of the treaties registered each year with the United Nations are in this form. Although the exchange of notes began life as an informal means of concluding a treaty, it is now used at all levels and for any subject. It is the *act of exchange* that constitutes consent to be bound if the notes provide that the exchange shall have that effect, or if it is otherwise established that the states have so agreed (Article 13). But quite often the notes will provide that the agreement constituted by the exchange of notes will not *enter into force* until each party has informed the other that its constitutional formalities (or such like) have been completed. This amounts to a sort of ratification.

Although the notes are often signed by ambassadors or other officials, they can be signed by ministers. They can be on matters of national importance[32] or the mundane.[33] Although they are often self-standing, they can be supplementary to another treaty. They are frequently used to amend a treaty.

In the vast majority of cases, the exchange is between two states. Although it can be between more than two,[34] this can cause technical problems that may outweigh the advantages of this procedure unless there are good political reasons.[35]

Ratification

Ratification is defined by the Convention as 'the international act so named whereby a State establishes on the international plane its consent to be bound by a treaty'

[29] 2042 UNTS 586 No. 35326; 34 ILM (1995) 43. [30] 38 ILM (1999) 1465.

[31] 2262 UNTS 253 No. 40296; 41 ILM (2002) 1. [32] See Lend-Lease Agreements p. 36.

[33] Such as the transfer of a hut in Antarctica: UK–Uruguay Exchange of Notes 1997, 2038 UNTS 263 No. 35251; UKTS (1998) No. 16. See also Appendix E.

[34] See the double exchange of notes between Saudi Arabia and Qatar and Bahrain, pp. 29–30.

[35] For multiple exchanges of notes, see p. 111; on exchange of notes generally, p. 36.

(Article 2(1)(b)), although, as already explained above, it is not the only way in which a state can express its consent to be bound. The most common misconception about ratification is that it is a constitutional process. It is definitely *not*. As the definition makes clear, *it is an 'international' act carried out on the 'international' plane.* Although parliamentary approval of a treaty may well be required – and be referred to, most misleadingly, as 'ratification' – that is a quite different (and entirely domestic) process. This is mostly reported incorrectly by newspapers when they say that the US Congress or Senate has 'ratified' a treaty. Congress (or rather the Senate) may have *approved* the treaty, albeit with reservations, so that the president (i.e., the head of state) may now sign the instrument of ratification.[36]

Ratification consists of (1) the execution of an *instrument of ratification* by the executive and (2) either its exchange for the instrument of ratification of the other state (bilateral treaty) or its lodging with the depositary (multilateral treaty).

The normal reason for *requiring* ratification is that, after the adoption and signature of a treaty, one or more of the negotiating states will need time before it can give its consent to be bound. There can be various reasons for this. First, the treaty may require legislation. This should always be done before the treaty enters into force for the state, otherwise it risks being in breach of its treaty obligations. Sometimes a state will ratify before the necessary legislation has been enacted. This may be done so that it can say that it has been one of the first to ratify, and thereby gain kudos at home and abroad. Although the stratagem may also have the beneficial effect of encouraging other states to ratify early, it is inherently risky since the treaty might enter into force before the state has been able to enact the legislation. Second, even if no legislation is needed, the constitution may require parliamentary approval of the treaty, or some other procedure like publication, before the treaty can be ratified. Third, even if no legislative or other constitutional process has to be gone through, the state may need time to consider the implications of the treaty. That a state has taken part – even an active part – in the negotiations does not necessarily mean that it is enthusiastic about the subject matter, or the text that was finally agreed, or there may have been a change of government following the negotiation process . The breathing space provided by the ratification process allows time for sober reflection before the instrument of ratification is lodged.

Most bilateral treaties now either provide that they shall be subject to ratification, or dispense with this requirement by providing that they shall enter into force on signature, upon a specified date or event, or, rarely, on a date to be agreed. These days even less formal instruments, such as exchanges of notes, can have similar, though simpler, ratification provisions (see p. 114). But the need for ratification is generally much greater for multilateral treaties.

36 The president's right to sign the instrument of ratification is to be found in the US Constitution.

Article 14(1) of the Convention provides that the consent of a state to be bound by a treaty is expressed by ratification when:

(a) the treaty so provides: this is the norm when ratification is required, and usually follows signature, though an express provision for signature is not always included;
(b) it is otherwise established that the negotiating states were agreed that ratification would be required: this may be evidenced by a collateral agreement or in the *travaux*. Today, that would be unusual: if a treaty is silent on the question of ratification, there is a (albeit rebuttable) *presumption* that it is *not* needed;
(c) the representative of the state has signed the treaty 'subject to ratification': this is a unilateral act, but is occasionally expressly provided for in the treaty. Where the treaty provides that it will enter into force on signature or at a specified time, a signature expressed to be subject to ratification amounts to a *conditional signature*. However, unlike a signature *ad referendum*, the consent of the state to be bound will operate only as from the date of actual ratification, although in the interim the signature *may* have various legal effects; or
(d) the intention of the state to sign subject to ratification appears from the full powers of its representative or was expressed during the negotiations.

If the treaty provides expressly that signature must be followed by ratification, it is not necessary for a representative to specify that his or her signature is subject to ratification, though this is sometimes done in ignorance.

It is another common misconception that, once a treaty has been ratified, then it is legally binding on the ratifying state. But the situation is quite different from the coming into force of legislation. Expressing consent to be bound, in itself, does not make the treaty binding on the state. *The treaty also has to enter into force for that state.* When that happens, the state becomes a 'party' to the treaty (Article 2(1)(g)). Whether, and when, ratification will bring the treaty into force for the state will depend on the provisions of the treaty.

Exchange or Deposit of Instruments of Ratification

Article 16 (which also applies to 'acceptance' and 'approval': see pp. 120–121) specifies that, unless the treaty provides otherwise, the consent of a state to be bound is established by one of the following:

(a) The *exchange* of instruments of ratification between the contracting states. This is normally only for bilateral treaties. Unless the states want to emphasise the importance of the occasion, no ceremony is necessary, with the exchange taking place in one of the foreign ministries and at whatever level is felt appropriate. Unless the treaty is of high political importance, the exchange would usually be effected by the head of the treaty department of the foreign ministry and a member of staff of the other state's embassy. Full powers are not needed. Although the exchange does not have to be simultaneous, this is almost invariably the practice. If it is not to be simultaneous, the effective date of the exchange will be the date on which the latter of the two instruments is received. If, as is usually the case, the treaty was signed in one of the states, it is the custom for the exchange to take place in the other state. The host state for the exchange should produce two originals of a certificate of exchange (sometimes called a *procès-verbal* or protocol).[37] The text of the certificate, including any foreign language text, should be agreed in advance. The certificate is signed when the instruments are exchanged, and the representative of the other state takes away the original instrument in which their state is given 'precedence'. The certificate is not published. See the example of a draft exchange of instruments of ratification in Appendix M.

(b) The *deposit* of an instrument of ratification with the depositary of the treaty.[38] This is the normal practice for multilateral treaties.

(c) The *notification* of the instrument of ratification to the other contracting state or states or to the depositary, if so agreed. This is a simplified form of exchange or deposit, but is best avoided in the interests of certainty and simplicity. It is hardly, if ever, now done.

Consent to be bound is effective from the date of exchange, deposit or receipt of notification. That date is the date of ratification, no other; and certainly not the date on which any parliamentary approval is given. Whether, and if so, when, the treaty enters into force for the ratifying state will depend on when the treaty enters into force and the relevant provisions of the treaty governing ratification and entry into force: see Chapter 9.

Conditional Ratification?

Ratification must be unconditional; it cannot be made dependent on the receipt or deposit of other instruments of ratification, unless the treaty provides for this. This does not, however, prevent reservations being attached to the ratification,[39] or even the withdrawal of the instrument before entry into force.[40]

No Obligation to Ratify

Signature of a treaty imposes no legal obligation to ratify, though a state should refrain from signature if it has little intention of ratifying.[41]

[37] Not to be confused with a treaty named 'Protocol'. [38] As to the depositary, see Chapter 18.
[39] See Chapter 8. [40] See pp. 129–130. [41] See also pp. 127–129 on Article 18.

Period for Ratification

It is not usual to set a deadline for ratification, and some multilateral treaties are ratified (or more usually acceded to) many years later. Although the Genocide Convention was originally a US idea, the United States did not ratify the Genocide Convention 1948[42] until 1988, due to hold-ups in the US Senate. Following the break-up of the Soviet Union, the Baltic states (not regarding themselves as successor states to the Soviet Union) acceded to many treaties, including some nearly fifty years old. Libya and the United Kingdom acceded to the Hague Convention on the Pacific Settlement of Disputes 1907 respectively some sixty-five and eighty years later.[43]

Ratification of Part of a Treaty

A state may consent to be bound by part of a (multilateral) treaty, provided this is permitted by the treaty or the other contracting states agree (Article 17(1)). Some multilateral treaties provide that on ratification a state is required to choose between certain options, in which case the choice must be made then if the ratification is to be effective (Article 17(2)). The Conventional Weapons Convention 1980 has three *original* protocols,[44] and requires that on depositing an instrument of ratification a state must notify its consent to be bound by at least two of them. If this is not done, the instrument will not be effective. The notification should be included in, or accompany, the instrument. This case should be distinguished from provisions or related instruments (such as an optional protocol), which give a state an option that it is free to exercise or decline. This often relates to means of settling disputes arising under the treaty.

Instrument of Ratification

Who Can Sign?

The instrument of ratification has to be signed on behalf of the state. The international practice is for this to be done as for full powers, that is by the head of state, head of government or foreign minister ('qualified authorities'), depending on the constitution and practice of each state. If anyone else signs, full powers authorising that person to do so will have to be produced.[45] An instrument signed by a deputy or vice minister for foreign affairs will not be acceptable without full powers, unless it is clear that the minister is in charge of the foreign ministry *ad interim* or is acting foreign minister. Similarly, an instrument signed by another minister, including another cabinet minister, is *not* acceptable, even if the subject matter lies within their

42 78 UNTS 277 No. 1021; UKTS (1970) No. 58. See also W. Schabas, *Genocide in International Law* (2nd ed., Cambridge University Press, Cambridge 2009), 595–599.

43 205 CTS 233; UKTS (1971) No. 6. But the jurisdiction of the ICJ in the *Lockerbie* cases was *not* founded on the Hague Convention: see 37 ILM (1998) 587.

44 1342 UNTS 137 No. 22495; 19 ILM (1980) 1523; UKTS (1996) No. 105.

45 See Chapter 5.

responsibility, unless the instrument is accompanied by a declaration (in effect, full powers), signed by one of the qualified authorities, that under the law of the state the minister is authorised to bind the state in respect of the treaty.[46] So it is much simpler if one of the qualified authorities signs, usually the foreign minister.

Form and Content of an Instrument of Ratification

The form and content of an instrument of ratification is not laid down by the Convention. However, since Article 2(1)(b) defines ratification as 'the international act so named whereby a State establishes on the international plane its consent to be bound by a treaty', the instrument must give clear and unambiguous expression to that intention. It is not enough to say that the necessary steps for the purpose of ratification have been taken or suchlike. The instrument of ratification must therefore: (1) identify the treaty by its title and the date when, and place where, it was concluded; (2) give the name and title of the person signing the instrument; and (3) say when and where the instrument was issued.

The instrument can be in the form of a letter. An unsigned instrument is not acceptable, even if it bears the seal of one of the qualified authorities, since it is important to ensure that the act of ratification has been approved *personally* at the proper level. However, in exceptional circumstances the practice of the UN Secretary-General (as depositary of many multilateral treaties) is to accept a letter or email from a permanent representative to the United Nations, accompanied by a scanned copy of the signed instrument, confirming that the original will be deposited as soon as it is received in the mission.[47] But if the instrument is not received within a few days, the Secretary-General may refuse to treat the state as having ratified, and simply wait for the instrument to arrive.

There is no rule as to the language in which the instrument must be drawn up, but it is obviously sensible to use an official language of the depositary. But even if the instrument is not in that language, it will still be acceptable. However, the depositary may not be able to acknowledge receipt until it has had the text translated to see exactly what it is and what it contains. Thankfully, it is no longer the practice to attach a copy of the treaty to the instrument of ratification.

Appendix L gives as an example an instrument of ratification with the simplified wording used by the British Foreign Secretary. Occasionally, the depositing state will *misdescribe* the instrument: a state that has signed the treaty, but may deposit an instrument of 'accession'; a state that did not sign the treaty may deposit an instrument of 'ratification'. The depositary will then seek confirmation that the instrument should be treated as one of ratification or accession, as the case may be.

To be valid, an instrument must be deposited within the time limit (if any) prescribed by the treaty.

[46] UN Depositary Practice, paras. 22–23 and Annex XV thereto; see also p. 96.

[47] Cf. the similar practice to full powers, p. 97.

Place of Deposit of Instruments

Instruments should be deposited at the seat of government of the depositary state or, if the depositary is an international organisation, at its headquarters. A ceremony is held only if the event is important politically. Perhaps somewhat perversely, signature ceremonies are usually higher-profile occasions than the deposit of an instrument of ratification, which in most cases is handled fairly bureaucratically in terms of process, with the instrument being simply delivered to the depositary. This can be done by post. However, given the importance of the instrument, and the trouble that has been taken over it, it is prudent to deliver it by hand. Instruments have been known to be 'mislaid' in even the better-run foreign ministries or international organisations. It is also prudent to have checked in advance that the relevant section of the Foreign Ministry or international organisation is open at the proposed hour of deposit and able to receive the instrument.

Acknowledgement and Date of Deposit

The depositary will send the ratifying state a formal acknowledgement of receipt of the instrument, and notify the other parties and states entitled to become parties. Provided the instrument is valid and meets all the necessary conditions for effectiveness, the date of deposit will be given as the date the instrument is actually received by the depositary, except in the various circumstances mentioned above.

Acceptance or Approval

Consent to be bound can, if the treaty so provides, be expressed by 'acceptance' or 'approval' under conditions very similar to those that apply to ratification (Article 14(2)). There is no substantive difference between signature subject to acceptance or approval and signature subject to ratification. It is, in fact, now common for multilateral treaties to provide that they shall be 'subject to ratification, acceptance or approval'.

The use of acceptance or approval was developed in order to enable some states to avoid constitutional requirements to obtain parliamentary authority to ratify, particularly when the parliamentary process was described as 'ratification' and no clear distinction is drawn by the parliament or the constitution between that domestic process and ratification on the international plane.[48]

The rules applicable to ratification apply equally to acceptance or approval. Unless the treaty provides otherwise, acceptance or approval has the same legal effect as ratification. Expressing consent to be bound by acceptance or approval, but without prior signature, is analogous to accession (see pp. 121–123). For some

[48] See Article 2(2).

treaties, it is the only way to express consent. For example, treaties adopted within the FAO do not include provision for signature, consent being expressed by an instrument of acceptance.[49]

Provisional or Definitive Acceptance

Article 19(c) of the International Nickel Study Group Terms of Reference 1986[50] (actually a treaty) provides for a prospective party to give notice that it 'intends' to apply the treaty either 'provisionally, pending the conclusion of its internal procedures' or 'definitively'. Despite the clumsy wording, the last term amounts to acceptance, and the former to provisional acceptance (and provisional application) – in this context, equivalent to signature subject to ratification.

Accession

No state has a right to accede unless the treaty so provides or the parties agree to that state acceding to the treaty. Accordingly, Article 15 provides that accession is a means by which a state can consent to be bound by a treaty if:

(a) the treaty so provides;
(b) it is otherwise established that the negotiating states were agreed that consent could be so expressed; or
(c) all the parties have subsequently agreed that a state may express its consent by such means.[51]

Accession is primarily the means by which a state may become a party if, for whatever reason, it is unable to *sign* the treaty. This may be because, as in Article 81 of the Convention itself, the treaty restricts the right of signature to certain states or because there is a deadline for signature and it has passed. For a few treaties, accession may be the only means of becoming a party.[52]

In practice, accession is mainly relevant to multilateral treaties. Today, multilateral treaties that are subject to ratification – which is most of them – will almost always include an accession clause. Commonly, entry into force is conditional on the deposit of a certain number of instruments of ratification (or acceptance or approval) or accession. Article 84 of the Convention provides that it:

> shall enter into force on the thirtieth day following the date of deposit of the thirty-fifth instrument of ratification or accession.

[49] See Article X Compliance Agreement 1993: 2221 UNTS 120 No. 39486; 33 ILM (1994) 968.
[50] 1566 UNTS 29 No. 27296.
[51] That is, following entry into force: see the definition of 'party' in Article 2(1)(g).
[52] For example, the Protocol relating to the Status of Refugees 1967: 606 UNTS 267 No. 8791; UKTS (1969) No. 15.

If, however, the treaty provides that a state may accede only after a certain date or event (e.g., entry into force of the treaty), but an instrument of accession is received before then, the depositary will inform the state that the instrument will be held until that date has arrived or the event has occurred. Until then, the instrument will *not* be counted for the purposes of calculating whether the conditions for entry into force have been met.

Nowadays there is usually no requirement for the exercise of a right to accede to be delayed until the deadline for signature has passed.

Preconditions for Accession

As with the right to sign, the right to accede may be restricted to a specified category or categories of states, and may be made subject to conditions or the consent of other states. The conditions may be matters of fact, for example that the state is already a party to a specific treaty. Article 22 of the Antarctic Treaty Environmental Protocol 1991[53] provides that, after the deadline for signature, the Protocol is open for accession by any state that is a party to the Antarctic Treaty. The conditions may include a requirement that the parties are to determine collectively that they are satisfied that the applicant state has met certain conditions. Article XXIX of the Convention on the Conservation of Antarctic Marine Living Resources (CCAMLR) 1980 provides that the Convention:

> shall be open for accession by any State interested in research or harvesting activities in relation to the marine living resources to which [the] Convention applies.[54]

The parties have interpreted this as requiring them to reach a collective determination as to whether the applicant state is truly interested in such activities. In practice, the CCAMLR Secretariat circulates a note about the applicant state, and if no party objects, the application is deemed to be accepted.

The CoE Framework Convention for the Protection of National Minorities 1995 provides that after its entry into force:

> the Committee of Ministers of the Council of Europe may *invite* to accede to the Convention ... any non-member State of the Council of Europe ...[55]

Even when the accession clause provides for invitations to accede, it is sometimes necessary to conclude a treaty (usually called a protocol) to formalise the accession

[53] 30 ILM (1991) 1460; UKTS (1999) No. 6.
[54] 1329 UNTS 47 No. 22301; 19 ILM (1980) 837; UKTS (1982) No. 48; TIAS 10240.
[55] 2151 UNTS 243 No. 37548; 34 ILM (1995) 353; UKTS (1998) No. 42; ETS No. 157: see Article 29(1). See also Article 33 CoE Criminal Law Convention on Corruption 1999, 2216 UNTS 225 No. 39391; 38 ILM (1999) 505; ETS No. 173.

and make any consequential modifications to the principal treaty. This will often be needed if the treaty concerns a collaborative project.[56]

Sometimes the accession clause of a multilateral treaty may be excessively complicated.[57] This may be due to political problems.

There are instances of the parties to a bilateral treaty consenting to a third state acceding to it, thereby making it multilateral. The France–Germany Ultra-High-Flux Reactor Convention 1967[58] provides, in its final clauses, that:

> The present Convention shall be open to accession by third States. Any accession shall require the consent of the signatory Governments. The conditions of accession shall be the subject of an agreement between the signatory Governments and the Government of the acceding State.

Note the term 'signatory Governments' in the above extract. There was a tendency for some European treaties on *defence* matters to be concluded by a limited number of states, and only once all of them had signed and ratified the treaty, and it had entered into force, were other states allowed to apply to the parties for their approval to accede.[59]

When a treaty has been amended or supplemented by later treaties, and it is necessary or desirable that an acceding state should be bound also by those treaties, when inviting a state to accede the parties will require as a condition for accession that the state consents to be bound by the later treaties as well. This can be done by a declaration in the instrument of accession that accession to the principal treaty constitutes accession to the other (listed) treaties also. But it is even better if the accession clause in the principal treaty includes such a condition.

Accession 'subject to ratification' does not amount to accession, but is equivalent to signature subject to ratification. It is now rarely found, and is probably due to a misunderstanding of the nature of accession.

The rules on deposit of instruments of ratification (or acceptance or approval) apply also to instruments of accession; and, unless the treaty provides otherwise, accession has the same effect as ratification.

Unless otherwise indicated, and for simplicity, in this book the terms 'ratification' and 'consent to be bound' are used to cover approval, acceptance or accession.

[56] The 1996 Protocol to the *Estonia* Agreement of 1995 in effect amended the principal Agreement to allow other states to accede to it (1947 UNTS 404 No. 32189; UKTS (1999) No. 74).

[57] See Article XXIII Food Aid Convention 1999: 2073 UNTS 138 No. 32022.

[58] Article IV: 821 UNTS 345 No. 11764; Agreement concerning UK Accession 1974: UKTS (1976) No. 31.

[59] See, e.g., Articles 55 and 56 Framework Agreement between France, FRG and others concerning the European Defence Industry 2000: 2184 UNTS 5 No. 38494; UKTS (2001) No. 33. The UK–France Agreement concerning the European Air Group 1998 (2067 UNTS 264 No. 35802; UKTS (1999) No. 10), Article 35, provides for other European states to accede to it by means of ad hoc protocols.

Any Other Agreed Means

Article 11 is a good example of the inherent flexibility of the law of treaties, as reflected in many parts of the Convention. It provides that the consent of a state to be bound may be expressed by any other agreed means. The agreement does not have to be express; it is enough for it to be implicit in the text of the treaty or otherwise established, for example by conduct. Thus, it is possible for a treaty to be concluded without signature,[60] and enter into force *instantly* for all the adopting states. The Text establishing the Preparatory Commission of the Comprehensive Nuclear-Test-Ban Treaty 1996[61] was adopted by a resolution of the states that had signed the CTBT, and was effective in international law immediately without any further act by those states.

A most ingenious device is the 'simplified procedure' of Article 5 of the Implementation Agreement 1994,[62] that relates to Part XI of UNCLOS 1982.[63] Though not expressed as such, the purpose of the Agreement is to amend Part XI in such a way as to enable industrialised states to become parties to the 1982 Convention. Because sixty-four states had ratified that Convention by the date of adoption of the Agreement, and therefore the Convention would enter into force four months later, *politically* there was an urgent need for a means for the (predominantly developing) contracting states (i.e., those that had not ratified the 1982 Convention) to establish their consent to be bound by the Agreement, but in a low-key manner. For some, there could have been domestic political problems if they had had to seek the approval of their parliaments to ratification of the Agreement so soon after they had approved ratification of the 1982 Convention. It was therefore agreed that, if a contracting state to that Convention merely signed the Agreement, it would be considered to have established its consent to be bound by the Agreement unless it notified the depositary, within twelve months of the adoption of the Agreement, that it would not avail itself of this simplified procedure.[64] It worked.

Although the original members of the United Nations had to sign and then ratify the UN Charter,[65] all other members have been admitted to the organisation in accordance with the procedure in Article 4 of the Charter, which includes making a Declaration of Acceptance of the obligations in the Charter.[66]

'Signatory', 'Party', 'Signed Up To' and 'Adherence'

In the media – and all too often even in foreign ministries – it is said that a state is a 'signatory' of a treaty, with the implication that it is a party. As will have been evident

[60] As to the lack of need for signature, see pp. 31–32. [61] UKTS (1999) No. 46.
[62] 1836 UNTS 42 No. 31364; 33 ILM (1994) 1313; UKTS (1999) No. 82.
[63] 1833 UNTS 3 No. 31363; 21 ILM (1982) 1261; UKTS (1999) No. 81.
[64] See D. Anderson, 'Further Efforts to Ensure Universal Participation in the UNCLOS', ICLQ 43 (1994) 886–893.
[65] UKTS (1946) No. 67, Articles 3 and 110. See also UN Multilateral Treaties, chapter I.1.
[66] See UN Multilateral Treaties, chapter I.2.

from this chapter, there are several ways in which consent to be bound can be expressed; signature is *only one* way, and is usually subject to ratification. Even when the signature has been ratified, that does not mean that the treaty has entered into force for that state. Only when that does happen would the state then be a 'party'.

'Signatory' is, therefore, a loose and misleading term, and should be avoided if at all possible. It should be used only when it is *abundantly clear* that it refers solely to the fact that a state has signed, nothing more. So to avoid misunderstandings, if one wants to say merely that a state has signed, it is still preferable to add that it is subject to ratification, if that is the case. If a state has ratified, one should say just that. When a treaty has entered into force for a state, including when the treaty enters into force on signature, one should always say that the state is a party. If one follows such practice, one ought to be understood, though one may well have to explain.

One also often hears a government minister saying that the state has 'signed up to' a treaty. In English, the expression usually means being bound legally, but not always. So, being a loose term, it should be avoided.

It may be more convenient to use a generic term to express the fact that a state has consented to be bound by saying, in English, that it has 'adhered' to a treaty. (Confusingly, the French for accession is '*adhesion*'.) But this should not be confused with the – now archaic – provisions in treaties for adhesion or adherence, which have now been replaced by accession clauses.[67]

The 'All States' and 'Vienna' Formulas

Until the mid-1950s a treaty intended to have universal application would have a final clause permitting 'all states' (or 'any state') to become a party. Since 1973, this has again been the normal formula.[68] Nevertheless, the depositary of a multilateral treaty may sometimes receive an instrument of ratification from an entity about which there is doubt or controversy as to whether it is a state. When the Internationally Protected Persons Convention was adopted in 1973, the UN General Assembly issued a general statement that the Secretary-General, in discharging his functions as depositary of a treaty with an 'all states' clause, would follow the practice of the General Assembly and, whenever advisable (i.e., in problematic cases), would request the opinion of the Assembly before receiving a signature or an instrument of ratification or accession.[69] Due to Cold War attitudes, from the mid-1950s to 1972 problems arose over the application of 'all states' clauses. At the time, there were some entities over which there were long and serious (and essentially political) disputes as to whether they

[67] See *O'Connell*, 229.

[68] See, e.g., Articles XVIII and XX Chemical Weapons Convention 1993: 1974 UNTS 317 No. 33757; 32 ILM (1993) 804; UKTS (1997) No. 45.

[69] See the commentary on the Convention by M. Wood, ICLQ 22 (1974) 791, 816–817; and UNJurYbk (1974) 157 and (1976) 186.

were states, for example the German Democratic Republic, North Korea and North Vietnam. To avoid differences over whether they had the necessary capacity to become party to a particular treaty, the so-called 'Vienna formula' was included in new treaties. Under it, a disputed entity was entitled to become a party only if it was a member of at least one of a number of specified international bodies.

It is not exactly clear when the Vienna formula was first used, but it is to be found in a simple form in the International Atomic Energy Agency (IAEA) Statute 1956.[70] A more elaborate formula seems to date from the four Geneva Law of the Sea Conventions 1958.[71] Article 81 of the VCLT itself is a typical example of the final, comprehensive form:

> The present Convention shall be open for signature by all States Members of the United Nations or of any of the specialised agencies or of the International Atomic Energy Agency or parties to the Statute of the International Court of Justice, or by any other State invited by the General Assembly of the United Nations to become a party.

Mercifully, there has been no need for the formula since 1973. Nevertheless, the Vienna formula is to be found in the important Climate Change Convention 1992,[72] and this caused a *real* problem. Although clearly a state, there was doubt whether, between 1992 and 1996, the Federal Republic of Yugoslavia (Serbia and Montenegro) was a member of the United Nations, its membership of the United Nations, and of the rest of the UN family of organisations, being legally equivocal. During that period, it was therefore not clear whether the Federal Republic of Yugoslavia could become a party to treaties containing the Vienna formula. The use of such an outmoded formula in 1992 for an important multilateral treaty would seem to have simply been a mistake.

Rights and Obligations Prior to Entry into Force

In the period prior to the entry into force of a treaty, the acts of adopting, signing and consenting to be bound will create certain rights and obligations for the negotiating and contracting states, and for any depositary. The most obvious relate to those matters that have to be attended to so that the treaty can enter into force. As from the moment the text is adopted, the provisions on depositary functions, authentication, consent to be bound, reservations and other matters necessarily arising before entry into force will apply (Article 24(4)). Other rights and obligations will arise during that interim period

[70] See Article XXI Statute of the IAEA: 276 UNTS 3 No. 3988; UKTS (1958) No. 19.

[71] See, e.g., Article 26 Convention on the Territorial Sea and the Contiguous Zone 1958: 516 UNTS 205 No. 7477; UKTS (1965) No. 3.

[72] See Article 20 UN Framework Convention on Climate Change 1992: 1771 UNTS 107 No. 30822; 31 ILM (1992) 851; UKTS (1995) No. 28.

if the Convention or the treaty in question so provides, such as in relation to a preparatory commission.

Obligation Not to Defeat the Object and Purpose of a Treaty Prior to Its Entry into Force (Article 18)

Article 18 requires a state 'to refrain from acts that would defeat the object and purpose of a treaty' when:

(a) it has signed the treaty ... subject to ratification, acceptance or approval, until it shall have made its intention clear not to become a party to the treaty; or
(b) it has expressed its consent to be bound by the treaty, pending the entry into force of the treaty and provided that such entry into force is not unduly delayed.

It is sometimes argued that a state that has not yet even ratified a treaty must, in accordance with Article 18, nevertheless comply with it, or at least do nothing inconsistent with its provisions. This is clearly wrong, since the act of ratification would then have little or no purpose, the obligation to perform the treaty then *not* being dependent on ratification and entry into force.

Subparagraph (a) is straightforward, and there is a high-profile example. Even though the US administration at the time had signed the Rome Statute 1998 on 31 December 2000,[73] the subsequent US administration did not like the Statute. Since, under the rule in Article 18, the legal effect of *simple signature*[74] by the United States was that it had an obligation to refrain from acts that would defeat the object and purpose of the Statute until it had made clear its intention not to ratify it, the United States needed to send a diplomatic note to the depositary saying that it did not intend to become a party. This it did on 6 May 2002.[75] The legal effect is similar to the withdrawal of an instrument of ratification before entry into force.

When a treaty enters into force on the signature of the negotiating states signing at the same time, the legal effect of their signature is established at that point. However, if the treaty enters into force only after all (or a minimum number of) states have signed (which is only likely to occur with a plurilateral treaty), it is possible that a state could 'withdraw' its signature before the treaty enters into force. Although withdrawal of a signature could not be done *physically*, a diplomatic note to the depositary that the signature of the state 'shall be considered as having been withdrawn' has the same legal effect as the withdrawal of an instrument of ratification before entry into force. Another way in which the legal effect of signature might be nullified would be if the act of signature were invalid, though the chances of that occurring are likely to be extremely rare.[76]

Subparagraph (b) is rather more difficult to apply. Once a state has expressed its consent to be bound (e.g., has ratified), the obligation to refrain from acts that would

[73] 2187 UNTS 91 No. 38544; 37 ILM (1998) 998; UKTS (2002) No. 35.
[74] That is, not *definitive* signature.
[75] UN Multilateral Treaties, chapter XVIII.10, note to US entry.
[76] See Chapter 17 (Invalidity).

defeat the object and purpose of the treaty continues pending its entry into force, provided that event is 'not unduly delayed'. There is uncertainty both as to the extent of the obligation and, in particular, the proviso. What is certain is that only by examining the treaty in question in the light of all the circumstances can one determine whether the provision might apply. There is virtually no practice but, given the manner in which it is worded, the discussions in the ILC[77] and the views of writers,[78] it may be possible to formulate the following propositions.

A state is not required to comply in any *general* sense with a treaty or its object and purpose before it enters into force. The obligation is only to 'refrain' (a weak term) from acts that would 'defeat' (a strong term) the object and purpose of the treaty.[79] The state must not, therefore, do anything that would prevent it from being able to fully comply with the treaty once it has entered into force. It follows, therefore, that it does not have to abstain from all acts that will be prohibited after entry into force. But the state must not do an act that would (not merely 'might') invalidate the basic purpose of the treaty. Thus, if the treaty obligations are premised on the status quo at the time of signature, doing something before entry into force that alters the status quo in a way that would prevent the state from performing the treaty would be a breach of the article. The test is objective, and it is not necessary to prove bad faith. In the following examples there would probably be a breach of the obligation:

(1) The treaty provides for the return of objects, which are then destroyed by the possessor state before entry into force.
(2) The treaty provides for territory to be ceded. Before entry into force, the ceding state transfers part of the territory to a third state.
(3) Several states sign a treaty subject to ratification, undertaking to reduce their existing armed forces by one-third. Entry into force is not unduly delayed. After ratification but before entry into force, a state announces a long-term programme to, say, double its forces. The position would be different if the state had made the statement after signature but before ratification: this would in effect amount to an expression of its intention not to become a party.[80]

[77] See, in particular, the *Yearbook of the International Law Commission* (1965) Pt I, 87–99 and 262–263 and Pt II, 43–45.

[78] P. McDade, 'The Interim Obligation between Signature and Ratification', *NILR* (1985) 5–47; J. Klabbers, 'How to Defeat a Treaty's Object and Purpose Pending Entry into Force: Toward Manifest Intent', *Vanderbilt Journal of Transnational Law* (2001) 283–331; D. Jones, 'The CTBT', *International Law and Politics* 39 (2007) 1007–1046; P. Palchetti, 'Article 18 of the 1969 Vienna Convention: A Vague and Ineffective Obligation or a Useful Means for Strengthening Legal Cooperation?', in E. Cannizzaro (ed.), *The Law of Treaties Beyond the Vienna Convention* (Oxford University Press, Oxford 2011), 25–36.

[79] On the meaning of 'object and purpose', see Chapter 8, pp. 147–148; and in the context of reservations, Guideline 3.1.5, Guide to Practice on Reservations to Treaties, Report of the ILC on the Work of its 63rd session, 2011, UNGA 66th Session, Supplement No. 10, Addendum 1, Doc. A/66/10/Add. 1, 352–359.

[80] See also *O'Connell*, 222–224.

These are fairly obvious examples. A Greco-Turkish Mixed Arbitral Tribunal in 1928 held that a Turkish seizure of Greek property before the entry into force for Turkey of the Treaty of Lausanne[81] was invalid, since if the treaty had then been in force it would have been a material breach.[82] This view is supported by the *travaux* of Article 18.

Withdrawal of Consent to Be Bound before Entry into Force

A question that sometimes arises (though fortunately very rarely) is whether a state that has consented to be bound may nevertheless withdraw its consent before the treaty enters into force. The answer does not depend on whether the treaty is bilateral or multilateral; though if a state has expressed its consent to be bound by a bilateral treaty by signature, and the other state has already signed, it is less easy to see how this could be 'withdrawn' unless the treaty has by then not entered into force.

What little authority is available is conflicting, and there is scant state practice. But, in principle, there would seem to be no reason why it cannot be done given certain circumstances. The consent is to be bound once the treaty has entered into force, not before. At the Vienna Conference, one delegate referred to the 'sovereign right of a State to withdraw from the treaty at any time before it finally became binding'.[83] No delegate challenged this assertion. In 1952 Greece withdrew an instrument of acceptance deposited in 1950. After the treaty had *later* entered into force, Greece 'reconfirmed' its acceptance. In 1958, Spain withdrew an instrument of accession two months after it had been deposited, but *before* the treaty had entered into force. At the same time, it deposited a new instrument containing a reservation. This was accepted. In 1999 and 2000, Italy and Luxembourg, respectively, withdrew their instruments of ratification of the Fish Stocks Agreement 1995, which had been deposited prematurely.[84] They later ratified it along with their fellow EU members. In each case, the UN Secretary-General notified the other states concerned. There were no objections. It has long been the practice of the UN Secretary-General to regard as permissible the withdrawal of consent before the entry into force of a treaty, on the understanding that until entry into force states are not definitively bound.[85] In the context of the UK's withdrawal from the European Union, the UK withdrew its instrument of ratification of the Agreement on a Unified Patent Court.[86]

[81] Treaty of Peace with Turkey (Treaty of Lausanne): UKTS (1923) No. 16. [82] 4 ILR 395.

[83] Official Records, 19th Meeting, 100. The delegate was from the Ukraine SSR, and at that time (1968) was, in reality, speaking for the Soviet Union.

[84] See UN Multilateral Treaties, chapter XXI.7, notes for Italy and Luxembourg.

[85] UN Depositary Practice, paras. 157–158.

[86] OJ 2013/C 175/01: the instrument was withdrawn on 20 July 2020. As at 31 July 2022, the Agreement had not yet entered into force.

The obligation under Article 18 does not prohibit a state from withdrawing an instrument. The obligation is to refrain from acts that would defeat the object and purpose of the treaty before its entry into force for the state. It relates, therefore, to the *substance* of the treaty, rather than to the procedure by which the state consents to be bound or by which the treaty enters into force. Mere withdrawal of an instrument, in itself, will not be a breach of the obligation in Article 18. But even if there are no legal consequences of withdrawing an instrument, it could be damaging *politically*. The deposit of an instrument of ratification is a solemn act.[87] Even if a new government coming to power does not like the treaty, that may not be a good reason to withdraw consent. The consent given by the previous government was given on behalf of the *state*, which usually continues in being despite the change of government. In giving consent to be bound, a government engages the honour not just of itself, but also of the state.

Withdrawal and Re-ratification?

See page 170 as to whether a state can withdraw from a treaty only for the purpose of re-ratifying with a new reservation.

Unratified Treaties

The International Court of Justice (ICJ) has held that an unratified treaty may constitute an accurate expression of the understanding of the states at the time of signature, and represented evidence of their views as to the factual extent of one side's authority.[88]

Development of Treaties

It is convenient to deal with this topic here. As we shall see, the inclusion of a built-in, compulsory amendment procedure enables a treaty to be adjusted more easily to meet changing needs. This is especially so for procedures by which detailed, technical annexes are to be amended. But in addition to a need for amendments to be made simply and quickly, there is sometimes a need for provisions by which a *legal regime* created by the treaty can develop. The procedures that have been devised are in no way outside the ambit of the Convention, its rules being broad and flexible enough to allow for many different types of regime. This can be done in three main ways:

(1) framework treaties;
(2) legally binding measures adopted by organs of international organisations; and
(3) jurisprudence of tribunals established by the treaty.

[87] See also p. 180.
[88] *Maritime Delimitation and Territorial Questions between Qatar and Bahrain* (Merits), ICJ Reports (2001) 40, at 66–68, paras. 80–91, esp. para. 89; 40 ILM (2001) 847.

A treaty may also develop in other ways that do not involve the creation of legal rights and obligations, such as by the adoption of guidelines and codes of conduct, but these are outside the scope of this book.

Framework Treaties

The term 'framework treaty' is a relatively recent invention. It describes a multilateral treaty that is no different in its legal effect from other treaties. The term is no more than a description of a type of treaty that provides a framework for later, and more detailed, treaties (often called protocols) or national legislation, which elaborates the principles declared in the framework treaty.

Measures

'Measures' is only an easy way of labelling *subsidiary instruments* made under a treaty. When establishing an international organisation, it is not unusual for the constitution of the organisation to give the power to impose on the member states legally binding *measures* by which the object and purpose of the organisation can be more effectively achieved.[89] The UN Charter is the most obvious example. If, under chapter VII of the Charter, the Security Council determines that there is a threat to international peace and security, it can impose measures to maintain or restore this. These can include a demand that an aggressor state leave territory it has occupied, the imposition of economic and other sanctions, the authorisation for the use of force or the establishment of international criminal tribunals. Under Articles 25 and 48 of the Charter, all members of the United Nations have a legal obligation to carry out such measures. Although the measures usually apply to particular situations (e.g., Bosnia and Herzegovina or Iraq), nevertheless, by its actions over a period, and especially since the invasion of Kuwait in 1990, the Security Council has created important precedents. As a result, the parameters within which the Council may take measures have been more clearly defined.

The Antarctic Treaty 1959 is short in length and short on detail.[90] There was, therefore, a need for it to include a dynamic element. Article IX provides for those parties that conduct substantial scientific research activity in Antarctica (the so-called consultative parties), in practice acting by consensus, to *recommend* to their governments measures in furtherance of the principles and objectives of the treaty. Under Article IX(4) the measures 'shall become effective' when they have been formally 'approved' by the governments of *all* the consultative parties.[91] In recent years,

[89] Such a procedure does *not* result in treaties, despite what is often said.

[90] 402 UNTS 71 No. 5778; UKTS (1961) No. 97.

[91] This can take many years. Measure 1 (2003) to establish a permanent Antarctic Treaty Secretariat is now in force. Until entry into force, the Secretariat acted on the basis that the Measure, and the Headquarters Agreement with Argentina, were being applied provisionally. Thus, financial contributions to the Secretariat had to be voluntary: see 26 ATCM, Final Report 2003, at: https://documents.ats.aq/atcm26/fr/atcm26_fr001_e.pdf.

measures adopted by the Antarctic Treaty Consultative Meeting (ATCM) have been subject to one of the procedures contained in Articles 6(1) and 8(2) of Annex V of the Antarctic Treaty Environmental Protocol.[92] Both provide generally for deemed approval after ninety days from adoption. Under Article IX(6) of the CCAMLR 1980, it is expressly provided that measures adopted by the CCAMLR Commission, by consensus, become binding on those parties that are members of the Commission 180 days after they have been notified to them, except that a member can opt out by making an objection within ninety days.[93]

Chapter VII decisions of the UN Security Council, measures under the Antarctic Treaty and CCAMLR, International Civil Aviation Organization (ICAO) standards and EU law, though binding in international law, may, of course, still need to be implemented in domestic law.

Jurisprudence of International Tribunals

As part of a treaty regime, states may establish an international court or tribunal to help further the object and purpose of the treaty. This has certainly been the task of the European Court of Human Rights, which has translated the general human rights principles of the European Convention on Human Rights into a highly developed body of jurisprudence. The Court of Justice of the European Union performs a similar role. Both courts – like courts the world over, international or domestic – have developed the regimes created by constituent instruments, sometimes in ways that may not have been foreseen by their authors.

[92] At the 42nd meeting (Prague 2019), 12 measures were adopted; and at the 43rd meeting (Paris 2021), 23 were adopted.

[93] See n. 54. Other examples of treaties which enable the adoption of measures include Articles 37, 38 and 54(1) Chicago Convention; Article 22 Universal Postal Union Constitution; and of course, the EU Treaties (TEU and TFEU).

8

Reservations

> The subject of reservations to multilateral treaties is one of unusual – in fact baffling – complexity.

> a matter of considerable obscurity in the realm of juristic speculation.

These depressing views by the eminent international lawyers, Hersch Lauterpacht and Daniel O'Connell in 1953 and 1970, respectively, are even truer today.[1] The last word had not been said in Articles 19–23 of the Convention. As is apparent from the vast amount that has been written on the subject, a spirited debate has developed on how those articles should be applied, especially the effect of an objection to a reservation on the ground that it is contrary to the object and purpose of the treaty: an issue seen as particularly relevant to human rights treaties.

It would be wrong to think that the problems are just theoretical. Since the Second World War, and especially during the last quarter of the twentieth century and the years that followed, there has been an enormous increase in the number and complexity of multilateral treaties on all subjects, and in the number of states adhering to them. In 1945 the United Nations had 51 members; by July 2022 it had 193. In the twenty years from 1975 to 1995 just one state, the United Kingdom, became a party to some 330 multilateral treaties, and made reservations to 45 of them.

Every week foreign ministries are notified of new reservations. They have to consider whether they are acceptable and, if not, what to do about them. Officials, including legal advisers, can be hampered by the misunderstandings and uncertainties that surround the subject. These can cause problems also for depositaries. On the other side of the coin, foreign ministries will have to consider carefully whether their state should make reservations to treaties they wish to ratify. Yet there are few decisions of international or national courts and tribunals on reservations.[2] Although there are some problems with

[1] YBILC (1953) vol. II (A/CN.4/63, https://legal.un.org/ilc/), 124, comment on draft Article 9; *O'Connell*, 230. To these comments one can now add that of the ILC's Special Rapporteur, Alain Pellet: 'the topic brings with it an emotional charge at the political level which I had underestimated and which made things even more complicated'. See A. Pellet, 'The ILC Guide to Practice on Reservations to Treaties: A General Presentation by the Special Rapporteur', EJIL 24(4) (2013) 1061–1097, 1063.

[2] For an instructive exception, see the *Case concerning the Delimitation of the Continental Shelf between UK and France*, Decision 30 June 1977 and Decision 14 March 1978, Court of Arbitration, 54 ILR 6, and the detailed discussion of it by *Sinclair*, 70–77.

reservations to treaties, the lack of judgments about them may indicate that *practical* problems with reservations may not loom quite as large as the extensive literature might suggest.

This chapter will explain, as far as possible in practical terms, the role played by reservations, the application of the Convention's rules, some outstanding issues and ways in which some of the problems can, even today, be managed better. It draws heavily on the ILC *Guide to Practice*,[3] which is, as the title and the word 'guidelines'[4] indicate, not a binding instrument but a *vade mecum*.[5]

But first, a word on interpretative declarations and political declarations, which it is also helpful to deal with here.

Interpretative Declarations

A state may seek to adjust the way in which a treaty will apply to it by means of interpretative declarations or reservations. An interpretative declaration may be defined as:

> a unilateral statement, however phrased or named, made by a State or an international organization, whereby that State or that organization purports to specify or clarify the meaning or scope of a treaty or of certain of its provisions.[6]

Interpretative declarations are widely used. Genuine interpretative declarations differ from reservations in that they 'specify or clarify the meaning or scope of a treaty', while reservations purport 'to exclude or to modify the legal effect of certain provisions' of a treaty.[7] Interpretative declarations should also be distinguished from optional or mandatory declarations made under some treaties.[8]

Interpretative declarations are not a recent invention. The first may have been made by the United Kingdom in respect of an instrument adopted at the Congress of Vienna in 1815.[9] During the course of the negotiation of a multilateral treaty, there will often be differences of view as to the meaning of a particular provision. If these cannot be resolved, a delegation may make a formal statement expressing the interpretation

[3] Guide to Practice on Reservations to Treaties, YBILC 2011, Vol. II, Part Three A/CN.4/SER.A/2011/ADD.1 (Part 3) and Corr.1 and 2 (in this chapter referred to as the *ILC Guide to Practice or ILC Guide*). For an account of the ILC's work by the Special Rapporteur, see Pellet (n. 1).

[4] The guidelines in the *ILC Guide to Practice* are referred to in this chapter simply as '*Guidelines*', normally followed by the specific number.

[5] Introduction to the *ILC Guide to Practice* (n. 3), Introduction, para. 4.

[6] *Guideline* 1.2.

[7] For the definition of 'reservation', see p. 141. See also the Commentary on *Guideline* 1.5, paras. 16–19.

[8] See P. Kohona (then Head of the UN Treaty Section), 'Some Notable Developments in the Practice of the UN Secretary-General as Depositary of Multilateral Treaties: Reservations and Declarations', AJIL (2005) 433–450, 448. On transitional opt-outs, see Article 124 Rome Statute. See also *Guideline* 1.5.3, para. 1.

[9] 64 CTS 454; 2 BFSP 3.

favoured by its government. If a summary record is made of the proceedings, this statement should appear in it. It then becomes part of the negotiating history (*travaux*). If the interpretation is important to the declarant state – and it usually is – that state may feel it necessary or desirable to repeat its interpretation at the time of signature or ratification. But an interpretative declaration formulated when signing a treaty does not require subsequent confirmation when a state or an international organisation expresses its consent to be bound by the treaty.[10]

The purpose of an interpretative declaration is often to establish an interpretation of the treaty that is consistent with the domestic law of the state concerned. When ratifying the Rights of the Child Convention 1989,[11] the United Kingdom made several declarations, one of which interpreted the references to 'parents' to mean:

> only those persons who, as a matter of national law, are treated as parents. This includes cases where the law regards a child as having only one parent, for example, where a child has been adopted by one person only, and in certain cases where a child is conceived other than as a result of sexual intercourse by the woman who gives birth to it [e.g., by *in vitro* fertilisation by donor] and she is treated as the only parent.[12]

This was designed to reflect UK domestic legislation, but was also a useful elaboration of a difficult term.[13]

However, there are occasions when signatory states or parties wish to oppose[14] the interpretation put forward by another state. When acceding to the Vienna Convention, Syria declared that in Article 52 (coercion) the reference to 'force' included economic and political coercion. Other parties formally opposed this.[15] When so doing, the opposing state may either implicitly acknowledge that the interpretative declaration is indeed a declaration rather than a reservation, but one it does not approve; or it may seek to characterise the declaration as a reservation (a process referred to in the *ILC Guide* as 'recharacterization'[16]), and respond to it as such. In principle, recharacterization does not so much directly engage the content of the declaration as

[10] *Guideline* 2.4.6. [11] 1577 UNTS 3 No. 27531; 28 ILM (1989) 1448; UKTS (1992) No. 44.

[12] See *UN Multilateral Treaties*, chapter IV.11.

[13] Human Fertilisation and Embryology Act 1990, sections 27–29. For details of UK practice in making interpretative declarations, see BYIL 68 (1997) 482–485. For a problematic Australian declaration to the Rome Statute, see Kohona (n. 8), 440.

[14] On the use of the terms 'approve' or 'oppose' in relation to interpretative declarations, see Pellet (n. 1), 1085, note 148.

[15] *UN Multilateral Treaties*, chapter XXIII.1. See also the Declaration on the Prohibition of Military, Political or Economic Coercion in the Conclusion of Treaties, attached to the Final Act of the Vienna Conference; and *Sinclair*, 65–68. In *Maritime Delimitation in the Black Sea (Romania* v. *Ukraine)*, ICJ Reports (2009) 61, at 78, para. 42, the ICJ considered the effect of Romania's declaration concerning Article 121 UNCLOS.

[16] *Guideline* 2.9.3: '"Recharacterization" of an interpretative declaration means a unilateral statement made by a State or an international organization in reaction to an interpretative declaration in respect of a treaty formulated by another State or another international organization, whereby the former State or organization purports to treat the declaration as a reservation.'

challenge its essential nature and legal effects,[17] but the opposing state, in its response, may do both at the same time.

However, the vast majority of interpretative declarations do not produce any response.[18] There are relatively few examples of states opposing such declarations, and there are even fewer examples of states expressly approving them.[19] If other parties do not make conflicting declarations or indicate their disagreement, what effect does this have? In the case of *reservations*, subject to the terms of Article 20(5) of the Convention, silence may be taken as consent. The *ILC Guide* recommends a different approach in the case of *interpretative declarations*. Under *Guideline* 2.9.8, an approval of, or an opposition to, an interpretative declaration shall not be presumed,[20] and under *Guideline* 2.9.9, an approval of an interpretative declaration shall not be inferred from the mere silence of a state or an international organisation.[21]

Subject to the above, an interpretative declaration is likely to become an element to consider in the interpretation of the treaty, and, provided it is not a disguised reservation,[22] the rules on interpretation in Articles 31 and 32 VCLT would apply to it. In principle, an interpretative declaration made in connection with the conclusion of a treaty might be considered under Article 31(2)(b) as part of the context, while an interpretative declaration made during the course of negotiation is more likely to be considered under Article 32 as part of the preparatory work, and thus among the supplementary means of interpretation.[23] But the precise effect of a statement regarding the interpretation of a provision will depend on all the circumstances.[24]

If the interpretative declaration is made in the context of the conclusion of the treaty (on adoption of the Final Act, or on signature or ratification), the declarant state will normally wish to ensure that it is properly recorded and published. Other states, however, even if they do not object to the declaration, may seek to ensure that it retains the (limited) status of an interpretative declaration (i.e., a unilateral statement) and does not become an integral part of the agreement. In cases where a

[17] *Gardiner*, 105.

[18] As to other declarations made on ratification of the Vienna Convention, see *Sinclair*, 63–68.

[19] *Guideline* 2.9.2, and commentary, para. 1.

[20] This to be read with *Guideline* 2.9.8, para. 2, which states: 'Notwithstanding guidelines 2.9.1 and 2.9.2, an approval of an interpretative declaration or an opposition thereto may be inferred, in exceptional cases, from the conduct of the States or international organizations concerned, taking into account all relevant circumstances.'

[21] See the discussion in the commentary on *Guideline* 2.9.8 on the extent to which (if it all) the conduct of a state may constitute acceptance.

[22] See the definition of 'conditional interpretative declaration' in *Guideline* 1.4, and pp. 139–141. See also D. M. McRae, 'Legal Effect of Interpretative Declarations', BYIL 49 (1978) 155–173, drawing a distinction between a 'simple interpretative declaration' and a 'qualified interpretative declaration'.

[23] See *Gardiner*, chapter 3.6, 105.

[24] '. . . the legal significance of an interpretative declaration must always depend on the particular circumstances in which it is made': Waldock as Special Rapporteur on the law of treaties, YBILC (1965) vol. II, 49, para. 2, quoted in *Gardiner*, 111–112.

Secretariat or depositary is involved, they too will be alert to this point, but whether one is representing the declarant or another state, it is always worth checking. The declarations made in connection with the Treaty of Lisbon are annexed to the Final Act of the Intergovernmental Conference which adopted the Treaty and divided it into sections, with Part C recording the declarations made by individual EU member states, or a group of EU member states. These were published along with the Final Act (and the Treaty) in the Official Journal, the UN Treaty Series and, for example, the UK Treaty Series.[25]

The need to consider how a declaration is properly recorded and published (if appropriate) is also relevant in the case of other statements and declarations which may be made by states, including political declarations, declarations of territorial extension, and declarations designating authorities and others, each of which will need handling in a different way.[26]

The definition of an interpretative declaration in the *ILC Guide*, unlike the definition of a reservation in the VCLT, does not include any temporal limitation on the making of the declaration.[27] But that does not necessarily mean that an interpretative declaration can be made at any time.[28] First, this may be formally prohibited by the treaty itself.[29] Second, a conditional interpretative declaration would necessarily be limited to the time of signature, ratification, acceptance or accession, or else it would cast unacceptable doubt on the existence and scope of treaty obligations.[30] And third, a declarant state would be precluded from modifying the original declaration where it has already formulated an interpretation which its partners have taken as a basis or were entitled (by estoppel) to take as a basis. Some declarations, however, might need updating to keep in line with other developments.[31]

It is possible for a party to make an interpretative declaration with regard to a bilateral treaty.[32] This does not give rise to the same difficulty of principle as with making a reservation to a bilateral treaty, since it is not purporting to exclude or modify the application of a treaty provision (at least if the declaration is genuinely

[25] 2702 UNTS 3 No. 47938, OJ C 306, 17.12.2007, 1, and OJ C 326, 26.10.2012, 1; UKTS (2010) No. 7.

[26] See *Gardiner*, chapter 3.4, 101; see also *Guideline* 1.5 and the commentary thereto.

[27] See *Guideline* 2.4.4.

[28] See the commentary on *Guideline* 2.4.4, paras. 1–6, and on *Guideline* 1.2, paras. 21–34.

[29] But see *Guideline* 2.4.7 (where a treaty states that an interpretative declaration may be formulated only at specified times).

[30] See *Guideline* 1.4 (Conditional interpretative declarations), and the commentary on *Guideline* 1.2, para. 31 and on *Guideline* 1.4, para. 14.

[31] For example, the UK declaration accompanying accession to the EC defining UK nationals for the purposes of EC law. This was replaced in 1982 following changes in UK nationality law. None of the other member states objected to the new declaration, and the European Court of Justice (ECJ) upheld it. The declaration was subsequently referred to in Declaration No. 63 annexed to the Final Act of the Conference adopting the Treaty of Lisbon.

[32] See *Guideline* 1.6.2.

interpretative).[33] The United States has been the most active. In the period from 1975 to 1995, it attached interpretative declarations to instruments of ratification of twenty-eight bilateral treaties.[34] US practice is to give the other state the text of the declaration before the exchange of instruments of ratification. This gives both parties an opportunity to agree on how to deal with the matter. The US instrument of ratification of the UK–US Cayman Islands Mutual Legal Assistance Treaty 1986[35] included certain unilateral 'understandings'. An interpretative statement accompanied the UK instrument of ratification to the effect that the United Kingdom regarded the US understandings as not modifying the obligations under the treaty. This procedure had been agreed in advance.

Guideline 1.6.3 specifies that the interpretation resulting from an interpretative declaration made in respect of a bilateral treaty by a state (or an international organisation) party to the treaty and accepted by the other party constitutes an authentic interpretation of that treaty. But often the other party will stay silent. Sometimes the declarant state is making the declaration either because the politics demands it, or because it has accepted the other party's wording of a particular provision, and wishes to assert its own view of its legal effect. Both states are aware of the sensitivity. The non-declarant party is prepared not to openly oppose the declaration, since this might prejudice the overall deal, yet it does not want to openly accept it.[36]

Political Declarations

When signing or ratifying a multilateral treaty, a state may make a declaration that is not intended to have any legal effect, or at least not in respect of the treaty itself. This type of declaration may be a statement of the general policy of the state towards the subject matter of the treaty, or a disclaimer that ratification does not signify recognition of a particular party as a state. Some, for example, have intimated that ratifying a particular treaty that Israel has already ratified does not imply that the state recognises Israel or is entering into relations with it.[37] The UN Secretary-General discourages statements made for political purposes only, though they will circulate and record them (and any responses) if the declarant state insists.[38]

[33] See the commentary on *Guideline* 1.6.1, and on *Guideline* 1.6.2.

[34] See also *Whiteman*, vol. 14, 164–170.

[35] UKTS (1990) No. 82; 1648 UNTS 179 No. 28332.

[36] See, for example, the context of a unilateral declaration which the UK made on 11 March 2019 in connection with a previous version of the Protocol on Ireland/Northern Ireland, which was to form part of the EU–UK Withdrawal Agreement (see n. 41). The UK Attorney General gave written advice to the prime minister and made a statement to parliament concerning this and a related joint instrument: www.parliament.uk/business/news/2019/march/attorney-generals-statement-on-joint-instrument-and-unilateral-declaration/; and Hansard, 12 March 2019, Col. 193.

[37] See also *Guideline* 1.5.1 (Statements of non-recognition).

[38] See Kohona (n. 8), 447–448.

Political declarations in this sense may vary in their significance but most are single statements by a single party on a particular aspect of a treaty being signed or ratified. These should be distinguished from a 'Political Declaration' in the sense of a lengthier, more substantial document agreed between those adopting the declaration that contains political (non-binding) commitments, either made in the context of a specific treaty,[39] or incorporated in a free-standing instrument.[40] The Political Declaration made by the European Union and the United Kingdom in the context of the Agreement on the withdrawal of the United Kingdom from the EU and EURATOM[41] was (as the word 'Political' clearly signals) not a treaty, but nevertheless a significant document which constituted the framework for the future relationship. The Withdrawal Agreement provided that the parties would 'use their best endeavours, in good faith and in full respect of their respective legal orders, to take the necessary steps to negotiate expeditiously the agreements governing their future relationship referred to in the Political Declaration'.[42]

Disguised Reservations and Conditional Interpretative Declarations

To determine whether a unilateral statement is a reservation or an interpretative declaration, the statement should be:

> interpreted in good faith in accordance with the ordinary meaning to be given to its terms, with a view to identifying therefrom the intention of its author, in light of the treaty to which it refers.[43]

The phrasing or name of a unilateral statement provides an indication of the purported legal effect.[44] In many cases, if a declaration is intended to be a reservation,

[39] See, for example, the UK–Morocco Political Declaration, made on 26 October 2019 upon agreement of the text of the Association Agreement between the two countries: www.gov.uk/government/publications/uk-morocco-political-declaration/uk-morocco-political-declaration-2.

[40] See, for example, the Political Declaration on HIV and AIDS, adopted by resolution of the General Assembly, 8 July 2011 (A/RES/65/277).

[41] OJ C 3841, 12.11.2019, 1–177; UKTS (2020) No. 3; Political declaration setting out the framework for the future relationship between the EU and the UK (OJ C 3841, 12.11.2019, 178–193), referred to in Article 184 of the Withdrawal Agreement as 'the Political Declaration of 17.10.2019'.

[42] Article 184 Withdrawal Agreement. See also the evidence of Michel Barnier, Head of the EU Task Force for Relations with the United Kingdom, to the House of Lords Select Committee on the EU, 23 June 2020, as part of his response to Q1: 'I am told, "The political declaration is not a treaty". We are well aware of that, but it is the basis for the treaty.'

[43] *Guideline* 1.3.1.

[44] *Guideline* 1.3.2. States use a wide variety of terms to describe their unilateral statements: see, for example, the 'understandings', 'interpretations', 'views', 'declarations', etc. made by the UK on ratification of the Protocol Additional to the Geneva Conventions 1949, and relating to the Protection of Victims of International Armed Conflicts (Protocol I) 1977: 1125 UNTS 3 No. 17512; 36 ILM (1997) 1391; UKTS (1999) No. 29 (with the text at 74–76).

its terms will leave no doubt, being either headed 'reservation' or prefaced by words such as 'the Government of Freedonia reserves'.[45] In other cases, a state (or international organisation) may make a declaration that is in fact an attempt 'to exclude or to modify the legal effect of certain provisions of the treaty in their application to that State'.[46] This is referred to below as a disguised reservation: a declaration which is, in fact, a reservation and which should be treated under the rules applying to reservations.

Specifically, a state (or international organisation) may, when making a declaration, in effect attach a *condition* to its adherence to the treaty, either expressly or implicitly. This may amount to a 'conditional interpretative declaration', which the *ILC Guide* defines as:

> a unilateral statement formulated by a State or an international organization when signing, ratifying, formally confirming, accepting, approving or acceding to a treaty, or by a State when making a notification of succession to a treaty, whereby the State or international organization subjects its consent to be bound by the treaty to a specific interpretation of the treaty or of certain provisions thereof.[47]

Conditional interpretative declarations are, according to the *ILC Guide*, subject to the rules on reservations.[48]

It is in fact only rarely that the conditional nature of an interpretative declaration is clearly apparent from the wording used.[49] It is not uncommon for what is in fact a reservation to be described as an 'understanding', 'explanation' or 'observation'. If a state makes its acceptance of certain provisions on the 'understanding' and so on that they are to be interpreted in a particular way, that may, depending on the circumstances, amount to a reservation. The situation is complicated by the fact that such terms are used also for *genuine* interpretative declarations.

A state or international organisation may characterise a reservation as an interpretative declaration because the treaty prohibits reservations or because it is politically more acceptable for a state not to appear to be attaching conditions to its participation in a treaty or modifying its effect. But, as the definition of reservation makes clear, it does not matter how the declaration is phrased or what name is given to it; one must look at the substance. The *ILC Guide* gives many examples of conditional interpretative declarations.[50] The following are examples of declarations which might be considered more generally as disguised reservations.

[45] See, e.g., the numerous declarations made by parties to the ICCPR (*UN Multilateral Treaties*, chapter IV.4).

[46] As in the definition of a reservation in Article 2(1)(d) VCLT.

[47] *Guideline* 1.4, para. 1.

[48] *Guideline* 1.4, para. 2. See also the commentary on *Guideline* 4.7.1 (Clarification of the terms of the treaty by an interpretative declaration), paras. 1–10.

[49] Commentary on *Guideline* 1.4, para. 8.

[50] Commentary on *Guideline* 1.4, paras. 3–11.

Bulgaria's ratification of the TIR Convention 1975[51] was accompanied by a 'declaration' denying the right of economic unions to become parties to the Convention. The member states of the European Economic Community (as it was then called), and the Community itself, responded by pointing out that the TIR Convention allowed for such participation; that the declaration had the appearance of a reservation; and that the TIR Convention prohibited reservations, except to the dispute settlement article.[52] On ratifying the Seabed Arms Control Treaty 1971,[53] Yugoslavia made a declaration to the effect that if a party wished to exercise inspection rights under the treaty about the continental shelf of another party, it had to give it advance notice. The United Kingdom responded that it could not accept this as a valid interpretation and that, insofar as it was intended to be a reservation, the United Kingdom formally objected to it on the ground that it was incompatible with the object and purpose of the treaty.[54] UNCLOS 1982 prohibits reservations except where expressly permitted, but allows a state to make interpretative 'declarations or statements', provided these do not 'purport to exclude or modify the legal effect of the provisions of this Convention in their application to that State'.[55] Many declarations have been made to UNCLOS, and many have been objected to as being reservations.[56]

On ratification of the Chemical Weapons Convention 1993,[57] the United States stated that, for the purposes of the Annex on Implementation and Verification, it would be a 'condition' that no sample collected by an inspection team could be removed from the United States for analysis. The Annex does not envisage any such restriction. Although not labelled 'reservation', the statement, and in particular the use of the term 'condition', clearly went beyond interpretation and amounted to a reservation.

Reservations

Article 2(1)(d) of the Vienna Convention defines a reservation as:

> a unilateral statement, however phrased or named, made by a State, when signing, ratifying, accepting, approving or acceding to a treaty, whereby it purports to exclude or to modify the legal effect of certain provisions of the treaty in their application to that State.

[51] 1079 UNTS 89 No. 16510; UKTS (1983) No. 56. See the Declaration by Bulgaria in *UN Multilateral Treaties*, chapter XI.A-16.

[52] See *UN Multilateral Treaties*, chapter XI.A-16, Objections. For some examples of UK responses to declarations, see BYIL 68 (1997) 485–486.

[53] 955 UNTS 115 No. 13678; 10 ILM (1971) 145; UKTS (1973) No. 13.

[54] See UKTS (1975) No. 125, 9–11.

[55] See Articles 309 and 310 (1833 UNTS 397 No. 31363; 21 ILM (1982) 1261; UKTS (1999) No. 81).

[56] See *UN Multilateral Treaties*, chapter XXI.6. For the UK objections, see BYIL 68 (1997) 494–495. See also L. Nelson, 'Declarations, Statements and "Disguised Reservations" with respect to the Convention on the Law of the Sea', ICLQ 50 (2001) 767–786.

[57] 1974 UNTS 317 No. 33757; 32 ILM (1993) 804; UKTS (1997) No. 45.

Although a reservation is 'unilateral' in the sense that it has not been agreed by the negotiating states, two or more states can make the same reservation. Reservations must be distinguished from 'derogations'. The latter are statements specifically authorised by a treaty by which a party is able to exclude certain provisions in their application to it during a particular period, such as a public emergency.[58]

Reservations must also be clearly distinguished from declarations by a state on ratification (or subsequently) whereby it extends the treaty to some or all of its overseas territories. However, when making such a declaration of extension, a state may formulate reservations which it proposes to apply specifically in respect of the specified territory or territories.[59]

Bilateral Treaties

The Convention does not generally distinguish between bilateral and multilateral treaties, even for reservations. One has therefore to look to basic principles and state practice when examining the question of reservations and interpretative declarations made in connection with bilateral treaties. Although the Convention does not say so, a 'reservation', as that term is defined in Article 2(1)(d), cannot be made to a bilateral treaty given the nature of such a treaty. Since there are only two parties, a bilateral treaty is more like a contract, *all* the terms of which must be agreed before it can bind the parties. Making a 'reservation' to a bilateral treaty amounts to a request for a modification of it, usually in favour of the requesting state. The treaty cannot therefore be binding unless and until the other state accepts the 'reservation', either expressly or tacitly, or the reserving state agrees to drop the 'reservation'.

The United States has a long history of making its ratification of bilateral treaties conditional on modifications being made. This is due to the power given to the Senate by the Constitution.[60] Because the US president needs Senate approval ('Advice and Consent') before ratifying certain treaties, the Senate will sometimes give its approval only on condition that the president obtains a modification to the treaty. This is often misleadingly described by the Senate as a 'reservation'. It has happened over one hundred times since the first one in 1795, and at least thirteen times between 1975 and 1985,[61] with nine of the thirteen treaties being double taxation agreements. Although, in theory, the acceptance of the other state could be tacit, this does not seem to happen. The US Senate approved the UK–US Supplementary Extradition Treaty

[58] Article 4(3) ICCPR 1966: 999 UNTS 171 No. 14668; 6 ILM (1967) 368; UKTS (1977) No. 6; and Article 15 ECHR 1950: 213 UNTS 221 No. 2889; UKTS (1953) No. 71; ETS No. 5.

[59] See *Guideline* 1.1.4: 'A unilateral statement by which a State, when extending the application of a treaty to a territory, purports to exclude or to modify the legal effect of certain provisions of the treaty in relation to that territory constitutes a reservation.'

[60] See p. 145 on the Senate's attitude to 'no reservations' articles in multilateral treaties.

[61] A 'proviso' attached to Senate approval of a bilateral treaty has legal effect, if any, only in US domestic law, and is therefore *not* included in the instrument of ratification: see D. Hollis, M. Blakeslee and B. Ederington (eds.), *National Treaty Law and Practice* (Martinus Nijhoff, Leiden 2005), 774–776.

1985[62] on condition that certain amendments were made. The US government having informed the UK government of this, it was decided to amend the treaty by an exchange of notes. The US note recorded the Senate's condition and attached the articles of the treaty as they would read if so amended. The note explained that the president could not execute the instrument of ratification unless the amendments were made, and asked if they would be acceptable to the UK government. The UK note confirmed that the amendments were acceptable and instruments of ratification were finally exchanged in December 1986. Other states do not make their acceptance of bilateral treaties conditional, except for treaties with the United States, and then generally in response to a US 'reservation'.

If a legislature refuses to approve a bilateral treaty or to pass implementing legislation, the correct course is for the government to seek to renegotiate the treaty, or at least part of it.

Multilateral Treaties

The need to make reservations stems from the nature of the multilateral treaty-making process. A contract is usually between two, or at least a limited number of, parties, and is made under the law of one state. In contrast, even when states are part of the same continent (or even the same island), they very often have their own domestic legal systems, varying national policies and different languages. The problems these pose for the successful negotiation of even a regional treaty are multiplied when the treaty is intended to have general application, as do most treaties adopted in the United Nations or the so-called UN specialised agencies. In the United Nations, multilateral treaties can be negotiated by nearly 200 states. Reaching agreement on a text requires compromises in order to accommodate all their different interests and concerns. Now that most multilateral treaties are adopted by consensus, inevitably some, or even many, of the negotiating states will be dissatisfied with at least some aspects of the resulting text. But, for political reasons, a state may be reluctant to stand in the way of reaching consensus, and may even sign a treaty despite some unhappiness at the result. If it is greatly dissatisfied, it will have the option of not becoming a party. If this would be difficult politically, a state may seek to adjust certain provisions *in their application to it* so as to make it possible for it to become a party: that is, it will formulate and enter reservations. Sometimes a legislature will require such adjustments as a condition of its consent to ratification. We shall later see some of the problems this can cause.

But one should not exaggerate the problem. Except perhaps for some human rights treaties, reservations are generally not so numerous or so extensive as to jeopardise the effectiveness of a treaty, though in some cases this may be because states that have real difficulty simply decide not to become parties. Despite what has been written on

[62] 1556 UNTS 369 No. 15811; UKTS (1988) No. 6; TIAS 12050.

the subject, most reservations can be dealt with adequately by the application of Articles 19–23.

Reservations Are Generally *Not* Prohibited

There is nothing inherently wicked or even undesirable in formulating a reservation to a multilateral treaty. It would be quite wrong to think that the world is divided into reserving states and objecting states. As with diplomatic relations – where every state is both a sending state and a receiving state – many states both make reservations and object to reservations, though in fact reservations are generally not objected to. In many, if not most cases the purpose of the reservation is merely to adjust the reserving state's obligations under the treaty to conform to its domestic law where, for political, cultural or social reasons, it is not feasible or desirable to change the law. Many states have made reservations to the Convention on the Rights of the Child 1989.[63] The United Kingdom made several detailed ones, some of which were made only in respect of application to its overseas territories.[64] There have been no objections.

It is also important to note that all the rules on reservations in the VCLT (and enumerated in the *ILC Guide*) are not peremptory by nature, meaning that states and international organisations are able to derogate from them by the provision of a specific regime in an individual convention.[65]

These realities need to be emphasised, since they are sometimes obscured by the great debate about the legal effect of prohibited reservations and objections to them, which we will come to later.

Article 19 states the basic rule that a state *may* formulate a reservation *unless:*

(a) the reservation is prohibited by the treaty;
(b) the treaty provides that only specified reservations, which do not include the reservation in question, may be made; or
(c) in cases not falling under subparagraphs (a) and (b), the reservation is incompatible with the object and purpose of the treaty [the so-called 'compatibility test'].

Although only paragraph (a) expressly uses the term 'prohibited', we will use that term also when referring to paragraphs (b) and (c), since, clearly, they also deal with prohibited reservations. We will examine each paragraph in turn.

Exception (a): the Reservation Is Prohibited by the Treaty

It is increasingly common for treaties, such as the Rome Statute 1998,[66] to provide expressly that reservations are not permitted. This can cause problems, in particular for

[63] See n. 11. [64] See *UN Multilateral Treaties*, chapter IV.11. [65] See Pellet (n. 1), 1074 and 1077.
[66] 2187 UNTS 91 No. 38544; 37 ILM (1998) 998; UKTS (2002) No. 35.

the United States, given the way that the Senate jealously guards its power to refuse or give conditional approval to those treaties that have to be submitted to it.[67] When approving the ratification of the Fish Stocks Agreement 1995,[68] the Senate criticised the 'no reservations' clause in Article 42 because it had:

> the effect of inhibiting the Senate from exercising its constitutional duty to give advice and consent to a treaty, and the Senate's approval of this treaty should not be construed as a precedent for acquiescence to future treaties containing such a provision.[69]

The International Labour Organization (ILO) Constitution[70] prohibits the making of reservations to the ILO Conventions. This is because of the unique trilateral negotiating structure of the ILO: trades unions, employers' associations and governments.[71] There may, however, be some scope for (genuine) interpretative declarations.

Exception (b): the Treaty Provides that Only Specified Reservations May Be Made

In the course of the negotiation of a treaty, it may become evident that it will not be possible to reach consensus unless certain states are given the possibility of, in effect, opting out of one or more provisions. Although the treaty could be silent on the question of reservations (and many are), this can be most unsatisfactory. The permissibility of a reservation will then depend on whether it satisfies the compatibility test in exception (c), the application of which is difficult and uncertain (see below). It is, therefore, preferable to specify expressly the matters on which reservations are permitted. Examples include the following:

(1) A contracting party may exclude certain specific subjects from the scope of the treaty. The Revised General Act for the Pacific Settlement of International Disputes 1949[72] lists the type of disputes (e.g., territorial) that a state can, by a reservation, exclude from the settlement procedures of the General Act as it would apply to that state. The Optional (Second) Protocol 1989 to the International Covenant on Civil and Political Rights (ICCPR),[73] Article 2, permits a reservation to be made to allow for capital punishment in the case of serious military offences in wartime. Of the present ninety parties, five made and maintained that reservation; other related reservations have been withdrawn.[74]
(2) A reservation may be made in respect of one or more specified articles, such as an article providing for the submission of disputes about the interpretation or

[67] The United States is *not* a party to the Rome Statute.
[68] 2167 UNTS 3 No. 37924; 34 ILM (1995) 1542; UKTS (2004) No. 19. [69] AJIL (1996) 647.
[70] See www.ilo.org for the up-to-date text. [71] See AJIL Supp. 29 (1935) 843–844.
[72] 71 UNTS 101 No. 912. [73] 1642 UNTS 414 No. 14668, 29 ILM (1990) 1465; UKTS (2000) No. 39.
[74] *UN Multilateral Treaties*, chapter IV.12.

application of the treaty to the ICJ or other settlement mechanism. The TIR Convention 1975[75] prohibits all reservations, except to the article on dispute settlement. The Bonn Convention on the Conservation of Migratory Species of Wild Animals 1979,[76] Article XIV, prohibits general reservations, but allows specific reservations to be made, which, for the reserving party, have the effect of removing certain species from the lists in the appendices to the Convention. The CoE Regional or Minority Languages Charter 1992,[77] Article 21(1), provides that no reservation may be made except to Article 7(2)–(5).

(3) A treaty may provide that reservations may be made only in respect of certain rights and obligations. The Convention on the Recognition and Enforcement of Decisions relating to the Maintenance Obligations 1973[78] prohibits reservations, except for some which are specified with great precision.

(4) Exceptionally, the treaty provides that only one (named) party (the United Kingdom, for example) may make a specified reservation.[79]

A provision that reservations may be made to articles other than certain specified ones means that a reservation to an article which is not so specified will be subject to the compatibility test. The CoE Convention on Nationality 1997,[80] Article 29(1), states this expressly in providing that, with the exception of certain chapters, reservations may be made to the rest of the Convention as long as they are compatible with its object and purpose.

Whether a reservation is permissible under exceptions (a) or (b) will depend on interpretation of the treaty.

Exception (c): Exceptions (a) and (b) Do Not Apply, and the Reservation Is Incompatible with the Object and Purpose of the Treaty (Compatibility Test)

It is relatively easy to determine whether a reservation is expressly or impliedly prohibited under exceptions (a) or (b). But when a treaty is silent on the matter of reservations, it can be extremely difficult to assess whether a reservation passes the compatibility test. *Guideline* 3.1.5 gives a general steer:

> A reservation is incompatible with the object and purpose of the treaty if it affects an essential element of the treaty that is necessary to its general tenor, in such a way that the reservation impairs the *raison d'être* of the treaty.

[75] See n. 51. [76] 19 ILM (1980) 15; UKTS (1990) No. 87.

[77] 2044 UNTS 577 No. 35358; ETS No. 148. See also Article 8 CoE Convention on Reduction of Cases of Multiple Nationality: 634 UNTS 222 No. 9065; UKTS (1971) No. 88; ETS No. 43.

[78] 1021 UNTS 209 No. 15001; UKTS (1980) No. 49 (Articles 26 and 34).

[79] See Article 32(1)(b) European Convention on Transfrontier Television 1989: 2206 UNTS 312 No. 33611; 28 ILM (1989) 859; ETS No. 132; UKTS (1993) No. 22. Amending Protocol 1998: ETS No. 171.

[80] 2135 UNTS 189 No. 37248; 37 ILM (1998) 44; ETS No. 166.

A few points on this are worth drawing from the *ILC Guide*.[81] The concept of 'object and purpose' in the Convention is not confined to reservations.[82] Although there is no definition of the concept in the other provisions, it can be inferred that it does not require a detailed dissection of the treaty, but rather an extraction of the treaty's 'essence' or 'overall mission'.[83] The term 'essential element' is not necessarily limited to a specific provision. An 'essential element' may be a norm, a right or an obligation.[84] In an endeavour to avoid too high a 'threshold', the ILC chose the adjective 'necessary' in preference to the stronger term 'indispensable', and decided on the verb 'impair' (rather than 'deprive') to apply to the '*raison d'être*' of the treaty.[85]

As for methodology, drawing on the wording of Article 31, *Guideline* 3.1.5.1 states:

> The object and purpose of the treaty is to be determined in good faith, taking account of the terms of the treaty in their context, in particular the title and the preamble of the treaty. Recourse may also be had to the preparatory work of the treaty and the circumstances of its conclusion and, where appropriate, the subsequent practice of the parties.

The *Guide* lists certain types of reservations which pose particular problems in assessing compatibility with the object and purpose, and recommends an approach in respect of each to mitigate them.[86] These reservations are:

- vague or general reservations;
- reservations to a provision reflecting a customary rule;[87]
- reservations to provisions concerning rights from which no derogation is permissible under any circumstances;
- reservations relating to internal law (including specific rules of an international organisation);
- reservations to treaties containing numerous interdependent rights and obligations; and
- reservations to treaty provisions concerning dispute settlement or the monitoring of the implementation of the treaty.

81 *ILC Guide*, 211–218.

82 See Articles 18, 19(c), 20(2), 31(1), 33(4), 41(1)(b)(ii), 58(1)(b)(ii), and 60(3)(b).

83 Commentary on the Guideline 3.1.5, para. 2.

84 That is a norm, right or an obligation 'which, interpreted in context, is essential to the general tenor of the treaty and whose exclusion or modification would compromise the treaty's *raison d'être*': commentary on *Guideline* 3.1.5, para. 14(a).

85 Commentary on *Guideline* 3.1.5, para. 14(c). The formulation in *Guideline* 3.1.5 seeks to strike an acceptable balance between the need to preserve the integrity of the treaty and the concern to facilitate the broadest possible participation in multilateral conventions: para. 13.

86 *Guidelines* 3.1.5.2–3.1.5.7.

87 There was a passionate debate in the ILC concerning reservations to provisions reflecting a peremptory norm (*jus cogens*). The commentary on *Guideline* 3.1.5.3 reflects the differing positions. See also *Guideline* 4.4.3, paras. 1 and 2; and Pellet (n. 1), 1088–1089.

When a treaty has quite a narrow focus, it should be relatively easy to identify its object and purpose. This is so for the short Physical Protection of Nuclear Material Convention 1979.[88] On its accession in 2000, Pakistan entered a reservation excluding nuclear material in domestic use, storage or transport from the Convention, which is designed to protect *all* nuclear material used for peaceful purposes.[89] Despite several objections, the reservation was not withdrawn. As treaties become longer and more complex, identifying the object and purpose of a treaty is more difficult. Applying the compatibility test to a human rights treaty such as the ICCPR, which also covers a wide range of subjects, can be difficult as well.[90]

Since the VCLT is itself a treaty, one can make reservations to it; but, as its final clauses do not include a reservations article, a reservation is subject to the compatibility test. Some reservations have been made.[91] In 1997, Guatemala made certain reservations that called into question important and well-established rules of customary international law that the Convention codified. In particular, it said that the rule in Article 27 (internal law may not be invoked as justification for failure to perform a treaty) would not apply with respect to the Guatemalan Constitution. Since the rule is so fundamental to the law of treaties, the reservation plainly failed the compatibility test and some states lodged objections to it.[92]

Acceptance of and Objection to Reservations

Definitions of Acceptance and Objection

While the meaning of acceptance is amplified in Article 20(5),[93] the term 'objection' is not defined in the Convention. This gap is filled by *Guideline* 2.6.1, which reads:

> 'Objection' means a unilateral statement, however phrased or named, made by a State or an international organization in response to a reservation formulated by another State or international organization, whereby the former State or organization purports to preclude the reservation from having its intended effects or otherwise opposes the reservation.

Grounds for Objection

A point that is often overlooked is that, even when a reservation is *not prohibited* under Article 19(a), (b) or (c), it does not mean that other contracting states cannot object to

88 1456 UNTS 101 No. 24631; 18 ILM (1979) 1319; UKTS (1995) No. 61.

89 See www.iaea.org.

90 See J. Klabbers, 'Some Problems Regarding the Object and Purpose of Treaties', *Finnish YBIL* (1997) 138–160.

91 See *UN Multilateral Treaties*, chapter XXIII.1.

92 See also the reservations by Peru to Articles 11,12 and 25 VCLT, which seemed to contradict Article 27; and the objections to them (*UN Multilateral Treaties*, chapter XXIII.1).

93 For Article 20(5), see pp. 152–153.

it on the ground that its effect would be contrary to general international law (e.g., an allegedly excessive assertion of extraterritorial jurisdiction) or, in fact, on *any* ground.[94] No reasons for an objection have to be given, though they often are. Even if the basis for the objection is *pure policy*, it will have the same effect as an objection on *legal grounds*. By formulating a reservation, the reserving state is consenting to be bound subject to a condition laid down by it. It makes an offer that is subject to acceptance by the other contracting states. It will not, therefore, be legally effective in relation to another contracting state unless that state has accepted it either expressly or by necessary implication. The only exception is when a reservation has been expressly authorised by the treaty (Article 20(1)). In practice, most objections seem to be made on the ground that a reservation is prohibited, and often because it fails the compatibility test. But we will look first at Article 20(2) and 20(3) of the Convention.

Plurilateral Treaties

The term 'plurilateral' is probably used only in international law. It describes a treaty negotiated between a limited number of states with a particular interest in the subject matter.[95] Article 20(2) provides that, if it appears from the object and purpose of the treaty that the application of it in its entirety, and between all the parties, is an essential condition for the consent of each of them to be bound by it, any reservation will require the acceptance of all the parties. Examples might include the Antarctic Treaty 1959,[96] which created a special regime for which the integrity of the treaty is vital. The distinct possibility of reservations concerning claims and counterclaims to sovereignty in parts of Antarctica was avoided by a saving provision, Article IV, protecting the various legal positions.

Constituent Instrument of an International Organisation

Where a treaty creates the constitution of an international organisation, it is also essential to preserve its integrity. Article 20(3) provides that a reservation to such a treaty will require the acceptance of the competent organ of the organisation – usually a general conference, or assembly, of the members – unless the constituent instrument otherwise provides. The constituent treaties of the (now) European Union are accompanied by national declarations, agreed in advance, which adjust the detailed application of each instrument to the particular circumstances of individual member states.

[94] See *Guideline* 2.6.2. [95] See pp. 11–12.
[96] 402 UNTS 71 No. 5778; UKTS (1961) No. 97; www.ats.aq.

All Other Cases

We will examine the rules of the Convention on acceptance of and objection to reservations, and then some issues that have been raised about them. But first, some history.[97]

The Law on Acceptance and Objection before the Convention

Before 1951, generally the rule for acceptance of a reservation was unanimity. Just as the adoption of a treaty always used to require the agreement of all the negotiating states, so a reservation was effective only if it had been accepted by all, expressly or tacitly, and usually *before* signature.[98] There was, however, a regional exception in pan-American practice, which, while preserving the requirement of other states' consent to a reservation, allowed the possibility that a multilateral treaty could apply between a state which made a reservation (the reserving state) and other states which accepted it, and would not apply between the reserving state and other states which did not accept it.[99]

In 1951 the UN General Assembly asked the ICJ for an Advisory Opinion about certain reservations that had been made to the Genocide Convention 1948. The pan-American practice was influential in shaping the Court's thinking.[100] The Opinion, reached by only seven votes to five, resulted in the following guidance:

(1) If a reservation has been objected to by one or more parties, but not by others, the reserving state will be a party, provided the reservation is compatible with the object and purpose of the treaty.
(2) If a party objects to a reservation because it considers it incompatible with the object and purpose, that party may consider the reserving state as *not* a party.
(3) If a party accepts a reservation as being compatible with the object and purpose, it may consider the reserving state as a party.[101]

The UN General Assembly asked the Secretary-General to conform his practice to the Advisory Opinion, so that when, as depositary, he received reservations or objections in respect of new multilateral treaties concluded under UN auspices, he would not consider their legal effect. Instead, he would communicate them to all states concerned, leaving each to draw its own conclusions.

At first the compatibility test was criticised as being subjective and unworkable, and it was thought by some that points (2) and (3) would lead to fragmentation of

[97] For an account of the historical background to the Convention articles, see *Sinclair*, 54–63.
[98] See AJIL Supp. 29 (1935) 843–912.
[99] See the report approved by the Council of the Panamerican Union, 4 May 1932, YBILC (1965) vol. II, 79; *Corten and Klein*, 410–411.
[100] See *Corten and Klein*, 411.
[101] *Reservations to the Convention on the Prevention and Punishment of the Crime of Genocide*, Advisory Opinion, ICJ Reports (1951) 15; 18 ILR 364.

multilateral treaties. But during the period 1951–1962, when the ILC was studying reservations as part of its work on the law of treaties, the process of decolonisation quickened and it became clear that the much greater number of potential parties to multilateral treaties made adherence to the unanimity principle impractical. So a more flexible system was devised. The basic approach taken by the Court, and followed by the General Assembly, found favour with the ILC, which recognised that the difficulty with the compatibility test lay not so much in the test itself, but in the process by which it was applied.[102]

The Rules of the Convention Relating to Acceptance and Objection

Article 20(4) sets out the residual rules to be applied when one is *not* dealing with an expressly authorised reservation, a plurilateral treaty or the constituent instrument of an international organisation. The rules were intended to be a flexible means of accommodating the different needs of the reserving state and the other contracting states:

(a) *acceptance* by another contracting state of a reservation constitutes the reserving state a party to the treaty *in relation to that other state* if or when the treaty is in force for those states;
(b) an *objection* by another contracting state to a reservation does not preclude the entry into force of the treaty as between the objecting and reserving states *unless a contrary intention is definitely expressed by the objecting state;*[103]
(c) an act expressing a state's consent to be bound by the treaty and containing a reservation is effective as soon as *at least one other contracting state* has accepted the reservation.[104]

It is rare for a contrary intention (paragraph (b)) to be 'definitely' (i.e., explicitly) expressed. The most noteworthy example may be the general – and sharp – objection by the Netherlands to the reservations to the Genocide Convention made by communist countries, some developing countries and the United States, in which they

[102] See YBILC (1953) vol. II (A/CN.4/63) or at https://legal.un.org/ilc/publications/yearbooks/english/ilc_1953_v2.pdf, 124, comments on Alternative draft A, paras. 1 and 2.

[103] In relation to Article 21(3), see further pp. 153–154.

[104] Emphasis added. However, the practice of the UN Secretary-General as depositary has been to include in the number of instruments required for entry into force all those that have been accepted for deposit, whether or not they are accompanied by reservations and whether or not those reservations have met with objections (*Summary of Practice of the Secretary-General as Depositary of Multilateral Treaties* (ST/LEG/7/Rev.1), para. 184). In view of this, the ILC, while confirming the rule in Article 20(4)(c), stated in *Guideline* 4.2.2. para. 2: 'The author of the reservation may, however, be included at a date prior to the establishment of the reservation in the number of contracting States and contracting organizations required for the treaty to enter into force, if no contracting State or contracting organization is opposed.' See A. Pellet and D. Müller, 'Reservations to Treaties: An Objection to a Reservation is Definitely not an Acceptance', in E. Cannizzaro (ed.), *The Law of Treaties beyond the Vienna Convention* (Oxford University Press, Oxford 2011), 37–59.

refused to accept the jurisdiction of the ICJ over disputes between the parties. The Netherlands stated that it did 'not deem any State which has made or which will make such reservation a party to the Convention'.[105] But, as we shall see, in many cases an objecting state will say expressly that it will nevertheless regard the treaty as in force between it and the reserving state.

Article 20(5) provides that acceptance of a reservation can be *tacit*. For the purposes of Articles 20(2) and (4), and unless the treaty otherwise provides:

> a reservation is considered to have been accepted by a State if it shall have raised no objection to the reservation by the end of a period of twelve months after it was notified of the reservation or by the date on which it expressed its consent to be bound by the treaty, whichever is later.

The combined effect of that provision and paragraph 20(4)(c) is that the reserving state will become a contracting state unless *all* the other contracting states (1) object to the reservation and (2) explicitly object to the reserving state becoming a contracting state. Yet this will never happen. Under the ILC's 1966 draft articles on the law of treaties, a mere objection to the reservation would have precluded the treaty entering into force between the reserving and objecting states. Instead of this, the Convention which emerged from the Vienna Conference puts the onus on the objecting state both to express its objection and, if it does not want the treaty to enter into force between it and the reserving state, to say so explicitly. In putting this responsibility on the objecting state, the Conference did not take sufficiently into account the actual practice of states. It would be wrong to think that every foreign ministry agonises over every reservation notified to it; even in the best-managed of them, reservations are not always given the attention they deserve. There are many other matters to attend to, and reservations may not be seen as a priority. If one studies any list of reservations, it is surprising how few states object, even though a clearly objectionable reservation has been made. As O'Connell said as long ago as 1970:

> the almost universal failure of States to object to reservations, whether implicitly permitted or not, is the basic reason for the juristic bewilderment that has confounded this subject.[106]

Even more striking is the absence of express acceptances.

It is thus possible that not every party to a multilateral treaty will be bound by the treaty to every other party. A reserving state, Utopia, may be a party to a treaty in relation to Ruritania (which raised no objection), but not Freedonia (which did, and said expressly that it precluded the treaty entering into force between it and Utopia), even though Ruritania and Freedonia may themselves be mutually bound. However,

[105] See *UN Multilateral Treaties*, chapter IV.1. [106] *O'Connell*, 235.

although such a result is not surprising when the reservation is permissible, as we shall also see, it is arguable that the scheme of Article 20(4) and (5) does *not* apply when the reservation is prohibited, *including* when it has been objected to by only one contracting state on the ground that it fails the compatibility test.

The Legal Effect of Reservations and Objections to Reservations

Article 21(1) sets out the rules governing the legal effects of a reservation that has been 'established with regard to another party in accordance with articles 19, 20 and 23'. *Guidelines* 4.1.1–4.1.3 seek to clarify the concept of an 'established' reservation by essentially requiring the following conditions to be satisfied:[107]

(i) it must be formulated in accordance with the required form and procedure;
(ii) it must be permissible; and
(iii) it must be accepted by the required number of contracting states or international organizations.

So, in essence, an 'established' reservation is a valid and accepted reservation, which should be distinguished from a valid reservation to which an objection has been made.[108] According to the Convention, an 'established' reservation:

(a) modifies for the reserving state *in its relations with that other party* the provisions of the treaty to which the reservation relates to the extent of the reservation; and
(b) modifies those provisions to the same extent for *that other party* in its relations with the reserving state.[109]

But the reservation does not modify the provisions of the treaty for the other parties to the treaty as between themselves (Article 21(2)).

There is nothing exceptional in these rules, which reflect the consensual nature of the relations between the parties – each is only bound to the extent to which it has agreed to be bound – so that an effective reservation will operate reciprocally between the party that made it and any other party that has not objected to it, modifying the treaty to the extent of the reservation for them both in their mutual relations. But as between the *other* parties, the treaty is unaffected.

Article 21(3) provides that, when an objecting state has not opposed the entry into force of the treaty between itself and the reserving state, the *provisions* to which the reservation relates do not apply as between the two states to the extent of the reservation.[110] This deals with the situation where an objecting state does not indicate 'definitely' that the reservation will preclude the entry into force of the treaty as between

[107] This is the Special Rapporteur's own summary of the 'general idea' of these Guidelines: Pellet (n. 1), 1090.
[108] See the commentary under *Guideline* 4.1, para. 2.
[109] Article 21(1). See further *Guidelines* 4.2.4 and 4.2.5.
[110] See the amplification of this in *Guideline* 4.3.6.

the two states (see Article 20(4)(b)).[111] This is often referred to as an objection with 'minimum effect'.

Where an objecting state definitely intends that its objection should preclude entry into force between itself and the reserving state (an objection with 'maximum effect'), that is the effect.[112] Where the objecting state purports to achieve not only that the reservation objected to is not valid but also that, as a result, the treaty as a whole applies *ipso facto* in the relations between the two states (an objection with 'super-maximum effect'), the author of a *valid* reservation is not required to comply with the provisions of the treaty without the benefit of its reservation.[113]

Permissibility v. Opposability

One of the more contentious issues is whether the regime constructed by Articles 20 and 21 applies to all reservations. Certainly, it works satisfactorily with respect to permissible reservations. But if one attempts to apply it to reservations prohibited under Article 19(a), (b) or (c), problems arise. Nevertheless, there is a view that there is nothing in the scheme that precludes its application to a prohibited reservation, provided it has been accepted under Article 20(4) – which, as we have just seen, under Article 20(5) can be done, and usually is done, tacitly, with the reserving state becoming a party in relation to those states that do not object.

The proponents of 'permissibility' hold that a reservation incompatible with the object and purpose of the treaty is invalid and without legal effect, and therefore a nullity, regardless of whether others states accept or object. 'Permissibility' is thus a preliminary issue which depends upon the interpretation of the treaty.[114] The proponents of opposability, on the other hand, hold that 'the validity of a reservation depends solely on the acceptance of the reservation by another contracting State' and therefore view Article 19(c) (the compatibility test) 'as a mere doctrinal assertion, which may serve as a basis for guidance to States regarding acceptance of reservations, but not more than that'.[115]

The argument for opposability must necessarily seek to draw a distinction between reservations prohibited by Article 19(a) and (b) and those prohibited by Article 19(c), on the basis that the question of whether a reservation passes the compatibility test is a matter for each contracting state. But Article 19 makes no such distinction. It authorises the formulation of reservations subject to three exceptions. It is unlikely that Articles 20 and 21 were intended to apply to reservations that Article 19 says may

[111] See the detailed discussion on this point in the award in the 1977 *UK-France Continental Shelf Arbitration*, in *Sinclair*, 76–77. See also *Guideline* 2.6.7.

[112] See *Guideline* 4.3.5. See also Guideline 4.3.7 and commentary, 289–290, in relation to an objection with 'intermediate effect'.

[113] *Guideline* 4.3.8. See also Pellet (n. 1), 1091–1092; Pellet and Müller (n. 104).

[114] See D. Bowett, 'Reservations to Non-Restricted Multilateral Treaties', BYIL 48 (1977) 67–90, 88, quoted in *Guide*, general commentary under *Guideline* 3, para. 4.

[115] J. M. Ruda, 'Reservations to Treaties', Hague Receuil 146 1975-III 95–218, at 190, quoted in *Guide*, general commentary under *Guideline* 3, para. 4.

not be made. It is not provided that, if a treaty prohibits the making of reservations, or allows only specified ones, a contracting state could nevertheless accept (usually tacitly) a reservation expressly prohibited by the treaty.

According to the *ILC Guide*, a reservation may be invalid either because it does not comply with the correct form and procedure or because it is impermissible (or both).[116] On the latter aspect (impermissibility), the *Guide* draws no distinction between reservations which are impermissible on the grounds of Article 19(a) and (b) and those impermissible on the ground of Article 19(c) (incompatibility with the object and purpose).[117] It further proposes that acceptance of an impermissible reservation by a contracting state or by a contracting organisation shall not affect the impermissibility of the reservation.[118] In other words, acceptance cannot cure the impermissibility.[119]

The question then arises as to the consequences of the impermissibility or other invalidity. On this, the *ILC Guide* states that a reservation that does not meet the conditions of *formal validity* and *permissibility* set out in Parts 2 and 3 of the *Guide* is null and void, and therefore devoid of any legal effect.[120] This nullity is not dependent on the reaction of another individual contracting state or contracting organisation.[121] The *Guide* thus, to this extent, follows the 'permissibility' approach.

Whether this reflects state practice, however, is unclear.[122] States do object to reservations they regard as invalid, no doubt out of concern that, unless they do so, an invalid reservation may be treated as valid.[123] It may be only the objection that lays bare that a reservation is incompatible with the object and purpose since, unlike the tests in Article 19(a) and (b), the compatibility test in Article 19(c) requires an element of subjective assessment. The reactions of other states to a reservation may, in fact, influence courts in determining its validity.[124] But because, according to the scheme in the *Guide*, impermissibility and nullity do not depend upon the filing of an objection, it leads to uncertainty, not least for the reserving state as to the nature of its treaty relations.

Severability

This leads inevitably to a further question: *can one sever a prohibited reservation*? If a state has made a prohibited reservation, is it then bound by the treaty, but without the

[116] Commentary under *Guideline* 4.5.1, para. 2. [117] *Guideline* 3.3.1.

[118] *Guideline* 3.3.3. The aim of this particular Guideline, however, is not to determine the effects of acceptance of a reservation by a state, but simply to establish that, if the reservation in question is impermissible, it remains impermissible despite that acceptance: commentary para. 5.

[119] *Guide*, 244, para. 2. [120] *Guideline* 4.5.1.

[121] *Guideline* 4.5.2, para. 1. See, however, the commentary under *Guideline* 3.3.3, 411, para. 8 *et seq*: 'The question remains, however, whether collective acceptance of an otherwise impermissible reservation is possible'.

[122] See E. T. Swaine, 'Treaty Reservations', in *Hollis, Oxford Guide*, 284–306, 292–294.

[123] *Guideline* 4.5.2, para. 2, notwithstanding the nullity *ab initio* of an invalid reservation, encourages a state or an international organisation which considers that a reservation is invalid to formulate a reasoned objection as soon as possible.

[124] Commentary, *Guideline* 4.5.2, paras. 4–6, and the cases referred to there.

benefit of the reservation? Or does the invalidity of the reservation nullify the reserving state's consent to be bound by the treaty, so that it is not a party?[125]

In some cases, the government of the reserving state will have obtained parliamentary approval for ratification only on condition that the reservation is made. Following the stance taken in 1982 by the European Commission on Human Rights,[126] the European Court of Human Rights in *Belilos*[127] (in 1988) held that a declaration by Switzerland on ratifying the European Convention on Human Rights 1950 (ECHR)[128] was an invalid reservation, but that it could be disregarded as Switzerland remained bound by the ECHR in full. Although Switzerland had the option of withdrawing from the ECHR, it did not do so – no doubt for good political reasons.

The Court came to a similar decision in 1995 in *Loizidou* (Preliminary Objections),[129] holding that Turkey was bound by its acceptance of the right of individual petition and of the jurisdiction of the Court, but without the invalid reservations attached to those acceptances. *Belilos* and *Loizidou*, however, need to be seen in the light of the particular circumstances. The issue arose within a regional system dedicated to adherence to common social and political values. As the Court said in *Loizidou*, the ECHR has a special character and must be interpreted in the light of contemporary conditions, its enforcement machinery, and its object and purpose. Also, although the Court applied the rules on interpretation in Articles 31 and 32, it did *not* refer to the Convention's rules on reservations.

The objections to the reservations made in 1997 by Guatemala to the VCLT[130] itself show a divergence of views by states on the question of whether a *prohibited* reservation can be disregarded. Austria and Germany said that their objections did not preclude the entry into force of the Convention between them and Guatemala, so leaving ambiguous the effect of the reservation on Guatemala's obligations under the Convention. The United Kingdom did not say what effect its objection would have. In contrast, Denmark, Finland and Sweden each said that, although their objections did not preclude the entry into force of the Convention between them and Guatemala, it would be 'without Guatemala benefiting from these reservations'. This approach went further than *Belilos*, in that there were no special circumstances as in *Belilos*, and it ignored the plain fact that the reserving state had made it clear that it was willing to be bound only subject to a condition.[131]

[125] See generally Swaine (n. 122), 297–303.

[126] See *Temeltasch* v. *Switzerland* Application no. 9116/80, Report of 5 May 1982, (1983) 88 ILR 619. Since 1998, the Commission has been combined into one institution, the European Court of Human Rights.

[127] ECHR Pubs. Series A, Vol. 132 (1988); (1988) 10 EHRR 466; 88 ILR 635; S. Marks, 'Reservations Unhinged: The Belilos Case Before the European Court of Human Rights', ICLQ 39 (1990) 300–327; I. Cameron and F. Horn, 'Reservations to the ECHR: The Belilos Case', Ger YBIL (1990) 69–129.

[128] Amended by subsequent Protocols: consolidated text at CoE website.

[129] ECHR Pubs. Series A, Vol. 310 (1995); (1995) 20 EHRR 99; 103 ILR 621.

[130] See *UN Multilateral Treaties*, chapter XXIII.1.

[131] See also the objection by Denmark to reservations by Yemen to CERD (*UN Multilateral Treaties*, chapter IV.2).

The *ILC Guide* strikes a middle route between the main approaches.[132] It proposes that the status of the author of an invalid reservation depends on *the intention expressed* by the reserving state (or international organisation) on whether it intends to be bound by the treaty without the benefit of the reservation or whether it considers that it is not bound by the treaty. The *Guide* suggests that, unless the reserving state has expressed a contrary intention or such an intention is otherwise established, that state is considered a contracting state without the benefit of the reservation. The reserving state may, however, express at any time its intention not to be bound by the treaty without the benefit of the reservation.[133]

Reservations to Human Rights Treaties

Article 28(2) of the Convention on the Elimination of All Forms of Discrimination against Women (CEDAW) 1979[134] provides merely that reservations incompatible with its object and purpose *shall not be permitted*. This formula seems to have become the norm for later UN human rights treaties.[135] But, in the case of a human rights treaty, there may be weighty political reasons why a state is reluctant to object to the entry into force of the treaty between it and a reserving state, even when it has objected to the reservation on the ground that it fails the compatibility test. Such treaties have become enormously important from the second half of the twentieth century on. For the parties, they create not only a network of mutual bilateral undertakings, but also rules of behaviour for each party in its treatment of persons for whom it is responsible. It is understandable that most objecting states are reluctant to take the position that such treaties will not be in force between it and the reserving state unless and until the reservation is withdrawn. As fellow parties, they may feel better able to persuade the reserving state to bring its laws and practices into line with the treaty, and withdraw the reservation. In fact, when faced with a questionable reservation, most parties to human rights treaties remain silent. And those that do express views formally, frequently take differing positions.

The question arises whether reservations to human rights treaties should be treated differently from those made in respect of other treaties. The argument for is that human rights treaties are essentially non-reciprocal; they require full application since they do not lend themselves to reservations; and contrary to other treaties, their integrity is guaranteed by special bodies.[136] The argument against is that the non-reciprocal nature of obligations is a feature of treaties in other areas, such as

[132] *Guideline* 4.5.3, which this paragraph summarises.

[133] *Guideline* 4.5.3, para. 4, adds: 'If a treaty monitoring body expresses the view that a reservation is invalid and the reserving State or international organization intends not to be bound by the treaty without the benefit of the reservation, it should express its intention to that effect within a period of twelve months from the date at which the treaty monitoring body made its assessment.'

[134] 1249 UNTS 13 No. 20378; 19 ILM (1980) 33; UKTS (1989) No. 2.

[135] See, e.g., Article 51(2) Convention on the Rights of the Child 1989 (n. 11).

[136] Pellet (n. 1), 1079.

environmental law; the reciprocal element is not indispensable for the Convention framework of reservations; there are many other treaties with interdependent rights; and while the existence of treaty-monitoring bodies is a peculiarity of human rights treaties, it is not a necessary element of these instruments, nor an 'exclusive' peculiarity, nor an argument to modify the generally applicable reservations regime.[137]

In the case of the ICCPR, the Human Rights Committee stated in its General Comment No. 24 that:

> In an instrument which articulates very many civil and political rights, each of the many articles, and indeed their interplay, secures the objectives of the Covenant. The object and purpose of the Covenant is to create legally binding standards for human rights by defining certain civil and political rights and placing them in a framework of obligations which are legally binding for those States which ratify; and to provide an efficacious supervisory machinery for the obligations undertaken.

While this comment might suggest that any reservation to a substantive right in the Covenant would be invalid, that is not the practice of states, and the Committee itself goes on to set criteria for determining whether a reservation would be incompatible with the object and purpose.[138] Having noted this, the *ILC Guide* goes on to argue that, while the object and purpose of human rights treaties are complex, and these treaties are characterised by the global nature of the rights they intend to protect, nevertheless, some of the protected rights may be more essential than others, and even in the case of essential rights, one cannot rule out that a reservation dealing with certain limited aspects of the implementation of the right in question may be permissible.[139]

The *ILC Guide* therefore proposes to treat human rights treaties in a more general category of treaties with interdependent rights and obligations whose difficulties are recognised. *Guideline* 3.1.5.6 thus states:

> To assess the compatibility of a reservation with the object and purpose of a treaty containing numerous interdependent rights and obligations, account shall be taken of that interdependence as well as the importance that the provision to which the reservation relates has within the general tenor of the treaty, and the extent of the impact that the reservation has on the treaty.

Reservations Relating to Internal Law

The tendency to adopt differing positions in response to reservations is illustrated by the variety of responses by some western European states to the following general reservation made by the United States in 1988 to the Genocide Convention:

[137] Pellet (n. 1), 1080–1081. [138] Commentary under *Guideline* 3.1.5.6, para. 3.
[139] Commentary under *Guideline* 3.1.5.6, para. 5.

> nothing in the Convention requires or authorises legislation or other action by the United States of America prohibited by the Constitution of the United States as interpreted by the United States.[140]

That such a 'constitutional reservation' should be made was not surprising. For some years the US Senate had authorised the president to ratify human rights treaties only if they made it clear that the US Constitution would prevail over them. Denmark, Finland, Greece, Ireland, Norway and Sweden objected that the reservation was contrary to the general rule that a party may not invoke its internal law as justification for failure to perform a treaty (Article 27), but, apart from Sweden, they did not specify the legal effect of their objection. Sweden said its objection 'does not constitute an obstacle to the entry into force of the Convention between Sweden and the United States'. Such a statement is regularly found in objections to human rights treaties and illustrates the political dilemma faced by the objecting state. Italy and the United Kingdom objected that the reservation 'creates uncertainty as to the extent of the obligations which the Government of the United States is prepared to assume with regard to the Convention'.[141] Yet neither said what were the legal consequences. The Netherlands objected on both of the two last grounds, but did not specify any legal consequences. In contrast, Spain did not object, but interpreted the reservation to mean that legislation or other action by the United States would continue to be in accordance with the Convention. There was also inconsistency in the responses by such states when a similar constitutional reservation was made by the United States with respect to the Torture Convention.[142]

Yet Article 27 is not in the part of the Convention that deals with reservations and should not, therefore, be relied upon to found an objection to a reservation; in fact, it is usually because the internal law of the state is incompatible with the treaty that a reservation is made. Article 27 applies only once the reserving state's obligations under the treaty have been determined.[143]

When other states have made such constitutional reservations, the responses have also been inconsistent, and the attitude of the United States to constitutional reservations made by other states can be intriguing. In response to a reservation by Colombia to the Vienna Drugs Convention 1988[144] that it would be contrary to its constitution for Colombia to extradite its own nationals, the United States objected that the statement 'purports to subordinate Colombia's obligations under the Convention to its Constitution'.[145]

[140] *UN Multilateral Treaties*, chapter IV.2. [141] *UN Multilateral Treaties*, chapter IV.2.

[142] *UN Multilateral Treaties*, chapter IV.9. EU member states now try – with varying degrees of success – to coordinate their responses to reservations by other states by discussions in their public international law committee (COJUR).

[143] See the commentary under *Guideline* 3.1.5.5, paras. 1–6.

[144] 1582 UNTS 165 No. 27627; 28 ILM (1989) 493; UKTS (1992) No. 26.

[145] See *UN Multilateral Treaties*, chapter IV.19.

Since constitutional reservations make it difficult, if not impossible, to determine their effect on the reserving state's obligations, the United Kingdom has adopted a temporising, non-committal approach. In response to four constitutional reservations made in 1990 by the Republic of Korea to the ICCPR 1966,[146] the United Kingdom stated that it was:

> not however able to take a position on these purported reservations in the absence of a sufficient indication of their intended effect, in accordance with the terms of the Vienna Convention on the Law of Treaties and the practice of the parties to the Covenant. Pending receipt of such indication, the Government of the United Kingdom reserve their rights under the Covenant in their entirety.[147]

The effect of this statement is to suspend the time limit for making objections until the reserving state has made clear the effect of the reservation. The hope was that the reservation would be withdrawn or at least made specific. Within two years Korea had withdrawn two of the reservations.[148]

The *ILC Guide* draws a distinction between reservations justifying themselves by considerations arising from internal law which are 'clearly expressed and sufficiently detailed', and reservations formulated by reference to internal law in general or to whole sections of such law without any further detail ('vague or general reservations'), which are discussed in the next section.[149] In respect of *detailed* reservations relating to internal law, the *ILC Guide* proposes that a reservation made by a state in order to preserve the integrity of specific rules of its internal law may be formulated only insofar as it does not affect an essential element of the treaty nor its general tenor.[150]

Vague or General Reservations

Reservations which seek to subordinate a human rights treaty to domestic law *in a general manner* have been made not only in the type of cases mentioned in the previous section but also in cases which make reference to Islamic law. For example, when ratifying the Rights of the Child Convention 1989,[151] Iran reserved the right 'not to apply any provisions or articles of the Convention that are incompatible with Islamic laws'. This, and similar reservations to that Convention by some other Muslim states, were objected to in 1991 by certain western European states, generally on the ground that the reservations cast doubt on the commitment of the reserving state to the object and purpose of the Convention. But in each case the objecting state said that the objection did not preclude the entry into force of the Convention between it and the reserving state.[152] The reservations were not withdrawn. However, objections can lead

[146] 999 UNTS 171 No. 14668; 6 ILM (1967) 368; UKTS (1977) No. 6.
[147] *UN Multilateral Treaties*, chapter IV.4, UK objections 24 May 1991.
[148] *UN Multilateral Treaties*, chapter IV.4.
[149] See the Commentary under *Guideline* 3.1.5.5, paras. 1–2; and under *Guideline* 3.1.5.2.
[150] *Guideline* 3.1.5.5. [151] See n. 11. [152] *UN Multilateral Treaties*, chapter IV.11.

to withdrawal or modification of some reservations. In 1995, Malaysia attached reservations to its accession to CEDAW 1979,[153] which were to the effect that certain of its provisions would not apply if they conflicted with *Sharia* law or the Malaysian Constitution. Following some objections, in 1998 the reservations were partially withdrawn.[154]

The *ILC Guide* takes the view that the difficulty of reservations relating to *Sharia* law arises not from their religious origin but from their vague and general formulation.[155] It therefore addresses the issue in that light through *Guideline* 3.1.5.2, encouraging reservations to be worded in such a way as to allow their meaning to be understood, in order to assess in particular their compatibility with the object and purpose of the treaty.

Treaty-Monitoring Bodies

The problem of determining whether a reservation is permissible, and in particular whether it passes the compatibility test, is further compounded by the absence in most cases of a standing tribunal or other organ with competence to decide such matters. Regional human rights treaties, such as the European Convention on Human Rights[156] or the American Convention on Human Rights,[157] have a standing court. Most modern universal human rights treaties establish no more than a committee of - albeit mostly distinguished and independent - experts to monitor the way in which the parties carry out their obligations. The best known is the Human Rights Committee established by the ICCPR 1966 referred to above.[158] The role of its eighteen members is to scrutinise and comment on periodic reports by the parties to the Covenant on their implementation of it; to consider complaints from parties about alleged violations by other parties; and to examine communications (petitions) from individuals alleging violations, provided the party said to be at fault has recognised the competence of the Committee for this purpose.

The Committee is not empowered to give decisions binding on the parties. Nevertheless, in 1994, in its General Comment No. 24, in the course of expressing views on the problem of reservations, the Committee said that it must necessarily take a view as to the status and effect of a reservation if this is needed in order to carry out its functions under the Covenant, in particular considering reports from parties. The

[153] See n. 134.

[154] *UN Multilateral Treaties*, chapter IV.8. See also the reservations made to CEDAW in the early twenty-first century by certain Muslim states, and objections to them by certain Western states.

[155] See Pellet (n. 1), 1088; and the Commentary under *Guideline* 3.1.5.2.

[156] See n. 128.

[157] 1144 UNTS 144 No. 17955; 9 ILM (1970) 673.

[158] See p. 409 and n. 58; see also www.ohchr.org/en/hrbodies/ccpr/pages/ccprindex.aspx. The Committee should not be confused with the UN Human Rights Council (HRC), which was established in 2006 to replace the Commission on Human Rights (CHR), which, even then, was often confused with the Human Rights Committee because its acronym shared the same letters as that of the Committee, albeit in a different order.

Committee gave the impression that it could in such circumstances make an authoritative determination. This view was severely criticised on the grounds that the Committee could not be equated to an international court or tribunal, which reaches decisions on the basis of the facts found by it and after hearing full legal argument from both sides.[159]

The *ILC Guide* includes a series of guidelines in relation to treaty-monitoring bodies.[160] It acknowledges that a treaty monitoring body may, for the purpose of discharging the functions entrusted to it, assess the permissibility of reservations formulated by a state or an international organisation, but its assessment has no greater legal effect than that of the act which contains it. The *Guide* encourages the reserving states and international organisations to give consideration to that body's assessment of the permissibility of the reservations. It emphasises that the competence of the body is without prejudice to the competence of the contracting states or organisations themselves to assess the permissibility of reservations to the relevant treaty, or to that of dispute settlement bodies competent to interpret or apply the treaty.

With reference to severability, *Guideline* 4.5.3 adds:

> If a treaty monitoring body expresses the view that a reservation is invalid and the reserving State or international organization intends not to be bound by the treaty without the benefit of the reservation, it should express its intention to that effect within a period of twelve months from the date at which the treaty monitoring body made its assessment.

Some Ways of Minimising the Problem of Reservations

Express Provision in the Treaty

The problems of reservations may be lessened, or even avoided, if provision is made in each new treaty, but this is nothing new. In 1961, McNair urged that states should insert into multilateral treaties express provisions on reservations.[161] Unfortunately, all too many treaties are simply silent on the matter: sometimes because no agreement could be reached; sometimes because it was not seen as important enough, the matter being dealt with anyway by the VCLT 1969; and, sometimes because the problem was just not considered.

The seemingly intractable problem of determining whether a reservation is incompatible with the object and purpose of a treaty was faced over forty years ago. Article

159 See 34 ILM (1995) 839. See also R. Goodman, 'Human Rights Treaties, Invalid Reservations, and State Consent', AJIL (2002) 531–560.

160 *Guidelines* 3.2.1–3.2.4, together with *Guideline* 4.5.3, para. 4, and the commentary under these *Guidelines*.

161 *McNair*, 169–170. For early examples of express provisions, see AJIL Supp. 29 (1935) 844–846.

20(1) of CERD[162] provides that the depositary shall circulate all reservations and any objections notified within ninety days. Paragraph (2) provides that a reservation incompatible with the object and purpose of the Convention, or that would inhibit the functioning of any bodies established by the Convention, shall not be permitted. It then provides that:

> A reservation shall be considered incompatible or inhibitive if at least two-thirds of the States Parties to the Convention object to it.

Several (mostly western European) objections have been lodged.[163] Although many refer to paragraph (2), there has never been a two-thirds majority.[164] But it is not clear if that specific provision had the effect of replacing the general rule on objections, as reflected in Articles 19–21 of the VCLT. Some of the objections appear to assume that the two-thirds rule merely supplemented the general rule. Either way, there must be doubt as to whether the objections had their intended legal effect.

The European Agreement concerning the Work of Crews of Vehicles Engaged in International Road Transport 1970 (AETR II)[165] provides that:

> If . . . a State enters a [non-authorised] reservation . . . the Secretary-General of the United Nations shall communicate the reservation to [the contracting states]. The reservation shall be deemed to be accepted if *none* of the said States has, within six months after such communication, expressed its opposition to acceptance of the reservation. *Otherwise, the reservation shall not be admitted, and, if the State which entered the reservation does not withdraw it, the deposit of that State's instrument of ratification or accession shall be without effect.*

The Convention on Psychotropic Substances 1971[166] authorises certain reservations to be made and provides that:

> A State which desires to become a party but wishes to be authorised to make [non-authorised] reservations . . . may inform the Secretary-General of such intention. Unless by the end of twelve months after the date of the Secretary-General's communication of the reservation concerned, this reservation has been objected to by one third of the [contracting states] . . . it shall be deemed to be permitted, it being understood, however, that States which have objected to the reservation need not assume towards the reserving State any legal obligation under this Convention which is affected by the reservation.

162 669 UNTS 195 No. 9464, UKTS (1967) No. 77.

163 See *UN Multilateral Treaties*, chapter IV.2.

164 See *Democratic Republic of the Congo* v. *Rwanda* (Provisional Measures), Order of 10 July 2002, ICJ Reports (2002) 219, at 243–244, paras. 64–67; 41 ILM (2002) 1175. The two-thirds is presumably calculated as at the date of the reservation: see p. 281.

165 Concluded at Geneva, 1 July 1970: 993 UNTS 143 No. 14533, Article 21(2).

166 1019 UNTS 175 No. 14956; 10 ILM (1971) 261; UKTS (1993) No. 51, Article 32(3).

A more recent, and certainly tough formulation is found in the FAO Compliance Agreement 1993:[167]

> Acceptance of this Agreement may be made subject to reservations which shall become effective only upon *unanimous* acceptance by all parties to this Agreement. The Director-General [of FAO] shall notify forthwith all parties of any reservation. Parties not having replied within three months from the date of notification shall be deemed to have accepted the reservation. Failing such [i.e., unanimous] acceptance, the State or regional economic organisation making the reservation *shall not become a party to this Agreement.*

If the outcome envisaged in the final sentence happens, the reserving state could, of course, either withdraw the reservation before the end of the three months or deposit a fresh acceptance without the reservation.

Reservations Permitted Only in Respect of Annexes

Another approach is to permit reservations only in respect of the annexes to a treaty, or certain of them. This is a relatively recent development, and is to be found particularly in arms control treaties. Article XXII of the Chemical Weapons Convention 1993 (CWC) (now in force) prohibits reservations to the CWC itself, but allows them to be made in respect of its annexes, provided the reservations are compatible with the object and purpose of the CWC.[168] The CTBT 1996 (which probably will never be in force) prohibits reservations to the treaty and its annexes, but allows reservations to the protocol to the treaty (and the annexes to the protocol), provided they are not incompatible with the object and purpose of the treaty.[169] In both treaties, the attachments contain very detailed provisions which may need certain adjustment in their application by some contracting states.

Express Acceptance

Article 18 of the Paris Convention on Third Party Liability in the Field of Nuclear Energy 1960[170] provides that reservations may be made 'at any time *prior to* ratification', but shall be admissible only if the terms of the reservations 'have been expressly accepted by the Signatories', with the exception of signatories that have not ratified within twelve months of the reservation having been notified to them by the depositary. Such a provision is now exceptional.

[167] 2221 UNTS 120 No. 39486; 33 ILM (1994) 968, Article XII. [168] See n. 57.
[169] 35 ILM (1996) 1439, Article XV. [170] 956 UNTS 251 No. 13706; UKTS (1968) No. 69.

Procedure

The procedural provisions in Article 23 of the VCLT are important, since the *chapeau* to Article 21(1) makes it clear that, in order to have legal effect, a reservation must be established in accordance with not only Articles 19 and 20, but also with Article 23. Some of these procedures may not reflect customary international law, especially the time limit in Article 20(5) which the UN Secretary-General now applies and can thus be regarded as established practice.

Procedure for the Making of Reservations

A statement made during the negotiation of the treaty or on its adoption, even if recorded formally, must be made again if it is to be effective as a reservation. The *chapeau* to Article 19 provides that a reservation may be formulated when signing, ratifying, accepting, approving or acceding to a treaty, but does not prohibit a reservation being made at another time if this is provided for in the treaty. A reservation made on signature could, in principle, be written under or next to the signature. But, unless the reservation is *very* brief, it is much more usual to give the text separately to the depositary at the time of signature. It is then deemed to accompany the signature. In fact, the UN Secretary-General strongly discourages writing the reservation on to the treaty itself, since the text of the reservation may be either too long or illegible, or both. It is, therefore, highly advisable to put it into a first- or third-person diplomatic note handed over to the depositary at the time of signature.

Today, most treaties that expressly mention reservations provide for them to be made upon ratification. Therefore, if it is made on or before signature of a treaty that is subject to ratification, *to be effective it must be formally confirmed by the reserving state when expressing its consent to be bound*, the reservation then being considered to have been made on the date of such confirmation (Article 23(2)). This latter provision is important for the purposes of calculating the start of the twelve-month period specified in Article 20(5). A different rule can apply to the constituent instruments of an international organisation (Article 5). For example, reservations to amendments to the International Telecommunication Union (ITU) constituent treaties can be made only at the time of adoption of the amendment.[171]

A reservation, or an express acceptance of a reservation, must be made in writing and communicated (in practice, by the depositary) to the contracting states and other states entitled to become parties to the treaty (Article 23(1)). Typically, the reservation will be contained in a note or letter from a diplomatic representative of the reserving state, and this should be referred to in the instrument of ratification. If the

[171] 1825 UNTS 331 No. 31251; UKTS (1996) No. 24, Article 32, para. 16 (446), at p. 63 UKTS text, or see at: www.itu.int (amended by the Instruments adopted November 1998, UK Misc. Series (2016) No. 2).

reservation is in a separate note, which is not referred to in the instrument, or if the person signing the note is not one of the qualified authorities,[172] they may need to produce either special or general full powers.[173] This is a firm requirement of the UN Secretary-General and is generally followed by other depositaries.

Procedure for Objecting to Reservations

An objection[174] will, of course, have no effect if the reservation is one that is expressly authorised by the treaty (Article 20(1)).

To be effective, an objection to a reservation cannot be made until the objector is a contracting state (i.e., has consented to be bound by the treaty, even though it is not yet in force), but thereafter it can object to any reservations, past or future. The objection must be made in writing to the depositary, and then communicated (in practice by the depositary) to the other contracting states and other states entitled to become parties to the treaty (Article 23(1)). If an objection is made to a reservation made on signature subject to ratification, and before the reservation has been confirmed on ratification, the objection does not have to be confirmed (Article 23(3)). An objection can also be expressed in general terms so as to apply also to other reservations made in the same terms in the future.[175]

Article 20(5) provides that, except when objecting to a reservation to the constituent instrument of an international organisation or where the treaty otherwise provides, a reservation is considered to have been accepted by a state if it has raised no objection within twelve months after it was notified of the reservation or by the date it expressed its consent to be bound by the treaty, whichever is later. This provision does not apply to the Convention itself because of its non-retroactivity clause (Article 4). Although the rule may not reflect customary international law, it is now established practice.[176] If the meaning and effect of the reservation is not clear, the period will not start to run until they have been satisfactorily clarified by the reserving state.

Withdrawal of Reservations and of Objections to Reservations

Reservations are from time to time withdrawn.[177] Sometimes this is done in response to objections from other contracting states; sometimes because conditions have changed. With the end of the Cold War, several former Eastern-bloc states withdrew

[172] That is, head of state, head of government or foreign minister.

[173] See Chapter 5. The CoE and the OAS accept reservations in letters from permanent representatives: see Kohona (n. 8), 434–435, text to notes 15 and 16.

[174] See the definition of 'objection' in *Guideline* 2.6.1, reproduced at p. 148.

[175] See pp. 151–152 on the objection by the Netherlands to a common reservation to the Genocide Convention.

[176] *UN Depositary Practice*, paras. 213–214.

[177] See the withdrawal by the Republic of Korea of reservations to articles of the ICCPR (*UN Multilateral Treaties*, chapter IV.4, footnote to entry for the Republic of Korea).

their reservations to dispute settlement clauses, such as Article 66 of the Convention itself.[178] Since a reservation can be withdrawn, it is possible also to modify or even replace a reservation, provided the result is to restrict its effect.[179]

Withdrawal of a reservation or an objection is regulated by Articles 22 and 23(4). Withdrawal must be done in writing, usually to the depositary, who will notify the contracting states. Unless the treaty provides otherwise, withdrawal of a reservation or objection can be done at any time, and the consent of a state that has accepted a reservation is not necessary for its withdrawal (and would anyway be impractical given that most acceptances are tacit). Unless the treaty otherwise provides, or it is otherwise agreed, the withdrawal of a reservation becomes operative in relation to another contracting state when notice of it has been received by that state.[180]

Although the Convention deals with the withdrawal of reservations or objections, it does not contain provisions concerning the withdrawal of the acceptance of a reservation. This is neither authorised nor prohibited. *Guideline* 2.8.13 seeks to clarify this issue by providing that 'the acceptance of a reservation cannot be withdrawn or amended'. This is justified on the basis that first, in respect of tacit acceptance, this would undermine the principle of Article 20(5); and in respect of express acceptance, the effect of such acceptance is the entry into force of the treaty between the reserving state and accepting state subject to the reservation: to call the legal consequences into question *a posteriori* would seriously undermine legal certainty and the status of the treaty between the two parties, if not more widely.[181]

Functions of the Depositary in Relation to Reservations

The UN Secretary-General is the depositary of many more multilateral treaties than any other international organisation or state.[182] The holder of that office has nearly eighty years of experience as a depositary of multilateral treaties, which is therefore invaluable and followed in most respects by other depositaries. When acting as a depositary they must, of course, act entirely impartially. Although the law relating to reservations has continued to develop since 1969, it develops through the practice of states. It is, therefore, important that this is reflected in the practice of depositaries.

The Secretary-General's practice is now to send all depositary notifications – not just on reservations and objections – by email on the same day as they are processed to those signing in to the automated subscription services through the United Nations Treaty Collection website at https://treaties.un.org. Depositary notifications are also

[178] See *UN Multilateral Treaties*, notes to chapter XXIII.1.
[179] See p. 169, in the section on 'Late reservations'.
[180] See *Armed Activities on the Territory of the Congo (New Application: 2002) (Democratic Republic of the Congo* v. *Rwanda)*, Jurisdiction and Admissibility, Judgment, ICJ Reports (2006) 6, at 22–29, paras. 29–55; 45 ILM (2006) 271.
[181] See the Commentary on *Guideline* 2.8.13.
[182] See generally, Kohona (n. 8).

posted on this website. This makes it easier for states to consider reservations in good time.

When the Secretary-General receives an objection to a reservation, but it does not specify whether it precludes the entry into force of the treaty between the objecting and reserving states, they do not, despite the presumption in Article 20(4)(b), pronounce upon the legal effect of the objection as between the states concerned. Nor do they refuse an objection received after the twelve-month deadline provided for by Article 20(5), though when circulating the text they describe it as a 'communication'.

Functions of the Depositary in Relation to Treaties with Express Provisions on Reservations

If a treaty contains provisions on reservations, the depositary will be guided by them when considering whether to accept a signature or instrument accompanied by a reservation. If the treaty *expressly* forbids all reservations or reservations to specific articles, or *expressly* authorises reservations to specific articles only, the depositary must follow those provisions. Except for those cases where there is a question as to whether the reservation is compatible with the object and purpose of the treaty, if in the opinion of the depositary a reservation is prohibited, the depositary should first query it with the reserving state. Alternatively, the depositary can circulate the statement to the interested states, leaving it to them to decide if it amounts to a reservation. Article 309 of UNCLOS 1982 prohibits reservations. On ratifying the Convention the Philippines expressed various 'understandings'. The UN Secretary-General, as depositary, circulated the understandings and received a number of objections that the understandings were reservations.[183]

Functions of the Depositary in Relation to Treaties Silent as to Reservations

Since December 1959, the UN Secretary-General, when acting as depositary of a treaty that is silent as to reservations (in respect of which it is therefore permissible to make reservations provided they satisfy the compatibility test), merely communicates to the states concerned the text of the reservations, and later any objections to them, but without commenting on the legal effect of either.[184] It is also the practice of the UN Secretary-General to ignore the possibility that a reservation that might be invalid might render void the consent of the reserving state to be bound; and in calculating whether the necessary minimum number of instruments have been deposited for the

[183] *UN Multilateral Treaties*, chapter XXI.6: see, e.g., the Australian objection and the Philippines' response; and *UN Depositary Practice*, paras. 194–196.

[184] *UN Depositary Practice*, paras. 173–181.

treaty to enter into force, they take no account of the possible effect of a possibly invalid reservation.[185]

Late Reservations

The Convention does not authorise (or even envisage) the making of reservations after a state has ratified (see the definition of reservation in Article 2(1)(e) and the terms of Article 19). Being made after ratification, a late reservation cannot be effective unless it is accepted by the contracting parties expressly or, perhaps, tacitly. Previously, the UN Secretary-General's practice as depositary had been to stipulate ninety days as the period within which a state could object to a late reservation. However, since the issue can involve complex issues of law and policy, they have come to consider this period too short. Since April 2000, the practice of the Secretary-General has therefore been that, *provided* the treaty either does not prohibit reservations or the substance of the late reservation is authorised specifically by the treaty, they will circulate it and, if no objection to it is received within twelve months of the date of circulation, they will 'accept it in deposit' (a quaint term which simply means: treat it as a valid reservation).[186] The revised procedure is an improvement. The Secretary-General's practice deviates from the strict requirements of the Convention, but reflects the fact that, if *no* state objects to such a late reservation, it would be unrealistic to insist on rejecting it. The twelve-month period is consistent with Article 20(5). If an objection is received after the twelve-month period, it is circulated by the Secretary-General only as a 'communication'.

The same practice is applied by the Secretary-General when a reserving state withdraws an original reservation and tries to substitute a new or modified reservation.[187] The UN Secretary-General will circulate the text. If *no* objection has been received within twelve months, they treat this as tacit acceptance of the new or modified reservation.[188]

The *ILC Guide* proposes that a state or an international organisation may not formulate a reservation to a treaty after expressing its consent to be bound by the treaty, unless the treaty otherwise provides or none of the other contracting states and contracting organisations opposes the late formulation of the reservation.[189] Unless the treaty otherwise provides or the well-established practice followed by the depositary differs, the late formulation of a reservation shall be deemed to have been accepted only if no contracting state or contracting organisation has opposed such

[185] *UN Depositary Practice*, paras. 184–188. [186] See UN Treaty Handbook, para. 3.5.3 and Annex 2.

[187] *Guideline* 2.3.4 proposes: 'The modification of an existing reservation for the purpose of widening its scope is subject to the rules applicable to the late formulation of a reservation. If such a modification is opposed, the initial reservation remains unchanged'.

[188] UN Treaty Handbook, para. 3.5.8 and Annex 2. [189] *Guideline* 2.3.

formulation after the expiry of the twelve-month period following the date on which notification was received.[190]

Can a Reservation Be Made on 'Re-accession'?

The practice of the UN Secretary-General does not indicate just how late a reservation can be made, though it seems that if a state does not make it within twelve months of ratification, it may well feel that it must resort to other means, such as withdrawing from the treaty (assuming this is permissible) and immediately 're-acceding' to it with the reservation. This is what Trinidad and Tobago did in 1998. It had become a party to the ICCPR 1966 in 1978, and to the (first) Optional Protocol to it in 1980.[191] Parties to the Protocol agree to individuals communicating with (i.e., petitioning) the Human Rights Committee established by the Covenant. By 1998, Trinidad and Tobago had decided that this procedure was being increasingly 'abused' by prisoners sentenced to death. It therefore gave the required three months' notice to withdraw from the Protocol, but at the same time deposited an instrument of accession to it, to take effect three months later. The new instrument included a reservation that the Human Rights Committee would *not* be competent to receive and consider communications from such prisoners.[192]

Although the withdrawal from the Optional Protocol was in itself valid, the right to make the reservation in this way is legally questionable. For a party to withdraw and then 're-accede' solely for the purpose of making a reservation which it did not make originally, and which, if made as a late reservation, is unlikely to have been accepted, is open to serious objection. The stratagem can be viewed as a *single* transaction, the only purpose of which is to enter a late reservation, the effectiveness of which can therefore be defeated by a *single* objection. Following objections to its stratagem, Trinidad and Tobago withdrew from the Protocol in 2000.[193] Guyana copied the stratagem in 1999. There were only three objections,[194] and Guyana did not withdraw from the Protocol.

In 1967, Sweden ratified the Council of Europe Convention on Reduction of Cases of Multiple Nationality,[195] but denounced it in 2002, re-acceding to it the next day with a declaration limiting its obligations to those of chapter II. Article 7 permits such a declaration (in practice, a reservation) to be made, but only when consenting to be bound. But there were no objections from the other parties, which must be deemed to have acquiesced. There were nevertheless some polite mutterings, Nordic and otherwise.

[190] *Guideline* 2.3.1. [191] See n. 58.
[192] See *UN Multilateral Treaties*, chapter IV.5, reservation by Trinidad and Tobago and note to it.
[193] See *UN Multilateral Treaties*, chapter IV, see note to Trinidad and Tobago's accession.
[194] See *UN Multilateral Treaties*, chapter IV, note to Guyana's accession. [195] See n. 77.

9

Entry into Force

The treaty becomes international law after 40 countries have ratified it.[1]

This suggestion that *all* states are bound by a (multilateral) treaty once it has entered into force is a common misconception, even among diplomats. When a treaty has entered into force, it binds *only* those states that have consented to be bound by it. A treaty is therefore not like national legislation which, once in force, applies to all to whom it is directed. A treaty is much closer to a contract. But if the treaty reflects rules of customary international law, a non-party can be bound by those rules, though only as *customary international law*: it is not a party to the treaty. (For the position of third states, see Chapter 14.)

Each of the states for which a treaty is in force is a 'party' (Article 2(1)(g)). Thereafter it should *never* be referred to by the – uninformative and misleading – term 'signatory'. But it must also be remembered that, when a state expresses its consent to be bound, it does not necessarily mean that the treaty will enter into force for it at that point: it will depend on whether the treaty is already in force for the states that have already consented to be bound or whether further consents are needed to bring it into force. A state's consent may, of course, have the effect of bringing the treaty into force if it is the last one needed to do that.

However, none of this means that a treaty will have no legal effects before it enters into force. Certain of its provisions have to apply from the moment it is adopted, such as those on authentication of the text, the right to participate, reservations, entry into force and depositary functions (Article 24(4)).

Express Provisions

A treaty enters into force in such manner and on such date as provided for in the treaty or as the negotiating states may agree (Article 24(1)). There are various methods.

[1] *The Times*, 26 June 1998, on the Landmines Convention.

(1) On ratification (or analogous procedure) by both (or all) signatory states

If a multilateral treaty requires ratification by all the negotiating states, entry into force may be expressed to be on, or at a specific time after, the deposit of the last instrument of ratification. The Europol Convention 1995,[2] Article 45(1), provides that:

> This Convention shall enter into force on the first day of the month following the expiry of a three-month period after the notification [that it has completed its constitutional requirements] by the Member State which, being a member of the European Union *on the date of adoption by the Council of the Act drawing up this Convention*, is the last to fulfil that formality.

This apparently elaborate formula is essential. First, it ensures that the treaty cannot enter into force until all member states have consented to be bound. Second, it has the effect of excluding from that calculation any *new* member states. Since the treaty gives them the right to accede at any time, without the emphasised words entry into force could be delayed for many years if new states join the EU before all the member states at the time of the adoption of the treaty have consented to be bound. Third, without the special formula, the treaty might not enter into force at all if not all *new* member states were to consent to be bound. Some non-EU treaties fall into this trap.[3] An alternative is for the treaty to prohibit accession by new member states until the treaty is in force or simply not to count their accession for the purpose of entry into force.

(2) On ratification (or, occasionally, signature) by a minimum number of the negotiating states

The minimum number for a multilateral treaty is two. The four Geneva Conventions of 1949, their Additional Protocols of 1977[4] and other treaties on international humanitarian law require only *two* ratifications before they enter into force. Although the treaty will at first bind only the two states, this reflects the nature of such treaties, the purpose of which is to protect military personnel of the parties to a conflict and civilians.

A humanitarian law treaty therefore creates, in effect, a network of bilateral treaties between its parties. But for most multilateral treaties the number for entry into force is rather larger, sometimes much more than the thirty-five needed to bring the VCLT into

[2] 2156 UNTS 200 No. 37663; UKTS (2000) No. 103. The UK's participation in Europol is now governed by Part Three, Title V, EU–UK Trade and Cooperation Agreement 2020: UKTS (2021) No. 8; OJ L 149, 30.04.2021.

[3] See Article 4, Protocol No. 11 ECHR: 2061 UNTS 12 No. 2889; 33 ILM (1994) 960; UKTS (1999) No. 33; ETS No. 155. Similar problems can occur with amendments: see pp. 277–279.

[4] Geneva Conventions: 75 UNTS 3 Nos. 970–973; UKTS (1958) No. 39; Additional Protocols: 1125 UNTS 3 No. 17512; 16 ILM (1977) 1391; UKTS (1999) Nos. 29 and 30.

force. UNCLOS 1982[5] needed sixty ratifications, as did the Rome Statute 1998.[6] A large number is usually chosen to ensure that the treaty has received a broad measure of acceptance before it enters into force. This will be important if it requires parties to make significant financial contributions to a new international organisation. In the case of UNCLOS, this aim was *not* realised because the industrialised states did not ratify until after entry into force, and then only after UNCLOS had, in effect, been amended by the Implementation Agreement 1994.[7] The 1984 Protocol amending the Chicago Convention 1944 required 102 ratifications (a high number and something of a novelty). So it was not surprising that it did not enter into force until 1998.[8]

Certain treaties to which international organisations are parties, in particular regional economic integration organisations, such as the European Union, provide that, in addition to its member states, the organisation can become a party in its own right, except that its instrument of ratification shall *not* be counted in addition to those deposited by its member states.[9]

(3) Conditional on the ratification (or, occasionally, signature) of certain states specified by number, name or category

The Nuclear Non-Proliferation Treaty 1968 provided for entry into force after ratification by forty signatory states, including ratification by the three depositary states: the Soviet Union, the United Kingdom and the United States.[10] The entry into force of the Protocol to the 1979 Convention on Long-Range Transboundary Air Pollution (EMEP) 1984 required ratification by nineteen states and organisations within the geographical scope of the Protocol, which, being Europe, meant that the instruments deposited by Canada and the United States before the entry into force of the Protocol did not count for that purpose.[11] The Comprehensive Nuclear-Test-Ban Treaty 1996 cannot enter into force until all forty-four states named in Annex 2 to the treaty have ratified.[12] Article 27(3) of the EU Convention on Mutual Assistance in Criminal Matters 2000[13] provides that the Convention shall enter into force after eight states, which were EU member states *at the time of adoption of the Convention*, have consented to be bound.

[5] 1833 UNTS 3 No. 31363; 21 ILM (1982) 1261; UKTS (1999) No. 81.

[6] 2187 UNTS 91 No. 38544; 37 ILM (1998) 998; UKTS (2002) No. 35.

[7] 1836 UNTS 42 No. 31364; 33 ILM (1994) 1313; UKTS (1999) No. 82.

[8] 1984 Protocol: 2122 UNTS 337 No. 36983; 23 ILM (1984) 705; UKTS (1999) No. 68.

[9] See Article 305(1)(f) of and Article 8 of Annex IX to UNCLOS (n. 5); and Article XI(2) Compliance Agreement 1993: 2221 UNTS 120 No. 39486; 33 ILM (1994) 968. Nor can the organisation and its member states usually have more votes in aggregate than the total votes of the member states.

[10] 729 UNTS 161 No. 10485; 7 ILM (1968) 809; UKTS (1970) No. 88; TIAS 6839. See also Article XIV(3) Outer Space Treaty 1967: 610 UNTS 205 No. 8843; 6 ILM (1967) 386; UKTS (1968) No. 10; TIAS 6347.

[11] 1480 UNTS 216 No. 25247; 27 ILM (1988) 701; UKTS (1988) No. 75: see Article 10(1)(a) of the Protocol. See also Article 6 Implementation Agreement 1994 (n. 7).

[12] 35 ILM (1996) 1439. [13] OJ 12.07.2000 No. C 197/3.

(4) As in (2) or (3) above, but the minimum number of states or organisations must also fulfil other conditions

These conditions are often financial, economic or scientific. They are designed to ensure that the treaty does not enter into force until the states that have a significant interest in the subject matter have ratified or, as in the case of commodity agreements, there is a balance between producing and consuming states. Article 10(1)(b) of the EMEP (see (3) above) imposed a further condition for entry into force: that the aggregate of the UN assessment rates for the European states that ratified had to exceed 40 per cent. The Montreal Protocol on Substances that Deplete the Ozone Layer 1987 had a similar provision, entry into force being dependent on eleven ratifications 'representing at least two-thirds of the 1986 estimated global consumption of the controlled substances' [i.e., CFCs].[14] Since the Protocol did not define 'estimated global consumption', the UN Secretary-General, as depositary, notified the entry into force of the Protocol only after having obtained confirmation, in the form of data provided by the states concerned, that the necessary conditions for entry into force had been met.[15] The Kyoto Protocol 1997 could enter into force only when it had received fifty-five ratifications, including the parties listed in Annex I who accounted for at least 55 per cent of the total carbon dioxide emissions for 1990. In practice, this required either Russia or the United States to ratify, which Russia did in 2004, the Protocol entering into force the following year.[16] The United States never ratified.

(5) On the exchange of instruments of ratification (bilateral treaty)

The parties to a bilateral treaty may agree that it enters into force when instruments of ratification are exchanged by the two parties.

(6) On notification by each signatory state to the other (or others) of the completion of its constitutional requirements

This formula can be used even if the other state (or some of the other states) does not (or do not) have to satisfy any such requirements, in which case the notification is a formality. The notification is usually by a third-person diplomatic note. Again, this is more common for bilateral treaties or multilateral treaties that are between only a few states.

[14] 1522 UNTS 3 No. 26369; 26 ILM (1987) 1550; UKTS (1990) No. 19.

[15] See also Article 15 OECD Bribery Convention 1997: 2802 UNTS 228 No. 49274; UKTS (2000) No. 107; 37 ILM (1998) 1. See further examples in *UN Depositary Practice*, paras. 226–232.

[16] 2303 UNTS 162 No. 30822; UKTS (2005) No. 6.

(7) In the case of an exchange of notes, on the date of the reply note

In the case of a treaty constituted by an exchange of notes, on the date of the reply note, though a further stage (such as in (6) above) is frequently added.

(8) In the case of an exchange of notes, on a date later than the reply note

An exchange of notes may specify that it will enter into force on a date later than that of the reply note.

(9) On a date specified in the treaty

The parties are free to specify a date later than that of signature or even for the treaty to operate retrospectively. Because of the difficulties in getting multilateral treaties ratified, it is unusual for them to specify a date for entry into force. But inserting a specific date may serve a political purpose by encouraging states – or, perhaps more to the point, their parliaments – to meet the deadline. Such a provision is therefore usually subject to a proviso. Article 16 of the Montreal Protocol on Substances that Deplete the Ozone Layer 1987 provided that it would enter into force on 1 January 1989, but only if by then it had been ratified by eleven states or regional economic integration organisations, and certain other conditions had been satisfied.[17] Article 5 of the UK–Poland Agreement on the Prepayment of Certain Obligations by Poland 2005[18] is unclear as to its meaning or effect:

> This Agreement shall enter into force on the day of signing, in line with the laws applicable to each of the parties.

(10) On a date to be agreed

The (UK–Netherlands) Lockerbie Agreement 1998, concerning a Scottish trial in the Netherlands for those accused of the Lockerbie bombing, provided that it would enter into force on a date to be agreed.[19]

(11) On a date later than the treaty envisages

Paragraph 19(a) of the International Nickel Study Group Terms of Reference 1986[20] provided that the treaty would enter into force once at least fifteen states, which in total accounted for over 50 per cent of the world trade in nickel, had consented to be bound.

[17] See n. 14. [18] UKTS (2005) No. 17.

[19] Article 29(1): 2062 UNTS 82 No. 35699; 38 ILM (1999) 926; UKTS (1999) No. 43. It entered into force on 8 January 1999. See also p. 290.

[20] 1566 UNTS 29 No. 27296. The treaty is strangely worded, but the above text translates it into more normal treaty language.

But subparagraph (b) provided that, if the treaty had not entered into force by 20 September 1986, those who had consented would meet to decide whether or not the treaty should enter into force between them. It therefore entered into force on 23 May 1990.

(12) On signature only by all the negotiating states

This is common for bilateral treaties when they do not have to be approved by parliaments (see Appendix B), and is sometimes found in treaties between a few states (plurilateral treaties), even when the subject is of major importance, such as the Dayton Agreement 1995[21] or the London Agreement 1945, which established the Nuremberg Tribunal.[22]

Other Provisions

There can be other, even more complex, entry into force provisions, especially for amendment treaties. Careful drafting is required when it is desired that, before the amendment treaty enters into force, all the parties to the original treaty are also bound by the amendment treaty. Article 35 of the 1998 Protocol amending the CoE Convention on Transfrontier Television 1989[23] gets it right, albeit tortuously, but, even then, not quite:

(1) This Protocol shall enter into force on the first day of the month following the date on which the *last of the parties to the* [1989] *Convention* has deposited its instrument of acceptance . . . [So, this is not limited to the parties as at the time of adoption of the amending treaty.]
(2) However, this Protocol shall enter into force following the expiry of a period of two years after the date on which it has been opened to acceptance, unless a Party to the [1998] Convention has notified . . . an objection to its entry into force. The right to make an objection shall be reserved to those States or the European [Union] which expressed their consent to be bound by the Convention prior to the expiry of a period of three months after the opening for acceptance of this Protocol.
(3) Should such an objection be notified, the Protocol shall enter into force on the first day of the month following the date on which the Party to the Convention which has notified the objection has deposited its instrument of acceptance.

Article 35 provides that it shall enter into force once all the parties to the Convention have accepted the Protocol. But this is followed by a proviso that the Protocol shall

[21] 35 ILM (1996) 75. See also Article 2(3) EU Convention on Mutual Assistance in Criminal Matters 2000 (n. 13).
[22] 82 UNTS 279 No. 251; UKTS (1946) No. 27.
[23] 2206 UNTS 312 No. 33611; 28 ILM (1989) 859; ETS No. 132; UKTS (1993) No. 22; and amending Protocol 1998: ETS No. 171.

nevertheless enter into force in two years (tacit acceptance),[24] unless a party to the Convention has formally objected to this. The right to object is limited to those parties to the Convention who had consented to be bound by it before the expiry of three months from when the Protocol was opened for acceptance. This restriction to existing parties to the Convention is to prevent a state, which later consents to be bound by the Convention, from objecting to the entry into force of the Protocol. But if a valid objection is notified, the Protocol will not enter into force until the objecting state accepts the Protocol. Luckily, there were none.

No Provision or Agreement on Entry into Force

If the treaty has no express provision on entry into force, and there is no other agreement about it between the negotiating states, the treaty will enter into force as soon as all those states have consented to be bound (Article 24(2)). The Iraq–United Nations Memorandum of Understanding 1996 (actually a treaty) had no provision for ratification or entry into force.[25] Entry into force may be implicit. No express provisions were needed in the UK–Norway Brent Spar Agreement 1995[26] concerning the disposal of the Brent Spar offshore installation, since it contains only assurances by the United Kingdom about the eventual disposal of the installation.

Date of Entry into Force

In the case of multilateral treaties it is usual to provide that the *date* of entry into force will be a specified number of days, weeks or months following the deposit of the last instrument of ratification which is needed to bring the treaty into force (see, e.g., Article 84(1) of the VCLT itself). The period may be of any length, but the normal range is from thirty days to twelve months. This breathing space gives the depositary time to notify the contracting states of the forthcoming entry into force. In addition, contracting states may need time to bring into effect implementing legislation that they have previously enacted (or even to enact it). It also allows time for other necessary preparations.

One must be careful in calculating the date of entry into force. If the period is *thirty days* following deposit of the last necessary instrument, the time runs from the day *after* the date of that deposit. So, if the deposit date is 14 January, the treaty will enter into force on 13 February. If the period is *one month*, it will run from the date of deposit. If that is 14 January, the treaty will enter into force on 14 February, the same

[24] The CoE has used this tacit acceptance procedure before: see the Explanatory Report on Article 35 of the 1998 Protocol at: https://rm.coe.int/09000016800cce42.

[25] MOU on the Implementation of Security Council Resolution 986 (1995): 1926 UNTS 9 No. 32851; 35 ILM (1996) 1097.

[26] Exchange of Notes: UKTS (1995) No. 65; 2033 UNTS 203 No. 35102, but no text. For the termination of the treaty, see a further Exchange of Notes 1998: UKTS (1998) No. 46.

date one month later. When there is no corresponding date (e.g., no '30 February' or '31 April'), the treaty will enter into force on the last day of *that* month, that being the nearest corresponding day.[27]

Another formula provides that the treaty shall enter into force 'on the first day of the second [or third] month' following the deposit of the last instrument of ratification needed for entry into force. The CoE Framework Convention for the Protection of National Minorities 1995 provides that it:

> shall enter into force on the first day of the month following the expiration of a period of three months after the date on which twelve Member States of the Council of Europe have expressed their consent to be bound.[28]

This (apparently convoluted) way of saying that the treaty will enter into force after three *complete calendar months* have passed nevertheless has the merit of certainty, leaving no doubt as to precisely when the treaty will enter into force.

In the case of a bilateral treaty, it is good practice to confirm the date of entry into force in the Certificate of Exchange of Instruments of Ratification. Once instruments have been exchanged, it is not usual to provide for any further delay before entry into force.

Ratification after the Treaty Has Entered into Force

When a state ratifies after the entry into force of the treaty, it will enter into force for that state on the date of deposit of its instrument, unless the treaty otherwise provides (Article 24(3)). So a multilateral treaty will usually provide that it will enter into force for such a state once a specified period has elapsed following deposit. This is often the same period as for the original entry into force of the treaty, and gives time for the depositary to notify the existing parties. Particular care must be taken in drafting the clause; and there is a surprising range of them. One should try to avoid a formula such as:

> The present Convention shall enter into force three months after the date on which [twenty] states have deposited their instruments of ratification. For each state which *thereafter* [or *subsequently*] ratifies, the present Convention shall come into force three months after deposit of its instrument of ratification.

In this example it is not clear if 'thereafter' (or 'subsequently') refers to (a) the date of fulfilment of the *conditions* for entry into force (i.e., the date when the minimum number of instruments has been received) or (b) the *actual date* of entry

[27] *UN Depositary Practice*, para. 236. [28] 34 ILM (1995) 353; ETS No. 157; UKTS (1998) No. 42.

into force, which is usually later. It has been the consistent practice of the UN Secretary-General, when acting as depositary, to interpret such terms in accordance with alternative (a), and most treaties now adopt the formula found in Article 84(2) VCLT:[29]

(1) The present Convention shall enter into force on the thirtieth day following the date of deposit of the thirty-fifth instrument of ratification or accession.
(2) For each State ratifying or acceding to the Convention *after the deposit of the thirty- fifth instrument of ratification or accession*, the Convention shall enter into force on the thirtieth day after deposit by such State of its instrument of ratification or accession.

Similar problems arise with denunciation clauses.

Who Determines the Date of Entry into Force?

In the case of a multilateral treaty, the date on which it will enter into force is normally determined by the depositary, who will notify the parties and other states concerned by a formal note. If there are doubts whether the conditions for entry into force have been met, the depositary may have to consult the interested states.

Time of Entry into Force

On occasion, it may even be necessary to determine the precise time on a given day that the treaty will enter into force.[30] In the overwhelming majority of cases, a treaty is expressed to enter into force after a certain number of days have elapsed following the deposit of the two instruments of ratification (bilateral) or of a specified number of instruments (multilateral). Then there can be no doubt that the treaty will enter into force at the first moment of the day so identified (a well-known domestic law principle). There could, however, be a problem with a bilateral treaty if, instead of providing that it shall enter into force on the 'date' of the exchange of instruments of ratification, it provides that it shall enter into force on their 'exchange' or provisions having similar effect.[31] When the problem can be foreseen, it is therefore preferable to cover the point in the treaty. This is especially so when – as is often the case with bilateral treaties – the parties inhabit different time zones. Very similar, and very practical problems can arise with termination clauses.

[29] *UN Depositary Practice*, paras. 244–245.
[30] *McNair*, 198–199, cites a perceived time problem with the Treaty of Versailles 1919 (225 CTS 188; UKTS (1919) No. 4). But its final clauses provided for it to enter into force 'from the *date* of [the] first procès-verbal' recording the deposit of certain ratifications. So, the exact time of the signing of the *procès-verbal* was not relevant.
[31] See *Blix and Emerson*, 75–82, examples 2, 8, 9, 12–14, 23 and 26.

Date Relevant to Provisions within the Treaty

When drafting a treaty which provides, for example, for the transfer of rights, it is important to make clear if the rights are those existing at the date of adoption, signature or entry into force, or at some other date.[32]

Effect of Withdrawal of an Instrument or Extinction of a State

In calculating whether the minimum number of instruments of ratification needed to bring a treaty into force have been deposited, the depositary should discount any that have been withdrawn. But if the instrument is withdrawn *after* deposit of the last instrument needed to bring the treaty into force, it appears to have been the practice of the UN Secretary-General not to regard the withdrawal as affecting satisfaction of the conditions for entry into force. Thus, if, say, forty ratifications are needed for entry into force, the conditions would be satisfied even if one of the forty is then withdrawn *before* entry into force.[33] This may, however, be too literal an approach, and consequently not a correct application of the essential premise that all conditions for entry into force must have been satisfied. One of the conditions, albeit implicit, must surely be that on entry into force there will still be the minimum number of parties, that is forty, *not* thirty-nine.

The same considerations apply if a ratifying state should cease to exist, as does happen.

Reservations Attached to Instruments

The depositary does not necessarily have to disregard any ratification containing reservations to which other contracting states may have objected. In the case of the VCLT itself, several of the first thirty-five instruments of ratification needed for it to enter into force contained reservations to which objections had been lodged. The UN Secretary-General, as depositary, consulted the contracting states, stating his assumption that, for the purpose of calculating the date of entry into force, account should be taken of all thirty-five instruments. No one objected.[34]

Provisional Application

The subject of Article 25 is sometimes described loosely as provisional *entry into force*. This may be because the draft article prepared by the ILC so described it, but, as Article 25 makes clear, it is concerned only with the *application* of a treaty on a provisional basis. To speak of provisional entry into force is confusing, and could

[32] *McNair*, 204–205. [33] *UN Depositary Practice*, para. 159. [34] *Sinclair*, 45.

mislead one into believing that the treaty is already in force, albeit on some kind of conditional basis.

In August 2021 the ILC completed a study of provisional application, resulting in draft guidelines (referred to in this chapter as the *Guidelines*) and a draft annex constituting the Guide to Provisional Application of Treaties.[35] Following a debate in the Sixth Committee the following autumn, in which delegations commented on the Guide,[36] the General Assembly adopted a resolution taking note of the Guide and bringing it to the attention of states and international organisations.[37]

At the time the VCLT was adopted, provisional application clauses were relatively rare.[38] The growing need for them has arisen from a combination of political pressure to bring treaties that are subject to ratification into operation early, and the problem of doing just that. The problem is especially difficult for treaties adopted within the United Nations or the specialised agencies, since they require a substantial number of ratifications for entry into force. The VCLT required the relatively small number of thirty-five, but, as we have seen, the 1984 Protocol amending the Chicago Convention 1944 needed 102.[39]

Some states have constitutions which do not allow provisional application, often because full treaty procedures (including obtaining parliamentary approval[40]) need to be completed before the state can apply any obligation in a treaty (or certain types of treaty), even if provisionally. Sometimes, however, it is worth exploring whether such a requirement amounts to a block on provisional application per se, or rather a block on applying the treaty before completion of all domestic treaty procedures. Even if one state has to complete procedures sufficient, in effect, for it to ratify the treaty, there may still be advantage in provisional application if the other state is not ready to ratify but is in a position to provisionally apply. In addition, some states may say initially that provisional application is 'not possible' but further probing reveals that it is not necessarily constitutionally impossible, but rather a departure from normal practice which involves procedural or political difficulties. In that case again, depending on the significance of the treaty and the imperative for its early application, it may be possible to surmount these. But ultimately, provisional application is

[35] Guide to Provisional Application of Treaties, Report of the ILC on the work of its 72nd session, 2021, UNGA 76th Session, Supplement No. 10, Doc. A/76/10. This is to be distinguished from the Guide to Practice on Reservations to Treaties referred to extensively in Chapter 8 (n. 3).

[36] Topical summary of the discussion held in the Sixth Committee of the General Assembly during its seventy-sixth session, prepared by the Secretariat, A/CN.4/746, 28 February 2022.

[37] UNGA Resolution 76/113, 9 December 2021, A/RES/76/113.

[38] See *Blix and Emerson*, 84–86; and A. Quast Mersch, *Provisionally Applied Treaties: Their Binding Force and Legal Nature* (Brill, Leiden 2012).

[39] See also Article 45 Energy Charter Treaty 1994: 2080 UNTS 100 No. 36116; 34 ILM (1995) 373; UKTS (2000) No. 78; www.encharter.org.

[40] See R. Lefeber, 'The Provisional Application of Treaties', in J. Klabbers and R. Lefeber (eds.), *Essays on the Law of Treaties* (Kluwer Law, The Hague 1998), 81–96, 89–90.

an optional process which some states accept and some do not, and even those which accept the practice may in a specific case only do so reluctantly.[41]

Article 25(1) provides that a treaty is applied provisionally pending its entry into force if it so provides or if the negotiating states have in some other manner so agreed. *Guideline* 4 amplifies this latter point:

> In addition to the case where the treaty so provides, the provisional application of a treaty or a part of a treaty may be agreed between the States or international organizations concerned through:
>
> (a) a separate treaty; or
> (b) any other means or arrangements, including:
>   (i) a resolution, decision or other act adopted by an international organization or at an intergovernmental conference, in accordance with the rules of such organization or conference, reflecting the agreement of the States or international organizations concerned;
>   (ii) a declaration by a State or by an international organization that is accepted by the other States or international organizations concerned.

In the case of a bilateral agreement, the treaty itself may include a provision relating to provisional application, but it is by no means unusual for this to be dealt with in a separate instrument or exchange of notes accompanying the treaty. In either case, provisional application may take effect either upon signature or at a later date following a further procedure which is specified in the treaty provision or in the separate instrument. A state or international organisation may need a further procedure, even before provisionally applying, if, for example, it first has to put in place new legislation or other measures to give effect to any of the treaty provisions; or indeed, as explained above, one side may have to complete its full treaty procedures.

In the case of a multilateral treaty, the text of which is adopted by an international conference, the obligation of a state to apply the treaty provisionally may be created by its participation in its adoption. If there is no clause, the obligation may arise if the state supports provisional application, usually by voting for a resolution to that effect. A state that does not so vote, or does not join a consensus, will be under no such obligation. And should a treaty clause or a resolution be expressed to apply only to signatory states, it will not apply to a negotiating state until it has signed. Provisional application terminates with the entry into force of the treaty between the states concerned. The date from which a treaty is to be applied provisionally can be the date of adoption or signature, or whatever the negotiating states can agree on. The most famous – but hugely atypical – example of provisional application of a multilateral agreement is the

[41] See the final preambular paragraph of UNGA Resolution 76/113 (n. 37): '*Underlining* the essentially voluntary and optional nature of the provisional application of treaties'. See also the report of the Sixth Committee discussion (n. 36), para. 148: 'It was also recalled that the provisional application of a treaty was an exception and meant to facilitate but not replace the entry into force of a treaty. It was also emphasized that the mechanism of provisional application should not be abused.'

General Agreement on Tariffs and Trade 1947 (GATT), which was applied provisionally for decades by a Protocol of Provisional Application.[42]

It is possible to provisionally apply only a part of the treaty. This needs to be clearly specified in the relevant provision or instrument. It may also be advisable to specify, if there is a lack of clarity, whether certain provisions in the treaty which refer to entry into force, such as those relating to periods of time or the establishment of dispute settlement mechanisms, should be construed as if they referred to provisional application.

As intimated in the opening paragraph of this section, the legal effect of provisional application is not the same as entry into force, which constitutes a conclusive consent to be bound. Nevertheless, as *Guideline* 6 states:

> The provisional application of a treaty or a part of a treaty produces a legally binding obligation to apply the treaty or a part thereof between the States or international organizations concerned, except to the extent that the treaty otherwise provides or it is otherwise agreed. Such treaty or part of a treaty that is being applied provisionally must be performed in good faith.

Provisional application by a state terminates with the entry into force of the treaty for that state. Unless the treaty provides, or the negotiating states have agreed otherwise, provisional application is also terminated with respect to a state if it notifies the other states between which it is being applied provisionally of its intention not to become a party to the treaty (Article 25(2)).[43]

The period of provisional application can be limited. The (OSCE) Treaty on Open Skies 1992[44] provides that certain of its provisions shall be provisionally applied, and that:

> This provisional application shall be effective for a period of 12 months from the date when this Treaty is opened for signature. In the event that this Treaty does not enter into force before the period of provisional application expires, that period may be extended if all the signatory States so decide. The period of provisional application shall in any event terminate when this Treaty enters into force. However, the States Parties may then decide to extend the period of provisional application in respect of signatory States that have not ratified this Treaty.

The whole treaty was provisionally applied from 1992 until its entry into force in 2002.

Article 7 of the Implementation Agreement 1994,[45] relating to Part XI of UNCLOS 1982, is unusual in that it provided that if the Agreement had not entered into force by

[42] 55 UNTS 194 No. 814 (b); Protocol of Provisional Application: 55 UNTS 308 No. 814 (c).

[43] For further guidance in relation to termination, see *Guideline* 9. See also Chapter 16, pp. 312–314.

[44] UKTS (2002) No. 27, Article XVIII, section 1.

[45] See n. 7. See also D. Anderson, 'Legal Implications of the Entry into Force of the UN Convention on the Law of the Sea', ICLQ 44 (1995) 313–326; and p. 124 and p. 173.

16 November 1994 (which it did not), it would be applied provisionally by states that had agreed to its adoption, or had signed it, *unless they notified the depositary otherwise.* In other words, this amounted to *implied* consent to provisional application, but with an opt-out. Out of seventy-nine signatories of the Agreement, seventeen opted out.

An alternative is to provide in the Final Act that:

> The Meeting agreed that it was desirable to ensure the effective implementation at an early date of the provisions of the Protocol. Pending entry into force of the Protocol it was agreed that it was *desirable* for all Contracting Parties to the Antarctic Treaty to apply Annexes I–IV, *in accordance with their legal systems and to the extent practicable,* and to take individually such steps to enable it to occur as soon as possible.

The treaty in question, the Antarctic Treaty Environmental Protocol 1991,[46] required ratification by all twenty-six negotiating states to enter into force. Because of this, and the complexities of the implementing legislation, entry into force was delayed for six years. Practical implementation during the period before entry into force was patchy at best. But this would have been so with or without the exhortation in the Final Act. The inclusion of the phrase 'in accordance with their legal systems and to the extent practicable', or something similar, is found in many provisional application clauses in multilateral treaties, such as that in the Implementation Agreement.

The problem of the length of time that a measure adopted under some treaties can take to come into force is well illustrated by Measure 1 (2003) adopted by the Antarctic Treaty Consultative Parties. Its purpose was to establish a permanent Antarctic Treaty Secretariat with a Headquarters Agreement with Argentina. Because such measures may take some years to enter into force,[47] the Secretariat acted on the basis that, in accordance with Decision 2 (2003), Measure 1 (2003) would be applied provisionally. This also meant that during this period the financial contributions to the Secretariat budget had to be voluntary.

Treaties that provide for a uniform regime (like those concluded within the Universal Postal Union for things like envelope sizes) are, in practice, often applied by the membership long before they enter into force, as well as by states that never become members. This is simply because it is in the common interest that such matters should be handled uniformly.

Preparatory Commissions

A further approach that is increasingly being employed is to establish a preparatory commission ('prepcom') once a treaty has been adopted. This is usually a body, composed of all the negotiating or signatory states, entrusted with the task of making

46 30 ILM (1991) 1460; UKTS (1999) No. 6; [1998] ATS 6.

47 On measures adopted by the Antarctic Treaty Consultative Meeting (ATCM), see pp. 131–132.

the necessary arrangements for when the treaty enters into force. For example, although a monitoring body established by the treaty will not be able to meet formally until the treaty has entered into force, it is desirable that draft rules of procedure should be prepared, secretariat staff engaged, premises found and, perhaps most important of all, financial arrangements agreed.

The need for a prepcom is particularly acute when the treaty establishes an international body that needs to be able to begin work as soon as the treaty enters into force. The prepcom for the GATT was the Interim Commission for the International Trade Organization (ICITO), which was established by a resolution of the UN Conference on Trade and Development and Employment 1947–48.[48] A prepcom was established for UNCLOS 1982 and met for many years. The Final Act of the 1998 Conference on the Establishment of an International Criminal Court adopted a resolution requesting that the UN General Assembly establish a Preparatory Commission for the Court. Its tasks included drafting rules of procedure, a headquarters agreement, financial regulations, privileges and immunities, and a budget for the first financial year.[49] This prepcom followed a pattern set by the United Nations itself in 1945,[50] and as a matter of law was no more than a committee assisted by a temporary secretariat.

The 1996 CTBT[51] provides for an elaborate verification and monitoring regime, involving the establishment of numerous monitoring stations throughout the world. This requires not only their construction, but also the drafting and negotiation of bilateral agreements, with provisions for privileges and immunities.[52] For this purpose, later in 1996 a meeting of the signatory states adopted a resolution which approved a supplementary treaty.[53] This established a prepcom composed of representatives of all signatory states but which has legal personality, with a Provisional Technical Secretariat to serve it, and imposed various financial obligations on the signatory states pending entry into force of the CTBT. Since the entry into force of the CTBT still seems far off, the work of the Secretariat has been increasingly important.

Retroactive Effect of a Treaty

A treaty does not have retroactive effect so as to bind a party with respect to any act or fact that took place, or any situation that ceased to exist, before its entry into force for that party, unless this is provided for in the treaty (Article 28). A treaty can, of

48 Cmd. 7375.

49 UN Doc. A/CONF.183/C.1/L.76/Add. 14; 37 ILM (1998) 1002. For the UNGA resolution, see A/RES/53/105.

50 See L. M. Goodrich, E. Hambro and A. P. Simons, *Charter of the United Nations* (3rd ed., Columbia University Press, New York 1969), 8–9.

51 See n. 12. 52 See, e.g., the UK–CTBT Prepcom Agreement 1999: UKTS (2004) No. 35.

53 The full title is Text on the Establishment of a Preparatory Commission for the Comprehensive Nuclear Test-Ban Treaty Organization 1996: UKTS (1999) No. 46.

course, apply to a pre-existing act, fact or situation that continues after entry into force.[54] An international court or tribunal may, under the dispute settlement clause of a treaty, have jurisdiction over matters occurring before entry into force of the treaty.

However, if a treaty provides that certain substantive[55] obligations shall take effect on a certain date, but the treaty does not enter into force until after that date, the obligations will be legally binding only from the date of entry into force of the treaty.

Revival of a Treaty

When a treaty has been terminated by one, both or all parties, the parties (or some of them) can always agree to revive it. Unless modifications are necessary, only a short, simple treaty (perhaps an exchange of notes) is needed.

The treaty constituted by the Exchange of Notes of 9 and 17 March 2000[56] between Brazil (acting on behalf of the United Kingdom) and the FRY revived the UK–Yugoslavia Air Services Agreement 1959,[57] which the United Kingdom had 'terminated' in 1998. The Exchange of Notes took immediate effect on 17 March 2000. At the time the United Kingdom had no direct diplomatic relations with the FRY, but there was a mutual wish to resume flights in anticipation of the resumption of relations.

[54] The UK–Brazil Agreement on the Transfer of Prisoners 1998 (UKTS (2002) No. 23) applies to the enforcement of sentences imposed before or after entry into force. See also the UK–UN Agreement on the Enforcement of Sentences of the ICTY 2004: 2252 UNTS 30 No. 40107; UKTS (2004) No. 20.

[55] Not the procedural matters mentioned in Article 24(4).

[56] UKTS (2000) No. 96.

[57] 359 UNTS 340 No. 5151; UKTS (1960) No. 10.

10

Treaties and Domestic Law

Treaties are made to be performed.[1]

It should not be assumed that, once a treaty has entered into force for a state, it is then in force *in* that state; in other words, that it has become part of its law. The point is of particular importance for treaties that accord rights to individuals, such as human rights treaties, where the rights are intended to be exercised by them (and sometimes by corporations or companies). International law and domestic law (the law in force within a state; sometimes termed 'municipal', 'internal' or 'national' law) operate on different planes. International law is concerned with the rights and obligations of states and other international legal persons, such as international organisations. When a treaty provides for rights or obligations to be conferred on persons (legal or natural), they can usually be given effect *only* if they are made part of the domestic law of each party, and with provisions for their enforcement. A good example is the immunities and privileges granted to diplomatic missions and their staff by the Vienna Convention on Diplomatic Relations 1961.[2] For them to be fully effective, the *domestic* law of the receiving state must accord the required immunities and privileges. Similarly, even though under a treaty, such as the European Convention on Human Rights 1950[3] or a bilateral investment treaty (BIT), a person can eventually take a state to an international court or tribunal for an alleged breach of his or her rights, actually enforcing a decision may well require that the state's domestic law recognises the award and will enforce it.

Whether rights and obligations created by a treaty need to be enforceable in domestic law, and, if so, whether in fact they are, is a matter of concern to both the public international lawyer and the domestic lawyer. If the lawyer works in a foreign ministry, they and their diplomatic colleagues will want to know what, if any, effect a treaty under negotiation will need to have in domestic law; and, in particular, whether new legislation will be necessary. When another ministry is conducting the negotiations, its officials will have (or should have) the same concerns. All those involved with the negotiation of a treaty need to assure themselves that, if their state should become a

[1] *Reuter*, para. 44.
[2] 500 UNTS 95 No. 7310; UKTS (1965) No. 19. See the (UK) Diplomatic Privileges Act 1964.
[3] Amended by subsequent Protocols: consolidated text at CoE website.

party, there will be no domestic legal obstacle to its negotiation of that treaty or to its full implementation, since any non-implementation could have adverse consequences, international and domestic, and legal and political.

How a treaty is implemented in domestic law is not specified in the Convention. Treaty obligations rest on the states parties. It is, therefore, the state that has to ensure that the obligations can be implemented domestically. This means that all state organs, including the judiciary, state agencies and other public bodies, and, depending on the nature of the obligation, private persons and bodies, must, if necessary, be bound by domestic law in such a way that the treaty obligations can be carried out. Fresh or amending legislation may be needed, and problems can arise for federal states.[4]

Duty to Perform Treaties

Article 26 contains the fundamental principle of the law of treaties: *pacta sunt servanda:*

> Every treaty in force is binding upon the parties to it and must be performed in good faith.

Pacta sunt servanda embodies a rule that is an elementary and universally agreed principle fundamental to all legal systems, and is of prime importance for the stability of treaty relations. The oft-quoted Latin phrase means no more than that a treaty is legally binding and so must be performed by the parties to it. The third preamble to the Convention notes that 'the principles of free consent and of good faith and the *pacta sunt servanda* rule are universally recognised'. In its Commentary on draft Article 23 (later Article 26), the ILC saw the phrase as representing 'the fundamental principle of the law of treaties', and that the principle of good faith is a legal principle that forms an integral part of the *pacta sunt servanda* rule.[5] A simple illustration of the application of the good faith principle was the approach of the members of the United Nations to the change of name of two permanent members of the Security Council, the Republic of China and the Union of Soviet Socialist Republics, whose original names are mentioned explicitly in the UN Charter, which was *not* changed. In other words, like most domestic law today, international law looks more to the substance than the form.

The *pacta sunt servanda* rule is qualified so as to apply only to a treaty that is 'in force'. A state that has signed a treaty subject to ratification, or otherwise expressed

[4] For some vivid examples of such problems, see R. Higgins, 'The Concept of "The State"', in L. Boisson de Chazournes and V. Gowlland-Debbas (eds.), *The International Legal System in Quest of Equity and Universality* (Martinus Nijhoff, The Hague 2001), 547–561.

[5] *Gabčíkovo-Nagymaros Project (Hungary/Slovakia)*, ICJ Reports (1997) 7, 65 and 79, paras. 114 and 142; 27 ILM (1988) 162; 116 ILR 1.

consent to be bound by a treaty, even though the treaty has not yet entered into force, has only a very limited obligation under Article 18. Similarly, the *pacta sunt servanda* rule does not apply if the invalidity of the treaty is established. But to do this is by no means easy, there being a natural presumption that every treaty is valid (see Article 42), so that it is difficult to rebut.[6] International courts and tribunals seek to avoid anything that would unnecessarily undermine the stability of treaty relations and the continuation in force of treaties as the natural order of things. The *pacta sunt servanda* rule is also restricted to treaties as they are defined in Article 2(1)(a): a *treaty* is an international agreement 'governed by international law'. This excludes instruments that the participants do not intend should be governed by international law (non-binding instruments).

It goes without saying that, if a party to a treaty does not perform it, that will, to the extent of the non-performance, be a breach of its international obligations to the other party or parties. A breach that is 'material' entitles another party to invoke it as a ground for termination of the treaty or suspending its operation in whole or in part (Article 60).

Article 26 is followed by its corollary, Article 27: a party may not invoke the provisions of its internal (i.e., domestic) law as justification for its failure to perform a treaty.[7] Thus, if a new law, or a modification to existing law, is needed in order to carry out the obligations on the state by the time it consents to be bound by the treaty, a negotiating state should ensure that this is done *at least* by the time that the treaty enters into force for it. If this is not done, not only will the state risk being in breach of its treaty obligations, but it will also be liable in international law to another party if, as a result, that party, or its nationals, is later damaged. Although it may be tempting, a state cannot plead that it is waiting for its legislature to legislate. Even if the treaty does not enter into force for the state at the time it consents to be bound, the date of entry into force may come earlier than expected. It is therefore desirable that any necessary legislation is made *before the state gives its consent to be bound* (e.g., ratification), though the actual coming into force of the legislation may be postponed until the entry into force of the treaty.

A state cannot plead a change of government to excuse failure to implement a treaty. Since the treaty is entered into on behalf of the *state*, the new government must also perform the treaty. Nor is it at all easy for a state to plead successfully that a treaty is invalid because its consent to be bound was expressed in violation of its own law.[8]

[6] See Chapter 17.

[7] For this purpose, internal law includes, e.g. (supranational) EU law. See pp. 159–160 regarding objections to a reservation on the ground that it is incompatible with Article 27.

[8] Article 27 refers to the obligation of a state to perform a treaty which is in force. The second sentence of the Article states that this rule is without prejudice to Article 46. Article 46 relates to the competence to conclude a treaty in the first place. See *Villiger*, 373; and Chapter 17, pp. 321–324.

Constitutional Provisions

Some treaties, such as treaties of alliance (or, for that matter, the Convention itself), should not need to have effect in the domestic law of the parties. But given the subject matter of treaties today, many do need to be given such effect. It may, for example, be necessary to create new criminal offences. How this is done depends on the way in which treaties are dealt with in the constitution of each state, the Convention wisely not attempting to provide guidance. Although no two constitutions are identical, there are two general approaches to how states deal with treaties: 'dualism' and 'monism'. Even in states that take the dualist approach to treaties, customary international law is regarded as part of domestic law, though legislation (e.g., conferring jurisdiction and imposing penalties) may still be needed to make the treaty truly effective. The two terms are general descriptions of the way in which treaties are dealt with in a state's domestic law.

It must be stressed, however, that both approaches are doctrines that have been developed in an attempt to explain the general approaches by states. Although monism is often presented as the opposite of dualism, this is misleading. If one examines even a small selection of constitutions, it soon becomes apparent that many contain both dualist and monist elements. In this matter the constitutional practices of states make up a spectrum. At one end is found the United Kingdom, which has perhaps the purist form of dualism; at the other end might be said to be Switzerland, which has perhaps the most developed form of monism. In between these two extremes there are many variations.[9] It is necessary, however, to be familiar with the different approaches, since constitutional constraints on one of the negotiating states *may* (I put it no higher than that) affect the way in which final clauses are drawn, especially in respect of ratification, entry into force and provisional application, or may even suggest that a non-binding instrument may be preferable to a treaty. Monist and dualist countries seem to get along without mentioning the process under which each has to labour.

A brief description of the monist approach will be given, with some examples. This will be followed by an explanation of the dualist approach. The constitutional practice of the United Kingdom will be dealt with in some detail. Not only is it the prime example of dualism, but it has been followed (albeit with some variations) in almost all other Commonwealth states, which amount to over a quarter of all states. This section will end with a description of how treaties are dealt with in the US Constitution, which combines both approaches, and needs to be better understood given the importance of the United States for treaty making.

[9] See the useful accounts of how the constitutions of nineteen states deal with treaties in D. B. Hollis, M. R. Blakeslee and L. B. Ederington (eds.), *National Treaty Law and Practice* (Martinus Nijhoff, Leiden 2005); A. P. Blaustein and G. H. Flanz (eds.), *Constitutions of the Countries of the World: A Series of Updated Texts, Constitutional Chronologies and Annotated Bibliographies* (looseleaf) (Oceana Publications, Dobbs Ferry, NY 1971–).

Monism[10]

The essence of the monist approach is that a treaty may, without legislation, become part of domestic law once it has been concluded in accordance with the constitution and has entered into force for the state. When legislation is not needed, such treaties are commonly described as 'self-executing'. However, as we shall see, in many cases legislation will be needed. Although there are *many* variations in how the monist approach is expressed in constitutions, three main features are common to most. First, although the constitution requires the treaty to have first been approved by parliament, there are exceptions for certain types of treaties or certain circumstances. Second, a distinction is made between treaties according to their nature or subject matter, some regarded as being self-executing, others requiring legislation before they can have full effect in domestic law. Third, a self-executing treaty may constitute supreme law and override any inconsistent domestic legislation, whether existing or future, though in some states where parliament is supreme, later legislation can override a self-executing treaty.

France

In France,[11] the executive has sole responsibility for concluding treaties. But in view of the supremacy of treaties under the Constitution over French law (Article 55 of the Constitution), the National Assembly and the Senate should authorise ratification if the treaty concerns peace, trade, an international organisation that has the power to restrict the exercise of French sovereignty, that is for individual status or territory, or if the treaty would modify existing legislation or have new legislative effect. Authorisation is given in the form of a statute (*loi*). The parliamentary vote ensures the due process of approval of the treaty and, should the parliament fail to vote in favour, the executive would not be authorised to ratify a treaty or approve an agreement. Furthermore, if a treaty falling within Article 55 does not get parliamentary approval, it could be challenged before an administrative court. Although there are now more matters for which authorisation should be sought, the executive has complete discretion as to whether to seek it.

The Conseil constitutionnel has authority to pronounce on whether a treaty conforms to the Constitution, but only if the president, prime minister, president of the Senate, president of the National Assembly or sixty members of either of the latter two bodies refer it to the Conseil constitutionnel (Article 54 of the Constitution). Those treaties authorised by the National Assembly and the Senate must be published in the *Journal Officiel* within one month. They then prevail over existing or later legislation (i.e., are self-executing). Until so published, a treaty cannot

[10] From the theory that denies any duality of mind and matter; hence, international law and domestic law are not separate, though the former is supreme. See further, *Crawford/Brownlie*, 45–47; *Shaw*, 111–114.

[11] Hollis *et al.* (n. 9), 253–316.

be applied by the courts, but once published the courts will apply it from the date the treaty entered into force for France. If the terms of a (non-self-executing) treaty are not clear, a court will not apply them. Nor will they do so if the terms are not capable of being applied as domestic law without new legislation (i.e., are not self-executing), such as those of the Convention on the Rights of the Child 1989.[12]

Germany

In Germany,[13] under the Constitution (Basic Law) the conclusion of treaties is the responsibility of the executive, though the Foreign Relations Committee of parliament is informed when a treaty is concluded. Only a limited number of categories of treaties need the consent of parliament before they can be ratified, namely treaties that regulate the political relations of the Federation or relate to subjects of federal legislation. Even in those cases, parliament cannot amend the treaty, impose conditions or require reservations to be made. Its approval is given by a law. Whether a treaty needs the consent of parliament is ultimately a matter for the Constitutional Court, but if the Foreign Relations Committee considers that the consent of parliament is needed, in practice it will be sought. The law approving ratification of the treaty also has the effect of making the treaty part of German law with effect from the day the treaty enters into force for Germany. If the treaty would affect existing laws or require new legislation, a separate law has to be enacted. In so far as the *Länder* have power to legislate, they may, with the consent of the Federal Government, conclude treaties with foreign states.[14]

The Netherlands

The basic constitutional rule in the Netherlands[15] is that all treaties need the approval of parliament. Parliamentary approval of a treaty can be express or tacit, though a treaty that would conflict with the Constitution always requires express approval. The Kingdom Act of 1994[16] provides several defined exceptions to the rule that treaties require parliamentary approval: if this is laid down by Act of Parliament for such treaties; if the treaty is only to implement an already approved treaty; if the treaty imposes no substantial financial obligations on the state and has been concluded for a period not exceeding one year (extension of the period being possible); if it is to

[12] 1577 UNTS 3 No. 27531; 28 ILM (1989) 1448; UKTS (1992) No. 44.

[13] Hollis *et al.* (n. 9), 317–348; S. Kadelbach, 'International Treaties and the German Constitution', in C. A. Bradley (ed.), *The Oxford Handbook of Comparative Foreign Relations Law* (Oxford University Press, Oxford 2019), 173–190.

[14] See Article 32.2 Basic Law; and p. 80.

[15] Hollis *et al.* (n. 9), 483–536.

[16] The Kingdom Act of 7 July 1994 containing regulations on the approval and publication of treaties and the publication of decisions of international organisations (*Rijkswet van 7 juli 1994, houdende regeling betreffende de goedkeuring en bekendmaking van verdragen en de bekendmaking van besluiten van volkenrechtelijke organisaties*).

extend a treaty which is about to expire; if it is to amend an annex which is an integral part of an approved treaty and the contents of which aim to implement the provisions of that approved treaty; or, in exceptional circumstances of a compelling nature, if it is in the interests of the state that it should remain secret or confidential. This last exception is surprising in view of Article 102 of the UN Charter. If provisions of a treaty are binding on all persons by virtue of their contents, they prevail over existing or future legislation. The foreign minister must periodically submit to parliament a list of all treaties under negotiation, unless the negotiations are confidential.[17]

Poland

Under Article 91 of the Polish Constitution of 1997, a treaty, once it has been ratified and promulgated in the Journal of Laws of the Republic of Poland (*Dziennik Ustaw*), and has entered into force for Poland, constitutes part of the domestic legal order and applies directly, unless its application depends on the enactment of a statute. If a treaty is ratified with prior consent granted by statute, it has precedence over other statutes if such an agreement cannot be reconciled with the provisions of such statutes. If an agreement establishing an international organisation and ratified by the Republic of Poland so provides, the laws established by it shall be applied directly and have precedence in the event of a conflict of laws.

Russia[18]

In 1995 Russia adopted a new Federal Law on International Treaties.[19] The law goes into considerable detail about the respective roles of the executive and the legislature, and various other organs and agencies of the state. This is due to the complex constitutional structure of the Russian Federation. The law closely follows the Convention, its main interest for present purposes being in the procedures for approval of treaties, and their place in domestic law. The conclusion of treaties is the exclusive responsibility of the executive, but certain categories are required to be made subject to ratification, which, in turn, requires the approval of parliament (the State Duma and the Federal Assembly) by means of a federal law. These include treaties that will need new laws or changes to existing laws, and treaties concerning human rights, territorial demarcation, defence and international security, and participation in international organisations if this would involve transfer of powers of the Russian Federation or if decisions of the organs of the organisation would be binding

[17] J. Klabbers, 'The New Dutch Law on the Approval of Treaties', ICLQ 44 (1995) 629–643.

[18] Hollis *et al.* (n. 9), 537–580.

[19] 34 ILM (1995) 1373; W. E. Butler, *International Law in the Russian Legal System* (Oxford University Press, New York 2020); R. Mullerson, M. Fitzmaurice and M. Andenas (eds.), *Constitutional Reform and International Law in Central and Eastern Europe* (Kluwer Law, The Hague 1998), 259–278 and 295–317 (text of the law). See also I. Lukashuk, 'Treaties in the Legal System of Russia', Ger YBIL (1997) 141–163.

on the Federation. Provided the treaty has not entered into force for Russia, the Constitutional Court has the power to pronounce on whether it conforms to the Constitution.

Treaties are an integral part of the Russian legal system, and prevail over inconsistent domestic law. With effect from 4 July 2020 the Constitution was amended to give the Constitutional Court considerable power to review decisions and judgments of international treaty-based courts and arbitral tribunals for the conformity of these judgments and decisions to the Russian Constitution. The 1995 Federal Law was amended accordingly. A treaty has direct effect if it is in force for Russia, has been published there officially and does not require legislation in order to implement it.

Switzerland

Under the Swiss Constitution,[20] the treaty-making power is vested in the Confederation. The Federal Council (i.e., the executive) is thus entitled to conclude treaties, even on matters within the competence of the constituent units of the Confederation (the cantons).[21] Although the Constitution provides for the Federal Assembly to approve treaties, in constitutional practice about half are not specifically approved by the Federal Assembly; the Federal Council concluding such 'executive agreements',[22] provided the Federal Assembly has authorised it beforehand, either expressly or implicitly, or if they concern a matter of minor importance that does not primarily affect individuals. In other cases, if the matter is urgent, the Federal Council may apply a treaty provisionally, but cannot ratify it without the approval of the Federal Assembly.

In practice, the Federal Council has a large measure of discretion as to whether to submit a treaty to the Assembly for approval.[23] When it does so, this has to be done between signature and ratification. The treaty will be accompanied by the text of any reservations that the Federal Council proposes to make. The Federal Assembly may reformulate them, and add or delete new ones. A treaty approved by the Federal Assembly that is of indefinite duration and not capable of being denounced, that provides for participation in an international organisation or concerns multilateral law making, must be submitted to a referendum of all Swiss citizens, if 50,000 citizens or eight cantons so demand. (Until 2000, other treaties were submitted to a referendum if both houses of the Federal Parliament (the Federal Assembly and the Council of States) so decided.) Since 1977, adherence to a collective security treaty or to a treaty establishing a supranational body must be submitted to a referendum of Swiss

[20] Hollis *et al.* (n. 9), 627–685. [21] See p. 80 on treaty making by the cantons.
[22] See US 'executive agreements'.
[23] To allow the Assembly to exercise a certain control over how the Federal Council makes use of its delegated authority to conclude treaties, the latter has to submit an annual report to the Assembly, containing all the treaties it has concluded during the year.

citizens and the cantons. A majority of the citizens and cantons (notably Geneva) voted in 1986 against joining the United Nations, though Switzerland eventually joined as the 190th member in 2002, only just ahead of the brand new state of Timor Leste.

Once a treaty enters into force for Switzerland, it becomes part of Swiss law; there is no need for it to be formally incorporated. This is so whether or not the Federal Assembly has specifically approved the treaty. Treaties prevail over inconsistent law, existing or future. However, according to some case law of the Federal Tribunal (Supreme Court), parliament can enact a law that is inconsistent with a treaty to which Switzerland is bound provided this is done deliberately, though there is a growing tendency in the jurisprudence of the Federal Tribunal in favour of recognising the primacy of treaties. Once it has become part of the law, a treaty can be invoked before domestic courts, provided it is self-executing. For this purpose, the treaty must be precise enough for the courts to apply it. Whether a treaty is self-executing will depend on its nature and purpose.

Dualism

Under the dualist approach, the constitution of the state accords no special status to treaties; the rights and obligations created by them have no effect in domestic law *unless legislation is in force to give effect to them*. When the legislation is specifically made for this purpose, the rights and obligations are then said to be 'incorporated' into domestic law. This approach reflects, on the one hand, the constitutional power of the executive generally to bind itself to a treaty without the prior consent of the legislature and, on the other hand, the supreme power of the legislature under the constitution to make laws. In the United Kingdom, this division of powers was a product of the seventeenth-century constitutional struggle between the king and Parliament. This resulted in the power to legislate being almost completely vested in Parliament, yet with the Crown retaining in common law certain 'royal prerogatives' (the right to act without the consent of Parliament),[24] which include the conduct of foreign relations and the making of treaties.[25]

With dualism, the provisions of a treaty that have been incorporated into domestic law *have the status only of domestic law*, and can be amended or repealed by later legislation. If such action were to result in breach of the treaty, there would be *no* remedy in domestic law since there would have been no violation of it.[26] The attraction of this approach is much greater certainty as to the effect that the treaty

[24] Parliament can limit prerogative powers, and the exercise of a few are subject to statutory restrictions.
[25] This particular division of powers was inherited by most former colonies of the United Kingdom, the United States being the usual exception.
[26] See Lord Bingham in *R.* v. *Lyons* [2002] UKHL 44, at 14; [2003] 1 AC 976.

has (or does not have) in domestic law. Nevertheless, in certain limited circumstances the courts will have regard to unincorporated treaties.[27]

In the case of *Miller No. 1*,[28] the UK Supreme Court considered whether Ministers acting under the prerogative could lawfully give a formal notice of withdrawal from the European Union without prior legislation being enacted by Parliament to amend the European Communities Act 1972, which gave effect to the EU treaties in UK law. Two constitutional principles were at issue: the first, that the conduct of the UK's foreign relations is part of the executive's prerogative power; and the second that, unless permitted by primary legislation, the prerogative power does not enable Ministers to change statute law or common law.[29] The majority of the Court decided that legislation was required to amend the 1972 Act, given the particular circumstances and nature of that Act.

UK Constitutional Practice

The various methods by which treaties may be incorporated into domestic law can perhaps be better understood by an explanation of the constitutional practice of the United Kingdom. The treaty-making power of the Crown is exercised by the Secretary of State for Foreign, Commonwealth and Development Affairs (foreign minister). Although there was no requirement for Parliament to consent to the Crown entering into a treaty, under constitutional practice (now changed for the United Kingdom) a treaty that was subject to ratification or analogous procedure (known as the 'Ponsonby Rule') was 'laid before' (notified to) Parliament, with a short explanatory memorandum, for twenty-one days while Parliament was sitting. That was so that Parliament could be informed of the treaty. The Ponsonby Rule (so-called after the Parliamentary Secretary for Foreign Affairs when it was introduced in 1924), is described in some detail as all, or some, of the Rule may still be used in existing as well as former UK overseas territories.

Parliament could debate a treaty if it wished, but this seldom happened unless legislation was needed or the treaty was of major political importance, in which case the government would normally arrange for a debate anyway.[30] If a parliamentary select committee needed more than twenty-one days to inquire into a particular

[27] See S. Fatima, 'The Domestic Application of International Law in British Courts', in Bradley (n. 13), 485–500. See also p. 200.

[28] *R. (on the application of Miller and another)* v. *Secretary of State for Exiting the European Union* [2017] UKSC 5, UK Supreme Court.

[29] See Fatima (n. 27), 489–490.

[30] See also C. Warbrick, 'Current Developments, Public International Law, I. Treaties', ICLQ 49 (2000) 944–953; and J. Harrington, 'Scrutiny and Approval: the Role of Westminster-style Parliaments in Treaty-making', ICLQ 55 (2006) 121–160, 126–131.

treaty, the government would usually agree to this. Extra-parliamentary consultations were also held.[31] This informal procedure worked well. But in the United Kingdom, the Ponsonby Rule was replaced by the Constitutional Reform and Governance Act 2010.[32]

Under a dualist constitution, no provisions of a treaty can have effect in domestic law without specific legislation. In the UK, this can take four main forms:

(1) An Act of Parliament for the purpose of incorporating the treaty into the law of the United Kingdom. The text of the whole or part[33] of the treaty may be scheduled to the Act, which will provide that those provisions of the treaty set out in the schedule 'shall have the force of law in the United Kingdom'. But even when treaty provisions are scheduled to an Act, they will not necessarily become part of the law. For example, the Geneva Conventions Act 1957, as amended by the Geneva Conventions (Amendment) Act 1995, has annexed to it the (complete) text of the four Geneva Conventions of 1949 and the two Additional Protocols of 1977, but the Act does not provide that their provisions shall have the force of law in the United Kingdom.[34] The main purpose of the Act is to enable 'grave breaches' of the Conventions to be prosecuted, and to protect the Red Cross emblem. Scheduling the texts therefore enables those provisions to be seen in context. The other provisions of the Conventions are implemented by administrative means, including disciplinary regulations of the armed forces. The 1995 Act provides that, if the United Kingdom makes any reservations or declarations when ratifying either of the two Additional Protocols, an Order in Council may certify that they have been made and that the scheduled Protocol shall be interpreted subject to, and in accordance with, such reservations and declarations.[35]

In contrast, none of the treaty may be scheduled. Instead, the Act makes such changes to the law as are necessary to give effect to the treaty.[36] The Act may, for example, simply authorise expenditure required by the treaty. In such cases, it may or may not declare that its purpose is to give effect to the treaty. This can have implications for the interpretation of the legislation (see below).

[31] See Harrington (n. 30), 130.

[32] See J. Barrett, 'The United Kingdom and Parliamentary Scrutiny of Treaties: Recent Reforms', ICLQ 60 (2011) 225–245.

[33] Compare the Diplomatic Privileges Act 1964 (part of the treaty) with the Consular Relations Act 1968 (whole of the treaty). See also section 50 of, and Schedule 8 to, the International Criminal Court Act 2001, which set out the definitions of the offences as in the Rome Statute.

[34] See *Cheng* v. *Conn, Inspector of Taxes* [1968] 1 AER 779; and P. Rowe and M. A. Meyer, 'The Geneva Conventions (Amendment) Act 1995: A Generally Minimalist Approach', ICLQ 45 (1996) 476–484.

[35] Section 4(7), inserting new section 7(3) in the 1957 Act. An Order was made: SI 1998 No. 1754.

[36] See the State Immunity Act 1978, which mainly implements the CoE Convention on State Immunity 1972: 1495 UNTS 182 No. 25699; 11 ILM (1972) 470; UKTS (1979) No. 74.

Alternatively, an Act may require that rules made under it conform to a treaty.[37]

(2) An Act of Parliament conferring all the powers necessary to carry out obligations under existing or future treaties.[38] Generally, bilateral air services agreements can be concluded without the need each time for fresh legislation since existing legislation, both primary and secondary, is sufficient to implement the agreements. But it may not be obvious that this is the reason for an Act or part of it.[39]

(3) An Act of Parliament that provides a framework within which secondary legislation can be made to give effect to a certain category of treaty, often bilateral. The Act can:

(a) authorise the Crown to make *secondary legislation making the text of the treaty part of domestic law*. This is usually done by a statutory instrument to which the text of the treaty is attached. Such legislation is made, for example, for bilateral double taxation conventions[40] and certain social security conventions;[41] or

(b) authorise the Crown to make *secondary legislation to implement obligations imposed by certain categories of treaty*. The treaty is not attached to the secondary legislation. Instead, its provisions are transformed into the language of the Act, and, if necessary, elaborated. Typical of this method is the International Organisations Act 1968, under which Orders in Council are made to give effect to treaties conferring privileges and immunities on international organisations and tribunals, and persons connected with them.[42] The Orders have to be approved, in draft, by both Houses of Parliament (affirmative resolution procedure). This requires a short debate in each House; or

(c) enact in primary legislation all the provisions necessary for the implementation of a treaty in domestic law, and *authorise the Crown by statutory instrument to designate countries to which those provisions should be applied*, together with any adaptations. This is the case, for example, in respect of extradition treaties.[43]

(4) Orders on some matters may not be subject to any parliamentary procedure, particularly if, unlike diplomatic immunity, they do not have the effect of restricting the rights of the ordinary citizen. They cannot be revoked except by

[37] See Section 2 Asylum and Immigration Appeals Act 1993, which requires that the Immigration Rules be consistent with the Refugees Convention 1951, as amended by the 1967 Protocol.

[38] See also para. (c) below.

[39] See *Salomon* v. *Commissioner of Customs and Excise* [1967] 2 QB 116, at 127 (C).

[40] See Section 2 Taxation (International and Other Provisions) Act 2010; and, e.g., SI 2013/3143 (Netherlands).

[41] See Section 179 Social Security Administration Act 1992; and, e.g., SI 2020/1597 (Norway).

[42] See the Tribunal for the Law of the Sea (Immunities and Privileges) Order 1996, SI 1996/272.

[43] See Section 193 Extradition Act 2003.

another Order or by Act of Parliament. The United Nations Act 1946 has only one (short) substantive section, which empowers the Crown to make such provision in Orders in Council as are 'necessary or expedient' to enable measures adopted by the United Nations Security Council to be effectively applied. The power is used extensively to implement measures adopted by the Security Council under chapter VII of the UN Charter, which can include economic and other sanctions, the establishment of ad hoc international criminal tribunals, and associated privileges and immunities. In 1998 an Order was made to enable a Scottish court to hold a trial in the Netherlands of the two Libyans accused of the sabotage of flight PA 103 at Lockerbie in 1988.[44] Although the Orders are notified to Parliament, they are not subject to any parliamentary procedure, and so can be made and brought into effect quickly, if necessary on the day they are made. This is important for the effectiveness of a sanctions regime.

Since treaties are not supreme law in the United Kingdom, even if they have been incorporated, Parliament, being the supreme body in the British Constitution, can enact legislation that is inconsistent with treaty obligations.[45] There have been instances of UK legislation being held by the European Court of Human Rights to be in breach of the ECHR.[46] Parliament has in such cases passed new or amending legislation. It has no *constitutional* duty to do so, but under Article 46(1) of the ECHR, as amended, the United Kingdom has an obligation in international law to comply with the judgments in cases to which it is a party. Provisions of the ECHR have now effectively been incorporated into the law of the United Kingdom by the Human Rights Act 1998.[47] The Act requires courts and public bodies to apply existing and future legislation as far as possible in a way that is compatible with rights under the ECHR. Under section 4, if a court determines that a legislative provision is incompatible with such a right, it may make a 'declaration of incompatibility'.[48] Under section 10, subsidiary legislation may then be made (there is no legal obligation on Parliament to do so) to remove the incompatibility, including an incompatibility determined by the European Court of Human Rights. Section 19 requires a bill for an Act of Parliament to be accompanied by a Statement regarding its compatibility with rights under the ECHR.

44 The High Court of Justiciary (Proceedings in the Netherlands) (United Nations) Order 1998, SI 1998/2251, implementing Security Council Resolution 1192 (1998). See also UN Doc. S/1998/795, which includes the draft of the Order and the Netherlands–UK Agreement.

45 See *R. (Norris)* v. *Home Secretary* [2006] EWHC (Admin) 280.

46 Amended by subsequent Protocols: consolidated text at CoE website.

47 Text also in 38 ILM (1999) 464. See also Lord Bingham in *R. (Al-Skeini)* v. *Secretary of State for Defence* [2007] UKHL 26; [2008] 1 AC 153 (HL).

48 See *Bellinger* v. *Bellinger* [2003] UKHL 21, Lord Nicholls, paras. 50–55; [2003] AC 467; *Smith* v. *Scott* [2007] SCLR 268. A declaration or determination of incompatibility (by the UK court or the ECtHR) does not affect the validity or operation of the law. It is for Parliament to decide how to address the issue.

Interpretation and Application of Treaties by UK Courts

Despite the dualist system, international law has been increasingly applied by the UK courts. In interpreting and applying treaties, they have developed certain principles alleviating some of the apparent strictness of dualism, which might tentatively be outlined as follows:[49]

(1) If the language of legislation implementing a treaty is unambiguous, the courts should not look behind the legislation at an unincorporated treaty.[50]
(2) If the language is ambiguous, the court will look at the treaty, if necessary all of it. It will do this even if the legislation does not mention the treaty.[51]
(3) Ambiguous legislation will be interpreted in the way that is most consistent with the international obligations of the United Kingdom, including unincorporated treaties (such as the ECHR even before it was incorporated).[52]
(4) This extends also to a presumption (again only in the case of ambiguous legislation) that primary and secondary legislation is to be construed in a manner consistent with fundamental rights, the nature and scope of which may be affected by customary international law or unincorporated treaties.[53]
(5) Insofar as a treaty is to be interpreted (if, for example, it has been incorporated by attaching all or part of it to legislation), the courts should interpret it according to the rules of international law, in particular Articles 31–33 VCLT (even though the Convention has not been incorporated).[54]

But the position is very fluid and the case law is evolving. One particular area of uncertainty concerns the courts' approach to the way in which a government policy or a government decision takes account of unincorporated treaties.[55]

Scotland

The arrangements for Scotland are a helpful illustration of the handling of treaties by the devolved administrations. Under the Scotland Act 1998, Ministers of the Scottish government may enjoy competence in relation to the observation or implementation of

[49] For fuller analysis, see Fatima (n. 27), 485–500; S. Fatima, *International Law and Foreign Affairs in English Courts* (Hart Publishing, Oxford and Portland, Oregon 2023).
[50] *Salomon* (n. 39), 143–144. And, if the text of the statute is narrower than that of the treaty to which it purports to give effect, the court must follow the statute: *R. (Pepushi)* v. *Crown Prosecution Service* [2004] EWHC (Admin) 798, para. 31.
[51] See *Salomon* (n. 39), 143; *The Jade* [1976] 1 AER 920.
[52] See *Salomon* (n. 39), 144; *Garland* v. *British Rail Engineering* [1983] 2 AC 751, 771. See also *Shaw*, 129–137.
[53] *R. (Al-Saadoon)* v. *Secretary of State for Defence* [2016] EWCA Civ 811, paras. 198–200, but note the limitations.
[54] See *Basfar* v. *Wong* [2022] UKSC 20, para. 16; *Gardiner*, 144–149.
[55] See *Heathrow Airport Ltd and others* v. *Her Majesty's Treasury* [2021] EWCA Civ 783; *R. (Friends of the Earth)* v. *Secretary of State for Transport (Heathrow Airport)* [2020] UKSC 52.

the United Kingdom's treaty obligations on matters which have been devolved to Scotland or where powers have been conferred on Scottish Ministers. Although the UK Parliament retains the power to legislate to implement international obligations on any subject, whether it or the Scottish Parliament should enact implementing legislation for Scotland is, in practice, a matter for consultation in each case between the UK government and the Scottish Government and Scottish Parliament. For this purpose the UK Parliament will not normally, without the consent of the relevant devolved legislature, legislate with regard to devolved matters.[56] Scotland may not, however, legislate for the implementation of international conventions in a manner which is outside the competence of the Scottish Parliament.[57]

There is also a power in the Scotland Act for the Secretary of State to intervene to prohibit Scottish Parliament legislation being submitted for Royal Assent if the Secretary of State has reasonable grounds to believe that the Bill contains provisions which would be incompatible with any international obligations.[58] Similarly, if the Secretary of State has reasonable grounds to believe that any proposed action by a member of the Scottish government would be incompatible with an international obligation, the Secretary of State has the power to direct that such action is not taken. There is a similar power to require that action is taken by a member of the Scottish government to give effect to an international obligation.[59] These powers have not been used to date.

Guidelines on international relations, in the form of a 'concordat', have been drawn up by the Foreign, Commonwealth and Development Office (FCDO) and the Scottish and other administrations.[60]

Other Dualist States[61]

Naturally, those Commonwealth states that had been under the sovereignty of the United Kingdom, which is almost all of the other fifty-five such states, have constitutions that embody the dualist approach. Even when the constitutions have been changed, most still follow the same approach.[62] The South African Constitution, however, has

[56] In relation to Scotland, see section 28(8) Scotland Act 1998 and Devolution Guidance Note 10 at: https://assets.publishing.service.gov.uk/government/uploads/system/uploads/attachment_data/file/60985/post-devolution-primary-scotland.pdf.

[57] See *Reference – UN Convention on the Rights of the Child (Incorporation) (Scotland) Bill etc.* [2021] UKSC 42, UK Supreme Court.

[58] Section 35 Scotland Act 1998. [59] Section 58 Scotland Act 1998.

[60] See D, Concordat on International Relations (under Memorandum of Understanding and Supplementary Agreements), October 2013, at: https://assets.publishing.service.gov.uk/government/uploads/system/uploads/attachment_data/file/316157/MoU_between_the_UK_and_the_Devolved_Administrations.pdf.

[61] See B. Opeskin, 'Constitutional Modelling: The Domestic Effect of International Law in Commonwealth Countries: Part I', *Public Law* (2000) 607–626, 622–626; M. Gobbi, 'Drafting Techniques for Implementing Treaties in New Zealand', *Statute Law Review* (2000) 71–103.

[62] For an account of how two Commonwealth federal states (Australia and Canada) deal with treaties, see Harrington (n. 30), 131–141. On Canada, see also Hollis *et al.* (n. 9), 91–122.

both monist and dualist elements, which are uneasy bedfellows. It provides that ratification of (important) treaties needs the approval of the National Assembly and the National Council of the Provinces. A treaty forms part of the law of South Africa if it is 'self-executing' and is not inconsistent with the Constitution or an Act.[63] Applying this test may not be easy. In many cases, implementing legislation will also be needed. Other treaties become part of the law only when legislation makes them so. Denmark,[64] other Nordic states and Israel[65] also follow a dualist approach.

Is One Approach Better?

This is a question fraught with danger. One can argue long about the relative merits of the monist and dualist approaches. The workings of dualist systems may, from the above account, seem to be more complicated. This may be because dualist procedure has been described in greater detail. A value of dualism is greater certainty and precision. In a dualist system, whether a treaty is part of domestic law depends on whether legislation has been made to make it so: if no legislation has been made, it is not part of domestic law. This puts a burden on government to decide, before it ratifies, whether legislation will be needed, which requires a detailed examination of the treaty. Thus the onus is on government and parliament, rather than the citizen or the courts, to determine how far the treaty is to be part of domestic law. Under a monist system it may be many years after the treaty entered into force for a state that such a determination is made, and then by a court deciding, usually on an application by a citizen, if a provision is self-executing. Of course, the advantages of dualism will be lost if the government is not diligent in vetting treaties before ratification, but in UK practice that is unlikely.

The United States

The way that treaties are dealt with under the Constitution of the United States embodies aspects of both dualist and monist approaches, and so has rightly been described as 'remarkably complex'.[66] Any non-American lawyer who has to deal with the status of a treaty in US law would be well advised to consult a good New York or

63 Article 231. See Blaustein and Flanz (n. 9). See also Hollis *et al.* (n. 9), 581–626.

64 F. G. Jacobs and Roberts (eds.), *The Effect of Treaties in Domestic Law* (Sweet & Maxwell, London 1987), 29–38.

65 Hollis *et al.* (n. 9), 386–413.

66 J. Jackson, in Jacobs and Roberts (n. 64), 141–169. See also J. Galbraith, 'International Agreements and US Foreign Relations Law', in Bradley (n. 13), 157–171; C. A. Bradley, *International Law in the US Legal System* (2nd ed., Oxford University Press, New York 2015); L. Henkin, *Foreign Affairs and the US Constitution* (2nd ed., Clarendon Press, Oxford 1996); S. A. Riesenfeld and F. M. Abbott, *Parliamentary Participation in the Making and Operation of Treaties* (Martinus Nihoff, Dordrecht 1994), 205–328; Hollis *et al.* (n. 9), 765–822.

Washington DC law firm. Under Article II, section 2(2) of the Constitution the president may ratify a 'Treaty' only with the 'Advice and Consent' of the Senate, signified by the affirmative vote of two-thirds of the members present. (Although only the president can ratify a treaty, this Senate process is sometimes misleadingly referred to as 'ratification'.) These days, the Senate will sometimes withhold its approval. In the case of universal treaties, between 1993 and 2000 the Senate rejected some 25 per cent.[67]

Although the Constitution mentions only one type of international agreement ('a Treaty'), from its earliest days an alternative form has been employed by the US government in order to avoid the problems inherent in obtaining Senate approval. They are termed 'executive agreements'. This is because there is sufficient authority for the executive to conclude such agreements; they do not have to be submitted to the Senate. But they are regarded by both the US government and other states as treaties for the purposes of *international law*.[68] Unless otherwise indicated, a reference in the following pages to a 'treaty' includes an executive agreement; and a reference to a 'Treaty' (with a capital 'T') is only to a treaty that requires the approval of the Senate before the president can ratify it.

Most treaties entered into by the United States have been, and still are, executive agreements, and can be broken down roughly into four categories:[69]

(1) those which have prior authorisation from Congress;
(2) those subsequently authorised by Congress;
(3) those entered into by the president in exercise of his executive power (a controversial and ill-defined area); and
(4) those authorised by a previous Treaty or executive agreement.

Under a federal statute, known as the 'Case Act',[70] all executive agreements have to be notified to Congress within sixty days of entry into force, and published annually.

Treaties as the Law of the Land

Under Article VI, section 2 of the Constitution all treaties are the 'supreme law of the land'. This has been interpreted by the Supreme Court as applying also to executive agreements that have been authorised by Congress. The provision is often, and misleadingly, described as making treaties 'self-executing'. By this is meant that the treaty,

[67] D. Sloss, 'International Agreements and the Political Safeguards of Federalism', *Stanford Law Review* 55 (2003) 1984–1985.

[68] For a full account of 'executive agreements', see O. A. Hathaway, C. A. Bradley and J. Goldsmith, 'The Failed Transparency Regime for Executive Agreements: An Empirical and Normative Analysis', *Harvard Law Review* 134(2) (2020) 629–725.

[69] See generally Bradley (n. 66), 78–93.

[70] US Code, Title 1, §112b, 11 ILM (1972) 1117; 18 ILM (1979) 82; Hollis *et al.* (n. 9), 798–799; Galbraith (n. 66), 182.

once it has entered into force, is directly applicable as if it were an Act of Congress. Contrary to what is sometimes asserted, whether a particular provision is self-executing does not depend on whether it is in a treaty or an executive agreement.[71] The concept has led inevitably to considerable confusion and uncertainty, since there is no sure method for determining whether a provision is or is not self-executing. The matter has ultimately to be decided *in each case* by the US courts. There is now considerable jurisprudence, but it is not easy, even for American lawyers, to advise whether a particular provision is self-executing. The crucial factor is the text of the treaty or executive agreement, although the intention of the parties will also be given weight. In some cases, the other party to a treaty may have to intervene in legal proceedings in the United States to protect its position. However, a treaty will not be self-executing if it clearly envisages implementing legislation. But that is the exception; usually it is necessary to consider various factors, such as language and purpose, the specific circumstances, the nature of the obligations, and the implications of permitting a private right of action without the need for legislation.

Hierarchy of Norms

If a treaty or executive agreement is part of the law of the land, it may come into conflict with US domestic law. Whenever possible the courts will seek to reconcile the two, but that is not always feasible. When this happens the residuary rules are as follows:

(1) Treaties prevail over common law.
(2) Treaties prevail over state law.
(3) The Constitution prevails over *all* treaties. This rule may, in part, have led in recent years to the Senate requiring the president to attach a reservation when ratifying certain human rights treaties to the effect that:

> Nothing in the treaty requires or authorises legislation or other action by the United States of America prohibited by the Constitution of the United States as interpreted by the United States.

(4) In the case of a conflict between a treaty and an Act of Congress, the later in time prevails.[72] However, there is still considerable uncertainty over whether a later executive agreement prevails. The judicial decisions do not give a clear guide,

[71] In some cases, the United States has made a declaration that a treaty is 'non-self-executing'. See *UN Multilateral Treaties*, chapters IV.2 (Racial Discrimination), IV.4 (ICCPR) and IV.9 (Torture); D. Sloss, 'The Domestication of International Human Rights: Non-Self-executing Declarations and Human Rights Treaties', *Yale Journal of International Law* (1999) 129–221. See Hollis *et al.* (n. 9), 798–799; D. B. Hollis and C. M. Vázquez, 'Treaty Self-Execution as "Foreign" Foreign Relations Law', in Bradley (n. 13), 467–484, 468–471.

[72] For useful examples, see D. Vogts, 'The United States and its Treaties: Observance and Breach', AJIL (2001) 313–334, 319–320.

though it is probably fair to say that, generally, an executive agreement concluded in exercise of the executive power of the president will not prevail only over a prior Act of Congress.

Interpretation of Treaties by US Courts

When a court in the United States is called upon to interpret a treaty, it sometimes has regard less to the text and more to the intention of the parties. The object and purpose is looked at closely (in this, a US court follows a similar approach to that which it adopts for the interpretation of legislation, where the 'legislative history' may be examined in depth). The court will give weight to an interpretation given by the US government in *amicus curiae* briefs[73] and, when applicable, to any understanding expressed by the Senate when giving its advice and consent.

Implementation by the Federal States of the United States

The performance of treaties by federal states can give rise to special problems. Although Article 29 provides that, unless there is a different intention, a treaty is binding upon each party in respect of its entire territory, it may be difficult for a federal government to ensure that a treaty is fully implemented in all the constituent units. This may be because under a federal constitution certain functions, such as taxation and criminal justice, are often shared with state bodies. If they have to legislate, there could be delays or even obstruction. The federal constitution may therefore provide for such matters to be vested exclusively in the federal government when powers have to be exercised in performance of a treaty obligation; or, under a monist-type constitution, a treaty once ratified may override inconsistent state law. It may be partly for this reason that human rights treaties are submitted to the US Senate, so that once they have eventually been approved by it, and have entered into force for the United States, they clearly prevail over state law.

Although, in principle, executive agreements also override state law, in practice it is not always easy for the US government to convince state governments and legislatures that they are obliged to comply with them.[74] This happens most frequently with provisions for exemption from taxes. The problem is not caused by the nature of the instrument requiring action by the states, but by the jealous guarding by those states of what they see as their rights. It is due to such problems that in the UK–US Air

[73] In the United States, a written statement filed with the court by someone who is not a party to the case but has an interest in the outcome and wishes to influence the court's decision.

[74] For some good examples, see Higgins (n. 4), 552–558.

Services Agreement 1977 ('Bermuda 2') (which was an executive agreement) the obligation to exempt airlines from dues and taxes was limited to 'best efforts'.[75] However, the award in the *UK–US Heathrow User Charges* Arbitration, 1988–94, invested this formula, at least in respect of aircraft user charges, with rather more substance than perhaps either state had intended.[76]

75 1079 UNTS 21 No. 16509; UKTS (1977) No. 76. See Article 8(5).

76 (1994) 102 ILR 215, 290–295, Article 10.

11

Territorial Application

It comes with the territory.[1]

Article 29 of the Convention provides for a flexible approach to territorial scope:

> Unless a different intention appears from the treaty or is otherwise established, a treaty is binding upon each party in respect of its entire territory.

Because of its very nature, in order to be effective, a treaty such as the UN Charter has to apply to all the territory of the parties. Other treaties will, by their terms, identify explicitly or by necessary implication the territory of the parties to which they relate.[2] The relationship between jurisdiction and territoriality is a complex one. The proviso at the start of Article 29 ('unless a different intention appears from the treaty or is otherwise established') is broad enough to allow the parties to establish the extraterritorial application of a treaty if they so intend. But in itself Article 29 neither supports nor undermines extraterritoriality.[3]

Some treaties clearly apply to the activities of a party or its nationals outside its territory. A party to the Antarctic Treaty 1959,[4] which applies to the area south of 60° S latitude, is required to apply that treaty to its nationals in that area. But even that treaty and its sister treaties, as well as many other treaties, have to have legal force also in the metropolitan territory of the parties. The Antarctic Treaty Environmental Protocol 1991[5] applies to the Antarctic Treaty area, but requires controls over the organisation of Antarctic expeditions to be exercised in the territory of a party. In fact, all treaties will require some action within the territory of the parties, though not always legislation.

The European Convention on Human Rights 1950[6] protects the rights of everyone within the territory of a party or 'subject to its jurisdiction', thus including persons who

[1] Arthur Miller, *Death of a Salesman* (1949), 'Requiem'.

[2] See Article 27 of the CoE Convention on Extradition 1957: 359 UNTS 273 No. 5146; UKTS (1991) No. 97.

[3] S. Karagiannis, 'The Relationship(s) between Treaties and Territory', in *Hollis, Oxford Guide*, 309–335, 327.

[4] 402 UNTS 71 No. 5778; UKTS (1961) No. 97; www.ats.aq. Some of the parties to the treaty have territory within the area, but their sovereignty is not necessarily recognised by other parties, or by non-parties: see *Aust Handbook*, 328 *et seq*.

[5] 30 ILM (1991) 1460; UKTS (1999) No. 6; [1998] ATS 6; www.ats.aq.

[6] Amended by subsequent Protocols: consolidated text at www.echr.coe.int/Pages/home.aspx?p=basictexts&c.

are not nationals of the party but are within its jurisdiction. This has been interpreted, for example, to include cases where a party 'exercises effective control of an area outside its national territory'[7] or where it exercises some of the 'public powers normally to be exercised by a sovereign government'.[8] Under the ECHR, a state party may also be accountable for acts performed through its agents operating, whether lawfully or unlawfully, in the territory of another state. This is potentially wide enough to include members of a state's armed forces or its diplomats.[9]

'Territory' – though not defined in the VCLT – embraces all the land, internal waters and territorial sea, and the airspace above them, over which a party has sovereignty.[10] Unless it appears otherwise from the treaty, references to territory do not include the continental shelf, exclusive economic zone or fishery zones, over which a state has no sovereignty but does have certain sovereign rights.[11]

In the absence of an express definition or other contrary intention, the territory thus comprises the metropolitan territory of a state and any other territory under its sovereignty. It is common these days, however, in certain types of bilateral agreement such as trade agreements, for the parties to provide a definition of 'territory', so as to avoid any ambiguity. Hence, the Japan–Australia Free Trade Agreement 2015 defines the 'Area' as, for Australia:

> the Commonwealth of Australia:
>
> (A) excluding all external territories other than the Territory of Norfolk Island, the Territory of Christmas Island, the Territory of Cocos (Keeling) Islands, the Territory of Ashmore and Cartier Islands, the Territory of Heard Island and McDonald Islands, and the Coral Sea Islands Territory; and
>
> (B) Australia's territorial sea, contiguous zone, exclusive economic zone and continental shelf, over which Australia exercises sovereign rights or jurisdiction in accordance with international law.[12]

Similarly, the UK–Australia Free Trade Agreement defines the territory of the United Kingdom as:

> for the United Kingdom:
>
> (i) the territory of the United Kingdom of Great Britain and Northern Ireland including its territorial sea and airspace;

7 *Loizidou* v. *Turkey (Preliminary Objections)*, ECHR Pubs. Series A, Vol. 310 (1995), at para. 62; (1995) 20 EHRR 99; 103 ILR 621.

8 *Al-Skeini and others* v. *United Kingdom*, App. No. 55721/07, [2011] ECHR 55721/07, at para. 149, with a reference to the 'exceptional circumstances'.

9 See Karagiannis (n. 3), 334.

10 The ILC Commentary on the Convention notes that the expression 'entire territory of each party' includes 'all the land and appurtenant territorial waters and air space which constitute the territory of the State': YBILC (1966) vol. II, 213, para. (3).

11 See *Villiger*, 392.

12 Article 1.2(d), Japan–Australia Economic Partnership Agreement 2014: [2015] ATS 2.

(ii) all the areas beyond the territorial sea of the United Kingdom, including the sea-bed and subsoil of those areas, over which the United Kingdom may exercise sovereign rights or jurisdiction in accordance with international law;
(iii) the Bailiwicks of Guernsey and Jersey and the Isle of Man (including their airspace and the territorial sea adjacent to them), territories for whose international relations the United Kingdom is responsible, as regards [specified chapters];
(iv) any territory for whose international relations the United Kingdom is responsible and to which this Agreement is extended in accordance with Article 32.4 (Territorial Extension – Final Provisions).[13]

There are a number of things to note in these provisions: first, the way in which territorial sea, airspace and areas beyond the territorial sea are dealt with; second, the importance of including the phrase 'in accordance with international law' – it is generally not sufficient to have a definition which allows a party to define these areas only with reference to their domestic law;[14] third, the express inclusion (and exclusion) of certain non-metropolitan territories; and fourth, in relation to the UK definition, the express provision allowing further extension of the Agreement to such territories subject to a specified procedure.[15]

Non-metropolitan territories, which were previously referred to as 'dependent territories' or 'dependencies', are today generally called 'overseas territories'.[16] In treaties, as above, they are often referred to as 'territories for the international relations of which a state is responsible', or similar. Whether the territory of a state is treated as metropolitan or overseas is a matter for the constitution of the state. Under the French Constitution, there are some *départements* of France that are thousands of kilometres from metropolitan France. In contrast, the British territories of the Channel Islands and the Isle of Man, though not that far from the UK mainland, are not actually part of the United Kingdom.

It is sometimes implicit in the terms of a treaty that it applies only to the metropolitan territory. The Channel Tunnel Treaty (France–United Kingdom) 1986 can, for obvious geographical reasons, apply only to the metropolitan territory of the two states.[17] On the other hand, a treaty may apply only to an overseas territory or territories. The express scope of the Agreement establishing the South Pacific Commission 1947 (now the Pacific Community) is such that it applies only to the South Pacific territories of the parties.[18] The area of application of CCAMLR 1980 is

13 Article 1.4, UK–Australia Free Trade Agreement 2021: [2022] ATNIF 3; UK Country Series, Australia (2022) No. 1.

14 In the Japan–Australia Agreement (n. 12), the 'Area' is defined in respect of Japan as: 'the territory of Japan, and all the area beyond its territorial sea, including the sea-bed and subsoil thereof, over which Japan exercises sovereign rights or jurisdiction *in accordance with international law and the laws and regulations of Japan*'. In addition, at the end of the respective definitions, there is a Note which states: 'Nothing in this subparagraph shall affect the rights and obligations of the Parties under international law, including those under the United Nations Convention on the Law of the Sea done at Montego Bay on 10 December 1982.'

15 On these last two points, see further under 'Territorial extension clauses' below.

16 See *Oppenheim*, 275, paras. 84 *et seq.*

17 1497 UNTS 335 No. 25792; UKTS (1992) No. 15.

18 97 UNTS 227 No. 1352; UKTS (1952) No. 21. See Article II.

defined in a way that covers the Antarctic and sub-Antarctic territories of the parties.[19] Even though Guadeloupe is a *département* of France, the France–UK Agreement on Maritime Delimitation concerning Montserrat and Guadeloupe 1996,[20] regarding the delimitation of the two maritime areas in the Caribbean, naturally does not apply to territory in Europe of the two states.[21]

Today, most multilateral treaties will be silent as to their territorial scope. This is not usually a problem unless a party has overseas territories and the content of the treaty is capable of applying to them. Then one will need to know if the treaty does apply to them, particularly if legislation will be needed to implement it. The VCLT does not attempt to provide an answer. Article 29 merely lays down a flexible rule: a treaty is binding upon each party in respect of its entire territory, *unless a different intention appears from the treaty or is otherwise established.* That intention can be established in various ways.

Territorial Extension Clauses

Bilateral Treaties

If a bilateral treaty is silent as to its territorial scope, in principle it will extend to all the territory of the parties unless its subject matter or nature dictates otherwise. Since there is no established practice as for multilateral treaties (see below), it is therefore advisable that a bilateral treaty, which, on the face of it, could apply also to the non-metropolitan territory of a party, has an express territorial clause, as illustrated above.

Many bilateral treaties have provisions for *extending* them to overseas territories. They are typically found in treaties on matters such as double taxation, extradition, narcotic drugs, mutual legal assistance and investment protection. The UK–South Africa Agreement for the Promotion and Protection of Investments 1994 (a BIT),[22] provides that, in addition to the United Kingdom:[23]

> At the time of ratification of this Agreement, or at any time thereafter, the provisions of this Agreement may be *extended to such territories for whose international relations the Government of the United Kingdom are responsible*[24] as may be agreed between the Contracting Parties in an Exchange of Notes.[25]

[19] 1329 UNTS 71 No. 22301; 19 ILM (1980) 837; UKTS (1982) No. 48; TIAS 10240.

[20] 2084 UNTS 66 No. 36143; UKTS (1997) No. 28.

[21] See also the UK–Spain Agreement on Taxation and the Protection of Financial Interests regarding Gibraltar 2019, which applies only to Gibraltar (Chapter 4, n. 105).

[22] UKTS (1998) No. 35. [23] See p. 214 on the meaning of the 'United Kingdom'.

[24] The government of the United Kingdom is referred to in the plural since, in strict constitutional terms, it consists only of ministers advising the monarch. But it is rather pedantic to insist on this point in treaties.

[25] See, for example, the UK–Uzbekistan Exchange of Notes 1999 (2197 UNTS 415 No. 31724; UKTS (2002) No. 16), extending to the Isle of Man and the Bailiwicks of Guernsey and Jersey the IPPA 1993 (2197 UNTS 415 No. 31724; UKTS (1994) No. 8).

Multilateral Treaties

Before the era of decolonisation, it was common to include a territorial application clause in multilateral treaties, such as Article XII of the Genocide Convention 1948, which states:

> Any Contracting Party may at any time, by notification addressed to the Secretary-General of the United Nations, *extend* the application of the present Convention to *all or any of the territories for the conduct of whose foreign relations that Contracting Party is responsible.*[26]

The emphasised words are wide enough to include territory over which a party does not have sovereignty, such as a protected state.

Alternatively, some treaties have an article under which a state could exclude all or some of its territory from their scope. Very occasionally, a relatively old multilateral treaty will provide expressly that it 'shall apply to all territories for whose international relations a contracting State is responsible, except those which are excluded by such State by written notice to the depositary of this Convention either at the time of ratification, acceptance or approval *or subsequently*'.[27] Although most clauses like this are therefore found in relatively old treaties, they demonstrate the need for any state that has overseas territories to consider whether it needs to say anything about them on ratification of any treaty, multilateral or bilateral.

From the 1960s, both types of 'colonial clause' fell out of favour, especially for treaties negotiated within the United Nations or the so-called UN specialised agencies. In contrast, treaties concluded within the (more homogeneous) Council of Europe have always included territorial application clauses. Newly independent states, and those of the then Soviet bloc, argued that such clauses were an unacceptable acknowledgement of colonialism. Therefore, other, less provocative means were adopted by which states could extend (or not) treaties to their overseas territories. As the objection to territorial extension clauses was political, other states acquiesced in this, though the clauses became more acceptable with the end of the Cold War, and with most overseas territories that wished to secure independence having achieved it.

Article 30 of the Convention on Temporary Admission 1990,[28] adopted under the auspices of the Customs Co-operation Council (since 1994, the World Customs Organization), provides that:

> (1) Any Contracting Party may, at the time of signing this Convention without reservation of ratification or of depositing its instrument of ratification or accession, *or at any time thereafter*, declare by notification given to the

[26] 78 UNTS 277 No. 1021; UKTS (1970) No. 58. For other examples, see *Blix and Emerson*, 156–162.

[27] See Article 70 of the International Centre for Settlement of Investment Disputes (ICSID) Convention 1965: 575 UNTS 159 No. 8359; 4 ILM (1965) 532; UKTS (1967) No. 25. See also the Convention on the Recovery Abroad of Maintenance 1956: 268 UNTS 3 No. 3850; UKTS (1975) No. 85, Article 12.

[28] 1762 UNTS 121 No. 30667; UKTS (1999) No. 60.

depositary that this Convention shall *extend to all or any of the territories for whose international relations it is responsible.* Such notification shall take effect three months after the date of the receipt thereof by the depositary. However, this Convention shall not apply to the territories named in the notification before this Convention has entered into force for the Contracting Party concerned.

(2) Any Contracting Party which has made a notification under paragraph 1 of this Article extending this Convention to any territory for whose international relations it is responsible may notify the depositary, under the procedure of Article 31 [denunciation] of this Convention, *that the territory in question will no longer apply this Convention.*

The drafting of this clause is somewhat ponderous, but nevertheless it has the merit of stating precisely what has to be done and its legal effect. Although some other clauses may be rather simpler, this one correctly and comprehensively reflects well-established practice, in particular that an extension can be made on or at any time after ratification, and can be changed. Such clauses are now more likely to be found in treaties on matters that involve existing domestic legislation, such as customs matters and extradition, where it cannot be assumed that overseas territories will be able to implement a treaty, or even that they will want to have it applied to them, most inhabited overseas territories now having a considerable degree of internal self-government.

Certain multilateral treaties enable parties to conclude bilateral treaties extending the treaty to all or some of the overseas territories of one or both parties.[29]

Article 22 of the UN Educational, Scientific and Cultural Organization (UNESCO) Cultural Property Convention 1970[30] requires the parties to consult their overseas territories on or before ratification with a view to securing the Convention's application to them, and to so notify the UNESCO Director-General in due course.

Article 35(8) of the ILO Constitution is unusual in that it requires members to give reasons if they do not extend an ILO Convention to one or more of their overseas territories.[31]

Transfer of an Overseas Territory

A question that has not been decided is whether a treaty that has been extended by a state to an overseas territory continues to apply to a part of the territory that is later split off to form a new, separate overseas territory of the same state, either alone or with territory taken from another overseas territory of the same state. In either case, the new territory remains an overseas territory of the same state. Different considerations would apply if the territory was transferred to another state.

[29] See, e.g., the UK–Hungary Exchange of Notes concerning the Extension of the European Convention on Extradition to Certain Dependent Territories 1995–1996: 2115 UNTS 38 No. 36781; UKTS (2000) No. 29.

[30] 823 UNTS 231 No. 11806.

[31] See www.ilo.org for the up-to-date text.

Could the principles on succession of states to treaties be applied by analogy? The situation is rather different. For example, if the part of the territory transferred had no permanent population, and the new or consolidated territory is similarly uninhabited, many treaties that had previously been extended to the territory, part of which has been transferred, might not be appropriate for the new or consolidated overseas territory. The answer may well depend on whether a declaration is made by the state concerned extending the treaty to the new overseas territory, the absence of a declaration perhaps raising a presumption that the treaties would not apply. Any other rule could lead to much uncertainty.[32]

Declaration on Signature or Ratification

When a treaty does not by its nature obviously apply to all the territory of a party, yet is silent as to its territorial scope and lacks a territorial clause, there is a well-established practice by which a state indicates to which, if any, of its overseas territories the treaty will be extended. The state makes its position clear, at the time of signature or ratification,[33] either that the treaty applies only to the metropolitan territory or that it extends also to a specified overseas territory or territories.[34] If necessary, the ratification may be extended later by means of a diplomatic note to the depositary that specifies further territories.

Unlike the case of a reservation, the purpose of a declaration regarding territorial scope is not to exclude certain provisions of the treaty, but to establish a different intention for the purposes of Article 29. That article recognises that a treaty will not be binding in respect of the entire territory of a state if a different intention appears from the treaty 'or is otherwise established'. The UN Secretary-General has long taken the view that the constant practice of certain states in respect of territorial application, and acquiescence by other states, has established a different intention for the purposes of Article 29.[35] Today, as in the past, many territories are small (some *very* small),[36] but most have internal self-government. Given their circumstances, they do not necessarily want, or need, every multilateral treaty to apply to them. One should contrast this state practice with the reservations made by federations regarding the implementation of treaties by their metropolitan political subdivisions (see below).[37]

[32] See R. v. *Secretary of State, ex parte Quark Fishing* [2005] UKHL 57, Bingham LJ, at paras. [21]–[27].

[33] Since the declaration is *not* a reservation (see p. 142), one made on signature that is subject to ratification does *not* have to be confirmed on ratification: see p. 165.

[34] For the text of two UK declarations included in instruments of accession, see BYIL 68 (1997) 478–480.

[35] *UN Depositary Practice*, paras. 284–285. In the early years of the twenty-first century, the former Head of the UN Treaty Section seems to have cast some doubt on this position: P. Kohona, 'Some Notable Developments in the Practice of the UN Secretary-General as Depositary of Multilateral Treaties', AJIL (2005) 433–450, 445–446.

[36] Pitcairn has about only forty inhabitants.

[37] See below on UK practice.

Since 1967, when expressing consent to be bound by a multilateral treaty the United Kingdom has followed a consistent practice of declaring in writing to the depositary to which, if any, of its overseas territories the treaty will extend. If it is to apply, at least for the moment, only to the metropolitan United Kingdom, the instrument of ratification will state that the treaty will apply to 'the United Kingdom of Great Britain and Northern Ireland'. That name requires a little excursion into history. It derives from the uniting in 1801 of the kingdoms of Great Britain (England, Wales and Scotland) and of Ireland,[38] the reference to 'Ireland' being changed in 1922 to 'Northern Ireland' on the independence of the rest of the island.

The government of the United Kingdom consults fully with the governments of each of its overseas territories (including the Crown Dependencies)[39] on whether a treaty should be extended to them. This process, as well as the drafting and enactment of any necessary implementing legislation for them, can be lengthy. Any such necessary implementing legislation will either be made by the United Kingdom or by the territories themselves, in the former case usually by an Order in Council extending to the territories concerned, with suitable modifications, the provisions of the Act by which the United Kingdom implemented the treaty.[40] The United Kingdom will therefore ratify the treaty either for the United Kingdom of Great Britain and Northern Ireland, or also for all or certain of its overseas territories. The extension to any overseas territories will be effective as from the date of receipt of the notification of extension by the depositary of the treaty.

When extending to a territory, and subject to its terms, any reservations or declarations made on ratification will apply to that territory, unless otherwise specified in the notification to the depositary; additional or modified reservations and declarations may also be attached.[41] However, if the original reservations or declarations were not included in the instrument of ratification but in a note accompanying it, it may be prudent to repeat the reservations or declarations (with or without any changes) in the note extending the ratification to the territory.

The UK practice is shared by other states with overseas territories, including Denmark and the Netherlands, and has not been challenged by other states or depositaries.

[38] Some assert that the term 'United Kingdom' was created by the Act for the Union of England and Scotland 1707 as the United Kingdom of Great Britain. Whoever is right, the fact is that, even today, some governments of other developed states persist in referring to the United Kingdom, wrongly, as 'Great Britain'.

[39] The Bailiwick of Guernsey, the Bailiwick of Jersey, and the Isle of Man (or, put another way, the Channel Islands and the Isle of Man).

[40] See, e.g., the Antarctic Act 1994 (Overseas Territories) Order 1995 (SI 1995 No. 490).

[41] As was the case when the United Kingdom extended the Convention on the Rights of the Child to certain of its territories (*UN Multilateral Treaties*, chapter IV.11).

In December 1999, the United Kingdom sought to ratify the Fish Stocks Agreement 1995[42] in respect of certain of its overseas territories but *not* its metropolitan territory. The United Kingdom was constrained by its then European Community (EC) obligations from ratifying in respect of its metropolitan territory until the EC and all the member states were ready to ratify en masse; the United Kingdom had earlier signed the Agreement on behalf of overseas territories before it signed on behalf of its metropolitan territory. After receiving clarification on 10 December 2001 of the reason for the somewhat unusual procedure – in particular that ratification in respect of overseas territories would be of benefit to them – the UN Secretary-General accepted the ratification as of that date, and the Agreement thereupon entered into force. The EC (now the European Union) and its member states finally ratified the Agreement two years later.[43]

The Crown Dependencies of the Isle of Man and the Channel Islands

The Isle of Man and Channel Islands, which comprise the Bailiwick of Jersey and the Bailiwick of Guernsey (which in turn comprises the jurisdictions of Guernsey, Alderney and Sark), are internally self-governing 'Dependencies' of the Crown included in the geographical area known as the 'British Islands'.[44] To distinguish them from the overseas territories (which used to be referred to as the 'Dependent Territories'), they should be referred to as the 'Crown Dependencies' (CDs).

The CDs have autonomy in their domestic affairs and each jurisdiction has its own legislative assembly, administrative, fiscal and legal system, and courts of law. The Crown, via the Privy Council, is responsible for the CDs' good government; and the UK government is responsible for their defence and international relations. The CDs work directly with UK government departments on areas of common policy; however, the UK Ministry of Justice has oversight of the UK's constitutional relationship with them and has done since 2001. (Prior to 2001 the Home Office held oversight.)

In international law the CDs are *not* recognised as sovereign states in their own right but as 'territories for which the United Kingdom is responsible'. As such they cannot sign up to international agreements under their own aegis but can have the UK's ratification of such instruments extended to them either at the point when the UK ratifies, accedes to or accepts an international agreement, or at a later date. In cases where the UK is planning to ratify a particular convention or treaty, the CDs are consulted about whether they wish to have it extended to them.

Where appropriate, a CD may be entrusted by the UK with the authority to negotiate and conclude specific international agreements themselves, as they have been, for example, in the case of Tax Information Exchange Agreements (TIEAs) and

[42] 2167 UNTS 3 No. 37924; 34 ILM (1995) 1542; UKTS (2004) No. 19.

[43] See *UN Multilateral Treaties*, chapter XXI.7, note 5 (United Kingdom). See also Kohona (n. 35), 446–447.

[44] The Interpretation Act 1978, Schedule 1.

Double Taxation Agreements (DTAs) with third countries. Any entrustment to a CD is given on the understanding that the government of the CD supplies evidence to the Ministry of Justice that the government with whom the CD is negotiating is content to conclude the treaty directly with the government of the CD, and that the UK requires the CD to submit the text of the draft treaty for approval by the UK before signature. This also applies to future proposals to negotiate or conclude amendments to any agreement text previously concluded under entrustment.

Relevant CD agreements with third countries are considered treaties by virtue of the grant of an entrustment, by the issuing of a Letter of Entrustment, from the UK to the CD in question authorising the CD to negotiate and conclude specific agreements. This fact may be referred to in the preamble of the treaty itself. The UK registers agreements concluded by CDs under entrustment under Article 102 of the UN Charter, since the UK remains responsible in international law for any obligations entered into by the CDs.

Because the UK overseas territories and the CDs do not have international legal personalities separate from the UK, it is not possible for the UK to enter into internationally legally binding agreements with them, or for overseas territories and CDs to do so among themselves, and such arrangements should take the form of an MOU.

DTAs and TIEAs concluded between the UK and individual CDs and overseas territories, or among CDs and overseas territories, are *not* treaties. These are only domestic arrangements between the UK and CDs and overseas territories and have MOU (non-legally binding) status despite being drafted using treaty terminology. The UK has, however, legislated to give effect to the terms of its DTAs with the CDs and overseas territories in exactly the same way as it gives effect, through *domestic* legislation, to double taxation treaties. So the arrangement has the force of law in the UK. There are also examples of DTAs between the UK and other states that are not treaties but non-binding instruments[45] that are given effect through domestic legislation.

Application of a Treaty to an Overseas Territory Alone

It is possible for a treaty to apply only to an overseas territory. This is more usual for bilateral treaties and can happen in two ways. The 'parent' state can become a party to the treaty solely in respect of the territory. Alternatively, the state can authorise the territory to enter into a treaty, or a category of treaties, in its own name. In the case of the United Kingdom, this is done by an 'instrument of entrustment' granted to the government of the territory. Of course, the other party can decline to deal only with the territory and, whichever the method, the parent state will remain ultimately

[45] See Chapter 3.

responsible for ensuring that the territory fully implements the treaty, and for any breach of it.

The parent state may also denounce a treaty in respect of its metropolitan territory, so leaving the extension to the overseas territory (or territories) in effect. This could happen if the treaty has been amended and the parent state wishes to become a party to the amended treaty, but its overseas territory (or territories) either does not yet have the legislation in place to implement the amended treaty, or does not want it to be extended to it (or them).

Objections to Territorial Extensions

Sometimes a contracting state objects to an extension of a treaty to an overseas territory. This is usually because of a dispute over sovereignty of the territory. Argentina regularly objects to the extension by the United Kingdom of treaties to the Falkland Islands, South Georgia and the South Sandwich Islands, and the British Antarctic Territory, to all of which Argentina asserts territorial claims. In such a case, the depositary, usually the UN Secretary-General, will circulate the text of the objection and any response.[46]

Political Subdivisions of the Metropolitan Territory

Many states, such as federations, have a constitution that divides the metropolitan territory into political subdivisions. Even when it is only the federation that can be party to treaties, their implementation may require action by the governments and legislatures of the subdivisions; yet the federation remains responsible in international law for the due performance of all treaties of which it is a party.[47] Under Article 36(1)(b) of the Vienna Convention on Consular Relations (VCCR) 1963, a person accused of a crime who is an alien must be informed of their right to communicate with a consulate of their state.[48] In the case of *Breard*,[49] a Paraguayan national arrested for murder in the US state of Virginia, the defendant was not told of this right, and was convicted and sentenced to death. On an application by Paraguay in 1998, the ICJ indicated, as a provisional measure, that the United States should take all measures at its disposal to ensure that Breard was not executed pending the Court's final decision.[50] The State Department therefore sought a stay of execution,

[46] *UN Depositary Practice*, para. 183.

[47] See, generally, B. R. Opeskin, 'Federal States in the International Legal Order', NILR (1996) 353–386; B. R. Opeskin, 'International Law and Federal States', in B. R. Opeskin and D. R. Rothwell (eds.), *International Law and Australian Federalism* (Melbourne University Press, Melbourne 1997), 1–33.

[48] 596 UNTS 261 No. 8638; UKTS (1973) No. 14; TIAS 8620.

[49] *Breard* v. *Greene*, 523 U.S. 371 (1998).

[50] *Vienna Convention on Consular Relations (Paraguay* v. *United States of America)*, Provisional Measures, Order of 9 April 1998, ICJ Reports (1998) 248; 118 ILR 1; 37 ILM (1998) 810 (ICJ) and 824 (US Supreme Court). See also AJIL (1998) 666–712; AJIL (1999) 170–174.

but the US Supreme Court declined to intervene and the execution was carried out. The case was later settled.[51]

Some treaties expressly provide that their provisions 'extend to all parts of federal States without any limitation or exception'.[52] If a treaty ratified by the Australian government requires legislation by the Australian states, and they refuse, the Australian government would still be internationally responsible.[53] There are certain methods by which these problems can be reduced: territorial clauses, federal clauses and federal reservations.

Territorial Clauses

Article 93(1) of the Convention on Contracts for the International Sale of Goods 1980[54] provides that:

> If a Contracting State has two or more territorial units in which, according to its constitution, different systems of law are applicable in relation to matters dealt with in this Convention, it may, at the time of signature, ratification, acceptance, approval or accession, declare that this Convention is to extend to all its territorial units or only to one or more of them, and may amend its declaration by submitting another declaration at any time.

When acceding to that Convention, Canada declared that it would extend it to nine of its then provinces and territories, and the following year added the other three.[55]

Where it is possible to agree on the inclusion of the clause, the above example represents the modern formula.[56] The clause is also a territorial application clause, though expressed in a way that applies also to political subdivisions of the metropolitan territory.[57] Use of the clause is mostly confined to treaties on commercial law, private law or private international law, such as those concluded within the UN Commission on International Trade Law (UNCITRAL) and the Institute for the Unification of

[51] A similar application to the ICJ was made by Germany against the United States on 2 March 1999: *LaGrand (Germany* v. *United States of America)*, Judgment, ICJ Reports (2001) 9; 40 ILM (2001) 1069; 118 ILR 37. See also *Avena and Other Mexican Nationals (Mexico* v. *United States of America)*, Judgment, ICJ Reports (2004) 12; 43 ILM (2004) 581, and, especially, the case of *Medellin*, where in 2008 the US Supreme Court refused to intervene as a judgment of the ICJ is not directly enforceable as domestic law in the courts of a US state: see *Medellin* v. *Texas*, 552 US 491 (2008), 128 S.Ct 1346 (2008), No. 06-984, 25 March 2008; and *Request for Interpretation of the Judgment of 31 March 2004 in the Case concerning Avena and Other Mexican Nationals (Mexico* v. *United States of America)*, Provisional Measures, Order of 16 July 2008, ICJ Reports (2008) 311.

[52] ICCPR 1966: 999 UNTS 171 No. 14668; 6 ILM (1967) 368; UKTS (1977) No. 6, Article 50.

[53] *R.* v. *Burgess, ex parte Henry* (1936) 55 CLR 608; *Commonwealth* v. *Tasmania (Tasman Dam case)* (1983) 158 CLR 1; 46 ALR 625; 68 ILR 266.

[54] 1489 UNTS 3 No. 25567; 19 ILM (1980) 671.

[55] See *UN Multilateral Treaties*, chapter X.10, for the Canadian declarations. Since 1 April 1999 there has been a thirteenth province, Nunavut, created from part of the Northwest Territories.

[56] For earlier examples, see Opeskin, 'Federal States in the International Legal Order' (n. 47).

[57] Australia has not extended to Western Australia the ICSID Convention 1965 (n. 27).

Private Law (UNIDROIT).[58] It reflects the fact that in a federation the subdivisions often regulate such matters. Although this clause has been criticised less than the clause that is discussed next, it has been viewed as detrimental to those treaties that depend for their effectiveness on their uniform application.

Federal Clauses

Article 34 of the UNESCO Convention concerning the Protection of the World Cultural and Natural Heritage 1972[59] provides:

> The following provisions shall apply to those State Parties to this Convention which have a federal or non-unitary constitutional system:
>
> (a) with regard to the provisions of this Convention, the implementation of which comes under the legislative jurisdiction of the federal or central legislative power, the obligations of the federal or central government shall be the same as for States Parties which are not federal States;
> (b) with regard to the provisions of this Convention, the implementation of which comes under the legislative jurisdiction of individual constituent states, countries, provinces or cantons that are not obliged by the constitutional system of the federation to take legislative measures, the federal government shall inform the competent authorities of such states, countries, provinces or cantons of the said provision, with its recommendation for their adoption.

These provisions limit the obligation of a federal state party when certain matters are outside its constitutional power. Although such clauses are not popular with unitary states, they do make it easier for federations to become parties. This is especially so if the constitution takes a dualist approach, in which treaties are not the supreme law. But they have the disadvantage of creating uncertainty as to the extent of the obligations undertaken by the federation, and can result in unequal treatment between the parties.[60] In 1999, Australia announced that it had no plans to seek federal clauses in future treaties. Instead, it would continue to make a federal statement or declaration (see below) on signature, as appropriate.[61]

Federal Reservations or Statements

It is only in the last fifty or so years that federations have sought to use reservations to deal with their problems in participating in treaties. In 1988, Canada made the

[58] See Article 40 Hague Convention on the Civil Aspects of International Child Abduction 1980: 1343 UNTS 89 No. 22514; UKTS (1986) No. 66. UNCITRAL is a UN body, but despite its name, UNIDROIT is not.
[59] 1037 UNTS 151 No. 15511; 11 ILM (1972) 1358; UKTS (1985) No. 2; TIAS 82250.
[60] For other examples, see Opeskin, 'Federal States in the International Legal Order' (n. 47), 370–374.
[61] *Review of the Treaty-making Process*, August 1999, see at: www8.austlii.edu.au/au/other/dfat/reference_documents/#sect13.

following reservation to the Espoo Convention on Transboundary Environmental Impact Assessment 1991:[62]

> In as much as under the Canadian constitutional system legislative jurisdiction in respect of environmental assessment is divided between the provinces and the Federal Government, the Government of Canada in ratifying this Convention makes a reservation in respect of proposed activities ... that fall outside of federal legislative jurisdiction exercised in respect of environmental assessment.[63] Where federal legislative power extends to the implementation of treaties (as in Australia, India and the United States),[64] a federal reservation expressed in such terms would be improper.

An alternative course is for a federation to make a statement on ratification explaining *how* the treaty will be implemented within the federal structure. In 1984, Australia replaced its federal reservation to the ICCPR with a 'Declaration':

> Australia has a federal constitutional system in which legislative, executive and judicial powers are shared or distributed between the Commonwealth and the constituent states. The implementation of the treaty throughout Australia will be effected by the Commonwealth, state and territory authorities having regard to their respective constitutional powers and arrangements concerning their exercise.[65]

Since the statement does not purport to exclude or modify the treaty in its application to the state, it is not objectionable, and the Australian government remains internationally responsible for implementation of the treaty.

Hong Kong and Macao Special Administrative Regions

Before Hong Kong was returned to China, the United Kingdom had extended many treaties to Hong Kong. The way these were dealt with on handover is described below. Section XI of Annex I to the Joint Declaration (and Article 153 of the Basic Law – the Hong Kong Special Administrative Region (HKSAR) Constitution) provides that after handover:

> The application to the HKSAR of international agreements to which the People's Republic of China is or becomes a party shall be decided by the Central People's Government, *in accordance with the circumstances and needs of the HKSAR, and after seeking the views of the HKSAR Government.*[66]

[62] 1989 UNTS 309 No. 34028; 30 ILM (1991) 802.

[63] *UN Multilateral Treaties*, chapter XXVII.4. See also the objections and notes.

[64] See also the relevant US 'understanding' on ratifying the Racial Discrimination Convention, the ICCPR and the Torture Convention (*UN Multilateral Treaties*, chapters IV.2, 4 and 9, respectively). See also pp. 217–218 on 'Political subdivisions of metropolitan territory'.

[65] *UN Multilateral Treaties*, chapter IV.4.

[66] See pp. 84–87, chapter 4: the Basic Law can be found at: www.basiclaw.gov.hk/en/index/.

The words emphasised are in recognition of the 'high degree of autonomy' to which the HKSAR is entitled under the regime established by the Joint Declaration and the Basic Law. It is also similar to the situation before handover when, in accordance with the general practice of the United Kingdom, Hong Kong was consulted about the extension of treaties. Only in an exceptional case would a treaty have been extended to Hong Kong against its objections.

The Chinese note of 20 June 1997 to the UN Secretary-General envisaged, in respect of treaties that were not listed in the note but to which China was then or would become a party, that if it were decided to apply them to the HKSAR, the Central People's Government (CPG) would separately carry out the formalities.[67] This is a reference to the above provisions of the Joint Declaration and the Basic Law, pursuant to which China may, following consultations with the HKSAR, accept the obligations of a treaty in respect of the rest of China *separately* from its acceptance on behalf of the HKSAR. For the avoidance of doubt, the note also states that no separate formalities will need to be carried out by the CPG 'with respect to treaties which fall within the category of foreign affairs or defence or which, owing to their nature and provisions, must apply to the entire territory of a State'. However, even in those areas, to the extent that implementing legislation will be needed in the HKSAR to give effect to such treaties, the HKSAR will need to be consulted in order that the legislation can be made in good time. Thus, sometimes China will postpone application to the HKSAR of a treaty until the HKSAR has enacted the necessary implementing legislation.[68] The HKSAR retains the dualist approach to giving effect to treaties in domestic law.

Occasionally, China will adhere to a treaty in respect of the HKSAR alone.[69] Where necessary, the provision of a treaty on its territorial application will provide that the treaty shall apply 'in relation to the Hong Kong Special Administrative Region of the People's Republic of China, to such region'. This makes it clear that it has no application to the rest of China.[70]

A bilateral treaty between the HKSAR and a foreign state will often be expressed to apply to the 'Hong Kong Special Administrative Region: Hong Kong Island, Kowloon and the New Territories'.[71]

[67] *UN Multilateral Treaties* (Introduction), entry for China, Note 2, para. IV.

[68] See Kohona (n. 35), 44–46.

[69] For example, the Oil Pollution Fund Protocol 1992: UKTS (1996) No. 87. Further example of treaties that are applicable to the HKSAR but not to so-called mainland China can be found at www.doj.gov.hk/en/external/treaties.html.

[70] See the UK–HKSAR Agreement for Surrender of Fugitive Offenders 1997: 2038 UNTS 71 No. 35239; UKTS (1998) No. 30. The UK government suspended the operation of the treaty on 20 July 2020, Hansard Vol. 678, Col. 1832.

[71] See Article 1(b), UK–HKSAR IPPA 1998: 2115 UNTS 84 No. 36783; UKTS (2000) No. 9.

12

Successive Treaties

> The question of conflict between treaties, or incompatibility of treaties with one another, is a complicated matter and it cannot be said that clear guidance has yet come from judicial or arbitral sources.[1]

McNair's view cited above may lead the reader to turn to Chapter 13; and it has to be said that, although the relationship between successive treaties can be immensely difficult, it does not cause daily consternation in the legal departments of foreign ministries. But since McNair wrote in 1961, the topic has gained in importance.[2] Because of the greater number and complexity of multilateral treaties, particularly on the environment, questions increasingly arise as to the relationship between successive treaties. In recent years, more has been written on the problem.[3] But it is the sort of puzzle that is difficult to study in the abstract; it can be done properly only in relation to actual treaties and real problems. This chapter will therefore concentrate more on what rules there are and practical ways of seeking to overcome future problems.

There should be no problem when the parties to both treaties – whether bilateral or multilateral – are identical. If the earlier treaty is not considered as terminated or suspended (Article 59), the earlier treaty applies only to the extent that its terms are compatible with those of the later treaty (Article 30(3)).

Problems can occur when two or more multilateral treaties deal in whole or in part with the same subject matter but the parties to them are not identical. When drafting the final clauses of a multilateral treaty, it is therefore important to consider whether anything might be said about the relationship between it and existing or future treaties

[1] *McNair*, 219, deals with the subject in only four pages, and in the context of the validity of treaties.

[2] *Sinclair*, 93–98, has a typically incisive survey of the topic. See also *Oppenheim*, 1211–1216, paras. 590–592; and the short but thought-provoking passage in *Reuter*, paras. 200–203. For a more recent examination of the question, and a useful bibliography, see J. Mus, 'Conflicts between Treaties in International Law', NILR (1998) 208–232. See also A. Boyle and C. Chinkin, *The Making of International Law* (Oxford University Press, Oxford 2007).

[3] See, e.g., P. Vigni, 'The Interaction Between the Antarctic Treaty System and the Other Relevant Conventions Applicable to the Antarctic Area: A Practical Approach versus Theoretical Doctrines', *Max Planck Yearbook of UN Law* (Kluwer Law International, The Hague 2000), 481–542, 542; J. Klabbers, 'Moribund on the Fourth of July: the Court of Justice on Prior Agreements of the Member States', *European Law Review* (2001) 187–197.

dealing with the same subject matter. Essentially, the issue is not so much about whether states can conclude a later treaty, but which obligations have priority. Fortunately, many apparent conflicts can be resolved merely by interpretation of the treaties, particularly by applying the principle that a specific rule prevails over a general rule.

As will become apparent, these questions are related to the rules on amendment of treaties, particularly Article 41 (Agreements to modify multilateral treaties between certain of the parties only). This chapter should, therefore, be read with Chapter 15. Article 58 (Suspension of the operation of a multilateral treaty by agreement between certain of the parties only) and Article 59 (Termination or suspension of the operation of a treaty implied by the conclusion of a later treaty) are also relevant.

Bilateral Treaties

Problems should not arise with successive *bilateral* treaties between the same parties, even if there is an inconsistency. With careful interpretation, it should be possible to apply both treaties. Where this is not possible, the earlier treaty will be considered as terminated or suspended in accordance with Article 59. If the obligations in a treaty between State A and State B are incompatible with the obligations which State A has to State C under an earlier treaty, the obligations under the earlier treaty will be unaffected. State A will have to try to amend or terminate one or other of the treaties, or risk being in breach of one or both of them.

In order to facilitate interpretation, and to avoid obvious conflicts between obligations, parties to bilateral treaties often include express clauses (or phrases) of the type which feature in multilateral treaties. Mention is therefore made below, in the section on multilateral treaties, of similar provisions used in the bilateral sphere.

Where a new bilateral treaty covers similar or identical ground to an earlier treaty with the same country, the best course is to make clear in the new treaty whether the previous treaty is terminated as a whole, or, if part of the earlier treaty continues to apply, which of its provisions have been terminated or amended, and which are preserved. Hence Article 17.5 of the Agreement between Australia and Uruguay on the Promotion and Protection of Investments 2019[4] provides:

> The Parties agree that the 'Agreement between Australia and Uruguay on the Promotion and Protection of Investments', signed at Punta del Este on 3 September 2001 (hereafter the 'IPPA'), will terminate on the date of entry into force of this Agreement.[5]

[4] [2019] ATNIF 12.

[5] The following paragraph, Article 17.6, states for the avoidance of doubt: 'For greater certainty, the agreement of the Parties to terminate the IPPA in paragraph 5 shall, on the date of entry into force of this Agreement, supersede the provisions for termination contained in Article 15 (Entry into force, duration and termination) of the IPPA.'

Article 19.2 of the UK–Serbia Readmission Agreement 2022[6] also has express provision, although the effect of paragraph 1 (and the relationship between paragraphs 1 and 2) is slightly uncertain:

> 1. Nothing in this Agreement shall prevent the return of a person under other formal or informal arrangements which have been agreed in writing by the parties.
> 2. This agreement supersedes and replaces all previous agreements or arrangements between the parties relating to the subject matter of this agreement.

Article 77 of the UK–Switzerland Social Security Coordination Convention 2021[7] contains provisions which, first, continue to apply the previous bilateral agreement (the 1968 Convention) to certain Crown dependencies and, second, terminate the application of the 1968 Convention to England, Scotland, Wales and Northern Ireland, subject to the continuation of certain provisions which are specified in paragraph 3.

The UK–Norway Agreement of 2020 on the Continued Application and Amendment of a prior bilateral agreement (the 1961 Convention) on the Reciprocal Recognition and Enforcement of Judgments[8] is a good example of a specific mix of provisions covering (as the title implies) continued application, amendment and scope, with a view to making the effect of the prior agreement as clear as possible. In view of the UK's exit from the European Economic Area and the European Union, it was necessary potentially to revive provisions of the 1961 Convention which had been superseded by the Lugano Convention,[9] in the event that the UK had not successfully rejoined the Lugano Convention by the time of exit. But the provisions of the 1961 Convention had to be adapted and amended accordingly.

Sometimes the parties will adopt a more general approach, such as in paragraph 2 of the following article in the 2020 Customs Cooperation Agreement between the UK and China:[10]

> 1. The provisions of this Agreement shall not affect the obligations of the Contracting Parties under any other international agreement or convention.
> 2. Notwithstanding the provisions of paragraph 1, the provisions of this Agreement shall take precedence over the provisions of any bilateral agreement on customs cooperation and mutual administrative assistance which has been concluded between the United Kingdom and the People's Republic of China prior to the date this Agreement is signed, insofar as the provisions of the latter are incompatible with those of this Agreement.

How easy it will be to interpret this type of provision depends on the particular circumstances of the treaty relationship in the specific sphere. The advantage is that, at the time of negotiating the new agreement, it may avoid a separate negotiation in

[6] UK Country Series, Serbia (2022) No. 1.
[7] UK Country Series, Switzerland (2021) No. 4.
[8] UK Country Series, Norway (2020) No. 2.
[9] Convention on Jurisdiction and the Enforcement of Judgments in Civil and Commercial Matters 1988: 1659 UNTS (1992) No. 28551; UKTS (1992) No. 53.
[10] UKTS (2022) No. 3.

relation to the details of prior agreements. There may, for example, be a concern not to reopen other (perhaps sensitive) aspects of those agreements and to focus only on new provisions. But if conflicting views emerge in the future, a solution will depend more heavily on consultation and goodwill.

Multilateral Treaties

Even relatively modern treaties can cause enormous difficulties when the original treaty is being drafted and insufficient thought is given to anticipating, and providing for, future changes. The Convention on the Establishment of an International Fund for Compensation for Oil Pollution Damage 1971[11] had to be amended by a Protocol in 1992.[12] Some of the difficulties experienced then are reflected in Article 28, which is hardly a model of lucid drafting, including as it does the following:

> (5) A State which is a party to this Protocol but is not a party to the 1971 Fund Convention shall be bound by the provisions of the 1971 Fund Convention as amended by this Protocol in relation to other parties hereto, but shall not be bound by the provisions of the 1971 Fund Convention in relation to parties thereto.
>
> (6) Any instrument of ratification, acceptance, approval or accession deposited after the entry into force of an amendment to the 1971 Fund Convention as amended by this Protocol shall be deemed to apply to the Convention *so amended, as modified by such amendment.*

Article 4 of the Implementation Agreement 1994,[13] which effectively amends UNCLOS[14] and was adopted before UNCLOS had entered into force, provides that:

> (1) After adoption of this Agreement, any instrument of ratification or formal confirmation of or accession to [UNCLOS] shall also represent consent to be bound by this Agreement.
>
> (2) No State or entity may establish its consent to be bound by this Agreement unless it has previously established or establishes at the same time its consent to be bound by [UNCLOS].

Paragraph (2) is unexceptional. But despite what it apparently says, paragraph (1) cannot bind those sixty-four states that, *before* the adoption of the Agreement, had consented to be bound by UNCLOS. It may be, however, that the opening words apply to states that consented to be bound by UNCLOS only after the adoption of the Agreement. Those that had earlier consented to be bound by UNCLOS would be bound by the Agreement only if they did so in accordance with its Article 4(3), or if they had acquiesced in the application to them of paragraph (1).

[11] 1110 UNTS 57 No. 17146; UKTS (1978) No. 95. [12] UKTS (1996) No. 87.

[13] 1836 UNTS 42 No. 31364; 33 ILM (1994) 1313; UKTS (1999) No. 82.

[14] 1833 UNTS 397 No. 31363; 21 ILM (1982) 1261; UKTS (1999) No. 81.

Article 30 of the VCLT seeks primarily to address the general problem, though not entirely satisfactorily given the developments in multilateral treaty making since 1969 (see below). Prevention being better than cure, today a multilateral treaty may contain a clause (called a 'conflict clause' by the ILC)[15] that seeks to regulate the relationship between it and another treaty or treaties. The clause may concern a prior treaty, a future treaty or any (unspecified) treaty existing or future. Although the interpretation and application of such clauses is not always simple, especially when the treaties are not adopted within the same international organisation, or are for different purposes,[16] they may be better than nothing. A number, mostly from the 1950s and 1960s, are to be found in *Blix and Emerson*. Here are some more, and mostly more recent, examples.

Express Provisions

When drafting a treaty one should always consider whether there should be a provision on its relationship to other treaties. Though sometimes unnecessary, they can still be included out of caution. Article 11(7) of the Rome Convention for the Suppression of Unlawful Acts against the Safety of Maritime Navigation 1988[17] provides that:

> With respect to the offences as defined in this Convention, the provisions of all extradition treaties and arrangements applicable between States Parties are modified as between States Parties to the extent that they are incompatible with this Convention.

The effect of this article is to deem the offences to be included in existing extradition treaties between the states parties. There would not seem to be any conflict between those treaties and the Rome Convention (see Article 30(3) of the 1969 Convention). Nevertheless, the provision has been included in later counterterrorism conventions, perhaps more for the avoidance of doubt.[18]

The Treaty Prevails over All Other Treaties, Past and Future

The prime example of this kind of clause is Article 103 of the UN Charter:

> In the event of a conflict between the obligations of the Members of the United Nations under the present Charter and their obligations under any other international agreement, their obligations under the present Charter shall prevail.

15 YBILC (1966) vol. II, 214.

16 See Article XIV Convention on International Trade in Endangered Species of Wild Flora and Fauna (CITES Convention) 1973: 993 UNTS 243 No. 14537; UKTS (1976) No. 101.

17 1678 UNTS 222 No. 29004; 27 ILM (1988) 672; UKTS (1995) No. 64; [1993] ATS 10.

18 See, e.g., Article 11(5) Convention for the Suppression of the Financing of Terrorism 1999: 2178 UNTS 229 No. 38349; 39 ILM (2000) 268; UKTS (2002) No. 28; [2002] ATS 23.

The application of Article 103 is comprehensive ('any other international agreement'). It applies to new members in respect of their existing, not just future, obligations.[19] It applies also to members with regard to their agreements with non-members, though the extent to which it affects the rights of non-members is a question of little practical importance now that virtually all states are members of the UN.

UN Charter obligations include measures imposed on members by the Security Council (UNSC) under chapter VII.[20] In Resolution 787 (1992), paragraph 13, the UNSC reaffirmed that Danube riparian states had to take necessary measures to ensure that shipping on the river did not breach the sanctions regime established by Resolutions 713 (1991) and 757 (1992), some riparian states having asserted that their obligations under the freedom of navigation provisions of the Belgrade Convention 1948[21] were not affected by the regime.

The interpretation and application of Article 103 was before the ICJ in the *Lockerbie (Libya* v. *United Kingdom)* (Provisional Measures) decision in 1992,[22] in which a crucial issue was whether the obligations of members under Resolution 748 (1992), and other chapter VII measures concerning Libya, prevailed over members' obligations under the Montreal Convention on Aircraft Sabotage 1971.[23] In 1992, the Court had decided that, in accordance with Article 103, the obligation to carry out the decisions of the Security Council prevailed over obligations under any other treaty, including the Aircraft Sabotage Convention, and therefore that prima facie the Charter obligation extended to Resolution 748. The Court did not therefore determine the issue definitively, and the proceedings carried on for another eleven years before being discontinued by consent in 2003.

In the bilateral sphere, the EU–UK Trade and Cooperation Agreement includes a specific saving for the UN Charter:[24]

[19] L. M. Goodrich, E. Hambro and A. P. Simons, *Charter of the United Nations* (3rd ed., Columbia University Press, New York 1969), 614.

[20] See also B. Simma (ed.), *The Charter of the United Nations: A Commentary* (3rd ed., Oxford University Press, Oxford 2012), 795, 1340 (obligations extend to authorisations) and 1377; and *R. (Al-Jedda)* v. *Secretary of State for Defence* [2008] 1 AC 332, in which the House of Lords held that the authorisation in UNSC Resolution 1546 (2004) to detain prevailed over obligations under Article 5 ECHR. Later, on 7 July 2011, the Grand Chamber of the ECtHR reversed the decision of the House of Lords; see *Al-Jedda* v. *United Kingdom*: App. No. 27021/08, [2011] ECHR 27021/08.

[21] 33 UNTS 181 No. 518.

[22] *Questions of Interpretation and Application of the 1971 Montreal Convention arising from the Aerial Incident at Lockerbie (Libyan Arab Jamahiriya* v. *United Kingdom)* (Provisional Measures), Order of 14 April 1992, ICJ Reports (1992) 3, at 15, paras. 39 *et seq*; 31 ILM (1992) 662, 94 ILR 478. See also the dissenting opinion of Judge Schwebel in *Lockerbie (Libya* v. *United Kingdom)* (Preliminary Objections), Judgment, ICJ Reports (1998) 9, at 71; 37 ILM (1998) 507; 117 ILR 1 and 664 (Schwebel at 61).

[23] 1974 UNTS 177 No. 14118; UKTS (1974) No. 10.

[24] UKTS (2021) No. 8; OJ L 149, 30.04.2021: Article 415.

> Nothing in Titles I to XII of this Heading or Heading Six shall be construed:
>
> . . .
>
> (c) to prevent a Party from taking any action in pursuance of its obligations under the United Nations Charter for the maintenance of international peace and security.

One can also find in this and other trade and cooperation treaties an express clause whereby states acknowledge the primacy of obligations to fulfil Security Council resolutions in specific areas, particularly non-proliferation and illicit arms trade. Hence Article 2.13.4 of the Trans-Pacific Partnership reads:[25]

> Nothing in this Article shall be construed in a manner that would require a Party to grant an export licence, or that would prevent a Party from implementing its obligations or commitments under United Nations Security Council Resolutions, as well as multilateral non-proliferation regimes, including [specified non-proliferation and export control arrangements].[26]

Since there is no international organisation comparable to the United Nations in terms of its universality, purposes and powers, it would not be possible for treaties not involving the UN to adopt a clause as extensive in effect as Article 103. Its importance is recognised by Article 30(1) VCLT, which provides that the residuary rules in Article 30 are subject to Article 103.

The Treaty Is Subordinate to an Earlier One

The express purpose of the Fish Stocks Agreement 1995 is to implement provisions of UNCLOS.[27] Article 4 of the Agreement therefore provides that:

> Nothing in this Agreement shall prejudice the rights, jurisdiction and duties of States under [UNCLOS]. This Agreement shall be interpreted and applied in the context of and in a manner consistent with the [UNCLOS].[28]

A similar, though more extensive clause can be found in the *Titanic* Agreement 2003:[29]

> Nothing in this Agreement shall prejudice the rights, jurisdiction and duties of any State under international law as reflected in the 1982 United Nations Convention on the Law of the Sea, nor the present or future claims and legal views of any State concerning the law of the sea or the future development of international law regarding underwater cultural heritage.

[25] Signed at Auckland, 4 February 2016, now included in the CPTPP, with certain provisions suspended: see New Zealand Foreign Affairs and Trade website.

[26] See similarly Article 29 EU–UK Trade and Cooperation Agreement (n. 24). This has further reference to Security Council commitments in provisions relating to trade in illicit arms (Article 766) and counter-terrorism (Article 768).

[27] See n. 14. [28] See n. 42. See also Article 44 VCLT. [29] UKTS (2019) No. 8.

The Parties Shall Not Enter into Later Inconsistent Treaties

Article 8 of the North Atlantic Treaty 1949[30] provides:

> Each Party declares that none of the international engagements now in force between it and any other of the Parties or any third State is in conflict with the provisions of this Treaty, and undertakes not to enter into any international engagement in conflict with this Treaty.

The purpose of the clause is to maintain the integrity of the regime created by and under the treaty. It therefore prohibits parties from entering into any kind of inconsistent later treaties, whether bilateral or multilateral, with another party or a third party, but does not prohibit treaties that merely supplement the treaty. The treaty established the North Atlantic Treaty Organization (NATO) and is, in certain ways, more in the nature of a framework or 'umbrella' treaty. Under it the parties have concluded many multilateral and bilateral treaties (and even more MOUs) on defence matters.

Article 28 of the CoE Extradition Convention 1957[31] provides, in part:

> (1) This Convention shall, in respect of those countries to which it applies, supersede the provisions of any bilateral treaties, conventions or agreements[32] governing extradition between any two Contracting Parties.
> (2) The Contracting Parties may conclude between themselves bilateral or multilateral agreements *only* in order to supplement the provisions of this Convention or to facilitate the application of the principles contained herein.

Article 311(3) of UNCLOS[33] provides that:

> two or more parties may conclude agreements modifying the operation of UNCLOS *solely as between themselves, provided* that the agreements do not relate to a provision derogation from which is incompatible with the object and purpose of UNCLOS, affect the basic principles of UNCLOS, or affect the enjoyment of other parties to UNCLOS of their rights or the performance of their obligations.

The Parties Shall Consult in the Case of a Future Treaty on the Same Subject Matter

Article 9.2 of the *Titanic* Agreement provides:

> If a general multilateral Convention on the protection of underwater cultural heritage enters into force for all Parties, they shall consult to discuss the relationship between this Agreement and that Convention.

[30] 34 UNTS 243 No. 541; UKTS (1949) No. 56. [31] 359 UNTS 273 No. 5146; UKTS (1991) No. 97.

[32] The use of the three terms may be because the existing bilateral treaties were variously designated, yet para. (2) refers only to agreements.

[33] See n. 14.

This has the merit of a consensual deliberative approach, but the parties might in practice wish to get together earlier than entry into force of the Convention if there was a real risk of competing obligations. The convention in question might also cause problems even if only some of the parties were affected.

An Existing Treaty Shall Not Be Affected

Article 7 of the North Atlantic Treaty 1949[34] provides that the treaty shall not be interpreted as affecting rights and obligations under the UN Charter. This article was rather unnecessary in view of Article 103 of the UN Charter, and would appear to have been included more for (no doubt good and understandable) political reasons. Such provisions may be included either simply for reassurance or because of a risk of conflict between obligations under a new treaty and those under an existing treaty.

Given the wide scope of the Treaty of Rome 1957, which established the European Economic Community (now the European Union), a general provision was made in Article 234 for those treaties that had been concluded previously by member states with third states, and remained in force, but were *not* compatible with the EC Treaty:

> The rights and obligations resulting from agreements concluded before 1 January 1958 or, for acceding States, before the date of their accession, between one or more Member States on the one hand, and one or more third countries on the other, shall not be affected by the provisions of the Treaty.[35]

It is a useful assurance both to the member states and third states. The provision applied to all treaties, whatever the subject matter, which might affect the operation of the treaty. So an EU member state is not prevented from performing its *obligations* to non-EU parties under such treaties, but it must not assert *rights* under them if the effect would be incompatible with its obligations to other member states under the treaty. The article goes on to require member states to take 'all appropriate steps to eliminate' any incompatibility of treaty obligations.[36] The corollary is that, once they have joined the European Union, member states cannot then enter into treaties that are inconsistent with their EU obligations.[37]

Sometimes it is relatively easy to identify the relevant treaties, or at least some of them. The Antarctic Treaty Environmental Protocol 1991[38] seeks to protect the Antarctic environment in a comprehensive manner. However, because there already existed treaties and measures, mostly within the Antarctic Treaty System, which dealt

[34] See n. 30. [35] Now, in amended form, Article 351 TFEU: see consolidated version, [2008] OJ C115/47.

[36] See Klabbers (n. 3); P. Manzini, 'The Priority of Pre-Existing Treaties of EC Member States within the Framework of International Law', EJIL (2001) 781–792.

[37] See *Commission* v. *United Kingdom* (2002), Case C-466/98.

[38] 30 ILM (1991) 1460; UKTS (1999) No. 6; [1998] ATS 6.

with discrete aspects of the Antarctic environment, it was felt necessary to make it clear that these treaties would not be affected. Accordingly, Article 4(2) provides that:

> Nothing in this Protocol shall derogate from the rights and obligations of the Parties to this Protocol under the other international instruments in force within the Antarctic Treaty system.

The Final Act of the meeting at which the Protocol was adopted noted that nothing in the Protocol should derogate from the rights and obligations of parties under CCAMLR 1980, the Antarctic Seals Convention and the International Whaling Convention, and that the environmental impact assessment procedure provided for in the Protocol was not intended to apply to activities under those three conventions.

A formal interpretative Decision made by the negotiating states on adoption of the Energy Charter Treaty 1994[39] specified that, in the event of a conflict between it and the Svalbard Treaty 1920,[40] the latter:

> shall prevail to the extent of the conflict, without prejudice to the positions of the Contracting Parties in respect of the Svalbard Treaty. In the event of such conflict or a dispute as to whether there is such conflict or as to its extent, Article 16 and Part V of the Energy Charter Treaty shall not apply.[41]

In the case of the Protocol on Ireland/Northern Ireland to the EU–UK Withdrawal Agreement from the EU,[42] Article 1.1 provides, in relation to the Good Friday or Belfast Agreement of 1998:[43]

> This Protocol is without prejudice to the provisions of the 1998 Agreement in respect of the constitutional status of Northern Ireland and the principle of consent, which provides that any change in that status can only be made with the consent of a majority of its people.

It adds further, in paragraph 3 of the same Article:

> This Protocol sets out arrangements necessary to address the unique circumstances on the island of Ireland, to maintain the necessary conditions for continued North–South cooperation, to avoid a hard border and to protect the 1998 Agreement in all its dimensions.

For regional economic organisations such as the European Union, both bilateral and multilateral treaties can raise issues of compatibility with rules applicable between the Member States, particularly in the case of Union law. There is, therefore, sometimes

[39] 2080 UNTS 100 No. 36116; 34 ILM (1995) 373; UKTS (2000) No. 78.
[40] 2 LNTS 8; UKTS (1924) No. 18; [1925] ATS 10.
[41] See T. W. Wälde (ed.), *The Energy Charter Treaty* (Kluwer Law, London 1996), 662.
[42] OJ C 3841, 12.11.2019, 1–177; UKTS (2020) No. 3.
[43] See Annex 1 UK–Ireland Agreement 1998: 2114 UNTS 473 No. 36776; 37 ILM (1998) 777; UKTS (2000) No. 50.

an express recognition that rules in a multilateral convention may conflict with those rules or may not reach the standard of integration already achieved between the members of the organisation. Hence, Article 3.4 of the Convention on the Facilitation of Border Crossing Procedures[44] states:

> This Convention shall not affect the rights and obligations resulting from other international agreements in which the Parties participate or from their membership in regional organizations for economic integration.

And Article 12.4 of the UN Convention on International Settlement Agreements Resulting from Mediation[45] provides:

> This Convention shall not prevail over conflicting rules of a regional economic integration organization, whether such rules were adopted or entered into force before or after this Convention: (a) if, under article 4, relief is sought in a State that is member of such an organization and all the States relevant under article 1, paragraph 1, are members of such an organization; or (b) as concerns the recognition or enforcement of judgments between member States of such an organization.

For Parties to the Treaty It Prevails over Earlier Treaties

Article 20 of the ILO Maternity Protection Convention 2000[46] provides that ratification of a convention that revises it shall, unless the new convention provides otherwise, *ipso facto* involve the immediate denunciation of the 2000 Convention if, and when, the new convention enters into force. This is a common provision in ILO conventions. However, this still leaves a problem if a party to the 2000 Convention does not become party to the revising convention.

By 1961 there were nine multilateral treaties concerning narcotic drugs. The Single Convention on Narcotic Drugs 1961[47] sought to replace all of them, and included this clause:

> The provisions of this Convention, upon its coming into force, shall, *as between the Parties hereto*, terminate and replace the provisions of the [nine] treaties.

The fact that the later treaty cannot deprive a state *that is not a party to it* of its rights under the earlier treaty is reflected in Article 30(4)(b) VCLT:

> When the parties to the later treaty do not include all the parties to the earlier one . . . as between a State party to both treaties and a State party to only one of

[44] Convention on the Facilitation of Border Crossing Procedures for Passengers etc. Carried by Rail 2019, at UN website.

[45] Also known as the Singapore Convention on Mediation 2018, at UNCITRAL website.

[46] Convention No. 183: 2181 UNTS 255 No. 38441; 39 ILM (2000) 2.

[47] 520 UNTS 151 No. 7515; UKTS (1965) No. 34: Article 44.

the treaties, the treaty to which both States are parties governs their mutual rights and obligations.

The Single Convention was amended by a Protocol in 1972,[48] and supplemented by the Convention on Psychotropic Substances 1971[49] and the Vienna Drugs Convention 1988.[50] Article 25 of the 1988 Convention provides that, for the parties to the Convention, it does not derogate from any rights enjoyed or obligations undertaken by them under the 1961 Convention, as amended by the Protocol, or under the 1971 Convention. This results in a number of possible permutations. Leaving aside the Protocol, let us assume that State A is a party to only the 1961 Convention, State B is a party to the 1961 and 1971 Conventions, and State C is a party to the 1971 and 1988 Conventions. Assuming that none of them denounce any of the conventions, *as between themselves* States A and B will be bound by the 1961 Convention and States B and C by the 1971 Convention, but States A and C will be bound by none of the three conventions. This can lead to most undesirable results when there is a need for uniformity of obligations. The situation is close to that produced by a series of amending treaties that have differing sets of parties. It is unavoidable unless there is a suitable amendment mechanism built into the initial treaty, though this may well not be possible politically.[51]

Compatible Supplementary Treaties Are Permitted

Article 73 of the VCCR 1963[52] provides that:

(1) The provisions of the present Convention shall not affect other international agreements in force as between States Parties to them.
(2) Nothing in the present Convention shall preclude States from concluding international agreements *confirming or supplementing or extending or amplifying* the provisions thereof.

Paragraph 1 preserves consular agreements (often called 'conventions') concluded before the parties to them become bound by the 1963 Convention. This was necessary since numerous consular agreements existed before the 1963 Convention was adopted, and it was not considered necessary, or desirable, for them to be replaced with the VCCR's uniform provisions. Instead, states should be free to enter into consular agreements that do not simply repeat those of the 1963 Convention. Paragraph 2 therefore enables parties to conclude supplementary consular agreements that do not derogate from the obligations of the 1963 Convention, but

48 976 UNTS 3 No. 14151; 11 ILM (1972) 804; UKTS (1979) No. 23. Consolidated text: 976 UNTS 105 No. 14152. See also *UN Multilateral Treaties*, chapter VI.18.
49 1019 UNTS 175 No. 14956; 10 ILM (1971) 261; UKTS (1993) No. 51.
50 1582 UNTS 165 No. 27627; 28 ILM (1989) 493; UKTS (1992) No. 26.
51 For how the amendment of UNCLOS was handled, see p. 124.
52 596 UNTS 261 No. 8638; UKTS (1973) No. 14; TIAS 6820.

prohibits, though by implication only, the conclusion of treaties that, by providing for more limited rights or obligations, would so derogate. These provisions are necessary because of the need for certain uniform minimum standards.[53]

Comprehensive Provisions

Given the importance of its subject matter, its universal application and the many existing treaties, both bilateral and multilateral, on the same topic, the drafters of UNCLOS[54] took care to ensure that its relationship to other treaties was clearly and precisely spelled out. Inspired by the VCLT,[55] Article 311 UNCLOS has three key provisions:

> (1) This Convention shall prevail, as between the States Parties, over the Geneva Conventions on the Law of the Sea of 29 April 1958.
> (2) This Convention shall not alter the rights and obligations of States Parties which arise from other agreements compatible with this Convention and which do not affect the enjoyment by other States Parties of their rights or the performance of their obligations under this Convention.
> (3) Two or more States Parties may conclude agreements modifying or suspending the operation of provisions of this Convention, applicable solely to the relations between them, provided that such agreements do not relate to a provision derogation from which is incompatible with the effective execution of the object and purpose of this Convention, provided further that such agreements shall not affect the application of the basic principles embodied herein, and that the provisions of such agreements do not affect the enjoyment by other States Parties of their rights or the performance of their obligations under this Convention.

The Best of Both Worlds

Article 16 of the Energy Charter Treaty 1994[56] provides that:

> Where two or more Contracting Parties have entered into a prior international agreement, *or enter into a subsequent international agreement*, whose terms *in either case* concern the subject matter of Part III [Investment Promotion and Protection] or V [Dispute Settlement] of this Treaty,

[53] See further L. T. Lee and J. Quigley, *Consular Law and Practice* (3rd ed., Oxford University Press, Oxford 2008).

[54] See n. 14.

[55] See M. Nordquist (ed.), *The United Nations Law of the Sea Convention: A Commentary*, Vol. V (Martinus Nijhoff, The Hague 1982), 229–243.

[56] See n. 39. Article 26(2) also gives an investor the option to submit disputes 'in accordance with any applicable, previously agreed dispute settlement procedure'. Given the liberal nature of the treaty, 'previously' would seem to refer to procedures agreed at any time before the dispute arose, not just those agreed before the treaty came into force.

(1) nothing in Part III or V of this Treaty shall be construed to derogate from any provision of such terms of the other agreement or from any right to dispute resolution with respect thereto under that agreement; and
(2) nothing in such terms of the other agreement shall be construed to derogate from any provision of Part III or V of this Treaty or from any right to dispute resolution with respect thereto under this Treaty,

where any such provision is more favourable to the Investor or Investment.

Neutral Provisions

Some treaties deal with the relationship with other treaties by not saying what would be the situation if there were to be a conflict of obligations. Others are not always clear what would happen. Three preambular paragraphs of the Rotterdam Convention on Hazardous Chemicals 1998[57] read:

Recognizing that trade and environment policies should be mutually supportive with a view to achieving sustainable development,
Emphasizing that nothing in this Convention shall be interpreted as implying any change in the rights and obligations of a Party under any existing international agreement applying to chemicals in international trade or to environmental protection,
Understanding that the above recital is not intended to create a hierarchy between this Convention and other international agreements.

The Residual Rules of Article 30

The relationship with other treaties relating to the same subject matter, including future treaties, should always be borne in mind when drafting a new treaty. If the negotiating states can reach agreement on the matter, it may be desirable to include a clause in the new treaty clarifying its interrelation with an earlier or later treaty to avoid problems in the future. But if the treaty remains silent on its interrelation with other treaties concerning the same subject matter, one is left with the rules in Article 30.[58] In that sense, and though it is not expressed as such, the rules in Article 30 are residual.[59]

Article 30 is worth setting out in full:

(1) Subject to Article 103 of the Charter of the United Nations, the rights and obligations of States parties to successive treaties relating to the same subject matter shall be determined in accordance with the following paragraphs.

[57] 2244 UNTS 393 No. 39973; 38 ILM (1999) 1; UKTS (2004) No. 46.
[58] Mus (n. 2), 213 note 25. See also E. Vierdag, 'The Time of the Conclusion of a Multilateral Treaty: Article 30', BYIL 59 (1988) 75–111. Some other articles, such as Articles 40, 41, 53, 59 and 60, may also be relevant,
[59] *Sinclair*, 97.

(2) When a treaty specifies that it is subject to, or that it is not to be considered as incompatible with, an earlier or later treaty, the provisions of that other treaty prevail.[60]

(3) When all the parties to the earlier treaty are parties also to the later treaty but the earlier treaty is not terminated or suspended in operation under Article 59, the earlier treaty applies only to the extent that its provisions are compatible with those of the later treaty.

(5) When the parties to the later treaty do not include all the parties to the earlier one:

 (a) as between States parties to both treaties the same rule applies as in paragraph 3;

 (b) as between a State party to both treaties and a State party to only one of the treaties, the treaty to which both States are parties governs their mutual rights and obligations.

(5) Paragraph 4 is without prejudice to Article 41, or to any question of the termination or suspension of the operation of a treaty under Article 60 or to any question of responsibility which may arise for a State from the conclusion or application of a treaty the provisions of which are incompatible with the obligations towards another State under another treaty.

Particular points to note include the following:

(1) The article applies only if both treaties are in force and in operation, not when one of the treaties has been terminated or its operation suspended by implication under Article 59.[61]

(2) The rules in paragraph 4 determine the mutual rights and obligations of the particular parties in each situation *only as between themselves*; they do not relieve any party of international responsibility for concluding or applying a treaty the provisions of which are incompatible with its obligations towards *another* state under *another* treaty.[62] If the rights of a party to another treaty are infringed, all the normal consequences of breach of treaty will follow. The injured party may terminate or suspend the operation of the treaty under Article 60 or invoke the international responsibility of the infringing party. On the other hand, nothing in paragraph 4 prevents some of the parties to a multilateral treaty concluding an agreement to modify it among themselves provided the conditions in Article 41 are met (paragraph 5).

[60] See Article XIII London Dumping Convention 1972: 1046 UNTS 120 No. 15749; 11 ILM (1972) 1294; UKTS (1976) No. 43.

[61] The relationship between Article 30 and 59 is discussed further in Chapter 16, pp. 299–300. The two sections should be read together.

[62] In this connection, see the judgment of the ECJ in *Commission* v. *United Kingdom* (2002) (Case C-466/98) holding that, by concluding the UK–US Air Services Agreement 1977, the United Kingdom was in breach of Article 52 Treaty of Rome (now Article 49 TFEU).

(3) In determining which treaty is the earlier and which the later, the relevant date is the date of adoption, not entry into force (see the reference in Article 59(1) to the conclusion of a later treaty).

(4) The obligations under Article 30 apply to a state only as from the date it becomes a party to the treaty.

(5) The meaning of the expression 'relating to the same subject matter' is not clear. The present author would favour an interpretation which allowed an assessment of the 'subject matter' in light of the whole content and context of the treaties in question:[63] in other words, not the narrowest interpretation but equally not tangential.[64] The issue has been of significance in international investment arbitrations arising out of bilateral investment treaties between EU member states (so-called 'intra-EU BITs') and in related domestic enforcement and set-aside proceedings, particularly following the *Achmea* judgment of the CJEU.[65] In *Achmea*, the Court held that intra-EU BITs were incompatible with the TFEU for reasons of EU law.[66]

(6) In practice, in the author's experience, states will primarily seek to resolve issues concerning incompatibility of successive treaties by negotiation. Unless the issue is contentious (which it may be, as in relation to investment disputes under intra-EU investment agreements), parties will most likely approach the matter pragmatically, looking at all possible ways to apply Articles 30 and/or 59, including ways of interpreting the treaties, or clarifying the issue by an exchange of notes or other instrument, to achieve the certainty they desire.

[63] Anthony Aust in the previous edition stated on this point: 'The meaning of the expression "relating to the same subject matter" is not clear, but should probably be construed strictly, so that the article would not apply when a general treaty impinges indirectly on the content of a particular provision of an earlier treaty.' In the same vein, see *Sinclair*, 98. But see *Dörr and Schmalenbach*, 544–545.

[64] See Vierdag (n. 58), 100: '[t]he requirement that the instruments must relate to the same subject matter seems to raise extremely difficult problems in theory, but may turn out not to be so very difficult in practice. If an attempted simultaneous application of two rules to one set of facts or actions leads to incompatible results it can safely be assumed that the test of sameness is satisfied.' See also Fragmentation of International Law: Report of the Study Group of the International Law Commission, finalized by Martti Koskenniemi, A/CN.4/L.682, 13 April 2006, paras. 23–25, 117 and 254.

[65] *Slovak Republic* v. *Achmea BV*, ECLI:EU:C:2018:158.

[66] See Ł. Kułaga, 'Implementing Achmea: The Quest for Fundamental Change in International Investment Law', *Polish Yearbook of International Law* (2019) 227–250, and cases cited at 229–231. The vast majority of investment tribunals to have addressed the issue of compatibility between intra-EU BITs, or Article 26 of the Energy Charter Treaty as between EU member states, and EU law have done so by reference to Articles 30 and 59 VCLT, and have found that those international investment agreements do not cover the 'same subject matter'. As a result, they have almost without exception accepted jurisdiction over claims based on these instruments.

13

Interpretation

> the interpretation of documents is to some extent an art, not an exact science.[1]

This understatement by the International Law Commission[2] will come as no surprise to any lawyer, domestic or international. It is especially true for treaties, which are the product of negotiations leading to compromises to reconcile, often wide, differences. Then an international court has to make some sense of the text. For multilateral treaties, the greater the number of negotiating states, the greater the need for imaginative and subtle drafting to satisfy competing interests and concerns. The process inevitably produces some wording that is unclear or ambiguous. Despite the care lavished on drafting, and accumulated experience, there is no treaty that cannot raise some question of interpretation.[3] Most disputes submitted to international adjudication involve some problem of treaty interpretation. Just as construing legislation is the constant concern of the domestic practitioner, treaty interpretation forms a significant part of the day-to-day work of a foreign ministry legal adviser. So it would be wrong to think that only international courts and tribunals interpret treaties. And, increasingly, domestic courts are faced with issues that involve their interpretation.[4] For many years, one of the most common has been the meaning of 'accident' in the Warsaw Convention 1929 and its successive treaties.[5] For example, courts have had to interpret the meaning of accident in light of such issues as deep vein thrombosis or coffee spillage.[6]

[1] ILC Commentary on draft Articles 27 and 28, para. (4).

[2] See at: http://untreaty.un.org/ilc/reports/reports.htm; A. Watts, *The International Law Commission 1949–1998*, vol. II (Oxford University Press, Oxford 1999), 609–823.

[3] See *Gardiner*. For earlier works, see *Sinclair*, 114–158; M. Bos, 'Theory and Practice of Treaty Interpretation', NILR (1990) 31–38, 135–170; M. K. Yasseen, 'L'interprétation des traités d'après la Convention de Vienne sur le droit des traités', *Hague Recueil* 151 (1976-III) 1–114.

[4] On the interpretation and application of treaties by UK courts, see Chapter 10, p. 200.

[5] 137 LNTS 11; UKTS (1933) No. 11: on amendments, see notes 3 and 4, Chapter 14.

[6] On deep vein thrombosis, see *Dizon* v. *Asiana Airlines* 240 F. Supp. 3d 1036, 1038–39 (C.D. Cal. 2017); *Rodriguez* v. *Ansett Australia Ltd.* F.3d 914 (9th Cir. 2004); *Deep Vein Thrombosis and Air Travel Group* Litigation [2006] 1 AER 786; *Povey* v. *Qantas* [2005] HCA 33; and on coffee spillage, see *GN* v. *ZU*, CJEU Case C-532/18, judgment of 19 December 2019.

A small, but nevertheless troublesome, example of a practical interpretation problem is to be found in the CTBT.[7] Article XIV(2) envisages a conference being convened if the CTBT has not entered into force 'three years after the date of *the anniversary of* its opening for signature'. Some states argued that the italicised words above referred to the date twelve months after the opening for signature, and therefore the required period was one-plus-three years; others asserted that the words were tautological and must be a clear mistake, and that the period was therefore only three years. We will come back to this as we examine Articles 31 and 32 of the VCLT. (Article 33 is considered at the end of this chapter.)

Approaches to Interpretation

In its Commentary on the drafts of what were to become Articles 31 and 32,[8] the ILC surveyed the differing views of jurists on whether there were any rules of international law governing the interpretation of treaties, and if so, what they were. The Commission rejected the view that, in interpreting a treaty, one must give greater weight to one particular factor, such as the text ('textual' or 'literal' approach), or the supposed intentions of the parties or the object and purpose of the treaty ('effective' or 'teleological' approach). Reliance on one to the detriment of the others was contrary to the jurisprudence of the ICJ.[9] Placing undue emphasis on the text, without regard to what the parties intended; or on what the parties intended, regardless of the text; or on the perceived object and purpose in order to make the treaty more 'effective', irrespective of the intentions of the parties, is unlikely to produce a satisfactory result.[10]

McNair was also suitably sceptical about various doctrines of interpretation espoused by his fellow jurists. His views on interpretation, and those of O'Connell, still contain much good sense.[11] The ILC very sensibly avoided a doctrinaire approach. In what are two of the most elegantly drafted articles, it formulated what it regarded as the comparatively few general principles governing treaty interpretation. The ICJ considers that the principles embodied in Articles 31 and 32 reflect customary international law,[12] and other international courts and tribunals, for

[7] 35 ILM (1996) 1439 or www.ctbto.org. Unfortunately, the treaty is unlikely ever to enter into force.

[8] See draft Articles 27 and 28, and *Sinclair*, 115–119.

[9] On this, see H. Thirlway, 'The Law and Procedure of the International Court of Justice 1960–1989', BYIL 62 (1991) 16–17, and generally, 16–75.

[10] On the 'effective' approach, see *O'Connell*, 253–255. See also a useful summary of the law, though more in the context of human rights treaties and advocating an 'interactive' (i.e., a more teleological) approach, in J. Hathaway, *The Rights of Refugees Under International Law* (Cambridge University Press, Cambridge 2005), 48–74.

[11] *McNair*, 364–473; *O'Connell*, 251–265.

[12] *Libya* v. *Chad*, ICJ Reports (1994) 6, at 15, para. 21. *Kasikili/Sedudu Island (Botswana* v. *Namibia)*, ICJ Reports (1999) 1045, at 1059, para. 18; 39 ILM (2000) 310; 119 ILR 467; M. Shaw, 'Case Concerning Kasikili/Sedudu Island (Botswana v. Namibia)', ICLQ 49 (2000) 964–978. See also the ILC Draft

example the WTO Appellate Body, have followed this.[13] The two articles (and especially Article 31) also contain much of practical value to the treaty maker or to anyone involved in implementing a treaty.

Special Areas

The VCLT provisions remain the yardstick for interpretation of treaties. International tribunals and panels generally state that they base their decisions on the Convention rules, and many bilateral (and plurilateral) trade agreements specifically acknowledge these, for example Article 31.13.4 of the United States–Canada–Mexico Agreement,[14] Article 28.12.3 of the Trans-Pacific Partnership Agreement,[15] Article 29.17 of the EU–Canada Trade Agreement[16] and Article 4 of the EU–UK Trade and Cooperation Agreement.[17] But as different areas of law have developed over the years, some with their own dispute settlement systems, it is possible to discern within these particular approaches to interpretation. Examples are the WTO,[18] investment treaties[19] and tax treaties, the European Union, the European Court of Human Rights[20] and other

Conclusions on subsequent agreements and subsequent practice in relation to the interpretation of treaties, *ILC Yearbook* 2018, vol. II (Part Two) (in this chapter referred to as ILC Conclusions). Conclusion 2.1 states: 'These rules also apply as customary international law.'

[13] For more detail and references, see para. (4) of the commentary to Conclusion 2. See generally A. Orakhelashvili, 'The Recent Practice on the Principles of Treaty Interpretation', in A. Orakhelashvili and S. Williams (eds.), *40 Years of the Vienna Convention on the Law of Treaties* (BIICL, London 2010), 117–154.

[14] 30 November 2018: at USTR website. Article 31.13.4 provides: 'The panel shall interpret this Agreement in accordance with customary rules of interpretation of public international law, as reflected in Articles 31 and 32 of the *Vienna Convention on the Law of Treaties*, done at Vienna on May 23, 1969.'

[15] See New Zealand Foreign Affairs and Trade website. Article 28.12.3 goes on to say: 'With respect to any provision of the WTO Agreement that has been incorporated into this Agreement, the panel shall also consider relevant interpretations in reports of panels and the WTO Appellate Body adopted by the WTO Dispute Settlement Body.'

[16] EU–Canada Comprehensive Economic and Trade Agreement (CETA) 2016: OJ L 11, 14.1.2017, 23–1079.

[17] UKTS (2021) No. 8; OJ L 149, 30.04.21.

[18] See G. Abi-Saab, 'The Appellate Body and Treaty Interpretation', in M. Fitzmaurice, O. Elias and P. Merkouris (eds.), *Treaty Interpretation and the Vienna Convention on the Law of Treaties: 30 Years On* (Martinus Nijhoff, Leiden, Boston 2010), 99–109; B. Stern, 'Interpretation in International Trade Law', in Fitzmaurice *et al.* above, 111–128; M. Fitzmaurice and P. Merkouris, 'Canons of Treaty Interpretation: Selected Case Studies from the World Trade Organization and the North America Free Trade Agreement', in Fitzmaurice *et al.* above, 153–237; A. Qureshi, *Interpreting WTO Agreements* (Cambridge University Press, Cambridge 2015); I. van Damme, 'Jurisdiction, Applicable Law, and Interpretation', in D. Bethlehem, D. McRae, R. Neufeld and I. van Damme (eds.), *The Oxford Handbook of International Trade Law* (Oxford University Press, Oxford 2009), 298–343; I. van Damme, *Treaty Interpretation by the WTO Appellate Body* (Oxford University Press, Oxford 2009).

[19] See C. Schreuer, 'Diversity and Harmonization of Treaty Interpretation', in Fitzmaurice *et al.* (n. 18), 129–151; T. Gazzini, 'Interpretation of (Allegedly) Self-Judging Clauses in Bilateral Investment Treaties', in Fitzmaurice *et al.* (n. 18), 239–254.

[20] See M. Fitzmaurice, 'Dynamic (Evolutive) Interpretation of Treaties and the European Court of Human Rights', in Orakhelashvili and Williams (n. 13), 55–95; G. Letsas, 'Intentionalism and the Interpretation of the ECHR', in Fitzmaurice *et al.* (n. 18), 257–272; D. J. Harris, E. Bates and C. Buckley, *Harris, O'Boyle and*

human rights bodies,[21] constitutive treaties of international organisations,[22] and the ICJ itself. So the lawyer, when faced with an issue of interpretation, needs to ask in what area of law this arises, what is the relevant tribunal or court, and how has this previously approached interpretative issues. This requires specialists in the particular areas to opine in detail, though this chapter gives a broad overview and refers to recent literature. Sometimes it is possible to discern a particular approach through detailed analysis of past judgments, but each case depends on its own particular facts.

Approaches to Interpretation within Treaties

Many treaties will not establish a specific standing mechanism for interpretation of their provisions, though some treaties (particularly those in areas with complex, detailed or sensitive provisions, such as trade) will provide that disputes about the interpretation or application of the treaty may be referred to a panel or joint committee established under the treaty, or to an international court or tribunal, for settlement. Where a bilateral or multilateral treaty provides for meetings of the parties, or for a committee or commission, such bodies may play a role in interpreting the treaty.

Article 21(c) of the European Transfrontier Television Convention 1989, for example, empowers the Standing Committee (on which each party is represented) to 'examine, at the request of one or more parties, questions concerning the interpretation of the Convention'.[23] The committee takes decisions by a three-quarters majority of the members present. The EU–UK Withdrawal Agreement provides for disputes concerning the interpretation of the Agreement to be referred first to a Joint Committee of the Parties, and if not resolved, then to an arbitration panel. However, disputes concerning the interpretation of Union law are to be referred to the CJEU. In the case of the Trans-Pacific Partnership, the functions of the Commission established under Article 27.1, composed of government representatives of each party at the level of ministers or senior officials, include issuing interpretation of the provisions of the Agreement. There are, in addition, full dispute settlement procedures.

Some treaties provide that they shall be interpreted by reference to the provisions of another, relevant treaty. Article 11(1) of the Organisation for the Prohibition of Chemical Weapons (OPCW)–UK Privileges and Immunities Agreement

Warbrick: Law of the European Convention on Human Rights (Oxford University Press, Oxford 2018), 3–24; G. Letsas, *A Theory of Interpretation of the European Convention on Human Rights* (Oxford University Press, Oxford 2007).

21 B. Çalı, 'Specialized Rules of Treaty Interpretation: Human Rights', in *Hollis, Oxford Guide*, 504–523; D. Moeckli and N. D. White, 'Treaties as 'Living Instruments', in M. J. Bowman and D. Kritsiotis (eds.), *Conceptual and Contextual Perspectives on the Modern Law of Treaties* (Cambridge University Press, Cambridge 2018).

22 C. Brölmann, 'Specialized Rules of Treaty Interpretation: International Organizations', in *Hollis, Oxford Guide*, 524–542.

23 2206 UNTS 312 No. 33611; 28 ILM (1989) 859; UKTS (1993) No. 22; ETS No. 132.

2000 provides that the provisions of the Agreement shall be interpreted in the light of the functions that the Chemical Weapons Convention 1993 entrusts to the OPCW.[24]

Articles 31 and 32 VCLT

Whatever the mechanism by which a dispute about the interpretation or application of a treaty is determined, the body will most often be guided by the rules in Articles 31 and 32. Articles 31 and 32 read as follows:

Article 31: General Rule of Interpretation

(1) A treaty shall be interpreted in good faith in accordance with the ordinary meaning to be given to the terms of the treaty in their context and in the light of its object and purpose.
(2) The context for the purpose of the interpretation of a treaty shall comprise, in addition to the text, including its preamble and annexes:
   (a) any agreement relating to the treaty which was made between all the parties in connexion with the conclusion of the treaty;
   (b) any instrument which was made by one or more parties in connexion with the conclusion of the treaty and accepted by the other parties as an instrument related to the treaty.
(3) There shall be taken into account, together with the context:
   (a) any subsequent agreement between the parties regarding the interpretation of the treaty or the application of its provisions;
   (b) any subsequent practice in the application of the treaty which establishes the agreement of the parties regarding its interpretation;
   (c) any relevant rules of international law applicable in the relations between the parties.
(4) A special meaning shall be given to a term if it is established that the parties so intended.

Article 32: Supplementary Means of Interpretation

Recourse may be had to supplementary means of interpretation, including the preparatory work of the treaty and the circumstances of its conclusion, in order to confirm the meaning resulting from the application of Article 31, or to determine the meaning when the interpretation according to Article 31:

(a) leaves the meaning ambiguous or obscure; or
(b) leads to a result which is manifestly absurd or unreasonable.

Let us now examine those two articles in detail.[25]

[24] UK–OPCW Agreement on the Privileges and Immunities of the OPCW 2000: 2207 UNTS 16 No. 39170; UKTS (2002) No. 31.

[25] See also M. Villiger, 'The Rules on Interpretation: Misgivings, Misunderstandings, Miscarriage? The "Crucible" Intended by the International Law Commission', in E. Cannizzaro (ed.), *The Law of Treaties beyond the Vienna Convention* (Oxford University Press, Oxford 2011), 105–122.

Article 31: General Rule of Interpretation

Article 31 is entitled '*general rule* of interpretation'. The fact that the singular is used for the word 'rule' indicates that the whole article comes under this heading and that neither one paragraph nor another by itself constitutes the general rule. This is supported by the ILC Commentary on the draft Articles.[26]

Paragraph (1) requires one to consider three main elements: the text, its context, and the object and purpose of the treaty. Paragraph (2) amplifies what is meant by 'context'. Paragraph (3) directs that, together with the context, there shall be taken into account any subsequent agreement regarding the interpretation of the treaty and any subsequent practice in the application of its provisions. Although formulated as a rule, the Convention provisions are to be applied flexibly, with an appreciation of the context and circumstances of the point to be interpreted.[27] As the ILC has stated:

> The interpretation of a treaty consists of a single combined operation, which places appropriate emphasis on the various means of interpretation indicated, respectively, in articles 31 and 32.[28]

Paragraph (1): good faith, ordinary meaning to be given to the terms of the treaty in their context and in the light of its object and purpose

The first concept – interpretation *in good faith* – flows directly from the principle of *pacta sunt servanda* enshrined in Article 26. Interpretation is part of the performance of the treaty and, therefore, the process of examining the relevant materials and assessing them must be done in good faith. The next concept is *ordinary meaning* ('interpreted ... in accordance with the ordinary meaning'), since it is reasonable to assume, at least until the contrary is established, that the ordinary meaning is most likely to reflect what the parties intended. As McNair put it, the task of interpretation is:

> the duty of giving effect to the expressed intention of the parties, that is, their intention *as expressed in the words used by them in the light of the surrounding circumstances.*[29]

[26] ILC Commentary, under draft Articles 27 and 28, para. (8), YBILC (1966) vol. II, 219–220.

[27] See R. Gardiner, 'The Vienna Convention Rules on Treaty Interpretation', in *Hollis, Oxford Guide*, 459–488, at 465, quoting Waldock: 'The Commission was fully conscious ... of the undesirability – if not impossibility – of confining the process of interpretation within rigid rules, and the provisions of [the draft articles] ... do not appear to constitute a code of rules incompatible with the required degree of flexibility ... any "principles" found by the Commission to be "rules" of interpretation have the character of "guidelines" since their application in a particular case depends so much on the appreciation of the context and the circumstances of the point to be interpreted.' Sir Humphrey Waldock, Special Rapporteur, Sixth Report on the Law of Treaties, YBILC (1966) vol. II, 51, at 94.

[28] ILC Conclusion 2.5. [29] *McNair*, 365 (emphasis in the original).

But interpretation according to the natural and ordinary meaning of the words employed is not an absolute one:

> Where such a method of interpretation results in a meaning incompatible with the spirit, purpose and context of the clause or instrument in which the words are contained, no reliance can be validly placed on it.[30]

The determination of the ordinary meaning therefore cannot be done in the abstract, only in the *context* of the treaty and in the light of its *object and purpose*. The concept of the *context* is amplified in Article 31(2). The latter concept, as we have seen in relation to reservations to treaties, can be elusive. Even though the *object and purpose* may be taken sequentially in the analysis,[31] it is no less important and is not to be taken merely as a check, but rather to shed light on the 'ordinary meaning'. The concept of object and purpose includes a teleological element and an element of 'effectiveness', but it does not make the Convention rule as a whole teleological.[32] Nor can it be used to alter the clear meaning of a term of the treaty.[33]

Paragraph (2): Context

This paragraph specifies what comprises the context. We all think we know what an 'aircraft' is, but when a treaty uses that term, does it include all aircraft, civil *and* military, and what about microlights, hovercraft or balloons?[34] Any term can be fully understood only by considering the context in which it is employed. Does the term 'public official', as used in Article 1(1) of the Torture Convention 1984,[35] include a head of state?[36]

One must look at the treaty as a whole, including the preamble and any annexes. For example, Article I of the Comprehensive Nuclear-Test-Ban Treaty 1996[37] prohibits 'any nuclear weapon test explosion *or any other nuclear explosion*'. This apparently all-inclusive formula might lead one to conclude that the CTBT also bans the use of nuclear weapons. This thought is, however, quickly dispelled by the aspirations for nuclear disarmament expressed in the preamble, and by the unambiguous title of the treaty.

[30] *South West Africa Cases*, Preliminary Objections, Judgment, ICJ Reports (1962) 319, at 336, cited in *Arbitral Award of 31 July 1989 (Guinea-Bissau* v. *Senegal)*, ICJ Reports (1991) 53, at 69–70, para. 48; see *Gardiner*, 184–196.

[31] See, e.g., *Kasikili/Sedudu Island (Botswana* v. *Namibia)* (n. 12), at 1072–1074, paras. 43–45; Shaw (n. 12), 964–978.

[32] See the discussion in *Gardiner*, 211, and generally 211–222.

[33] See *Gardiner*, 219.

[34] The English Court of Appeal held that a hot-air balloon was an aircraft for the purposes of the Warsaw Convention, see *Laroche* v. *Spirit of Adventure* [2009] EWCA Civ. 12. In Annex 7 to the Chicago Convention, the definition of 'aircraft' excludes hovercraft: '*Aircraft* Any machine that can derive support in the atmosphere from the reactions of the air other than the reactions of the air against the earth's surface.'

[35] 1465 UNTS 85 No. 24841; 23 ILM (1984) 1027; UKTS (1991) No. 107.

[36] See *R.* v. *Bow St Magistrates' Court, ex parte Pinochet (No. 3)* [2000] 1 AC 147; [1999] 2 AER 97; [1999] 2 WLR 827; 38 ILM (1999) 581; 119 ILR 135.

[37] See n. 7.

In the example given at the beginning of this chapter, also taken from the CTBT, paragraph (2) of Article XIV must be seen in the context of the preceding and succeeding paragraphs:

> (1) This Treaty shall enter into force . . . in no case earlier than two years *after its opening for signature.*
> (2) If this Treaty has not entered into force three years after the date of *the anniversary of its opening for signature,* the Depositary shall convene a Conference . . .
> (3) . . . this process shall be repeated at subsequent anniversaries of the opening for signature.

The absence of any reference in paragraph (1) to the *anniversary* of the opening for signature might suggest that inclusion of that term in paragraph (2) was deliberate and, therefore, effect must be given to it (this is an example of interpretation *a contrario).* However, the phrase 'subsequent anniversaries' in paragraph (3) would make perfect sense even if paragraph (2) had no reference at all to anniversary, the phrase in paragraph (3) clearly being a reference to the anniversaries of the opening for signature, which will occur *after* the conference has been convened. If it had really been intended that the conference would be convened only after four years, why did it not say so explicitly? The meaning of paragraph (2) does lack clarity.

Paragraph (2) of Article 31 is most important for treaty making. It provides that, in addition to the text, including the preamble and annexes, the context comprises the following:

> (a) any agreement relating to the treaty which was made between all the parties in connexion with the conclusion of the treaty.

The agreement does not have to be part of the treaty, or be itself a treaty (international law has no *acte contraire* doctrine), but it must be a clear expression of the intention of the parties. A good example is to be found in the Final Act of the conference that adopted the CCAMLR 1980.[38] Attached to the Final Act is a formal statement regarding certain islands within the area of application of CCAMLR. The purpose of the statement is to permit these islands to be taken out of the normal application of CCAMLR. The statement was read out by the chairman of the conference, and so is known as the 'Chairman's Statement'. The Final Act records that no objection was made to the statement (it having been carefully negotiated during the conference).[39] When the Convention on the Prohibition of Military or Any Other Hostile Use of Environmental Modification Techniques (ENMOD Convention) 1976[40] was negotiated, a series of 'understandings' were agreed

[38] 1329 UNTS 71 No. 22301; 19 ILM (1980) 837; UKTS (1982) No. 48; TIAS 10240.

[39] See also the Final Act of the Conference that adopted the Refugees Convention 1951 (189 UNTS 137 No. 2545; UKTS (1954) No. 39).

[40] 1108 UNTS 151 No. 17119; 16 ILM (1977) 16; TIAS 9614.

regarding its interpretation or application. The UN Convention on Jurisdictional Immunities of States and their Property 2004[41] has an (integral) annex with important 'understandings' with respect to certain of its provisions.

Such instruments should not be seen only as an aid to interpretation, but also as a valuable tool of the treaty maker. At least as a matter of law, there is often no reason why the content of an instrument could not have been put into the treaty. One reason for employing such devices is therefore political. One or more parties may insist on a particular point, but others, while accepting that it has to be made, may find it politically awkward to have it in the treaty itself, but could agree to it being made in a separate document, which is expressed to be made by certain negotiating states or by the chairman of the conference. The need for such devices has increased with the greater use of consensus in the adoption of treaties. But sometimes they are used simply for convenience. An agreed minute or exchange of letters regarding the detailed application of terms used in a treaty may be neater than overloading the treaty with lengthy definitions.[42] They may also provide useful assurances on the effect of certain provisions or confirmation of their interpretation.[43]

The explanatory reports approved by the government experts involved in drafting conventions of the Council of Europe, and adopted at the same time as the conventions and published with them, provide an invaluable guide to their interpretation and should be seen as part of the 'context' in which the conventions were concluded.[44] As such, they must be distinguished from 'official' commentaries, which are produced later and, depending on the circumstances, may come to be regarded as authoritative. The *Handbook on Procedures and Criteria for Determining Refugee Status,* published by the UN High Commissioner for Refugees (UNHCR), is generally treated as an authoritative commentary on the Refugees Convention 1951 and practice under it, and is often referred to by domestic courts and tribunals.[45] Commentaries published by other organisations, such as those by the International Committee of the Red Cross (ICRC) on the Geneva Conventions 1949, can also be influential.[46]

41 A/RES/59/38; 44 ILM (2005) 801. The convention is not yet in force: it needs thirty ratifications, or similar. By late 2022 it had twenty-three parties. The text was based on a draft by the ILC: see Watts (n. 3) vol. III, 1999–2103. The ILC draft, ILC Commentary and the reports of the Ad Hoc Committee of the 6th Committee, and of that Committee itself, will also be relevant to the interpretation of the convention.

42 See the exchange of interpretative letters accompanying the UK–US Air Services Agreement 1977 (1079 UNTS 21 No. 16509; UKTS (1977) No. 76).

43 See, for example, the various side-letters in connection with the United States–Mexico–Canada Agreement (n. 14) (a trilateral agreement), some of which are between two of the parties only.

44 *Sinclair*, 129–130. For an example, see 33 ILM (1994) 943.

45 See *Adan* [1999] 3 WLR 1244. See Hathaway (n. 10), 54 note 146.

46 Commentaries on the Geneva Conventions (ICRC): GC I (Cambridge University Press 2016); GC II (Cambridge University Press 2017); GC III (Cambridge University Press 2021).

(b) any instrument made by one or more parties in connexion with the conclusion of the treaty and accepted by the other parties as an instrument related to the treaty.

The Dayton Agreement 1995 included many such instruments.[47] The need for acceptance distinguishes this case from unilateral interpretative declarations made by a state when signing or ratifying. It is common practice for European Union treaties (and its predecessor constituent treaties) to have various instruments associated with them that have been produced by one or more member states, the texts having been agreed during the negotiation of the treaty.[48] They are also made in connection with bilateral treaties. The US–USSR 'START' Treaty 1991[49] was accompanied by many assurances and explanations in correspondence between the parties and in joint and national declarations.

Paragraph (3): Subsequent Agreements and Subsequent Practice

Subsequent agreements

Subparagraph (a) provides that, together with the context, there shall be taken into account any 'subsequent agreement' between the parties regarding the interpretation of the treaty or the application of its provisions.[50] Given that the parties can agree later to amend or modify the treaty, they can also subsequently agree on an authoritative interpretation of its terms. Sometimes this can amount, in effect, to an amendment. Subsequent agreements and subsequent practice can be distinguished on the basis whether an agreement of the parties can be identified as such, in a common act, or whether it is necessary to identify an agreement through individual acts that in their combination demonstrate a common position.[51] Both subsequent agreements and subsequent practice may also be relevant to the question whether the meaning of a treaty term can evolve over time.[52]

47 35 ILM (1996) 75. 48 See Chapter 8, pp. 136–137.

49 31 ILM (1992) 246). See also the Quadripartite Agreement 1971: 880 UNTS 124 No. 12621; 10 ILM (1971) 895; UKTS (1972) No. 111.

50 ILC Conclusion 3 states: 'Subsequent agreements and subsequent practice under article 31, paragraph 3 (*a*) and (*b*), being objective evidence of the understanding of the parties as to the meaning of the treaty, are authentic means of interpretation, in the application of the general rule of treaty interpretation reflected in article 31.'

51 ILC Commentary to Conclusion 4, para. (10). It goes on to say: '"A subsequent agreement" under article 31, paragraph 3 (*a*), must therefore be "reached" and presupposes a deliberate common act or undertaking by the parties, even if it consists of individual acts by which they manifest their common understanding regarding the interpretation of the treaty or the application of its provisions.' Para. (11) reads: '"Subsequent practice" under article 31, paragraph 3 (*b*), on the other hand, encompasses all (other) relevant forms of subsequent conduct by the parties to a treaty that contribute to the identification of an agreement, or "understanding", of the parties regarding the interpretation of the treaty. It is, however, possible that "practice" and "agreement" coincide in specific cases and cannot be distinguished…'

52 See pp. 252–255, where the evolutionary principle is discussed, and ILC Conclusion 8.

For a subsequent agreement, there is no need for a further treaty,[53] since the paragraph refers deliberately to an 'agreement', not to a treaty. Provided the purpose is clear, the agreement can take various forms,[54] including a decision adopted by a meeting of the parties.[55] It requires a common understanding regarding the interpretation of a treaty which the parties are aware of and accept. Though it will be taken into account, such an agreement need not be legally binding.[56] The weight of a subsequent agreement or subsequent practice as a means of interpretation under Article 31(3) depends, inter alia, on its clarity and specificity.[57]

The Treaty of Rome 1957 establishing the European Economic Community, as amended, refers to the 'ECU' (European currency unit). When, in 1995, the member states decided to replace the ECU with the 'euro', instead of amending the EC Treaty, which would have involved a lengthy ratification procedure and parliamentary scrutiny, the heads of state and government of the member states recorded in the 'Conclusions' of their meeting in Madrid that:

> The specific name Euro will be used instead of the generic term 'ECU' used in the Treaty to refer to the European currency unit. The Governments of the fifteen Member States have achieved the common agreement that this decision is the agreed and definitive interpretation of the relevant Treaty provisions.[58]

Under the Ramsar Wetlands Convention 1971,[59] as amended in 1982 to include an amendment clause, the acceptance of 'two-thirds of the Contracting Parties' is needed for an amendment to come into force. However, it was not clear if the phrase referred to the contracting parties at the time the amendment was adopted, or at any given moment. Therefore, at a conference of the parties in 1990, a resolution was adopted that it should be interpreted to refer to the time of adoption of the amendment.

[53] But see the UK–Czech Republic Exchange of Notes 1996 regarding the Interpretation of the Consular Convention of 1975: 1967 UNTS 224 No. 33638; UKTS (1997) No. 5: 'for the purposes of paragraph 3, Article 31 of the Vienna Convention on the Law of Treaties'.

[54] ILC Conclusion 6.2. But the instrument in question has to reach a certain threshold: see the example cited in the ILC Commentary, para. (15), 35, where the Court of Final Appeal, Hong Kong, rejected a booklet concerning immigration regulations and practices as evidence of a subsequent agreement, since the purpose of the booklet was not to 'interpret or to apply' (in this case) the UK–China Joint Declaration within the meaning of article 31, paragraph 3(a). Hong Kong, China, Court of Final Appeal, *Ng Ka Ling and Others* v. *Director of Immigration* [1999] 1 HKLRD 315.

[55] See the case of *Seaboard World Airlines Inc.* v. *Department of Trade* [1976] 1 Lloyd's Rep 42, cited by *Gardiner*, 249, a dispute concerning a bilateral agreement on air services, where the judge relied on discussion between representatives of the UK and US governments recorded in an attachment to a 'Memorandum Summarising a Portion of the Discussions'.

[56] ILC Conclusion 10. [57] ILC Conclusion 9.1.

[58] Conclusions of the Madrid European Council 1995 (*Bulletin of the EU*, 12 (1995) 10). For another example, see D. Howarth, 'The Compromise on Denmark and the Treaty on European Union: A Legal and Political Analysis', *Common Market Law Review* 31 (1994) 765–805.

[59] 996 UNTS 245 No. 14583; 11 ILM (1972) 963; UKTS (1976) No. 34 (for consolidated text, see UKTS (1996) No. 13). See M. Bowman, 'The Multilateral Treaty Amendment Process: A Case Study', ICLQ 44 (1995) 540–559, 552.

Under Article 1.F(c) of the Refugees Convention 1951,[60] if there are 'serious reasons' for considering that a person is 'guilty of acts contrary to the purposes and principles of the United Nations', they are not entitled to refugee status. On 17 December 1996, the UN General Assembly adopted, without a vote, a Declaration that terrorism is contrary to the purposes and principles of the United Nations.[61] This can be seen as a subsequent agreement about the interpretation of the UN Charter, and thus also of the Refugees Convention. It does not amount to an amendment of the Convention, nor is it legally binding. Nevertheless, it carries considerable weight in the interpretation of the Convention, and should therefore be taken into account also by national courts and tribunals.

Article IX(1) of the Antarctic Treaty 1959[62] provides for certain of the parties (known as 'consultative parties') to *recommend* to their governments *measures* in furtherance of the principles and objectives of the treaty. Article IX(4) provides that the measures 'shall become effective' when they have been 'approved' by all of the consultative parties. Between 1961 and 1995 over 200 measures were recommended. But, until 1995, there had been a misunderstanding, and a consequent misapplication, of Article IX(1). From the very beginning, the consultative parties had adopted instruments termed 'recommendations', of which the majority were no more than exhortatory, ephemeral or procedural. Nevertheless, they were treated as measures subject to the full approval procedure of Article IX(4). This resulted in most recommendations not becoming 'effective' until many years after their adoption. This unsatisfactory situation was corrected in 1995, when the consultative parties agreed that in future they would recommend under Article IX(1) only 'measures' properly so called (i.e., intended to be legally binding). In future, other matters would be the subject of 'decisions' or 'resolutions', and would be effective on their adoption at the annual ATCM. This agreement was embodied in Decision 1 of the 1995 ATCM.[63] The new arrangements were explained by the proposers to be a subsequent agreement for the purposes of Article 31(3)(a).

More generally, the ILC draft Conclusions specify that the legal effect of a decision adopted within the framework of a Conference of States Parties depends primarily on the treaty and any applicable rules of procedure. Depending on the circumstances, such a decision may embody, explicitly or implicitly, a subsequent agreement under Article 31(3)(a), or give rise to subsequent practice under Article 31(3)(b), or to other subsequent practice under Article 32.[64] Conclusion 11.3 adds:

> A decision adopted within the framework of a Conference of States Parties embodies a subsequent agreement or subsequent practice under article 31, paragraph 3, insofar as it expresses agreement in substance between the parties

[60] See n. 39. [61] A/RES/51/210. [62] 402 UNTS 71 No. 5778; UKTS (1961) No. 97; www.ats.aq.
[63] 35 ILM (1996) 1188. [64] ILC Conclusion 11.2.

> regarding the interpretation of a treaty, regardless of the form and the procedure by which the decision was adopted, including adoption by consensus.

The example cited above in respect of Article IX(1) of the Antarctic Treaty and the ATCM is more in the nature of corrective action, the earlier examples amounting more to modifications of, or amendments to, the treaties. Foreign ministry legal advisers are familiar with the question: how can we modify a treaty without amending it? Even if the treaty does have a built-in amendment procedure, the process can be lengthy and uncertain, especially if it is a multilateral treaty and any amendment is subject to ratification. Much will depend on the circumstances, but, particularly where the modification is essentially procedural, it may be possible to embody it in an agreement as to the application of the treaty. This technique is particularly useful if there is a need to fill a lacuna, to update a term or to postpone the operation of a provision. The time for the first election of judges of ITLOS was specified in UNCLOS 1982, but since that date turned out to be premature, the election was postponed by a consensus decision of a meeting of the parties, the decision being recorded in the record of the meeting.[65] Such means should be used cautiously and sparingly, however. The distinction between application and amendment is not always easy to draw.

Subsequent Practice

Subparagraph (b) provides that, together with the context, there shall be taken into account any subsequent practice in the application of the treaty which establishes the agreement of the parties regarding its interpretation. This is a most important element in the interpretation of any treaty, and reference to practice is well established in the jurisprudence of international tribunals. However precise a text appears to be, the way in which it is actually applied by the parties is usually a good indication of what they understand it to mean, provided the practice is consistent and is common to, or accepted, expressly or tacitly, by both or all parties. In its Award in the *US–UK Heathrow User Charges* Arbitration, the Tribunal found that a 1983 UK–US MOU was of value as 'consensual subsequent practice' by the parties.[66] In *Kasikili/Sedudu Island (Botswana* v. *Namibia)*,[67] the ICJ examined the evidence of subsequent state practice.[68]

Some of the principles outlined above in respect of subsequent agreements include guidance on subsequent practice.[69] In addition, it is important to note that subsequent practice is not only relevant to Article 31(3)(b). Recourse may be had to other subsequent practice in the application of the treaty as a supplementary means of

[65] SPLOS/3, 28 February 1995. [66] 102 ILR 215, 353, paras. 6.7–6.8.
[67] See (n. 12) at 1075–1096, paras. 47–80; Shaw (n. 12), 973–975.
[68] See H. Fox, 'Article 31(3)(a) and (b) of the Vienna Convention and the Kasikili/Sedudu Island Case', in Fitzmaurice *et al.* (n. 18), 59–74.
[69] See, in particular, ILC Conclusions 3, 4 and 6, mentioned on pp. 247–248.

interpretation under Article 32.[70] As already noted, the weight of subsequent practice under Article 31(3)(b) depends, inter alia, on its clarity and specificity.[71] It also depends on whether and how it is repeated.[72]

Subsequent practice under Article 31(3)(b) must be conduct 'in the application of the treaty'. The ILC Commentary states that this includes:

> not only official acts at the international or at the internal level that serve to apply the treaty, including to respect or to ensure the fulfilment of treaty obligations, but also, *inter alia*, official statements regarding its interpretation, such as statements at a diplomatic conference, statements in the course of a legal dispute, or judgments of domestic courts; official communications to which the treaty gives rise; or the enactment of domestic legislation or the conclusion of international agreements for the purpose of implementing a treaty even before any specific act of application takes place at the internal or at the international level.[73]

Subsequent practice under Articles 31 and 32 may consist of any conduct in the application of a treaty which is attributable to a party to the treaty under international law.[74] Other conduct, including by non-state actors, does not constitute subsequent practice under Articles 31 and 32. Such conduct may, however, be relevant when assessing the subsequent practice of parties to a treaty.[75]

On the face of it, Article 5 of the Chicago Convention 1944,[76] which governs charter air services, does not require a charter airline to obtain permission to land en route, but for many years it has been a requirement that charter airlines seek permission to land in all cases, and the article is now so interpreted.

Perhaps the best, and most often quoted, example of interpretation by subsequent practice is the way in which members of the United Nations have interpreted and applied Article 27(3) of the UN Charter. This provides that decisions of the Security Council on non-procedural matters shall be made by the 'affirmative' vote of nine of its members 'including the *concurring votes* of the permanent members'. Although at first sight this would appear clearly to mean that all five permanent members must cast an affirmative vote, the practice of the Council from as early as 1946 was to interpret 'concurring' as meaning just 'not objecting'. Therefore, if a permanent member wishes

70 ILC Conclusion 2.4. See also Conclusions 4.2 and 4.3: '2. A "subsequent practice" as an authentic means of interpretation under article 31, paragraph 3 (*b*), consists of conduct in the application of a treaty, after its conclusion, which establishes the agreement of the parties regarding the interpretation of the treaty. 3. A "subsequent practice" as a supplementary means of interpretation under article 32 consists of conduct by one or more parties in the application of the treaty, after its conclusion.'

71 ILC Conclusion 9.1. 72 ILC Conclusion 9.2.

73 ILC Commentary on Conclusion 4.2, para. (18). See also *Gardiner*, 257–259, for analysis of conduct that may amount to practice of states in terms of executive, legislative and judicial acts.

74 ILC Conclusion 5.1.

75 ILC Conclusion 5.2. See the ILC Commentary on Conclusion 5 for further analysis.

76 15 UNTS 295 No. 102; UKTS (1953) No. 8. See B. Cheng, 'Air Law', in *Encyclopedia of Public International Law*, vol. 1 (North-Holland, Amsterdam 1992), 69, para. 5.

to block a decision, it is not enough for it to abstain, or even be absent; it must cast a negative vote (known colloquially as 'the veto'). Thus, during the early stages of the Korean War in 1950 the Soviet representative was, by staying away from meetings of the Council, not able to prevent the Council taking action.[77] The practice was upheld by the ICJ in *Namibia (South West Africa) (Legal Consequences for States of the Continued Presence of South Africa)*,[78] even though it is clear from the *travaux* of the Charter that it was not what had been originally intended by the members most directly affected: the permanent members.[79]

It is not necessary to show that each party has engaged in a practice, only that all have accepted it, albeit tacitly.

Relevant Rules of International Law

Article 31(3)(c) provides that there shall be taken into account, 'together with the context':

> any relevant rules of international law applicable in the relations between the parties.

This confirms that a treaty must be interpreted also in the wider context of general international law, but it can be misunderstood. In *Oil Platforms* (Merits),[80] the ICJ controversially used the provision as a peg on which to hang the whole corpus of international law on the use of force. In her separate opinion President Higgins pointed out that, in applying the provision, the Court should also have had regard to the 'context' of the treaty that gave jurisdiction to the Court and that was limited to economic and commercial matters.[81]

In certain cases, reaching an interpretation that is consistent with the intentions (or perceived intentions) of the parties may require regard to be had not only to international law at the time the treaty was concluded, but also to contemporary law (the 'inter-temporal rule').[82] On this, in its report on *Fragmentation of International Law*, the ILC stated in 2006:

[77] S. D. Bailey and S. Daws, *The Procedure of the United Nations Security Council* (3rd ed., Oxford University Press, Oxford 1998), 257.

[78] ICJ Reports (1971) 3, at 21–22, paras. 20–22; 49 ILR 2.

[79] See L. M. Goodrich, E. Hambro and A. P. Simons, *The Charter of the United Nations* (3rd ed., Columbia University Press, New York 1969), 229.

[80] ICJ Reports (2003) 161, at 182–184, paras. 41–45; 42 ILM (2003) 1334.

[81] See Separate Opinion of Judge Higgins at paras. 45 *et seq.*; and the note by A. Orakhelashvili, 53 ICLQ (2004) 753–761.

[82] See *Gardiner*, 291–295; P. Sands and J. Commission, 'Treaty, Custom and Time: Interpretation/ Application', in M. Fitzmaurice *et al.* (n. 18), 39–58; *Sinclair*, 138–140; Thirlway (n. 9), 57–60; R. Higgins, 'Some Observations on the Inter-temporal Rule in International Law', in J. Makarczyk (ed.), *Theory of International Law at the Threshold of the 21st Century* (Kluwer Law, The Hague 1996), 173–181; R. Higgins, 'Time and the Law: International Perspectives on an Old Problem', ICLQ 46 (1997) 50–120; Shaw (n. 12), 964–978.

> *Inter-temporality*. International law is a dynamic legal system. A treaty may convey whether in applying article 31(3)(c) the interpreter should refer only to rules of international law in force at the time of the conclusion of the treaty or may also take into account subsequent changes in the law. Moreover, the meaning of a treaty provision may also be affected by subsequent developments, especially where there are subsequent developments in customary law and general principles of law.[83]

It is also helpful to consider the inter-temporal rule through the perspective of what might be considered separate principles: the principle of contemporaneous interpretation (that the terms of a treaty are to be interpreted as they were understood at the time of the conclusion of the treaty); and the principle of evolutionary interpretation (that the terms of a treaty are to be interpreted as they are understood at the time of the interpretation of the treaty).[84] In choosing the former, judicial bodies have often relied on logic and common sense. When favouring the latter, certain factors may be identifiable, depending on the nature of the court or tribunal adjudicating, such as whether the terms are 'by definition evolutionary' or 'generic', or the treaty was entered into for a very long period, or is multilateral as opposed to bilateral, or is a human rights treaty.[85] After an examination of the relevant case law, Professor Dupuy concludes that the ICJ:

> only allows for a dynamic interpretation of a treaty where justified by notions and concepts in the terms of the treaty from which it may be inferred that the text is open to considerations of factual or legal evolution after the conclusion of the treaty.[86]

But other courts and tribunals may adopt different approaches depending upon the instrument and the context.

As for the role of subsequent agreements and subsequent practice in respect of evolutionary interpretation, ILC Conclusion 8, which is entitled 'Interpretation of treaty terms as capable of evolving over time', states:

[83] Fragmentation of International Law, Report of the ILC on the Work of its 58th session, 2006, UNGA 66th Session, Doc. A/61/10, A/CN.4/SER.A/2006/Add.l (Part 2), 175–184, at 180, para. (22). See also the majority of the UK Supreme Court in *Basfar* v. *Wong* [2020] UKSC 20, para. 67: 'The principle that developments in international law since the conclusion of a treaty should be taken into account in interpreting its terms is not only supported by the general presumption in favour of evolutionary interpretation; it is also required by article 31(3)(c) of the Treaties Convention.'

[84] See P. Tzeng, 'The Principles of Contemporaneous and Evolutionary Interpretation', in J. Klingler, Y. Parkhomenko and C. Salonidis (eds.), *Between the Lines of the Vienna Convention? Canons and Other Principles of Interpretation in Public International Law* (Kluwer Law International, Alphen aan den Rijn 2019), 387–422, at 387.

[85] This is drawn from Tzeng (n. 84), 418. See *Award in the Arbitration regarding the Iron Rhine ('Ijzeren Rijn') Railway between the Kingdom of Belgium and the Kingdom of the Netherlands*, 27 RIAA (2005) 35, 72–75, paras. 77–84.

[86] P.-M. Dupuy, 'Evolutionary Interpretation of Treaties: Between Memory and Prophecy', in Cannizzaro (n. 25), 123–137.

> Subsequent agreements and subsequent practice under article 31 and 32 may assist in determining whether or not the presumed intention of the parties upon the conclusion of the treaty was to give a term used a meaning which is capable of evolving over time.[87]

In the case of *Tyrer* v. *United Kingdom* the European Court of Human Rights took the view that the Convention[88] was a 'living instrument' to be 'interpreted in light of present-day conditions'.[89] In the case of *Magyar Helsinki Bizottság* v. *Hungary*,[90] the Court relied on subsequent practice to accord recognition, under certain conditions, to a right of freedom of information. But the Court has drawn certain limits to evolutionary interpretation. It has:

> not been prepared to derive from treaty instruments rights that were not included there at the outset, and it has been careful not to apply evolutionary interpretation to provisions that are determinative of the scope of other provisions of the treaty instrument.[91]

Article 31(3)(c) refers to any relevant rules of international law applicable in the relations *between the parties*. Four possibilities have been identified:[92] all parties to the treaty being interpreted must be parties to any other treaty being used; all parties to the dispute over interpretation must be parties to any other treaty being used; a rule being invoked from any other treaty must be shown to be a customary rule; a rule being invoked in another treaty must have been implicitly accepted or tolerated by all parties to the treaty under interpretation. Which of these prevails is unresolved.[93] But, similarly in its report on *Fragmentation of International Law*, the ILC stated in 2006:

> *Application of other treaty rules.* Article 31(3)(c) also requires the interpreter to consider other treaty-based rules so as to arrive at a consistent meaning. Such other rules are of particular relevance where parties to the treaty under interpretation are also parties to the other treaty, where the treaty rule has passed into or expresses customary international law or where they provide evidence of

[87] The Commentary explains, at para. (4), 181: 'Draft conclusion 8 [3] should not be read as taking any position regarding the appropriateness of a more contemporaneous or a more evolutive approach to treaty interpretation in general. Draft conclusion 8 [3] rather emphasizes that subsequent agreements and subsequent practice, as any other means of treaty interpretation, can support both a contemporaneous and an evolutive interpretation (or, as it is often called, evolutionary interpretation), where appropriate. The Commission, therefore, concluded that these means of treaty interpretation "may assist in determining whether or not" an evolutive interpretation is appropriate with regard to a particular treaty term.' See more fully the Commentary, 181–188.

[88] Amended by subsequent Protocols: consolidated text at CoE website.

[89] 5856/72, 58 ILR 339, at 353.

[90] 18030/11 ECHR 2016.

[91] E. Bjorge and R. Kolb, 'The Interpretation of Treaties over Time', in *Hollis, Oxford Guide*, 489–503, at 499.

[92] C. McLachlan, 'The Principle of Systematic Integration and Article 31(3)(c) of the Vienna Convention', ICLQ 54 (2005) 279–319.

[93] See the analysis in *Gardiner*, 310–317.

the common understanding of the parties as to the object and purpose of the treaty under interpretation or as to the meaning of a particular term.[94]

Special Meaning

A special meaning must be given to a term if it is established that the parties so intended (paragraph (4)).[95] The most obvious way they can do this is by defining a term in the 'definitions' article of the treaty.[96] Notwithstanding the apparent meaning of a term in its context, it is open to a party to invoke any special meaning, but the burden of proof of a special meaning will rest on that party.[97] In the passage in the 'Chairman's Statement' in the Final Act of the Conference on CCAMLR[98] which refers to islands 'over which the existence of State sovereignty is recognised by all Contracting Parties', the word 'existence' was carefully chosen to indicate that the passage also covered islands where sovereignty is disputed, such as South Georgia and the South Sandwich Islands.

Article 32: Supplementary Means of Interpretation

Supplementary means, such as the preparatory work of the treaty (*travaux*) and the circumstances of its conclusion, are not included in Article 31. That article is limited to the primary purpose for interpreting a treaty: an elucidation of the meaning of the text, not a fresh investigation as to the supposed intentions of the parties. Furthermore, *travaux* are by their nature less authentic than the other elements, often being incomplete and misleading.[99] Nevertheless, Article 32 provides that recourse may be had to supplementary elements to 'confirm' the meaning resulting from the application of Article 31.[100]

International tribunals (and those appearing before them) have for long had recourse to the *travaux* for this purpose.[101] In the *Lockerbie* proceedings, the United Kingdom maintained that it was not intended that the UN Charter should give the ICJ a power

[94] Fragmentation of International Law (n. 83), 180, para. (21).
[95] See *Gardiner*, 334: 'The notion of special meaning includes two distinct categories. One is the meaning which a term has in a particular area of human endeavour; the other is a particular meaning given by someone using a term that differs from the more common meaning or meanings. . . . The Vienna rules cover both situations.'
[96] See, e.g., the definition of 'aircraft' in Annex 7 to the Chicago Convention referred to in n. 34.
[97] See *Sinclair*, 126–127; Thirlway (n. 9), 27–29. [98] See n. 38. See also p. 245.
[99] See generally on the role of *travaux* in the context of Article 32, D. Mortenson, 'The Travaux of Travaux: Is the Vienna Convention Hostile to Drafting History?', AJIL (2013) 780–822; P. Merkouris, '"Third Party" Considerations and "Corrective Interpretation" in the Interpretative Use of Travaux Préparatoires – Is it Fahrenheit 451 for Preparatory Work?', in Fitzmaurice *et al.* (n. 18), 75–95; and R. Gardiner, 'The Role of Preparatory Work in Treaty Interpretation', in Orakhelashvili and Williams (n. 13), 97–116.
[100] See generally L. Sbolci, 'Supplementary Means of Interpretation', in Cannizzaro (n. 25), 145–163.
[101] See, e.g., *McNair*, 413 note 3, and 422 note 4; and the example of the use of the *travaux* of the VCCR 1963 in M. Mennecke and C. Tams, 'The Right to Consular Assistance under International Law', Ger YBIL

of judicial review over Security Council decisions, and that this was supported by the *travaux* of the Charter.[102]

The rest of Article 32 provides that recourse may also be had to the same supplementary means of interpretation when reliance on the primary means produces an interpretation that (a) leaves the meaning 'ambiguous or obscure' or (b) leads to a result that is 'manifestly absurd or unreasonable'. In this case, the purpose is not to confirm the meaning, but to determine it.

It has been suggested that, even when the ordinary meaning appears to be clear, if it is evident from the *travaux* that the ordinary meaning does not represent the intention of the parties, the primary duty in Article 31(1) to interpret a treaty in good faith requires a court to 'correct' the ordinary meaning.[103] It is, however, important to differentiate the case where supplementary means are used to *confirm* a meaning reached by applying the general rule, and the case where they are used to *determine* the meaning of a treaty provision.[104] Professor Gardiner suggests that:

> in the latter case supplementary means (most commonly preparatory work) may only be used if the result of deploying the general rule leaves the meaning ambiguous or obscure or produces a result which is manifestly absurd or unreasonable. These preconditions do *not* apply to use of preparatory work to confirm the meaning reached by application of the general rule, nor to its use for general understanding of the treaty.[105]

The ILC did not seek to define what is included in the *travaux*, but it is generally understood to include written material, such as successive drafts of the treaty, conference records,[106] explanatory statements by an expert consultant at a codification conference, uncontested interpretative statements by the chairman of a drafting committee and ILC Commentaries: in O'Connell's words, 'the amorphous mass of documentation which goes under the name *travaux préparatoires*'.[107] The value of the material will depend on several factors, the most important being authenticity, completeness and availability. The summary record of a conference prepared by an independent and skilled secretariat, such as that of the United Nations, will carry more weight than an unagreed record produced by a host state or a participating state.

42 (1999) 192–241, 223–224; *O'Connell*, 263; *Kasikili/Sedudu Island (Botswana* v. *Namibia)* (n. 12), at 1074, para. 46.

[102] See *Lockerbie (Libya* v. *United Kingdom)* (Preliminary Objections), ICJ Reports (1998) 9, at 24–27, paras. 41–48; 37 ILM (1998) 587; 117 ILR 1 and 664, and the dissenting opinion of President Schwebel. See also the oral submissions of the Lord Advocate (CR 97/17, para. 5.46), Verbatim Record 1997/17.

[103] S. Schwebel, 'May Preparatory Work be Used to Correct Rather than Confirm the "Clear" Meaning of a Treaty Provision?', in Makarczyk (n. 82), 541–547.

[104] *Gardiner*, 409. [105] *Gardiner*, 409.

[106] For a good example of UN practice, see the reports of the negotiation of the International Convention for the Suppression of the Financing of Terrorism 1997, UN Docs A/54/37, A/C.6/54/L.2 and A/54/ 615.

[107] *O'Connell*, 263. See *Kasikili/Sedudu Island (Botswana* v. *Namibia)* (n. 12), at 1074–1075, para. 46.

However, even the records of a conference served by an independent and expert secretariat will generally not tell the whole story. The most important parts of a negotiation, and of drafting, often take place informally with no agreed record being kept. The negotiations at the Third United Nations Law of the Sea Conference, which met intermittently from December 1973 until the adoption of UNCLOS 1982, are a good example. The reason why a particular compromise formula was adopted, and what it was intended to mean, may be difficult to establish.[108] This will be especially so if the form of words was deliberately chosen to overcome a near-irreconcilable difference of substance.

The final drafting of new Article 3 *bis* (prohibition on use of force against civil aircraft) of the Chicago Convention 1944 was done by hectic, highly visible and informal (*literally* back-of-the-envelope) negotiations during a mayoral reception held near the end of a three-week conference. As a result, it shows all the signs of the last-minute compromises that are needed to reach consensus. Here is the key paragraph:

> The Contracting States recognise that every State must refrain from resorting to the use of weapons against civil aircraft in flight and that, in case of interception, the lives of persons on board and the safety of aircraft must not be endangered. This provision shall not be interpreted as modifying in any way the rights and obligations of States set forth in the Charter of the United Nations.[109]

In fact, the purpose of the second sentence is to indicate, albeit obliquely, that force may be used against a civil aircraft if it is done in proper exercise of the inherent right of self-defence, as reflected in Article 51 of the UN Charter.

Here is an example of even more tortuous drafting:

> The activities of armed forces during an armed conflict, as those terms are understood under international humanitarian law, which are governed by that law, are not governed by this Convention, and the activities undertaken by the military forces of a State in the exercise of their official duties, inasmuch as they are governed by other rules of international law, are not governed by this Convention.

This opaque text in Article 19(2) of the Terrorist Bombings Convention 1997[110] reflects a sharp difference of opinion on the extent to which acts by members of armed forces should be subject to that convention. The formula does not paper over the cracks very well.

108 See, e.g., E. Denza, *Diplomatic Law* (4th ed., Oxford University Press, Oxford 2016), 123 *et seq.*, regarding whether legal process can be served on a diplomatic mission.

109 23 ILM (1984) 705; UKTS (1999) No. 68.

110 2149 UNTS 284 No. 37517; 37 ILM (1998) 251; UKTS (2001) No. 31; [2002] ATS 17.

Travaux must therefore always be approached with care. Their investigation is time-consuming, their usefulness often being marginal and very seldom decisive.

In the case of a multilateral treaty that is open to states that did not take part in its negotiation, the *travaux* can probably be invoked in a dispute to which they are parties, at least if they have been published or are otherwise available. Any other rule would be extremely inconvenient given the number of new states that emerged after the Second World War, and the quantity of multilateral treaties made since then to which states have subsequently become parties.[111]

An examination of the *travaux* did not resolve the question of interpretation posed by Article XIV(2) of the CTBT mentioned at the start of this chapter, the official records of the Conference on Disarmament not throwing any light on the matter. But it was agreed eventually that the inclusion of the phrase 'the anniversary of' before the reference to the opening for signature was simply a mistake; the words should have been omitted. This would have brought the provision into line with the rest of the article. Because of an oversight, this was not done.

Other Supplementary Means of Interpretation

Article 32 gives only examples of the principal supplementary means of interpretation. It may also be legitimate to look at other treaties on the same subject matter adopted either before or after the one in question that use the same or similar terms. It is also legitimate to assume that the parties to a treaty did not intend that it would be incompatible with customary international law.[112]

There are several other means of interpretation (often referred to as 'canons of interpretation'),[113] though it is not always easy to distinguish them from familiar legal techniques that are based on simple common sense or grammatical rules. Many derive from principles of domestic law, especially Roman law. *Oppenheim* lists the most important, as well as giving a wealth of examples of their application and other sources.[114] It will therefore be enough to mention briefly some of the more useful, remembering always that none of them should be followed slavishly, being no more than *possible* aids to interpretation. Most relate to discovering the ordinary meaning.

(1) *A contrario*: the ICCPR 1966 has no denunciation clause, but its (first) Optional Protocol (adopted at the same time) does. One can therefore argue that it was not intended that a party would have the right to withdraw from the Covenant. This is interpretation *a contrario*. Article IV of the Genocide Convention 1948[115]

[111] Paragraph 20 of the ILC Commentary to draft article 28: YBILC 1966, vol. II, 223; *Sinclair*, 142–144.
[112] *O'Connell*, 261. [113] See Klingler *et al.* (n. 84).
[114] 1269–1282, paras. 631–633. See also the detailed analysis of each of the main canons in Klingler *et al.* (n. 84).
[115] 78 UNTS 277 No. 1021; UKTS (1970) No. 58.

provides that heads of state can be prosecuted for genocide in the country where the crime was committed or before an international tribunal. Article 27 of the Rome Statute 1998 provides expressly that a head of state is subject to the jurisdiction of the ICC.[116] Since neither the Hostages Convention 1979[117] nor the Torture Convention 1984[118] have such provisions, it could be argued that it could not have been intended that those treaties should apply to heads of state. But in these two latter examples, this argument on its own is unlikely to be decisive.

(2) Acquiescence: if a party has made plain its understanding of the meaning of a provision, and it later applies it in that sense without objection, other parties may not be able to insist on a different interpretation. Article 31(3)(b) might also apply.

(3) *Effet utile* (principle of effectiveness): provisions should be interpreted so as to have an effective meaning. This may be adopted narrowly in the sense of the related principle, *ut res magis valeat quam pereat*: if various interpretations of a provision are possible, the one that does not deprive that provision of its meaning will be pursued.[119] Or it may be adopted more broadly to justify giving a maximum effect to treaty provisions, or to give maximum effectiveness to the intentions of the parties; or by stressing the need to give ambiguous provisions an effective meaning in the context of the other provisions of a treaty or, more broadly, in the context of international law in general.[120]

(4) *Contra proferentem*: if it is possible to interpret a provision in two ways, the meaning that is less favourable to the party that proposed it, or for whose benefit it was included, should be adopted. The principle is applied more often to standard contracts; it is rarer for a treaty (and especially a multilateral treaty) to contain a provision for which only one party is clearly responsible.[121]

[116] 2187 UNTS 91 No. 38544; 37 ILM (1998) 998; UKTS (2002) No. 35.

[117] 1316 UNTS 205 No. 21931; 18 ILM (1979) 1460; UKTS (1983) No. 81.

[118] 1465 UNTS 85 No. 24841; 23 ILM (1984) 1027; UKTS (1991) No. 107.

[119] See C. Braumann and A. Reinisch, '*Effet Utile*', in Klingler *et al.* (n. 84), 47–72, at 48. This analyses the relationship between the principle of *effet utile* and Article 31 VCLT, and interpretations guided by *effet utile* in practice. The principle has been discussed in decisions by, for example, the ICJ, ICSID tribunals, the WTO Appellate Body, the Inter-American Court of Human Rights and the European Court of Human Rights. On the last of these, see also D. Rietiker, 'The Principle of "Effectiveness" in the Recent Jurisprudence of the European Court of Human Rights', *Nordic Journal of International Law* 79 (2010) 245–277; G. Serghides, 'The Principle of Effectiveness in the European Convention on Human Rights, in Particular its Relationship to the Other Convention Principles', *Hague Yearbook of International Law* 30 (2017) 1–16.

[120] Braumann and Reinisch (n. 119), 49.

[121] See P. d'Argent, '*Contra Preferentem*', in Klingler *et al.* (n. 84), 241–258. He states at 252–253: 'However, the silence of the Vienna Convention on *contra preferentem* did not mark its demise: litigants continue to refer to it in support of their arguments, while various separate or dissenting opinions have relied on it. Some tribunals have expressly alluded to it, although to the best of the author's knowledge, none have applied it as such to justify a specific interpretation of a treaty: rather, tribunals have found it inapplicable in the case they had to settle.'

(5) *Ejusdem generis*: when general words follow special words, the general words are limited by the *genus* (class) indicated by the special words.[122] Taking as an example Article I of the CTBT, in the phrase 'any nuclear weapon test explosion *or any other nuclear explosion*' the scope of the italicised words is limited by the preceding words, thereby excluding from the CTBT the actual use of nuclear weapons.
(6) *Expressio unius est exclusio alterius:* when something is stated expressly in the treaty, any similar matter omitted from the treaty is presumed to have been omitted intentionally.[123]
(7) *Ex abundante cautela*: a seemingly redundant word may be explained as simply an excess of caution by the drafter.[124]
(8) *Lex posterior derogat legi priori*: when two rules apply to the same matter, the later in time prevails.
(9) *Lex specialis derogat legi generali*: a *specific* rule prevails over a general rule.[125] This rule has been applied when considering the applicability of a body of law in one area (e.g., armed conflict) with that in another (e.g., human rights).[126]

All these supplementary means of interpretation need to be used with special care. They are no more than aids to interpretation, and might well produce wrong results if followed slavishly.

Manifestly Absurd or Unreasonable

Even if the words of the treaty are clear, if applying them would lead to a result that would be manifestly absurd or unreasonable (to adopt the language in Article 32(b)),

122 See F. Baetens, 'Ejusdem Generis and Noscitur a Sociis', in Klingler *et al.* (n. 84), 133–159. The latter principle holds that the meaning of an unclear word or phrase, especially one on a list, should be determined by the words immediately surrounding it. The article concludes (at 157): 'Despite the number of references to it, and with the exception of the interpretation of MFN clauses, *ejusdem generis* is not an influential canon in most areas of international law. The *noscitur a sociis* canon has apparently never been explicitly applied at the international level, so its influence is negligible.'

123 See J. Klingler, '*Expressio Unius Est Exclusio Alterius*', in Klingler *et al.* (n. 84), 73–114. This carefully analyses cases where the principle has been applied or rejected. It comments at the outset (at 75): 'Expressions of caution, if not outright scepticism, are appropriately widespread. Indeed, if there is a common theme in the jurisprudence, it is that the canon "must always be applied with great care", for it "is not of universal application".'

124 See A. Macdonald, '*Ex Abundante Cautela*', in Klingler *et al.* (n. 84), 115–131. This observes (at 121) that bilateral investment treaties are the main area in which this principle has been applied to treaties, rather than to other types of text (see 121–126 for the analysis).

125 Or the rule may be reframed negatively as '*generalia specialibus non derogant*', general rules do not derogate from special rules. See D. Pulkowski, '*Lex Specialis Derogat Legi Generali/Generalia Specialibus Non Derogant*', in Klingler *et al.* (n. 84), 161–196.

126 See *Legality of the Threat or Use of Nuclear Weapons*, Advisory Opinion, ICJ Reports (1996) 226, at 240, para. 25; *Legal Consequences of the Construction of a Wall in the Occupied Palestinian Territory*, Advisory Opinion, ICJ Reports (2004) 136, at 178, para. 106; and Pulkowski (n. 125), 191–195.

the parties must seek another interpretation. When, in 1971, the government of the People's Republic of China replaced the government of the Republic of China as the representative of China in the United Nations, there was never any question of the specific reference in Article 23(1) of the UN Charter to 'the Republic of China' having to be amended. A similar approach was followed in 1991 when, with the gaining of independence by various Soviet republics, the 'Union of Soviet Socialist Republics' (also specifically mentioned in Article 23(1)) was renamed the Russian Federation and lost much of its territory.[127] Any other approach would have led to manifestly unacceptable results.

Implied Terms

Although it is not for an international tribunal to revise a treaty by reading into it provisions that it does not contain,[128] except by necessary implication, it is sometimes necessary to imply a term, and this has been the approach of the ICJ (though it will not 'revise' a treaty on the pretext that it has found an omission)[129] and the European Court of Human Rights.[130] Courts and tribunals have on occasion considered the question of implied powers either of an international organisation or of the court or tribunal itself.[131] The notion of implied powers in this context has a 'degree of normativity' in the interpretation of constituent instruments, although 'perhaps not yet reaching the status of a customary norm or general principle of law'.[132]

Here is an example that, like most cases of interpretation, did not end up in court. At the end of the Falklands conflict in 1982 there was not enough accommodation in the territory for the approximately 10,000 Argentine prisoners of war (POWs) captured on land in the final stages, the tents intended for them having been lost at sea when the ship carrying them was sunk by enemy action. Following consultations by the United Kingdom with the ICRC, it was decided that the POWs could be kept on merchant ships and warships in Falklands waters until they could be repatriated. Article 22 of the Third Geneva Convention[133] clearly prohibits holding on ships POWs who are captured on land, but given that the primary object and purpose of that Convention is the welfare of POWs, one could properly imply a term to the effect

[127] See http://treaties.un.org/Pages/HistoricalInfo.aspx, notes to entries for China and the Russian Federation.

[128] See *Gardiner*, 165–167, and the cases cited there.

[129] See S. Rosenne, *The Law and Practice of the International Court of Justice* (3rd ed., Martinus Nijhoff, The Hague 1997), 172–173. And see Thirlway (n. 9), 42–43.

[130] See *McNair*, chapter 26; and A. H. Robertson and J. G. Merrills, *Human Rights in Europe* (Manchester University Press, Manchester 2001).

[131] See, for example, *Reparation for Injuries Suffered in the Service of the United Nations*, Advisory Opinion, ICJ Reports (1949) 174, at 182: 'Under international law, the Organization must be deemed to have those powers which, though not expressly provided in the Charter, are conferred upon it by necessary implication as being essential to the performance of its duties.'

[132] A. D. Mitchell and T. Voon, 'The Rule of Necessary Implication', in Klingler *et al.* (n. 84), 331–357, at 334.

[133] 75 UNTS 3 No. 972; UKTS (1958) No. 39.

that when, for reasons beyond its control, a party to a conflict is unable to comply with Article 22, it may hold POWs on ships if that is preferable to leaving them on land without sufficient protection from the elements. Good interpretation is often no more than the application of common sense.

A treaty is interpreted in a way that is consistent with the general rules of international law (*lex generalis*), *unless* the treaty, by express words or necessary implication, provides otherwise, though due to its nature *jus cogens* could, of course, not be displaced. Thus, one has to look at the treaty *as a whole*, plus all other relevant materials, assessing their respective weight and value.

Interpretation of Treaties in More Than One Language

Most treaties, bilateral as well as multilateral, are bilingual or plurilingual. The exceptions are mostly very old treaties or treaties between states that share the same first language, or official or working language.[134] Even then, a (non-authentic) text in another language may be produced for certain purposes. It is also quite common for two states with different languages to negotiate a treaty in a third language (these days often English), and for the only authentic text to be in that language. Ironically, these include even cultural agreements.[135] The language of one or more of the negotiating states may not be widely spoken, and to produce a draft, and hold the negotiations, in that language may be unduly burdensome. Bilateral negotiations are therefore frequently held in the language of only one of the states or in a third language common to both.

This may be reflected in the languages in which a treaty is concluded and in the choice of a language text to prevail in the case of a difference. The Holy See–Israel Fundamental Agreement 1993 is in English and Hebrew, the English prevailing in case of divergence.[136] Similarly, the Israel–Jordan Peace Agreement 1994 has equally authentic texts in Arabic, English and Hebrew, but again the English text prevails.[137] Air services negotiations are frequently conducted only in English, even if that is not the first language of either delegation. But it is the *lingua franca* of the world of aviation, not just of pilots, and so, sometimes, an English text will prevail[138] or the text will be in English only.[139] The *Estonia* Agreement 1995[140] between Estonia, Finland and Sweden was concluded *only* in English.

[134] For example, see the e-ASEAN Framework Agreement 2000: 40 ILM (2001) 516.

[135] Japan–Pakistan Cultural Agreement 1957 (325 UNTS 22 No. 4692); Finland–Netherlands Cultural Agreement 1988 (1540 UNTS 257 No. 26718).

[136] 1775 UNTS 182 No. 30925; 33 ILM (1994) 154.

[137] 2042 UNTS 586 No. 35326; 34 ILM (1995) 43.

[138] Netherlands–Saudi Arabia Air Transport Agreement 1985: 1480 UNTS 143 No. 25244. See also the Poland–UK Agreement on the Prepayment of Certain Obligations 2005: UKTS (2005) No. 17.

[139] UK–Bahrain Agreement 1998: 2067 UNTS 152 No. 35799; UKTS (1999) No. 4. The Jordan–US Agreement on a Free Trade Area 2000 is in English only. Although an authentic Arabic text has been prepared, the English text will prevail in case of any discrepancy (41 ILM (2002) 63).

[140] 1890 UNTS 176 No. 32189. See also 1947 UNTS 404 No. 32189; UKTS (1999) No. 74 (Additional Protocol on UK accession).

Occasionally, when the treaty has been negotiated in one of the two equally authoritative languages, and neither will prevail in case of a difference, the other language text may be prepared only after the treaty is signed, and this can in practice lead to delay in entry into force.[141] The UK–EU Trade and Cooperation Agreement was signed on 30 December 2020, with some urgency just before the end of the transition period.[142] The text had been negotiated in English, and only an English text was ready upon signature. Article 780 provided that all language versions would be subject to a process of final legal-linguistic revision by 30 April 2021. It went on to provide:

> The language versions resulting from the above process of final legal-linguistic revision shall replace *ab initio* the signed versions of the Agreement and shall be established as authentic and definitive by exchange of diplomatic notes between the Parties.

Multilateral negotiations are most likely to be held in more than one language, though there are notable exceptions. All but the most formal sessions of the fifty-seven-member OSCE are held only in English, and the OSCE Convention on Conciliation and Arbitration of 1992[143] was negotiated on the basis of an English draft. Although the proceedings of the General Assembly of the United Nations and its committees are conducted in the six official languages, informal meetings (of which there are many) are often held, and drafting done, only in English.

The reasons for using one language in multilateral negotiations are various, and will depend on the circumstances. The cost of translation and simultaneous interpretation is an important factor. Even when these can be afforded, it is sometimes easier, and therefore quicker, to hold negotiations in one language. On the other hand, technical reasons (or national policies) may require that negotiations are conducted in other languages or at least that the resulting treaty is in several. This can lead to treaties, particularly regional treaties, being produced in numerous languages. An extreme example is the 1997 Protocol further amending the Eurocontrol Convention of 1960.[144] This is in no less than nineteen European languages, all of which are equally authentic, even though it was negotiated on the basis of only English and French texts.

[141] See the UK–Lithuania Agreement on International Road Transport 1994: UKTS (2005) No. 34. The UK–Kazakhstan Convention for the Avoidance of Double Taxation 1994 provides for an equally authentic Kazakh text to be prepared. Although the Agreement entered into force in 1996, a Protocol agreeing the Kazakh text was concluded only in 1998: see UKTS (1999) No. 25, 65.

[142] See n. 17. The treaty was provisionally applied pending entry into force. The 'transition or implementation period' was a period established under Article 126 *et seq.* of the EU–UK Withdrawal Agreement during which, save as otherwise provided, Union law was applicable to and in the UK. It expired on 31 December 2020.

[143] 1842 UNTS 151 No. 31413; 32 ILM (1993) 557.

[144] 523 UNTS 117 No. 7557; UKTS (1963) No. 39; amending Protocols 1981: UKTS (1987) No. 2; and 1997: text in UK Misc. Series (2002) No. 15.

Fortunately, it provides that in the case of divergence between the different language versions the French text prevails, as the original treaty provided.

Treaties that have been concluded in more than one language can cause problems of interpretation if there are material differences between the language texts. These can be to some extent avoided if, before the texts are authenticated, there is a thorough combing through of the texts (as part of the process known, appropriately, as the *toilettage finale* or perhaps less elegantly, 'scrubbing') to clean them up and straighten out inconsistencies. This has the added advantage that one usually discovers at least minor errors, and sometimes major substantive problems. The process is most easily done with bilateral treaties. In practice, the translations of multilateral treaties are done by translators who, though highly professional, will not have been at the negotiations and may not necessarily appreciate all the nuances of the final text. When the negotiations have been primarily on the basis of a draft in one language, it is essential that the states into whose mother tongue the text is to be translated check the translations meticulously.

But if, despite all these efforts, there is a discrepancy, the problem may be largely overcome if the treaty provides that, in the case of inconsistency, the text in one language shall prevail. The 1955 Protocol to amend the Warsaw Convention 1929 has three authentic texts – English, French and Spanish – but provides that 'in the case of any inconsistency, the text in the French language, *in which language the Convention was drawn up*, shall prevail'.[145] Because the Warsaw Convention was concluded so long ago, has been amended several times and is specifically designed to be given effect in domestic law, consistency in its interpretation is of prime importance. This can only be achieved by maintaining the French text of the Convention, and the amendments to it, as the authoritative (i.e., only true) text, even if this causes difficulties for judges in non-French-speaking countries.[146] The British legislation implementing amendments to the Convention therefore schedules both the French and English texts.[147]

When a treaty is not one in a line of treaties on the same matter, it may still be prudent to provide for one language to be authoritative. The Kuwait Regional Marine Environment Convention 1978 was concluded in Arabic, English and Persian, but provides that in the case of divergence the English text prevails.[148] The Convention was almost certainly drafted and negotiated primarily, or even exclusively, in English.

Article 112 of the Interim Agreement with a view to an Economic Partnership between the SADC EPA States and the European Community (now the Union), initialled on 23 November 2007, provides that all the EC (now EU) official languages

[145] 478 UNTS 371 No. 6943; UKTS (1967) No. 62.

[146] R. Gardiner, 'Treaty Interpretation in the English Courts since Fothergill v. Monarch Airlines', ICLQ 44 (1995) 620–628.

[147] Carriage by Air Act 1961 and Carriage by Air (Supplementary Provisions) Act 1962.

[148] 1140 UNTS 155 No. 17898; 17 ILM (1978) 511.

shall be equally authoritative, but in the event of a 'contradiction' reference shall be made to the text in which the Agreement was negotiated (namely, English).[149]

Article 33

These treaty practices are reflected in Article 33.[150] Unless the treaty provides, or the parties otherwise agree, that in the case of divergence between the texts a particular text shall prevail, the text is equally 'authoritative' in each language in which it has been authenticated (paragraph 1). Some treaties are silent on the matter of authenticity. A treaty concluded by an exchange of notes in different languages does not make any provision that one language text will prevail, though one waits in hope for the day that a UK–US treaty does so. In the absence of any provision to the contrary, each text is equally authentic. The most usual practice is to state expressly in the treaty if the various language texts are equally authentic (see, e.g., Article 85 of the VCLT itself).

If a version of a treaty is produced in a language other than those in which the treaty has been authenticated (e.g., an 'official' text or one made for the purposes of registration with the United Nations), it is not an authentic text unless the treaty so provides or the parties so agree (paragraph 2).

If there are two or more authentic texts, the normal rules of interpretation in Articles 31 and 32 remain the starting point. Although discrepancies between different language texts can complicate interpretation, when the meaning is ambiguous or obscure in one text, it may be clearer in another, and so there may be no need to attempt to reconcile them. Paragraph 3 of Article 33 reflects this approach: the terms of a treaty are presumed to have the same meaning in each authentic text.[151]

Paragraph 4 lays down the residual rule that, provided there is no provision for a particular text to prevail, when a comparison of the authentic texts discloses a difference of meaning that the application of Articles 31 and 32 does not remove, one must adopt the meaning that best reconciles the texts. In *France* v. *Commission*,[152] the European Court of Justice (ECJ) interpreted Article 228 of the Treaty of Rome by considering the authentic English, Danish, Dutch, French and German texts.

Of course, in most cases each party will use only one authentic language version of the treaty (as it is entitled to do under paragraph 3), and if there are discrepancies they may never come to light. But this does not mean that the most restrictive

[149] OJ L 319, 04.12.2009, 3, at 31.

[150] See the useful article by C. Kuner, 'The Interpretation of Multilateral Treaties: Comparison of Texts versus the Presumption of Similar Meaning', ICLQ 40 (1991) 953–964, though it somewhat overstates the scale of the problem. As regards the *Young Loan* Arbitration 1980 (59 ILR 495), see *Sinclair*, 121–122, 143–144 and 150–152.

[151] The ICJ applied Article 33(3) in *Kasikili/Sedudu Island (Botswana* v. *Namibia)* (n. 12), at 1062, para. 25.

[152] Case C-327/91; [1994] ECR I-3641; 101 ILR 29.

interpretation, or the lowest common denominator, must be adopted.[153] Nor does it mean that each language text will carry the same weight. If the treaty was negotiated and drafted in only one of the authentic languages, it is natural to place more reliance on that text, particularly if it is unambiguous. This approach is not incompatible with paragraph 4, and the jurisprudence of the ICJ would seem to support it in suitable cases.[154] The Dayton Agreement 1995 was negotiated entirely in English, even though there are supposed to be authentic texts in Bosnian, Croatian and Serbian.[155] The European Space Agency Convention 1975 was concluded in seven 'equally authentic' languages. The Convention provides for texts to be drawn up in other official languages of the member states and 'authenticated by a unanimous decision of all Member States'. In this particular case, although such texts are equally authentic, in practice they may not carry quite the same weight as the original language texts. In other cases, the treaty may be concluded in one authentic, 'neutral', language (such as English or French) and provide for 'official' (but non-authentic) translations into the languages of the parties to be made later. The Convention on Temporary Admission 1990[156] has two authentic texts, English and French, but makes provision for 'authoritative translations' into Arabic, Chinese, Russian and Spanish.[157]

[153] ILC Commentary, 225–226, para. (8); *Sinclair*, 149–151. [154] *Sinclair*, 147–152. [155] See n. 47.
[156] 1762 UNTS 121 No. 30667; UKTS (1999) No. 60. [157] Article 34.

14

Third States

Who is the third who walks always beside you?[1]

In relation to a treaty, a third state[2] is 'a State not a party to the treaty' (Article 2(1)(h)). A range of states falls within this definition, from one that is not eligible to become a party to a state that has ratified but for which the treaty is not yet in force. Third states should not be confused with *objects* of international law, such as corporations and individuals. Although some treaties confer important rights on them, that does *not* make them third parties. While the rules in the Convention rest firmly on the sovereignty and independence of states, similar rules apply in the law of contract, and, as with them, the third state probably has to be identifiable either by name or as a member of a certain class or as answering to a particular description.

General Rule

The general rule is rather obvious: a treaty does not create either obligations or rights for a third state without its consent (Article 34). Thus, a treaty, whether bilateral or multilateral, cannot, by its own force, impose an obligation on a third state, or modify in any way the legal rights of a third state, without that state's consent.[3] For the same reason, a right cannot arise for a third state from a treaty that makes no provision for that state, either specifically or by necessary inference.

Articles 35 and 36 elaborate the general rule by setting out those circumstances in which a treaty can apply to a third state.

Treaties Providing for Obligations for Third States

Two conditions must be satisfied before a state can be bound by an *obligation* arising from a provision in a treaty to which it is *not* a party: first, the parties must intend the provision to be the means of establishing the obligation of the third state; second, the

[1] T. S. Eliot, *The Waste Land* (1922), Pt 5.

[2] For an exhaustive account of this subject, see M. Fitzmaurice, 'Third Parties and the Law of Treaties', *Max Planck Yearbook of UN Law* (Kluwer Law International, The Hague 2002), 37–137.

[3] This is reflected, for example, in Article 351 of the Treaty on the Functioning of the European Union (previously Article 234 of the Treaty of Rome 1957, for which, see 298 UNTS 3 No. 4300).

third state must have expressly accepted the obligation in writing (Article 35). Conduct consistent with acceptance of the obligation will not, of itself, bind the third state. And even when a third state has accepted an obligation in a treaty, it does *not* become a party to the treaty.

Treaties Providing for Rights for Third States

There is nothing in international law which prevents two or more states creating by treaty a *right* in favour of a third state. An intention to create only a *benefit* (such as an agreement between the parties to restrict noxious emissions which will, as a matter of fact, also benefit a third state) does not confer any right on the third state. Whether states have created a right for a third state depends on their intention. Thus, a right arises for a third state (or a group of states to which it belongs) from a provision of a treaty if the parties to it so intend *and* the third state assents. But since the right accorded to the third state does not require it to do anything, its assent is presumed as long as the contrary is not indicated, unless the treaty provides otherwise (Article 36(1)).

Peace treaties concluded after the First and Second World Wars provided for the defeated states to waive claims arising out of the wars in favour of certain states that were not parties to the peace treaties. Article 109 of the Treaty of Versailles[4] contained stipulations in favour of Denmark, and Articles 358 and 374 in favour of Switzerland.

When exercising a right conferred on it, the third state must comply with the conditions for its exercise provided for in the treaty or established in conformity with it (Article 36(2)). The latter phrase takes account of the fact that the conditions may be laid down in a supplementary instrument or, if consistent with the treaty, unilaterally by a party. Provisions on freedom of navigation on specific international rivers or waterways are usually subject to the right of the territorial state to lay down conditions for its exercise. Similarly, Article 35(2) of the UN Charter gives a state that is not a member of the United Nations the right to bring a dispute to which it is a party to the attention of the Security Council or the General Assembly, provided it accepts in advance for the purposes of the dispute the obligations of peaceful settlement of disputes provided for in the Charter.

Erga omnes Status or Regime

Obligations *erga omnes* were defined in the *Barcelona Traction* case in 1970 as obligations in whose observance 'all States can be held to have a legal interest'.[5]

[4] CTS 188; UKTS (1919) No. 4. See H. Thirlway, 'The Law and Procedure of the International Court of Justice', BYIL 63 (1992) 43–47.

[5] *Barcelona Traction, Light and Power Company, Limited*, Judgment, ICJ Reports (1970) 3, at 32, para. 33.

The concept is recognised in the ILC Draft Articles on State Responsibility.[6] The notion of *erga omnes partes* obligations means those which stem from an international treaty,[7] whereas *erga omnes* obligations denote universally recognised obligations of international customary law owed to the international community as a whole.[8] There is a substantial overlap with the concept of *jus cogens*,[9] but in the treaty context specific *erga omnes partes* obligations, which do not necessarily reflect peremptory norms, might be considered to have distinctive value.

Certain treaties have in this sense been considered as creating a status or regime valid *erga omnes*.[10] Examples include treaties that provide for neutralisation or demilitarisation of a certain territory or area, such as Svalbard[11] or outer space;[12] for freedom of navigation in international waterways, such as the Suez Canal (Constantinople Convention 1888),[13] the Turkish (or Black Sea) Straits (Montreux Convention 1936)[14] and the Straits of Magellan;[15] or for a regime for a special area. The Antarctic Treaty 1959[16] has been given as an example of the latter, since it creates a unique (or objective) regime for the area south of latitude 60° S, even though it has only forty-six parties (and of which only twenty-eight have decision-making powers under the treaty), but they come from all continents and include most of the major politically and economically important states.[17] It has been suggested that the *Estonia* Agreement may create an objective regime.[18]

The VCLT does not deal with *erga omnes* rights and obligations as such. The ILC considered that the rule in Article 36(1), by which a right can be accorded to 'all States', and the process recognised by Article 38 (see below), furnished a sufficient legal basis for the establishment of treaty rights and obligations valid *erga omnes*.

6 Articles 42 and 48, Draft articles on responsibility of States for Internationally Wrongful Acts, ILC Report 2001, A/56/10, 20–143.

7 See the Commentary to Article 48, Draft articles on responsibility (n. 6), 126, para. 6.

8 *Dörr and Schmalenbach*, 482–483 and note 126.

9 On *jus cogens*, see Chapter 17, pp. 328–329. On the overlap and distinction between *jus cogens* and *erga omnes*, see *Dörr and Schmalenbach*, 1005–1006; C. Tams, *Enforcing Obligations Erga Omnes in International Law* (Cambridge University Press, Cambridge 2005), 139–157; P. Picone, 'The Distinction between Jus Cogens and Obligations Erga Omnes', in E. Cannizzaro (ed.), *The Law of Treaties beyond the Vienna Convention* (Oxford University Press, Oxford 2011), 411–424.

10 See M. Ragazzi, *The Concept of International Obligations Erga Omnes* (Oxford University Press, Oxford 1997), 24–27; Commentary to Article 48, Draft articles on responsibility (n. 6), 126, para. 7.

11 2 LNTS 8; UKTS (1924) No. 18; [1925] ATS 10.

12 610 UNTS 205 No. 8843; 6 ILM (1967) 386; UKTS (1968) No. 10; TIAS 6347.

13 Convention Respecting the Free Navigation of the Suez Maritime Canal 171 CTS 241.

14 Convention regarding the Regime of the Straits 173 LNTS 213; UKTS (1937) No. 30.

15 Boundary Treaty between Argentina and Chile 159 CTS 45.

16 402 UNTS 71 No. 5778; UKTS (1961) No. 97; www.ats.aq. For Antarctic law, see A. Watts, *International Law and the Antarctic Treaty System* (Grotius Publications: Cambridge 1992).

17 For a detailed argument for regarding the Antarctic Treaty as creating an objective regime, see Watts (n. 16), 295–298.

18 1890 UNTS 176 No. 32189; UKTS (1999) No. 74; J. Klabbers, 'Les cimetières marins sont-ils établis comme des régimes objectifs', *Collection Espaces et Ressources Maritimes* 11 (1997) 121–133.

Revocation or Modification of Obligations or Rights of Third States

When an *obligation* has arisen for a third state in conformity with Article 35, unless it has been agreed otherwise, the obligation may be revoked or modified only with the consent of the parties *and* the third state (Article 37(1)). The initiative for revocation may come from the third state, in which case the consent of the parties to the treaty is necessary; but if they wish to renounce their right to call for the performance by the third state of the obligation, the consent of the third state would be a formality. On the other hand, the third state's obligations may involve a complex relationship with the parties to the treaty, and possibly involve also the rights of the third state. It is therefore desirable that any change in the obligations should be by mutual consent.

When the parties create *rights* in favour of a third state, especially in matters such as freedom of navigation in international waterways or transit through territory, it is desirable that such rights should have a measure of solidity and firmness. The parties may not therefore revoke or modify rights if it is established that they were intended not to be revocable or subject to modification without the consent of the third state (Article 37(2)).

If the parties wish to have such options, they can provide for this in the treaty, or by other means, when creating them. If they have not done so, and if the treaty creates a status or regime that is valid *erga omnes,* there is a presumption that the right cannot be changed without the consent of third states.

There is no need to provide for revocation by the third state of its rights, since it can always decline to exercise them.

Rules in a Treaty Becoming Binding on Third States through International Custom

A treaty may formulate a rule or establish a regime which later becomes generally accepted by states that are not parties to the treaty. Nothing in Articles 34–37 precludes a rule set forth in a treaty from becoming binding upon a third state, though as a rule of customary international law (Article 38). In respect of the rules of land warfare in the Hague Conventions 1899 and 1907, the Nuremberg Tribunal decided that by 1939 the rules 'were regarded as being declaratory of the laws and customs of war'.[19] Similarly, a treaty purporting to codify customary law may come to be regarded as representing the customary rules. The VCLT is itself a very good example. These are not cases where a treaty has legal effects for third states: for them the binding force of the rules remains custom. It was, nevertheless, decided to include Article 38 so as to make it clear that nothing in the immediately preceding articles precluded such a result.

[19] *International Military Tribunal*, vol. XXII, 497, quoted in R. Woetzel, *The Nuremberg Trials in International Law* (Stevens, London 1960), 497.

Third-State Nationals and Some Others

Even though State C is not party to a bilateral or multilateral treaty to which States A and B are parties, a national of State C who is present in one of the other two states may still be subject to the treaty. For example, a bilateral extradition treaty provides for the surrender of a person who is in the territory of one party to the other party. This is *irrespective* of their nationality, except that – perhaps rather ironically – sometimes the requested state has reserved the right not to surrender its own nationals. A similar situation exists under multilateral counterterrorism treaties, though an own national who cannot be extradited can still be prosecuted even if the alleged offence occurred abroad. Similarly, under the Rome Statute 1998, a national of a state that is not a party to the Statute may still be surrendered to the ICC.[20] The Court could have jurisdiction over a national of a state that is not a party to the Statute if the crime was committed in the territory of a party or was referred to the ICC by the Security Council.

[20] 2187 UNTS 91 No. 38544; 37 ILM (1998) 998; UKTS (2002) No. 35.

15

Amendment

I must make amends.[1]

The amendment of treaties is of infinitely more concern than any question of their possible invalidity (Chapter 17). A subject of great practical importance, amendment always needs to be thought about seriously when drafting or negotiating, especially a multilateral treaty: afterwards is just too late. Although amending a bilateral treaty is not technically difficult, amending a multilateral treaty can raise a multitude of problems, both technical and political. In domestic law, most contracts are between two parties and are relatively short-lived. In contrast, a multilateral treaty may have as many as 190 or so parties, and be of unlimited duration. These factors lead to three basic problems. First, the process of agreeing on amendments and then bringing them into force can be as difficult as negotiating and bringing into force the original treaty, and sometimes even more troublesome. Second, because of their long life, multilateral treaties are more likely to need amendment. Third, because of an inadequate amendment provision (or, indeed, no provision) in the original treaty, most amendments do not bind all the parties to that treaty.

Before the watershed of the Second World War, treaty amendment usually required unanimity. It was relatively rare for a multilateral treaty to have a built-in amendment procedure, and when it did, the procedure would normally incorporate the unanimity rule. But because of the difficulty of obtaining unanimity, a practice gradually developed by which amendments entered into force between only those states willing to accept them. This meant the original treaty remained in force between the parties which did not accept the amendment, and between those which accepted and those that did not, but the amended treaty applied as between the parties that accepted the amendment.

This unsatisfactory state of affairs is made worse when there is a series of amending treaties. The Warsaw Convention 1929[2] was amended by Protocols in 1955 and 1971, and by four Additional Protocols in 1975, and then supplemented by a Convention in 1961, some of which are still not in force.[3] The parties to the various amending and

[1] Janis Joplin, 'Mercedes Benz' (1970) (song). [2] 137 LNTS 11; UKTS (1933) No. 11.

[3] For the Warsaw Convention and the later treaties, see D. McClean (ed.), *Shawcross and Beaumont: Air Law* (LexisNexis, London 1997–), chapter 33, under 'Development of the Warsaw System', and Appendix B (for the text of the relevant Conventions and Protocols).

supplementing instruments vary; some states remain parties to just the Warsaw Convention; some to that Convention and to one or more of the other instruments; and some to one or more of those instruments only.[4] This has resulted in the international limits of liability of an airline to its passengers being dependent primarily on which treaty obligations have been accepted by the state concerned, instead of a *uniform* regime applying throughout international aviation, as the Warsaw Convention had intended, or even one that reflected US legislation. Establishing which version of the Warsaw Convention applies can sometimes be very difficult, especially for national courts, and it is they that have usually to enforce the regime.[5] The Montreal Convention for the Unification of Certain Rules for International Carriage by Air 1999 was a courageous attempt to replace the Warsaw system, but has the same drawbacks.[6]

The ILC was well aware of these problems, but, no doubt wisely, did not attempt to suggest solutions. Instead, the VCLT lays down certain basic rules. Article 39 states the general rule regarding the amendment of treaties, whether bilateral or multilateral: a treaty may be amended by 'agreement' between the parties. The use of this word recognises that it is perfectly possible to amend a treaty by an agreement that does not itself constitute a treaty or, possibly, by an oral agreement, the legal force of which is preserved by Article 3. A treaty may also be in effect amended by a subsequent agreement between the parties regarding the interpretation or application of the treaty (Article 31(3)(a)). Despite an amendment procedure having been built into it, the Convention on International Trade in Endangered Species of Wild Flora and Fauna (CITES Convention) 1973 was effectively modified by a resolution of the Conference of the Parties in 1986.[7] Subsequent practice in the application of a treaty by one or more parties may also have the effect of modifying it if there is tacit or implied consent to it by the other party or parties.[8] This is possible only if it, or they, had the opportunity to raise objections to a regular course of conduct, but did not do so.[9]

Although an amending treaty is often called a 'protocol', the title is not legally significant. An amending treaty, being distinct legally from the treaty it amends, is not subject to any amendment procedure laid down in the treaty itself. International law

4 For the status of the relevant Conventions and Agreements, see *Shawcross and Beaumont* (n. 3), Appendix A.

5 EU member states also have to apply EU Regulation 2027/97 (OJ L 285, 17.10.1997) as amended by Regulation 889/2002 (OJ L 140, 30.5.2002).

6 2242 UNTS 350 No. 39917; UKTS (2004) No. 44.

7 993 UNTS 243 No. 14537; 12 ILM (1973) 1085; UKTS (1976) No. 101; 27 UST 1087; TIAS 82249. See the Proceedings of the Sixth Meeting of the Conference of the Parties (Doc. 6.19; Res. 6.2.4) at: www.cites.org.

8 The draft conclusions of the ILC (YBILC (2018) vol. II, chapter IV, 11–116) on subsequent agreements and subsequent practice in the application of a treaty are cautious in their approach to the possible amending effect of either: see draft conclusion 7.3; and I. Buga, 'Subsequent Practice and Treaty Modification', in M. J. Bowman and D. Kritsiotis (eds.), *Conceptual and Contextual Perspectives on the Modern Law of Treaties* (Cambridge University Press, Cambridge 2018), 363–391.

9 See pp. 250–254. See also *United States* v. *France* (1963), 38 ILR 182, 248–255; *United States* v. *Italy* (1965), 45 ILR 393; and *Egypt* v. *Israel (Taba Arbitration)* (1988), 80 ILR 224.

does not contain a principle of *acte contraire*. In other words, there is no general legal requirement that changes to a treaty be made through the same process or by an act of the same nature as the original instrument.[10]

Bilateral Treaties

Naturally, bilateral treaties can be amended more easily than multilateral. The parties can always agree to an amendment: the only question is the form in which it is to be expressed. Sometimes the treaty will contain an amendment clause. Here is a simple example from an air services agreement:

> Any amendments or modifications of this Agreement agreed by the Contracting Parties shall come into effect when *confirmed* by an Exchange of Notes.[11]

Similar provisions are found in many other air services agreements. They leave the procedure for *adopting* the amendment to be determined by the parties, the agreement to amend coming into effect when confirmed by an exchange of notes. The amendment will often, for such agreements, be recorded first in an NBI such as an MOU, which may also provide for the amendment to be put into effect 'administratively' pending confirmation. The provision for confirmation by an exchange of notes is a prudent means of ensuring that not only will each amendment be properly recorded, but that there will be no doubt that the decision to amend is legally binding. This is important since, as has been pointed out, it is not necessary for an amendment to be in writing. But it is undesirable to effect amendments to treaties orally, or by other informal means such as an NBI, unless this is later confirmed formally. Otherwise, there may be doubt as to what was agreed, or as to its legal effect or, indeed, whether anything had been finally agreed. After all, that is why one has treaties. Formal confirmation is also a good way of testing that the amendment will work in relation to the rest of the treaty, and whether any consequential changes need to be made.

For agreements outside the field of air services, amendment will normally be effected by proceeding straight to a binding exchange of notes.[12] A provision for amendment may, in addition, stipulate when such an exchange would enter into force, albeit with the possibility that the parties can agree otherwise in the exchange itself. Thus, Article 22.2 of the UK–Japan Customs Co-operation Agreement 2021 provides:

> This Agreement may be amended by mutual consent of the Contracting Parties through diplomatic notes exchanged between them. Amendments shall enter into force on the first day of the month following the date on which the

[10] J. Brunée, 'Treaty Amendments', in *Hollis, Oxford Guide*, 336–354, 339.

[11] UK–US Air Services Agreement 1977 (1079 UNTS 21 No. 16509; UKTS (1977) No. 76).

[12] For other examples of provisions amending bilateral agreements, see *Blix and Emerson*, 223–225.

> diplomatic notes are exchanged between them except as otherwise agreed by the Contracting Parties.[13]

Or the original treaty may stipulate that amendments shall enter into force on the date of receipt of the last notification by the parties that their internal procedures for approval have been completed.[14]

There may be reasons why an amendment clause is not wanted or is not desirable. It may not be wise politically to contemplate amendments to a treaty that establishes a border. But if both parties want to amend such a treaty, they can, of course, do so. The advantage of an amendment clause is that the means by which the amendment is to be done is agreed from the start. But should the means not be suitable, the parties can simply ignore it and amend the treaty in any way they can agree on.[15]

Multilateral Treaties: Residual Rules

Many multilateral treaties have specific amendment procedures, which are examined in the next main section below. But there are multilateral treaties, including quite modern ones, which have no built-in amendment procedures. And even where there is a procedure, it is either not comprehensive or does not cover all eventualities. One has then to fall back on the residual rules in Articles 40 and 41.

Proposal to Amend a Treaty as between All the Parties

Under the residual rules, any proposal to amend a multilateral treaty as between all the parties must be notified to all the 'contracting states' (i.e., those that have consented to be bound by the treaty, even if it is not yet in force). Each of them has the right to take part in the decision on the action (if any) that should be taken, and to participate in the negotiation and conclusion of any amendment treaty (Article 40(1) and (2)). There can be problems in determining exactly which are the contracting states, and in excluding a state that is regarded as not suitable (e.g., an aggressor). In an extreme case, it may be possible to avoid such problems only by some of the states negotiating a new treaty incorporating the amendments, and withdrawing from the original.

[13] UKTS (2021) No. 5.

[14] See, for example, Article 20 UK–Switzerland Agreement on Police Cooperation 2020: UKTS (2022) No. 2. A variation on the same lines is Article 23.3 UK–EAEC Agreement between the UK and the European Atomic Energy Community for Cooperation on the Safe and Peaceful Uses of Nuclear Energy 2020 (UKTS (2021) No. 10), which provides: 'Any amendment shall enter into force on the date specified by the Parties, by an exchange of diplomatic notes between the Parties or through their competent authorities, as appropriate, that their respective internal procedures necessary for its entry into force have been completed.'

[15] See the UK–Norway Frigg Field Agreement 2001 (UKTS (2001) No. 43) which amended the 1976 Agreement (UKTS (1977) No. 113). The amended Agreement was then replaced by a consolidated text (UKTS (2002) No. 21). See also the UK–Paraguay Exchange of Notes 1993: UKTS (2001) No. 42.

Every state entitled to become a party to the treaty is also entitled to become a party to the treaty as amended (Article 40(3)). This would apply to a state that had taken part in the conclusion of the treaty but had not yet expressed its consent to be bound. An amending agreement does not bind a party to the treaty that does not become a party to the amending agreement (Article 40(4)). As between such a party and a party to the amending agreement, only the *unamended* treaty applies.

It is not uncommon for a state to consent to be bound by a treaty for which an amending agreement is already in force, but for that state not to indicate whether it intends to be bound by the amending agreement(s). Article 40(5) reflects the established (and sensible) practice of the UN Secretary-General: unless the state expresses a different intention, it is considered to be a party to the treaty as amended, and any party to the treaty that is not bound by an amending agreement is regarded as a party to the *unamended* treaty. This rule is reflected in the 1972 Protocol amending the Single Convention on Narcotic Drugs 1961,[16] which provides that any state that becomes a party to the Convention after the entry into force of the Protocol shall, unless it expresses a different intention, be considered a party to the amended Convention, but as a party to the unamended Convention in relation to any party to the Convention that is not a party to the Protocol.

Agreement to Modify a Multilateral Treaty between Certain Parties Only

There are instances where some of the parties to a treaty make an agreement for the purpose of modifying the treaty only as between themselves. Such an *inter se* agreement may have an aim and effect incompatible with the object and purpose of the treaty. If so, in relation to the other parties to the treaty, it may amount to a breach. But an *inter se* agreement is permissible if the possibility of such a modification is provided for in the treaty (Article 41(1)(a)). Alternatively, provided the modification is not prohibited by the treaty, an *inter se* agreement is permissible if it meets *both* of two conditions. First, it must not prejudice the rights or add to the burdens of the other parties. Second, it must not relate to a provision derogation from which would be incompatible with the effective execution of the object and purpose of the treaty as a whole (Article 41(1)(b)). It could, therefore, be permissible for some of the parties to an environmental treaty to enter into an agreement to enforce *higher* standards than required by the treaty. Unless the possibility of the proposed *inter se* agreement is provided for in the treaty, and the treaty does not provide for notification, the prospective parties to an *inter se* agreement must notify the other parties to the treaty of their intention and of the modification (Article 41(2)). The provisions of Article 30(4) (application of successive treaties relating to the same subject matter)

[16] Convention: 520 UNTS 151 No. 7515; UKTS (1965) No. 34; Protocol: 976 UNTS 3 No. 14151; 11 ILM (1972) 804; UKTS (1979) No. 23; consolidated text: 976 UNTS 105 No. 14152.

will *not* apply if an agreement to amend satisfies the conditions in Article 41 (see the saving provision in Article 30(5)).

Multilateral Treaties: Specific Amendment Procedures

The tremendous increase in multilateral treaty making, the advent of multilateral treaties of great complexity and the constantly changing needs of international society have made it essential to include in most multilateral treaties an *effective* mechanism for their amendment.

Issues Normally Covered by Amendment Provisions

The amendment procedures built into treaties in recent years are often elaborate. No two are the same, each being tailored to suit the particular needs of the organisation or treaty,[17] but they usually provide for:

(1) the number of parties, or votes in the plenary body or meeting, needed to support an amendment before it has to be put to all the parties;
(2) the majority needed for adoption of the amendment;
(3) whether the adopted amendment needs to be ratified or accepted (some treaties enable technical annexes to be amended simply by a decision of a body or meeting);
(4) if so, the number of parties which need to ratify or accept for the amendment to come into force;
(5) where ratification or acceptance is not required, whether the amendment can be adopted by tacit agreement; and
(6) whether the amendment also binds those parties which have not ratified or accepted it.

These points can be illustrated by looking at two examples: the Compliance Agreement 1993,[18] and the Comprehensive Nuclear-Test-Ban Treaty 1996.[19] Further examples of multilateral treaty amendment provisions follow.

Compliance Agreement 1993: Requirement for Acceptance

Under Article XIII of the Compliance Agreement 1993 a proposed amendment requires the approval of the FAO Conference by two-thirds of the votes cast, and enters into

[17] *Blix and Emerson*, 225–239, have many examples from before 1966. See also the UN Handbook of Final Clauses, available at: https://treaties.un.org.

[18] 2221 UNTS 120 No. 39486; 33 ILM (1994) 968.

[19] 35 ILM (1996) 1439. The CTBT may never enter into force, though not because of the amendment provisions. Its Article VII is modelled on Article XV of the Chemical Weapons Convention 1993 (1974 UNTS 317 No. 33757; 32 ILM (1993) 804; UKTS (1997) No. 45).

force after acceptance by two-thirds of the parties.[20] However, if an amendment involves new obligations for parties (which is assumed unless the Conference decides otherwise by consensus), it comes into force for each party only when it has been accepted by that party. The subject matter of the Agreement is not only important, but contentious. The less than comprehensive binding amendment procedure reflects the familiar reluctance of states to be bound by amendments they do not formally accept. Article 9 of the Vienna Convention for the Protection of the Ozone Layer 1985[21] has – no doubt for similar reasons – a similar procedure. To be more effective, any amendments are therefore likely to need approval by consensus.

Comprehensive Nuclear-Test-Ban Treaty 1996: Different Procedures for 'Amendments' and 'Changes'

Contrast the Compliance Agreement procedure with Article VII of the CTBT 1996.[22] This is more complex and makes a distinction between 'amendments' and 'changes', which are specified under paragraph 7 of Article VII as changes to certain parts of the Protocol and Annexes 1 and 2 relating only to matters of an 'administrative and technical nature' (but which are still amendments as a matter of treaty law). Of particular interest is the accelerated procedure for 'changes'.

Any party can propose amendments (as distinct from 'changes') to the CTBT. If a majority of the parties support consideration of the proposal, a conference must be held. At the conference, an amendment is adopted by the vote of a simple majority of the parties, provided no party casts a negative vote. The amendment then enters into force for *all* parties thirty days after *all those parties that voted for the amendment* have deposited instruments of ratification.

As for 'changes' to parts of the Protocol and its Annexes (but *not* the CTBT itself) which relate only to administrative or technical matters, any party may make a proposal. After the proposal has been evaluated by the Director-General, it is examined by the Executive Council. If the Council recommends adoption of the change, it is 'considered approved' if no party objects within ninety days. If the Executive Council recommends rejection, it is considered rejected if no party objects within ninety days. But if a party objects to a recommendation to adopt or to reject a proposal, the proposal must be considered by the next conference of the parties. If consensus cannot be reached, a decision is taken by a two-thirds majority of the parties present and voting at the conference. Changes that have been adopted by any of these procedures enter into force 180 days after they have been notified to the parties, and *all* are bound. This longer period is to give time for the parties to make arrangements for the implementation of the change, such as modifying legislation.

[20] For the FAO acceptance procedure, see pp. 32 and 121.
[21] 1513 UNTS 324 No. 26164; 26 ILM (1987) 1529; UKTS (1990) No. 1.
[22] See n. 19.

The tacit procedure for minor changes to the Protocol and its Annexes enables them to become effective more quickly than substantive amendments to the treaty, since there is no need for the changes to be ratified. This procedure avoids the delay that is inevitably caused by having to submit amendments to a ratification process, though some constitutions may require that all recommendations for amendment or changes be scrutinised in some way by parliament. In any case, all amendments and changes that are adopted should be published by each party. Once in force, they should be registered by the depositary with the UN Secretary-General.

Amendments by Joint Committees or Similar Bodies

Many bilateral treaties (and to a lesser extent, multilateral treaties) provide for the establishment of a Joint Committee or similar body, which in general supervises the operation of the treaty. As part of its tasks, it may propose or adopt amendments to the treaty, often of a technical nature, by means of a simplified procedure. Hence the Trade Committee under the UK–Ukraine Political, Free Trade and Strategic Partnership Agreement 2021 may update or amend the Annexes to Title IV of the Agreement.[23] Normally, the powers to amend in such cases are limited to amendment of defined parts or annexes of an agreement. As for the procedure, Article 405.1 states:

> [The Committee] shall adopt its decisions and recommendations by agreement between the Parties and following completion of the Parties' respective internal procedures.

Express Provisions Concerning New Parties

Article 20 of the Rome Convention for the Suppression of Unlawful Acts against the Safety of Maritime Navigation 1988[24] envisages possible amendments, and provides that after the entry into force of an amendment any *new* party shall be deemed to be bound by the Convention as so amended.

Amendment by Consensus

Paragraph 18 of the International Nickel Study Group Terms of Reference 1986[25] (actually a treaty) provides that it may be amended only 'by consensus', no further procedure being specified.

[23] Article 404.7: UKTS (2022) No. 1.
[24] 1678 UNTS 222 No. 29004; 27 ILM (1988) 672; UKTS (1995) No. 64; [1993] ATS 10.
[25] 1566 UNTS 29 No. 27296.

Automatically and Comprehensively Binding Amendment Mechanisms

Some treaties establishing international organisations ('constituent instruments') have built-in amendment procedures under which, once an amendment has been approved by a specified percentage of the members, it is binding on *all* members. Article 108 of the UN Charter 1945[26] has perhaps the most succinct and elegant procedure:

> Amendments to the present Charter shall come into force for *all* Members of the United Nations when they have been adopted by a vote of two-thirds of the members of the General Assembly and ratified in accordance with their respective constitutional processes by two-thirds of the Members of the United Nations, including all the permanent members of the Security Council.

Despite the sting in the tail of Article 108, the enormous advantage of the procedure is that, once an amendment has entered into force, it binds *even those who neither voted for nor ratified it*. In this sense, it may very properly be described as 'automatically and comprehensively binding'. Article 34(2) of the INMARSAT Convention 1976[27] is even more blunt about the effect of its amendment procedure:

> Upon entry into force, the amendment shall become binding upon all Parties and all Signatories, including those which have not accepted it.

Interestingly, Article 121 of the Rome Statute 1998[28] provides that for an amendment to be adopted at the Assembly of the States Parties, or a review conference, it requires either consensus or a two-thirds majority of the states parties. It then enters into force for *all* states parties one year after seven-eighths of them have ratified the amendment, subject to certain qualifications for those which have not accepted it. There are, for example, special provisions for amendments to Articles 5–8 (crimes within the ICC's jurisdiction).[29]

Article 8(3) of the Locarno Agreement on Industrial Designs 1968[30] provides that any amendment (other than to financial obligations) to Articles 5, 6, 7 or 8 which are accepted by the required majority:

> shall bind all the countries which are members of the Special Union at the time the amendment enters into force, *or* which become members thereof at a subsequent date.

Deemed Acceptance of Amendment

A simpler way of speeding the entry into force of an amendment for all the parties is Article 21(3) of the celebrated Customs Treatment of Pool Containers Convention

[26] 1 UNTS (1946) xvi; UKTS (1946) No. 67.
[27] 1143 UNTS 105 No. 17948; 15 ILM (1976) 1051; UKTS (1979) No. 94; TIAS 9605.
[28] 2187 UNTS 91 No. 38544; 37 ILM (1998) 998; UKTS (2002) No. 35.
[29] See Article 121.5 and 6.
[30] 828 UNTS 437 No. 11853; UKTS (2004) No. 4.

1994.[31] It provides that any amendment recommended by the Committee established by that Convention:

> shall enter into force with respect to all Contracting Parties three months after the expiry of a period of eighteen months ... if no objection to the recommended amendment has been notified during that period to the Depositary by a Contracting Party.

The Percentage Problem

Some amendment clauses provide for entry into force of an amendment after a specified percentage of 'the parties' have ratified it, but do not say to *which* parties the percentage has to be applied. Since, generally, one cannot imply that it excludes those that became parties after adoption of the amendment, it is therefore important to exclude them expressly. If this is not done, the percentage must be applied to the parties from time to time. Thus, if a number of states become parties after adoption of the amendment, even more parties will have to ratify before the amendment can enter into force (entry into force clauses can have similar problems). Unfortunately, the drafters of several treaties have fallen into this trap. Article 20 of the Physical Protection of Nuclear Material Convention 1980[32] provides that the amendment shall enter into force 'after two thirds of the States Parties have deposited their instruments of ratification'. The same mistake was made in the Ramsar Wetlands Convention 1971[33] when, ironically, it was amended in 1982 to include an amendment article. Article XIII(4) of the Compliance Agreement 1993[34] also has the same error. A way to avoid the problem is to use a simple formula, such as that in Article XVII of the INTELSAT Agreement 1971:[35]

> An amendment ... shall enter into force ... after the Depositary has received notice of approval ... from ... two thirds of the States *which were parties as of the date upon* [sic] *which the amendment was approved.*

No Effective Amendment Procedure

Many (usually older) built-in amendment procedures contain no automatic element. Under Article XVI of the European Space Agency (ESA) Convention 1975,[36] any member state can recommend an amendment, but it will enter into force only if all

31 2000 UNTS 289 No. 34301; UKTS (2004) No. 13.

32 1456 UNTS 101 No. 24631; 18 ILM (1979) 1319; UKTS (1995) No. 61.

33 996 UNTS 245 No. 14583; 11 ILM (1972) 963; UKTS (1976) No. 34 (for the consolidated text, see UKTS (1996) No. 13).

34 See n. 18.

35 1220 UNTS 22 No. 19677; 10 ILM (1971) 909; UKTS (1973) No. 80. See at: www.intelsat.com.

36 1297 UNTS 161 No. 21524; 14 ILM (1975) 864; UKTS (1981) No. 30. See also Article 17 EUMETSAT Convention: UKTS (1990) No. 32.

member states ratify it. This is no more than a formalisation of the basic rule on amendment in Article 39 of the VCLT, and is therefore no more effective.

The problem caused by the absence of any built-in amendment procedure in the Warsaw Convention, and its several successor treaties, has already been described. The Montreal Convention 1999[37] attempted to rectify the problem. Article 55 provides that this Convention prevails over the Warsaw Convention 1929 and its successor treaties. However, this will apply only to those states that ratify the new Convention. Fortunately, the Montreal Convention now has over 130 parties. But, once again, and most fittingly, it has no amendment clause.

Other Aspects of Amendments

Amendments to Plurilateral Treaties

When the treaty is plurilateral, it is usual for all parties to ratify any amendment before it can enter into force. Article 58(1) of the Framework Agreement concerning the European Defence Industry 2000[38] provides that any proposed amendment requires the written agreement of 'all the parties', and shall enter into force when 'all *those* parties' have ratified it. This is fine in principle, except that it does not clearly identify who 'all the parties' are. The Agreement had six signatory states, and entered into force once two of them had ratified. It would, therefore, seem to mean all the parties at the time the amendment had been agreed, though this could be the original two only. That this appears to be so is confirmed by the further provision that any amendment that enters into force 'before all six signatory States have become parties, shall be binding on the other signatory States when they become parties'.

Review Clauses

Article 109 of the UN Charter provides for its review. It is, however, no different in substance from Article 108 as regards the process for the adoption and entry into force of an amendment resulting from a review, the only additional provisions being those for the calling of a general conference for the purpose of reviewing the Charter. The ILC saw no essential *legal* difference in the processes of amendment and review, regarding amendment as including review. Article 26 of CEDAW 1979 provides simply that a party may request revision of the Convention, and the UN Secretary-General shall decide upon the steps to be taken, 'if any'. There are numerous other precedents.[39]

[37] See n. 6. [38] 2184 UNTS 5 No. 38494; UKTS (2001) No. 33.

[39] For some earlier examples, see *Blix and Emerson*, 240–245; *UN Depositary Practice*, para. 251.

Replacement of Original Treaty

Sometimes the amendments are so numerous or extensive that it may be better to replace the whole of the original treaty with a new one. Alternatively, a consolidated text showing the treaty as amended should be agreed and produced for information. If the amendments have the effect of replacing the original treaty and any previous amendments to it, another approach is to require any party to the amendment treaty to denounce all the previous treaties with effect from the date the new treaty enters into effect for that party.[40] The replacement treaty may provide that its entry into force for a party shall be deemed to amount to denunciation of the original treaty.

Supplementary Treaties

It is important to distinguish between treaties that *amend* and treaties that *supplement*. The right to become a party to a supplementary treaty is not necessarily limited to parties to the earlier treaty. The supplementary treaty, although linked to the earlier treaty, may well stand alone and may not need the parties to it to be parties to the earlier treaty in order to be effective. The Protocol relating to the Status of Refugees 1967 does not amend the Refugees Convention 1951, but requires the parties to the Protocol to apply the substantive provisions of the Convention, as broadened by the Protocol. It is, in effect, open to all states.[41] Although it does not amend the Antarctic Treaty 1959, because the provisions of the Protocol on Environmental Protection 1991 are so closely related to that treaty and because of the need to preserve the integrity of the Antarctic Treaty System, the Protocol provides, in effect, that once it has entered into force (as it did, in 1998), a party to the Antarctic Treaty can be accepted as a Consultative Party under that treaty (with the right to take part in decision making) only if it first becomes a party to the Protocol.[42]

Amendment before Entry into Force

It may be necessary to adopt amendments to a multilateral treaty even before the treaty has entered into force. In 1958 a Protocol to amend the Olive Oil Agreement

[40] See Article 17(5) of the Protocol of 2002 amending the Athens Convention 1974 (1463 UNTS 40 No. 24817; UKTS (2014) No. 14) and previous amending Protocols (www.imo.org). See also Article 14(2) of the CoE European Convention on the Protection of the Archaeological Heritage (revised) 1992 (1966 UNTS 305 No. 33612; UKTS (2002) No. 29; ETS No. 143), which requires a party to the 1969 Convention on the same subject (799 UNTS 227 No. 11212; UKTS (1973) No. 26; ETS No. 66) to denounce it by the time that it becomes a party to the later Convention.

[41] Convention: 189 UNTS 137 No. 2545 and UKTS (1954) No. 39; Protocol: 606 UNTS 267 No. 8791; UKTS (1969) No. 15.

[42] 30 ILM (1991) 1460; UKTS (1999) No. 6; [1998] ATS 6 (Article 22(4)).

1956 was adopted before that Agreement had entered into force, which it did in 1959 as so amended.

A more famous example is the Implementation Agreement 1994 (relating to the Implementation of Part XI of UNCLOS).[43] Industrialised states would not adhere to that Convention since the provisions in Part XI on mining of the deep seabed had become unacceptable to them. The Convention could therefore have entered into force with mostly developing states as parties. Such a situation would have been very unsatisfactory, not only to the over sixty developing states that would then have had to pay all the costs of the elaborate institutions established by the Convention, but also because it would have denied the Convention its universal character. There was, however, understandable reluctance by those developing states that had already ratified the Convention to amend it (or at least to be seen to do so) before it had entered into force.

After difficult and lengthy negotiations, it was agreed to supplement the Convention with an Agreement.[44] By Article 1 the parties to the Agreement 'undertake to *implement* Part XI in accordance with this Agreement'. For this purpose, the Annex to the Agreement is an integral part of it and contains what are, in effect, amendments to Part IX. Furthermore, the parties agree that the provisions of the Agreement and Part IX 'shall be interpreted and applied together as a single instrument', and that in the case of any inconsistency '*the provisions of this Agreement shall prevail*' (Article 2). The Agreement also provides, in Article 4, that any ratification and so on of the Convention following adoption of the Agreement would represent consent to be bound by the Agreement; and that one cannot become a party to the Agreement without being a party to the Convention.

This has been kindly described as an 'imaginative' development in the law of treaties, since the provision could not, as such, bind those states that had ratified the Convention before the adoption of the Agreement.[45] But as the Agreement was the only sensible way of resolving the problem, and since none of those states have objected, they must be regarded as having acquiesced. A simplified procedure by which existing parties to the Convention can express consent to be bound without having to ratify the Agreement is also provided. The Agreement, adopted on 28 July 1994, was applied provisionally with effect from 16 November 1994 (the date on which the Convention entered into force) and finally entered into force in 1996.

It is not uncommon for bilateral treaties to be amended before they have entered into force.

[43] 1836 UNTS 42 No. 31364; 33 ILM (1994) 1313; UKTS (1999) No. 82.

[44] See D. Anderson, 'Further Efforts to Ensure Universal Participation in the United Nations Convention on the Law of the Sea', ICLQ 43 (1994) 886–893.

[45] R. R. Churchill and A. V. Lowe, *The Law of the Sea* (3rd ed., Manchester University Press, Manchester 1999), 20–21.

Implementation of Amendments

Where parties are not required to ratify an amendment for it to enter into force for them, they must nevertheless take any necessary steps to implement the amendment (including any legislation) should it enter into force. This is particularly important for parties with a 'dualist' constitution. It is, therefore, desirable when enacting legislation to implement a treaty that is likely to last for a long time, and need amendment, to provide for a simple and quick means of amending or supplementing the legislation, if possible by secondary legislation.[46]

[46] See, e.g., the broad power to make secondary legislation given by the (UK) Antarctic Act 1994, section 25.

16

Duration and Termination

En toute chose il faut considérer la fin.[1]

The length of this chapter demonstrates that this is an important topic, though it is often neglected. Consideration of the duration and termination of a new treaty should not be left until the end of negotiations. Not only may the necessary provisions raise difficult technical questions, but they can also raise sensitive policy issues which should be discussed earlier rather than later in the negotiations. But first, a note on terminology.

Denunciation denotes a unilateral act by which a party terminates its participation in a treaty; lawful denunciation of a *bilateral* treaty *terminates* it. Although denunciation is also used in relation to a multilateral treaty, the better term is *withdrawal*, since withdrawal from a multilateral treaty will not, normally, result in its termination. While 'denunciation' is used in relation to treaties as a technical term, non-lawyers may see it as carrying undertones of its ordinary, condemnatory meaning. For this reason it should be avoided, if at all possible, 'termination' being a much better word.

Part V of the Convention, Articles 42–45 and 54–64, set out the various circumstances in which a treaty can be denounced or terminated, or its operation suspended, other than on grounds of invalidity (for which, see the – much shorter – Chapter 17). Unless the treaty otherwise provides, a party claiming that it is not bound by the treaty has the onus of establishing this. To be effective, denunciation, termination or suspension may take place only as a result of the application of the provisions of the treaty itself or of provisions of the Convention (Article 42(2)). The provisions of Part V therefore exclude other grounds for denunciation, withdrawal or suspension, although debate continues as to whether desuetude and obsolescence,[2] or the emergence of a new customary rule,[3] or the concept of

[1] 'In all matters one must think of the end', La Fontaine, *Fables*, III.5, 'Le Renard et le Bouc'.
[2] See pp. 316–317, and the references in that section.
[3] That is, a new customary rule providing a separate ground for termination, as distinct from a new peremptory norm of international law which required termination of the treaty, as provided by Article 64 of the Convention. See *Kolb*, 208; *Corten and Klein*, 1025–1026.

exceptio inadimpleti contractus,[4] or full performance[5] might be considered as providing a separate basis.

These days, most treaties contain provisions on duration and termination, often in the same article. But when there are none, one must consider not only the relevant article in Part V, but other articles in that Part which govern the conditions for applying the article, such as Articles 65–68 concerning the procedure to be followed. Certain other articles of the Convention may also be relevant, for example, Article 5, if the treaty is the constituent instrument of an international organisation.

Express Provisions on Termination or Withdrawal

A treaty may terminate, or a party may withdraw from it, in conformity with its provisions (Article 54(a)). In practice, most difficulties arise over the drafting of a suitable clause or its interpretation, or when a party seeks to terminate or suspend the operation of a treaty on the ground of breach by another party. Although one occasionally finds a treaty that makes provision only for its duration, or only for denunciation or withdrawal, or that is silent on all such matters, it is more usual to find a clause providing for both duration and termination. This is so whether the treaty is bilateral or multilateral. The following examples illustrate the great variety of clauses.[6]

Indefinite Duration with Right to Terminate

Many *bilateral* treaties make no provision for duration, and their subject matter is such that they could remain in force indefinitely. But since it is possible that either of the parties may want to terminate it at some time, they include a termination clause. Typically, this provides that:

> Either party may terminate this treaty by means of a written notice to the other party. Termination shall take effect six months following the date of notification.[7]

[4] Also called the 'exception of non-performance', which permits the performance of an obligation to be withheld if the other party has failed to perform the same or a related obligation: see D. Azaria, 'Exception of Non-Performance', *MPEPIL* (2015); B. Simma and C. J. Tams, 'Reacting against Treaty Breaches', in *Hollis, Oxford Guide*, 568–594, at 572 note 15; *Dörr and Schmalenbach*, 1118; M. Fitzmaurice, 'Angst of the Exceptio Inadimplenti Non Est Adimplendum in International Law', in L. Bartels and F. Paddeu (eds.), *Exceptions in International Law* (Oxford University Press, Oxford 2020), 285–304; M. Xiouri, *The Breach of a Treaty: State Responses in International Law* (Brill Nijhoff, Leiden, Boston 2021), 54–68.

[5] See p. 316; *Corten and Klein*, 1026–1027.

[6] See also *Blix and Emerson*, 96–113.

[7] UK–US Treaty on Mutual Legal Assistance in Criminal Matters 1994, as amended by an Exchange of Notes 2001: 1967 UNTS 102 No. 33632 and 2114 UNTS 392 No. 36773; UKTS (1997) No. 14 and (2002) No. 8.

Air services agreements can last for many decades because they are usually in general terms, can be amended easily and can be supplemented by NBIs. Most will contain the following provision:

> Either Contracting Party may at any time give notice in writing to the other Contracting Party of its decision to terminate this Agreement. Such notice shall be simultaneously communicated to the International Civil Aviation Organisation. This Agreement shall terminate *at midnight (at the place of receipt of the notice) immediately before the first anniversary of the date of receipt of the notice by the other Contracting Party*, unless the notice is withdrawn by agreement before the end of this period. In the absence of acknowledgement of receipt by the other Contracting Party, the notice shall be deemed to have been received 14 days after receipt of the notice by the International Civil Aviation Organisation.

This rather elaborate (but common) formula in the UK–Azerbaijan Air Services Agreement 1994[8] is necessary because of the special nature of the subject matter. An air services agreement provides the framework for important legal and commercial relations between two states and their airlines. It is essential to be able to determine *precisely* when termination will take effect. Unlike most other treaties, the effect of termination on this type of commerce can be immediate: once the agreement has terminated, the aircraft of each state will have no treaty right to land in or take off from the other state with fare-paying passengers or cargo. Although termination takes effect on the expiration of the last day that the agreement is in force (i.e., at midnight),[9] because the parties to an air services agreement will often be in different time zones, there is a need to know exactly when termination will take effect, in particular *whose* midnight.

It is, of course, always open to the parties to agree to terminate a treaty early.[10] Most *multilateral* treaties of unlimited duration will allow a party an unconditional right to withdraw. In this the Terrorist Bombings Convention 1997[11] is typical of practice within the United Nations. Article 23 of this Convention reads:

> (1) Any State Party may denounce this Convention by written notification to the Secretary-General of the United Nations.
> (2) Denunciation shall take effect one year following the date on which notification is received by the Secretary-General of the United Nations.

Other multilateral treaties place certain limitations on when a party may withdraw. Article 13(1) of the European Synchrotron Radiation Facility Convention 1988[12] was concluded:

8 1892 UNTS 140 No. 32208; UKTS (1995) No. 20.

9 See *McNair*, 198–199.

10 See the UK–Moldova Exchange of Notes 1999 terminating a UK–USSR Agreement of 1964: 2139 UNTS 348 No. 37317; UKTS (2000) No. 83, Moldova having succeeded to the treaty (see pp. 378–379).

11 2149 UNTS 284 No. 37517; 37 ILM (1998) 251; UKTS (2001) No. 57; [2002] ATS 17.

12 See: www.esrf.eu.

> for an initial period ending on 31 December 2007 and shall remain in force after that date. It may be denounced with three years notice, such notice to be given to the [Depositary]. Withdrawal can only take effect on 31 December 2007 or at the end of each successive period of three years.

Article 18(1) of the Civil LORAN C Navigation System Agreement 1992[13] provides that:

> After the expiry of ten years from the date of entry into force of this Agreement, any Party may denounce the Agreement within the first six months of the eleventh year. Such denunciation . . . shall take effect at the end of the financial year following the financial year in which the said notice has been received by the Depositary, or at such later date as may be specified in the notice.

This is tightly drawn, but it is not clear if the 'later date' has to be at the end of another financial year, though this would seem to be the intention. Paragraph (2) provides that if a party does not denounce in accordance with paragraph (1), it remains bound by the Agreement for further consecutive periods of seven years following the expiry of the first ten-year period, unless it denounces it in the same way as provided for in paragraph (1).

Conventions adopted within the ILO often require a lengthy period of notice and impose strict conditions on when notice can be given. For example, ILO Conventions 163–166 of 1987, concerning seafarers' welfare, each provide that a member state cannot give notice of denunciation until ten years after each Convention 'first comes into force' (i.e., not just for the member state concerned); and if a member state does not denounce it within twelve months of the expiration of that ten-year period, it cannot denounce until the expiration of a *further* ten-year period, and so on and so on.[14]

In this case, in calculating the precise date when denunciation will take effect, similar considerations apply as for entry into force.

Under Article 58 (previously 65), paragraph 1, of the ECHR 1950,[15] after it has been a party for five years a state may denounce the Convention by giving six months' notice. However, paragraph 2 has a saving clause:

> Such denunciation shall not have the effect of releasing the High Contracting Party concerned from its obligations under the Convention in respect of *any act which*, being capable of constituting a violation of such obligations, *may have been performed by it before the date at which the denunciation became effective.*

[13] 1774 UNTS 476 No. 30919.

[14] No. 163: 1580 UNTS 162 No. 27583; 26 ILM (1987) 633–667; No. 164: 1592 UNTS 13 No. 27864; No. 165: 1690 UNTS 437 No. 29148; No. 166: 1644 UNTS 311 No. 28256.

[15] Amended by subsequent Protocols: consolidated text at CoE website.

Duration for a Fixed Period with Possibility of Extension

The United Kingdom–Russia Agreement on Provision of Assistance for the Destruction of Chemical Weapons 2001 was expressed to expire on 31 March 2004, unless extended by agreement.[16] The Lockerbie Agreement 1998 provides in Article 29 that:

> (1) This Agreement shall enter into force on a date to be agreed by the Parties, provided that they may agree in the meantime to apply provisionally any of its provisions.
> (2) . . . this Agreement shall remain in force for one year from its entry into force, with the possibility of extending it by mutual agreement.[17]

The one-year period was chosen to avoid delay. Under the Dutch law on treaties, some treaties which are for no more than a year do not have to be submitted to parliament for approval, though extension of the period may be possible.[18] Nevertheless, the provision that the Agreement would enter into force on a date to be agreed was to reduce the likelihood of the need for the term of the agreement to be extended, though this was eventually done.

Indefinite Duration with Conditional Right to Withdraw

Article X(1) of the Nuclear Non-Proliferation Treaty 1968 provides for withdrawal by a party, albeit subject to very special conditions:

> Each Party shall in exercising its national sovereignty have the right to withdraw from the Treaty if it decides that extraordinary events, related to the subject matter of this Treaty, have jeopardised the supreme interests of its country. It shall give notice of such withdrawal to all other Parties to the Treaty and the United Nations Security Council three months in advance. Such notice shall include a statement of the extraordinary events it regards as having jeopardised its supreme interests.[19]

Even though this provision gives discretion to the withdrawing party ('if it decides'), given that a treaty must be performed in good faith, the party must indicate the factual grounds for its decision. Furthermore, the extraordinary events must be 'related to the subject matter of this Convention'. The need for these elements is made clear by the requirement for the party to state what these extraordinary events are.

[16] 2188 UNTS 174 No. 38567; UKTS (2002) No. 14.
[17] 2062 UNTS 82 No. 35699; 38 ILM (1999) 926; UKTS (1999) No. 43; UN Doc. S/1995/795.
[18] In the event, the Agreement was submitted for approval.
[19] UNTS 161 No. 10485; 7 ILM (1968) 809; UKTS (1970) No. 88; TIAS 6839. See also the Chemical Weapons Convention 1993 (1974 UNTS 317 No. 33757; 32 ILM (1993) 804; UKTS (1997) No. 45), Article XVI, the substance of which is the same.

On 12 March 1993 the Democratic People's Republic of Korea (DPRK or North Korea), following a period of non-cooperation with the IAEA with regard to the safeguards agreement required by the NPT, gave three months' notice of withdrawal from the NPT. It gave as the reason US military exercises (which according to the DPRK threatened it with nuclear war) and the conduct of the IAEA. The three depositaries of the NPT (Russia, the United Kingdom and the United States)[20] issued a joint statement which questioned whether, as required by the NPT, the DPRK's reasons were 'extraordinary events related to the subject matter' of the NPT. The Security Council, in Resolution 825 (1993), called upon the DPRK to reconsider its decision. Following DPRK–US talks, and just before the end of the three months, on 11 June 1993 the DPRK and the United States announced that the DPRK 'had decided unilaterally to suspend as long as it considers necessary the effectuation of its withdrawal'.[21] But on 10 January 2003 the DPRK, referring to its previous notice of withdrawal, informed the Security Council that it would withdraw immediately from the NPT because of the critical US-inspired IAEA resolution of 6 January 2003 which reflected the 'vicious hostile policy' of the United States towards the DPRK. There were subsequent steps in the Security Council, and the holding of six-party talks, but the issue remains unresolved.

Duration until a Specific Event

The Egypt–United Nations UN Emergency Force Agreement 1957[22] provided for it to remain in force until the departure of UNEF (UN Emergency Force) from Egypt, the date to be determined by the UN Secretary-General and the government of Egypt.

Duration for a Specified Period of Years with No Provision for Extension or Withdrawal

This is unusual. The UK–USSR Exchange of Notes on Inspection Rights relating to the INF Treaty[23] was entered into for thirteen years from the date of entry into force of the treaty, with no provision for termination or extension. The Death of Missing Persons Convention 1950[24] provided for it to be valid for five years from its entry into force, but, perhaps not surprisingly, two Protocols were later concluded to extend that Convention.

20 See below on the reason for such triple depositaries.

21 See UN Docs S/25405; S/25515; S/RES/825 (1993).

22 260 UNTS 62 No. 3704: see para. 44.

23 1658 UNTS 382 No. 28537; UKTS (1991) No. 30.

24 119 UNTS 99 No. 1610; Protocol 1957: 258 UNTS 392 No. 1610; further Protocol, 15 January 1967: 588 UNTS 290 No. 1610.

Extension of Treaties

A treaty for a fixed period may sometimes include a procedure for extending its duration. Article XXV of the Food Aid Convention 1999[25] provides for it to remain in force until 30 June 2002 unless extended by the Food Aid Committee for successive periods of up to two years.

Alternatively, the parties can always agree ad hoc to an extension. This can be done by another treaty. It can also be done by less formal means, such as by a resolution of all the parties, even if this is not provided for in the treaty. This is not necessarily simple. The term of the International Coffee Agreement 1994[26] was due to expire on 30 September 1999. It was extended for a further two years by Resolution 384 of the International Coffee Council, the governing body established by the Agreement on which all the parties are represented. The extension would apply only to those parties that had formally notified their acceptance by 30 September 1999, provided those parties represented at least twenty exporting members (i.e., parties) holding a majority of the votes of the exporting members *and* at least ten importing members holding a majority of the votes of the importing members. In the case of both groups, an undertaking received by 30 September 1999 to apply the extended Agreement provisionally would be regarded as equal in effect to a formal acceptance.[27] The extended Agreement was then replaced by the International Coffee Agreement 2001.[28]

Comprehensive Clauses

When the parties are not sure how long they envisage the treaty lasting, they will often include a clause that provides for an initial term that can be extended, either expressly or tacitly, as well as for withdrawal. Such flexible provisions enable the parties to keep their options open, and are normally found in bilateral treaties. The UK–Slovenia Cultural Co-operation Agreement 1993[29] provides that it:

> shall remain in force for a period of five years and *thereafter* shall remain in force until the expiry of six months from the date on which either Contracting Party shall have given written notice of termination to the other through the diplomatic channel.

This example does not, however, make clear *when* notice of termination may be given. The placing of 'thereafter' after 'period of five years' might imply that it can be given only after five years have elapsed, but this would mean that the minimum term would

[25] 2073 UNTS 138 No. 32022. See also *UN Multilateral Treaties*, chapter XIX.41.c.

[26] 1827 UNTS 3 No. 31252; UKTS (1995) No. 101.

[27] See *UN Multilateral Treaties*, chapter XIX.40.a.

[28] 2161 UNTS 312 No. 37769. See also *UN Multilateral Treaties*, chapter XIX.43. A further agreement, the International Coffee Agreement 2007, was adopted in 2007: 2734 UNTS 101 No. 48333; UK Misc. Series (2019) No. 28.

[29] 1919 UNTS 4 No. 32760; UKTS (1996) No. 14, Article 18. See also Article 14(2) of the UK–FRY Agreement on Educational etc. Co-operation 2002: UKTS (2004) No. 2.

be five and a half years, a rather curious result. Although one might argue that the notice may be given at any time before the end of the five years to take effect *on or after* the expiry of the five years.[30] A clause that puts the matter beyond doubt is as follows:

> This Agreement shall terminate on 31 December 1998 upon notification by either party *not less than six months before this date* that it is opposed to renewal; otherwise the Agreement's duration shall be extended automatically for periods of one year, subject to notification of opposition to renewal by either party *not less than six months before the end of any one-year period.*[31]

However, it might have been better if the clause had ended there, for the next paragraph provides:

> This Agreement may be terminated by denunciation by either party. The party wishing to denounce the Agreement shall notify the other of this step not less than *one year* before the intended date of termination.

Since this paragraph stands alone, it must mean that the Agreement could be terminated at any time, even before 31 December 1998, provided twelve months' notice was given. If so, it would have been clearer if the paragraph had at least begun:

> Notwithstanding the provisions of paragraph 1, this Agreement may be terminated at any time . . .

That example shows just how easy it is to formulate imprecise clauses. The UK–France Film Co-Production Agreement 1994[32] gets it right – almost:

> This Agreement shall remain in force initially for a period of eighteen months from the date of its entry into force. Either Contracting Party wishing to terminate it shall give written notice to the other [at least] three months before the end of that period and the Agreement shall then terminate at the end of the eighteen months. If no such notice is given, the Agreement shall automatically remain in force for successive periods each of eighteen months, unless written notice to terminate is given by either contracting party *at least* three months before the end of any period of eighteen months, in which case it shall terminate at the end of that period.

Given the wording of the second sentence, the words in square brackets seem to have been omitted by mistake. Of course, even if a clause does not specify 'at least X months' or 'not less than X months', but merely says that 'X months' notice must be given, the notice can be given more than X months before the date on which it is meant to take effect, provided that date is stated in the notice.

[30] See also the UK–Qatar Treaty of Friendship 1971: 824 UNTS 93 No. 11810; UKTS (1972) No. 4.

[31] UK–European Space Agency Ascension Island Ariane Station Agreement 1989 (1640 UNTS 168 No. 28188; UKTS (1990) No. 27), Article 90. The name of the island was most fitting.

[32] 1913 UNTS 288 No. 32650; UKTS (1995) No. 82.

It would therefore be better to provide something on the lines that the treaty will remain in force for X years and be automatically renewed for further periods of X (or Y) years, unless notice is given at least Z months prior to the expiration of the first or any succeeding period of X (or Y) years.[33] Or one might provide that the treaty shall terminate on X months' notice before the end of any calendar year, to take effect on the first day of the following calendar year. Here is one example:

> This agreement has been concluded for a period of five years and comes into force on signature. Either side may give notice of termination of this agreement not less than one year before it is due to expire. Failing such notice the agreement shall remain in force for further periods of five years at a time unless notice of termination is given by either side not less than one year before the end of each five-year period.[34]

Differing Termination Formulas

Because of the nature of their subject, some bilateral treaties have to provide termination provisions that reflect the parties' differing legislation. For example, not all states have the same fiscal year: for many it is the calendar year; for the United Kingdom it is (for a typically historic reason) from 6 April to the following 5 April.[35]

Duration for an Indefinite Period with No Withdrawal Clause

Article 11 of the Treaty of Nice 2001 (an EC/EU constituent treaty) provided that it was concluded for an unlimited period.[36] But the Treaty on European Union was subsequently amended by the Lisbon Treaty to include a withdrawal clause.[37]

Transitional Provisions

If a treaty concerning a cooperative project is *bilateral*, it will usually contain a transitional provision which keeps the treaty alive until the project has been completed and provides for certain obligations to continue indefinitely:

[33] See the UK–US Agreement for Co-operation in Research etc. of Weapons Detection 2002: UKTS (2005) No. 23, Article 16(1).

[34] UK–USSR Agreed Minute on Co-operation in Agricultural Research 1965: 543 UNTS 78 No. 7897; UKTS (1965) No. 36. See also the UK–Ireland Agreement on the Reciprocal Holding of Oil Stocks 2005: UKTS (2005) No. 20, Article 10.

[35] See Article 30 Australia–UK Double Taxation Convention 2003: 2258 UNTS 119 No. 40224; UKTS (2004) No. 5.

[36] Treaty of Nice amending the TEU, the treaties establishing the European Communities etc., 2001; 2701 UNTS 3 No. 47937; UKTS (2003) No. 22; OJ C 80/1 10.4.2001.

[37] Article 50 TEU: OJ C 326, 26.10.2012, 1; UKTS (2010) No. 7.

> The termination of this Agreement shall not affect the carrying out of any project or programme undertaken under this Agreement and not fully executed at the time of termination of this Agreement.[38]

A BIT[39] will provide that, in respect of investments made while the BIT is in force, its provisions will continue in effect with respect to those investments for a certain period (usually ten or fifteen years) *after* the date of termination.[40]

Sometimes the withdrawal of a party from a *multilateral* treaty may cause financial problems for the remaining parties. Some treaties anticipate this and provide for such consequences.[41] Since these consequences can be complex, and will probably be dependent largely on the circumstances at the time of withdrawal, the clause will be in general terms.[42] Article 317(2) of UNCLOS provides that:

> A State shall not be discharged by reason of the denunciation [of this Convention] from the financial and contractual obligations which accrued while it was a party to this Convention, nor shall the denunciation affect any right, obligation or legal situation of that State created through the execution of this Convention before its termination for that State.[43]

Sometimes negotiating states agree that it is impossible to lay down the arrangements for termination, even in outline, before the event. The agreements between Norway and the United Kingdom relating to the exploitation of several oil and gas fields are of indefinite duration, and each provide that the two governments 'may amend or terminate this Agreement at any time by agreement', so leaving the conditions to be agreed at the time and in the light of the situation then.[44] The European Synchrotron Radiation Facility Convention 1988 provides – optimistically – that:

> The conditions and effects of withdrawal or termination, in particular the costs, shall be settled by agreement among the Contracting Parties before ... withdrawal or termination.[45]

[38] UK–South Africa Agreement on Co-operation in Science and Technology 1995 (1914 UNTS 6 No. 32659; UKTS (1995) No. 62); see also the ESA–UK Ascension Island Agreement (n. 31), Article 10.

[39] UK BITs are often called Investment Promotion and Protection Agreements (IPPAs).

[40] UK–Venezuela Agreement for the Promotion and Protection of Investments 1995 (1957 UNTS 76 No. 33501; UKTS (1996) No. 83). See also the texts of model BITs in R. Dolzer and M. Stevens, *Bilateral Investment Treaties* (Martinus Nijhoff, The Hague 1995).

[41] See ESA–UK Ascension Island Agreement (n. 31), Article 10.

[42] For example, Article XXIV ESA Convention 1975 (1297 UNTS 161 No. 21524; 14 ILM (1975) 864; UKTS (1981) No. 30); and Articles 21 and 30 INMARSAT Convention 1976 (1143 UNTS 105 No. 17948; 15 ILM (1976) 1051; UKTS (1979) No. 94; TIAS 9605).

[43] 1833 UNTS 397 No. 31363; 21 ILM (1982) 1261; UKTS (1999) No. 81.

[44] For example, Article 24(2) UK–Norway Murchison Field Agreement 1979 (1249 UNTS 174 No. 20387; UKTS (1981) No. 39).

[45] See n. 12.

Termination or Withdrawal by Consent

A treaty may, of course, be terminated, or a party may withdraw from it, at any time by consent of all the parties (Article 54(b)). This can be done even if the treaty provides for a minimum period of notice.[46] Although individual parties may have to take into account their own constitutional requirements, the parties are free to choose the form their consent will take. The ILC did not accept that the civil law principle of *acte contraire* (a rule can be altered only by a rule of the same legal nature) applied. Although it is desirable that the parties' consent is formalised in writing, the agreement of the parties does not have to be in the same form as the treaty (cf. amendment of a treaty other than by another treaty). If the treaty creates rights for a third state in accordance with Article 36, or an obligation has arisen for a third state from the treaty in accordance with Article 37, the consent of the third state may also be needed. That does not have to be expressed in any particular form.

Article 54(b) imposes one precondition, applicable only to a multilateral treaty: before taking action the parties must consult the contracting states, that is states that have consented to be bound but for which the treaty is not yet in force. By the same means, the parties may suspend the operation of the treaty (Article 57(b)).

Although these provisions would appear to envisage the power to terminate or suspend the whole treaty, the parties are, of course, free to agree to terminate or suspend only a part or parts of it.

The operation of all or some of the provisions of a multilateral treaty may be *suspended* by agreement between only certain parties if this is done in accordance with Article 58, the terms of which are substantially similar to Article 41 (agreement to modify a multilateral treaty between certain parties only). The United States has concluded over one hundred bilateral treaties (including with parties to the Rome Statute) under which the other state agrees not to surrender US military personnel, government officials, or civilian employees or contractors to the ICC.[47] Whether such treaties are compatible with the Rome Statute is questionable. The purpose of its Article 98(2), under which the treaties purport to be made, was to preserve the status of forces and similar agreements, not to shield the nationals of states that are not party to the ICC (which includes the United States) from ICC jurisdiction.[48]

[46] See the UK–Armenia Exchange of Notes 1996 terminating a UK–USSR Agreement 1964: 2068 UNTS 4 No. 35808; UKTS (1998) No. 57.

[47] See, e.g., the US–Uzbekistan Agreement 2002: 42 ILM (2003) 39. For a summary of the United States' attitude towards the Court, including the bilateral agreements, see W. Schabas, *An Introduction to the International Criminal Court* (6th ed., Cambridge University Press, Cambridge 2020), 25–31. For the Statute, see 2187 UNTS 91 No. 38544; 37 ILM (1998) 998; UKTS (2002) No. 35.

[48] See M. Cherif Bassiouni, *Introduction to International Criminal Law: Second Revised Edition* (Martinus Nijhoff, Leiden, Boston 2013), 703–705; R. Cryer, D. Robinson and S. Vasiliev, *An Introduction to International Criminal Law and Procedure* (4th ed., Cambridge University Press, Cambridge 2019), 165–167.

Reduction of Parties below the Number Necessary for Entry into Force

In the past at least, a few multilateral treaties provided that they would terminate if the number of parties fell below a certain number. Although the ILC did not cite an example, it thought it desirable to make it clear that if the number of parties were to fall below the number required for entry into force, this would not affect the continuance of the treaty, unless the treaty provided otherwise (Article 55).[49] If the remaining parties are unhappy with the situation – which may leave them with a greater financial burden – they would generally be free to withdraw, individually or collectively, or to join together and conclude a new treaty.

No Provision for Termination or Withdrawal

Some general law-making conventions are naturally silent as to their duration, but, perhaps surprisingly, they have provisions for withdrawal: for example, the Genocide Convention 1948[50] and the Geneva Conventions 1949.[51] Does this mean that when other similar conventions (including the VCLT itself) or other treaties, bilateral or multilateral, are silent as to their duration and have no provision for withdrawal, one cannot imply a right? In such cases, Article 56(1) *prohibits* a party from denouncing or withdrawing *unless*:

(a) it is established that the parties intended to admit the possibility of denunciation or withdrawal; or
(b) a right of denunciation or withdrawal may be implied by the nature of the treaty.

It must also give the other party or parties at least twelve months' notice of its intention (Article 56(2)). As the grounds for justifying withdrawal are expressed as an exception, the onus of establishing that the exception applies lies with the party wishing to withdraw.

Since it is now very common to include provisions on withdrawal, when a treaty is silent about the matter it may be that much harder for a party to establish the grounds for the exception. A party will *not* be able to withdraw from a treaty transferring territory or establishing a boundary (see Article 62(2)(a)), except in the (highly unlikely) event of the treaty allowing for this. (The same may apply in the case of some codification conventions.) Although Article 317(1) of UNCLOS permits denunciation, its predecessors did not.[52] When, in 1971, Senegal purported to denounce two of the Geneva Conventions 1958, several parties objected that this was not possible.[53]

[49] See pp. 129–130 on the effect of withdrawal of consent to be bound before entry into force.
[50] 78 UNTS 277 No. 1021; UKTS (1970) No. 58. [51] 75 UNTS 3 Nos. 970–973; UKTS (1958) No. 39.
[52] See n. 43.
[53] See, e.g., *UN Multilateral Treaties*, chapter XXI.1, Convention on the Territorial Sea and the Contiguous Zone, note 6 regarding the purported denunciation by Senegal; *Sinclair*, 187.

In any event, in many cases the rules in such codification conventions reflect, or have become accepted as, customary international law, so withdrawal might make little or no legal difference. Article 317(3) of UNCLOS confirms that denunciation:

> shall not in any way affect the duty of any State Party to fulfil any obligation embodied in this Convention to which it would be subject under international law independently of this Convention.[54]

Other treaties that are unlikely to be capable of withdrawal are peace treaties and disarmament treaties, and those establishing permanent regimes, such as for the Suez Canal. Many universal human rights treaties *do* provide for withdrawal. But in the case of the ICCPR 1966, the Human Rights Committee established under it has expressed its view that the omission of such a right, as well as the nature of the Covenant, precludes the existence of the right.[55] Although the views of the Committee are not determinative of the matter, and must *sometimes* be treated with caution,[56] they would seem to be correct in this case.[57] In August 1997, the DPRK gave notice of withdrawal from the ICCPR. The UN Secretary-General informed the DPRK that it could not withdraw unless all the other parties consented.[58] The DPRK *appears* to have accepted this.

Treaties that, by their nature, are more likely to fall within the exception in Article 56(1)(b) are treaties of alliance, commercial or trading agreements, cultural relations agreements, treaties of arbitration or judicial settlement, and constituent instruments of international organisations.[59] The commercial character of a treaty will, however, not be decisive, particularly when the treaty concerns a joint endeavour.

It will usually be possible to withdraw from a general treaty for the settlement of disputes between the parties even when it has no withdrawal provision. This is consistent with the consensual nature of international jurisdiction: a state can be made subject to the jurisdiction of an international court or tribunal only if it consents, either in advance or ad hoc. Moreover, states have withdrawn from optional protocols on dispute settlement to several UN treaties without (at least legal) objection even when they contain no provision for this.[60] Declarations under Article 36 of the Statute of the International Court of Justice (which is an integral part of the UN Charter) can be, and have been, withdrawn. However, another party or parties will be able to invoke the

[54] See n. 43.
[55] General Comment No. 26 (61), adopted on 8 December 1997, CCPR/C/21/Rev. 1/Add. 8/Rev. 1. The text is in 34 ILM (1995) 839.
[56] The Human Rights Committee (established a long time ago by the ICCPR) should not be confused with the Human Rights Council – with which it shares the same acronym: HRC.
[57] See also above pp. 258–259 on the *a contrario* argument.
[58] See *UN Multilateral Treaties*, chapter IV.4, note on the DPRK (note 8).
[59] See the discussion in *Dörr and Schmalenbach*, 1050–1052; *Corten and Klein*, 1272–1273; *Villiger*, 703; L. R. Helfer, 'Terminating Treaties', in *Hollis, Oxford Guide*, 624–640, at 628–629.
[60] See, e.g., *UN Multilateral Treaties*, chapter III.8 (note on the United States) on the immediate withdrawal of the United States from the Optional Protocol concerning the Compulsory Settlement of Disputes to the VCCR 1963: 596 UNTS 487 No. 8640; UKTS (1973) No. 14.

jurisdiction of the Court or tribunal during any period of notice in order to deal with an existing dispute.[61]

Even where the treaty has no express provision on duration or termination, the position will be different if there is an inherent time factor conditioning the application of the treaty. Thus, the ICJ rejected the contention of Iceland that it could denounce a treaty with the United Kingdom of 1961 that provided that either party could have recourse to the Court if Iceland purported to extend its fishery limits. Since the right to invoke the jurisdiction of the Court was deferred until the occurrence of such a well-defined future event, the treaty could *not* be denounced by Iceland *before* that event had occurred.[62]

Termination or Suspension by Conclusion of a Later Treaty

Two or more states conclude a treaty on the same subject matter as an earlier treaty to which they are parties, but the terms of the treaties are not compatible. In the absence of an express provision, what effect is there on the earlier treaty? If the parties to both treaties are identical, they are competent to abrogate the earlier one, and should include an express provision to this effect in the later treaty. The same would apply even if the parties to the later treaty are not the same as for the earlier one, provided that they include *all* the parties to the earlier one. But can the conclusion of the later treaty *impliedly* terminate the earlier one? Article 59(1) provides that if *all* the parties to the earlier treaty are also parties to the later one, *and* the two treaties relate to the same subject matter, the earlier treaty will be terminated if:

(a) it appears from the later treaty or is otherwise established that the parties intended that the matter should be governed by that treaty; or
(b) the provisions of the later treaty are so far incompatible with those of the earlier one that the two treaties are not capable of being applied at the same time.

The question is, therefore, one of interpretation of the two treaties to determine what the parties intended. Although a later treaty for a fixed term will not necessarily abrogate an earlier treaty with a longer or indefinite duration, there is likely to be a presumption that the parties intended that effect. The earlier treaty will be considered as suspended in operation only if it appears from the later treaty, or it is otherwise established, that that was the intention of the parties (Article 59(2)).[63]

[61] H. Thirlway, 'The Law and Procedure of the International Court of Justice 1960–1989', BYIL 63(1) (1992) 63–71.

[62] *Fisheries Jurisdiction (United Kingdom* v. *Iceland)* (Merits), ICJ Reports (1974) 3, at 12–15, paras. 25–29; 55 ILR 238; Thirlway (n. 61), 64–65.

[63] The fact that Article 59(2) does not include a second limb as does Article 59(1)(b) probably makes no difference in interpretation of the two paragraphs. See *Dörr and Schmalenbach*, 1092–1093.

The relationship between Article 59 and Article 30 is important and potentially difficult.[64] On the face of the text, the latter deals only with the *priority* of inconsistent obligations in treaties when there is no doubt that *both are in force*. It therefore comes into play only once it has been determined, by the application of the rules in Article 59, that the parties did not intend to abrogate or suspend the earlier treaty. But, in practice, when faced with potential incompatibility, states will often consider the two provisions together and explore their flexibility. There may be policy reasons, for example, why a state would not want to consider an earlier treaty *automatically* terminated; or would want to consider it *suspended* rather than *terminated*; or would not want to consider it even terminated or suspended at all (in its entirety) if there are provisions of the earlier treaty which it wishes to regard as still applicable, or which it may wish to revive after a period of non-application. States will therefore look at their legal options in light of these policy considerations.

The issue of the application of both Articles has arisen in the aftermath of the *Achmea* case, in which the CJEU held that intra-EU BITs were incompatible, for reasons of EU law, with the TFEU.[65] On 5 May 2020, twenty-three EU member states (excepting Ireland, Finland, Austria and Sweden) signed an Agreement for the Termination of BITs between EU Member States, which had the effect of terminating more than 130 such treaties.[66] The preamble to the Agreement referred to both Union law and the rules of customary international law as codified in the VCLT (but not specifically to Articles 30 or 59). Further action to terminate the BITs has also been taken by some EU member states and by the United Kingdom bilaterally.[67] The question of post-termination responsibility of states is a continuing point of discussion.[68]

Termination or Suspension for Breach[69]

Relationship between Treaty Law Responses and Countermeasures

A breach of a treaty may entitle another party to terminate or withdraw from the treaty, or suspend its operation in accordance with the Convention provisions. But

[64] For discussion of Article 30, see pp. 235–237.

[65] *Slovak Republic* v. *Achmea BV*, ECLI:EU:C:2018:158. See Ł. Kułaga, 'Implementing Achmea: The Quest for Fundamental Change in International Investment Law', *Polish Yearbook of International Law* (2019) 227–250.

[66] OJ L 169, 29.5.2020, 1–41. For a list of the treaties, see Annex A. For comment, see J. Tropper, 'The 2020 Termination Agreement of Intra-EU BITs and Its Effect on Investment Arbitration in the EU – A Public International Law Analysis of the Termination Agreement', *Austrian Yearbook on International Arbitration* 16 (2022) 301–340.

[67] Kułaga (n. 65), 231.

[68] See A. Reinisch and S. Mansour Fallah, 'Post-Termination Responsibility of States? – The Impact of Amendment/Modification, Suspension and Termination of Investment Treaties on (Vested) Rights of Investors', *ICSID Review – Foreign Investment Law Journal* 37 (2022) 101–120.

[69] See, generally, S. Rosenne, *Breach of Treaty* (Cambridge University Press, Cambridge 1985).

the Convention rules may not be the only determinant of a state's response. Article 73 of the Convention provides that its provisions do not prejudge any question that may arise in regard to a treaty from the international responsibility of a state. And the law of state responsibility may permit countermeasures to be taken in response to an internationally wrongful act, which may be constituted by a breach of either a treaty or non-treaty obligation.[70]

Although treaty law responses and countermeasures may be deployed in response to the same situation, they serve subtly different purposes. Countermeasures are temporary measures aiming to compel the defaulting state to cease its violation of international law and/or restore the situation that would have existed had there been no such violation. Treaty law responses aim at remedying the situation in which the balance of rights and obligations within a treaty relationship has been upset due to a prior breach by a defaulting state.[71] While countermeasures require proportionality, this principle is not expressly written into the Convention rules.[72] The issue of countermeasures is discussed further in Chapter 20.[73]

The following section deals with the Convention rules in relation to a material breach (Article 60). In *Gabčíkovo*,[74] the ICJ held that in many respects Articles 60–62 represented customary international law.

Bilateral Treaties

A 'material' breach of a bilateral treaty by one party entitles the other to invoke it as a ground for terminating the treaty or suspending its operation in whole or in part (Article 60(1)) (see below for the definition of 'material'). The use of 'invoke' means that a party may not simply declare a treaty at an end because of a perceived breach. Subject to such right as it may have to take countermeasures, Article 33 of the UN Charter requires the party to seek a peaceful settlement of the dispute, and, more particularly, the parties should follow the procedure in Articles 65–68 of the Convention. To entitle a party to invoke a material breach, the breach must be of the treaty itself, not of another treaty or of rules of general international law.[75] The effective termination in 1998 of the United Kingdom–Yugoslavia Agreement concerning Air Services 1959[76] was explained by the British foreign minister as having

[70] On the definition of an internationally wrongful act, see Article 2 Draft Articles on the Responsibility of States for Internationally Wrongful Acts, YBILC (2001) vol. II, Part Two, 34 (www.un.org/law/ilc); see also para. (7) of the Commentary on that Article, at 35. On countermeasures, see draft Articles 49–54.

[71] F. Capotorti, 'L'extinction et la suspension de traités', RCADI 134 (1971) 417–581, at 548–549. For discussion of the relationship between the law of treaties and the law of state responsibility on this aspect, see Simma and Tams (n. 4), 572–574; *Corten and Klein*, 1354; Xiouri (n. 4), 15–37; C. J. Tams, 'Regulating Treaty Breaches', in M. J. Bowman and D. Kritsiotis (eds.), *Conceptual and Contextual Perspectives on the Modern Law of Treaties* (Cambridge University Press, Cambridge 2018), 440–467.

[72] See the discussion in Simma and Tams (n. 4), 577–578.

[73] See pp. 366–369.

[74] ICJ Reports (1997) 3, at 38, para. 46; 37 ILM (1998) 162; 116 ILR 1.

[75] *Gabčíkovo* (n. 74), at 65, para. 106.

[76] 359 UNTS 340 No. 5151; UKTS (1960) No. 10.

been done on 'moral and political grounds' (i.e., not legal grounds), following an escalation of violence in Kosovo, President Slobodan Milošević having 'forfeited' his right to the twelve months' notice required by the Agreement.[77] A party which is itself already in breach, and has prevented the other party from complying with the treaty, cannot invoke the resulting breaches by that other party.[78] Finally, if relying on the Convention rules, the injured party can take action only in respect of the same bilateral treaty of which the material breach is alleged, not in respect of another treaty, even if that treaty is closely related.[79]

Multilateral Treaties

Multilateral treaties pose different problems, since a material breach by one party may not necessarily directly affect all other parties, but their interests must also be taken into account. Article 60(2) therefore deals with three different situations:

(1) The other parties, by unanimous agreement, are entitled to suspend the operation of the treaty in whole or in part, or to terminate it, in the relations between themselves and the defaulting state, or to terminate or suspend the operation of the treaty completely. It is not clear if in taking such action the other parties must follow the procedure in Articles 65–68.[80]

(2) A party 'specially affected' by the breach may invoke it as a ground for suspending the operation of the treaty in whole or in part in the relations between itself and the defaulting state.[81]

(3) If the treaty is 'of such a character' that a material breach 'radically changes the position of every party with respect to the further performance of its obligations under the treaty', any party (other than the defaulting party) may invoke the breach as a ground for *suspending* the operation of the treaty in whole or in part with respect to itself. This provision is designed to deal with certain special types of treaty, such as disarmament treaties, where a breach by one party could undermine the whole treaty regime. In such a case, the provisions in (1) and (2) above may not adequately protect the interests of an individual party, which could not suspend the performance of its own obligations in relation to the defaulting party without at the same time breaching its obligations to the other parties; yet if it

[77] BYIL 70 (1999) 554–556. Notice of termination was given on 9 September 1998, but a flight ban was imposed by the United Kingdom a week later. (The treaty was revived in 2000, see p. 186.) This somewhat unusual case needs to be distinguished from that of unilateral suspension of the UK–USSR ASA (p. 304).

[78] *Gabčíkovo* (n. 74), at 67, para. 110.

[79] See Simma and Tams (n. 4), 577; *Dörr and Schmalenbach*, 1110; *Corten and Klein*, 1371.

[80] See *Sinclair*, 189; *Oppenheim*, 1302, para. 649, note 5; *Corten and Klein*, 1375; *Dörr and Schmalenbach*, 1113. The previous author, Anthony Aust, added in the Third Edition: 'though given the reason for those articles there would seem good reason why they should'. The present author is inclined to the view that the responses taken under Article 60(2)(a) are not subject to the procedural requirements in Articles 65–68.

[81] For discussion of 'specially affected', see *Corten and Klein*, 1364–1365; *Dörr and Schmalenbach*, 1114.

does not do so, it may be unable to protect itself against the threat resulting from, for example, rearmament by the defaulting state.

Material Breach

Determining what is a 'material breach' depends on the precise facts and circumstances of each case. Article 60(3) defines it as:

> (a) a repudiation of the treaty not sanctioned by the present Convention; or
> (b) the violation of a provision 'essential to the accomplishment of the object and purpose of the treaty.

Fitzmaurice's draft articles had included the term 'fundamental' breach, but this was replaced by the term 'material' breach by Waldock, his successor as Special Rapporteur, so as to cover provisions which the parties considered to be essential despite their ancillary character.[82] A breach under Article 60(3)(b) can, therefore, be constituted by the breach of an important ancillary provision.[83] If a party to the CWC 1993[84] obstructs the conduct on its territory of international inspections to verify that it is complying with that Convention, this could be a material breach since the inspection regime is a key means of monitoring compliance with the CWC.

While paragraph (a) of Article 60(3) concerns rejection of the treaty as a whole,[85] paragraph (b) concerns the violation of a particular provision. But sometimes the two may be difficult to distinguish, or at least they may be invoked simultaneously.[86]

Article 60(4) preserves the rights of the parties under any specific provisions of the treaty that would apply in the event of breach. Article 60(5) makes it clear that Article 60(1)–(3) does not apply to breach of provisions in treaties relating to the protection of the human person and, in particular, provisions prohibiting any form of reprisals against persons protected by such treaties. Although the drafters had in mind the Geneva Conventions of 1949, the paragraph would apply equally to other conventions of a humanitarian character, including possibly human rights treaties,[87] since they

82 See ILC Commentary, YBILC (1966) vol. II, 255, para. 9; and Waldock's Second Report, YBILC (1963), vol. II, 75, para. 11. See *Corten and Klein*, 1358–1360; and *Dörr and Schmalenbach*, 1100–1101.

83 On the issue of 'gravity', see also Xiouri (n. 4), 97–100; Simma and Tams (n. 4), *Hollis, Oxford Guide*, 575; Tams (n. 71), 446–449.

84 See n. 19.

85 *Arbitration between the Republic of Croatia and the Republic of Slovenia*, Partial Award, 30 June 2016, PCA Case No. 2012-04, para. 213; *Villiger*, 742.

86 *Namibia (South West Africa) (Legal Consequences for States of the Continued Presence of South Africa)*, Advisory Opinion, ICJ Reports (1971) 3, at 47, para. 95. See also Xiouri (n. 4), 92–97.

87 The previous author, Anthony Aust, in the Third Edition, was more definitive on this point, stating: 'the paragraph would apply equally to other conventions of a humanitarian character, or human rights treaties, since they create rights intended to protect individuals irrespective of the conduct of the parties to each other'. The present author would interpret Article 60(5) more restrictively, on the basis that the key word is 'humanitarian', and the wording of the phrase 'the protection of the human person contained in treaties of a humanitarian character' suggests that 'treaties of a humanitarian character' is the determinative category of

create rights intended to protect individuals irrespective of the conduct of the parties to each other.

The concept of 'material breach' was deliberately adopted by the UN Security Council in certain of its acts in relation to Iraq. In Resolution 707 (1991), paragraph 1, Iraq's serious violations of the weapons of mass destruction provisions in Resolution 687 (1991) were said to constitute material breaches of the ceasefire (as embodied in the Resolution) and provisions of the Council essential for the restoration of peace and security in the region.[88]

Fundamental Breach

It is doubtful whether the concept of fundamental breach exists within the framework of treaty rules. As stated above, the term 'fundamental breach' in the draft articles of the Convention was consciously replaced by 'material breach'.[89] A flagrant breach of the object and purpose of a treaty may still constitute a material breach and, if so, this would entitle a state to respond to such a breach within the Convention rules.[90] But insofar as a state may wish to respond outside these rules to what it regards as a 'fundamental breach' of a treaty, this has to be considered within the field of countermeasures.[91]

On 1 September 1983, Korean Airlines flight KAL 007 was unlawfully shot down by Soviet forces. Several states with air services agreements with the Soviet Union unilaterally, and for varying periods, suspended the agreements with immediate effect, so preventing Russian airline Aeroflot from landing in their territory, and vice versa. It was argued they were entitled to do so because the Soviet action undermined the fundamental basis of every air services agreement: that each party would ensure the safety of the other party's aircraft.[92] Only the previous year, in response to the failure of Afghanistan to extradite or prosecute the alleged hijackers of a Pakistan airliner contrary to its obligations under the Hague (Hijacking) Convention 1970,[93] certain states had terminated their air services agreements with Afghanistan, but only by giving the twelve months' notice required under them.[94] Despite acrimonious discussions between Western states, no agreement could be reached that the breach

treaties, rather than human rights treaties at large. See the discussion in *Corten and Klein*, 1366–1368; *Dörr and Schmalenbach*, 1122; and *Villiger*, 747.

88 See Resolution 768 (1990), para. 2; Resolution 1441 (2002), para. 1. See also Resolution 1696 (2006).

89 See p. 303.

90 See *Military and Paramilitary Activities in and against Nicaragua (Nicaragua* v. *United States of America)*, Merits, ICJ Reports (1986) 14, at 138, paras. 275–276; *Corten and Klein*, 1360.

91 See *Dörr and Schmalenbach*, 1107.

92 See G. Richard, 'KAL 007: The Legal Fallout', *Annals of Air and Space Law* (1984) 146–162, 150; K. Chamberlain, 'Collective Suspension of Air Services', ICLQ 32 (1983) 616–632, 630–631.

93 Convention for the Suppression of Unlawful Seizure of Aircraft 1970: 860 UNTS 105 No. 12325; UKTS (1972) No. 39.

94 Chamberlain (n. 92), 626–628.

by Afghanistan had been so fundamental as to justify immediate suspension of air services.

Supervening Impossibility of Performance

If an *object* which is 'indispensable' for the execution of a treaty disappears permanently or is destroyed, thereby making the performance of the treaty impossible, it is hardly surprising that a party can invoke this as a ground for terminating or withdrawing from the treaty, and Article 61(1) so provides. The rule has been much criticised,[95] and there are few precedents.[96] In its judgment in *Gabčíkovo*, the ICJ held that the object of the relevant treaty had not definitively ceased to exist, there being means in the treaty by which the parties could negotiate necessary adjustments.[97] The ILC mentioned as possible examples of impossibility of performance the submergence of an island (which global warming *may* now make a practical possibility), the drying up of a river (though this may not be permanent) or the destruction of a dam by an earthquake. Another example might be the loss by fire of national treasures which one state has loaned to another. As *Gabčíkovo* made clear, serious financial difficulties would not be enough.[98] The total extinction of the international personality of one of the parties has also been suggested, but was not included because it also involves issues of state succession, which the Commission was not then addressing. If the impossibility of performance is temporary, it is only ground for suspension.

At the end of the Falklands conflict in 1982, all the tents shipped down to the area, and intended for Argentine POWs, were lost at sea due to Argentine action. This unfortunate occurrence can be properly regarded as a good ground for the temporary suspension of the provision in Article 22 of the Third Geneva Convention 1949, which prohibits the holding of POWs on ships, it being the only way to protect the over 10,000 POWs from the Falklands' abominable weather.

Impossibility of performance may not be invoked by a party if it is the result of a breach by it either of an obligation under the treaty (as was the case with Hungary in *Gabčíkovo*)[99] or of any other international obligation owed to any other party to the treaty (Article 61(2)).

The concept of supervening impossibility of performance in treaty law is related to, but distinguishable from, the concept of *force majeure* under the law of state

[95] See *Sinclair*, 191–192.

[96] See also the Draft articles on the Responsibility of States for Internationally Wrongful Acts, ILC Commentary on Article 23, paras. (4) and (5), in J. Crawford, *The International Law Commission's Articles on State Responsibility* (Cambridge University Press, Cambridge 2002), 170–173.

[97] See n. 74, at 63–64, paras. 102–103; 116 ILR 1; 37 ILM (1998) 162. The 'object' was the Gabčíkovo-Nagymaros Project, the construction and operation of a system of locks along the Danube.

[98] See p. 63, para. 102. [99] At p. 64, para. 103.

responsibility.[100] Article 61 enables a state to terminate or suspend its obligations, thus preventing the breach of any international obligation, whereas *force majeure* operates as a defence to preclude the wrongfulness of the treaty violation.[101]

Fundamental Change of Circumstances *(rebus sic stantibus)*

The principle that a person may no longer be bound by a contract if there has been a fundamental change in the circumstances that existed at the time it was signed (in English common law, the doctrine of frustration) has been acknowledged to apply also to treaties. But there has been a lively debate about the conditions under which it could be invoked. Because the concept was abused in the past, particularly between the First and Second World Wars, Article 62 was drawn in restrictive terms. On the other hand, the ILC did not limit it, as had been suggested by some writers, to treaties with unlimited duration and no termination clause, though the Commission noted that, since most treaties now have either express duration or termination clauses, today the scope for invoking the article is more limited.

Paragraph 1

Paragraph 1 of Article 62 defines strictly the (cumulative) conditions under which a change of circumstances may be invoked. It may *not* be invoked as a ground for terminating or withdrawing from a treaty *unless*:

(1) the change is of circumstances existing at the time of the conclusion of the treaty;
(2) the change is 'fundamental';
(3) the change was not foreseen by the parties (i.e., when they concluded the treaty);
(4) the existence of the circumstances constituted 'an essential basis of the consent of the parties to be bound by the treaty'; and
(5) the effect of the change was 'radically to transform the extent of the obligations still to be performed under the treaty'.

The application of the principle is thus strictly circumscribed. A state may not invoke its own conduct. Whether a change of policy by the government of one party would be enough would depend entirely on the circumstances,[102] but certainly only if the

[100] See the discussion in M. Fitzmaurice, 'Exceptional Circumstances and Treaty Commitments', in *Hollis, Oxford Guide*, 595–623, at 618–621; J. Crawford, *State Responsibility* (Cambridge University Press, Cambridge 2013), 295–301.

[101] See *Dörr and Schmalenbach*, 1141. See also Article 23 Draft Articles on the Responsibility of States for Internationally Wrongful Acts (n. 70): 'The wrongfulness of an act of a State not in conformity with an international obligation of that State is precluded if the act is due to *force majeure*, that is the occurrence of an irresistible force or of an unforeseen event, beyond the control of the State, making it materially impossible in the circumstances to perform the obligation.'

[102] See the discussion in J. Kułaga, 'A Renaissance of the Doctrine of *Rebus Sic Stantibus*?', ICLQ 69 (2020) 477–497, 492–497.

effect were to alter fundamentally a circumstance that constituted an essential basis of the consent of the parties to the treaty.

The principle has been *invoked* many times, and recognised by treaties.[103] But it has rarely been *applied* by an international tribunal,[104] though no tribunal has denied its existence.[105] Article 62 was considered by the ICJ in *Fisheries Jurisdiction (United Kingdom* v. *Iceland)* (Merits).[106] The Court found that the article was declaratory of customary international law. In *Gabčíkovo*, the same Court rejected Hungary's argument that profound political changes that diminish the economic viability of a project, progress in environmental knowledge or the development of new norms of international environmental law constituted a fundamental change of circumstances. The Court emphasised that the stability of treaty relations requires Article 62 to be applied only in exceptional cases.[107]

In *Racke*,[108] the ECJ upheld a Decision of the Council of Ministers in 1991, which denounced the operation of the EC–Yugoslavia Cooperation Agreement 1980. The Court accepted that, since the changed conditions in Yugoslavia could amount to a fundamental change of circumstances, in adopting the Decision the Council of Ministers had *not* made 'a manifest error of assessment'. The Court did not consider the international law point in depth, but rather approached the case as one of judicial review of action taken under EC law (as it was then). The Court said, in effect, that the Council had not been clearly wrong; but it did not go as far as saying the Council had been right to apply the principle.

If the principle is to be invoked successfully, this needs to be done without delay. Otherwise, the party may be deemed to have acquiesced in the treaty remaining in force (see Article 45(b)).

Paragraph 2

In addition to the strict conditions for the application of the principle, paragraph 2 of Article 62 makes two exceptions. First, the principle cannot be invoked if the treaty establishes a boundary, that term being used so as to include treaties which cede territory, not merely delimit a boundary. The ILC resisted suggestions that the exception might be inconsistent with the principle of self-determination, but accepted

[103] *Oppenheim*, 1305, para. 651 note 2.

[104] See *Racke* (1998) Case C-162/96; [1998] ECR I-3688; 37 ILM (1998) 1128; 117 ILR 263 and the discussion in Fitzmaurice (n. 100), 607–611. She comments at 612: 'It may thus be said that the doctrine of fundamental change of circumstances is an exception in international law, used very sparingly by States and treated with great circumspection by the ICJ.'

[105] See *Oppenheim*, 1307, para. 651, note 8; and *Free Zones*, PCIJ Reports (1932), Series A/B, No. 46, 156–158; 6 AD 363, 365.

[106] See n. 62, at 17–18, para. 36. See *Sinclair*, 195–196; and Thirlway (n. 61). For examples of state practice, see *McNair*, 681–691; O. Lissitzyn, 'Treaties and Changed Circumstances', AJIL (1967) 895–922, 905–908; A. Vamvoukos, *Termination of Treaties in International Law* (Clarendon Press, Oxford 1985).

[107] See n. 74, at 64, para. 104.

[108] See n. 104, paras. 53–59. See also AJIL (1999) 205–209.

that the operation of that principle was not excluded in any case where the conditions for its legitimate operation existed.[109] Second, the principle cannot be invoked if the fundamental change is the result of a breach by the party invoking it either of an obligation under the treaty or any other international obligation owed to any other party to the treaty. This is an application of the general principle of law that a person cannot take advantage of their own wrongdoing, which is applicable to any of the grounds for termination that might be invoked. It is mentioned here, and in Article 61 (impossibility of performance), because of the risk that the grounds dealt with by them might well result from a breach of treaty.

Paragraph 3

If the ground can be invoked, it may also be invoked as a ground for suspending the operation of the treaty.

Procedure

It would be wrong to think that this heading of section 4 of Part V of the Convention means that the content is less important than that of the preceding sections, though it might be less exciting. The ILC was concerned that the grounds for termination or suspension might be invoked as a pretext for shrugging off inconvenient treaty obligations. When one of the grounds is invoked, whether it is justified will essentially turn upon the facts and particular circumstances, the determination or appreciation of which may well be controversial; if the facts are agreed, then it is more likely that the parties will be able to agree to modify or terminate the treaty. The danger for the security of treaties is particularly great if the ground invoked is based on an alleged material breach or fundamental change of circumstances, both of which can produce a substantial degree of subjectivity.

In *Gabčíkovo*, the ICJ recognised that Articles 65–67 *generally* reflect customary international law and contain certain procedural principles, which are based on the obligation to act in good faith.[110] But the commentaries express some doubts about the extent to which *the detail* of Articles 65–67 represents customary international law, particularly Article 66, and generally there is a dearth of state practice.[111] The issue can be important, particularly in light of the number of reservations (and objections) which have been made in respect of these articles.[112]

[109] ILC Commentary on draft Article 59, para. (11). [110] See n. 74, at 66–67, para. 109.

[111] See *Dörr and Schmalenbach*, 1213–1214, 1234, 1254; *Corten and Klein*, 1486–1490, 1515–1516, 1548–1550; *Villiger*, 813, 843–844.

[112] See, for example, the reservation of the USSR (now Russian Federation) in respect of Article 66, and disputes concerning Articles 53 or 64; and the objection of the United Kingdom: 'With respect to any other reservation the intention of which is to exclude the application, in whole or in part, of the provisions of article 66, to which the United Kingdom has already objected or which is made after the reservation by the Government of the Union of Soviet Socialist Republics, the United Kingdom will not

Article 65 is a key provision, its procedural safeguards being designed to deter states from arbitrary action, though it is often not followed.[113] A party wishing to invoke provisions in Part V in order to terminate, withdraw from or suspend the operation of a treaty must notify the other parties of its claim. The notification must be in writing (Article 67(1)) and indicate the measure proposed to be taken and the reasons for it. The other parties must be given time to reply. Except in cases of special urgency, this must not be less than three months from receipt of the notification. If no party raises any objection within the notice period, the proposed measure can be carried out in the manner provided for in Article 67 (see below).

However, if an objection is raised, Article 65(3) provides that the parties are under an obligation to seek a solution through the means indicated in Article 33 of the UN Charter by, for example, negotiation, mediation or arbitration,[114] although existing agreements between the parties on dispute settlement remain unaffected. A party may, by way of answer to a demand by another party that it perform the treaty, or to a complaint that it is in breach, also make a notification under Article 65(5). A party may not have invoked the ground in question before being confronted with the complaint, but the failure to make prior notification does not prevent that party from making it in answer to a complaint. This is, however, without prejudice to Article 45, concerning the effect of inaction in debarring a party from invoking a ground.[115]

Article 66

Article 66 did not figure among the ILC's draft articles. It was included at the Vienna Conference in order to strengthen Article 65(3), which would have been little more than a pious hope if the parties in dispute were not already bound by a mechanism for settling their disputes. A number of states were not prepared to accept articles which they saw as progressive development of treaty law without procedural safeguards.[116] Paragraph (b) of Article 66 provides for conciliation of most disputes under Part V. Paragraph (a) deals only with *jus cogens* disputes.

Instruments for Termination, Withdrawal or Suspension

The withdrawal from a treaty, or the threat to do so, is sometimes made in a public speech not addressed directly to the other states concerned. To avoid any uncertainty as to the status of the announcement, Article 67 provides that any act terminating,

consider its treaty relations with the State which has formulated or will formulate such a reservation as including those provisions of Part V of the Convention with regard to which the application of article 66 is rejected by the reservation.'

113 See pp. 366–369 about countermeasures. 114 See *Aust Handbook*, chapter 22.

115 See *Case Concerning Armed Activities on the Territory of the Congo (New Application: 2002) (Democratic Republic of the Congo* v. *Rwanda)*, Jurisdiction and Admissibility, Judgment, ICJ Reports (2006) 3, at 51–52, para. 125.

116 For the history of the negotiation of Article 66, see *Sinclair*, 226–232. See also *UN Multilateral Treaties*, chapter XXI.6, for the several reservations about Article 66 and the objections to them.

withdrawing from or suspending the operation of a treaty under Article 65(2) or (3) must be done by an instrument communicated to the other party or parties. Because of the importance of the effect of such an act, the article provides also that, unless the instrument is signed by the head of state, head of government or foreign minister, the representative of the state communicating it can be called upon to produce full powers. No special form of words is needed.[117]

If the instrument does not specify the date on which it is to become effective, the date will be calculated in accordance with the withdrawal provisions of the treaty. It is, however, normal practice to specify the date. This must be calculated in accordance with the period of notice prescribed in the treaty, though a longer period may, by agreement, be specified. It is as well, in the case of a multilateral treaty, to check any date with the depositary and/or Secretariat.

A notification under Article 65, or an instrument under Article 67, may be revoked at any time before it takes effect (Article 68).[118] In the case of the UK's withdrawal from the European Union, the CJEU was asked to consider whether the UK's notification to that effect under Article 50 of the Treaty on European Union[119] could be withdrawn prior to the end of the two-year period specified in that Article. The Court determined that it could, basing its reasoning primarily on principles of EU law, but also referencing the VCLT provisions.[120] This point is to be distinguished from the domestic constitutional issue arising in the case of *Miller No. 1*,[121] where the applicant successfully challenged the submission of the notification of withdrawal (in this particular case) without an Act of Parliament.

Consequences of Termination, Withdrawal or Suspension

Article 70 does not deal with any question of state responsibility if, for example, a treaty has been terminated because of the breach of it by another party; and many treaties, including law-making treaties, do not contain provisions on the consequences of termination. But a treaty, whether bilateral or multilateral, pursuant to which acts are likely to be taking place at or after termination may, as the opening words of Article 70(1) recognise, have transitional provisions applying the treaty in whole or in part to such acts even after termination. Thus, Article 65(2) of the ECHR 1950[122] provides that denunciation shall not release a party from its obligations in

[117] See also examples in *Blix and Emerson*, 114–116.
[118] See AJIL (1996) 826; *Whiteman*, vol. 14, 446–448.
[119] 2702 UNTS 3 No. 47938, OJ C 306, 17.12.2007, 1, and OJ C 326, 26.10.2012, 1; UKTS (2010) No. 7
[120] *Wightman and others* v. *Secretary of State for Exiting the European Union*, Case C-621/18, ECLI:EU:C:2018:999, in particular paras. 70–71.
[121] *R. (on the application of Miller and another)* v. *Secretary of State for Exiting the European Union* [2017] UKSC 5, UK Supreme Court.
[122] Amended by subsequent Protocols: consolidated text at CoE website. It is now Art. 58 in the amended Convention.

respect of any acts which, being capable of constituting a violation of those obligations, may have been done before the denunciation becomes effective.

Following Russia's invasion of Ukraine in February 2022, the Committee of Ministers of the Council of Europe decided that the Russian Federation was in serious violation of its obligations under Article 3 of the Statute of the Council of Europe and should cease to be a member of the organisation.[123] A further Resolution adopted by the Committee of Ministers spelt out the legal and financial consequences of that decision, which included that Russia would cease to be party to the ECHR on 16 September 2022.[124] It went on to say:

> In line with the Resolution of 22 March 2022 of the European Court of Human Rights, the Court remains competent to deal with applications directed against the Russian Federation in relation to acts or omissions capable of constituting a violation of the Convention provided that they occurred until 16 September 2022. The Committee of Ministers will continue to supervise the execution of the judgments and friendly settlements concerned and the Russian Federation is required to implement them. The Russian Federation is to continue to participate in the meetings of the Committee of Ministers when the latter supervises the execution of judgments with a view to providing and receiving information concerning the judgments where it is the respondent or applicant State, without the right to participate in the adoption of decisions by the Committee nor to vote.[125]

In respect of other conventions and protocols, the Resolution determined that Russia would cease to be party to those which were open only to members of the Council of Europe. Russia would, however, continue to be party to those treaties concluded within the framework of the Council of Europe to which it had expressed its consent to be bound, and which were open to accession by non-member states.[126]

Suspension or termination of a treaty will not apply retrospectively to provisions on the settlement of disputes.[127] Transitional provisions are especially important when the

[123] Resolution CM/Res (2022)2 on the cessation of the membership of the Russian Federation to the Council of Europe (adopted by the Committee of Ministers on 16 March 2022 at the 1428ter meeting of the Ministers' Deputies). On 15 March 2022, the Government of the Russian Federation had in fact informed the Secretary-General of its withdrawal from the Council of Europe in accordance with the Statute of the Council of Europe and of its intention to denounce the ECHR.

[124] Resolution CM/Res (2022)3 on legal and financial consequences of the cessation of membership of the Russian Federation in the Council of Europe (adopted by the Committee of Ministers on 23 March 2022 at the 1429bis meeting of the Ministers' Deputies). See also Article 58(3) ECHR.

[125] Para. 7, Resolution CM/Res (2022)3.

[126] See also *Speaking points*, Mr Jörg Polakiewicz, Russia's expulsion from the Council of Europe – communication to the 62nd meeting of the Committee of Legal Advisers on Public International Law (CAHDI), Strasbourg (hybrid), 24 March 2022.

[127] See *Fisheries Jurisdiction* n. 62, at 15–16, para. 29; *United States Diplomatic and Consular Staff in Tehran*, Judgment, ICJ Reports (1980) 3, at 28, para. 54; 61 ILR 502.

treaty deals with a project that involves joint financing. Such provisions have to be tailor-made to suit the circumstances of the particular treaty, and can be complex.[128]

Article 70(1) provides, somewhat obviously, that in the absence of any transitional provisions, if a treaty is terminated under its provisions or in accordance with the Convention, the parties are released from any obligation further to perform it, but that this does not affect any right, obligation or legal situation 'of the parties' created through the execution of the treaty before its termination. The words in quotes are to make clear that the provision is not concerned with the question of vested interests of individuals.

No rule is laid down in the Convention to deal with the situation where a treaty has been terminated because of supervening impossibility of its performance (Article 61), yet has been partially executed by one party only. Given the difficulties that would be likely to be experienced in such a situation, very sensibly the matter is left to the good faith of the parties.

During a period of suspension the parties must refrain from acts tending to obstruct the resumption of the operation of the treaty (Article 72(2)).

Termination of Provisional Application

In Chapter 9 it was already noted that provisional application by a state terminates with the entry into force of the treaty in the relations between the states concerned.[129] Unless the treaty provides or the negotiating states have agreed otherwise, provisional application is also terminated with respect to a state if it notifies the other states between which it is being applied provisionally of its intention not to become a party to the treaty (Article 25(2)).[130]

In practice, treaties will often include express provision on termination of provisional application, even if it is a clause reiterating this principle along the following lines:

> The provisional application of this Treaty [or article(s)...] shall terminate upon its entry into force for a State [an international organization] that is applying it provisionally or if that State [international organization] notifies the other State [international organization] [Depositary] of its intention not to become a party to the Treaty.[131]

128 See Article XXIV ESA Convention 1975 (n. 42); and Articles 29 and 30 INMARSAT Convention 1976 (n. 42). See also on BITs, p. 295.

129 See *Guideline* 9.1, Guide to Provisional Application of Treaties, Report of the ILC on the work of its 72nd session, 2021, UNGA 76th Session, Supplement No. 10, Doc. A/76/10, at 55 (in this chapter referred to as *Guideline* and normally followed by the specific number).

130 See also *Guideline* 9.2, Guide to Provisional Application of Treaties (n. 129).

131 Draft model clause 1, para. 2, Draft model clauses on provisional application of treaties, Report of the ILC on the Work of its 71st session, 2019, UNGA 74th Session, Supplement No. 10, Doc. A/74/10, at 353. See also the other similar termination clauses cited in footnote 7, 354.

In the context of exit from the EU, the United Kingdom made increased use of provisional application to ensure that the treaties it had negotiated to replace EU treaties with non-EU countries were applicable immediately upon the expiry of the eleven month transition period after exit;[132] it was not always possible for both sides to ratify these treaties and bring them into force by the requisite date. Many of these treaties therefore included not only a provision allowing for provisional application but also a provision relating to its termination. This would often specify a period of notice for such termination, which was short enough to terminate a treaty quickly in the event of issues arising concerning its ratification, but long enough to avoid disruption to trade or other transactions. An example is to be found in the UK–Israel Trade and Partnership Agreement:

> 5. A Party may terminate the provisional application of this Agreement, or provisions of it, by written notification to the other Party. Such termination shall take effect on the first day of the third month following the notification.
>
> 6. The provisional application of this Agreement shall terminate upon its entry into force.[133]

ILC *Guideline* 9.3 affirms that, unless the treaty otherwise provides or it is otherwise agreed, a state or international organisation may invoke other grounds for terminating provisional application, in which case it shall notify the other state or international organisation concerned.[134] This appears to apply both to a state that wishes to terminate its own provisional application and to a state that wishes to invoke a ground for suspending or terminating another state's provisional application. This is particularly relevant if a party to the treaty (or a provisionally applying state) should consider another provisionally applying state to have committed a material breach of the treaty. Hence, for example, the provisional application of the Energy Charter Treaty[135] in relation to Belarus was suspended by the Contracting Parties because of a material breach of Article 18 of the Treaty.[136]

The Commentary to the ILC Guide to Provisional Application notes that there is flexibility on the timeframe for notification.[137] In some cases there may be need for

[132] To cover the continued application to the UK of EU agreements with other countries during the transition period, the European Union undertook to notify the other parties to the agreements that during the transition period the UK was to be treated as a Member State for the purposes of these agreements: Article 127 UK–EU Withdrawal Agreement and the asterisk thereto: OJ C 3841, 12.11.2019, 1–177; UKTS (2020) No. 3.

[133] Article 9.5 and 9.6, UK–Israel Trade and Partnership Agreement, UK Country Series, Israel (2019) No. 1.

[134] Guide to Provisional Application of Treaties (n. 129), 55.

[135] 2080 UNTS 100 No. 36116; 34 ILM (1995) 373; UKTS (2000) No. 78.

[136] Ad Hoc Energy Charter Conference, 24 June 2022: see Energy Charter Secretariat website. See also Proposal for a Council Decision on the position to be taken on behalf of the European Union at the Extraordinary Conference of the Energy Charter Treaty on 24th June 2022, COM(2022)293 final, 13 June 2022.

[137] Para. (9), Commentary on *Guideline* 9 (n. 129), 83.

sufficient advance notice. In others, the suspension or termination may take place immediately upon receipt of the notification. The Commentary also notes that the procedural requirements stipulated in the Convention for the termination of treaties already in force do not apply generally to the termination of provisional application.[138]

Miscellaneous

Articles 43–45 contain some general considerations.

Obligations Imposed by International Law Independently of a Treaty

The termination or suspension of a treaty, or withdrawal of a party, does not affect the duty of a state to fulfil any obligation in the treaty to which it would be subject under other international law (Article 43). For example, many of the substantive provisions of the four Geneva Conventions of 1949 are now accepted as representing customary international law. Thus, if a party were to withdraw from the Conventions, or any one of them, it would still be bound by customary international law to respect their substantive rules. This is reflected in each of the four Conventions, which provide that denunciation shall in no way impair the obligations of the parties to a conflict under general international law.[139] Similarly, Article 318(3) of UNCLOS[140] provides that:

> denunciation shall not in any way affect the duty of any State Party to fulfil any obligation embodied in this Convention to which it would be subject under international law independently of this Convention.

Separability of Treaty Provisions

In the past it was thought that if one party had the right to terminate a treaty on the ground that another party was in breach, it could do so only in respect of certain provisions, but not if termination was based on other grounds. Article 44(1) makes no such distinction. If a treaty provides a right to withdraw or to suspend its operation, this may be exercised only with respect to the *whole* treaty, unless the treaty provides or the parties agree otherwise. Paragraph 2 provides that where no such right is included, a party may invoke a ground recognised in the Convention only with respect to the *whole* treaty, except as provided in paragraph 3, or in Article 60 (termination for breach). Paragraph 3 permits separability if the ground relates *solely to particular clauses*. It may be invoked only with respect to those clauses if *all three* conditions are met:

[138] Para. (10), Commentary on *Guideline* 9 (n. 129), 83.
[139] See, e.g., Article 142 Third Geneva Convention (75 UNTS 3 No. 972; UKTS (1959) No. 39), and *Aust Handbook*, 237, about the so-called *Martens* clause.
[140] See n. 43.

(a) the clauses are separable from the remainder of the treaty with regard to their application, in that it must be possible to sever them without affecting the clauses which remain; *and*
(b) it appears from the treaty, or is otherwise established, that acceptance of the clauses was not an essential basis of the consent of the other party or parties to be bound by the treaty as a whole (this condition is the most difficult to apply, requiring an examination of the subject matter of the clauses, their relationship to the other clauses, and perhaps also the *travaux* and the circumstances of the conclusion of the treaty); *and*
(c) continued performance of the remainder of the treaty would not be unjust. Severance might affect the balance of the treaty; and an examination under condition (b) would not necessarily take into account how the balance of interests might have changed over the years the treaty has been operated.

Paragraphs 4 and 5 are relevant only to invalidity.

Loss of Rights by Acquiescence

A state may not invoke certain grounds for terminating, withdrawing from or suspending the operation of a treaty if, after it had become aware of the facts, it either (a) expressly agreed that the treaty remain in force or continue in operation, or (b) by reason of its conduct it must be considered as having acquiesced in its maintenance in force or in operation (Article 45). The article applies to grounds under Articles 46–50, 60 and 62.

Can a Party Validly Withdraw from a Treaty and Then Accede to It?

One can envisage reasons why a state may wish to withdraw from a multilateral treaty and then rejoin it; the United Kingdom once withdrew from UNESCO, only resuming its membership several years later. Probably the only reason a state would withdraw from a treaty, but then *immediately* accede to it, would be to make a reservation it had not made before. Although certain latitude may be allowed to states that make late reservations, this particular stratagem appears highly questionable.

Other Grounds for Termination

Article 42(2) makes it clear that a treaty may be terminated only as a result of the application of its provisions or those of the Convention. The ILC has been criticised for excluding from the draft Convention other suggested grounds of termination.[141] However, those usually mentioned may not really be grounds for termination. They include the following.

[141] *Sinclair*, 163–165.

By Implication

The Agreement regarding the Financial Support of the North Atlantic Ice Patrol 1956[142] appears to have been effectively terminated by the entry into force on 1 July 2002 of the Rules for the Management etc. of the North Atlantic Ice Patrol adopted pursuant to the Safety of Life at Sea Convention 1974 (SOLAS).[143] The Rules are binding on all the parties to the 1956 Agreement, but are incompatible with it.

Full Performance or Execution

This may seem too obvious a case to need mention, but if *all* the provisions of a treaty have been carried out, and none of them has any residual purpose, then one may say that the treaty has terminated by its execution. The UK–Egypt Tutankhamen Agreement 1971[144] for the loan for six months of the priceless treasures could fall into this category. A treaty for the transfer of territory is executed once the transfer has taken place in accordance with its terms, unless it has conditions that continue to apply to the parties in respect of the territory. In any event, the actual transfer of the territory will have continuing legal effects. The simplest procedure is to have an exchange of notes either terminating the treaty or confirming that nothing more needs to be done.

Once there has been full repayment under a bilateral loan or debt agreement, all obligations have been fulfilled. Although the parties could record this in a short agreement terminating the treaty, it is sufficient if the lender sends a diplomatic note to the borrower confirming that all the monies have been paid, and that the agreement is therefore terminated. The UN Secretary-General, with whom the treaty should have been registered, should be sent a copy of the note.

Desuetude (disuse) or Obsolescence[145]

Although the ILC did not dismiss these as grounds, because it considered the basis for them to be the consent of the parties as evidenced by their conduct, it saw no need for separate treatment.[146] In 1990 Austria declared that certain provisions of the Austrian

142 256 UNTS 171 No. 3627; UKTS (1956) No. 43; TIAS 3597.

143 1184 UNTS 278 No. 18961; UKTS (1980) No. 46 (subject to further amendments). See www.imo.org.

144 824 UNTS 71 No. 11809; UKTS (1972) No. 19.

145 See M. G. Kohen, 'Desuetude and Obsolescence of Treaties', in E. Cannizzaro (ed.), *The Law of Treaties beyond the Vienna Convention* (Oxford University Press, Oxford 2011), 350–359; *McNair*, 516–518 and 681–691.

146 But see Thirlway (n. 61), 94–96, with reference to the *Nuclear Tests* cases, ICJ Reports (1974), 253 and 457. See also the *UK–France Continental Shelf Arbitration* (1977), 54 ILR 6, at 47, with reference to the Continental Shelf Convention of 1958, where the Tribunal said: 'only the most conclusive indications of the intention of the parties to the 1958 Convention to regard it as terminated could warrant this Court in treating it as obsolete and inapplicable as between [France and the United Kingdom]'.

State Treaty 1955[147] had become obsolete. There were no objections.[148] In the case of a bilateral treaty it is, however, desirable for the parties to record their agreement that the treaty has become obsolete, thus avoiding any doubt on the matter. The simplest procedure is to have an exchange of notes either terminating the treaty or confirming that the parties do not consider it as any longer in force. Otherwise, there is always the danger that some enthusiast will want to celebrate the anniversary of a forgotten and long-overtaken treaty, such as the Oliver Cromwell–Queen Christina Treaty of Peace 1654,[149] which nobody had bothered to terminate formally. Its 350th anniversary was marked by an elaborate and expensive ceremony at Uppsala in April 2004 attended by the British Lord Chancellor, albeit without his elaborate robes of office.

Extinction of the International Legal Personality of a Party

These days this is more likely to occur when two states join to form one state (Yemen), or a state splits into two or more new states (Yugoslavia). This could, of course, also amount to a supervening impossibility of performance, or a fundamental change of circumstances or, perhaps more likely, simply raise a question of treaty succession (see Chapter 21).

Severance of Diplomatic or Consular Relations

The severance of diplomatic or consular relations between parties to a treaty does not affect the legal relations established between them by the treaty, except insofar as the existence of diplomatic or consular relations is indispensable for the application of the treaty (Article 63). The rule applies both to bilateral and multilateral treaties. In fact, the severance of diplomatic relations may not make a substantial difference. The widespread practice of establishing so-called interest sections in the embassies of third states, and informal contacts at the United Nations and other international organisations, means that, depending on the level of staffing of the interest sections, fairly normal relations can be maintained.[150] Diplomatic relations between Iraq and the United Kingdom were broken off in 1990 following the invasion of Kuwait. Nevertheless, between then and 2002 Iraq applied at least three times under the UK–Iraq Extradition Treaty 1932[151] for the extradition of Iraqi nationals, with the

[147] 217 UNTS 223 No. 2949; UKTS (1957) No. 58; TIAS 3298.

[148] D. Kennedy and L. Specht, 'Austrian Membership in the European Communities', *Harvard International Law Journal* (1990) 407–462.

[149] 1 BSP 691.

[150] E. Denza, *Diplomatic Law* (4th ed., Oxford University Press, Oxford 2016); *Oppenheim*, 1120, para. 523, note 4.

[151] 141 LNTS 277; UKTS (1933) No. 13.

applications and responses being transmitted through third states.[152] Naturally, each application was refused, but not on the basis that the treaty had been suspended.

Outbreak of Hostilities

Article 73 of the VCLT stipulates that the Convention provisions 'shall not prejudge any question that may arise in regard to a treaty . . . from the outbreak of hostilities between States'.[153] That does not mean that, in the event of an outbreak of hostilities, States disregard the VCLT. More on this below; but first, a bit of background.

In 1966 the ILC took the somewhat optimistic position that:

> in the international law of today the outbreak of hostilities between States must be considered as an entirely abnormal condition, and that the rules governing its legal consequences should not be regarded as forming part of the general rules of international law applicable in the normal relations between States.[154]

This may well have been a convenient way of dodging the issue, but there have been numerous international armed conflicts since 1945, and their legal effect on treaties is therefore important. When hostilities take place today between states, the preferred term is 'armed conflict', which also has the advantage of avoiding the technicalities attached to the concept of war.[155] All international armed conflicts are relevant whatever the legal basis for the use of force: self-defence, UN Security Council authorisation, humanitarian intervention or, indeed, an illegal use of force. In 2004 the UN General Assembly endorsed the decision of the ILC to study the issue. This resulted in a set of Draft Articles on the Effect of Armed Conflict on Treaties.[156] The Draft Articles are not to be regarded merely as a codification of customary law but contain elements of progressive development of international law.[157]

Draft Article 3 formulates a general principle:

> The existence of an armed conflict does not *ipso facto* terminate or suspend the operation of treaties:
>
> (*a*) as between States parties to the conflict;
> (*b*) as between a State party to the conflict and a State that is not.[158]

152 See also Article 74 VCLT about new treaties between the two states.

153 The full text is: 'The provisions of the present Convention shall not prejudge any question that may arise in regard to a treaty from a succession of States or from the international responsibility of a State or from the outbreak of hostilities between States.'

154 ILC Commentary on draft Article 69, para. (2).

155 *The Wimbledon* (1923), PCIJ Reports, Series A, No. 1, ICGJ 235; 2 AD 99; and see common Article 2 of the four Geneva Conventions 1949 (n. 51).

156 Report of the ILC on the Work of its 63rd session, 2011, UNGA 66th Session, Supplement No. 10, A/66/10, 106–130.

157 Y. Ronen, 'Treaties and Armed Conflict', in C. J. Tams, A. Tzanakopoulos and A. Zimmermann (eds.), *Research Handbook on the Law of Treaties* (Edward Elgar, Cheltenham UK, Northampton MA, USA 2014), 541–564, 545. See also *Dörr and Schmalenbach*, 1349–1350.

158 By way of historical background, see the view of McNair: *McNair*, 695–728.

According to further draft Articles, where a treaty itself contains provisions on its operation in situations of armed conflict, those provisions shall apply;[159] and the rules of international law on treaty interpretation are to be applied to establish whether a treaty is susceptible to termination, withdrawal or suspension in the event of an armed conflict.[160] In order to determine whether a treaty is susceptible, regard is to be had to all the relevant factors, including:

> (*a*) the nature of the treaty, in particular its subject matter, its object and purpose, its content and the number of parties to the treaty; and
>
> (*b*) the characteristics of the armed conflict, such as its territorial extent, its scale and intensity, its duration and, in the case of non-international armed conflict, also the degree of outside involvement.[161]

Paragraph (b) thus allows account to be taken of external factors and represents a departure from normal rules on interpretation.[162] An indicative list of treaties whose subject matter involves an implication that they continue in operation, in whole or in part, during an armed conflict is given in an Annex.[163]

The Draft Articles include a streamlined procedure for a state party to terminate or withdraw from a treaty, or suspend its operation, as a consequence of armed conflict.[164] But, reflecting the principle of Article 45 of the VCLT, a state may no longer do so if, after becoming aware of the facts, it shall have expressly agreed that the treaty remains in force or continues in operation; or it must by reason of its conduct be considered as having acquiesced in the continued operation of the treaty or in its maintenance in force.[165] In addition, a state committing aggression may not terminate[166] a treaty as a consequence of an armed conflict that results from the act of aggression if the effect would be to the benefit of that state.[167] Subsequent to an armed conflict, the states parties may regulate, on the basis of agreement, the revival of treaties terminated or suspended as a consequence of the armed conflict.[168]

The application of the Draft Articles in practice is not straightforward. One question which arises is the relationship between termination as a consequence of armed conflict and termination on Convention grounds.[169] Armed conflict raises issues of security and necessity which are not present in standard cases to which the Convention applies.[170] But Draft Article 18 makes clear that the Draft Articles are without prejudice to the

[159] Article 4. [160] Article 5. [161] Article 6. [162] Ronen (n. 157), 548.

[163] ILC Report, 2011 (n. 156), 119–120. The Annex is to be read with draft Article 7. For an assessment of the various categories, see *Dörr and Schmalenbach*, 1352–1357.

[164] Article 9. [165] Article 12.

[166] This also includes, as in the next paragraph, withdrawal or suspension. [167] Article 15.

[168] Article 13.1.

[169] See the discussion in Ronen (n. 158), 550–551; B. Zhi Peng Tan, 'The International Law Commission's Draft Articles on the Effects of Armed Conflicts on Treaties: Evaluating the Applicability of Impossibility of Performance and Fundamental Change', *Asian Journal of International Law* 3 (January 2013) 51–76; L. Caflisch, 'The Effect of Armed Conflict on Treaties: A Stocktaking', in N. Boschiero *et al.* (eds.), *International Courts and the Development of International Law* (Asser Press, The Hague 2013), 31–54; *Crawford/Brownlie*, 376.

[170] See *Dörr and Schmalenbach*, 1358–1359.

Convention rules. In the author's experience, many foreign ministry (and international organisation) lawyers will at least start their consideration by examining Articles 60–62[171] and principles such as the duty to notify. As for time periods, Draft Article 9 (Notification of intention to terminate etc.) allows the possibility of termination immediately upon receipt of a notification,[172] thus operating more flexibly than Article 65 of the Convention, though it also provides for the right of a notified state to object to the notification within a reasonable time, and an obligation to seek a solution through peaceful means.[173]

If a state which is party to the conflict has, through its actions, committed a gross violation of a constituent instrument of an international organisation, this may result in the other parties deciding that the state concerned should cease to be a member of that organisation. Hence, in March 2022 the Committee of Ministers decided that Russia should cease to be a member of the Council of Europe, and, as a result, it ceased to a party to the ECHR and certain other treaties which depended on its CoE membership.[174]

In the event of an armed conflict, treaty rules will be only one aspect to be considered. The rules of state responsibility, in particular the adoption of counter-measures or the application of necessity, will also be relevant.[175]

[171] That is to say, material breach, supervening impossibility of performance, and fundamental change of circumstances.

[172] See Article 9.2: 'The notification takes effect upon receipt by the other State party or States parties, unless it provides for a subsequent date.'

[173] Article 9.3–9.5. [174] For more detail, see p. 311. [175] See Chapter 20, pp. 366–370.

17

Invalidity

Groucho: 'That's what they call a sanity clause.'
Chico: 'You can't fool me; there ain't no Sanity Claus.'[1]

McNair devoted thirty-one pages to invalidity, even though he found little diplomatic or judicial (though abundant academic) authority on, for example, duress.[2] The Convention devotes as many as nine main articles to invalidity (Articles 46–53 and 64), although the ILC was well aware that invalidity was a rarity, there being a natural presumption that a treaty is valid, its continuance in force being the normal state of things. And the previous author Anthony Aust wrote that, in fifty-years of practice, he had only encountered one suggestion that a treaty might be invalid. This chapter is therefore shorter than most. It does, however, cover in more detail the issues of competence to conclude treaties (Article 46), coercion (Article 52) and peremptory norms (Article 53), which are attracting more interest in light of recent global developments.

Violation of Internal Law on Competence to Conclude Treaties

Article 46 is to be distinguished from Article 27, which provides that a party may not invoke a provision of its internal law as justifying its failure to perform a treaty. In other words, Article 27 concerns performance of a treaty once concluded, whereas Article 46 concerns the competence to conclude a treaty.[3] The wording of Article 46 clearly reflects the need for certainty in treaty relations:

> (1) A State may not invoke the fact that its consent to be bound by a treaty has been expressed in violation of a provision of *its* internal law regarding competence to conclude treaties as invalidating its consent *unless that violation was manifest and concerned a rule of its internal law of fundamental importance.*

[1] *A Night at the Opera* (film, 1935). [2] *McNair*, 206–236; *Sinclair*, 159–181 and 203–226.
[3] Generally on Article 46, see *Dörr and Schmalenbach*, 837–868; *Corten and Klein*, 1090–1101; *Villiger*, 583–594; *Oppenheim*, 1284–1288, para. 636; *Kolb*, 89–96; and for background of consideration in the ILC: YBILC 1963 II, 41–46; YBILC 1965 II 67–71; YBILC 1966 II, 240–242.

(2) A violation is manifest if it would be *objectively* evident to any State conducting itself in the matter in accordance with normal practice and in good faith.[4]

The provisions in both the 1969 and 1986 Conventions are expressed in negative form ('may not invoke . . . unless') to emphasise the exceptional character of the cases in which this ground might be invoked. The other emphasised words stress the difficulty of successfully invoking the rule. There are a number of procedures in treaty making, such as ratification, that have been specifically designed to enable a state to reflect fully before deciding whether or not to become a party, and to comply with any constitutional requirements.[5] States (or international organisations) are entitled to regard other treaty partners as having acted in good faith when their representatives express their consent to be bound.

Although the 'competence to conclude treaties' may be read as embracing both procedural and substantive limitations of the treaty-making power, minor technical and administrative defects will not meet the threshold. Even the question whether the parliament of the relevant state (State A) should have been consulted, although of fundamental importance, may not be manifest because states may treat various treaties in different ways and their systems may allow flexibility. If the representatives of State A are giving plausible explanations as to why they are following a particular domestic procedure, it is hard for its treaty partner, State B, to go behind that. There is no general obligation to be familiar with other states' constitutions.[6] In the context of withdrawal from the EU, where there was pressure on the UK and its treaty partners to bring into force as many 'continuity' agreements[7] at the end of the transition period[8] as possible, partners would sometimes say they could follow a particular domestic procedure to facilitate the process. If the suggestion was prima facie convincing, there was no reason to contest it.[9] But if the issue does arise, the outcome could be significant.[10]

[4] There is a parallel provision in Article 46 of the 1986 Vienna Convention.

[5] See *Cameroon* v. *Nigeria* (Merits), ICJ Reports (2002) 303, at 429–431, paras. 262–268.

[6] 'In this regard the Court notes that there is no general legal obligation for States to keep themselves informed of legislative and constitutional developments in other States which are or may become important for the international relations of these States': *Land and Maritime Boundary between Cameroon and Nigeria (Cameroon* v. *Nigeria: Equitorial Guinea intervening)* ICJ Reports (2002) 303, at 430, para. 266. See also *Maritime Delimitation in the Indian Ocean (Somalia* v. *Kenya)*, Preliminary Objections, Judgment, ICJ Reports (2017) 3, at 23, paras. 48–49.

[7] That is, new treaties concluded by the UK in its own name to replicate, where appropriate, treaties previously concluded by the EU, which before exit had applied to the UK as an EU member.

[8] The 'transition or implementation period' was a period established under Article 126 *et seq.* of the EU–UK Withdrawal Agreement 2020 during which, save as otherwise provided, Union law was applicable to and in the UK. It expired on 31 December 2020.

[9] There were, in fact, no problems.

[10] See the invocation of Article 46 in the US Senate with regard to the Sinai II Agreements, signed on 4 September 1975 (Agreement between Egypt and Israel on Sinai and Suez Canal, and Protocol), 14 ILM 1975 1450, and US–Israel Early Warning System Agreement 1975 (26 UST 2271); US–Israel Memorandum of Understanding 1975 (32 UST 2150); and the Panama Canal Treaties between the USA and Panama (including Panama Canal Treaty and Treaty concerning the Permanent Neutrality and Operation of the

The question is probably most likely to come up where there is a third party or institutional challenge to the treaty after entry into force (that is, a challenge through domestic courts or an international court/tribunal such as the CJEU);[11] or a change of government (a new government looking for a reason to extract itself from prior commitments); or an authoritarian regime (a strong leader or executive having power de facto to override rules, or lack of clarity about the leader's or executive's powers de jure); or weak rule of law (constitutional defects less likely to surface or more easily brushed aside).[12] Even then, in all these cases there are still reasons why the threshold for a state invoking invalidity will be hard to meet. One of the more difficult circumstances might be where the *question* whether there is a violation of internal law is manifest but it is not manifest that there is actually such a *violation*.[13]

The judgment of the ECJ in *France* v. *Commission*[14] is instructive. The Court held that the European Community (as it then was) had concluded a treaty with the United States in contravention of internal EC rules governing the competence of various EC organs to conclude treaties. However, the Court did not decide that the treaty was not binding on the EC in international law.[15] Given the complexity of EC (now EU) internal rules, if the EU were to enter into a treaty in breach of those rules, any internal irregularity would hardly be manifest. It is therefore unlikely that the EU could invoke any rule of customary international law that might be reflected in Article 46 or the equivalent article in the 1986 Convention.

This was confirmed in 2006 when the ECJ held that the EC had no internal legal base for concluding the EC–US Processing and Transfer of PNR Data by Air Carriers

Panama Canal, done at Washington, 7 September 1977), 1280 UNTS 3 No. 21086; 1161 UNTS 177 No. 18342; discussed in T. Meron, 'Article 46 of the Vienna Convention on the Law of Treaties (*Ultra Vires* Treaties)', BYIL 49 (1978) 175–199.

11 See the case of *France* v. *Commission*, Case C-327/91, [1994] ECR I-3641; 101 ILR 29.

12 For cases often referred to when discussing issues of competence and constitutional rules, see *Award in an Arbitration between France and Switzerland* (1912) 11 RIAA 411; *George Pinson* (1928) 5 RIAA 327; *Rio Martin* (1924) 2 RIAA 724; *Eastern Greenland case* (concerning a unilateral statement), PCIJ (1933), Series A/B. No. 53, 56–71 and 91; *Free Zones case*, PCIJ, Series A/B. No. 46, 170; *Attorney General of Israel* v. *Kamiar* (1967) Supreme Court (Israel), 44 ILR 197, 268; *Delimitation of Maritime Boundary between Guinea-Bissau and Senegal (Guinea-Bissau* v. *Senegal)* (1989), 20 RIAA 119, para. 56; 83 ILR 1; *V* v. *Regierungsrat des Kantons St Gallen*, 1994, Federal Court (Switzerland), ATF 120 Ib 360, 365–366; *Loan Agreement between Italy and Costa Rica (Italy* v. *Costa Rica)*, 1998 25 RIAA 23, paras. 27, 44–45; *Harksen* v. *President of South Africa* (2000), 132 ILR 565–566, paras. 26–27, South African Constitutional Court; *Cameroon* v. *Nigeria* (n. 6), at 426–431, paras. 253–267; *Somalia* v. *Kenya* (n. 6), at 23–24, paras. 47–50. See the discussion and quotation of many of these cases in *Dörr and Schmalenbach*, 849–858.

13 See Meron (n. 10), p. 191: 'But the fact that a claim of violation has gained notoriety does not mean that the violation – if any – is necessarily a manifest one.'

14 See n. 11.

15 In cases where the CJEU (previously the ECJ) has found that the EU has breached some internal rule in concluding a treaty, it has sought to preserve the effect of the treaty in question on grounds of legal certainty where the immediate effects of annulling that act would give rise to serious negative consequences: see *Commission* v. *Council*, C-28/12, EU:C:2015:282, para. 60 and the case law cited; *Commission* v. *Council (Agreement with Kazakhstan)*, C-244/17, EU:C:2018:662, para. 51.

to the US Homeland Security Department Agreement 2004.[16] But, in paragraph 90, the Court recognised that the EC could not rely on its own law to justify not fulfilling the Agreement. It noted, however, that the EC could terminate the Agreement by giving ninety days' notice, and gave the EC time to renegotiate the Agreement so that it would comply with EC (now EU) law. A new Agreement was later signed, and, pending its entry into force, was applied provisionally.

It is also unlikely that, if an EU member state enters into a treaty in breach of EU law, that would entitle the member state to invoke Article 46. In *Commission* v. *United Kingdom*,[17] the ECJ (now CJEU) held that a member state could not enter into a treaty (in this case, a new air services agreement with the United States) that infringed existing obligations under EC (as it then was) law. But since a non-member state cannot be expected to know all the intricacies of EC/EU law, the violation would not seem to be manifest.

Violation of Specific Restrictions on Authority to Express Consent

An omission by the representative of a state to observe a specific (internal) restriction on their authority to express the consent of their state to be bound may not be invoked as invalidating that consent, unless the restriction was previously notified to the other negotiating state or states (Article 47). Moreover, this rule is limited to those cases where the treaty is not subject to ratification or similar process, since in that case the state would have an opportunity to repudiate any unauthorised act of its representative.

Error

Because the treaty-making process is such that the risk of material errors is reduced to the minimum, almost all the recorded cases where error has been invoked to invalidate a treaty have concerned mistakes in maps.[18] Sometimes a further treaty disposed of the matter; sometimes the error was treated more as affecting the application of the treaty rather than its validity, and the matter settled by arbitration. A state may invoke an error as invalidating its consent to be bound if the error relates to a fact or situation which was assumed by the state to exist at the time when the treaty was concluded, and formed an *essential* basis of its consent to be bound, provided that it did not contribute to the error by its own conduct, and if the circumstances were not such as to put it on notice of a possible error (Article 48). (This formula was taken

[16] *European Parliament* v. *Council* (Judgment), Cases C-317/04 and C-318/04, 30 May 2006. For the Agreement, see OJ 2004, L 183, 83.

[17] (2002) Case C-466/98.

[18] See *Oppenheim*, 1288, para. 638.

from the *Temple of Preah Vihear* decision.)[19] The following additional points should be noted:

(1) the error cannot for this purpose be one of law, although it is not always easy to draw a line between law and fact;[20]
(2) the error can be mutual or unilateral;
(3) the error does not make the treaty void automatically: the ground must first be invoked. But if invalidity is established, the treaty will be void *ab initio* (from the start);
(4) an error that relates only to the wording of the text does not affect its validity, and failure by one party to read properly the final text will not be a ground for invoking Article 48; the only recourse is to the correction procedures of Article 79.

Fraud

It is heartening that no clear case of fraud being used to procure the conclusion of a treaty has ever been cited. Nevertheless, if a state were to be induced to conclude a treaty by the fraudulent conduct of another negotiating state, the first state may invoke the fraud as invalidating its consent to be bound (Article 49). The expression 'fraudulent conduct' includes any deliberately false statements, misrepresentations or other deceitful proceedings by which a state is induced to give consent that it would not otherwise give. The detailed connotations given to the concept of fraud in domestic law are not necessarily applicable. Fraud may be invoked with respect to particular clauses only, provided they are separable and are not essential to the treaty, and it would not be unjust to continue performance of the rest of the treaty (Article 44(4)).

Fraudulent misrepresentation of a material fact which induced an error would likely be caught by the provisions on error.

Corruption

If the consent of a state to be bound by a treaty has been procured through the corruption of its representative by another negotiating state, directly or indirectly, the first state may invoke that as invalidating its consent (Article 50). But the state may only rely on acts calculated to exercise a substantial influence on the disposition of its representative to conclude the treaty; a small courtesy or favour is not enough. It is unlikely that Article 50 could be invoked if the treaty is subject to ratification. As with

[19] *Temple of Preah Vihear (Cambodia* v. *Thailand)*, Merits, ICJ Reports (1962) 6, at 26; 33 ILR 48.

[20] See H. Thirlway, 'The Law and Procedure of the International Court of Justice', BYIL 63 (1992) 27–28. The different consequences of a mistake of law and of fact are now less distinct in English law: *Kleinwort Benson* v. *Lincoln City Council* [1998] 3 WLR 1095.

fraud, corruption may be invoked either with respect to the whole treaty or, subject to conditions, to particular clauses (Article 44(4)). Surprisingly, perhaps, there does not appear to be any recorded example of such corruption.

Coercion of a Representative of a State (Duress)

If a state's consent to be bound has been procured by coercion of its *representative* by acts or threats directed against them, the consent is without any legal effect (Article 51). Even if it were possible to separate out provisions of the treaty to which the state would have no objection, this is not permitted: the whole treaty will be void (Article 44(5)). The acts or threats, such as a physical threat to the representative or their family, or blackmail (more likely), must affect the representative as an individual, not as the representative of their state. Such coercion is therefore unlikely to be used in order to procure ratification. There have been a few cases of personal coercion, such as the extreme pressure put on the president and foreign minister of Czechoslovakia in 1939 to get them to sign the treaty creating a German protectorate over Bohemia and Moravia.[21]

Coercion of a State by the Threat or Use of Force

Article 52 provides that a treaty is void if its conclusion has been procured by the threat or use of force in violation of the principles of international law embodied in the UN Charter. No separation of the provisions of the treaty is permitted (Article 44(5)). The principle, as set out in Article 2(4) of the UN Charter, does not include economic or political pressure.[22] Since the prohibition of the use of force is a rule of general international law of universal application, Article 52 applies also to those very few states that are still not members of the United Nations. The article does not itself have any retrospective effect (Article 4), but, since the Charter is regarded as setting out modern customary law on the use of force, the rule laid down in Article 52 recognises, by implication, that it will apply to all treaties concluded at least since the entry into force of the Charter.[23] The Czechoslovakia–Germany Nationality Treaty 1938, which gave effect to provisions of the notorious Munich Agreement, may have been void because of the enormous pressure put on the Czech government.[24]

[21] *Oppenheim*, 1290, para. 641, note 1.

[22] *Oppenheim*, 1290, para. 641, note 5; *Sinclair*, 177–179, including his discussion of the Declaration on the Prohibition of Military, Political or Economic Coercion in the Conclusion of Treaties, which was attached to the Final Act of the Vienna Conference.

[23] See also *Fisheries Jurisdiction (United Kingdom* v. *Iceland)* (Jurisdiction), ICJ Reports (1973) 3, at 14, para. 24; 55 ILR 183.

[24] As to the Munich Agreement, see *Oppenheim*, 1291, para. 641, note 8.

Article 52 does not apply to the threat or use of *lawful* force. The agreement concerning the restoration of the government of President Aristide, signed in Port au Prince on 18 September 1994 by the provisional president of Haiti and former US President Jimmy Carter, on behalf of US President Bill Clinton, might at first sight appear to have been obtained by the threat of unlawful force, since at the time US bombers were in the air on their way to Haiti. However, on 16 October 1993 the Security Council had adopted Resolution 875, which authorised the use of force to restore the legitimate government of Haiti.

It has been suggested that the FRY–NATO Kumanovo Military Technical Agreement 1999[25] was void because the FRY had concluded it under the threat of force by NATO states,[26] and therefore the UN Security Council, even acting under chapter VII of the Charter, could not by Resolution 1244 (1999) validate the Agreement if it was void *ab initio*. But the resolution was more than simply political endorsement of the Agreement, and amounted to implicit recognition that the Agreement had not been procured by any threat or use of force inconsistent with the principles of the United Nations.

Peace Treaties

It might seem as if a peace treaty must involve some degree of coercion of the vanquished by the victor. The starting point must be that a peace treaty forced on a state that has been the victim of aggression would be void. There is also an obligation upon states not to recognise illegal situations resulting from a serious breach of a peremptory norm.[27] This may, however, present practical challenges for bringing a war resulting from aggression to an end,[28] and challenge to the validity of peace treaties is rare.[29] The VCLT provides expressly that its provisions are without prejudice to any obligation in relation to a treaty that may arise for an aggressor

[25] 38 ILM (1999) 1217.

[26] See E. Milano, 'Security Council Action in the Balkans: Reviewing the Legality of Kosovo's Territorial Status', EJIL (2003) 999–1022.

[27] See Conclusion 19 and Commentary on the draft Conclusions on 'Identification and legal consequences of peremptory norms of general international law (*jus cogens*)': Report of the ILC on the work of its 73rd session, 2022, UNGA 77th session, Supplement no. 10, Doc A/77/10, 11-89, at 70–79. *Legal Consequences of the Construction of a Wall in the Occupied Palestinian Territory*, Advisory Opinion, ICJ Reports (2004) 136, at 200, para. 159. See also the next section below on treaties and peremptory norms.

[28] See K. Schmalenbach and A. Prantl, 'How to End an Illegal War?', *Völkerrechtsblog*, 21.04.2022; M. Kohen and M. Hébié, 'Peace Agreements and Territorial Change', in M. Weller, M. Retter and A. Varga, *International Law and Peace Settlements* (Cambridge University Press, Cambridge 2021), 432–446; *Dörr and Schmalenbach*, 946–953, 957–958.

[29] See S. Forlati, 'Coercion as a Ground Affecting the Validity of Peace Treaties', in E. Cannizzaro (ed.), *The Law of Treaties Beyond the Vienna Convention* (Oxford University Press, Oxford 2011), 320–332.

state in consequence of measures taken in conformity with the UN Charter with reference to that state's aggression (Article 75).

Conflict with a Peremptory Norm of General International Law *(jus cogens)*

A treaty is void if, at the time of its conclusion, it conflicts with a peremptory norm of general international law.[30] The concept of *jus cogens* (peremptory norm of general international law) was controversial at the time of the Vienna Conference. Now it is more the scope and applicability of the concept which is debated.[31] *Jus cogens* is defined in Article 53 for the purposes of the Convention as:

> a norm accepted and recognised by the international community of States as a whole as a norm from which no derogation is permitted and which can be modified only by a subsequent norm of general international law having the same character.[32]

The concept has to be considered in light of Draft Conclusions adopted by the ILC in 2022,[33] which concern the identification and legal consequences of peremptory norms.

As far as identification is concerned, Conclusion 4 states that it is necessary to establish that the norm in question meets the following criteria:

(a) it is a norm of general international law; and
(b) it is accepted and recognised by the international community of States as a whole as a norm from which no derogation is permitted and which can be modified only by a subsequent norm of general international law having the same character.

To identify a norm as a peremptory norm, there must be evidence that the norm is accepted and recognised as such.[34] This means acceptance and recognition by the international community of states as a whole, though a very large majority will suffice.[35] If only part of a treaty conflicts with an existing *jus cogens*, the whole of the treaty is void, not just the offending part (Article 44(5)).

[30] Article 53. On the legal consequences for treaties, see D. Costelloe, *Legal Consequences of Peremptory Norms in International Law* (Cambridge University Press, Cambridge 2017), 54–94; A. Orakhelashvili, *Peremptory Norms in International Law* (Oxford University Press, Oxford 2008), 133–204.

[31] For an in-depth discussion of *jus cogens* before and at the time of the adoption of the Vienna Convention, see *Sinclair*, 203–226.

[32] The definition in ILC Conclusion 3 (n. 27) tracks this.

[33] Report of the ILC 2022, Doc. A/77/10 (n. 27).

[34] Conclusion 6. Evidence may include public statements made on behalf of States; official publications; government legal opinions; diplomatic correspondence; legislative and administrative acts; decisions of national courts; treaty provisions; and resolutions adopted by an international organization or at an intergovernmental conference (Conclusion 8).

[35] Conclusion 7.1 and 7.2.

The annex to the ILC Draft Conclusions gives a non-exhaustive list of peremptory norms. These are: the prohibition of aggression;[36] the prohibition of genocide;[37] the prohibition of crimes against humanity; the basic rules of international humanitarian law; the prohibition of racial discrimination and apartheid; the prohibition of slavery; the prohibition of torture; and the right of self-determination.[38]

Article 53 has no retrospective effect (Article 4). It must, however, be read with Article 64, which provides that, if a new peremptory norm of general international law emerges, any *existing* treaty that is in conflict with that norm '*becomes* void and terminates'. Since this provision is not retrospective, the treaty is invalid only as from the time that the new norm has been established.

Since the vast majority of the rules of international law do not have the character of *jus cogens*, states are free to contract out of them; and a treaty that conflicts with general international law is, therefore, not necessarily void. Similarly, if a treaty provides that no derogation from it is permitted, but later a party concludes a treaty that conflicts with it, the latter treaty is not void, although the party may be liable for breach of the earlier treaty.

The consequences of the invalidity of a treaty that conflicts with *jus cogens* under Articles 53 or 64 are dealt with in Article 71.

Unequal Treaties

So-called 'unequal' (or 'Leonine') treaties are those that are generally said to have been forced upon a weaker state by a stronger one.[39] Neither McNair nor the Convention mentions them, and the idea that such treaties may in some way be invalid has never been accepted in international law. Sinha cites the Treaty of Berlin 1885,[40] by which European powers carved up Africa, as possibly void for inequality,[41]

[36] See the Commentary on Draft Conclusion 23, ILC Report (n. 27), 86 (para. 7). For discussion of the term 'aggression' rather than 'use of force', see O. Corten and V. Koutroulis, 'The Jus Cogens Status of the Prohibition on the Use of Force: What Is Its Scope and Why Does It Matter?', in D. Tladi (ed.), *Peremptory Norms of International Law (Jus Cogens): Disquisitions and Disputations* (Brill Nijhoff, Leiden 2021), 629–667. On the issue of apparent derogations in respect of the use of force, see also S. T. Helmersen, 'The Prohibition of the Use of Force as Jus Cogens: Explaining Apparent Derogations', *Netherlands International Law Review* 61 (2014) 167–193.

[37] In respect of genocide, slavery and torture, see *Furandzija* [1998] ICTY, paras. 147–157; 121 ILR 213.

[38] On ICJ jurisprudence, see C. Maia, 'Jus Cogens and (In)Application of the 1969 Vienna Convention on the Law of Treaties in the Jurisprudence of the International Court of Justice', in Tladi (n. 36), 342–365.

[39] See M. Craven and M. Fitzmaurice (eds.), *Interrogating the Treaty* (Wolf Legal, Nijmegen 2005), 43–80 (Craven) and 81–85 (Aust); L. Caflisch, 'Unequal Treaties', Ger YBIL (1992) 52–80; *Corten and Klein*, 1027; *Dörr and Schmalenbach*, 944.

[40] General Act of the Conference on West Africa, done at Berlin, 26 February 1885.

[41] S. Sinha, 'Perspective of the Newly Independent States and the Binding Quality of International Law', ICLQ 14 (1965) 121–131, 123.

though this is not the position of African states today.[42] Writings about unequal treaties have relied much on nineteenth-century treaties, such as the so-called capitulation agreements.[43] Some writers were also influenced by the effect of decolonisation and, to some extent, the apparently liberal views of Soviet and other jurists.[44] Yet it is a cornerstone of international law that all states are equal: that is, equal before the law, even if not equal economically, militarily or diplomatically. Very few states, including developed states, can be said to be equal in those areas. The UK–US Lend-Lease Agreements 1940[45] were obviously between a state in a very weak position and one infinitely stronger in every way.

To allow a state to avoid its treaty obligations on the ground of inequality of power would seriously undermine the stability of treaty relations. The idea could anyway only be relevant to bilateral treaties; proving that one or more of the states negotiating a multilateral treaty unduly influenced the others could be an impossible task, especially these days when most multilateral treaties are adopted by consensus. The presumption that treaties are valid is not easy to rebut, especially if one cannot find facts to satisfy one of the several specific grounds of invalidity that the Convention does recognise.

Consequences of Invalidity (Other Than for *jus cogens*)

With the exception of *jus cogens*, the invalidity of a treaty is rooted in the invalidity of the *consent* of a party to be bound. If it is a bilateral treaty, it will be void *ab initio* and its provisions will never have had legal force (Article 69(1)). If it is a multilateral treaty, an invalid consent will normally mean that the treaty will nevertheless remain valid for the other parties (Article 69(4)). Article 69 is concerned only with the immediate legal effects of the invalidity of a treaty: it does not deal with any question of state responsibility (see Article 73) arising from the act which was the cause of the invalidity, such as fraud or coercion.

Nevertheless, since the parties may have been performing acts under an invalid treaty for some years in good faith, each party can require another party as far as possible to re-establish in their mutual relations the position that would have existed if the acts performed under the treaty had not been performed, that is to say, to re-establish the *status quo ante*; and if an act performed in good faith under an invalid treaty is not otherwise unlawful, it will not be rendered unlawful by the invalidity of

[42] See the Constitutive Act of the African Union, Article 4(6): 2158 UNTS 3 No. 37733, or at: www.african-union.org.

[43] See *McNair*, 514, 527–531 and 662–664; H. Chiu, 'Communist China's Attitude towards International Law', AJIL (1966) 245–267.

[44] See Caflisch (n. 39); I. Detter (aka Princess Frankopan), 'The Problem of Unequal Treaties', ICLQ 15 (1966) 1069–1089, 1081–1082.

[45] 203 LNTS 201 and 204 LNTS 15; UKTS (1940) No. 21 and (1941) No. 2. See also *Territorial Dispute (Libya v. Chad)*, ICJ Reports (1994) 6, at 19–20, paras. 34-36; 100 ILR 1.

the treaty (Article 69(2)). But a party whose fraud, corruption or coercion was the cause of the invalidity cannot benefit from these provisions (Article 69(3)).

Procedure

Article 65 is a key provision, its procedural safeguards being designed to deter states from arbitrary action. In particular, a party wishing to invoke any of the grounds for impeaching the validity of a treaty must notify the other parties. The procedure in respect of termination applies equally to cases of invalidity.

There is an additional provision for cases of *jus cogens*. Article 66 did not figure among the final draft articles produced by the ILC, but was included at the Vienna Conference in order to strengthen the obligation in Article 65(3) to seek a peaceful solution. That obligation would have had little substance if the parties in dispute were not already bound by a mechanism for settling their disputes. A number of states were not prepared to include an article representing such a development in the law of treaties without some procedural safeguards.[46] Article 66(a) thus provides that, if a dispute as to the applicability of the *jus cogens* rules (Articles 53 and 64) to a particular treaty cannot be resolved in accordance with procedure laid down in Article 65(3), any party to the dispute may invoke the compulsory jurisdiction of the ICJ, unless the parties agree to arbitration. In contrast, Article 66(b) provides only for conciliation of other disputes under Part V. On ratifying the Convention, some states have sought to exclude the compulsory effect of Article 66(a), and other states have rejected these attempts.[47]

General Points

In each case it is for a party to establish that the necessary grounds for invalidity exist. To do this it should apply the provisions of the Convention (Article 42(1)). In all cases one must consider not only the article dealing with the particular ground invoked, but also other provisions in Part V, and the rest of the Convention, that govern the conditions for applying the article in question, including the special procedures laid down in Articles 65–68. Articles 44 and 45 contain some other general considerations. The comments on them in Chapter 16 also apply, where relevant, to cases of invalidity, subject to the following points.

Separability of Treaty Provisions

Article 44(4) lays down a different separability rule for cases of fraud and corruption. Article 44(5) rules out separability altogether in cases of coercion or where part of a treaty conflicts with an existing *jus cogens*.

[46] For the history of the negotiation of Article 66, see *Sinclair*, 226–232.

[47] See the reservations concerning Article 66(a), and the objections to them, in *UN Multilateral Treaties*, chapter XXIII.1; *Sinclair*, 65–68.

Loss of Rights by Acquiescence

Article 45 prevents a state from invoking grounds for invalidating a treaty if, after it had become aware of the facts, it either (a) expressly agreed that the treaty was valid or (b) by reason of its conduct must be considered as having acquiesced in the validity of the treaty. The article applies to grounds of invalidity under Articles 46–50 (lack of competence, restrictions on authority, error, fraud or corruption), but not to grounds for invalidity under Articles 51–53 and 64 (coercion or conflict with *jus cogens).*

18

The Depository

Neither a borrower nor a lender be.[1]

Had Shakespeare only taken a closer interest in treaty procedures, he would surely have had Polonius add: 'nor a depositary be'. This chapter will attempt to demystify the role of the depositary. Although not of much concern to others, and little appreciated, the exacting and onerous duties of a depositary are vital to the effective functioning of any multilateral treaty. Yet not all states, or even some international organisations, that act as depositaries are fully aware of their responsibilities or how they should be carried out. Their work can be made more difficult by simple lack of knowledge of the proper procedures.

The term 'depositary' means a person to whom something is entrusted. Even when used in the context of a treaty, it is sometimes wrongly spelt with an 'o' (depository), which means a storehouse, often for household furniture and the like.

Bilateral Treaties

A bilateral treaty is usually signed in duplicate, so that each of the contracting states keeps one signed original. In the most exceptional case of a bilateral treaty having only one original text, the contracting states would have to decide which of them should keep it. Alternatively, they could deposit it with a third state or an international organisation. The depositary would then provide both states with a copy certified to be true and accurate. Apart from that, there should be little more for the depositary of a *bilateral* treaty to do. But the depositary of a *multilateral* treaty often has much to do, in addition, of course, to registering it with the United Nations once it has entered into force.

Designation of the Depositary for a Multilateral Treaty

The increase in the number of parties to multilateral treaties led to the almost universal practice of designating a depositary for each treaty. The depositary plays an essential role throughout the life of the treaty in ensuring that the necessary formalities and

[1] William Shakespeare, *Hamlet*, I, iii, 75.

procedures are performed, and are properly recorded. The duties may appear at first sight to be routine, and although much of the work is of that nature, it is of vital importance, requiring a methodical approach, attention to detail and, needless to say, a responsible attitude. The designation of a depositary may be made by the negotiating states either in the treaty or in some other manner. The depositary may be one state (and very occasionally two or more), an international organisation or its chief administrative officer (Article 76(1)). Often these days the depositary for multilateral treaties is the UN Secretary-General or the chief administrative officer of another international organisation, as appropriate.

Failure to designate a depositary (as sometimes happens with plurilateral treaties)[2] may well lead to the all too common mistake of not registering the treaty with the United Nations, unless, of course, one of the states has agreed (preferably in the treaty) to do this.

A word of warning: when a state is a depositary, its duties should be carried out only by the foreign ministry. These days, when other ministries often take the lead in negotiating treaties on technical subjects, there may be a temptation for depositary functions to be 'subcontracted' to another ministry or public body which is responsible for the substance of the treaty. This should *never* happen. Depositary functions are the same whatever the subject matter of the treaty, and the necessary expertise should be found only in a foreign ministry or an international organisation, since they should have detailed experience of treaties and the proper procedures.

If a depositary state were itself to cease to exist, or become unwilling or unable to continue acting as depositary, no doubt the parties to the treaty would agree on a pragmatic solution. That might be to ask an international organisation, or a ministry of foreign affairs, to take over the role of depositary. For many treaties, it may involve receiving instruments of acceptance or written consent from all or some of the parties, and this may well turn out to be a long and involved process.

One or More States as Depositary

If a multilateral treaty has *not* been adopted within an international organisation or at a conference convened by one, it is customary (though not a rigid rule) for the treaty to be deposited with the state that hosted the conference. The UN Charter was adopted at the San Francisco Conference 1945, and provides for it to remain deposited in the archives of the US government.[3] The United Kingdom was depositary of the UNESCO Constitution[4] because the first preparatory meeting was held in

[2] The *Estonia* Agreement 1995 (1890 UNTS 176 No. 32189) has three original copies held by the three original parties: Estonia, Finland and Sweden. Later, the UK acceded to it under an Additional Protocol in 1996 (1947 UNTS 404 No. 32189; UKTS (1999) No. 74).

[3] Although the United States later agreed with the UN Secretary-General that he should be the depositary of amendments to the Charter.

[4] 4 UNTS 275 No. 52; UKTS (1961) No. 36 (subject to further amendments).

London. This 'tradition' is in recognition of the (not always easy) task that the host state has had to perform. It is also practical, the host state having probably provided most of the secretariat for the first conference and physically produced the final text of the treaty.

During the Cold War certain treaties, such as the Partial Test Ban Treaty (PTBT) 1963,[5] the Outer Space Treaty 1967[6] and the Nuclear Non-Proliferation Treaty 1968,[7] each had three depositaries: the Soviet Union (now the Russian Federation), the United Kingdom and the United States.[8] A state wishing to sign, ratify or accede to treaties with such provisions was (and still is) able to do so with any *one* of them. This arrangement was to avoid any embarrassment caused by differences between any one of the three depositaries and other states on the then question of the status of the German Democratic Republic (East Germany) and the right of the government of the People's Republic of China to represent China. Although contrary to normal practice, it was understood that, if it would embarrass a depositary to accept a signature or receive an instrument of ratification or accession from an entity that it did not recognise, it could decline to do so. Deposit of the instrument with one of the other depositaries that did recognise the entity would be sufficient. The arrangement also allowed a depositary that did not recognise an entity that had deposited an instrument with another of the depositaries to object (as a party, *not* as a depositary) to the entity taking part in any amendment conference. There is, at least at present, no need for such arrangements for new treaties.

Nevertheless, there are still a few entities that may be recognised as states by one state or a few states (sometimes for political or financial reasons), but not generally. Sometimes recognition has been withheld for political reasons, the Federal Republic of Yugoslavia having been an example. These may present problems for a depositary (see below on the duty to act impartially). In November 2011 the United Kingdom received Palestine's acceptance of the UNESCO Constitution,[9] despite the continued non-recognition of Palestine as a state by many states. This followed past precedent in accepting North Korea and East Germany, neither of which were then recognised by the West as states.

The Cambodia Agreement 1991[10] has two depositaries, France and Indonesia, simply, it seems, because they co-hosted the conference. The (OSCE) Open Skies

[5] 480 UNTS 43 No. 6964; UKTS (1964) No. 3; TIAS 5433.

[6] 610 UNTS 205 No. 8843; 6 ILM (1967) 386; UKTS (1968) No. 10; TIAS 6347.

[7] 729 UNTS 161 No. 10485; 7 ILM (1968) 809; UKTS (1970) No. 88; TIAS 6839.

[8] See E. Schwelb, 'The Nuclear Test Ban Treaty and International Law', AJIL (1964) 642–670, 651–653; *Oppenheim*, vol. I, 169–175, para. 50, note 6; UNJurYbk (1980) 207–208. There are many other treaties from the Cold War period that have three depositaries. The Protocol for the Suppression of Unlawful Acts of Violence at Airports 1988 (1589 UNTS 474 No. 14118; 27 ILM (1988) 627; UKTS (1991) No. 20), is unusual in that Article V(3) provides for the three states *and ICAO* to be depositaries.

[9] 4 UNTS 275 No. 52; UKTS (1946) No. 50 (subject to further amendments).

[10] 1663 UNTS 27 No. 28613; 31 ILM (1992) 182.

Treaty 1992 has two depositaries, Canada and Hungary.[11] This was merely symbolic, the treaty being about transparency in military matters between NATO members and former members of the Warsaw Pact. The depositaries of the Protocol for the Suppression of Unlawful Acts of Violence at Airports 1988[12] are a mixture of states and international organisations, being London, Moscow, Washington and the ICAO (in Montreal).

An International Organisation as Depositary

Most multilateral treaties are now adopted within an international organisation or at an international conference convened by one. Although there are some exceptions, the treaty will normally designate as depositary *the chief administrative officer* of the organisation. They will not normally agree to be depositary of a treaty with which their organisation has no substantial connection.[13] The designation of an international organisation *itself* as depositary should be made expressly and clearly in the treaty.[14] It would be a mistake to think that just because all treaties have to be *registered* with the United Nations, its Secretary-General is willing to be the depositary of any multilateral treaty.

The UN Secretary-General as Depositary

A treaty adopted within the United Nations, or at a conference convened by it, will usually include a provision that it shall be deposited with the UN Secretary-General. They may also agree to be the depositary of a non-UN treaty if satisfied that it is of worldwide interest; it would not interfere with the role of UN specialised agencies or other international organisations; and there are no provisions in the treaty (such as for the participation of certain non-state entities) that might be embarrassing for the Secretary-General politically. The Treaty Section of the UN Office of Legal Affairs should always be consulted well in advance, and, if the Secretary-General has agreed to be the depositary, the draft treaty, including its final clauses, must be submitted to the Treaty Section for review and comment *before* it is adopted. The Secretary-General will *not* agree to be a joint depositary, and normally will only agree to be depositary of a non-UN treaty if it is in all six authentic UN languages.

In carrying out depositary functions, the Secretary-General is guided also by any particular rules laid down by the UN General Assembly. Thus, when a treaty has an 'all states' participation clause, the Secretary-General will follow the resolutions and

[11] UKTS (2002) No. 27; A. Bloed (ed.), *The Conference on Security and Co-operation in Europe* (Kluwer Law, Dordrecht 1993), 1271. See Article XVII(1).

[12] 1589 UNTS 474 No. 14118; UKTS (1991) No. 20.

[13] *UN Depositary Practice*, paras. 28–30.

[14] See the Convention on the Marking of Plastic Explosives 1991: 30 ILM (1991) 726; UKTS (2000) No. 134. This rather buries the designation of ICAO as the depositary in Article XIII(2). It is better practice to specify the depositary more obviously, usually at the end of the treaty.

practice of the General Assembly in applying it and, where necessary, will ask the General Assembly for guidance before agreeing to receive the signature or an instrument of ratification from an entity where there is doubt as to whether it is a state.[15] The chief executive officers of the UN specialised agencies follow a similar practice, and their assemblies and general conferences tend to follow the lead given in such matters by the UN General Assembly. In practice, the Treaty Section of the Office of Legal Affairs in the UN Secretariat performs the depositary duties of the UN Secretary-General.

By May 2022, over 600 multilateral treaties had been deposited with the Secretary-General. No other international organisation is the depositary of so many. The UN publication *Multilateral Treaties Deposited with the Secretary-General* (referred to in this book as *UN Multilateral Treaties*) gives the status of those treaties (i.e., lists of parties, dates of entry into force, etc.). It is available online, where it is updated daily.

The *Summary of Practice of the Secretary-General as Depositary of Multilateral Treaties*[16] (referred to in this book as *UN Depositary Practice*) provides invaluable guidance on the depositary practice of the United Nations, and is a good guide for any depositary, whether an international organisation or a state. Last published in 1994, an updated version may be published on the UN website in due course.

Duty to Act Impartially

Multilateral treaties cause problems that require action by the depositary. It is a long-established, and fundamental, customary law principle that the functions of a depositary are, in the words of Article 76(2), 'international in character' and that the depositary is under an obligation 'to act impartially in their performance'.[17] A depositary should never substitute its own view for that of states; it is for states (and ultimately an international court or tribunal) to decide what are their treaty relations with other states.

This is especially important when the depositary was one of the negotiating states. A depositary *state* must at all times keep a very clear distinction between its views and national interests as a state and its functions as depositary. For example, problems can be caused by changes to the structure of a state or the emergence of a new state. When a depositary receives an instrument or communication from a state with which it has no diplomatic relations, or from an entity that it does not recognise as a state, or which it knows is not recognised by other states, it must *not* seek to pass judgement on the validity of the instrument or communication. If necessary, the depositary should circulate a note to the interested states (which are usually contracting states, signatory states and other states entitled to become parties to the treaty) about the

[15] *UN Depositary Practice*, paras. 82–87.
[16] At: https://treaties.un.org/doc/source/publications/practice/summary_english.pdf.
[17] Article 77(2) of the 1986 Convention has identical wording.

instrument or communication, but *without* comment. It is for those states to form a view as to the legal position.

On 21 June 1989 the Permanent Observer of Palestine to the United Nations lodged a purported instrument of accession of the 'State of Palestine' to the Geneva Conventions 1949. The depositary, Switzerland, circulated a note to the parties stating that, because of the uncertainty within the international community as to whether there was a State of Palestine, the depositary was not in a position to decide whether deposit of the instrument amounted to a valid act of accession. The instrument was therefore circulated for the information of the parties, leaving it to them to decide whether it could be accepted. There was no need for the parties to reply to the note. Given the circumstances and the neutral terms of the letter, silence could not have been taken as tacit acceptance of one view or the other. In the event, Palestine did not pursue the matter.[18]

When the depositary is the chief administrative officer of an international organisation, it may be necessary for the assembly of the organisation to be consulted about difficult cases. The UN Secretary-General is guided by the resolutions of the General Assembly and practice within the UN.

As we have seen, due to a drafting error there was doubt as to whether a conference could be held in 1999 or 2000 under the CTBT 1996. In the event, the contracting states agreed on 1999. Although under the CTBT the UN Secretary-General had the duty of convening the conference if a majority of the contracting states so requested, it was not for him to give an opinion as to the date unless asked to do so by the negotiating (not just the contracting) states.[19]

The corollary of the impartiality principle is that nothing that a state does as depositary will prejudice it *as a state*. By notifying the adherence to a treaty of an entity that it does not recognise, a depositary state does not thereby accord recognition to the entity. But its position as depositary does not prevent it from making known its position, as a state, in a *separate* communication to the other interested states.

A depositary may sometimes experience difficulties in issuing a list of contracting states – a task which should be done each time a new instrument of ratification, and so on, is received, the list being circulated to the contracting states and other states entitled to become parties. In the early 1990s the break-up of Yugoslavia and the gaining of independence by certain republics of the former Soviet Union caused problems for some depositaries. In 1994 the newly independent Ukraine lodged with the depositary state an instrument of *succession* to CCAMLR 1980[20] on the basis that it was a successor state to the Soviet Union, though the latter (as Russia) remained a

18 See also *Legal Consequences of the Construction of a Wall in the Occupied Palestinian Territory*, Advisory Opinion, ICJ Reports (2004) 136, 156–164, paras. 43–65; 43 ILM (2004) 1009.

19 See Article 2(1)(e) and (f) VCLT for the definitions of 'negotiating states' and 'contracting states'.

20 1329 UNTS 71 No. 22301; 19 ILM (1980) 837; UKTS (1982) No. 48; TIAS 10240.

party. The depositary duly notified the parties. Although five parties then claimed that, in view of the particular membership provisions in Article XXIX of CCAMLR, no state could become a party by *succession*, nevertheless the depositary accepted the instrument of *succession*. Although they had no objection to Ukraine becoming a party, as a matter of principle, and to prevent an undesirable precedent, the five parties then sent notes to the depositary indicating that they would treat the instrument as one of *accession*. The depositary then, rather grudgingly, notified all parties that Ukraine had become a party on the date of deposit of the instrument (not on the date of independence, as would have been appropriate in a case of succession), but without saying on what basis it had become a party.

But where it is indisputable that an instrument is unacceptable, the depositary *must* refuse it. In 1977 the depositary of the World Meteorological Organisation Convention[21] would not accept a purported instrument of accession from the 'Turkish Federated State of Cyprus' because it did not meet the (factual) precondition for participation: membership of the United Nations. This is clearly distinguishable from the case where there is a difference of view as to the status of an entity.

A difference between a state and the depositary as to the performance of the latter's functions can usually be resolved by informal contacts. When this is not possible, the depositary must bring the question to the attention of the interested states or, where appropriate, to the competent organ of the international organisation concerned (Article 77(2)). A treaty sometimes includes a specific provision on the settlement of such differences.[22]

Functions of the Depositary

In the past, when a treaty designated a depositary, it would list the depositary's functions, or at least some of them, and sometimes this is still done (see below). Subject to any provisions in the treaty, or as may be agreed by the contracting states, the principal functions are listed in Article 77(1):

(1) Keeping custody of the original text of the treaty and any full powers. (Before the invention of the typewriter, several *original* copies were made, and signed by all the plenipotentiaries, so that, rather like at a children's party, each could take away their very own signed original.)

[21] 77 UNTS 143 No. 998; UKTS (1950) No. 36.

[22] Article 22(3) Convention on Customs Treatment of Pool Containers 1994 (2000 UNTS 289 No. 34301; UKTS (2004) No. 13) provides that any difference between a party and the depositary as to the performance of its functions shall be brought to the attention of the other parties and signatories or to the Administrative Committee established by that Convention.

(2) Preparing certified copies of the original text and any further texts in such additional languages as may be required by the treaty,[23] and transmitting them to the parties and to 'the States entitled to become parties to the treaty' (which formula is not always easy to apply). A certified copy is usually needed by the negotiating states for the purposes of official publication and any parliamentary procedure that may be necessary. Unless the final act contains substantive provisions, normally neither it nor the signature pages are included in the certified copies.

(3) Receiving any signatures, and receiving and keeping custody of any instruments of ratification, acceptance, approval, accession or succession, any reservations or declarations, and all other notifications and communications relating to the treaty.

(4) Examining whether the signature, or any instrument, notification or communication relating to the treaty, is in due and proper form and, in case of doubt, bringing the matter to the attention of the state in question. If the instrument is in a foreign language, the depositary notes the date of deposit as the date on which it was received, but does not acknowledge receipt until the instrument has been translated and checked. It is therefore desirable that a state depositing an instrument in a language foreign to the depositary should provide a (suitable) translation (English or French will often be acceptable). Since it is *not* part of the functions of the depositary to adjudicate on the legal validity or effect of an instrument, notification or communication, if it appears that there may be an irregularity, the proper course is to draw the matter to the attention of the state concerned and, if that does not resolve the matter, to bring the question to the attention of the interested states or competent organ in accordance with Article 77(2).

(5) Informing the parties, and states entitled to become parties, of acts, notifications and communications relating to the treaty. This is elaborated in Article 78 (see below).

(6) Informing the states entitled to become parties to the treaty when the number of signatures or instruments of ratification, acceptance, approval or accession required for the entry into force of the treaty have been received or deposited. The date of entry into force of the treaty is a matter that requires the depositary to form a view as to the validity of the signatures received or instruments deposited in order to reach a view as to the date of entry into force. If the depositary's appreciation of the date were to be challenged (e.g., on the basis that an instrument was invalid), it would be bound to consult all interested states in accordance with Article 77(2).

[23] The Tampere Convention 1998 (2296 UNTS 5 No. 40906; UKTS (2005) No. 21) provides for six equally authentic language texts, but Article 17 directs the depositary to prepare three of them as soon as possible after signature.

(7) Following entry into force, registering the treaty with the Secretariat of the United Nations (see Article 80).
(8) Performing the functions specified in other provisions of the VCLT or the treaty, such as the convening of a review conference, though this may be regarded more as an administrative function (see below).

Now that depositary functions are so well established and largely codified in the Convention, it is enough simply to designate a depositary on the understanding that the duties will be performed in accordance with the law of treaties and established practice. Alternatively, the treaty can provide that the functions of the depositary shall be as set out in Part VII of the Vienna Convention on the Law of Treaties 1969.[24]

Nevertheless, including in the treaty a list of the depositary functions may provide a useful reminder or checklist, especially if the depositary is a state that is not so familiar with the duties of a depositary. The Lake Victoria Fisheries Organisation Convention 1994[25] lists the functions of the depositary as:

(1) sending true copies of the Convention to the contracting states;
(2) informing the contracting states of:
    (a) signature of the Convention and the deposit of instruments of ratification or accession;
    (b) the date of entry into force of the Convention;
    (c) proposals for amendments to the Convention and of the adoption of amendments;
    (d) notices of withdrawal from the organisation;
    (e) any other notification received from the contracting states; and
    (f) registration of the Convention with the United Nations.

Any list should, however, only be illustrative and *not* attempt to be exhaustive, since otherwise one is bound to leave out some task.

Notifications and Communications

Article 78 provides that, except as the treaty or the Convention otherwise provides, any notification or communication that the Convention requires a state to make:

(a) shall be made to the depositary or, if there is none, direct to the states for which it is intended;
(b) is considered as having been made only when it is received by the depositary or the states, as the case may be;

[24] See Article 22(2) Convention on Customs Treatment of Pool Containers (n. 22).
[25] 1930 UNTS 128 No. 32987; 36 ILM (1997) 671; Article XXII.

(c) if transmitted to a depositary, is considered received by the state for which it is intended only when that state has been informed by the depositary in accordance with Article 77(1)(e).

These rules are important for the calculation of time limits fixed by the Convention, including that in Article 20(5) for making objections to reservations, where this is applicable.

The reference in the *chapeau* of Article 78 – to the Convention 'otherwise providing' – is to prevent any misconception as to the relationship between that article and Article 16 (exchange or deposit of instruments of ratification, etc.) and Article 24 (entry into force). Although the depositary has a duty to notify states of the deposit of an instrument of ratification, that is only for the purpose of information; the notification is not a *substantive* part of the transaction by which the depositing state establishes treaty relations with the other states. The act of deposit will have the legal effect provided for under the treaty even if the notification of it by the depositary is delayed or overlooked, as happens sometimes. Similarly, late notification by the depositary of the date of entry into force will *not* affect that date.

The Depositary as a State

Being the depositary of a treaty does not prevent a state from becoming party to that treaty, though it has no obligation, legal, political or moral, to become a party. It is therefore good practice for a depositary state to maintain a very clear distinction between the two roles. This is especially important if, as will often be the case, the same official is responsible for, say, both preparing and depositing the instrument of ratification of their state, and then, but as the depositary official, receiving and recording receipt of the instrument. Steps must be taken to avoid simple mistakes: if the depositary state ratifies the treaty, one must not forget the need to include the name of that state in the list of states that have ratified. A depositary state should therefore treat itself as if it were just another state. Its officials do not have to go quite as far as sending diplomatic notes to themselves; it is enough if a memorandum concerning an act by the depositary state (signature, ratification, etc.) is recorded and filed in the same way as the acts of other states.

Sometimes a depositary state will receive an instrument via one of its own diplomatic missions. Even if it is forwarded promptly, the date on which it should be considered to have been received by the depositary could be crucial. The best practice is to treat the date of physical receipt by the treaty section of the foreign ministry of the depositary state as the date of actual receipt.

Correction of Errors

Unfortunately, it is increasingly common for errors to occur in the texts of treaties. This happens with both bilateral and multilateral treaties, though the problem is getting worse for multilateral treaties due to their greater length and complexity, as well as the time pressure under which they are negotiated. The errors may be typographical, spelling, punctuation, numbering or cross-referencing, or a lack of concordance between the authentic language texts. It may be a simple drafting mistake, such as use of inconsistent terminology. But correcting anything which is more than an obvious 'physical' error, or mistake of spelling or numbering, may affect the substance. Punctuation is an aspect of grammar that is perhaps more crucial for some languages, including English, than others that have more certain grammatical rules. Occasionally an error of drafting, usually caused by lack of time to check the text before adoption or signature, can cause a substantive problem. In the form in which it had been adopted, the Rome Statute 1998 contained some incomplete cross-references that, if not corrected, might have had a substantive effect.[26]

Attention may be drawn to an error by a state or the depositary. If there is a dispute as to whether there is an error, the problem may have to be decided in accordance with Article 48 (Error), *not* Article 79, which deals with corrections only when there is no dispute as to the existence of the error. It is more likely, however, that there will be no dispute that there is an error, merely a difference of opinion about how to deal with the matter.

In January 1997 the Preparatory Commission for the CTBT 1996 informed the negotiating states that the text of the attachments to the treaty contained several errors. The location or names of some monitoring stations were wrong, and in some cases the location had been found to be unsuitable. The errors did not come to light until after the authentic text had been prepared by the depositary (the UN Secretary-General) and would have been obvious only to someone with an intimate knowledge of the technical details. It was suggested that, once agreement had been reached by the negotiating states on what to do, the text could be 'corrected' in accordance with the procedure in Article 79 of the Convention. However, although corrections to the *details* of locations and names might be done in this way, to replace the entries for the locations that had been found to be unsuitable with others would amount to a substantive change, and could be done only by amending the text, if necessary before entry into force.

Since the subject of corrections is discrete, the reader is referred to the text of Article 79 in which the procedure for correcting errors is set out in detail. It is enough to draw attention to certain points:

(1) Paragraph 1 deals with the case where there is *no depositary*, as with bilateral and a few multilateral treaties, and applies even if the treaty has not yet entered into force (note the reference to 'the signatory states and the contracting states', rather than to the parties). The paragraph lays down a residuary rule, it being essentially

[26] 2187 UNTS 91 No. 38544; 37 ILM (1998) 998; UKTS (2002) No. 35. Article 121(5) about amendments should have cross-referred to Articles 6, 7 and 8 as well. It now does.

for the states concerned to decide what, if anything, to do about the error. In the case of a bilateral treaty there will normally be two original texts, possibly in two languages, whether the treaty is in a single instrument or an exchange of notes. Making corrections therefore needs to be done with particular care. If the error is only typographical, and the treaty has not yet been published, one method is for one foreign ministry to send the other, under cover of a third-person diplomatic note, a photocopy of the original texts with the corrections inserted clearly by hand. Once the corrections have been agreed, an authorised official of each side can then insert them in the original held by it, initialling each correction. (This is best done while sitting side by side.) If required by one of the states, the corrections can be confirmed by a further third-person note. But if the error is more than typographical or the treaty has been published, the most prudent course is for the agreed corrections to be set out in an exchange of notes (Appendix N). Since the notes will be recording only corrections, not amendments, the exchange should *not* be expressed to constitute an agreement (which could make the exchange itself a treaty). There is no need to publish the exchange, a corrigendum to the published text being sufficient.

(2) Paragraph 2 deals with the case where there *is a depositary*. It does not lay down a residuary rule, and applies even before the treaty has entered into force. Whether the depositary has been alerted to the error or discovered it itself, the depositary must initiate the correction procedure by notifying the signatory states and contracting states of the error and the proposed correction. In practice, the UN Secretary-General will communicate proposed corrections to all states that participated in the elaboration of the treaty, even though only the signatory and contracting states have the right to object to a correction.[27] No rule is laid down in the Convention, or otherwise, as to the legal effect of an objection to a proposed correction, though when an objection is not soundly based, the depositary can usually negotiate its withdrawal.[28] (The United Nations follows customary practice in usually specifying a ninety-day time limit for any objections, but will sometimes set a shorter one, especially if the errors were already well known to the states.) If there is no objection, an authorised official of the depositary makes the correction to the text of the deposited treaty, initialling each correction. The depositary then draws up a *procès-verbal* recording this,[29] and circulates it for information to the signatory and contracting states (when consulting the states it may be useful to include a draft *procès-verbal*). A specimen by a depositary state is at Appendix O.[30]

[27] *UN Depositary Practice*, paras. 53–54.

[28] *UN Depositary Practice*, paras. 61–62.

[29] See various examples of *Procès-Verbal* of Rectification by the UN Secretary-General in the *UN Treaty Collection* under *Texts of Recently Deposited Multilateral Treaties.*

[30] See also UKTS (1990) No. 32 (including a *Procès-Verbal* of Rectification to the EUMETSAT Convention) and UKTS (1992) No. 28 (*Procès-Verbal* of Rectification to the MOU for the Avoidance of Overlaps etc. relating to Deep Seabed Areas).

(3) The rules in paragraphs 1 and 2 apply also where there is a divergence between texts authenticated in more than one language. Although this can be due to simple errors in translation, sometimes the difference can raise a point of substance. This can happen when the treaty was negotiated in only one language and this has resulted in a misunderstanding.
(4) The corrected text is deemed to operate from the date of the original text, unless otherwise agreed.
(5) Where the error is found only in the certified copies of the treaty provided by the depositary (which is all that the interested states will usually hold), the depositary does not have to go through the procedure in paragraph (2): it is sufficient for it to execute a *procès-verbal* and communicate it to the interested states.

Administrative Functions

Although not strictly depositary functions, a depositary may also be entrusted by the treaty with functions such as maintaining a list of conciliators (see the Annex to the Convention) or convening meetings of the parties. But otherwise, when an international organisation is both the depositary of a treaty and also has responsibility for certain administrative functions under the treaty, it is important that the former are carried out by the treaty office and the latter by the other appropriate part or parts of the secretariat.

Under the PTBT,[31] the three states designated as the depositaries, the Soviet Union (now Russia), the United Kingdom and the United States, have the additional functions of circulating proposed amendments and convening amendment conferences. Although such functions are also often given to a depositary, they are more difficult for a state depositary to discharge, and even more difficult when these states are joint depositaries, as well as being parties to the treaty. The PTBT has an 'all states' participation clause that can cause the three depositaries a particularly acute problem when they are faced with the question, for example, of whether an entity is a state that has succeeded to the PTBT and is thus entitled to be invited to attend a review conference. An example would be the Federal Republic of Yugoslavia while it was in an international legal limbo.

As discussed earlier, the UN Secretary-General, as depositary of the CTBT 1996, might have been faced with the problem of whether to convene a conference in 1999 or 2000 if the contracting states had not reached agreement on this. In such circumstances, a wise depositary will consult the states concerned and do nothing until there is, hopefully, a consensus.

[31] See n. 5.

19

Registration and Publication

Order is heaven's first law.[1]

McNair emphasised the importance of registering and publishing treaties, and rightly saw the *United Nations Treaty Series* (UNTS) as 'an indispensable piece of international apparatus'.[2] Yet sometimes it can still be difficult to find the text of treaties, particularly recent ones. Although there are other ways of finding them using the Internet (even Google), the main place is still the UNTS. But, as we shall see, many treaties are never registered with the United Nations. A treaty cannot be registered until it is in force, and even when it has been registered, its publication in the UNTS may be delayed. And even once it is in the UNTS, there may be difficulty in searching for it, especially online, unless one knows the registration number. *So this book gives that number, whenever possible.*

This chapter will explain the procedure for registering a treaty; note the important improvements that have been made to the UNTS; discuss the legal effect of registration or non-registration; and offer suggestions on other ways of finding the texts of treaties, as well as information about treaty status.

Registration

Although the successful negotiation of a treaty may require secrecy, its existence requires openness. Abhorrence at the discovery, during and in the aftermath of the First World War, of secret treaties, and President Woodrow Wilson's call for 'open covenants', resulted in Article 18 of the Covenant of the League of Nations.[3] This required every new treaty entered into by any member of the League to be registered immediately with the Secretariat and published by it as soon as possible. Until registered, the treaty was not binding. No less than 4,834 treaties were registered. Article 102(1) of the UN Charter requires that 'every treaty and every international agreement' entered into by any member of the United Nations after the Charter comes into force be registered with the Secretariat as soon as possible, and then published by it. Article

[1] Alexander Pope (1688–1744), *An Essay on Man*, IV, 49. [2] *McNair*, 179.

[3] See also *McNair*, 179; B. Simma (ed.), *The Charter of the United Nations: A Commentary* (3rd ed., Oxford University Press, Oxford 2012), 2090 *et seq.*

80 of the VCLT also requires the parties to it to so register any treaty to which it is a party once it is in force. But failure to register does not affect the binding nature of a treaty that is in force for a party.

By the end of 2021 some 81,500 treaties had been submitted to the United Nations for registration; about 5 per cent were rejected. This was mainly because either the papers were incomplete, the treaty had not yet entered into force (see below) or it had already been submitted for registration by another party. Nevertheless, over 75,000 treaties have now been registered by the United Nations. Of these, over 28,000 were submitted by international organisations, including over 8,000 submitted for registration by the United Nations itself (see below on registration *ex officio*).

The term 'international agreement' was intended to embrace unilateral engagements of an international character made by one state in favour of another and accepted by the other state, implied acceptance being enough. The Secretariat therefore treats such engagements as international agreements.[4] Thus, declarations under Article 36(2) of the Statute of the International Court of Justice accepting its compulsory jurisdiction are registered. The unilateral declaration of 24 April 1957 by Egypt reaffirming its respect for the Constantinople Convention 1888,[5] and specifying the future arrangements for the Suez Canal, stated that it contained obligations and constituted an international instrument which would be registered with the United Nations, which it was.[6]

Article 83 of the Chicago Convention 1944[7] requires the parties to register new 'arrangements' with the ICAO Council, although there is no sanction for not registering. But the requirement does *not* avoid the need to register air services agreements with the United Nations.

Registration Regulations and Procedure

The UN General Assembly, in consultation with the Secretariat, has drawn up detailed regulations on registration.[8] The main rules are:

(1) A treaty is not registered *until it has entered into force for at least two parties*. This important precondition is sometimes overlooked. But there is no time limit for registration.

[4] M. Tabory, 'Registration of the Egypt–Israel Peace Treaty: Some Legal Aspects', ICLQ 32 (1983) 981–1003, 989.

[5] 171 CTS 241. [6] 265 UNTS 299 No. 3821; AJIL (1957) 673–675; *McNair*, 11.

[7] Cf. Article 81 Chicago Convention, which provides that all aeronautical agreements in existence on entry into force of the Convention are to be registered with the Council.

[8] 859 UNTS xii–xx: Resolution 97(i) adopted by the General Assembly, 14 December 1946, as modified by Resolutions 364(B)(iv), 482(v), 33/141A, 73/210 and 76/120, adopted by the General Assembly on 1 December 1949, 12 December 1959, 18 December 1978, 20 December 2018 and 9 December 2021, respectively. See the UN Treaty Handbook, chapter 5.

(2) Registration may be done by any party and relieves all other parties of the obligation to register.
(3) The United Nations must register *ex officio* every treaty which authorises the United Nations to register it, or which designates the United Nations as the depositary, or to which the United Nations and one or more UN members are parties. Treaties between the United Nations and another international organisation (or a non-UN member) are subject only to filing and recording (Articles 10 and 11 of the Regulations).
(4) All subsequent actions effecting changes in a treaty, such as a withdrawal or termination, must be registered. By May 2022, almost 132,000 such actions had been registered.
(3) A treaty that has already been terminated may still be registered.
(4) The date of receipt of the treaty by the Secretariat for registration, or the date of entry into force in the case of registration *ex officio*, is deemed to be the date of registration. Since the Secretariat has a duty to effect the registration of any treaty that is subject to registration and lodged with it for that purpose, the act of registration is regarded as that of the registering state, not of the Secretariat. This can be important if the status of the instrument is disputed.

To register a treaty one must submit certain documents to the Treaty Section of the Office of Legal Affairs of the United Nations:

(1) A copy of the treaty (certified true and complete) in *all* its authentic languages, together with all attachments (annexes, minutes, *procès-verbales*, etc.). Each should be of good quality, otherwise it may well not be good enough for the desktop publishing system used by the United Nations. It may be submitted in either hard copy or electronic format.
(2) Electronic copies should be sent by email to treatyregistration@un.org or submitted on CD or USB to the Treaty Section. They should be of high quality and transmitted in PDF or TIFF format (black and white, 300 dpi image resolution or higher, and G4 image compression method).
(3) If the treaty is not in English and/or French, a 'courtesy' translation into one or both languages should be supplied, if possible in the same form and with the same number of copies. Where available, courtesy translations of the text into any of the other official UN languages may also be supplied, in order to expedite translations into English and French.
(4) The text of any reservations or declarations.
(5) The certifying statement should include: a statement that it is a true and complete copy; the full title of the treaty; the date and place of conclusion; the date of entry into force; the method of entry into force (signature, ratification, approval, accession, notification, etc.); authentic languages; the language(s) of courtesy translations, if available; names of signatories, if available; and, in the case of multilateral treaties, a list of parties indicating the date of deposit of each party's

instrument of consent to be bound, the nature of such instrument (ratification, approval, acceptance, accession, etc.) and the date of entry into force of the treaty for each party, as well as certification of inclusion in the submission of all reservations, declarations and objections made by the parties.

The best source for up-to-date UN registration requirements is the website of the United Nations Treaty Collection, under 'Notes Verbales from the Legal Counsel relating to the Depositary Practice and the Registration and Publication of Treaties'.[9] This includes Notes on submission of treaties, completeness of registration submissions, registration requirements, publication requirements, translations, model instruments and information on the deposit of binding instruments.

The text of the treaty and related documents will appear electronically in the UN Treaty Collection online soon after registration in all the authentic languages, and later in the UNTS in all the authentic languages; if these do not include English and French, there will be translations into those languages. Translations into English and French, when available, are also made available online, for information, prior to publication in the UNTS. The best way to search for treaties which have not been fully published in the UNTS (those that have not been allocated a volume number) is to search under the title, or key words in the title.

It has been suggested that as many as 25 per cent of treaties are not submitted for registration.[10] There can be many reasons: ignorance of the requirement or of the rules or procedures; inertia; lack of human and technical resources; or simple oversight. Submitting a treaty for registration may require a lot of work: assembling the various language texts, including annexes and other attachments such as maps, and so on; preparing courtesy translations; and gathering the correct information to include in the certifying statements.

Some international organisations still, however, fail to register with the United Nations some treaties for which they are the depositary. Often a bilateral treaty is not registered because neither party has said that it would do it.

Associated Documents

Provided it meets the terms of the regulations, any document lodged with the Secretariat for registration will be registered. If the treaty provides that certain protocols, annexes, maps, and so on are integral to it, they must be registered, and they will normally be published with the treaty in the UNTS. Technical annexes to treaties or agreements where such annexes are frequently amended may not be published.[11]

It is the practice of the UN Treaty Section to delay registration while it asks the registering party to supply any missing documents. If a treaty presented for registration

[9] See the UN Treaty Collection website: https://treaties.un.org/pages/Resource.aspx?path=Publication/NV/Page1_en.xml.

[10] *Reuter*, note to para. 86.

[11] See further under 'Publication by the United Nations' below.

refers to a previous but unregistered treaty, knowledge of which treaty is necessary for the application of the new treaty, the practice of the Section is to ask the registering state to submit the previously unregistered treaty for registration and publication with the new treaty.[12]

However, states must take care over MOUs and other non-binding instruments (as they are defined in this book). As explained earlier, an MOU (or other non-binding instrument) can either stand alone or be supplementary to a treaty. It may be confidential and, of course, it is not a treaty. Therefore, before any MOU that is referred to in a treaty, or which is associated with it, is supplied to the Secretariat, it is important that its non-treaty *and* non-confidential status has been confirmed in writing by all the states concerned.

Joint Registration

On rare occasions the parties to a bilateral treaty will, as a political gesture, both submit it for registration. An example is the China–United Kingdom Joint Declaration on the Question of Hong Kong 1984.[13] But problems can arise if the two texts differ or if each party lodges a different set of associated documents. The difficulties were well illustrated in the (admittedly special) case of the Egypt–Israel Treaty of Peace 1979 (Camp David Accords),[14] which was accompanied by a complex set of minutes, letters and other documents. Since the parties could not agree which of these should be registered, the Secretariat registered and published separately the set of documents lodged by each party.

Article 80 of the Convention goes further than Article 102 of the UN Charter, in that it requires parties to the Convention to transmit treaties to the United Nations even if they are not UN members. If in the unlikely event these days none of the parties are UN members, the United Nations will not register the treaty as such, but will 'file and record' it, and publish it in Part II of the UNTS. A state that is neither a party to the Convention nor a member of the United Nations may nevertheless transmit a treaty to the United Nations, where it will also be filed and recorded, and published in Part II. Treaties concluded by overseas territories should, of course, be sent to the parent state for registration with the United Nations.

It is the invariable practice of the United Kingdom to submit bilateral treaties for registration, regardless of whether the other party has done so or intends to do so. The UN Treaty Section will register the first such treaty it receives, and will record the first state to submit the treaty for registration as the registering state. However,

[12] UNJurYbk (1979) 195–197.

[13] 1399 UNTS 33 No. 23391; 23 ILM (1984) 1366; UKTS (1985) No. 26. See also Article 12(3) UK–France Agreement concerning Fishing in the Bay of Granville 2000: 2269 UNTS 88 No. 40408; UKTS (2004) No. 9, which provides for joint submission by the parties for registration.

[14] 1136 UNTS 116 No. 17813 and 1138 UNTS 72 No. 17855; 18 ILM (1979) 362–389 and 530–536. See also Tabory (n. 4), esp. note 10.

registration by a party, in accordance with Article 1 of the UN regulations, relieves all other parties of the obligation to register and, similarly, registration by a depositary relieves all parties of the obligation to register.[15] Without prejudice to the right of any party to a treaty or international agreement to submit it for registration, if a treaty or international agreement designates one or more depositaries, any of the depositaries is encouraged to effect registration unless otherwise provided in the treaty or international agreement, or as agreed by its parties.

Legal Effect of Registration or Non-registration and Disputes

The UN Treaty Section will check that an instrument that is presented for registration is, on the face of it, a treaty. Now and then the Section has refused registration because it did not consider the instrument to be a treaty.[16] Although the vast majority of instruments presented for registration are without doubt treaties, some that would generally be regarded as MOUs are on rare occasions registered. Although over 1,900 instruments called 'memorandum of understanding' had been registered by May 2022, most of them are (probably) treaties. *But the act of registration, or the failure to register, as such, has no effect on the status of the instrument.* In registering an instrument, the Section does not pass any authoritative judgement on its status, and therefore registration does not confer on it any status that it does not already have.[17] When registration has been effected, the Section notifies only the registering party. In a small number of cases a party will register as a treaty an instrument that another party regards as an MOU or other non-binding instrument, yet the latter will probably remain unaware of the registration unless a dispute about the instrument were to arise.

When there is a dispute as to whether an instrument is a treaty, the fact that it has, or has not, been submitted for registration may, depending on the circumstances, be evidence of the intention of the states concerned as to its status. Article 102 of the UN Charter does not say on whom the obligation to register rests, and registration by one party (which is the norm) is evidence only that that party regards the instrument as a treaty. Nor is the lack of any protest at the registration necessarily evidence that the other party or parties accept that the instrument is a treaty, since states do not routinely monitor registrations. The Iraq–Kuwait Agreed Minutes 1963[18] (which formed the basis of the decision by the UN Security Council to help arrange for the

[15] Article 3.1, UN Regulations on registration (n. 8).

[16] *Repertory of Practice of United Nations Organs*, chapter XVI, Article 102; see at: www.un.org/law/repertory.

[17] See generally, D. Hutchinson, 'The Significance of the Registration or Non-registration of an International Agreement in Determining Whether or Not it is a Treaty', *Current Legal Problems* (1993) 257–290.

[18] 485 UNTS 321 No. 7063, and UNSC Resolution 687 (1991). See also M. H. Mendelson and S. C. Hulton, 'The Iraq-Kuwait Boundary', BYIL 64 (1993) 135–195; and by the same authors, 'La revendication par l'Iraq de la souveraineté sur le Koweit', *Annuaire français de droit international* 36 (1990) 195–227. The so-called Lusaka Agreement was submitted for registration even after proceedings in the ICJ had begun in *Armed*

common boundary to be demarcated) were registered by Kuwait in 1964. After its invasion of Kuwait in 1990, Iraq asserted, most unsuccessfully, that it had never been bound by the Agreed Minutes.[19] In *Qatar* v. *Bahrain* (Jurisdiction and Admissibility),[20] Qatar submitted for registration 'Minutes' of December 1990 (which it claimed constituted the agreement of the two states to submit their dispute to the ICJ) in June 1991, only ten days before it made its application to the Court commencing proceedings. The Court admitted the Minutes, since it found them to constitute a treaty, their status being unaffected by the objection as to its treaty status by Bahrain or the much delayed registration.

The intention of the parties as to the status of the instrument should be put beyond doubt by an express provision that it is (or is not) eligible for registration, as was done at the end of the Helsinki Final Act 1975.[21] It would be a bold step indeed for any court to disregard such a clear indication of the common position of the parties. But non-registration, at least on its own, is *not* evidence that the instrument is not a treaty.

Article 102(2) of the UN Charter provides that no party to any treaty entered into by a member of the United Nations which has not been registered may invoke it before any organ of the United Nations. However, the principal judicial organ of the United Nations, the ICJ, does not apply the provision strictly, or perhaps at all. In *Qatar* v. *Bahrain* (Jurisdiction and Admissibility),[22] the 1987 double Exchange of Letters, which the parties did agree constituted a treaty but which had *not* been registered, were invoked before the Court, which gave full regard to its terms. Other organs of the United Nations have on occasion allowed states to invoke an unregistered treaty; and it is unthinkable that the Security Council would ignore a treaty which is relevant to a matter of international peace and security just because it had not been registered. The sanction in Article 102(2) would appear from the practice of principal organs of the United Nations to be more honoured in the breach than in the observance.[23]

Publication

There is no rule of international law requiring a state to publish a treaty. Finding the text of a treaty, especially a new treaty (or even finding proof of its existence), is not always easy. The problem affects practitioners as much as scholars and students.

Activities on the Territory of the Congo (Democratic Republic of the Congo v. *Uganda)*, Judgment, ICJ Reports (2005) 168; 45 ILM (2006) 562. The ICJ did not bat an eyelid.

19 See Resolution 687 (1991), para. 2.

20 ICJ Reports (1994) 112, at 120–122, paras. 21–30, esp. 28–29; 33 ILM (1994) 1461; 102 ILR 9.

21 14 ILM (1975) 1293.

22 See n. 20, at 116–122, paras. 17–19, 22 and 29.

23 Shakespeare, *Hamlet*, I, iv, 14. See also Hutchinson (n. 17), 279; R. Higgins, *The Development of International Law through the Political Organs of the United Nations* (Oxford University Press, Oxford 1963), 334; *McNair*, 186–189.

Because a treaty cannot be published in the UNTS until it has entered into force and has been registered, and the publication of the UNTS is still some years behind, one has to rely heavily on governmental or commercial sources. The main reason for this delay is that many treaties are not in English and/or French (the two languages in which the text of the treaties must be published in the UNTS), and translations can take a significant time. As the root of the problem is the time it takes to translate treaties into English or French (or both), it is very helpful to the UN Treaty Section if, where necessary, courtesy translations into English and French (as appropriate), or at least into one of the official UN languages, are lodged at the same time as the registration application. To allow registered treaties to be publicly accessible pending publication in the UNTS, the UN Treaty Section makes available on its website,[24] promptly after registration, electronic copies of the authentic texts as submitted, accompanied by translations in English and/or French when available.

Publication by the United Nations

Article 102 of the UN Charter requires the Secretariat of the United Nations to publish treaties registered with it. It does this by publishing them in the single series of the UNTS, although it has the option not to publish in full (1) treaties of assistance and cooperation on financial, commercial, administrative or technical matters; (2) treaties relating to the organisation of conferences, seminars or meetings; (3) treaties that are published by a UN specialised or related agency (e.g., the IAEA); or (4) multilateral agreements that are to be published in a format similar to the UNTS by their depositaries.[25] Publication is done in all the authentic languages and, if these do not include English and French, with translations into those languages. By May 2022 the UNTS consisted of over 3,000 paper volumes, containing over 68,000 of the treaties that had been registered.

A treaty is generally registered within a few weeks of it being submitted for registration. Each month the website notches up to 120,000 visits.

The UN Secretary-General is now the depositary of 600 multilateral treaties. The annual publication *Multilateral Treaties Deposited with the Secretary-General* (in this book referred to as *UN Multilateral Treaties*) is an authoritative guide to the status of those treaties, containing as it does information on signatures, ratifications, accessions, successions, declarations, reservations, objections and entry into force. Since 2010 it has been published only electronically, in English and French, on the UN Treaty Collection website, which is updated every day. In addition, for some years now the certified true copies of the text of all multilateral treaties deposited with the

[24] See the UN Treaty Collection website: https://treaties.un.org/.

[25] Article 12.2, UN Regulations on registration (n. 8). In addition, as already mentioned on p. 349, technical annexes to treaties or agreements where technical annexes are frequently amended may also not be published.

Secretary-General have also been available on the same website well before their entry into force.

The website of the UN Treaty Collection is thus an invaluable source of information about treaties, though not the only one (see below). It can be accessed online at http://treaties.un.org.

Publication by States

Whether, or when, a treaty is published by a state is dependent on its constitution, legislation and practice. Publication may be in an official gazette or journal, or in an official treaty series. Although most states publish treaties, the extent to which this is done varies greatly, publication by most states not being comprehensive. The increasing number of treaties has led to some states dispensing with the publication of 'routine' treaties, such as those dealing with short-term aid projects. But where a treaty has to be submitted to parliament before it can be signed or ratified, it may well have to be published.

In the United Kingdom, all treaties that the United Kingdom concludes which are subject to ratification, accession, acceptance, approval or an analogous procedure, are laid before (i.e., formally presented to) Parliament in accordance with the statutory provisions of Part 2 of the Constitutional Reform and Governance Act 2010. That piece of legislation replaced the non-statutory constitutional practice (which worked perfectly well) and was known as the Ponsonby Rule. Prior to entry into force, such treaties are published as *Command Papers* in the *Country* or the *Miscellaneous Series.*

The United Kingdom treaty database contains records for more than 14,000 multilateral and bilateral treaties. Since 1892 every treaty has been laid before Parliament as a Command Paper and, when it has entered into force for the United Kingdom, has been published in the *United Kingdom Treaty Series* (UKTS). If it *enters into force on signature*, it will generally be published only in the UKTS, not in the *Country* or *Miscellaneous Series.* The UKTS is not published in volumes, each treaty being issued separately. Since 1973 only the English text of multilateral treaties (and since 2003 also bilateral treaties) has been published. Earlier British treaties dating back to at least 1812 can be found in *British and Foreign State Papers* (BFSP).

In contrast to some (chiefly monist) states, neither laying a treaty before the legislature (parliament) nor its publication in the UKTS has any legal effect; neither procedure makes the treaty part of the law of the United Kingdom.

Other Sources of Treaty Texts

A prime source of modern treaty texts is *International Legal Materials*, which has been published by the American Society of International Law since 1962. Published six times a year, it has become an invaluable source for texts of recently concluded treaties (and some non-binding instruments), whether bilateral or multilateral, which may be of general interest to public international lawyers, whether practitioners, academics or students. It is very often the quickest, or indeed the only way to find a new treaty or one whose entry into force, or publication in the UNTS, is considerably delayed.

For the text of treaties concluded between 1648 (Treaty of Westphalia) and 1919, the best source is the 231-volume *Consolidated Treaty Series* (CTS), though not all the treaties have been translated into English or French. For those concluded between 1919 and 1946, one should consult the 205-volume *League of Nations Treaty Series* (LNTS).[26]

Treaties and agreements that have entered into force for the United States are published in the *Treaties and Other International Acts Series* (TIAS) – the official publication format since 1945. Since 2006, TIAS prints of treaties and international agreements have been published in electronic form only, and can be found on the US Department of State website.[27] From 1982 until 2006, TIAS prints were published in 'slip' or pamphlet form by the Government Printing Office. From 1950 until 1982, they were compiled in bound volumes entitled *United States Treaties and Other International Agreements* (UST). These volumes are no longer published.

The many volumes of the *International Law Reports* (ILR), with its excellent (but out-of-date) index, are an important source for the decisions of courts and tribunals, both international and national, on treaty matters.

26 To be found co-located with the UNTS on the latter's website: https://treaties.un.org.

27 See US Department of State, How to Find Treaty and Agreement Texts: www.state.gov/finding-agreements/.

20

Dispute Settlement and Remedies

war settles *nothing* ... to win a war is as disastrous as to lose one![1]

This short chapter deals with the settlement of disputes and remedies. The subject is not specific to treaties, and has been dealt with more comprehensively in many other books. This chapter concentrates on those matters that are particularly relevant to treaties. While there are general processes which might be applied in cases of dispute or non-compliance (such as negotiations, conciliation or arbitration), there are also increasingly specific procedures which have been established in particular fields, such as trade, environment, law of the sea, human rights and investment arbitration.[2]

Voluntary Settlement

Negotiations and Consultations

When a treaty prescribes how disputes can be settled, it usually provides for a preliminary phase where the parties seek to settle the dispute by direct negotiations or consultations.[3] Even if the dispute is eventually referred to arbitration or judicial settlement, it is desirable that the points at issue should be better defined by such contacts. In fact, most disputes are settled through negotiation, and it may also be true that most disputes are not so intractable that the parties have to resort to more formal methods. One should treat with caution proposals for still further *general* treaties on dispute settlement. There are already sufficient methods for those states that wish to use them. And although formal methods of dispute settlement have an important role to play, they are usually no substitute for a carefully negotiated settlement.

Some treaties simply require the parties to consult, or convene a meeting, or settle through the diplomatic channel, without specifying any further procedure. Others require (or at least encourage) the parties to a dispute to enter into consultations or

[1] Agatha Christie, *An Autobiography* (1977), Pt. 10 (original emphasis).

[2] Specificity brings with it advantages of jurisprudence which takes into account the particular subject matter and context but also risks the fragmentation of international law.

[3] See, for example, Article 283 UNCLOS; Article 4 WTO Understanding on Rules and Procedures Governing the Settlement of Disputes: 33 ILM (1994) 1226; WTO | Dispute Settlement Understanding – legal text.

negotiations with a view to agreeing on or moving towards another method of settlement, if negotiations fail.[4] Some multilateral treaties may provide a number of mechanisms to assist with dispute settlement or non-implementation. For example, the 1992 Climate Change Convention provides for a subsidiary body for implementation, a multilateral consultative process and the more traditional paths of negotiation, conciliation or binding procedures.[5]

In the case of bilateral agreements, the more specific and binding mechanisms tend to be found in agreements with more specific obligations, particularly those directly affecting individual interests (such as trade or investment matters). Agreements which concern sensitive or security matters,[6] or which are of a more political or cooperative nature, or for which a binding dispute procedure might be unproductive or unnecessarily arduous, tend to have more general or diplomatic settlement processes.

Negotiations to settle a dispute must be implemented in good faith.[7] They must, therefore, be conducted purposefully. Negotiations can last as long as the parties wish, and may be stopped and resumed at any time. Some dispute settlement clauses, however, prescribe a time limit after which either party is free to invoke whatever third-party means of settlement is provided for in the treaty.[8]

If the negotiations are successful, it is essential that the parties record what has been agreed. The form will depend on the circumstances. It may involve an amendment to the treaty or a public statement. If the parties do not want publicity, they may record the terms of settlement in an unpublished non-binding agreement such as an MOU. For reasons already given, the MOU, though not itself legally binding, may nevertheless have legal consequences, as was demonstrated in the award in the *UK–US Heathrow User Charges* Arbitration.[9]

If the negotiations are not successful, one of the parties may decide to terminate the treaty. Since 1945, the United Kingdom has, because of unresolved disputes, terminated at least four air services agreements: with the Philippines (1953 and 1984), the United States (1976) and Lebanon (1981).[10] Sometimes a dispute

[4] See, for example, Articles 13–14 UK–US Air Transport Agreement 2020: UKTS (2021) No. 12.

[5] Articles, 10, 13 and 14: 1771 UNTS 107 No. 30822; 31 ILM (1992) 851; UKTS (1995) No. 28. See also P. Sands *et al.*, *Principles of International Environmental Law* (4th ed., Cambridge University Press: Cambridge 2018), 168 and generally 168–176.

[6] See, e.g., Article 15 UK–Turkey Security Agreement concerning the Protection of Defence Classified Information 2016: UKTS (2019) No. 6.

[7] See further *M/V Norstar (Panama* v. *Italy)*, Preliminary Objections, ITLOS Reports 2016, 44, 85–93, paras. 176–220; *Case Concerning the Detention of Three Ukrainian Naval Vessels (Ukraine* v. *Russian Federation)*, Provisional Measures, ITLOS Case No. 26, Order of 25 May 2019, 302–305, paras. 78–90; *Delimitation of the Maritime Boundary in the Atlantic Ocean (Ghana/Côte d'Ivoire)*, Judgment, ITLOS Reports 2017, 4, 166–167, paras. 627–628.

[8] See Article 14 UK–US Air Transport Agreement (n. 4).

[9] XXIV UNRIAA 1, esp. 130–134.

[10] A. Aust, 'Air Services Agreements: Current United Kingdom Procedures and Policies', *Air Law* (1985) 189–202, 198–199.

becomes so bad that termination and starting afresh is the only way out of the impasse. Of course, it does not mean that the dispute may not still be settled by reference to a third party, if the treaty provides for this (a disputes clause usually remains in force in relation to matters occurring before termination of the treaty), or if the parties agree to this course. But termination can have the advantage of drawing a line under the dispute, so enabling the parties to negotiate a new treaty to their mutual satisfaction.

Involvement of Third Parties

If it is not possible to settle a dispute by negotiation, it may be necessary to seek the help of a third party. Whether this will be successful, or indeed possible, will depend on various factors. One will be the degree of cooperation between the parties. Despite the existence of several general treaties on the settlement of disputes, in many cases there will be no agreement binding the parties to any means of third-party settlement for the particular dispute. It will then be necessary to negotiate - probably in unfavourable circumstances - an ad hoc agreement on a means of settlement. If the method is mediation or conciliation, unless the agreement provides for the parties to accept the recommendations of the third party (which is not usual), neither party will be bound by these methods.

Conciliation and Mediation

Conciliation may be provided for in the treaty itself or in a general treaty on the settlement of disputes to which the parties in dispute are both bound,[11] or it may be agreed ad hoc. The nature of conciliation is neatly expressed in the Annex to the VCLT, which provides for the conciliation of disputes between parties to the Convention in certain limited circumstances. Part of it provides that:

> (5) The [Conciliation] Commission may draw the attention of the parties to the dispute to any measures which might facilitate an amicable settlement.
> (6) The Commission shall hear the parties, examine the claims and objections, and make proposals to the parties with a view to reaching an amicable settlement of the dispute.

This formula became a model for multilateral treaties, in particular, for UNCLOS 1982.[12]

[11] The OSCE Convention on Conciliation and Arbitration (1842 UNTS 151 No. 31413; 32 ILM (1993) 557) provides for *compulsory* conciliation, though the outcome is not binding. See also Article 5 WTO Understanding on Rules and Procedures Governing the Settlement of Disputes (33 ILM (1994) 1226, or at WTO website) referred to at p. 356.

[12] 1833 UNTS 397 No. 31363; 21 ILM (1982) 1261; UKTS (1999) No. 81, Annex V, Articles 5 and 6.

The results of conciliation are almost invariably non-binding. Once again, the matter is well expressed in the Annex to the VCLT:

> (6) The report of the Commission, including any conclusions stated therein regarding the facts or questions of law, shall not be binding upon the parties and it shall have no other character than that of recommendations submitted for the consideration of the parties in order to facilitate an amicable settlement of the dispute.

There is no sharp dividing line between conciliation and mediation. Both involve the intervention of a third party to try to resolve the dispute. A mediator may act as an adjunct to negotiations, playing the role of an active participant, informally advancing fresh proposals and interpreting and transmitting each party's proposals to the other; in conciliation, the third person (or often a commission)[13] may assume a more formal role, investigating the details underlying the dispute, and making formal proposals for its resolution. But much depends upon the circumstances, the third person or commission, and the parties themselves.[14]

Conciliation and mediation feature in some dispute settlement mechanisms for trade disputes. Article 5 of the WTO Dispute Settlement Understanding provides that procedures of 'good offices, conciliation and mediation' may be undertaken voluntarily if the parties so agree.[15] An example in the bilateral sphere is the UK–Côte d'Ivoire Stepping Stone Economic Partnership Agreement, under which the parties may resort to a mediator before they have recourse to arbitration.[16]

Conciliation also features in environmental treaties (with mediation),[17] under certain provisions of UNCLOS 1982[18] and in investor–state disputes.[19] On the human rights side, the European Court of Human Rights may make itself available to the parties in an ECHR case with a view to securing a 'friendly settlement' of the matter.[20]

Compulsory Binding Settlement

In international law a state cannot be compelled to accept the jurisdiction of an international court or tribunal; it has to decide whether to consent to its jurisdiction, including in advance. The two principal characteristics of *compulsory binding* settlement are: (1) a *prior* agreement to submit disputes to a third party; and (2) that the decision of

13 See the Annex to the VCLT quoted above; and Article 14.6 Climate Change Convention (n. 5).

14 See J. Merrills and E. De Brabandere, *Merrills' International Dispute Settlement* (7th ed., Cambridge University Press: Cambridge 2022), 66; Sands *et al.* (n. 5), 170–172.

15 See n. 11.

16 Articles 47–49: UK Country Series, Côte d'Ivoire (2020) No. 1.

17 See Sands *et al.* (n. 5), 170–172.

18 See Merrills and Brabandere (n. 14), 281–284.

19 See Articles 28–35 Convention on the Settlement of Investment Disputes between States and Nationals of Other States: 575 UNTS 159 No. 8359; 4 ILM (1965) 524; UKTS (1967) No. 25.

20 Article 39 ECHR 1950, amended by subsequent Protocols: consolidated text at CoE website. For an account of bodies monitoring human rights treaties, see N. S. Rodley, 'The Role and Impact of Treaty Bodies', in D. Shelton (ed.), *The Oxford Handbook of International Human Rights Law* (Oxford University Press, Oxford 2013), 621–648.

the third party is *legally binding* on the parties in dispute. These two elements may be provided for in the treaty that is the subject of the dispute, in a general treaty on the settlement of disputes to which the parties in dispute are bound or ad hoc. But even if a treaty provides for a method of compulsory third-party settlement, unless the provision is tightly drafted, one party may, in practice, be able to delay the process (see below).

Arbitration

Arbitration is the submission of a dispute to a judge or judges, in principle chosen by the parties, which agree to accept and respect the judgment. The judges are termed 'arbitrators' and their judgment is referred to as an 'award'. Although some arbitrations are conducted by a single arbitrator, this is really suitable only for a relatively simple case involving a narrow, essentially factual point. It is normal to have only one arbitrator appointed by each party and one (or preferably three if the parties can agree on the extra expense) who is a 'neutral' arbitrator.

Although it may be more common to have no more than three arbitrators *in total*, this is not ideal since the chairman will then need the support of one of the national arbitrators in order to reach a decision. To do this, the chairman may well have to compromise. Three 'neutral' arbitrators do not face the same obstacles to reaching a correct decision.

If a party fails to appoint its national arbitrator, or there is no agreement on the choice of the neutral arbitrator or arbitrators, it is highly desirable to provide for the necessary appointments to be made by an eminent independent person (see below).

Many multilateral and bilateral treaties contain arbitration clauses, and more treaty disputes are decided by arbitration than by judicial settlement. Although it is unquantifiable, the possibility that another party to a treaty could take a dispute to arbitration can be an effective deterrent to a state contemplating breach of the treaty, especially a bilateral treaty. For this reason, many arbitrations about treaties concern genuine differences of view, not deliberate flouting of treaty obligations. The Abyei Arbitration 2008–09 was unusual, since it was between a state and part of that state, and was governed by the Optional Rules of the Permanent Court of Arbitration (PCA).[21]

Since arbitration is a consensual process, the parties must first agree that the dispute will be taken to arbitration. This can be done by the following methods:

(1) A treaty under which the parties agree to submit future disputes (not just about the interpretation or application of a treaty) to arbitration. The treaty can be multilateral or bilateral. The so-called Jay Treaty of 1794[22] between Great Britain (as it then was)[23] and the United States led to a series of arbitrations. The first multilateral treaties concerning dispute settlement (but without compulsory

[21] See ASIL ILIB, 16 September 2009. [22] 52 CTS 243.
[23] See p. 214 on the evolution of the United Kingdom.

settlement) were the Hague Conventions for the Pacific Settlement of International Disputes 1899 and 1907, which established the PCA.[24] They were followed by other such general treaties, though generally they have been little used.[25] Of particular importance in the field of investment disputes between a host state and a foreign investor is the Convention on the Settlement of Investment Disputes between States and Nationals of Other States.[26] States have sometimes entered into general bilateral treaties by which they agree to settle their disputes by arbitration, such as the UK–Switzerland Conciliation, Judicial Settlement and Arbitration Treaty 1965.[27]

(2) A clause in a treaty (known as a 'compromissory clause') under which the parties agree to submit all or part of their future disputes regarding the interpretation or application of the treaty to arbitration. In the past such clauses were usually drawn in general terms, and left most of the important details to be worked out only when one of the parties had invoked the clause. Many such clauses are to be found in treaties still in force. It is better, however, to put into the clause as much detail as possible, omitting only those matters that cannot easily be worked out until a dispute has arisen. Such an approach will avoid some of the considerable delay that will ensue if crucial matters, such as the method of appointment of the arbitrators, are not laid down with sufficient detail. The arbitration clause of the UK–US Air Services Agreement 1977,[28] which was invoked by the United States in 1988 over the dispute about the aircraft user charges at London Heathrow Airport,[29] contained fairly detailed provisions. But even they were soon found to be inadequate for what turned out to be a very long and complicated arbitration. The Rules of Procedure of the Arbitral Tribunal were modified several times during the course of the arbitration.

(3) A *compromis*. If there is no existing agreement, or if it does not contain enough detail, it will be necessary for the parties to conclude a treaty called a *compromis* (sometimes termed in English 'special agreement', even though the more elegant term, in English, is *compromis*, never 'compromise'). The *compromis* sets out all the details of the establishment and procedure of the arbitral tribunal. It usually covers:
- composition of the tribunal;
- appointment of its members, including the filling of vacancies;
- appointment of agents of the parties;
- question(s) to be decided;
- rules of procedure and methods of work;

[24] 187 CTS 410; UKTS (1901) No. 9; revised 1907: 205 CTS 233; UKTS (1971) No. 6. For details about the PCA, see www.pca-cpa.org.

[25] See the General Act 1928 (93 LNTS 343; UKTS (1931) No. 32), and the Revised General Act 1949 (71 UNTS 101 No. 912); CoE Convention for the Peaceful Settlement of Disputes 1957 (320 UNTS 243 No. 4646; ETS No. 23).

[26] See n. 19.

[27] 605 UNTS 205 No. 8765; 4 ILM (1965) 943; UKTS (1967) No. 42.

[28] 1079 UNTS 21 No. 16509; UKTS (1977) No. 76.

[29] See n. 9.

- language(s);
- applicable law;
- seat of the tribunal;
- appointment of the secretary of the tribunal and their staff;
- the binding nature of the award;
- costs.

It may not be necessary to cover all points. For example, the agreement may provide that the working methods of the tribunal will be determined by the tribunal itself. For an example of a *compromis*, see that between Botswana and Namibia, or the special agreement of Guatemala and Belize, to submit cases to the ICJ.[30]

A trap to be avoided is failure to provide for a third party to make the appointment of either a national or a neutral arbitrator if the appointment has not been made by the party concerned. There is just such an omission in Article 17 of the Jordan–United States Free Trade Area Agreement 2000,[31] there being no provision in case of a failure to appoint any member of a three-person arbitration panel. There may, however, be no need to include such a provision if the reference to arbitration is 'friendly'. Whether friendly or not, it is also essential to agree on precisely the subject matter of the dispute.

Judicial Settlement

The ICJ is the most prominent body providing for judicial settlement between states, but there are other significant judicial bodies with jurisdiction in specific areas of international law. Of particular note are the procedures which operate for disputes in international trade,[32] law of the sea,[33] regional human rights[34] and within the European Union (in respect of Union law).[35]

30 Botswana and Namibia: 119 ILR 467; 39 ILM (2000) 314–315; Guatemala and Belize: www.icj-cij.org/en/case/177/institution-proceedings.

31 41 ILM (2002) 63.

32 See P. Van den Bossche and W. Zdouc, *The Law and Policy of the World Trade Organization* (5th ed., Cambridge University Press, Cambridge 2022), 173–336; Merrills and De Brabandere (n. 14), 310–346; J. Pauwelyn and I. Van Damme, 'The World Trade Organization', in M. J. Bowman and D. Kritsiotis (eds.), *Conceptual and Contextual Perspectives on the Modern Law of Treaties* (Cambridge University Press, Cambridge 2018), 809–847.

33 See R. Churchill, 'The General Dispute Settlement System of the UN Convention on the Law of the Sea: Overview, Context, and Use', *Ocean Development & International Law* 48 (2017) 216–238; Merrills and De Brabandere (n. 14), 261–309.

34 See, for example, the ECtHR under the ECHR 1950 (n. 20); the Inter-American Court of Human Rights under the American Convention on Human Rights: 1144 UNTS 144 No. 17955; 9 ILM (1970) 673; the African Commission and the African Court on Human and Peoples' Rights (HPR) under the African Charter on HPR (1520 UNTS 217 No. 26363) and the 1998 Protocol to the Charter (at the Court's website); M. Fitzmaurice, 'Interpretation of Human Rights Treaties', in Shelton (n. 20), 739–771, 752–771; and S. Sheeran and N. Rodley (eds.), *Routledge Handbook of International Human Rights Law* (Routledge, London and New York 2016), Part IV, 405–520.

35 See Articles 251–281 TFEU: [2008] OJ C115/47.

International Court of Justice

Like an arbitral award, a judgment of the ICJ is binding on the parties, who can only be states. A state which considers that the other side has failed to implement the Court's judgment may bring the matter before the Security Council, which is empowered to recommend or decide upon measures to be taken to give effect to the judgment.[36] As a permanent body, the Court has certain advantages over an ad hoc arbitral tribunal. In addition, the jurisdiction of the more specialist international judicial bodies, such as the ITLOS,[37] is, in contrast to the ICJ, restricted by their constituent instruments to specific areas of law.

Being a permanent body, the ICJ has judges who are always available to hear cases. The parties do not have to pay anything towards the costs of the ICJ since, being the principal judicial organ of the United Nations (Article 92 of the UN Charter), the parties (who will almost always be UN members) already pay indirectly for the ICJ through their normal annual contributions to the UN budget. Although the ICJ has sometimes been criticised for being leisurely, it probably takes no more time to dispose of a complex case (and most cases coming before the ICJ are complex) than would an arbitral tribunal, yet at much less direct cost to the parties. Developing state litigants may also be able to have part of their legal costs met from a trust fund administered by the UN Secretary-General if the dispute is submitted to the ICJ by *compromis*. The scope of the jurisdictional competence of the ICJ will be known in advance, as will be its rules of procedure and methods of work. Moreover, since the ICJ has built up a body of jurisprudence, and the identity of judges will be known, states and their advisers may be better able to predict how the ICJ will deal with a case.

All these factors should, in principle, enable the proceedings to take place more quickly (provided that is what the parties want), and with less trouble and more cheaply. But given the ICJ's current increased workload, and because it is underfunded, some delays might still be experienced.

As with arbitration, a dispute can come before a standing court or tribunal only if the parties to the dispute have so agreed. Their agreement can be constituted in the following ways:

(1) By adherence to a general bilateral or multilateral treaty which provides for disputes between them to be referred, at the request of either, to the ICJ. Certain treaties of friendship provide for this. Iran successfully invoked the Iran–United States Treaty of Amity 1955[38] as the basis for the ICJ's jurisdiction to hear the dispute it had with the United States over attacks on its oil platforms.

[36] Article 94 UN Charter. [37] See www.itlos.org.

[38] UNTS 93 No. 4132; TIAS 3853. See *Oil Platforms (Iran* v. *United States of America)* (Preliminary Objection), Judgment, ICJ Reports (1996) 803, at 820, paras. 51–52; 42 ILM (2003) 1335.

Similarly, Nicaragua successfully invoked the US–Nicaragua Treaty of Friendship, Commerce and Navigation 1956.[39]

(2) By adherence to an optional protocol to the treaty, the interpretation or application of which is the subject of the dispute. Such a protocol is essentially a compromissory clause but, being a separate treaty, a party to the principal treaty will need to adhere to the protocol in order to accept the jurisdiction of the ICJ by this means. The Optional Protocol on Settlement of Disputes to the VCDR 1961[40] was invoked by the United States in its dispute with Iran over the Tehran hostages.[41] The Optional Protocol to the VCCR 1963[42] was invoked by Paraguay to take the United States to the ICJ.[43]

(3) By the compromissory clause of a treaty. The *Lockerbie* cases were brought by Libya under the compromissory clause of the Montreal Convention 1971.[44] On 4 May 2006 Argentina referred its dispute with Uruguay over the latter's use of the River Plate to the Court under Article 60 of the Argentina–Uruguay Statute of the River Uruguay 1975.[45]

(4) By the conclusion of a *compromis,* as in the *Kasikili/Sedudu Island* case.[46]

(5) By the making of reciprocal declarations under Article 36 of the Statute of the International Court of Justice accepting in advance the general jurisdiction of the Court to decide 'all cases that the parties refer to it and all matters specially provided for . . . in treaties and conventions in force'. Over seventy have been made by a wide geographical spread of states.[47] Most states that have made declarations have attached conditions to their acceptance of the general jurisdiction of the Court.[48] In order to confer jurisdiction on the Court over a dispute, the declarations of each party must match in all necessary particulars.

Failure to Provide for a Compulsory Dispute Settlement Mechanism

This was well illustrated in the *Southern Bluefin Tuna* case. Australia and New Zealand claimed Japan was in breach of the Southern Bluefin Tuna Conservation Convention 1993,[49] but Japan had not consented under its Article 16 to refer the

39 367 UNTS 3 No. 5224; *Military and Paramilitary Activities in and against Nicaragua (Nicaragua* v. *United States of America)* (Jurisdiction and Admissibility), Judgment, ICJ Reports (1984) 392, at 396–429, paras. 7–83; 76 ILR 104. See also ASIL ILIB, 3 February 2012, concerning the case of *Germany* v. *Italy.*

40 500 UNTS 241 No. 7312; UKTS (1965) No. 19.

41 *United States Diplomatic and Consular Staff in Tehran*, Judgment, ICJ Reports (1980) 3, at 24–28, paras. 45–55; 61 ILR 502.

42 596 UNTS 469 No. 8640, UKTS (1973) No. 14.

43 See the ICJ Press Release of 2011.

44 Article 14. See 974 UNTS 177 No. 14118; 10 ILM (1971) 10; UKTS (1974) No. 10.

45 1295 UNTS 340 No. 21425.

46 See n. 30, at 1049, para. 2.

47 J. Merrills, 'The Optional Clause Revisited', BYIL 64 (1993) 197.

48 A list of current declarations, including conditions, can be found in *UN Multilateral Treaties*, chapter I, and in the annual *Yearbook of the International Court of Justice.*

49 1819 UNTS 360 No. 31155.

dispute to the ICJ or arbitration. They therefore sought to have their claim heard by a tribunal established under Annex VII of UNCLOS 1982.[50] In 2000 the tribunal held that there was only one dispute, and it was under the 1993 Convention. Since Japan had not consented under that Convention to any means of compulsory dispute settlement, the tribunal had no jurisdiction.[51]

Remedies

> 'Tis a sharp remedy, but a sure one for all ills.

David Hume attributed this quote to Sir Walter Raleigh, who was reportedly referring to his own execution by the axe; most people then believed in an afterlife.

The use of force in response to a breach of treaty is now severely limited by the prohibition in Article 2(4) of the UN Charter on the threat or use of force in international relations. The victim state would be entitled to use force to repel the invader, Article 51 of the UN Charter preserving a state's inherent right of self-defence. But there are several more peaceful responses that a party can make to breach of a treaty. Here we enter into the broader realm of state responsibility, that is to say the responsibility in international law that a state bears for conduct in breach of its international obligations. Discussion of remedies for breach of a treaty will therefore be brief.[52]

Breach of any international obligation (not just breach of a treaty) constitutes an international wrong from which flow certain legal consequences in customary international law. The ILC did not deal with remedies in its draft articles on the law of treaties; but Article 73 of the Convention provides that its provisions do not prejudge any question that may arise about a treaty from the international responsibility of a state. Fortunately, after some fifty years, in 2001, the ILC produced a final set of draft articles to codify the law on state responsibility, and a detailed commentary on each.[53] They do, for the most part, reflect customary international law as it has developed over many years, though certain draft articles are controversial, particularly those on countermeasures.

A dispute about the interpretation or application of a treaty usually involves an allegation of a breach of the treaty; and many disputes involve mutual accusations of breach, as in *Gabčíkovo (Hungary* v. *Slovakia)*.[54] If a party to a treaty has been injured

[50] See n. 12.

[51] See 39 ILM (2000) 1359. On the problem of competing dispute settlement regimes, see B. Oxman, 'Complementary Agreements and Compulsory Jurisdiction', AJIL (2001) 277–312.

[52] As to the relationship between the law of treaties and the law of state responsibility, see *Rainbow Warrior (New Zealand* v. *France)* (1990) 82 ILR 499, at 547–551, paras. 72–75.

[53] See the ILC's 2001 Report, A/56/10, or see at: www.un.org/law/ilc. See also J. Crawford, *The International Law Commission's Articles on State Responsibility* (Cambridge University Press, Cambridge 2002).

[54] ICJ Reports (1997) 7; 37 ILM (1998) 162; 116 ILR 1.

by a breach of it by another party, in addition to the remedies that may be available under the VCLT, it may seek one or more of the following:

- cessation of the wrongful conduct;
- assurances and guarantees of non-repetition;
- reparation, including satisfaction, restitution in kind and compensation.

These options, and the complex law on state responsibility generally, is described in other works. But since a state is more likely to consider resorting to countermeasures as an initial reaction in response to an actual or perceived breach of treaty obligation, we will here deal at least with those, with a brief look at 'necessity'.

Countermeasures

(Unless otherwise indicated, specific articles cited in the rest of this chapter are to the ILC's final draft articles on state responsibility.[55])

Overwhelmingly, countermeasures[56] are resorted to in respect of alleged breaches of *bilateral* treaties, though they could also be employed if a party to a multilateral treaty considers that another party has, by breaching its obligations under the treaty, harmed it. We have seen how a material breach of a treaty may entitle another party to terminate or suspend the operation of the treaty in whole or in part, in which case the rules of the Convention will apply. The right to take countermeasures is also firmly established. The ability to take them is a most important means by which a state can respond effectively to breaches of its international rights, rather than relying solely on the lengthy processes of peaceful settlement and awards under them. Even if such methods are readily available, they may take years to produce a result (an international interim measure of protection (injunction) not being that easy to get or to enforce), and reparation (even if full and paid promptly) is seldom a fully satisfactory substitute for performance of the obligation. Given that enforcement of international law is not done within a legal system with a hierarchy of courts supported by sophisticated enforcement mechanisms, a state has sometimes to resort to self-help measures to protect its rights and those of its nationals. But by resorting to countermeasures, a state takes the risk that the action of the other state may be held to be lawful, thereby rendering the countermeasures themselves unlawful. The state taking the countermeasures also needs to consider at the outset, in a case where it is acting in response to a breach of a treaty, to what extent the treaty itself includes provision specifically precluding that action.

Countermeasures must be distinguished from reprisals (a term now properly used only in the context of the law of armed conflict), retorsion (a response not involving

[55] See n. 53.

[56] For a survey of the law, see F. I. Paddeu, 'Countermeasures', *MPEPIL* (2015); and B. Simma and C. J. Tams, 'Reacting against Treaty Breaches', in *Hollis, Oxford Guide*, 568–594, 585–594.

any breach of international law),[57] sanctions imposed under chapter VII of the UN Charter, or suspension or termination of a treaty.

Countermeasures consist of a state not performing certain of its international obligations towards another state that the first state considers has harmed it. But the measures are taken only for the purpose of inducing the other state to cease acting wrongfully and make full reparation (Article 49). If there is a good legal basis for taking countermeasures, they are not wrongful (Article 22). The classic example of countermeasures involves obligations under an air services agreement. The (mythical) agreement between T and France allows one airline of each state to operate a daily return flight between the two capitals using large capacity jets. But T Air later decides to fly with smaller aircraft, while Air France continues to fly larger aircraft. Although that is Air France's right under the agreement, T Air presses its government to deny Air France permission to land its large aircraft, and the T government does so. Then Air France asks its government to deny T Air permission to land more than three times a week in Paris until the T government allows Air France to land its daily large-capacity flights. The French government does so.[58] That is a classic countermeasure in response to a breach of treaty. Provided it is done in response to a breach of the air services agreement, and the measures taken are proportionate to the breach, they should be lawful.

Objects and Limits of Countermeasures

Article 49(1) emphasises that countermeasures are exceptional and limited; in particular, they must be necessary, and not a punishment. Countermeasures do not have to be reciprocal, in the sense of being limited to suspension of the performance of the same or a closely related obligation. In the above example, France cannot reply precisely in kind, though the countermeasure is directly related to an obligation under the air services agreement. Sometimes taking countermeasures in an unrelated field of activity may be unavoidable. A state cannot respond by breaching certain sacrosanct obligations (see below). Occasionally, a treaty may prohibit countermeasures or require their prior authorisation. Countermeasures must cease once they have had the desired effect (Article 49(2)), and must, as far as possible, be taken in such a way as to permit the resumption of performance of the responsible state's obligations, that is, be reversible (Article 49(3)).

Proportionality

Countermeasures must be 'commensurate with' (proportionate to) the injury suffered, taking into account 'the gravity of the wrongful act' and 'the rights in

[57] See *Shaw*, 991–992.

[58] For air services arbitrations: see *United States* v. *France* (1963), 38 ILR 182 and (1978) 54 ILR 303; and *United States* v. *Italy* (1965), 45 ILR 393.

question' (being those of both states) (Article 51). Proportionality is thus an essential requirement. If the countermeasures are excessive, the injured state will itself have committed an internationally wrongful act. In many cases there will be no exact equivalence between the acts of the responsible state and the countermeasures. But the more closely countermeasures are related to the breach, the more likely it is that they will be proportionate. It is usually sufficient for there to be rough approximation. So the suspension by the United States of all Air France flights between Paris and Los Angeles, in response to France's refusal to allow US airlines flying between Los Angeles and Paris to use a smaller aircraft for the section between London and Paris (known to the cognoscenti as a 'change of gauge'), was held to be not 'clearly disproportionate'.[59] But everything depends on the particular facts and circumstances.

Procedural Conditions

Resort to countermeasures is exceptional action. Therefore, before embarking on them the injured state should take the procedural steps set out in Article 52. However, since they may not represent customary international law, the conditional tense ('should', rather than 'shall' or 'must') will be used here. First, the injured state should call upon the responsible state to cease its wrongful act and make reparation. In practice, it is likely that this requirement will have already been met by discussions – albeit brief and heated – between the two states. Second, the injured state should notify the responsible state of its decision to take countermeasures, and offer to negotiate. Third, since in many situations these two requirements may take too long, Article 52(2) recognises that the injured state may take 'such urgent countermeasures as are necessary to preserve its rights'. The 'rights' referred to are both the right to take countermeasures and the primary rights that are the subject matter of the dispute. Fourth, the countermeasures should be suspended 'without undue delay' if the wrongful act has ceased, or if the dispute is 'pending' before an international court or tribunal that has jurisdiction to make decisions binding on the parties. The dispute will be 'pending' only once the court or tribunal is in a position to deal with the case. If it is an ad hoc tribunal set up pursuant to a treaty, the dispute will be pending only when the tribunal is actually constituted, and this can take months. This pending provision presupposes that the court or tribunal will have the power to order effective interim measures of protection. If the dispute has been referred by a *national* of the injured state to a tribunal, countermeasures would be justified only in exceptional cases. Fifth, countermeasures may be taken or continued if the responsible state fails to implement the dispute settlement procedures in good faith, such as

[59] *United States* v. *France* (1978), 54 ILR 303, para. 83. See also *Gabčíkovo* (n. 54), at 56–57, paras. 85 and 87.

non-cooperation in the establishment or procedure of a tribunal, non-compliance with an interim measures order or refusal to accept the final decision.[60] Countermeasures should, of course, be terminated as soon as the responsible state has complied with its obligations of cessation and reparation (Article 53).

It is possible that a state may lose its right to take countermeasures if it delays doing so for so long that it is deemed to have waived its right to take them.

Sacrosanct Obligations

Article 50 lists four obligations which must never be affected by countermeasures: (a) to refrain from the threat or use of force; (b) to protect fundamental human rights; (c) the prohibition in international humanitarian law of reprisals; and (d) peremptory norms of general international law *(jus cogens).* Article 50(2) lists two other obligations which have important functions in relation to the resolution of the dispute that has given rise to the threat or use of countermeasures, and which must therefore also be respected: (a) obligations under any dispute settlement procedure applicable between the two states; and (b) obligations to respect the inviolability of diplomatic or consular agents, premises, archives and documents.

Necessity

Like countermeasures, 'necessity' is a concept which belongs to the sphere of state responsibility but which states may also use to justify non-performance of a treaty obligation.[61] As with fundamental change of circumstances in the VCLT, the doctrine of necessity is formulated negatively. Under Article 25 of the draft articles, it may not be invoked unless the act:

(a) is the only way for the state to safeguard an essential interest against a grave and imminent peril; and
(b) does not seriously impair an essential interest of the state or states towards which the obligation exists, or of the international community as a whole.

In the *Gabčíkovo (Hungary* v. *Slovakia)* case, the ICJ rejected Hungary's plea of necessity, emphasising that such ground for precluding wrongfulness could only be

[60] As noted at p. 366, the state taking the countermeasures needs to consider at the outset, in a case where it is acting in response to a breach of a treaty, to what extent the treaty itself includes provision specifically precluding that action.

[61] On the uneasy relationship between this area of state responsibility and treaty law, see M. Fitzmaurice, 'The Law of Treaties, the Law of State Responsibility and the Non-performance of Treaty Obligations: A View from the Case Law', in M. J. Bowman and D. Kritsiotis (eds.), *Conceptual and Contextual Perspectives on the Modern Law of Treaties* (Cambridge University Press, Cambridge 2018), 748–789.

accepted on an exceptional basis.[62] It emphasised the conditions which are now in Article 25 – 'essential interest', 'grave and imminent' peril, the 'only way' to safeguard the interest – and the state invoking necessity must not itself have contributed to the situation of necessity.[63] These therefore set a very high bar.

[62] See n. 54, at 40, para. 51. [63] 40–41, para. 52.

21

Succession to Treaties

> The international lawyer seeking a way out of this marshland is as likely as ever to be led into the centre of the miry bog itself.[1]

Despite this warning ringing in our ears, we must explore this subject in some detail. This is particularly so as the topic is not covered by the 1969 Convention (see Article 73), but is the subject of a later, much less satisfactory, convention.[2] Yet when a new state has come into being by becoming truly independent, it is important to know *which* of the treaties, bilateral and multilateral, applied to it when it was part of another state, and which still apply to it. This is known as succession to treaties. It is not a question only for the immediate aftermath of the birth of the new state. It could also become an issue with other states many years later, and especially if the new state has taken few or no steps to clarify the legal position.

When a state becomes party to a treaty, a legal nexus (connection) is established between the treaty and the territory of that state. In the years following the end of the Second World War, problems arose chiefly when colonies became independent. After the end of the Cold War, and the subsequent fragmentation of some states, different, and very practical, problems of treaty succession arose, developing a body of recent state practice in addition to that from the era of decolonisation. As a guide to today's problems of treaty succession, the value of state practice before the Second World War must now be rather doubtful.

There is also the related Vienna Convention on Succession of States in respect of State Property, Archives and Debts 1983.[3]

Vienna Convention on Succession of States in Respect of Treaties 1978

The 1978 Convention[4] resulted from work done by the ILC.[5] By July 2022, only twenty-three states were parties. No permanent members of the Security Council are yet

[1] T. Maluwa, 'Succession to Treaties in Post-Independence Africa', *African Journal of International and Comparative Law* (1992) 791–815, 810.

[2] Vienna Convention on Succession of States in respect of Treaties: 1946 UNTS 3 No. 33356; 17 ILM (1978) 1488.

[3] 22 ILM (1983) 298. As at July 2022, seven countries have acceded. It is not yet in force.

[4] See n. 2.

[5] See A. Watts, *The International Law Commission 1949–1998*, vol. II (Oxford University Press, Oxford 1999), 987–1208 for an overview, the ILC draft articles and commentary, and the Convention. *Oppenheim* has a summary of the Convention at 237–240, para. 69.

parties. But, thanks to the new states of Eastern Europe becoming parties to it in the 1990s, the 1978 Convention eventually entered into force in 1996. Since the Socialist Federal Republic of Yugoslavia (SFRY) had ratified the Convention, Bosnia and Herzegovina, Croatia, Macedonia, Serbia and Montenegro, and Slovenia each deposited an instrument of *succession*.[6]

Why did it take so long for it to collect the fifteen ratifications needed for it to enter into force? Some states may not have seen its relevance or importance to them, the era of decolonisation having almost come to an end; and during the period from the Treaty of Versailles 1919 until the end of the Cold War, some seventy years later, the division of the territory of states (outside the context of decolonisation) was a relatively rare occurrence.

But there were other reasons. At the time when the draft articles were being developed by the ILC, most state practice related to former colonies and was not consistent. Consequently, those rules of the 1978 Convention which are concerned with newly independent states are excessively complex, yet do not give adequate weight to the abundant state practice of concluding devolution agreements or, more importantly, making declarations of succession. Moreover, decolonisation was almost at its end by 1978, and, unless the successor state were to agree otherwise, the 1978 Convention does not apply to a succession of states that occurred before its entry into force (6 November 1996). Nor did the rules in the 1978 Convention about the break-up of states reflect modern state practice, though admittedly at the time there was little on which to draw. Therefore, most states may be excused as having seen little advantage in becoming parties.

In short, the 1978 Convention is largely an example of the progressive development of international law rather than a codification of customary international law, and is therefore *not* a reliable guide to the customary law rules on treaty succession.[7] But its eventual entry into force, practice following the end of the Cold War and decisions of the ICJ may have breathed some life into certain of its provisions.

The rules of customary international law on the subject are not easy to determine. This is hardly surprising: the circumstances vary widely, and the subject is politically sensitive. In the case of a *bilateral treaty*, much depends on what can be agreed, expressly or tacitly, between the successor state and a *third* state. The interests and perceptions of a successor state may differ significantly from those of the predecessor

[6] See *UN Multilateral Treaties* (Historical Information) for the Czech Republic and Slovakia as successor states to Czechoslovakia.

[7] See G. Hafner and G. Novak, 'State Succession in Respect of Treaty Relationships', in *Hollis, Oxford Guide*, 383–413, 385–386; A. Zimmermann, 'La Convention de Vienne sur la succession d'Etats en matière de traités codification réussie ou échouée?', in G. Distefano, G. Gaggioli, A. Hêche (eds.), *La convention de Vienne de 1978 sur la succession d'États en matière de traités* (Bruylant, Paris 2016), 1547–1580; A. Zimmermann and J. G. Devaney, 'Succession to Treaties and the Inherent Limits of International Law', in C. J. Tams, A. Tzanakopoulos and A. Zimmermann (eds.), *Research Handbook on the Law of Treaties* (Edward Elgar, Cheltenham UK, Northampton MA USA 2014), 505–540, 508–509.

state (if it still exists). Where it is possible for the successor state and its predecessor state to reach an agreement on succession issues, this will be important to third states, even though they will not be bound by such agreement. Problems with bilateral treaties are most satisfactorily resolved on the basis of agreements between the successor state and the third state. The question of succession to *multilateral* treaties is a particularly uncertain and controversial area. Although recent state practice may prove to be of some value, for the moment it may be safer to say that there are only certain customary law principles; for the rest, there is evolving state practice. Such residual rules of customary international law as do exist play a secondary role.

General Principles[8]

Certain general principles can be deduced with reasonable confidence:

(1) A new state does not succeed automatically to a treaty if the subject matter is closely linked to the *political* relations of the predecessor state with the other party. It will usually, but not always, be a bilateral treaty, such as a treaty of alliance. Anyway, to remain in force it will need the third state to agree to it applying, preferably expressly.

(2) A new state will succeed, without any action by it, to treaties (or at least to the legal situation created by them) relating to matters such as the status of territory, boundaries or the navigation of rivers. Although this principle is well established, its exact extent is not.[9]

(3) When a state has been absorbed by another, such as the German Democratic Republic by the Federal Republic of Germany in 1990,[10] and South Vietnam by North Vietnam in 1976, almost all treaties entered into by the absorbed state will either simply lapse or their fate will need to be discussed with the other parties. Under the 'moving-boundary principle', treaties of the absorbing state will generally extend to the absorbed state. But when there is a true union of two states, such as that of the Republic of Yemen and the People's Democratic Republic of Yemen in 1990, most treaties will continue to bind the successor state, at least as regards that part of its territory for which the treaties were in force before the union.[11] This is also the approach of Article 31 of the 1978 Convention.[12]

[8] For a survey of useful practice since the end of the Cold War up to 1999, see J. Klabbers, M. Koskenniemi, O. Ribbelink and A. Zimmermann (eds.), *State Practice Regarding State Succession and Issues of Recognition* (Kluwer Law, The Hague 1999), 80–116.

[9] See *Oppenheim*, 213, para. 62(a); Articles 11 and 12, 1978 Convention (n. 2); the Commentary in Distefano *et al.* (eds.) (n. 7), J.-P. Pancracio (Article 11), 373–397; G. Distefano (Article 12), 399–458; and Hafner and Novak (n. 7), 405–406.

[10] See BYIL 68 (1997) 520–529.

[11] See *UN Multilateral Treaties*, chapter I.2, note to the entry for Yemen.

[12] See also the Commentary on this Article, A.-L. Graf-Brugère, in Distefano *et al.* (eds.) (n. 7), 1069–1100.

(4) A new state will not normally succeed automatically to multilateral treaties; a successor state is usually free to choose. The practice of the UN Secretary-General, as depositary of the Genocide Convention 1948 and nearly 600 other multilateral treaties, has been to leave new states free to decide whether to deposit an instrument of succession or accession.[13] Some states make a general declaration of succession. The FRY made such a declaration on 2 April 1992,[14] though it did so on the basis that it was the continuation of Yugoslavia, not a successor state, as most other states believed it to be. It was thus no more than a political statement, not a declaration of succession.[15] (The rule in Article 34 of the 1978 Convention was based on very limited and partial state practice.)

Some writers consider that treaties which embody or reflect generally accepted rules of international law (in particular, those concerned with human rights or international humanitarian law, i.e., 'good law') bind a successor state by virtue of the concept of the acquired rights of the inhabitants of the state.[16] There is, however, no good authority for this view.[17] The Human Rights Committee has suggested that: 'the rights enshrined in the [ICCPR 1966] belong to the people living in the territory of the State Party ... such protection devolves with the territory and continues to belong to them, notwithstanding ... State succession'.[18] An alternative view is that, insofar as such a human rights treaty represents rules of customary international law, a successor state will be bound by those rules, but only as a matter of customary international law. The ICJ avoided deciding the issue in its judgment in *Genocide Convention* (Preliminary Objections) in 1996,[19] concluding that the FRY was a party to the Genocide Convention 1948 because it had declared its intention to remain bound by the treaties to which the SFRY had been a party. But, even when a new state is bound by customary rules reflected in a human rights treaty, rather than the treaty itself,

[13] See, e.g., *UN Multilateral Treaties*, chapter IV.1; and W. Schabas, *Genocide in International Law* (2nd ed., Cambridge University Press, Cambridge 2009), 593–605. The Swiss and US governments follow a similar practice.

[14] UN Docs S/23877 and A/46/915.

[15] See M. Wood, 'Participation of Former Yugoslav States in the United Nations', *Max Planck Yearbook of UN Law* (Martinus Nijhoff, Leiden 1997), 231–258.

[16] See R. Mullerson, 'The Continuity and Succession of States, by Reference to the Former USSR and Yugoslavia', ICLQ 42 (1993) 473, 490–492. Mullerson, an Estonian, was the Soviet expert on the Human Rights Committee.

[17] See *Oppenheim*, 212–213, para. 62(a); Hafner and Novak (n. 7), 407–409, esp. note 220.

[18] General Comment No. 26 (61), 8 December 1997: CCPR/C/21/Rev.1/Add.8/Rev.1.

[19] *Application of the Convention on the Prevention and Punishment of the Crime of Genocide (Bosnia and Herzegovina* v. *FRY*), Preliminary Objections, Judgment, ICJ Reports (1996) 595, at 610–612, paras. 17–23; 115 ILR 442. But see the separate opinion of Judge Weeramantry, para. 17. The International Criminal Tribunal for the Former Yugoslavia Appeals Chamber in its 20 February 2001 judgment in *Celebici* (40 ILM (2001) 652, note 132) saw that 'the practice of international organisations (UN, ILO, ICRC) and States shows that there was a customary norm on succession de jure to general treaties, which applies automatically to human rights treaties'. This may be seen as limited to the circumstances of that particular criminal case, and not as an authoritative statement of general international law.

this will have important practical consequences. The state will not have the legal right to attend meetings of the states parties. Nor will it be under any legal obligation to report to any monitoring body established by the treaty. These factors are not unimportant.

(5) The transfer of part of the metropolitan territory of a state to another state will not usually involve succession of treaties unless the two states have agreed otherwise. Under the 'moving-boundary principle', when Alsace-Lorraine was returned to France at the end of the First World War, German treaties ceased to apply and French treaties once again applied to it as to the rest of France.[20]

(6) Article 6 of the 1978 Convention stipulates that its rules apply only to the effects of a succession of states occurring in conformity with international law, thus excluding situations which arise from the unlawful use of force.[21]

These general principles do not take one very far, but may be better understood by an examination of some of the more recent state practice.

Former Colonies and Other Overseas Territories

Although since the Second World War some hundred colonies or other overseas territories, such as protectorates, protected states and trust territories, have attained their independence, the practice of newly independent states has not been consistent. It is therefore not possible to promulgate a set of rules of customary international law on state succession applicable in such situations. The most one can do is to summarise the main approaches which have been taken.

There are two *theoretical* starting points.[22] The first is the nineteenth-century theory of universal succession, which persisted up to the 1960s. According to this, a new state inherited all the treaty rights and obligations of the former colonial power insofar as they had been applicable to the territory before independence. This approach was reflected in the *devolution agreements* entered into by Iraq in 1931 and by some former Asian colonies in the 1940s and 1950s.[23] From 1955, all former British colonies in West Africa, except for the Gambia, concluded devolution agreements with the United Kingdom. These provided that, as from the date of independence, all obligations and responsibilities of the United Kingdom that arose from 'any valid international instrument' would be assumed by the new state, 'insofar as such instruments may be held to have application' to it; and the rights and benefits previously enjoyed by the United Kingdom, by virtue of the application of such instruments to the former colony, would

[20] D. O'Connell, *Law of State Succession* (Cambridge University Press, Cambridge 1967), 221 and 374–381.

[21] See Hafner and Novak (n. 7), 387, including footnotes, esp. note 48; and Commentary on Article 6, G. Gaggioli, in G. Distefano *et al.* (eds.) (n. 7), 181–225.

[22] See also Hafner and Novak (n. 7), 388–389; Zimmermann and Devaney (n. 7), 516–518.

[23] UK–Iraq (UKTS (1931) No. 15); Netherlands–Indonesia 1949 (69 UNTS 266 No. 3); France–Vietnam 1954 (161 BFSP 649); UK–Malaya 1957 (163 BFSP 46).

be enjoyed by the new state. Although these agreements created a presumption that a treaty that *could* apply to the new state *would* apply to it, they naturally left many questions unanswered.[24] A devolution agreement could not, of course, bind a third state that is party to a devolved treaty (and especially a bilateral treaty) unless it consented, expressly or tacitly. Nevertheless, a devolution agreement was useful in serving as a formal and public statement of the general attitude of the new state towards its treaty obligations.

Although they did not enter into devolution agreements, most former French colonies in Africa regarded themselves as successors to pre-independence treaties, and made declarations to that effect that they notified to the UN Secretary-General.[25]

The other starting point is the so-called *clean slate* doctrine, under which the new state is free to pick and choose the treaties to which it will succeed. This approach was followed most famously by the United States when it gained its independence from the United Kingdom in the late eighteenth century. However, even when the clean-slate doctrine is applied, treaties that concern territorial rights, such as boundary treaties and those granting rights of navigation or passage, will usually bind the new state, for obvious reasons.

The doctrine has been applied in different ways. Following the so-called 'Nyerere Doctrine', a number of former British territories made unilateral declarations in which they undertook that, for a specified period following independence, they would continue to apply all treaties validly concluded by the United Kingdom unless abrogated or modified by agreement. After that period the new state would 'regard such of these treaties which could not by application of the rules of customary international law be regarded as otherwise surviving, as having terminated'.[26] Such declarations do not, however, in the longer term resolve all succession problems. Once the time limit has been reached, the effect of the declaration is uncertain unless the position of the new state in respect of all bilateral and multilateral treaties that might apply to it has by then been made clear. This is particularly so for treaties entered into expressly for the territory by the former colonial power, though the ICJ has held that they bind the new state.[27] Another clean-slate approach, adopted by Zambia in 1964, was to avoid any general commitment to confirm or deny the continuing applicability of treaties within any specific period of time.

When a clean-slate declaration has been made by a former British territory, it has been the (albeit legally unnecessary) practice of the United Kingdom to circulate to

[24] Maluwa (n. 1), 804.

[25] For the Malagasy Republic's declaration, see UN Doc. A/CN. 4/150, 117, para. 87; and Maluwa (n. 1), 792.

[26] See the Declaration by Malawi, 24 November 1964, in the ILA study, *The Effect of Independence on Treaties* (London 1965), 388; Maluwa (n. 1), 806–807; *Oppenheim*, 231, note 21.

[27] *Case concerning rights of United States Nationals in Morocco*, ICJ Reports (1952) 176, at 193–194; 19 ILR 255.

UN members a disclaimer of any continued responsibility for the treaties formerly applied by it to the territory.[28]

The matter can, of course, be put beyond doubt by a treaty between the former territory and the third state. A Bahamas–United States exchange of notes of 1978 confirmed that on independence the UK–US Extradition Treaty 1931,[29] which had been extended to the Bahamas by the United Kingdom, continued in force for the Bahamas and the United States.[30]

(Because of the special circumstances, the arrangements made by China and the United Kingdom for Hong Kong's treaties are described at the end of this chapter.)

The Two German States

The Federal Republic of Germany–German Democratic Republic (FRG–GDR) Unification Treaty 1990[31] provided that, in principle, most bilateral or multilateral treaties entered into by the FRG would apply to the whole of the unified state (moving-boundary principle), and for consultations with the other parties regarding treaties to which only the former GDR had been a party. Although other parties were not bound by the treaty, most tacitly accepted what had been agreed, the terms of which had been notified to all UN members and to the depositaries of multilateral treaties. Consultations with over 135 states resulted in their agreement that most of the GDR's bilateral treaties had lapsed. Treaties which the FRG and the GDR had with Czechoslovakia and Poland concerning borders were discussed with the other parties and various agreements reached. Germany became party to only a few multilateral treaties to which the GDR alone had been a party.[32]

The Former Soviet Union

Russia

The dramatic changes to the Union of Soviet Socialist Republics in 1991 had some similarity to the process of decolonisation in that several republics broke away and became independent states, yet the state that had exercised sovereignty over them *continued*, though under the name of the principal constituent part of the Soviet Union, the Russian Federation (or Russia for short). The process was, however, different from decolonisation in that the republics had been part of the Soviet

[28] For such a disclaimer in relation to Hong Kong, see below. [29] UKTS (1935) No. 18.

[30] See *Bowe* v. *United States* [1988] CLR (Const.) 157, 169–172, 188–189. The 1931 treaty was replaced by a new Bahamas–US Extradition Treaty in 1990.

[31] Treaty on the Establishment of German Unity, 31 August 1990, Articles 11 and 12: 30 ILM (1991) 457.

[32] See *UN Multilateral Treaties*, chapter I.2, note to entry for Germany; AJIL (1992) 152–173; D. Papenfuss, 'The Fate of the International Treaties of the German Democratic Republic within the Framework of German Unification', AJIL (1998) 469–488. See also Klabbers *et al.* (n. 8), 82–90.

Union. The continuation of the Soviet/Russian state was reflected most prominently in the United Nations and other international organisations where the name of the USSR was simply replaced by that of the Russian Federation without any requirement to apply for membership.[33] Nevertheless, Russia formally declared that it would continue to comply with all the international obligations entered into by the Soviet Union.[34] Since Russia's assertion that it was the continuation of the USSR had been accepted,[35] the declaration would seem to have had a purpose more political than legal.

Similarly, Russia sought to agree with certain states a list of the *bilateral* treaties that would continue to apply between them. This was desirable for the sake of good order. There were treaties entered into by the Soviet Union that in practice concerned only a part or parts of the Soviet Union that became independent, and therefore had no application to Russia.

Former Soviet Republics

The practice with regard to treaty succession of Armenia, Azerbaijan, Belarus, Georgia, Kazakhstan, Kyrgyzstan, Moldova, Tajikistan, Turkmenistan, Ukraine and Uzbekistan (the three Baltic states are dealt with below) is instructive, even though it is not consistent. At first the United States boldly asserted that, as successor states of the Soviet Union, the former republics were obliged by international law to fulfil the treaty obligations of the Soviet Union, and sought to make it a precondition for the establishment of diplomatic relations that they should commit themselves to fulfil those obligations.[36] Although the responses from most of the new states were suitably equivocal, diplomatic relations were soon established.

The United States then proceeded to conclude exchanges of notes with each of them concerning their succession to *bilateral* treaties between the United States and the former Soviet Union. The notes recorded that, following a review that had identified treaties that had expired or become obsolete, the parties *confirmed* that treaties dating from as long ago as 1854, and listed in an annex, would *continue* in force.[37] This formulation is perhaps more consistent with the continuity principle than with the clean-slate approach. The exchanges of notes recorded that the governments took 'as a point of departure' the continuity principle in Article 34 of the 1978 Convention. That article provides that, when a part or parts of the territory of a state

[33] Y. Z. Blum, 'Russia Takes Over the Soviet Union's Seat at the United Nations', EJIL 3 (1992) 354–361; Klabbers *et al.* (n. 8), 98–100.

[34] See the footnote to the entry for the Russian Federation in *UN Multilateral Treaties*, chapter I.1.

[35] BYIL 63 (1992) 652–654.

[36] P. Williams, 'The Treaty Obligations of the Successor States of the Former Soviet Union, Yugoslavia, and Czechoslovakia: Do They Continue in Force?', *Denver Journal of International Law and Policy* (1994) 1–37; and Klabbers *et al.* (n. 8), 100–102.

[37] See, e.g., AJIL (1995) 761–762.

separate to form one or more states, and whether or not the predecessor state continues to exist, any treaty in force at the date of succession in respect of the *entire* territory of the predecessor state continues in force in respect of each successor state so formed; and any treaty in force at the date of succession in respect only of *that part* of the territory of the predecessor state that has become a successor state continues in force in respect of that successor state alone. These rules do not apply if (a) the states concerned otherwise agree, or (b) it appears from the treaty or is otherwise established that the application of the treaty in respect of the successor state would be incompatible with the object and purpose of the treaty or would radically change the conditions for its operation. The article thus envisages the possibility of agreements between the new state and other states about which treaties would continue in force, the need for such agreements being amply demonstrated by the difficulty of otherwise applying the rules.[38]

The United Kingdom informed all the former republics of the Soviet Union that, as appropriate, it regarded all *bilateral* treaties to which the United Kingdom and the Soviet Union were parties immediately before the new states' independence as remaining in force between them and the United Kingdom.[39] The United Kingdom then concluded exchanges of notes with former republics confirming which UK–USSR bilateral treaties each republic had succeeded to and which were thus regarded as continuing in force with the United Kingdom, 'without prejudice to the possibility that other bilateral treaties might remain in force . . . in accordance with international law'.[40]

The practice of the former Soviet republics with regard to *multilateral* treaties was mixed and often unclear. For example, although the Soviet Union was a party to the VCLT 1969, Georgia, Kazakhstan, Moldova, Tajikistan, Turkmenistan and Uzbekistan *acceded* to it. On the other hand, in 1994 Ukraine purported to *succeed* to CCAMLR 1980[41] on the basis of succession to the Soviet Union which, as Russia, remained a party. But since that Convention laid down certain preconditions for accession, Finland, Norway, Sweden, the United Kingdom and the United States were unable to accept the validity of the instrument of succession. However, since Ukraine had fulfilled the conditions for accession, those states informed the depositary that they would treat the instrument as one of *accession*.[42]

The Baltic States

Since Estonia, Latvia and Lithuania had been annexed unlawfully by the Soviet Union in 1940, when they regained their independence in 1991 they did not regard

[38] On the break-up of the USSR, see also V. Bilkova, 'La succession aux traités internationaux suite à la dissolution des fédérations. ex-socialistes après 1990', in Distefano *et al.* (eds.) (n. 7), 1805–1852; Zimmermann and Devaney (n. 7), 525–526.

[39] BYIL 63 (1992) 652–655 and BYIL 68 (1997) 535–536.

[40] See, e.g., the UK–Ukraine Exchange of Notes 1999, listing ten treaties: UKTS (2000) No. 46.

[41] 1329 UNTS 47 No. 22301; 19 ILM (1980) 837; UKTS (1982) No. 48; TIAS 10240.

[42] See also p. 339.

themselves as successor states to the Soviet Union but as states that had regained their sovereignty. Each informed the UN Secretary-General that they did not regard themselves as parties by succession to any treaties entered into by the Soviet Union.[43] But, being *realistic*, they *then* acceded to many *multilateral* treaties to which the Soviet Union had been a party, and to which Russia continues to be a party. There was, however, a problem with *bilateral* treaties entered into by the Soviet Union during the period of unlawful occupation: to maintain that they had no relevance would have been to ignore the reality of fifty years. With admirable pragmatism, agreements were therefore reached with some neighbouring states to regard certain of those treaties as in force, at least for the time being; and some bilateral treaties entered into in the period between the First and Second World Wars, when the three states were first independent, were agreed to be still applicable, the rest being obsolete or irrelevant by the 1990s.[44]

Former Yugoslav Republics

By 1992 or 1993, with the exception of Serbia and Montenegro (see below for the complicated legal story), the constituent republics of the former *Socialist* Federal Republic of Yugoslavia had all been recognised as independent sovereign states. Although the dissolution of the SFRY was anything but amicable, it created similar succession questions to the break-up of Czechoslovakia (see below), though the attitude of Serbia and Montenegro, which relabelled itself the Federal Republic of Yugoslavia, was a considerable complication.[45]

Bosnia and Herzegovina, Croatia, Macedonia and Slovenia

Each of these four new states informed the UN Secretary-General that it considered itself bound, by virtue of state succession, to multilateral treaties to which the SFRY had been bound. The SFRY was a party to the 1978 Convention, and the four new states each deposited instruments of succession to it. In doing so, they were apparently guided by Article 9(1) of that Convention (the making of a unilateral declaration is not enough to make the successor a party to a treaty), as well as by Article 34 of the same Convention. They therefore lodged instruments of succession with the relevant depositaries. The United Nations gives as the date of succession the date of deposit of the instruments (see Article 23 of the 1978 Convention). This may be

[43] *UN Multilateral Treaties*, chapter I.2, see notes to the entries for the three states; Mullerson (n. 16), 480–487.
[44] See Klabbers *et al.* (n. 8), 96.
[45] See Wood (n. 15); Conference on Yugoslavia Arbitration Commission: Opinions on Questions Arising from the Dissolution of Yugoslavia: 31 ILM (1992) 1488.

because the dates on which each of the former Yugoslav republics became independent were not clear.

Former republics of the SFRY also entered into *bilateral* treaty succession arrangements with various other states. Croatia[46] and Slovenia[47] concluded exchanges of notes with the United Kingdom confirming which treaties (and some MOUs) remained in force (or in effect). Slovenia concluded such confirmations with over twenty states.[48]

The Federal Republic of Yugoslavia (Serbia and Montenegro)

Under its previous name, the Federal Republic of Yugoslavia (FRY), Serbia and Montenegro[49] asserted that it was the *continuation* of the SFRY, in the same way as Russia was the continuation of the Soviet Union. The other states that were former republics of the SFRY, as well as most third states, did not accept this, or the FRY claim to the seat of Yugoslavia in the United Nations and other international organisations.[50] In September 1992, the UN General Assembly decided that the FRY could not continue automatically the membership of the SFRY; that it should apply for membership; and that, therefore, it could not take part in the work of the General Assembly.[51] The consistent advice from successive UN Legal Counsel was that the effect of this decision was that the membership of 'Yugoslavia' was not terminated or suspended, but its practical consequence was that FRY representatives could no longer take part in the work of the General Assembly, its subsidiary organs, or conferences or meetings convened by the General Assembly.[52]

This assertion by the FRY of continuity was reflected in its attitude to treaties to which the SFRY had been a party. A formal FRY declaration of 27 April 1992 stated that the 'FRY, continuing the State, international legal and political personality of the SFRY, shall strictly abide by all the commitments that the SFRY assumed internationally.'[53] (This did at least accord with the wishes of the EU member states and other states that the FRY should abide by the international obligations of the SFRY, albeit as one of its successor states.) Other states were therefore faced with a dilemma: they wanted the FRY to respect the treaties, and especially human rights conventions, to

46 Third Supplementary List: UKTS (1997) No. 80.

47 Second Supplementary List: UKTS (1998) No. 39.

48 See Klabbers *et al.* (n. 8), 106–110.

49 In 2006 Montenegro became independent and joined the United Nations. See also *Genocide* (*Bosnia and Herzegovina* v. *Serbia and Montenegro*), ICJ Reports (2007) 43, at 73–76, paras. 67–79.

50 BYIL 63 (1992) 655–658. See also the reports of the Badinter Commission (92 ILR 162, 166, 194, 199, 202 and 206). The ICJ dodged the question in *Application of the Convention on the Prevention and Punishment of the Crime of Genocide (Bosnia and Herzegovina* v. *FRY*) (Provisional Measures), ICJ Reports (1993) 3, at 11–14, paras. 14–18; 32 ILM (1993) 888; 95 ILR 1.

51 See UNSC Resolutions 757 (1992), 777 (1992), 821 (1993) and 1074 (1996); UNGA Resolutions 47/1, 47/229 and 48/88; 31 ILM (1992) 1421.

52 See UN Doc. A/47/485. See also Wood (n. 15) and the many articles referred to.

53 See UN Doc. A/46/915 and *UN Multilateral Treaties*, Historical Information, entry for former Yugoslavia.

which the SFRY had been a party, but they could not accept the FRY as a party on the basis of continuation of statehood. It was not only a matter of principle: acceptance of the FRY's assertion of continuation could have an effect on the important question of succession to other rights and obligations of the SFRY, especially with regard to property and debts. The dilemma persisted even after the FRY was formally recognised as a state in 1996. It also caused problems for meetings of treaty parties in which the FRY wished to participate.

After the fall of Milošević in 2000, these problems were resolved. The FRY accepted that it was one of the successor states to the SFRY, and so was admitted as a *new* member of the United Nations on 1 November 2000. It then proceeded formally to succeed to the multilateral treaties to which the SFRY had been a party, or accede to others, such as the Climate Change Convention 1992.[54] On 12 March 2001, in various notes to the UN Secretary-General as depositary of many multilateral treaties, the FRY made over 240 notifications of succession to multilateral treaties and confirmed declarations made by the SFRY when signing or adhering to various treaties deposited with him.

When the United Kingdom recognised the FRY on 9 April 1996, a letter from the foreign secretary to the FRY president confirmed that 'as appropriate, we regard treaties and agreements in force to which the United Kingdom and the SFRY were parties as remaining in force between the United Kingdom and the FRY'.[55]

The problem of *bilateral* treaties was resolved pragmatically by some states separately agreeing with the FRY a list of those treaties between them and the SFRY that would remain in force. The United Kingdom signed on 3 April 1998 a 'record of a meeting' confirming this arrangement, to which was annexed a list of twenty-five treaties.[56]

The most one can say about treaty succession with regard to the FRY is that the situation has to be viewed and assessed in the light of its own particular facts.[57]

Between 1992 and the date when the FRY accepted that it was not the continuation of the SFRY and had not been a member of the United Nations, it had purported to take certain treaty actions which could only be done by a UN member, such as purporting to accept the general jurisdiction of the ICJ. This and similar matters were subsequently regularised.[58]

The preamble to the Agreement on Succession 2001[59] recognises that Bosnia and Herzegovina, Croatia, the Federal Republic of Yugoslavia, Macedonia (now North Macedonia) and Slovenia are 'the five successor States to the former Socialist Federal Republic of Yugoslavia'.

[54] See above on the problem caused by the Vienna formula in that Convention. Even though the SFRY had been a party to the Genocide Convention 1948, FRY *acceded* to it with a new reservation.

[55] BYIL 67 (1996) 707.

[56] See the entry for Yugoslavia, Federal Republic of, in the First Supplementary List of 1998: UKTS (1998) No. 28.

[57] Klabbers *et al.* (n. 8), 104–106. [58] See n. 53. [59] 2262 UNTS 253 No. 40296; 41 ILM (2002) 1.

Kosovo

Later, in 2008, Kosovo declared its independence from Serbia (of which it was an autonomous province). Kosovo has been recognised as a state by over one hundred countries, including EU states and the United States, but not by Serbia, China and Russia.[60] The ICJ declared in its Advisory Opinion in 2010 that the declaration of independence did not violate general international law.[61] This was potentially important because the 1978 Convention applies its rules only to the effects of a succession of states occurring in conformity with international law.[62] Kosovo's Constitution includes provision that:

> International agreements and other acts relating to international cooperation that are in effect on the day this Constitution enters into force will continue to be respected until such agreements or acts are renegotiated or withdrawn from in accordance with their terms or until they are superseded by new international agreements or acts covering the same subject areas and adopted pursuant to this Constitution.[63]

And its declaration of independence stated:

> We hereby undertake the international obligations of Kosovo, including those concluded on our behalf by [UNMIK – UN Interim Administration Mission in Kosovo] and treaty and other obligations of the former [SFRY] to which we are bound as a former constituent part, including the Vienna Conventions on diplomatic and consular relations.[64]

Following the declaration, Kosovo concluded exchanges of notes with a number of states concerning the continuity of treaties, for example with the United Kingdom, in respect of treaties to which the UK and UNMIK, and the UK and the SFRY, and as appropriate the FRY, were parties.[65]

Former Czechoslovakia

At midnight on 31 December 1992 Czechoslovakia was dissolved and was succeeded by two states: the Czech Republic and Slovakia. Both declared themselves to be successors to Czechoslovakia and committed to fulfilling its treaty and other international

60 See also pp. 83–84.
61 *Accordance with International Law of the Unilateral Declaration of Independence in Respect of Kosovo*, Advisory Opinion, ICJ Reports (2010) 403, at 452, para. 122.
62 Article 6. See also I. Panoussis, 'La Succession d'États aux Traités à l'Epreuve du Cas Kosovar', in Distefano *et al.* (eds.) (n. 7), 1853–1890, 1862.
63 Article 145 Kosovo Constitution: available at the Kosovo Assembly website.
64 Declaration of Independence (para. 9), 17 February 2008, http://news.bbc.co.uk/1/hi/world/europe/7249677.stm.
65 See Q. Qerimi and S. Krasniqi, 'Theories and Practice of State Succession to Bilateral Treaties: The Recent Experience in Kosovo', *German Law Journal* (2013) 1639–1659, 1640 and 1655.

obligations. Both sides consciously applied the rules in Article 34 of the 1978 Convention.[66] There was no suggestion that the Czech Republic, though the larger of the two states, was the continuation of Czechoslovakia.

The policy adopted by both states with regard to *multilateral* treaties to which Czechoslovakia had been a party was that each would be bound, as from the dissolution, by all of them, including any reservations or declarations. Both states regarded themselves as bound by virtue of a state succession that left them no discretion in the matter.[67] In addition, each state regarded itself as a signatory to all those multilateral treaties that had been signed, but not ratified, before the dissolution. The two states each sent notes to this effect to the UN Secretary-General and other depositaries, who circulated them to the interested states. No objections were raised.

Bilateral treaties entered into by Czechoslovakia were regarded by the two new states as continuing to apply, except insofar as it would not be appropriate. For example, the application of certain treaties had always been limited to the territory of Slovakia, in particular the 1977 treaty regarding the Danube Dam Project. In *Gabčíkovo (Hungary* v. *Slovakia)*,[68] the ICJ decided that Article 12 of the 1978 Convention (succession does not, as such, affect territorial regimes) reflected a rule of customary international law and applied to the treaty; thus, Slovakia's succession to Czechoslovakia did not affect the application of the treaty to Slovakia, it becoming binding on Slovakia alone on the dissolution of Czechoslovakia.

The Czech Republic and Slovakia each had discussions with certain states that had had bilateral treaties with Czechoslovakia. The main purpose was to seek confirmation that, unless there was a special reason, all the treaties would continue to apply to the new states. The discussions were also an opportunity to consider whether some treaties might be terminated or be replaced by new ones, particularly taking into account the political changes that had taken place with the end of the communist regime. In 1996, following a joint examination of bilateral agreements and 'arrangements' (i.e., MOUs), the Czech Republic and the United Kingdom entered into an exchange of notes confirming that eighteen treaties and MOUs, some dating from the 1920s, would be regarded as remaining in force or effect. The exchange was expressed to 'constitute *joint confirmation* of the position regarding bilateral agreements and arrangements between our two countries'. Accordingly, the exchange, not being a treaty, was not published as one and the United Nations was not informed. Instead, an information note was included in the *United Kingdom Treaty Series*.[69] By the end

[66] See above and *UN Multilateral Treaties* (Historical Information), entries for the Czech Republic and Slovakia; V. Mikulka, 'The Dissolution of Czech Republic and Succession in Respect of Treaties', in M. Mrak (ed.), *Succession of States* (Martinus Nijhoff, The Hague and Boston 1999), 109–125.

[67] Mikulka (n. 66), 47–48.

[68] ICJ Reports (1997) 7, at 69–73, paras. 116–124; 37 ILM (1998) 162; 116 ILR 1.

[69] See the Third Supplementary List for 1996: UKTS (1996) No. 96; BYIL 67 (1996) 755–759. For Slovakia, see a similar exchange of notes in 1999: UKTS (2000) No. 135, 31.

of 1998, the Czech Republic had made similar arrangements with some seventy states, and Slovakia had made over thirty.

The arrangements the Czech Republic made with Germany and Bosnia and Herzegovina included, respectively, some treaties between Czechoslovakia and the German Democratic Republic that had remained in force after reunification, and treaties between Czechoslovakia and the former SFRY.[70]

Multilateral Treaties: Role of the Depositary

If a successor state does not deposit an instrument of succession, the depositary is under no obligation to inquire as to its position. If asked by a successor state about procedure, a depositary should do no more than indicate the possible options. However, due to their particular position, when the UN Secretary-General is depositary of a multilateral treaty to which the predecessor state was a party, it is now their practice to write to the new state inviting it to confirm whether it considers itself to be bound by the treaty.

The depositary should, of course, notify the parties of any communication from the successor state and await their responses. Information issued by a depositary about the status of a treaty should distinguish between states which have deposited (1) instruments of ratification, acceptance or approval, (2) instruments of accession and (3) declarations of succession. In noting a succession in its records, the depositary should not delete the details of when and by what means the predecessor state became a party. This may be historically important.

'Yugoslavia'

The untidy status of the Federal Republic of Yugoslavia was also reflected for a period in its position with regard to multilateral treaties deposited with the UN Secretary-General. Since neither the UN General Assembly, nor any other intergovernmental organ representative of the (so-called) international community, nor any treaty organ with regard to a particular treaty, had taken a decision on this matter, the UN Secretary-General stated that he was not in a position to decide on disputed questions related to the participation of the FRY in a particular treaty for which he is depositary. And since the General Assembly had not terminated or suspended the membership of 'Yugoslavia' in the United Nations, the Secretary-General continued to list under 'Yugoslavia' treaty actions (ratifications etc.) by the SFRY *and* the FRY.[71] Following the fall of Milošević in 2000, the FRY applied for membership of the United Nations and was admitted. On 4 February 2003 it changed its name to Serbia and

[70] Mikulka (n. 66), 56–62; Klabbers *et al.* (n. 8), 110–112.

[71] Advice of the UN Legal Counsel annexed to ICAO Doc. A32-WP/175, 25 September 1998. See *UN Multilateral Treaties* (Historical Information), entry for Yugoslavia.

Montenegro, and drew up new constitutional arrangements, Montenegro becoming independent in 2006. Treaty actions undertaken by Yugoslavia were listed against the designation 'Serbia and Montenegro' until 2 June 2006. Treaty actions undertaken by the former Yugoslavia appear in footnotes, against the designation 'former Yugoslavia'.[72]

The five original successor states to the SFRY concluded the Agreement on Succession 2001 (but *not* succession to treaties), which entered into force in 2004.[73]

Date of Succession

There is no consistent practice as to the date on which succession takes effect, but the better (and logical) view is that it is the date of independence, the essence of succession to treaty rights and obligations being that the notification of succession is merely formal confirmation of what has already happened by operation of law, even though the confirmation may take some time in coming. But the matter may be treated differently when it is not possible to determine the exact date on which a new state came into being.[74] If the new state does not wish to be bound immediately, the correct course may be for it to accede when it is ready.

Domestic Implications of Treaty Succession

Treaty succession is not a subject of concern only to states and international lawyers; it can cause problems for others. Where a treaty has to be given effect in domestic law, the question of whether a new state has succeeded to it can cause a very real problem. The operation in domestic law of a treaty such as the Recovery Abroad of Maintenance Convention 1956,[75] or of the New York Convention on the Recognition and Enforcement of Foreign Arbitral Awards 1958,[76] will depend on whether the states concerned are parties to it. How that is decided depends on the relevant national legal system, but in all cases a decision has to be taken at the national level as to whether a state has succeeded to the treaty. In taking that decision, the national courts may look for guidance from government. But in some cases government will be in no position to give authoritative advice. There is no easy solution; each case has to be dealt with in the light of its own particular circumstances. In some ways, the problem of the FRY is not as difficult to deal with as some others where the position of the successor state is not clear. The FRY was clear that it was a party to all the treaties to which the SFRY had been a party: it was just that the FRY took a different view from others as to the *basis* on which it was a party. Thus, taking its cue from the

[72] See *UN Multilateral Treaties* (Historical Information), entry for Yugoslavia.
[73] See n. 59. Montenegro later made it six. [74] See above regarding the former Yugoslav republics.
[75] 268 UNTS 3 No. 3850; UKTS (1975) No. 85.
[76] 330 UNTS 3 No. 4739; UKTS (1976) No. 20; TIAS 6997.

judgment of the ICJ in the *Genocide Convention (Bosnia and Herzegovina* v. *Yugoslavia)* case, it should have been legitimate for a court to conclude that the FRY was a party to all treaties to which the SFRY had been a party.

Hong Kong and Macao

The circumstances of the handover of Hong Kong to China at midnight on 30 June 1997 were unique and do not provide much in the way of insight into the more usual treaty problems. But because the arrangements made for the continuation after the handover of Hong Kong's existing treaty relations are of interest beyond China and the United Kingdom, they are worth explaining in more detail. The regime for the Macao Special Administrative Region (SAR) is similar to that of the Hong Kong SAR.[77] Although both SARs are part of China, a special treaty regime – based on the principle of 'one country, two systems' – has been established for each of them.

Continued Application of Treaties

It was essential that there should be substantial continuity in Hong Kong's treaty relations after the handover. As the United Kingdom's most economically developed colony, and one of the world's larger economies, a considerable number of bilateral and multilateral treaties already applied to Hong Kong, either by virtue of their extension by the United Kingdom (over 200) or because Hong Kong had become a party in its own right. It was thus important for the future health and development of the Hong Kong economy that the framework of treaties within which Hong Kong operated should continue, and that there should be no doubt as to which treaties would continue to apply after the handover. The matter was therefore approached in a highly methodical way.

The future status of Hong Kong was agreed between China and the United Kingdom in a treaty of 19 December 1984, entitled Joint Declaration on the Question of Hong Kong.[78] After handover, Hong Kong would have the status of a SAR of China and be known as the 'Hong Kong Special Administrative Region' (HKSAR). It would be entitled to a high degree of autonomy, except in foreign and defence affairs, which are the responsibility of the Central People's Government (CPG). Although the governing principles with regard to treaties were laid down, there was no mention of 'succession', since that might imply that China had

[77] See the statements by China (n. 3) and Portugal, recorded in *UN Multilateral Treaties* (Historical Information).

[78] 1399 UNTS 33 No. 23391; 23 ILM (1984) 1366; UKTS (1985) No. 26. The Joint Declaration entered into force on 28 May 1985. See also P. Slinn, 'Le règlement sino-britannique de Hong-Kong', AFDI (1985) 167–190; and P. Slinn, 'Aspects juridiques du retour de Hong-Kong a la Chine', AFDI (1996) 273–295. See also BYIL 70 (1989) 593–598 and BYIL 68 (1997) 529–535.

previously validly ceded sovereignty to the United Kingdom, which China had never accepted. Section XI of Annex I to the Joint Declaration provides, in part, that:

> The application to the HKSAR of international agreements to which the People's Republic of China is or becomes a party shall be decided by the CPG, in accordance with the circumstances and needs of the HKSAR, and after seeking the views of the HKSAR Government. International agreements to which the People's Republic of China is not a party, but which are implemented in Hong Kong, may remain implemented in the HKSAR.

These general principles needed detailed elaboration by the Sino-British Joint Liaison Group (JLG) established by the Joint Declaration. The JLG was mandated in Annex II to the Joint Declaration with considering 'action to be taken by the two Governments to ensure the continued application of international rights and obligations affecting Hong Kong'. The JLG met until the end of 1999 as a forum in which the two governments were able to exchange views on matters relating to the implementation of the Joint Declaration. Multilateral and bilateral treaties were discussed separately.

Multilateral Treaties

Over a ten-year period, the JLG examined about 225 multilateral treaties and agreed that all but a handful would continue to apply to the HKSAR. The treaties examined were (a) treaties to which the United Kingdom was a party and which had been extended by the United Kingdom to Hong Kong, whether or not China was a party (in fact, it was not a party to over eighty treaties), but that would continue to apply to the HKSAR if China agreed, and (b) treaties to which China was a party but the United Kingdom was not.

The JLG also agreed on the mechanism by which the other parties to the treaties would be informed of what had been agreed. This was done in two parts. First, on 20 June 1997, shortly before the handover, China sent a diplomatic note to the UN Secretary-General (with a request that he bring it to the attention of the members of the United Nations and of the UN specialised agencies) notifying him that as from 1 July 1997 the treaties listed in Annex I to the note 'will be applied' to the HKSAR.[79] The Annex listed 127 multilateral treaties to which China was a party and which: (a) had applied to Hong Kong before 1 July 1997; or (b) because they concern foreign affairs (e.g., the UN Charter) or defence (e.g., disarmament treaties) had to apply to the entire territory of China; or (c) were not applied to Hong Kong before 1 July 1997, but which it had been decided should apply to the HKSAR as from that date (e.g., the revised Berne Copyright Convention). Annex II to the note listed eighty-seven treaties which already applied to Hong Kong, but to which China was not then a party. The note said

[79] 36 ILM (1997) 1675–1683, UKTS (1997) No. 80, 21–31. See also *UN Multilateral Treaties* (Historical Information), entries for China and the United Kingdom.

they 'would continue to apply' to the HKSAR as from 1 July 1997. The effect of Annex II was to make China a party to those treaties in respect of the HKSAR only.

The Chinese Note was matched by a Note to the UN Secretary-General from the United Kingdom stating that from 1 July 1997 the United Kingdom would cease to be responsible for the international rights and obligations arising from the application of treaties to Hong Kong.[80] A list of 231 treaties was annexed. This was seventeen more than listed in the Chinese Note, since the British Note included treaties which would no longer apply to the HKSAR.[81]

Second, China sent a separate Note to the depositary in respect of each treaty in which it explained the legal basis for the continued application of the treaty to the HKSAR: as from handover, treaties to which China was also a party 'will apply', the ones to which it was not a party 'will continue to apply', and China would assume responsibility for the international rights and obligations arising from the application of treaties to the HKSAR. The notes also specified the reservations and declarations which would apply to the HKSAR. These were for the most part the same as those that had been made previously in respect of Hong Kong, with suitable adaptations. Reservations and declarations made by China on becoming a party to them were not extended to the HKSAR, except where this had been agreed by the British and Chinese governments. China's reservations regarding provisions for the compulsory jurisdiction of the ICJ were extended to the HKSAR, as well as declarations about Taiwan. It was considered necessary for the parties to the treaties to be told formally of the continued application of reservations and declarations, and modifications to them, and since no party has objected, they are presumed to have acquiesced.

The Chinese Notes to the depositaries were matched by Notes from the United Kingdom by which it informed them that, as from 1 July 1997, it would cease to be responsible for the international rights and obligations arising from the application of treaties to Hong Kong. These included that most important human rights treaty the ICCPR 1966. China was not a party to it,[82] and it was therefore not included in Annex II to the Chinese Note to the Secretary-General regarding treaties which China had agreed would continue to apply to the HKSAR. However, in Annex I, section XIII of the Joint Declaration it is provided that the '*provisions* of [the Covenant] as applied to Hong Kong shall remain in force'. This was reiterated in the Chinese Note to the UN Secretary-General of 20 June 1997.[83] In addition, the Basic Law (the Constitution of the HKSAR) provides that the provisions of the Covenant 'shall be implemented through the laws of the [HKSAR]' (i.e., Article 39 of the Basic Law). Information on the implementation in the HKSAR of the provisions of the Covenant is prepared by

[80] 36 ILM (1997) 1684–1691; UKTS (1997) No. 80, 9–21; see BYIL 68 (1997) 536–537.

[81] See *UN Multilateral Treaties* (Historical Information), entries for China and the United Kingdom.

[82] In October 1998 China signed the Covenant, but has not yet ratified it.

[83] See *UN Multilateral Treaties* (Historical Information) entry for China, n. 13. See also the UK Note of 1 July 1997 in BYIL 68 (1997) 537–538.

the HKSAR and transmitted by the CPG to the Human Rights Committee established by the Covenant.

Thus, with a few exceptions, multilateral treaties that had applied to Hong Kong before handover continued to apply thereafter in all essential respects.

Bilateral Treaties with Third States

Bilateral treaties between the United Kingdom and third states (i.e., other than China) which had been extended to Hong Kong, and treaties concluded by Hong Kong under entrustment, could, under the terms of the Joint Declaration, have continued to apply to the HKSAR. It is not necessarily a matter of great concern to other parties if a state succeeds to the rights and obligations under a multilateral treaty. But a bilateral treaty is the result of (often intense) bargaining, particularly if the subject is economic or commercial relations, or if it involves important aspects of sovereignty. Thus, as with newly independent states, it could not be assumed that a third state would be willing to accept that a bilateral treaty would continue to apply to the HKSAR, even with any necessary technical adjustments. It was therefore agreed in the JLG that *none* of the then existing bilateral treaties with third states would apply to the HKSAR after handover. Instead, a process was agreed by which, following specific agreement in the JLG, Hong Kong was entrusted by the United Kingdom to negotiate and conclude directly with third states the bilateral treaties which it would need in the future. Such treaties would then apply to the HKSAR after handover.

Thus, before handover a substantial number of states concluded treaties with Hong Kong on such matters as air services, investment promotion and protection, surrender of fugitive offenders, mutual legal assistance in criminal matters and transfer of prisoners,[84] even though sometimes the third state already had a treaty on the same subject with China. In some cases the treaties, such as air services agreements, replaced treaties between the third state and the United Kingdom to the extent to which they had applied to Hong Kong. Most of the replacement treaties concluded by Hong Kong recited in their preamble that the government of Hong Kong was 'duly authorised to conclude this Agreement by the sovereign government which is responsible for its foreign affairs'. Since the handover more bilateral treaties have been entered into by the HKSAR.

Legal Effect of the Arrangements for Third States

The UN Secretary-General, as depositary of some fifty of the multilateral treaties applicable to the HKSAR, accepted that the arrangements are effective, as did other

[84] For example, the Hong Kong–US Agreement for the Surrender of Fugitive Offenders 1996 (which is now suspended): 36 ILM (1997) 844; the Hong Kong–US Agreement on the Transfer of Sentenced Persons 1997: 36 ILM (1997) 860; the Hong Kong–Japan IPPA 1997: 36 ILM (1997) 1425.

depositaries. The parties to various treaties also took the same view. No party to a multilateral treaty has objected to the continued application of a treaty to the HKSAR. For example, the Assembly of the International Oil Pollution Compensation Fund agreed that the International Oil Pollution Compensation Fund Convention 1971[85] could continue to apply to the HKSAR even though China is not a party. A similar attitude was exhibited by third states with respect to new bilateral treaties concluded by them with Hong Kong in the period leading up to the handover. Since they were all signed only after China had signified its approval in the JLG, and were designed to continue after the handover, they did not need further action by either China or the third state, and this was made abundantly clear to the negotiators of the third states.

A similar procedure was used for Macao.[86]

[85] 1110 UNTS 57 No. 17146; UKTS (1978) No. 95.

[86] See the statements by China and Portugal, recorded in *UN Multilateral Treaties* (Historical Information).

22

International Organisations

I don't want to belong to any club that would have me as a member.[1]

Given their importance for treaties, international organisations also deserve a separate chapter. There is no agreed definition of 'international organisation', but for present purposes it is an international legal entity created by a multilateral treaty, with international legal personality and principally with states as members. Such organisations are sometimes referred to as 'intergovernmental': see Article 2(1)(i).

International organisations grew out of the diplomatic conferences of the nineteenth century, as states sought more effective ways to deal with problems caused by the rapid development of international society.[2] Thus, the International Telegraphic (later Telecommunication) Union (ITU) and the Universal Postal Union (UPU) were founded in the 1860s. There are now countless international organisations, ranging from large ones with global responsibilities and virtually universal membership, such as the United Nations and so-called UN specialised agencies, to regional or international, but more narrowly focused organisations, such as the (very large) European Union and the (tiny) International Whaling Commission. Although they share certain characteristics, each international organisation is different and must be studied separately.

The importance of international organisations for treaties is fourfold. First, they are (generally) creations of treaties. Second, the international legal personality of the organisation is an important element. Third, being subjects of international law, they can, and do, conclude many treaties with other such subjects, both states and international organisations. Fourth, today most multilateral treaties are negotiated and concluded within international organisations or at conferences convened by them.

The European Union will be discussed at the end of the chapter, at pp. 412–414.

Establishment by Treaty

An international organisation is normally established by treaty, which is usually referred to as the constituent (or governing or founding) instrument, or sometimes

[1] Groucho Marx, *Groucho and Me* (New York, 1959), chapter 26.

[2] See J. Klabbers, *An Introduction to International Organizations Law* (4th ed., Cambridge University Press, Cambridge 2022), 16–23.

constitution, and will normally be for an indefinite period. The International Commission of Jurists (a legal entity only under Swiss law, and whose members are *not* states) is therefore *not* an international organisation as here defined.[3]

Many constituent instruments provide for their amendment or revision. Articles 108 and 109 of the UN Charter are the most effective, in that once an adopted amendment has been ratified by two-thirds of the UN membership, including all five permanent members, it comes into force for *all* members. However, for political reasons the only important amendment was in 1965 when the size of the Security Council was increased from its original eleven members to fifteen, and the majority needed to adopt a resolution (provided there is no veto by a permanent member) increased from seven to nine. A further increase has been actively discussed for over thirty years, but nothing has been decided due to the absence of any agreement on which states should be new permanent members (for every important candidate there is a credible rival); whether there might be some new and rotating permanent members; and the powers new permanent members would have.

Some constituent instruments have similar provisions (though without the permanent member hurdle), but some do not provide that, once adopted, an amendment will bind all members, though that may be implicit. Others provide that the amendment will bind only those who have ratified it. The constituent instrument of the International Civil Aviation Organization (ICAO) provides that the ICAO Assembly can provide that a member state that has not ratified an amendment to the constituent instrument, within a specified period after that amendment comes into force, shall cease to be a member.[4]

There are several international organisations that regularly replace their constituent instruments. Since the 1880s, the unions created by the Paris and Berne Conventions for the Protection of Industrial Property and of Literary and Artistic Works, respectively, have been revised on several occasions. Each is an amended version of the original Convention, which continues to exist, as does the union as constituted by the original Convention. When a state accedes to the most recent Convention, but is silent as to whether its accession is valid for previous Conventions, the practice of the unions is to regard the acceding state as having tacitly accepted the original Convention and all subsequent amendments.[5]

Interpretation of the Constituent Instrument

If the constituent instrument was concluded after the entry into force of the VCLT, that Convention will apply to it (Articles 4 and 5), insofar as the states parties to the

[3] See International Commission of Jurists/Commission international de juristes at: www.icj.org. It should *not* be confused with the International Court of Justice at www.icj-cij.org, which, of course, is the principal judicial organ of the United Nations.

[4] Article 94 Chicago Convention 1944: 15 UNTS 295 No. 102; UKTS (1953) No. 8; www.icao.int.

[5] For the texts of the Berne and Paris Conventions, see at: www.wipo.int.

instrument are parties to the Convention. If not, the Convention will apply only as customary international law.

When interpreting a constituent instrument, one needs also to take into account the relevant rules of the organisation (Article 5). In most cases, this will not be necessary, as Articles 31, 32 and 33 are normally adequate for the purposes of the constituent instruments of the United Nations (the Charter), and of other international organisations.

Constituent instruments have, however, been considered by the ICJ as treaties with 'certain special characteristics' or 'of a particular type'. So, in the Advisory Opinion on the legality of nuclear weapons, it stated:

> their object is to create new subjects of law endowed with a certain autonomy, to which the parties entrust the task of realizing common goals. Such treaties can raise specific problems of interpretation owing, *inter alia*, to their character which is conventional and at the same time institutional; the very nature of the organization created, the objectives which have been assigned to it by its founders, the imperatives associated with the effective performance of its functions, as well as its own practice, are all elements which may deserve special attention when the time comes to interpret these constituent treaties.[6]

It has been argued that, in its advisory opinion in *IMCO Maritime Safety Committee*,[7] the ICJ adopted a textual approach, though it also considered subsequent practice and the general purpose of the IMCO (now IMO) Convention. There is more evidence of a teleological approach in the *Reparation for Injuries Suffered*[8] and *Effects of Awards* cases,[9] and the *Nuclear Weapons Advisory Opinion* referred to above.[10] The last of these cases also draws out the relevance of the practice of the organisation,[11] a point picked up by Conclusion 12 of the ILC Conclusions on Subsequent Agreements and Subsequent Practice of 2018.[12] The situation varies, however, according to the constituent instrument and type of organisation, particularly in the case of a regional

6 *Legality of the Use by a State of Nuclear Weapons in Armed Conflict (Request by WHO)*, Advisory Opinion, ICJ Reports (1996) 66, 75, para. 19; 35 ILM (1996) 809; 110 ILR 1.

7 *Constitution of the Maritime Safety Committee of the Inter-Governmental Maritime Consultative Organization*, Advisory Opinion, ICJ Reports (1960) 150; 30 ILR 426.

8 *Reparation for Injuries Suffered in the Service of the United Nations*, Advisory Opinion, ICJ Reports (1949) 174; 16 ILR 318.

9 *Effects of Awards of Compensation made by the UN Administrative Tribunal*, Advisory Opinion, ICJ Reports (1954) 47, at 53.

10 See n. 6. See also C. Brölmann, 'Specialized Rules of Treaty Interpretation: International Organizations', in *Hollis, Oxford Guide*, 524–544, 526–533; *Gardiner*, 126–129, 282–285; N. Blokker, 'Constituent Instruments', in J. K Cogan, I. Hurd and I. Johnstone (eds.), *The Oxford Handbook of International Organizations* (Oxford University Press, Oxford 2016), 943–961; H. G. Schermers and N. M. Blokker, *International Institutional Law* (Brill Nijhoff, Leiden, Boston 2018), 871–885.

11 *Nuclear Weapons Advisory Opinion* (n. 6), 76, para. 21.

12 ILC Draft Conclusions on subsequent agreements and subsequent practice in relation to the interpretation of treaties, Report of the ILC on the Work of its 68th session, 2016, UNGA 71st Session, Supplement No. 10, A71/10, 118–240, 93–106.

international organisation such as the European Union (in respect of the TEU and TFEU),[13] where the CJEU (and other institutions) have established their own interpretative principles based on their view of the special nature of the EU legal order.[14]

Constituent instruments do not generally specify which organ of the organisation is competent to interpret them, though the obvious organ is the assembly of parties or an equivalent body. Yet, in the course of their work, other organs will sometimes have to take a view as to the meaning of a particular provision of the constituent instrument, and will usually do so without consulting the assembly of parties. Such practice will be important. The most famous example relates to the meaning of the so-called veto in the UN Security Council. The Council has had to decide in many cases whether it can determine, under Article 39 of the Charter, that there is a threat to international peace and security, so opening the way for the Council to then impose sanctions or authorise the use of force.

Some constituent instruments, however, give express power to one of its organs to interpret it authoritatively.[15] Financial agencies and commodity councils charge their executive organs with all questions of interpretation.[16] The Secretariat of an organisation (or its Legal Counsel) may often provide influential interpretations, which may take on a more authoritative nature if not contested.[17] In some cases, the constituent instrument may permit referral of a dispute concerning interpretation to a judicial organ, either for decision or for an advisory opinion.[18]

Article 20(3) VCLT provides that, unless the constituent instrument provides otherwise, a *reservation* to the instrument requires the acceptance of 'the competent organ' of the organisation. This is essential to preserve the integrity of the constituent instrument.

Membership

Each international organisation has its own provisions on membership. These usually involve a decision on an application for membership being taken by a specified majority of the members of a certain organ, or organs, of the organisation. The United Nations has an admission procedure involving a recommendation by the

[13] OJ C 326, 26.10.2012, 1; UKTS (2010) No. 7; and [2008] OJ C115/47.

[14] See *Gardiner*, 136–141; J. Klabbers, 'Straddling the Fence: The EU and International Law', in A. Arnull and D. Chalmers (eds.), *The Oxford Handbook of European Union Law* (Oxford University Press, Oxford 2015), 52–71; Case 26/62 *Van Gend & Loos* v. *Netherlands Internal Revenue Administration*, ECLI:EU:C:1963:1, at 12.

[15] See Article XIX Agreement of the International Monetary Fund 1945: 2 UNTS 39 No. 20, UKTS (1946) No. 21; Article IX(2) Agreement establishing the World Trade Organization 1994: 1867 UNTS 4 No. 31874; 33 ILM (1994) 1144; at WTO website.

[16] Schermers and Blokker (n. 10), 892.

[17] Schermers and Blokker (n. 10), 893–895.

[18] Schermers and Blokker (n. 10), 896–905.

Security Council (subject to the veto) and then a vote of two-thirds of the members of the General Assembly present and voting (Articles 4 and 18 of the UN Charter).

Certain organisations admit as members *non-state entities* on the basis that they are separate customs territories. Thus, China, Hong Kong (HKSAR)[19] and China, Macao, as well as Chinese Taipei (Taiwan), are full members of the World Trade Organization, as is China itself. Both China and the HKSAR are members of the International Textiles and Clothing Bureau, the World Tourist Organization and the World Meteorological Organization (WMO).[20] Some other organisations have a separate category of associate membership for overseas territories of its members. Many organisations allow non-member states, and some non-state entities, to be observers without the right to vote.

A new state will not succeed to membership of international organisations if the predecessor state still exists. There is no problem if a state continues the legal personality of an existing member, as with the USSR and the Russian Federation.[21] But, for example, twelve former Soviet republics each had to apply for UN membership, though Belarus (previously Byelorussian SSR) and Ukraine (previously Ukrainian SSR) were, for purely political reasons, already members of the United Nations in their own right, although not previously recognised by most states as sovereign until 1991.

The demise of Czechoslovakia raised a special problem because neither of the two successor states claimed to be the continuation of Czechoslovakia. Each therefore had to apply to join those organisations of which it wished to be a member. Where Czechoslovakia had been a member of certain bodies within a particular organisation, the two states agreed which of them should seek election to the seat, and this choice was generally respected and endorsed.[22]

If a new state is the result of the union of two states, and one or both was a member of the organisation before the union, the new state will usually be accepted as a member under its *new* name and without having to apply for membership. When the two Yemens joined together as one state, they retained one seat in the United Nations under the name of Yemen: no application for membership was required.

Withdrawal

Constituent instruments do not generally provide for a member to withdraw. But Article 56 provides that, when a treaty has no provision for withdrawal, there is a right to withdraw if it is established that the parties intended it or the right 'may be implied by the nature of the treaty'. Given the nature of a constituent instrument, that

[19] UK–China Joint Declaration on the Question of Hong Kong, section VI, Annex I.

[20] See also Chapter 4, pp. 84–87.

[21] See Y. Z. Blum, 'Russia takes over the Soviet Union's seat at the United Nations', EJIL 3 (1992) 354–361.

[22] A different procedure was adopted in respect of the ILO and ICAO: see Schermers and Blokker (n. 10), 102.

right is almost certainly implicit. This was the view of Waldock as Special Rapporteur,[23] and also the view of the committee of the San Francisco Conference which drew up the UN Charter and accepted it in plenary session.[24] Articles 5 and 6 of the Charter have provisions (never used) for suspending or expelling a member. Article 31 of the Constitutive Act of the African Union and Article 50 TEU allow a member of their respective organisations the right of withdrawal, subject to procedural conditions.[25] On 15 March 2022, following Russia's invasion of Ukraine in February 2022, Russia gave notice of withdrawal from the Council of Europe. The following day, the Committee of Ministers decided that Russia was in serious violation of its obligations under Article 3 of the Statute and should cease to be a member of the organisation.[26]

Withdrawal of the United Kingdom from the European Union

In a referendum held on 23 June 2016, the British people voted to leave the European Union. The UK government formally served notice of withdrawal under Article 50 TEU on 30 March 2017. Following this notification, the Union and the UK negotiated arrangements for withdrawal, which were set out in the EU–UK Withdrawal Agreement signed on 24 January 2020,[27] and, in parallel, a framework for the future relationship in the form of a Political Declaration.[28]

To allow time for the agreement on the future relationship to be negotiated, the Withdrawal Agreement included provision for a 'transition or implementation period' until 31 December 2020, during which, save as otherwise provided, Union law was applicable to and in the UK. This raised, however, a question as to how EU agreements with third countries (including multilateral agreements to which the EU was party) might continue to apply to the UK during that period. The UK for its part would be bound by these agreements by a special provision in the Withdrawal Agreement. But, unlike internal Union law, the continued application of international agreements in respect of the UK during the transition period required the consent, tacit agreement or acquiescence of the third-country treaty partners, or at least de facto application of the agreements by them.

[23] Second Report, YBILC (1963) vol. II, 69, para. 20. His draft article contained the qualification 'unless the usage of the organization otherwise prescribes': 64.

[24] See K. Widdows, 'The Unilateral Denunciation of Treaties Containing No Denunciation Clause', BYIL 53 (1982) 83–114, 98–102; *Dörr and Schmalenbach*, 1052–1053; Schermers and Blokker (n. 10), 108–120.

[25] African Union: 2158 UNTS 3 No. 37733, or at AU website; TEU: OJ C 326, 26.10.2012, 1; UKTS (2010) No. 7.

[26] Resolution CM/Res (2022)2 on the cessation of the membership of the Russian Federation to the Council of Europe (adopted by the Committee of Ministers on 16 March 2022 at the 1428ter meeting of the Ministers' Deputies). See p. 311.

[27] OJ C 3841, 12.11.2019, 1–177; UKTS (2020) No. 3. It came into force at midnight on 1 February 2020 Belgian time, and 2300 on 31 January 2020 UK time.

[28] See n. 27, 178–193.

The EU therefore undertook to notify the other parties to the agreements that during the transition period the UK was to be treated as a member state for the purposes of these agreements.[29] This notification took the form of a Note Verbale to states and international organisations which was issued by the EU shortly before the commencement of the transition period on 1 February 2020.[30] The legal theory underpinning this was never formalised, and different actors took different approaches, including the view that continued application de jure would require the express agreement of the third country. But, in practice, there were no material problems in the de facto application of the agreements during the transition period.

When the transition period expired at the end of 2020, all the EU's agreements with third countries ceased to apply to the UK. In anticipation of this, the UK had, immediately after the referendum in 2016, embarked on a substantial programme of treaty making, to ensure that it was able to replicate the more significant EU agreements by concluding new treaties with third countries in its own right. It also acceded, where necessary, in its own name to various multilateral agreements to which the EU had been party before the UK's withdrawal from the EU.

The UK's future relationship with the EU was encapsulated in three agreements signed on 30 December 2020, which were provisionally applied from 1 January 2021 to 30 April 2021: the EU–UK Trade and Cooperation Agreement;[31] the EU–UK Agreement concerning Security Procedures for Exchanging and Protecting Classified Information;[32] and the EAEC–UK Agreement for Cooperation on the Safe and Peaceful Uses of Nuclear Energy.[33] All three entered into force on 1 May 2021.

International Legal Personality

The most distinctive characteristic of an international organisation is that in *international law* it has legal personality separate from its members. In this regard it is rather like a company, which is legally separate from its shareholders. Having international legal personality makes the organisation a subject of international law, with rights and duties under it, including the ability to enter into treaties with other subjects of international law, whether they are member states, non-member states or other international organisations. Its constituent instrument may provide that it shall

[29] Article 127 UK–EU Withdrawal Agreement (n. 27) and the asterisk thereto. The actual wording in paragraph 5 of the Note Verbale issued by the EU was: 'the Union and Euratom notify parties to the international agreements referred to in point 4 above that, during the transition period, the United Kingdom is treated as a Member State of the Union and of Euratom for the purposes of these international agreements.' See https://ec.europa.eu/info/sites/default/files/model-note-verbale-international-partners_en.pdf.

[30] See notes 27 and 29.

[31] UKTS (2021) No. 8; OJ L 149, 30.4.2021.

[32] UKTS (2021) No. 9; OJ L 149, 30.4.2021.

[33] UKTS (2021) No. 10; OJ L 150, 30.4.2021.

have international legal personality. If it is a universal international organisation (membership open to all states), that provision is enough.

International legal personality may also be inferred from the purpose of the organisation, the powers given to it by its members and its practice.[34] Whether individual organs of an international organisation have a separate legal personality will turn on the particular organisation and organ in question. In principle, a treaty concluded by an international organisation will bind its subsidiary organs and, conversely, a treaty concluded by a subsidiary organ should bind the entire organisation.

Although originally there were doubts as to whether an international organisation had the power to enter into treaties with states or other international organisations, this is formally recognised by the eleventh paragraph of the preamble to the 1986 Vienna Convention,[35] which notes that:

> international organisations possess the capacity to conclude treaties which is necessary for the exercise of their functions and the fulfilment of their purposes.[36]

It is important that the organisation only concludes agreements in those areas in which it is competent to act.[37] Article 6 provides that 'the capacity of an international organization to conclude treaties is governed by the rules of that organization'. This means, in particular, 'the constituent instruments, decisions and resolutions adopted in accordance with them, and established practice of the organization'.[38] Sometimes the treaty-making power is expressly defined but sometimes it may be implied, for example in respect of the conclusion of headquarters agreements or, more significantly in the case of the European Union, to ensure consistency in the exercise of internal and external competence.[39]

The issue of accession of international organisations to law-making treaties may be particularly problematic, since it may raise questions concerning the organisation's capacity to perform all of the obligations or its autonomy as an organisation. An example of the former is the UN's decision not to accede to the 1949 Geneva

[34] *Reparation for Injuries Suffered* (n. 8). On the OSCE, see Schermers and Blokker (n. 10), 1032; M. S. Platise, C. Moser and A. Peters (eds.), *The Legal Framework of the OSCE* (Cambridge University Press, Cambridge 2019); and pp. 409–410.

[35] 25 ILM (1986) 543; A. Watts, *The International Law Commission 1949–1998*, vol. II (Oxford University Press, Oxford 1999), 950.

[36] On treaty-making by international organisations, see generally O. Elias, 'Who Can Make Treaties? International Organizations', in *Hollis, Oxford Guide*, 97–116.

[37] See the Third Report of the Special Rapporteur, YBILC (1974) vol. II, part I, 146, paras. 5–6. See further Elias (n. 36), 103–104.

[38] Article 2(1)(j).

[39] *Commission* v. *Council (AETR case)*, Case 22/70, ECR (1971) 263, 271; but see now Articles 3 and 4 TFEU. See also M. Cremona, 'Who Can Make Treaties? The European Union', in *Hollis, Oxford Guide*, 117–149, 121.

Conventions for the Protection of War Victims, and of the latter, the EU's possible accession to the ECHR, for which there is provision in Article 6(2) TEU.[40]

It is also important, in the case of multilateral treaties, that the treaty to which the international organisation wishes to become party is capable of being accepted or acceded to by the organisation in question. Some treaties may provide for only states, or certain states, to become parties;[41] or allow acceptance or accession by a specified organisation[42] or group of organisations;[43] or by regional economic integration organisations.[44] Where an international organisation becomes a party, special provision will often be required on issues like voting rights or financial contributions. And if the organisation (such as the European Union) is party to a multilateral treaty together with its member states, the division of competence may also need to be clarified.[45]

Treaties between States and International Organisations or between International Organisations: the 1986 Convention

Since the constituent treaty of an international organisation, and a treaty adopted *within* the organisation, are concluded by states, the VCLT applies to such instruments, but this is without prejudice to any relevant rules of the organisation (Article 5). Those rules may, for example, govern the procedure by which treaties are adopted within the organisation, how they are to be amended and the making of reservations.

Since the VCLT does not apply to treaties between states and international organisations or between international organisations, the UN General Assembly decided to adopt the 1986 Convention, applying to such treaties the provisions of the VCLT, suitably adapted. Although the 1986 Convention is not in force, there is no doubt that its substantive provisions, following so closely as they do those of the VCLT, are generally accepted as the applicable international law. Although the VCLT does not apply to a treaty between a state and an international organisation, the VCLT rules will apply to such a treaty as customary international law (insofar as the VCLT reflects such law): see Article 3(b).[46]

Where states that are parties to the VCLT are parties to a treaty to which other subjects of international law, in particular international organisations, are also parties,

[40] See Elias (n. 36), 111–113; P. Webb, 'Treaties and International Organizations: Uneasy Analogies', in C. J. Tams, A. Tzanakopoulos and A. Zimmermann (eds.), *Research Handbook on the Law of Treaties* (Edward Elgar, Cheltenham UK, Northampton MA USA 2014), 567–596, 577–579.

[41] See Articles 48, 50 VCDR 1961: 500 UNTS 95 No. 7310; UKTS (1965) No. 19.

[42] See Article 42 CoE Convention on Action against Trafficking in Human Beings: 2569 UNTS 33 No. 45795; UKTS (2012) No. 37; ETS No. 197, for the EU.

[43] See Article 82(c) 1986 Convention.

[44] See Article 29 Hague Convention on Choice of Agreements: 3110 UNTS No. 53483; UK Misc. Series (2018) No. 11.

[45] See pp. 412–413.

[46] See also *Brita GmbH* v. *Hauptzollamt Hamburg Hafen*, Case C-386/08, ECLI:EU:C:2010:91, para. 41.

as between the states parties it is the VCLT that applies, not customary international law (Article 3(c) VCLT). However, as we have already seen, the distinction between the rules of the VCLT and customary international law is now, in most areas, rather academic. As between states and international organisations, both or all of which are parties to the 1986 Convention, only that Convention would apply, though this would have little discernible practical importance given that the 1986 Convention mostly replicates the principles and rules of the VCLT; and, of course, the 1986 Convention is not yet in force.

To enter into force, the 1986 Convention needs thirty-five *states* to ratify it, yet nearly forty years on it is still not in force. Although it has attracted over forty ratifications, this does not include enough states; the other parties are international organisations, which do *not* count for the purpose of entry into force. The United Nations, and the mostly UN specialised agencies, have deposited 'instruments relating to an act of formal confirmation', the formula devised by the ILC and used in the 1986 Convention as a substitute for 'ratification'.[47] Why then is the 1986 Convention still not in force?

The scope of the 1986 Convention is clear from its title. After the Second World War there was an enormous increase in treaty making, in which international organisations played a large role, not only in convening treaty-making conferences, but also in concluding treaties with states or with other international organisations. A convention to codify the rules applicable to such treaties, and so complete the work begun by the VCLT, seemed also to be needed, or so it was thought at the time. The 1986 Convention follows the VCLT very closely. Indeed, until Article 73, the topics it covers are the same as in the VCLT. This is hardly surprising since, as the ILC acknowledged, the relationship between the two topics was extremely close; it therefore took each of the articles of the VCLT and made only those changes which were necessary to accommodate the different situation and needs of international organisations. In fact, the 1986 Convention is even closer to the text of the VCLT than were the Commission's final draft articles. Consequently, the 1986 Convention also reproduces any faults in the VCLT.[48]

The fact that the provisions of the 1986 Convention are so very close to those of the VCLT is almost certainly the principal reason why most states have not bothered to become parties. If the rules are essentially the same for all treaties, there would seem to be little point in making the effort to become a party, especially if the domestic process involves seeking the approval of the legislature. No state concludes that many treaties with international organisations, but when a state does, it can easily be guided by the organisation, and if necessary by the 1986 Convention, as to any different rules

[47] See Article 2 of the Convention and the ILC Commentary on the draft Article 2(1)(bis) in Watts (n. 35), 832.

[48] G. Gaja, 'The "New" Vienna Convention on Treaties', BYIL 58 (1987) 253–269, 254.

or practices that apply when dealing with the relevant international organisation. For this, it does not have to be a party to the 1986 Convention. Although that Convention was a worthy attempt at making the law of treaties more comprehensive, it did not meet a real need, and its provisions could just as well have been adopted as guidance rather than as a treaty. The 1986 Convention was adopted so easily because it was uncontentious.

In practice, international organisations (including those that have 'ratified' the 1986 Convention) generally consult, and refer only to, the VCLT, to which – ironically – only states can become parties, as reflecting customary international law. They see no particular need for the 1986 Convention, given that its substance is the same as the VCLT. In *France* v. *Commission*,[49] the European Court of Justice (now CJEU) considered the definition of treaty in Article 2(1)(a)(i) of the 1986 Convention, although the European Community (as it then was) had not 'ratified' that Convention, and the provision is the same in substance as Article 2(1)(a) VCLT.[50] Later the Court considered a similar matter without reference to either Convention.[51] In its *Opinion on the EEA Treaty*, the Court, in considering the exceptional character of the EC legal order, relied on the normal rules on treaty interpretation in Article 31 VCLT.[52] In *Brita GmbH* v. *Hauptzollamt Hamburg Hafen*, the CJEU applied the VCLT rules insofar as they reflected customary international law.[53] In *Council* v. *Front Polisario*, the CJEU made extensive reference to Articles 29–31 VCLT.[54] The Court also relied on that Convention (Articles 60 and 62, respectively) in *Portugal* v. *Council*[55] and in *Racke*.[56]

Negotiation of Multilateral Treaties

Treaties Adopted within an International Organisation

Article 9 VCLT does not, as such, deal with treaties drawn up within an international organisation, as distinct from those drawn up at an international conference, including those convened by an international organisation, but Article 5 provides that the Convention is without prejudice to any relevant rules of an international organisation. Accordingly, if the organisation has specific rules for the adoption of treaties, they will apply.

49 Case C-327/91: ECR I-3641, para. 25; 101 ILR 29.

50 See *Gardiner*, 137. Although the Court accepted that the agreement fell within the definition of the 1986 Convention, it did not refer to the interpretation provision of that Convention.

51 *France* v. *Commission* (2004), Case C-233/02, ECLI:EU:C:2004:173, paras. 38–46.

52 Opinion 1/91; 1991 ECR I-6079, point 14.

53 *Brita GmbH* v. *Hauptzollamt Hamburg Hafen* (n. 46).

54 Case C-104/16 P, *Council of the European Union* v. *Front Polisario* (21 December 2016), ECLI:EU:C:2016:973.

55 Case C-268/94, 1996 ECR I-6177, paras. 26–27.

56 Case C-162/96, 1998 ECR-I-3688; 117 ILR 399; 37 ILM (1998) 1128.

Not all of the approximately 600 treaties for which the UN Secretary-General is the depositary are produced by a UN process. They include subjects as diverse as immunities, human rights, refugees, drugs, slavery, health, trade, transport, law of the sea, law of treaties, outer space, disarmament and the environment. Since the Second World War, UN specialised agencies and certain other international organisations have been involved in the drafting, negotiation and conclusion of multilateral treaties.

Those multilateral treaties (more usually called 'conventions') that are produced *within the United Nations* are often adopted by the UN General Assembly (e.g., the ICCPR 1966)[57] after they have been negotiated in the Third Committee (human rights), or the Sixth Committee (legal), of the General Assembly, on which each UN member has a seat. If successful, the Committee recommends the treaty to the General Assembly for adoption, which is done by means of a resolution to which the text of the treaty is annexed.[58] The resolution will be adopted in accordance with the Rules of Procedure of the General Assembly, which for this purpose requires only a simple majority. But in practice, for good reasons, for many years now a draft treaty is not presented for adoption unless there is consensus or near consensus. Alternatively, treaties can be negotiated and adopted at a *diplomatic conference* convened by a resolution of the General Assembly (e.g., the Rome Statute 1998).[59] Preliminary work may well have been done in formal or informal meetings within the United Nations or by the ILC.

UN Sixth Committee

This Committee, like other main committees of the General Assembly, meets during the annual autumn session of the General Assembly, and intersessionally in committees and working groups. An important role of the Sixth Committee has been to elaborate conventions for adoption by the General Assembly, such as some counter-terrorism conventions.[60] It also oversees the work of the ILC by debating its annual report, commenting on its drafts and proposals for new topics, and deciding what form drafts for international instruments should take (convention, guidelines, model legislation, etc.), and whether the final drafting and negotiation should be done at a diplomatic conference or by the Committee itself.

57 999 UNTS 171 No. 14668; 6 ILM (1967) 368; UKTS (1977) No. 6. See UNGA Resolution 2200 (XXI), 1966.

58 See A/RES/52/164 adopting the Convention for the Suppression of Terrorist Bombings, 15 December 1997. For the Convention, see 2149 UNTS 284 No. 37517; 37 ILM (1998) 251; UKTS (2001) No. 57; [2002] ATS 17.

59 Rome Statute: 2187 UNTS 91 No. 38544; 37 ILM (1998) 998; UKTS (2002) No. 35. See A/RES/51/207, 16 January 1997.

60 See, e.g., the Convention on the Suppression of Financing of Terrorism 1999 (2178 UNTS 229 No. 38349; 39 ILM (2000) 268; UKTS (2002) 28; [2002] ATS 23), on the negotiation of which, see A. Aust, 'Counter-Terrorism: A New Approach', *Max Planck Yearbook of UN Law* (Kluwer Law International, The Hague 2001), 285–306.

UN International Law Commission

Established by the General Assembly,[61] the UN ILC[62] began work in 1949. It now has thirty-four members, elected by the General Assembly for five-year terms, mostly professors of international law or current or former foreign ministry legal advisers. It meets, in principle, for two five-week sessions each year in Geneva. For each topic, the Commission appoints one of its members as Special Rapporteur, who each year presents the Commission with a report on their research, including proposals and draft articles for a possible convention or other instrument, such as guidelines. The Commission each year reports to the General Assembly (in practice, to the Sixth Committee) on its work, with draft articles and commentaries on them. The Commission has been successful with the adoption of conventions originally drafted by it on, for example, the law of treaties and diplomatic relations, and with guidelines and draft articles (for example, on state responsibility), which in many respects form part of customary international law.

UN Specialised Agencies

Of the many UN specialised agencies,[63] the International Labour Organization (ILO) has probably adopted the most multilateral treaties, some 200 since its establishment in 1919. The International Maritime Organization (IMO) has adopted some thirty conventions (and numerous amendments and implementing instruments) promoting, in particular, the safety of merchant shipping. Other specialised agencies also active in treaty making are the FAO, ICAO, ITU, UNESCO, UPU, World Health Organization (WHO), World Intellectual Property Organization (WIPO), WMO and the so-called international financial institutions (IFIs): the International Bank for Reconstruction and Development (World Bank), International Finance Corporation (IFC) and International Monetary Fund (IMF). The IAEA is *not* a 'UN specialised agency', but it operates under the aegis of the United Nations and is regarded as one of the 'UN family'. It is responsible particularly for monitoring compliance with the Nuclear Non-Proliferation Treaty (NPT) 1968.[64]

Regional International Organisations

Regional international organisations, especially European ones, have also been forums for the production of many multilateral treaties. Established in 1949, the Council of Europe[65] now has forty-six members and has adopted over 200 multilateral

[61] UNGA Resolution 174 (11), 1947. [62] See P. S. Rao, 'International Law Commission', *MPEPIL* (2017).

[63] The so-called UN specialised agencies are *not* part of the United Nations.

[64] 729 UNTS 161 No. 10485, 7 ILM (1968) 809, UKTS (1970) 88, TIAS 6839.

[65] See www.coe.int; and S. Schmahl and M. Breuer (eds.), *The Council of Europe: Its Law and Policies* (Oxford University Press, Oxford 2017).

treaties, many on social issues and especially various aspects of human rights. The most important and influential treaty has been the European Convention on Human Rights 1950.[66] The European Union is covered in more detail below.

Responsibility for the acts of an International Organisation

Since an international organisation has international legal personality separate from its member states, it is responsible in international law for its own acts, including any wrongful act.[67] But several questions flow from this. What amounts to a wrongful act? What acts can be attributed to an organisation, as distinct from its member states? To what extent might the member states be liable as well? How does the position under international law relate to that under domestic law?

In 2011 the ILC adopted a separate set of draft articles on responsibility of international organisations.[68] The articles have been subject to criticism but have proved influential in state and judicial practice.[69] Under Article 10 ARIO, an international organisation is in breach of an international obligation when an act by it is not in conformity with what is required of it by that obligation, regardless of the origin or character of the obligation concerned. The latter phrase embraces obligations arising from a customary rule of international law, a treaty or a 'general principle applicable within the international legal order'.[70] It may, however, not always be clear how general principles apply to a particular organisation.[71]

The question of the attribution of acts to the international organisation, as distinct from its members or a third party acting with it, has arisen most acutely in the context of military operations.[72] Article 15 ARIO attributes responsibility to the organisation if it directs and controls a state or another international organisation in the commission of a wrongful act. Similarly, Article 7 proposes (in summary) that the conduct of an organ of a state or an international organisation that is placed at the disposal of another international organisation shall be considered an act of the latter organisation if the organisation exercises effective control over that conduct. The UN Secretary-General has adopted the criterion of 'effective control' with regard to joint

[66] UNTS 221 No. 2889; UKTS (1953) No. 71; ETS No. 5.
[67] See Article 3, ILC draft articles referred to in n. 68.
[68] Often referred to as 'ARIO': Responsibility of International Organisations, Report of the ILC on the Work of its 63rd session, 2011, UNGA 66th Session, Supplement No. 10, Addendum 1, Doc. A/66/10/Add. 1, 39–105.
[69] See Klabbers (n. 2), 314–317, Schermers and Blokker (n. 10), 1060–1065.
[70] See para. 2, Commentary on Article 10, at 63. See also *Interpretation of the Agreement of 25 March 1951 between the WHO and Egypt*, Advisory Opinion, ICJ Reports (1980) 73, at 89–90, para. 37.
[71] See Klabbers (n. 2), 324–327, Schermers and Blokker (n. 10), 1038–1039.
[72] See Klabbers (n. 2), 317–324, Schermers and Blokker (n. 10), 1052–1053, 1056–1058.

operations.[73] In the cases of *Behrami* and *Saramati*,[74] which concerned operations in Kosovo following the NATO intervention against Yugoslavia, certain actions of the Kosovo Force (KFOR)[75] were attributed, in principle, to the UN because the UN Security Council retained 'ultimate authority and control'.[76]

As for the responsibility of member states, Article 62 ARIO provides:

> a state member of an international organization is responsible for an internationally wrongful act of that organization if:
>
> (a) it has accepted responsibility for that act towards the injured party; or
> (b) it has led the injured party to rely on its responsibility.

This implies that the international organisation is solely responsible under international law for a breach of its obligations, unless its members have explicitly or implicitly accepted such responsibility.[77] A state may also incur responsibility where it has assisted a wrongful act, or directed it, or coerced the international organisation to commit it.[78] But even if a state is not directly liable, can it be liable in another way, for example by putting the organisation in funds to meet its liabilities ('indirect' responsibility), or through failing to do so if the organisation was in default ('secondary' responsibility)? There is scant authority for imposing such liability on member states and for lifting the 'corporate veil' in this way.[79] But sometimes member states may wish expressly to exclude liability. Article 3(4) of the Agreement establishing the International Fund for Agricultural Development 1976[80], for example, provides expressly that no member shall be liable by reason of its membership for acts or obligations of the Fund.

This relates to the question of the position of an international organisation under domestic law, since creditors are most likely to claim before domestic courts, as in the International Tin Council litigation in the 1980s.[81] The domestic law position will depend upon the particular domestic law of a particular country, albeit informed by international law. Most international organisations have conferred on them more or less total immunity from domestic jurisdiction,[82] so that, in practice, domestic legal remedies are generally not available anyway, and international dispute settlement mechanisms generally do not have jurisdiction over international organisations.

[73] See para. 9, Commentary on Article 7, at 58; and A/51/389, paras. 17–18.
[74] *Behrami* v. *France*, Application no. 71412/01; *Saramati* v. *France, Germany and Norway*, Application no. 78166/01, Grand Chamber, 2 May 2007: 133 ILR 1.
[75] Kosovo Force, NATO security presence in Kosovo.
[76] Paras. 140–141, *Behrami* v. *France* and *Saramati* v. *France* (n. 74).
[77] See P. Klein, 'Responsibility', in Cogan *et al.* (n. 10), 1034–1035.
[78] See Articles 58-61 ARIO.
[79] See Klabbers (n. 2), 327–330; Schermers and Blokker (n. 10), 1053–1055; Klein (n. 77), 1038.
[80] 1059 UNTS 191 No. 16041; 15 ILM (1976) 922; UKTS (1978) No. 41.
[81] See Klabbers (n. 2), 311-314.
[82] See Schermers and Blokker (n. 10), 1088–1089.

Dispute Settlement

A dispute between the members of an international organisation, or between the organisation and its members, about the interpretation or application of its constituent instrument can be settled in accordance with the relevant provisions (if any) of that instrument. Some, such as the treaties governing the World Trade Organization or the European Union, establish a more or less self-contained legal order within which the member states have to operate. The treaties therefore include elaborate procedures for settling disputes arising within that legal order. Other international organisations also have built-in disputes procedures. Articles 26–29 of the ILO Constitution provide for a commission of inquiry to hear complaints that a member state is not observing an ILO convention.[83] However, as with other disputes involving member states, it would be expected that they would first consult fully in an attempt to settle the matter.

Even if that is unsuccessful, it does not follow that the dispute settlement procedures (if any) of the organisation will be activated. There may be various reasons why members will not want to formalise the dispute. There are many disputes within international organisations that remain unresolved, largely because they are not so important (or at least not important to enough members) that they have to be resolved.

United Nations

It may seem surprising, but the UN Charter has no built-in procedure specifically for settling disputes between UN members about the Charter. There are differences of view, some long-standing, about the interpretation or application of the Charter, but these are dealt with by negotiations, mostly informal, and are often inconclusive. Some are on major issues (such as the effective exclusion of South Africa during its period of apartheid). Some are resolved, often by a compromise or 'fudge' (such as over the question of the arrears of South Africa's contributions following resumption of its seat). Others remain unresolved. Many matters are often best settled by a political fix rather than by the use of formal mechanisms.

However, under Article 96 of the UN Charter, the ICJ may be asked to give advisory opinions on, among other things, legal questions arising within the scope of the activities of the United Nations and the UN specialised agencies. Opinions have been given on treaties concerning the work of the organisation: for example, in 1988 the application of the headquarters agreement between the United Nations and the United States in relation to the observer mission of the Palestine Liberation Organization (PLO).[84] The Court can, if so requested, give an opinion very quickly –

[83] See www.ilo.org.

[84] See *Applicability of the Obligation to Arbitrate under Section 21 of the UN Headquarters Agreement 1947 (PLO case)*, ICJ Reports (1988) 12; 27 ILM (1988) 800; 82 ILR 300.

within eight weeks in the PLO case. The ICJ has given opinions on various other UN internal matters.[85] An opinion is not binding unless otherwise agreed, but an opinion can be persuasive legally and politically.[86]

UN Specialised Agencies

Most disputes within the UN specialised agencies are settled by negotiation, but, if there is a need to pursue a more formal procedure, in most of the agencies the dispute will be referred to one of the main organs; and if it cannot be settled, it may then be referred to arbitration or to the ICJ for an advisory opinion. ICAO and ILO have different procedures. The WTO has elaborate formal procedures for settling disputes between its members.

Staff Disputes

The constituent instruments of international organisations now usually provide how disputes between the organisation and staff members can be dealt with.[87] This is essential, since most international organisations have immunity from the jurisdiction of domestic courts. The United Nations now has a two-tier system consisting of the UN Disputes Tribunal and the UN Appeals Tribunal, established by the General Assembly, in place of the UN Administrative Tribunal. The ILO Administrative Tribunal also decides cases from some other specialised agencies.

Treaty-Monitoring Bodies

In certain fields (for example, human rights, environment,[88] and security), where full implementation on a mutual basis is particularly important, states have established systems to ascertain whether the parties are in compliance with their obligations. These normally involve the establishment of a committee or other body under the treaty which may variously gather information, consider complaints, produce reports and/or take steps to encourage implementation.

85 See www.icj-cij.org, go to Decisions, Advisory Cases, for example, *Admissions* cases, 1948 and 1950; *Reparation for Injuries Suffered* case, 1949; *Expenses* case, 1962; *Mazilu* case, 1989; and *Cumaraswamy* case, 1999.

86 Examples are *Legality of the Use by a State of Nuclear Weapons in Armed Conflict (Request by WHO)* (n. 6) and *Legal Consequences of the Construction of a Wall in the Occupied Palestinian Territory*, Advisory Opinion, ICJ Reports (2004) 136; 43 ILM (2004) 1009.

87 See C. Amerasinghe, *The Law of the International Civil Service: As Applied by International Administrative Tribunals*, vol. II (Clarendon Press, Oxford 1994); Klabbers (n. 2), 269–273.

88 For non-compliance procedures in the environmental field, see P. Sands, J. Peel, A. Fabra and R. Mackenzie, *Principles of International Environmental Law* (4th ed., Cambridge University Press, Cambridge 2018), 172–178.

An example in the human rights field is the eighteen-member Human Rights Committee (the Committee), which is responsible for enforcing the ICCPR 1966. The Committee is composed of nationals of the parties, mostly judges or professors of law, elected by a secret ballot of the parties to serve in a personal capacity for a four-year, renewable term. It operates, by consensus, in three ways:

(1) Considering reports by parties (within one year of becoming a party) on how they are implementing the ICCPR, and thereafter every five years. Representatives of each party are questioned about its report at a public hearing of the Committee.
(2) Receiving individual complaints. The (First) Optional Protocol to the ICCPR[89] enables the Committee to consider a 'communication' (petition) from an individual (not a legal person) who is subject to the jurisdiction of a party to the Protocol and who claims that they are the victim of a violation by that party of the ICCPR. The Committee's views are not binding and there is no prescribed sanction for ignoring them, the chief weapon of the Committee being publicity. A summary of its activities under the Protocol is published in the Committee's annual reports to the UN General Assembly.
(3) Issuing 'General Comments'. The Committee is empowered to issue General Comments on implementation of the ICCPR. So far, it has issued over thirty. Some have been on controversial issues, such as reservations to the ICCPR (GC 24).[90]

There are also committees to monitor the implementation of the Convention on the Elimination of all Forms of Racial Discrimination 1965 (CERD), the International Covenant on Economic, Social and Cultural Rights 1976 (ICESCR), the Convention on the Elimination of All Forms of Discrimination against Women 1979 (CEDAW) and the UN Convention against Torture Convention 1984 (UNCAT), the Convention on the Rights of the Child 1990 (CRC) and the Convention on the Rights of Persons with Disabilities 2008 (CRPD). They operate in a broadly similar fashion to the Committee (under the ICCPR), and include provisions for petitions, subject to the state concerned making the relevant declaration or ratifying the relevant optional protocol accepting the competence of the relevant committee to receive such petitions.[91]

Special Cases

In 1975 the Conference on Security and Co-operation in Europe (CSCE) adopted the Helsinki Final Act, a non-binding instrument. In 1994 it became the Organization for

[89] See n. 57.

[90] General Comment No. 26 (61), adopted on 8 December 1997, CCPR/C/21/Rev. 1/Add. 8/Rev.1. The text is in 34 ILM (1995) 839.

[91] For the annual reports of the HRC, and of other similar committees, see www.unhcr.ch.

Security and Co-operation in Europe (OSCE).[92] It has some fifty-seven 'participating states', mostly from Europe and central Asia (former Soviet republics), as well as Canada and the United States. Certain members, who did not want the OSCE to appear to be in competition with the United Nations, or even NATO, traditionally opposed making the OSCE treaty-based. Although the OSCE operates rather like an international organisation, it does not have international legal personality.[93] A convention to remedy this was drafted in 2006 but has not been adopted. To assist the OSCE's effectiveness, some states have, on a bilateral basis under their domestic law, accorded legal capacity to the OSCE, and certain privileges and immunities to it and persons associated with it.[94]

Decisions of the OSCE's various bodies are reached by consensus and are binding only politically. Their principal purpose is conflict prevention, crisis management, human rights, democracy building and post-conflict rehabilitation. It has also been a forum for the adoption of some important and complex multilateral treaties, such as the Treaty on Conventional Armed Forces in Europe 1990[95] and the Open Skies Treaty 1992.[96] The OSCE Convention on Conciliation and Arbitration 1992[97] entered into force in 1994. So far only thirty-four of the fifty-seven OSCE participating states have become parties, and they do not include either the United Kingdom or the United States. The Convention established a Court, which has so far not been used.

The Commonwealth (which developed from the British Empire and later the British Commonwealth of Nations) has no treaty basis, and continues as a voluntary association of over fifty-six states. It is effective in its own unique way. Membership is open to states that can show they meet eligibility criteria (including compliance with Commonwealth values, commitment to democracy and acceptance of the British monarch as 'Head of the Commonwealth') and are accepted by the existing members. They are presently the United Kingdom and overwhelmingly former territories in the UK's dependent empire, ranging from Canada to Tuvalu, though Cameroon (only part of which was once a British Trust Territory) and Mozambique (a former Portuguese colony surrounded by Commonwealth countries) became members some time after their independence. This was the case, too, for the most recent members – Rwanda, Togo and Gabon, who also lack a historical link to the British Empire. Some former UK territories (e.g., Myanmar) never joined. Ireland (formerly part of the United Kingdom) is not a member. Occasionally, members have been suspended (e.g., Nigeria from 1995 to 1999 and Fiji from 2009 to 2014) or decided voluntarily to leave (e.g., Zimbabwe). The Commonwealth Secretariat was established in 1965 by an

[92] See www.osce.org. [93] For a full discussion of the issues, see Platise *et al.* (n. 34).

[94] See the (UK) International Organisations Act 2005, section 4; and Schermers and Blokker (n. 10), 1032–1033.

[95] 30 ILM (1991) 1; UKTS (1993) No. 44. [96] UKTS (2002) No. 27.

[97] 1842 UNTS 151 No. 31413; 32 ILM (1993) 557.

'Agreed Memorandum' – in fact an MOU.[98] The Secretariat has been given legal capacity in UK law by the Commonwealth Secretariat Act 1966, and in the law of some other members.

The main purposes of the Commonwealth are to promote common goals and values around democracy and development; to constitute a forum for discussion of political, economic, social and legal issues affecting the membership; and to provide technical assistance on many matters, chiefly to developing country members. It does not enter into bilateral treaties or adopt multilateral treaties. However, it has been very active in devising legal machinery for the better functioning of civil and criminal law in Commonwealth countries. The various schemes relating to the rendition of fugitive offenders (i.e., extradition) within the Commonwealth have been contained in multilateral non-binding arrangements adopted by meetings of Commonwealth law ministers. Where the subject matter is reciprocal, the MOUs are generally implemented by matching (back-to-back) legislation in member countries. This practice is made easier by the fact that, overwhelmingly, Commonwealth countries share basically the same legal tradition and the English language.

The Commonwealth also encompasses a wide range of informal, professional and civil society organisations and activities outside the formal intergovernmental framework (e.g., the Commonwealth Lawyers Association, the Commonwealth Games). Many of these are supported by the Commonwealth Foundation, which was established by Commonwealth Heads of Government in 1965 in a parallel MOU to that of the Secretariat. It became a Charitable Trust under English law in March 1966.

The Antarctic Treaty 1959[99] did *not* establish an international organisation. Nor was there even a permanent secretariat to prepare and service annual meetings, each consultative party taking its turn to host the meeting and provide the secretariat. After forty years of this, the consultative parties decided that a permanent secretariat was needed. This began operating in 2004, albeit on a provisional basis, and the relevant decision came into force in 2009. Neither the Secretariat nor anybody established by the Antarctic Treaty purports to have international legal personality. The Secretariat has legal capacity only in the country of its seat, Argentina. There were some firm political objections to creating an 'Antarctic Treaty Organisation' with international legal personality, even on the model of its newer sister body, the CCAMLR Commission, created by the Antarctic Living Resources Conservation Convention 1980.[100]

Founded in 1873, the International Committee of the Red Cross (ICRC)[101] is a legal entity under Swiss law, and its permanent officials are Swiss nationals. States are not members. However, it has a special place internationally, being regarded with particular respect by governments and referred to in treaties, especially the Geneva

[98] 4 ILM (1965) 1108. [99] 402 UNTS 71 No. 5778; UKTS (1961) No. 97; www.ats.aq.
[100] 1329 UNTS 71 No. 22301; 19 ILM (1980) 837; UKTS (1982) No. 48; TIAS 10240.
[101] See www.icrc.org.

Conventions 1949. The International Red Cross/Crescent Movement is not part of the ICRC, but the umbrella body for national Red Cross/Red Crescent societies.

The European Union

The European Union is influential in the treaty field not only in terms of its bilateral relationships with other countries (for example, through trade, association and partnership agreements) but also as a member of international organisations (e.g., the WTO) and as a party to multilateral treaties (e.g., on trade, fisheries or law of the sea). Because of the special features of the EU legal order, and the division of competences between the EU and its member states, and even between its own institutions, its participation in treaties is sometimes not straightforward.

The Union and Euratom are accorded *legal capacity* by their respective constituent treaties, and the *international legal personality* of both the Union and Euratom is accepted by non-member states.[102] Accordingly, the two are able to enter into bilateral and multilateral treaties (and, of course, non-binding instruments)[103] with states and other international organisations. Both the Union and Euratom are party to some agreements.[104]

Member states have conferred legal powers (termed 'competences') on the Union in a large number of subject areas, including those where only the Union can act ('exclusive competence') and those where both the Union and member states may act ('shared competence').[105] Where there is exclusive competence, such as for the customs union, trade in goods and fisheries policy, the member states can no longer conclude treaties which deal with those subjects.[106] It is therefore the Union alone which can enter into such treaties, provided, of course, that the other parties accept the Union as a prospective party. But where competence is *shared* between the Union and its member states, such as on the internal market, the environment or transport, or straddles areas both within and outside Union competence, the Union and its member states may both become parties. In such a case, the treaty is known as a 'mixed agreement'. Under the EU Treaties it is for the High Representative to represent the Union on matters falling within the Common Foreign and Security Policy and for the Commission to represent the Union on other matters.[107]

[102] The European Economic Community had legal personality under Article 210 Treaty of Rome, and then the European Community under Article 281 Treaty Establishing the European Community. Although the European Union, established under the Maastricht Treaty 1992, concluded international agreements from 2001 onwards, it was only expressly accorded legal personality by the Lisbon Treaty, which entered into force on 1 December 2009: Article 47 TEU.

[103] See pp. 50–51. [104] See the EU–UK Trade and Cooperation Agreement 2020 (n. 31).

[105] Articles 2–4 TFEU. The member states may act in areas of shared competence only to the extent that the EU has not exercised its competence.

[106] See below concerning treaties entered into by member states before they joined the EU (or its previous incarnations).

[107] Articles 17.1 and 27.2 TEU.

In some cases where there is shared competence and the Union has not yet acted, member states can still conclude bilateral treaties with third states, or even with each other, though in doing so they must, of course, ensure that the treaty is consistent with EU law and does not encroach on areas where the Union (and its predecessors) has acted or otherwise occupied the field.

When an international organisation (such as the Union) and its member states both become parties to a treaty, the treaty will often include a special provision as to how the organisation and its member states are to exercise their rights and perform their obligations. It will, for example, provide that together they shall have no more votes than the total votes of the member states.[108]

There are treaties, such as ILO conventions, to which EU member states can be parties, but which do not permit an international organisation to be a party, even if it has competence for the subject. In such cases, those EU member states which are parties to the treaty have an obligation to act in the interests of the Union. But these internal matters are not of direct concern to the other parties.

As noted elsewhere, multilateral treaties, especially in fields such as the environment, trade and commodities, often provide for certain international organisations (often referred to as 'regional economic integration organisations' or REIOs) to become parties in their own right. UNCLOS 1982 permits international organisations to become parties if their member states have transferred competence, including the competence to enter into treaties, over matters governed by that Convention.[109] This applies to the Union because of its exclusive competence for fisheries policy. Some such treaties contain a provision under which the Union will make a 'declaration of competence' about the respective competences of itself and its member states with regard to the matters covered by the treaty.[110]

The internal procedures for the Union to conclude a treaty are set out in Title V TFEU.[111] It is for the Commission and High Representative to represent the Union in negotiations and for the Council to approve both the opening of negotiations and the signature and conclusion of agreements. It is important to note also the role of the European Parliament.[112] The Union may provisionally apply treaties.[113]

Other aspects of the EU's treaty making which have been touched on in other chapters include (1) its practice in respect of non-binding instruments;[114] (2) the

108 See Article 4, Annex IX UNCLOS: 1833 UNTS 397 No. 31363; 21 ILM (1982) 1261; UKTS (1999) No. 81. See CCAMLR (n. 100), Article XII.

109 See UNCLOS, Article 305(1)(f) and Annex IX.

110 See Article 5, Annex IX UNCLOS (n. 108); and Article 47 Fish Stocks Agreement 1995: 2167 UNTS 3 No. 37924; 34 ILM (1995) 1542; UKTS (2004) No. 19.

111 Articles 216–220.

112 See e.g., Article 218.6 and 218.10.

113 The three EU (and/or EAEC)–UK treaties signed on 30 December 2020 were all provisionally applied from 1 January 2021 to 30 April 2021: EU/EAEC–UK Trade and Cooperation Agreement (n. 31); EU–UK Agreement concerning Security Procedures (n. 32); EAEC-UK Agreement for Cooperation on the Safe and Peaceful Uses of Nuclear Energy (n. 33).

114 See pp. 50–51.

consequences of an error in internal procedures;[115] (3) agreements concluded by member states prior to the Treaty of Rome, or prior to their accession;[116] (4) the application between the EU and a third state of the VCLT as reflecting customary international law;[117] (5) the application of Articles 30 and 59 VCLT where intra-EU treaties conflict with the EU treaties;[118] and (6) the difficulty presented by treaties which might conflict with the autonomy of the EU legal order.[119]

115 See pp. 323–324. 116 See p. 230. 117 See pp. 400–402. 118 See p. 300.
119 See pp. 407 and 412.

23

Drafting and Final Clauses

> The party of the first part shall be known in this contract as 'the party of the first part'... the party of the second part shall be known in this contract as 'the party of the second part'.[1]

Although from an uproarious film, the quote is a useful reminder that lawyers are not always that good at drafting. The Greece–Former Yugoslav Republic of Macedonia Interim Accord 1995[2] refers to the parties only as 'the Party of the First Part' and 'the Party of the Second Part'. This was because Greece (which has a province called Macedonia) objected to the name 'Republic of Macedonia'. The full title is the Marx Brothers' formulation, and was therefore an imaginative way of breaking the impasse. When in a ticklish spot, such is the resourcefulness of the drafter.

This chapter will therefore describe the way in which treaties, and to some extent non-binding instruments, should be drafted, and what is good practice and what is not. It ends with some drafting tips. The views are inevitably subjective, though all are based on practical experience, including having to grapple with some thoroughly badly drafted treaties.

Treaties do not have to be in any particular form. But, with the principal exception of exchanges of notes (which are dealt with later in this chapter), most treaties consist of a single main instrument that follows a well-established pattern:

- title
- preamble
- main text
- final clauses
- *testimonium* and signature block
- attachments including annexes (if any).

Title

The title consists of two elements: the designation (name) of the treaty and its purpose.

[1] Otis B. Driftwood, aka Groucho Marx, in *A Night at the Opera* (film, 1935).
[2] 1891 UNTS 4 No. 32193; 34 ILM (1995) 1461, 1467.

Name

As has been mentioned, there is no consistent practice in the naming of treaties. Whereas agreement, convention and treaty are perhaps the most common names, other terms such as act, charter, covenant, pact and protocol are also used. Although a self-standing treaty is sometimes called a protocol, it is more common as a name for an amending or supplementary treaty, or an attachment to a treaty. And although a non-legally binding instrument like an MOU should never be called – at least formally – an agreement, some non-binding instruments have names like act, charter and protocol. In view of the importance of drawing *and* maintaining a clear distinction between treaties and non-binding instruments, one should try to reflect this in the name. For treaties, unequivocal terms, such as agreement, convention and treaty, should be used whenever possible. For non-binding instruments, names such as arrangement, memorandum of understanding or understanding should be used.

However, as previously mentioned, such names, in particular, memorandum of understanding, are also used for treaties. In the past, this may have been because the parties, for political reasons, did not want the treaty to appear too formal. Since there is no legal difference between treaties and treaties in simplified form – only between treaties and non-binding instruments – it is regrettable that, often for no good reason, some treaties are still being called memorandums of understanding. Conversely, it is storing up trouble if one tries to give a non-binding instrument a title more appropriate for a binding instrument, for example to make it seem more politically impressive.

Purpose

The title can include a simple description of the instrument's purposes, or be thoroughly bad. The descriptive titles of *multilateral* treaties are frequently far too long, and so inevitably a shorthand title is used for all but the most formal purposes. What is invariably referred to as the Fish Stocks Agreement[3] is actually the thirty-eight-word Agreement for the Implementation of the Provisions of United Nations Convention on the Law of the Sea of 10 December 1982 relating to the Conservation and Management of Straddling Fish Stocks and Highly Migratory Fish Stocks (with annexes) 1995. It is ironic that it supplements one of the longest and most important treaties of modern times, which happily enjoys the simple title of United Nations Convention on the Law of the Sea 1982.

The Fish Stocks Agreement title is not quite the worst example. The prize for that probably still goes to this thirty-nine-word title:

> Agreement concerning the Adoption of Uniform Technical Prescriptions for Wheeled Vehicles, Equipment and Parts which can be Fitted and/or Used on

[3] 2167 UNTS 3 No. 37924; 34 ILM (1995) 1542; UKTS (2004) No. 19.

> Wheeled Vehicles and the Conditions for Reciprocal Recognition of Approvals Granted on the Basis of these Prescriptions 1958.

Originally, it had only twenty-seven words, but this was later increased to thirty-nine.[4] One can only hope that those who have to implement the Agreement in practice use a more handy title, such as Road Vehicle Standards Agreement. In fact, sometimes the negotiating states will agree that, for most purposes, a treaty with a long-winded name will be known by a shorthand title.

We have already seen how some treaties, such as the General Framework Agreement for Peace in Bosnia and Herzegovina 1995, are known by the place where they were adopted, but not necessarily signed: hence the Dayton Agreement. Many treaties with long titles are referred to by a shorthand version of the title or an acronym. Thus, the Convention on the Prohibition of the Development, Production, Stockpiling and Use of Chemical Weapons and on their Destruction 1993 is spoken of as the Chemical Weapons Convention, or simply CWC. There is much to be said for the treaty or final act providing that the treaty may be referred to by a shorthand title.

The Comprehensive Nuclear-Test-Ban Treaty 1996 (the *full* title), or CTBT, is a good example of how things can be done better. Unless there is some important political reason for a long title (and in most cases it is not obvious that there is), it should be possible to capture the nature and purpose of a treaty in a few words, as was done for the Vienna Convention on the Law of Treaties 1969. As with so many aspects of treaties, that Convention is a sound and sensible model.

Titles pose less of a problem for *bilateral* treaties, if only because the parties are likely to be the only states affected by an impossibly long title. The ninety-seven word title of the Agreement between the UK and the Secretariat of the UN Framework Convention on Climate Change shows, however, that it can happen.[5] Unlike most multilateral treaties, bilateral treaties normally include in the title the full names of the parties. This is important if only to distinguish between the many bilateral treaties on the same subject. Thus a normal title will be:

> Agreement on Co-operation in the Field of Tourism between the Government of the United Kingdom of Great Britain and Northern Ireland and the Government of the Republic of Albania.[6]

There is no need to begin with the words 'Agreement on'. The treaty could have been entitled simply Tourism Agreement, since that is how it was referred to by those who had the challenging task of implementing it.

[4] 335 UNTS 211 No. 4789. See *UN Multilateral Treaties*, chapter XI. B.16, listing over 125 regulations made under it.

[5] In short, Agreement regarding the twenty-sixth session of the Conference of the Parties. The reference is UKTS (2021) No. 20.

[6] 1883 UNTS 214 No. 32030; UKTS (1994) No. 42. Reproduced as Appendix B.

But an even simpler formula is:

> Polaris Sales Agreement between the Government of the United Kingdom of Great Britain and Northern Ireland and the Government of the United States of America.[7]

Although the *full* names of the states should always be given in the title of a bilateral treaty, they can be abbreviated in the main text. As we have seen, there can sometimes be a problem if, for political reasons, the name used by one of the states is not acceptable to the other.[8] Previously, because of political sensitivities, the practice for a bilateral treaty between the Irish Republic and the United Kingdom had been for the title, preamble and *testimonium* of the original signed copy that was retained by the Republic to refer to 'the Government of *Ireland*' and 'the Government of the *United Kingdom*', and the original signed copy retained by the United Kingdom to refer to 'the Government of the United Kingdom *of Great Britain and Northern Ireland*' and 'the Government of *the Republic of* Ireland'.[9] Starting with the UK–Ireland Agreement of 10 April 1998,[10] the practice has been for *both* original copies to refer to the 'Republic of Ireland' and the 'United Kingdom of Great Britain and Northern Ireland'.[11]

Preamble

Bilateral Treaties

The preamble to a bilateral treaty will usually begin:

> The Government of Freedonia and the Government of Utopia ('the Parties')...

and end:

> *have agreed* as follows:

There is seldom need for more than a few preambular paragraphs, if any. In special cases it may be necessary to define who the parties are, especially when the treaty relates only to an overseas territory of a state.[12] As with multilateral treaties (see below), the preamble of a bilateral treaty may be a useful vehicle for recording either important points in the political or factual background or points which were of importance to one side in the negotiation but which the other side (or sides) would not accept as a

[7] 474 UNTS 49 No. 6871; UKTS (1963) No. 59.
[8] See the text to n. 2 on Macedonia.
[9] See the UK–Ireland Double Taxation Agreement 1976: 1056 UNTS 226 No. 15947; UKTS (1977) No. 42.
[10] UK–Ireland Agreement 1998: 2114 UNTS 473 No. 36776; 37 ILM (1998) 777; UKTS (2000) No. 50. As with earlier UK–Irish treaties on delicate political matters, the title does not mention the subject.
[11] For example, the 1998 Protocol to the UK–Ireland Double Taxation Agreement 1976 (2068 UNTS 277 No. 15947; UKTS (1999) No. 23).
[12] See Article 11 UK–France Agreement concerning Fishing in the Bay of Granville 2000 (2269 UNTS 88 No. 40408; UKTS (2004) No. 9). The overseas territory was Jersey, which is *not* part of the metropolitan United Kingdom.

substantive article in the text. The inclusion of a point in the preamble means that it forms part of the context for the purpose of interpretation.[13]

Preambular paragraphs in bilateral treaties may thus include:

(1) principles governing the bilateral relationship as a whole, or the particular part of the relationship covered by the treaty;[14]
(2) statements of political commitment, which may include language of importance to one party in particular;[15]
(3) helpful affirmation of a legal aspect of the relationship between the two parties;[16]
(4) confirmation that the treaty is without prejudice to other legal commitments;[17]
(5) the factual background, sometimes in detail where this is necessary;[18]
(6) reiteration of fields of other rights and obligations (such as labour, health or environmental protection) which form a relevant backcloth.[19]

Multilateral Treaties

There is a wide variety of ways in which multilateral treaties (and amending multilateral instruments) begin. The traditional introduction was:

> The States Parties to this Agreement/Convention/Treaty . . .

The term 'states parties' (the words are usually given initial capital letters in treaty texts) is used in the Convention itself, and generally in older multilateral treaties

[13] See Article 31 VCLT, particularly Article 31(2): 'The context for the purpose of the interpretation of a treaty shall comprise, in addition to the text, including its preamble and annexes . . .'.

[14] For example, the second preambular paragraph to the UK–Ukraine Political, Free Trade and Strategic Partnership Agreement 2020 (UKTS (2022) No. 1): 'COMMITTED to a close and lasting relationship that is based on common values, namely respect for democratic principles, the rule of law, good governance, human rights and fundamental freedoms, including the rights of persons belonging to national minorities, non-discrimination of persons belonging to minorities and respect for diversity, human dignity and commitment to the principles of a free market economy.'

[15] For example, preambular paragraphs 15–16 of the same UK–Ukraine Agreement (n. 14): 'RECOGNISING that Russia's hostile actions against Ukraine undermine Ukraine's sovereignty and territorial integrity in violation of international law; COMMITTED to strictly adhering to the policy of non-recognition of Russia's attempted annexation of the Autonomous Republic of Crimea and the city of Sevastopol.'

[16] For example, the first preambular paragraph to the UK–Canada Agreement on Trade Continuity 2020 (UK Country Series, Canada (2020) No. 1) implicitly confirmed that the EU–Canada Comprehensive Economic and Trade Agreement (CETA) would apply to the UK during the transition period provided for in the EU–UK Withdrawal Agreement 2020.

[17] For example, the fourth preambular paragraph to the UK–Kenya Agreement concerning Defence Cooperation 2021 (UK Country Series, Kenya (2021) No. 1): 'RECOGNISING that such cooperation shall be in accordance with their respective national policies and international best practices and shall not conflict with the domestic law of their respective states nor impair the commitments undertaken by their countries in the international field.'

[18] For example, the (probably too lengthy) preamble to the Agreement between the UK and the Secretariat of the UN Framework Convention on Climate Change (n. 5).

[19] For example, preambular paragraphs 11, 13 and 14 of the (plurilateral) US–Mexico–Canada Agreement: at USTR website.

concluded within or under the auspices of the United Nations or the UN specialised agencies. Similar terms are contracting parties, high contracting parties (e.g., in ICRC treaties), contracting states, contracting governments, signatory states, and partner governments, which may be more appropriate in particular circumstances. But increasingly other formulae are used, for example where international organisations or other subjects of international law may be parties. So, for example, the Paris Agreement on climate change starts simply:

> The Parties to this Agreement . . .[20]

Other introductory words may emphasise membership of an organisation ('The member states of the Council of Europe and other signatories hereto',[21] or 'Members of the World Trade Organization'[22]) or, if the instrument is adopted in the framework of an international conference or an international organisation, it may simply cite the relevant conference or organisation which has adopted the text ('The General Conference of the International Labour Organization',[23] or 'The General Conference of the United Nations Educational, Scientific and Cultural Organization'[24]). Some of the more technical Conventions or amendments may lead straight into the substantive provisions without such an introductory phrase.[25]

When the treaty is plurilateral (between only a few states), the preamble will often begin with the names of all the negotiating states. The Memorandum of Understanding (actually a treaty) on the Avoidance of Overlaps and Conflicts relating to Deep Seabed Areas 1991[26] begins with the names of the negotiating states and then provides that they shall be 'hereinafter referred to as the "Parties"'.[27] Despite the use of such a ponderous word as 'hereinafter', this formula is a useful way of simplifying the rest of the text of any treaty, not just a plurilateral treaty. Alternatively, after setting out the names of the parties, it is enough to add '("the Parties")'. Thereafter, one can use this term throughout the main text.

[20] UNTS No. 54113; UKTS (2017) No. 4. Similarly, 'The Parties to this Convention . . .' in the International Convention for the Control and Management of Ships' Ballast Water and Sediments, 2004 (as amended): UNTS No. 55544; UK Misc. Series (2021) No. 6.

[21] CoE Istanbul Convention: 3010 UNTS 107 No. 52313; UK Misc. Series (2022) No. 3.

[22] Protocol amending the Marrakesh Agreement 2014: UNTS No. A-31874; UK Misc. Series (2019) No. 1.

[23] ILO Violence and Harassment Convention, 2019 (No. 190): UK Misc. Series (2021) No. 7.

[24] More fully: 'The General Conference of the United Nations Educational, Scientific and Cultural Organization, meeting in Paris from 12 to 27 November 2019 at its 40th session . . .'. Global Convention on the Recognition of Qualifications concerning Higher Education 2019: UK Misc. Series (2021) No. 4.

[25] For example, The Geneva Act of The Hague Agreement Concerning the Registration of Industrial Designs 1999: UKTS (2018) No. 13.

[26] UKTS (1991) No. 52.

[27] It is similar where the plurilateral agreement is essentially bilateral in nature, with many parties on one side and a single party on the other. See, for example, the UK–CARIFORUM Economic Partnership Agreement: UK Misc. Series (2018) No. 18. Here the CARIFORUM States are listed by name, followed by 'hereinafter referred to as the "CARIFORUM States"', and then, after the UK: 'hereinafter jointly referred to as "the Parties"'.

Preambular Paragraphs

There is no rule or custom as to what the rest of the preamble should contain; everything depends on the circumstances. In fact, from the *legal* point of view there is no need to say more than:

> The Parties to this [Agreement], have agreed as follows ...

But if more needs to be said, the primary aim should be to introduce the main text of the treaty by including a few paragraphs about the background and the object and purpose of the treaty. Sometimes, however, the preamble contains what are essentially political statements.

As with bilateral agreements, it may also refer, though usually in a much watered-down version, to a matter which a negotiating state could not get included in the body of the treaty. As with UN resolutions, the preamble can be a most convenient place to put the leftovers of hopeless causes, both large and small, lost during the negotiating process. In this, it serves a valuable purpose. Often negotiations become bogged down over a point insisted on by one delegation, or a few. By suggesting that it might be dealt with by including 'a suitable form of words' (which will have to be agreed) in the preamble, further pointless arguments, and a possible negotiating impasse, *may* be avoided. The loser will be able to report to their government that, despite considerable pressure from others to exclude all mention of the point, they had been persuaded to include it in the preamble (i.e., right at the beginning). At the FAO Conference which adopted the Compliance Agreement 1993, a contentious issue was the problem of 'reflagging' of fishing vessels,[28] but because it was not possible to reach a consensus, oblique references to it were included in the preamble.[29] By such means the 'face' of a government, and even more importantly the credibility of its chief negotiator, may be saved.

But such a device should be used sparingly. The preamble is part of the context of the treaty for the purposes of interpretation (Article 31(2)) including for the determination of the object and purpose of the treaty. It is, therefore, important to ensure that preambular paragraphs are not inconsistent with the main text. The more one burdens the preamble with unnecessary but not always insubstantial material, the greater the danger that it will come to be relied on to support an unintended interpretation of the main text. In the negotiation of the UNGA resolution adopting the Terrorism Financing Convention 1999,[30] Syria pressed for the inclusion in the resolution of a reference to Resolution 46/51 (1991), the wording of which implied that terrorism might be acceptable in pursuit of self-determination. The Syrian proposal was rejected. Later resolutions, starting with 49/60 (1994), carried no such implication.

[28] The changing of the state of registry of a vessel, in this case to avoid fishing controls.

[29] 2221 UNTS 120 No. 39486; 33 ILM (1994) 968.

[30] 2178 UNTS 229 No. 38349; 39 ILM (2000) 268; UKTS (2002) No. 28.

While the aim of the lawyer is usually to keep the preamble as short as possible, one can discern a worrying trend towards ever longer preambles. In addition to the factors mentioned above, this may be due to a desire to give more copious citation of relevant legal instruments (for example, in the Istanbul Convention)[31] or to provide a full rationale for the underlying policy (as in the Protocol to Eliminate Illicit Trade in Tobacco Products 2013).[32]

A key objective of the chair should normally be to postpone detailed consideration of the preamble for as long as possible. Because it appears at the beginning, there is a natural – but misguided – tendency to start the negotiations by discussing it. This is a huge mistake. To start by discussing the preamble may be logical, but, as a French diplomatic friend and colleague once said, with all his native pragmatism: it is to put Descartes before the horse. Although preambles have their uses, their value is insignificant compared with the rest of the treaty. The final clauses – which are often not given the close attention they should be given – are considerably more important. Much time can be wasted discussing the preamble before the shape and content of the main text and the final clauses have been determined. A preamble should reflect the main text, not the other way around.

Each preambular paragraph begins with a participle such as 'recalling', 'recognising', 'noting', 'convinced', and suchlike. It is customary either to underline or italicise such opening words, but this is purely a matter of style. The preamble to the VCLT is a good model. As a purely *practical* matter, when a draft preamble contains several paragraphs it is useful to number them for ease of reference, the numbers being removed once the negotiations and drafting are complete.

The preamble, whatever its length, will normally end with a final paragraph:

> *Have agreed* as follows:

Non-binding Instruments

The preamble of an NBI will look similar to that of a treaty, except that the governments will normally be described by name or as 'the Participants'. Instead of the formula 'Have agreed as follows', the preamble should end 'Have reached the following understanding(s)', or 'Have decided' or, simply 'The Governments/Participants will'. Otherwise, the same advice on the preambular paragraphs themselves as outlined above in respect of treaties apply equally here. Because an NBI encapsulates political rather than legal commitments, it is perhaps natural that the preamble is seen by governments as an even greater opportunity to expound the political benefits (or defence) of a particular project,[33] but the tests of precision and necessity of wording are as much a virtue here as with treaties.

[31] See n. 21. [32] UNTS No. 55487; UK Misc. Series (2018) No. 5.

[33] See, for example, the preamble to the UK–Rwanda MOU for provision of an asylum partnership arrangement, signed at Kigali, 13 April 2022, available at: www.gov.uk/government/publications/memorandum-of-under

Main Text of Treaties

The main text is, of course, the heart of the treaty. Some suggestions on how to approach the drafting of it are at the end of this chapter. For the moment, we will concentrate on form and layout. One might be forgiven for thinking that the drafters of some multilateral treaties never actually have to use or advise on them. Treaties are tools of international life and so are in constant use; they should therefore be user-friendly. The problem is that they are becoming longer and more complex. The VCLT itself, with eighty-five relatively short articles, is now dwarfed by treaties such as UNCLOS 1982,[34] the Chemical Weapons Convention 1993[35] and the CTBT 1996.[36] UNCLOS has no less than 320 articles and 9, sometimes lengthy, annexes, yet it is quite easy to navigate. This is because each article is kept as short as possible and has a heading, as have the annexes.

The CWC is much more difficult to use. The fact that it has only twenty-four articles is misleading. Some are quite unnecessarily long. Article VIII consists of no less than fifty-one paragraphs. Article IX has twenty-five paragraphs. Others have nineteen and seventeen paragraphs. But that is not all. There are three (unnumbered) annexes. The most often consulted, the Annex on Implementation and Verification, has eleven parts, some of which stretch indecently to no less than eighty-six, sixty-nine, sixty-six, thirty-two (twice) and twenty-seven paragraphs. The difficulty in using the CWC was recognised at the time by the inclusion of a table of contents (see below) of the Annex referred to, though that is not a substitute for splitting it into more manageable bits. The same mistakes were made in the CTBT, which follows the form of the CWC. The article on verification has sixty-eight paragraphs and the one on the organisation has fifty-seven paragraphs. Although the CTBT has only two short annexes, it has a Protocol on Monitoring, which is split into three parts. The second has no less than 110 paragraphs.

Although one appreciates that complex subjects cannot be treated in short, simple treaties, that is no reason why they should not be reasonably easy to use, whether by lawyers, diplomats, legislators, technical experts or, indeed, even by students and members of the public. With mammoth articles it becomes that much more difficult to find or cite the relevant provision, and can lead to simple mistakes, especially inconsistencies. This is particularly so when there are no fewer than *nine* paragraphs *each* numbered '25', as in the CWC and its attachments. Dividing up an article or an annex with sub- and sub-subheadings is not the answer. Although it may give the appearance of order, it does not make the text any easier to deal with.

standing-mou-between-the-uk-and-rwanda/memorandum-of-understanding-between-the-government-of-the-united-kingdom-of-great-britain-and-northern-ireland-and-the-government-of-the-republic-of-r

[34] 1833 UNTS 397 No. 31363; 21 ILM (1982) 1261; UKTS (1999) No. 81.

[35] 1974 UNTS 317 No. 33757; 32 ILM (1993) 804; UKTS (1996) No. 45.

[36] 35 ILM (1996) 1439.

Sometimes treaties have been badly drafted because what began as short, simple articles were later added to many times, and during the process of (no doubt lengthy and difficult) negotiations no one had the energy, initiative or simple good sense to concern themselves with how the treaty would look or read; and by the time the negotiations were over there was no time left to recast the text. Although this may be understandable, a better laid-out text can be produced if a conscious effort is made from the *start*. Here are a few suggestions.

Layout

The layout and numbering of the VCLT (to which many drafters turn in time of need) is a good guide to the right way to do it. It consists of eighty-five articles, *each* with a heading. No article is longer than six paragraphs. The articles are grouped into eight 'parts', each with a short heading. These are then divided into 'sections'. The need for this latter grouping is marginal, though it does enable one to make reference to a group of articles on, say, reservations. But, in practice, it is simpler to refer to the numbers of the articles since they are always easier to find than a part, or a section of a part. Even if the published version of the Convention comes with a table of contents (see below), this is chiefly of use in finding a particular article or series of articles.

Headings

Even today one finds new treaties where the articles have no headings.[37] Even (perhaps especially) during drafting and negotiation, headings are extremely useful in helping to find one's way around the text, particularly if the numbers of the articles change during the negotiations.[38] Headings may be added at any time, provided it is understood that until the substance of the draft has been agreed, they are only provisional. (This can be emphasised by temporarily putting the headings in square brackets.) As with the preamble, there should be *no discussion* of the headings until the end of the negotiations: otherwise, much time may be wasted arguing over the wording of what is no more than a label. Although there can be arguments over exactly what should be in the heading, generally these are not serious, and should not discourage the drafters from inserting headings in the very first draft. Most headings can be very short. Those in the VCLT are rather different in that some of them are, in effect, summaries of the content of the articles (Article 18 being headed 'Obligation not to defeat the object and purpose of a treaty prior to its entry into force'), but for that reason they can in fact be rather useful.

[37] See, for example, the Paris Agreement (n. 20).
[38] On a way to avoid the problem of changing numbers, see below.

Numbering

The articles of the VCLT have Arabic numbers (1, 2, 3, etc.); the parts have Roman numerals (I, II, III, etc.); and the sections of the parts have Arabic numbers. In the past, it was customary to use Roman numerals for articles, and most regrettably, and inexplicably, they are still found even in new treaties. They should be avoided like the plague, especially if the treaty has many articles: up to thirty-nine is just about manageable but forty and beyond is more of a struggle.[39] For those without the benefit of a classical education, Article 79 VCLT is so much easier to find than Article LXXIX. Roman numerals can, as in the Convention, be used for numbering the parts (or chapters). Since there are only eight parts to the Convention and one Annex, this is acceptable; but when a treaty has more than one annex it may be better to use Arabic numbers for the parts of the main text and Roman numerals for the parts of the annexes, so distinguishing them clearly from the main text.

Paragraph Numbering

If necessary, articles should be divided into paragraphs, subparagraphs and sub-subparagraphs, in the following way:

1. A State whose vessels . . .
2. A State shall authorise . . .
3. Measures to be taken by a State in respect of vessels flying its flag shall include:
   (a) control of such vessels . . .;
   (b) establishment of regulations to:
      (i) apply terms . . .;
      (ii) prohibit fishing . . .;[40]

If an article has only one paragraph, that paragraph should *not* be numbered, and if it has subparagraphs, they should be numbered (a), (b), and so on *(not* 1, 2, 3, etc.). If sub-sub-subparagraphs are unavoidable, they should be numbered either (aa), (bb) or (A), (B), and so on. One should avoid all numbering which emulates that found in modern commercial contracts (1.1.1, 1.1.2, 1.2.1, etc.).[41] Not only is it inelegant, despite its seductive simplicity, but it is not as easy to use as one might think, as it can easily lead to errors, especially typographical, and amending provisions can be particularly tricky:

> In paragraph 4.4.7.6, the existing subparagraph .9 is renumbered as subparagraph .17 and in the renumbered subparagraph .17, the references to

[39] The Global Convention (n. 24) has articles up to XXV; the GATT 1947 has articles up to XXXVIII.
[40] See the Fish Stocks Agreement 1995 (n. 3).
[41] See the 1996 Protocol to the London Dumping Convention: 36 ILM (1997) 7.

paragraphs '4.4.7.6.2.2 and 4.4.7.6.3' are replaced by the references to paragraphs '4.4.7.6.7, 4.4.7.6.8 and 4.4.7.6.15'.[42]

Cross-references

If one is referring to an article of the treaty itself, or to a paragraph of that article, one should avoid pedantic cross-referencing, such as 'Article 4 *above*' or 'paragraph 6 *below*'. If there might really be doubt as to which particular article or paragraph is being referred to, one can always add 'of this treaty' or 'of this article'.

When the reference is to a paragraph or subparagraph of another article one should use the brief formula 'Article 4(6)(a)(i)' rather than 'sub-subparagraph (a)(i) of paragraph 6 of Article 4' or even 'Article 4, paragraph 6, sub-subparagraph (a)(i)'. The first (and *brief*) formula is more logical: one looks first for the article and then for the paragraph, and so on. It is both neater and clearer, and therefore much easier to use.

Footnotes

In the case of older treaties, it is not usual to find footnotes to a treaty text, except perhaps in the text as later published, and then only for *information*, such as a citation of a treaty mentioned in the text. But in more recent treaties the use of footnotes is increasingly widespread. There is nothing in principle against the inclusion of footnotes in a treaty provided there is no more suitable way of dealing with the matter. The ideal is that footnotes should be used sparingly and restricted to providing information to the reader which is more conveniently conveyed in this manner rather than in the body of the treaty, in the final act or in a resolution. But this ideal is more honoured in its breach.

The US–Mexico–Canada Agreement,[43] for example, contains numerous footnotes by way of clarification or interpretation, as do many other trade agreements.[44] There are also examples in multilateral treaties of the negotiating states recording Agreed Statements concerning certain provisions in footnotes against that provision, for example in the fourteen footnotes to the Marrakesh Treaty of 2013.[45] The UK–EU Withdrawal Agreement contains many footnotes specifying the relevant legislation referred to in the substantive text. It also includes an important 'asterisk' in the provisions relating to the transition period, whereby the European Union undertakes to notify the other parties to the agreements concluded by the Union that during the

[42] These are in fact amendments to the International Life-Saving (LSA) Appliances Code, part of the Amendments to the International Convention for the Safety of Life at Sea 1974 (SOLAS 1974), adopted between 2011 and 2013: UKTS (2020) No. 5 (Annex, para. 9, p. 6).

[43] See n. 19. [44] See, for example, the CPTPP.

[45] Marrakesh Treaty to Facilitate Access to Published Works for Persons Who Are Blind, Visually Impaired or Otherwise Print Disabled, 2013: UNTS No. 54134; UK Misc. Series (2019) No. 25.

transition period the United Kingdom is to be treated as a Member State for the purposes of these agreements.[46]

A footnote should *not*, however, be used to express the objection or reservation of one or more of the negotiating states to a provision, or explain that a particular phrase means something different in certain of the authentic languages.[47]

In some circumstances it may be necessary to clarify the status of the footnotes. Hence Article 34.2 of the US–Mexico–Canada Agreement provides:

> The annexes, appendices, and footnotes to this Agreement constitute an integral part of this Agreement.[48]

Non-binding Instruments

The points about layout and numbering apply generally to non-binding instruments (often MOUs) as well, except that one should use 'sections' or 'paragraphs' (with headings, of course), rather than 'articles', which should be used only for treaties.

Terminology

In order to make clear the intention to enter into a treaty, the established practice is to use, both in the main text and in annexes, well-understood terms which convey the intention that it will be a legally binding instrument rather than a non-binding instrument. The text should therefore use 'shall' (in French the present tense would be used), 'agree', and 'rights' and 'obligations'. A table contrasting the terminology which should be used for a treaty and for a non-binding instrument is at Appendix H. It may look strange, but it does work.

Most treaties have a list of definitions in the first or second article. Definitions help to keep the text simple and uncluttered by making it unnecessary to repeat long, descriptive phrases throughout the treaty. The VCLT once again shows how it should be done. Article 2 contains only nine definitions, but each is a model of precision combined with lucidity and conciseness.

Some drafters prefer to put all the definitions into the definitions article. Logic, order and consistency are desirable in drafting, but should not be applied slavishly. If a term

[46] Article 127 EU–UK Withdrawal Agreement and the asterisk thereto: OJ C 3841, 12.11.2019, 1–177; UKTS (2020) No. 3.

[47] See the 'Explanatory Notes' following Articles IX and XVI WTO Agreement 1994, and the attached Understanding on Rules and Procedures Governing the Settlement of Disputes (1867 UNTS 4 No. 31874; 33 ILM (1994) 1144). The footnote to the penultimate draft of Article 12 Disabilities Convention 2006 (A/60/232), which had said that in the Arabic, Chinese and Russian texts the term legal capacity referred to legal capacity for rights, rather than legal capacity to act, was eventually removed.

[48] See similarly Article 778 EU–UK Trade and Cooperation Agreement 2020: UKTS (2021) No. 8; OJ L 149, 30.4.2021; and Article 10 UK–Mexico Trade Continuity Agreement 2020: UK Country Series, Mexico (2021) No. 1.

needs to be defined, *but is used in only one article,* it is better to define it in *that* article and not in the definitions article, though the latter might have a cross-reference to the definition. Once again, the CWC shows how *not* to do it. Article II contains definitions of eleven terms used throughout the CWC. The twelfth definition contains (as it says so itself) definitions for the purposes of Article VI only. It would, therefore, have been more convenient, and sensible, if they had been included only in that article.

It is quite common in longer treaties, such as trade agreements, with a large number of Chapters covering distinct subjects, to find a general definitions section in the first Chapter, and a specific definitions section at the start of some of the separate Chapters.[49]

It is not easy to say when definitions should be added to the text as so much depends on the circumstances, but it will become apparent during the course of drafting and redrafting when they are needed. When preparing the initial draft, even if it is obvious that particular definitions will eventually be needed, it is better not to try to anticipate them, though a (blank) definition article should be included in the first draft as the first or second article. If this is not done, it will almost certainly be necessary later, and the rest of the text may well have to be renumbered throughout.

Privileges and Immunities

The subject of privileges and immunities is included here because, like final clauses, it is put at the end of a treaty, as well as being often regarded, albeit quite wrongly, as a routine matter. The topic is therefore rarely given proper attention at an early stage. Unlike final clauses, privileges and immunities are not solely the concern of foreign ministries. The subject, which includes conferring legal capacity on a new international organisation, exemptions from taxation and immunity from the jurisdiction of national courts, touches upon the rights of the ordinary citizen.[50] Moreover, the provisions will need implementing in domestic law, even if the rest of the treaty may not. Consultations with several ministries will almost certainly be necessary, and it is the task of the foreign ministry to coordinate this work. Since the process could be lengthy, ideally the provisions should be negotiated in parallel with the rest of the main text.

Although there are no model articles as such, one should try to follow as closely as possible the provisions in treaties on similar subjects.[51] If, as is usually the case, there need to be several articles, they may be put into an annex or protocol, or even a

[49] See, for example, the US–Mexico–Canada Agreement (n. 19); and the CPTPP.

[50] See Article VIII, paras. 48–51, and Pt. II, Section B, of the Verification Annex to the CWC (n. 35).

[51] For European treaties, a good starting point is Annex I to the ESA Convention 1975 (1297 UNTS 161 No. 21524; 14 ILM (1975) 864; UKTS (1981) No. 30), though more recent provisions should also be considered, depending on the subject matter of the treaty. For universal treaties, see, for example, the Protocol on the Privileges and Immunities of the International Seabed Authority 1998: 2214 UNTS 133 No. 39357; UKTS (2004) No. 25.

self-standing treaty. Non-binding instruments, principally in the defence field, sometimes make provision for privileges and immunities.

Table of Contents

Even though its preparation is a purely mechanical operation, unfortunately it is rare to find a table of contents even in a long and complex multilateral treaty. Notable exceptions are the Verification Annexes to the CWC and the CTBT. Since an unofficial table is sometimes added by a state when it publishes the treaty, there is no reason why a table should not more commonly be included in the adopted text, or why the negotiating states should not request, perhaps in the final act, that the depositary include a table of contents in the certified copy of the treaty that will be provided to them. As with the VCLT, it should be totally neutral, consisting only of the numbers of the parts, sections and articles, their respective headings and applicable page numbers of the certified text.

Final Clauses

Final clauses can be a painful trap for the unwary. Compared with the main body of a treaty, the final clauses may appear to anyone who is not a foreign ministry lawyer to be less important than the main body of the treaty – and in a sense they are. But, as should be apparent from earlier chapters,[52] final clauses do play an essential, if different, role from the main text. Unfortunately, they are not always given the care and attention they deserve, even though they are crucial to the smooth operation of any treaty. It may be because they come at the end that they are not always given the same careful thought as the main text, or even the preamble. Too often they are perceived as purely formal provisions which have only to be copied or adapted from another similar treaty. Although they are usually based on precedents – and once again the VCLT is a good *starting* point – it is vital that they are drafted with the needs of the particular treaty in mind. Although some clauses are truly technical, some will need important policy decisions by the negotiating states.

Now that so many treaties are negotiated by specialists rather than generalist diplomats and foreign ministry lawyers, the importance of final clauses may not always be fully appreciated, and their drafting done far too late. It is rare to find the first draft of a treaty with a full set of (or, for that matter, any) final clauses. This can lead to errors, some of which can be quite troublesome.[53] If a multilateral treaty is being negotiated within an international organisation or at a conference at which an

[52] See, e.g., those on consent to be bound, reservations, entry into force, amendment, and duration and termination.

[53] See p. 239 regarding the interpretation of Article XIV of the CTBT 1996.

international organisation provides the secretariat, the legal department of the organisation should provide the necessary expertise. Otherwise, delegations need to seek advice from their own foreign ministry lawyers at an early stage, and especially if the latter are not taking a direct part in the negotiations.

It is quite common to find a treaty accompanied by a protocol, which is itself a separate treaty. An optional protocol on dispute settlement is one example. Although the treaty and the optional protocol will be related, each being a treaty *in its own right*, each must have its own final clauses.

Final clauses can include articles on:

- relationship to other treaties
- settlement of disputes
- amendment and review*
- status of annexes
- signature*
- ratification*
- accession*
- entry into force*
- duration*
- withdrawal/termination*
- provisional application
- territorial application
- reservations*
- depositary*
- registration
- authentic texts.*

Those marked with an asterisk will be found in most multilateral treaties and in many bilateral treaties. Inclusion of the others will depend on the nature and content of the treaty. The length of the list illustrates the many different matters covered by final clauses, some of which, such as reservations, settlement of disputes, amendment, duration, termination and entry into force, may be of prime importance and raise difficult questions of policy (e.g., whether there should be a compulsory and comprehensive amendment and arbitration procedure). One article may deal with two or more subjects.

There are no rigid formulas for these various provisions, and therefore the examples given are not necessarily the 'right' ones. One of the problems is the very wide variety of final clauses. Earlier examples can be found in *Blix and Emerson*. In 1957 the United Nations published a *Handbook of Final Clauses* which may be updated from time to time.[54]

[54] See http://treaties.un.org/doc/source/publications/FC/English.pdf.

Non-binding Instruments

An MOU (non-binding instrument) will possibly have provisions on settlement of disputes, amendment, duration and withdrawal/termination. Signature and coming into operation or effect will normally be dealt with in a simplified *testimonium* at the end (see Appendix D). Where appropriate, what follows should be read with earlier chapters.

Relationship to Other Treaties

A provision on this matter will not always be needed for multilateral treaties, and rarely for bilateral treaties (see Chapter 12). If included, it may be placed right at the beginning[55] or towards the end.[56] Non-binding instruments seldom include an equivalent provision.

Settlement of Disputes

It is normal to find an article, or series of articles, on the settlement of disputes concerning the interpretation or application of the treaty, whether it is bilateral or multilateral. Such provisions can be long and complex and attract some sensitivity, as in the case of the EU–UK Withdrawal Agreement.[57] There are many precedents. Although they tend to follow a certain pattern, a negotiating state needs to give careful thought as to whether the procedure is appropriate to the particular agreement or fully reflects its interests.

A non-binding instrument will have either no such clause or one on the following lines:

> Any dispute regarding the interpretation or application of this MOU will be resolved by consultations between the Participants, and will not be referred to any national or international tribunal or third party for settlement.

Amendment and Revision

It is increasingly common to find a provision about amendment or revision. In the past there was a tendency not to think that far ahead. As a result, the amendment of treaties which included no such built-in provision caused, and continues to cause, considerable problems. Today's multilateral treaties are so complex, needing to be adjusted to meet changes, that an amendment clause is usually essential (see Chapter 15). It is common

[55] For example, Articles 1.2 and 1.3, US–Mexico–Canada Agreement (n. 19).

[56] For example, Article 71 Istanbul Convention (n. 21).

[57] See Title III of Part Six, Dispute Settlement, Articles 167–181 EU–UK Withdrawal Agreement, (n. 46); chapter 14 Dispute Settlement, Articles 289–311 (and chapter 15 Mediation Mechanism) UK–Ukraine Political, Free Trade and Strategic Partnership Agreement (n. 14).

in trade and related agreements for certain types of amendments to be made by a Joint Committee (or equivalent) established by the Parties.[58] These require careful drafting to determine precisely what amendments are within the scope of the Joint Committee's powers, and what procedures are to be followed, particularly in light of domestic processes, which may in certain cases require ratification (or equivalent) and informing (or obtaining the approval of) parliament.[59]

Non-binding instruments will sometimes have a clause providing that:

> This MOU may be amended at any time, in writing, by the mutual consent of the Participants. No amendment will have effect until signed by [both] [all] Participants.

Status of Annexes

When a treaty has an annex, it is normal to provide, though not necessarily in a separate article, that the annex is integral to the treaty (i.e., part of it). As a typical example, Article XVII of the CWC 1993 provides:

> The Annexes form an integral part of this Convention. Any reference to this Convention includes the Annexes.

Since there are often other documents produced at the time the treaty is adopted, such as agreed minutes, declarations and interpretative exchanges of notes, it is important to know whether they are an *integral part of the treaty* or merely associated with it. Unless there is an express provision that a particular document or documents are integral to the treaty,[60] the presumption is that they are *not*.

Signature[61]

Treaties do not have to be signed, and many, particularly bilateral treaties, do not have a separate article on signature, it being implicit from the terms of the *testimonium*.[62] But most multilateral treaties have a specific article on signature. The formula chosen depends on whether the treaty will enter into force on signature or is subject to

58 See, for example, Article 164 EU–UK Withdrawal Agreement (n. 46), and Decision No 1/2022 of the Joint Committee established by the Withdrawal Agreement of 21 February 2022: UKTS (2022) No. 4; OJ L 43/84, 24.02.2022; and Articles 8–9 UK–Switzerland Agreement on the Mutual Recognition of their Authorised Economic Operator Programmes 2021: UKTS (2022) No. 3.

59 See p. 279.

60 See, e.g., Article 12(1) UK–France Agreement concerning Fishing in the Bay of Granville (n. 12).

61 This section should be read with Chapter 7.

62 See the 1987 Agreement between six NATO members regarding inspections relating to the US–USSR Treaty on Elimination of Certain Missiles: 1658 UNTS 364 No. 28536; 27 ILM (1988) 60; UKTS (1991) No. 31.

ratification. A treaty adopted within or under the auspices of the United Nations, a UN specialised agency or other international organisation will usually provide:

> This [treaty] shall be open for signature by [all States] and shall remain open for signature at [place] from [date] until [date].

As indicated, the article of a multilateral treaty will normally set a deadline for signature. There is no *legal* requirement for this, the purpose being mainly political. Governments like to be able to say (particularly because a need for parliamentary approval or new legislation means that it will take some time to ratify the treaty) that they are 'a signatory'. Setting a deadline thus encourages those states to sign; and the more that sign, the greater the effect politically, including on those parliaments which have to approve the treaty before their states can ratify.

It is less common for a multilateral treaty to enter into force on signature, though this is provided for in some treaties that are between only a small number of states, provided no parliamentary procedure is needed before the treaties can enter into force for them all. Such a treaty will usually provide:

> This Agreement shall enter into force upon signature.

This simple formula assumes that the treaty will be signed by all on the same day, which will usually be the case for such treaties. Otherwise, the treaty will provide that it 'shall enter into force on the date of the last signature'.

A bilateral treaty is usually signed by both parties on the same day, and often provides for entry into force upon signature.

Ratification

When ratification is required for a multilateral treaty, a normal provision would be as in Article 82 VCLT:

> The present Convention is subject to ratification. The instruments of ratification shall be deposited with the [name of the depositary].

Sometimes the sentence about deposit of instruments of ratification is omitted, the matter being implicit from the article on the depositary. In the case of a *bilateral* treaty, a provision on ratification would read along the following lines:

> This [treaty] shall be ratified, and the instruments of ratification shall be exchanged at [place] as soon as possible.

But it is common now for parties to a bilateral agreement to bring a treaty into force by notification of completion of constitutional or domestic procedures, a procedure analogous to ratification. Hence, Article 783 EU–UK Trade and Cooperation Agreement[63] provides:

[63] See n. 48.

> This Agreement shall enter into force on the first day of the month following that in which both Parties have notified each other that they have completed their respective internal requirements and procedures for establishing their consent to be bound.

Accession

Accession is only relevant to multilateral treaties. Nowadays, those that are subject to ratification almost always include provision for accession during the period *before* entry into force and, depending on the terms of the accession article, a state will be able to accede after a specified date (e.g., the deadline for signature), or a specified event, or at any time (for examples and further details, see page 121).

Entry into Force

With a few exceptions, there will always be an express provision on entry into force. When there is none, it should be implicit from the terms of the treaty when entry into force will take place. Most provisions on entry into force will be straightforward, but sometimes entry into force will depend upon, or be subsequent to, another contingent event, not just (for example) on deposit of instruments of ratification or the last notification of completion of domestic procedures. In that case, the nature of the relationship between entry into force and that event will have to be carefully defined.[64] In addition, where the states are in different time zones, and the actual hour of entry into force is critical, the provision might specify at what hour in the respective countries the treaty will come into force.

Duration and Denunciation, Withdrawal or Termination

It is normal to provide for the duration of the treaty and the procedure by which a party may withdraw from it, or for the conditions under which it can be terminated,

[64] See, for example, Article 10 UK–Australia Agreement on Trade in Wine 2019: [2021] ATS No. 3; UK Country Series, Australia (2019) No. 1:

> 'This Agreement shall enter into force on the later of:
>
> (a) the date on which the EC-Australia Wine Agreement ceases to apply to the United Kingdom; or
> (b) the date of receipt of the later of the Parties' notifications confirming completion of their internal procedures.'

unless the treaty is such that that possibility is not envisaged. There are numerous examples of such clauses.

In a simple bilateral treaty the termination provision is often combined with other provisions:

> (1) Each Party shall notify the other of the completion of the constitutional formalities required by its laws for the entry into force of this Agreement. This Agreement shall enter into force on the first day of the month following the expiration of one calendar month after the date of the later of the two notifications.
> (2) It may be terminated by either Party by giving notice to the other through the diplomatic channel. It shall cease to be in force six months after the date of receipt of such notice.

Provisional Application

The parties may enable provisional application of a treaty either by including express provision in the treaty itself or by agreement 'in some other manner',[65] such as an exchange of notes. There is a wide variety of possible draft provisions for inclusion in a treaty depending on, for example, whether it is bilateral or multilateral, or whether it is to be provisionally applied upon signature or after a further procedure. The Annex to the ILC Guidelines on Provisional Application is a useful quarry of clauses used in both bilateral and multilateral agreements.[66] The UK made extensive use of provisional application in the context of its withdrawal from the EU to ensure that there was no gap between the application of previous (EU) agreements with third countries and new (UK) agreements. The provisions in these new agreements also provide helpful models.[67]

Territorial Application

When one or both of the states negotiating a bilateral treaty have overseas territories, a clause providing for the treaty to be extended to one or more of them may be included, but it is not essential for a multilateral treaty, or indeed even normal these days.

[65] See Article 25(1) VCLT; and pp. 182–183.

[66] Guide to Provisional Application of Treaties, Report of the ILC on the work of its 72nd session, 2021, UNGA 76th Session, Supplement No. 10, Doc. A/76/10, 55.

[67] See the following references for plurilateral or multilateral agreements in the UK Miscellaneous Series: (2019) Nos. 4, 15, 17, 18, 22, 28, 30, 31, 32; (2020) Nos. 3, 4, 8, 9; (2021) Nos. 2, 3; and for bilateral agreements in the UK Country Series: Albania (2021) No. 1; Ghana (2021) No. 1; Italy (2021) No. 1; Mexico (2021) No. 1; Switzerland (2021) No. 2; Netherlands (2021) No. 1; Norway (2020) No. 1. Even this is just a selection.

Reservations

Reservation clauses are found only in multilateral treaties, but not in all. When one is included, it may prohibit reservations:

> No reservations may be made to this Convention.

Alternatively, the clause will specify those categories of reservations which are permissible. The content of the clause will depend entirely on the rest of the treaty.

Depositary

A clause about the depositary is only necessary for a multilateral treaty. It may be a separate article near the end and, for example, provide that:

> The Secretary-General of the United Nations shall be the depositary of this Agreement.

It is advisable to have a depositary for a plurilateral treaty if this exceeds three or four parties. Needless to say, if articles in a plurilateral treaty refer to certain tasks being performed by a depositary, one should have a separate article designating the depositary.

An article designating a depositary may include an *illustrative* list of the depositary's functions, though this should not be necessary if the depositary is the head of the secretariat of a large international organisation that regularly acts as a depositary, and therefore needs no reminding of their duties. The main functions are set out in detail in Article 77. It may therefore be enough to specify only those functions which are peculiar to the treaty.

Often a separate article is dispensed with. Article 85 VCLT (Authentic texts) provides simply that the original of the Convention 'shall be deposited with the Secretary-General of the United Nations'. (For more details and examples, see Chapter 18.)

Registration

It is not legally necessary to provide that a treaty shall be registered, since under Article 102 of the UN Charter there is already an obligation to do so. For a *multilateral* treaty this is clearly the responsibility of the depositary (see Article 77(1)(g) VCLT), and it is normal to have a provision directing the depositary to register. Thus, Article XV of the Compliance Agreement 1993 provides that the FAO Director-General, as depositary, shall:

> arrange for the registration of this Agreement, upon its entry into force, with the Secretariat of the United Nations in accordance with Article 102 of the Charter of the United Nations.

The real advantage of such a clause is as a *reminder* to the depositary. The FAO formula is helpful since it contains the further useful reminder that the treaty cannot be registered until it has entered into force. It would also be useful if every *bilateral* treaty had an express provision saying *which* party would register it. All too many bilateral treaties are never registered, sometimes because each party assumes the other will do it.

Authentic Texts

Probably more than half of all modern treaties are in two or more languages, and these days multilateral treaties are very rarely in only one language. There is normally only one original copy of a multilateral treaty, which will contain all the authentic language texts. (See below about the *testimonium.)*

Testimonium

'*Testimonium*' is the Latin name for the last, formal part of a treaty beneath which the representatives sign. It is not essential, and a treaty adopted at an FAO Conference will not have one as FAO treaties are not signed.[68] The Landmines Convention 1997 dispensed with a *testimonium*, the signature article merely noting that the Convention was 'Done at Oslo, on 18 September 1997'. It is not clear if this was intentional.[69]

A *testimonium* consists of the following formal statement:

> In witness whereof the undersigned, being duly authorised [by their respective Governments], have signed this [Agreement].
>
> Done at [place], this [ ] day of [ ], two thousand and [ ].

The reference to being authorised by their respective governments can be omitted, and should be when a non-state entity is entitled to sign.

Sometimes the order of the two sentences is reversed, which would in fact appear to be the more logical order. The words 'In witness whereof' and 'Done' are often in capital letters, but this is purely a matter of style.

The VCLT uses the term 'undersigned Plenipotentiaries', which means that the representatives are invested with full powers. Although this is sometimes still found (e.g., the Fish Stocks Agreement 1995),[70] it is gradually falling into disuse. The term is anyway superfluous because of the inclusion of 'duly authorised'.

Then follow the 'signature blocks', that is the spaces in which representatives sign. Each block will begin with the words:

> For [the Government of] Atlantis:

[68] See Compliance Agreement 1993 (n. 29).

[69] 2056 UNTS 241 No. 35597; 36 ILM (1997) 1509; UKTS (1998) No. 18. See Article 15.

[70] See n. 3.

The name of the representative is *not* typed in. In the case of a multilateral treaty, the names of the states or governments are set out in alphabetical order according to the language of the treaty. When the treaty is in more than one language, the different language texts (including any annexes, but not the *testimonium*) will follow, one after the other. The treaty will then *end* with the *testimonium* written in each of the language versions. In UN practice, the states are then listed (in English alphabetical order) and there will be only *one* signature block. In other words, even when a multilateral treaty is in two or more languages, a representative signs only *one* original, and signs only *once*.

Bilateral Treaties

If the treaty is to be signed in only one language, the *testimonium* will read:

> In witness whereof the undersigned, being duly authorised thereto, have signed this [Agreement].
> Done in duplicate at [place], this [ ] day of [ ], two thousand and [ ].
> For the Government of [ ]: For the Government of [ ]:
> [signature] [signature]

In one of the originals the name of one of the parties will be put before the name of the other in the title, preamble, main text, *testimonium* and signature blocks; in the other original the name of the other party will be put first. This alternating in the texts is known as the *alternat*. Each representative will take away the original in which the name of his or her state is given precedence: a small, quintessentially diplomatic, touch.

If the treaty is in two languages the second sentence of the *testimonium* will read:

> Done in duplicate at [place], this [ ] day of [ ], two thousand [ ], in the [ ] and [ ] languages, both texts being equally authentic.

The two originals will each include both language versions. One of the originals will accord precedence to one of the states in *both* language versions, the precedence being reversed in the other original. Each representative will take away the original which gives precedence to their state. But if time is short, or it will not be easy to produce alternate texts in the two language versions (perhaps because one of the languages is 'difficult'), each party will be given precedence only in the versions of the text which are in its own language ('language precedence'). Fortunately, today's diplomacy has much more important concerns.[71] Note also that a bilateral treaty can be in three (or even more) languages.

It is no longer the practice to affix seals next to the signatures, except sometimes for heads of state treaties. In any case, today sealing has no legal significance.

[71] For an amusing account of the importance in the past of precedence and the *alternat*, see H. Nicolson, *The Congress of Vienna* (Methuen, London 1946), 217–220.

Increasingly in bilateral treaties the *testimonium* is omitted. The *testimonium* of the UN–Iraq Memorandum of Understanding 1998[72] on weapons inspections reads:

> Signed this 23rd day of February 1998 in Baghdad in two originals in the English language.

There are no final clauses, and no preamble. In matters of form at least, it is a model for bilateral treaties.

Non-binding Instruments

An MOU (non-binding instrument) does not have a *testimonium* as such. There is no standard form, but an MOU contained in a single document will usually end:

> The foregoing represents the understandings reached by the [Participants] [Governments].
>
> Signed in duplicate at [place], on [ ], in [one language] or [in the [ ] and [ ] languages, each text having equal validity.

There would then follow the same signature blocks as for a treaty.

Attachments

If a treaty has attachments, it will usually provide that they are integral. They will be named variously annex, protocol, appendix or schedule. Some treaties use more than one term. The CTBT 1996[73] has two integral Annexes (numbered 1 and 2) to the treaty itself and an (integral) Protocol with two Annexes of its own (*also* numbered 1 and 2). This is unnecessarily confusing since, when referring to an annex, one has to say always whether it is to the treaty or to the protocol. Unless there are good reasons for using different designations for the attachments to a treaty (and they may well be political reasons), if an attachment is an integral part of the treaty it should be called an annex; and if there are more than one, they should also be called annexes and numbered. To distinguish the provisions of annexes from provisions of the treaty, it may also be useful to number the annexes 'A', 'B', and so on.

Since some annexes are long and substantive, it is prudent to distinguish their provisions from those in the treaty itself. Since 'article' should always be used in the treaty, it should *not* be used in an annex. The Annex to the VCLT is divided into seven *paragraphs*. If the annex is much longer, it is better for it to be arranged as a series of 'sections', each containing as few paragraphs as possible and with a heading to each section. If desired, the sections can be grouped into chapters (or parts if the main text is divided into chapters, and vice versa). If it is necessary to have an attachment to an annex, it should be named appendix or schedule.

[72] 2005 UNTS 209 No. 34375; 37 ILM (1998) 501; UN Doc. S/1998/166. See also the Russia–Ukraine Treaty on Friendship, Cooperation and Partnership 1997: UN Doc. A/52/174.

[73] See n. 36.

The name 'protocol' should mostly be avoided, since it is used extensively as the title for amendment treaties (and sometimes even for first treaties), or for a treaty which is separate from, but related to, another new treaty. But sometimes a 'protocol' may be appropriate for an instrument forming part of a treaty but which contains substantive provisions on a separate and significant aspect, for example the Protocol to the Withdrawal Agreement on Ireland/Northern Ireland,[74] or Protocol 1 to the UK–Ukraine Political, Free Trade and Strategic Partnership Agreement concerning the Definition of 'Originating Products' and Methods of Administrative Cooperation.[75] Another example would be an Optional Protocol on Settlement of Disputes.[76]

Of course, there may be other instruments which, although associated with the treaty, are not either expressly or by necessary implication integral to it, such as resolutions attached to the final act. Although not part of the treaty as such, they may play a role in its interpretation.

Exchange of Notes: First Person Notes and Third Person Notes

An exchange of notes can constitute a treaty or a non-binding instrument. The difference in status is indicated solely by the wording. There is a lot of variation from one state to another on the finer points of drafting exchanges of notes but the broad principles are the same.

If an exchange of notes is in first-person form, it will usually be drafted in the form of an exchange between named individuals, that is, between an ambassador and a minister of the government of the state to which the ambassador is accredited, or between the permanent representative to an international organisation and the Secretary-General (or an office holder of senior level) of the organisation. But there are examples of exchanges between ministers[77] or between an Ambassador and a senior official.[78] 'First person' means that the individuals, although representing their governments, write in the introduction and conclusion in terms of 'I'.

A first-person exchange of notes which constitutes a treaty will, therefore, in addition to the usual treaty terminology in the body of the note (e.g., 'shall' rather than 'will'), have in the initiating note an opening paragraph ending with a formula such as:

[74] See n. 46. [75] See n. 14.

[76] For example, the Optional Protocol on the Compulsory Settlement of Disputes to the VCDR 1961 (500 UNTS 241 No. 7312; UKTS (1965) No. 19).

[77] For example, Spain–Chile Exchange of Notes on Participation in Municipal Elections 2009: 2647 UNTS 247 No. 47160.

[78] For example, between the UK Ambassador to Sweden and the Director-General for Legal Affairs at the Ministry of Foreign Affairs of Sweden, UK–Sweden Exchange of Notes concerning the Cessation of Responsibility for the Protection of Diplomatic and Consular Interests etc., 2014: UKTS (2016) No. 22.

> I therefore have the honour to *propose*[79] [on behalf of the Government of Utopia] the following:

The precise form of words will depend on the content. The first person note will then end with a formula like:

> If the foregoing *proposals* are acceptable to the Government of Freedonia, I have the honour to *propose* that this Note and your reply in that sense *shall constitute an Agreement* between our two Governments, which *shall enter into force* on the date of Your Excellency's reply.

(Traditionalists do not use a capital 'A' for agreement, but it is very common, and the point is of no importance. The same goes for 'state' and 'State'.)

The substance of the agreement constituted by the exchange of notes (in other words, the agreement that is proposed in the first note) will normally be included in the body of that note before the formal endings,[80] but sometimes the terms of the Agreement will be set out in an Annex or Attachment.[81] In the latter case, it is important that the notes are carefully drafted to ensure there is no ambiguity about what constitutes the agreement or about its date of entry into force.

The reply note will read:

> Your Excellency,
>
> I have the honour to refer to your Note No. [ ] dated [ ], which reads as follows:
>
> [*The main text of the first note is then set out. If the reply note is in another language, the text of the first note will not be set out in translation, instead it will be repeated exactly in the reply note.*]
>
> I have the honour to confirm that the foregoing *proposals* are acceptable to the Government of Freedonia, and your Excellency's Note and this reply *shall constitute an Agreement* between our two Governments in this matter, which *shall enter into force* on [today's date].

See the example in Appendix E.

It is good practice to repeat the main text of the initiating note. This avoids any doubt as to what has been agreed, *especially if the reply is to be in a different language.* It can sometimes be simpler for a bilateral treaty in two languages to be in the form of an exchange of notes. Although each state must check (extremely carefully) both language texts for accuracy, it may be simpler for each to produce the text for signature in its own language, especially when the two languages (e.g., French and Arabic) do not share the same alphabet. It is not customary to provide, as one usually would in a single instrument treaty, that both texts are equally authentic.

[79] Remember: all emphasis is the author's unless otherwise indicated.
[80] UK–Canada Exchange of Notes amending the Double Taxation Convention 2015: UKTS (2017) No. 10.
[81] See, for example, the UK–Sweden Exchange of Notes concerning the Assumption of Responsibility for the Protection of the Diplomatic and Consular Interests etc. 2012: UKTS (2012) No. 50.

It is also common to find a binding exchange of notes drafted in the form of the third person (as with a normal Note Verbale used for communication between an Embassy and the host government).[82] This will combine the normal introduction of a third-person note with the language making the proposal mentioned above, for example:

> The Embassy of Freedonia presents its compliments to the Ministry of Foreign Affairs of Utopia and has the honour to propose the following:

The ending will follow on the same lines:

> If the foregoing *proposals* are acceptable to the Government of Freedonia, the Embassy has the honour to *propose* that this Note and the Ministry's reply in that sense *shall constitute an Agreement* between the Government of Freedonia and the Government of Utopia, which *shall enter into force* on the date of the Ministry's reply.[83]

The note would then be stamped and initialled as would be normal for a Note Verbale. It is not usual to have a named signatory and a full signature, but there are examples where states have adopted this practice.

In the body of a *third-person* note, one should avoid reverting to the use of the first person ('I have the honour') or the second person ('you' or 'your'). For reasons of consistency, it is better that the third person is used throughout, with references therefore to 'the Embassy' and 'the Ministry' or 'the Government' as appropriate. Hence, for example, instead of referring to '*our* two Governments', it is normal to spell out the names of the two governments.

The reply from the Ministry should be drafted in the name of the Ministry and should not revert to the first person. The opening would therefore read:

> The Ministry of Foreign Affairs of the Republic of Utopia presents its compliments to the Embassy of Freedonia and has the honour to refer its Note No. [ ] dated [ ], which reads as follows:

After citing the text of the Embassy's note, the Ministry's reply would say:

> The Ministry has the honour to confirm that the foregoing proposals are acceptable to the Government of Utopia, and the Embassy's Note and this reply shall

[82] See, for example, Exchange of Notes to amend the UK–US Agreement for the Sharing of Visa, Immigration and Nationality Information 2020: UKTS (2021) No. 7; Finland–Russia Exchange of Notes concerning the Opening of a Border Crossing-Point 2001: 2472 UNTS 170 No. 31571; Exchange of Notes constituting an Arrangement between the FRG and the Netherlands on the Modification of an Annex etc. 2015: 3041 UNTS 98 No. 28022 (which, despite referring to an 'Arrangement', is in fact a binding agreement); Exchange of Notes constituting an Agreement amending the Host State Agreement between the Netherlands and the International Commission on Missing Persons 2017: UNTS No. 53068.

[83] This will be followed by the usual courtesy ending: 'The Embassy avails itself of this opportunity to renew to the Ministry the assurances of its highest consideration.'

> constitute an Agreement between the Government of Utopia and the Government of Freedonia in this matter, which shall enter into force on [today's date].

The courtesy ending would follow, then the stamp of the Ministry, which would be initialled. Both the proposal note and the reply note would state, beneath or alongside that, the place where the Note was issued and the date.

See the example in Appendix F.

Exchange of Letters

As with an exchange of notes, the form of an exchange of letters can be used equally for a binding or non-binding instrument. An exchange of letters should be in first-person form and the language used for a binding instrument will therefore be the same as for a binding first-person exchange of notes, save that any reference to 'Note' will be replaced by 'letter'.[84]

Non-binding Exchanges of Notes and Letters

In contrast, an exchange of notes which amounts to no more than a non-binding instrument will, in addition to employing non-binding terminology in the main text (e.g., 'will' rather than 'shall' etc.), have an opening paragraph referring to discussions between the two governments and ending with a formula such as:

> As a result of these discussions it is the *understanding* of the Government of Utopia that the following *arrangements will* apply:

The note will end with a formula such as:

> If the *arrangements* set out above are acceptable to the Government of Freedonia, I have the honour to *suggest* that this Note and Your Excellency's reply to that effect *will place on record the understanding* of our two Governments in this matter which *will come into effect* on [the date of your reply or another date].[85]

The reply note will read:

> Your Excellency,
>
> I have the honour to acknowledge receipt of your Note No. [ ] dated [ ] concerning [ ] and to *confirm* that the *arrangements* set out in your Note are acceptable to the Government of Freedonia, and that your Note and this reply will *place on record the understanding* of our two Governments in the matter, which *will come into effect* on [today's date or another date].

[84] See, for example, the UK–Belgium Exchange of Letters amending the Agreement relating to the Delimitation of the Continental Shelf 2013: UKTS (2016) No. 14.

[85] Please note that the italics are only for illustrative purposes.

Alternatively, and preferably, the main text of the first note can be repeated (if necessary in translation) in the reply (see the example in Appendix F). If the instrument is a non-binding exchange of letters, the only change necessary to the above is to replace 'Note' by 'letter'.

Procedure

Perhaps the most important practical advice is that one should ensure that the text of both notes (or letters) is agreed *well before the exchange takes place.* If this is not done, and one of the notes is found to be not quite correct, the side which discovers this may – depending on the seriousness of the error – have to draw it to the attention of the other side and try to persuade it to replace the note with a corrected one.

One way of seeing that the texts are fully agreed before they are exchanged is to ensure that the exchange is artificial, in the sense that the originating note is *not* sent to the other side, which then sends the reply note. Instead, they should be exchanged simultaneously at the foreign ministry. Doing it this way should ensure that no mistakes are made. No ceremony is usually necessary.

If the two notes are not agreed in advance, there may be discrepancies between the two notes or the reply may amount to a qualified response. Even if that is acceptable to the initiating state, it should then either send a further note confirming this or propose replacing the two notes with a fresh exchange. But this is untidy and therefore best avoided. *Agreeing the texts in draft should also ensure that there is no misunderstanding as to the status of the exchange (i.e., treaty or non-binding instrument).*

Drafting Techniques

> It was decided that the German reply to the British note should be written in English 'for fear of obscurity and misunderstanding if the note were translated in London'. The Chancellor asked the Kaiser to draw up the note, 'since I knew English best', the Kaiser recalled. 'I sat at the writing table in the adjutant's room, the other gentlemen stood around me. I would read a sentence from the British note aloud and sketch out an answer, which was, in turn, read aloud. Then criticisms were made left and right; one thought the sentence too complaisant, another too abrupt; it was thereupon remodelled, recast, improved and polished. The Chancellor particularly subjected my grammar and style to much torture, owing to his habit of probing things philosophically . . . After hours of work the note was finally finished and, having been passed a couple of times from hand to hand, and then read aloud by me half a dozen times more, it was signed.'[86]

That is how not to do it.

[86] From William II, *My Memoirs, 1878–1918*, London, 1922, 145, on the drafting on 29 January 1912 of a reply to a British note about naval and colonial matters.

It has been said many times that legal drafting is an art, not a science, yet there are certain guidelines which help and should avoid the dreadful torture inflicted on the Kaiser, even if he asked for it. Like any writing, drafting is a solitary pursuit – or at least it should be. No good first draft ever emerged from a committee, of even only two. As soon as another person looks over your shoulder, you are forced to compromise. This results in the first draft being less coherent than if you had done it alone. Even though your first, solitary draft will be imperfect, it will at least have the merit of being a text that, provided you follow the other suggestions below, should provide a better basis for the lengthy process of producing a treaty.

Legal drafting requires a disciplined ordering of material. Like managers, good drafters are born, not taught; but drafting technique can be improved by following some simple precepts. The basic rules for drafting treaties are essentially the same as for any legal instrument, whether a contract, legislation or a UN resolution:

(1) Keep it simple. The first draft should be as uncomplicated as possible; it will surely become more complex as the negotiations proceed.
(2) See the text as a whole. This is especially important during redrafting.
(3) Be consistent throughout the text. Do not use different words or formulations to say the same thing.
(4) Adopt one (clear) system of numbering, and keep to it.
(5) Try to avoid drafting in a language in which you are not really proficient. And even if you are fluent in that foreign language, *always* have it checked by someone who is a native speaker. Negotiating problems can be caused by a draft done by non-native speakers who have not had it properly checked.

How to Begin

The initial draft should be done *alone*. Sometimes it is more sensible for the initial draft to be done by the policy maker and then given to a legal adviser. The initial draft may be better done by hand rather than on a computer, though it is more a matter of personal preference, and age. If done by hand, use lined paper, double or treble spacing and generous margins. Write on one side only. Set aside time specially for the task. Draft at home if necessary.

Do not attempt to reinvent the wheel. Where possible, adapt precedents, but only if they are clearly right for the purpose and you fully understand them. Have your draft read by a disinterested person. If they cannot understand it, start again.

Style

Use short sentences. Avoid unnecessary words, especially adjectives. Try to limit the number of cross-references. Instead, repeat the provision unless it is long. If there is a need to refer to the same provision several times, consider making it into a definition (see the definition of 'party' in Article 2(1)(g) VCLT 1969). Avoid 'and/or' if what you really mean is 'both' or 'either'. Using simply 'or' will usually do the job.

Numbering

Include a correct numbering scheme in the first draft, otherwise it will be difficult to renumber properly later. Once the initial draft has been presented and amended with the addition of a new article, *do not change the numbering of the articles.* Unless the text becomes hopelessly complicated, leave renumbering until the end. The negotiations will go more smoothly if the representatives do not have to refer to 'Article 7, which used to be Article 5, and in the first draft was . . .'. If new articles have to be inserted, number them *5 bis*, 5ter, *5quater*, and so on or 5A, 5B, 5C and so on. If an article is deleted, *retain* the article number in the draft, but leave the body blank. Such practical techniques will also make it easier for everyone to follow their notes and reports of previous meetings, and will make new reports easier to follow.

Languages

If the draft is translated and there is no exact equivalent for a word, insert it after an *approximate* translation (e.g., *ordre publique* ('public order')), and say so.

Amendment/Consolidation

If the draft is of an amending treaty and the amendments are extensive, consider a replacement treaty, or at least attaching a consolidated text to the amending treaty or to the final act. The Final Act of the Conference of the States Parties to the Treaty on Conventional Armed Forces in Europe (CFE Treaty), which adopted the Agreement on Adaptation of the CFE Treaty,[87] noted that a consolidated version of the CFE Treaty, as amended by the Agreement on Adaptation, 'is being produced for information and to facilitate implementation'. Since the Agreement made the CFE Treaty even more complex, the consolidated text was essential.

The text of the Eurocontrol Convention 1960 was extensively amended by a Protocol in 1981, and a (non-authoritative) consolidated text of the amended Convention was (after much persuading) reluctantly attached to the Final Act of the amendment conference. Further amendments were made by a Protocol in 1997. This time, Article 1 replaced the Convention with a consolidated text (annexed to the Protocol) which incorporated all the previous and the new amendments.[88]

[87] For the treaty (which has not yet entered into force) see Agreement on Adaptation of the Treaty on Conventional Armed Forces in Europe. The Final Act does not seem to have been published.

[88] The Protocol was delayed due to a problem over Gibraltar. When that had been resolved, the Protocol could enter into force (UK Misc. Series (2002) No. 15). Other related texts are the Eurocontrol Convention 1960: 523 UNTS 117 No. 7557; UKTS (1963) No. 39; amending Protocol 1981: UKTS (1987) No. 2.

Substance

You can learn how to draft the substance only 'on the job'; and the more practice you get, the better you should be at drafting. Some of the simple techniques mentioned above should help. Hopefully, you will avoid some of the worst excesses of drafting, such as Article 4(1) of the Rome Convention for the Suppression of Unlawful Acts against the Safety of Maritime Navigation 1988:[89]

> This Convention applies if the ship is navigating or is scheduled to navigate into, through or from waters beyond the outer limit of the territorial sea of a single State, or the lateral limits of its territorial sea with adjacent States.

This is one of the more obscure treaty texts. In essence, what it tries to say is that the Convention applies only if there is an 'international element', and this could have been better expressed. The negotiations dealt with complex issues and there were lawyers experienced in UN affairs and lawyers expert in IMO shipping matters. But, because of lack of time, the final text prepared by the IMO Secretariat was adopted by the Rome Conference without any of the lawyers being able to check it properly.

Presenting the Draft

To present a draft in single spacing is thoughtless. It may save paper, but it is false economy since it will only annoy others (and you) by making the handling of the draft that much more difficult. One should *always* use double spacing and wide margins, and one side of the paper only. Although that doubles copying costs, it will be much appreciated by the reader, who will find it easier to read and annotate. Include – as a temporary measure – either explanatory notes or footnotes, or both, to the articles, including references to precedents. Avoid endnotes, which only irritate. Use square brackets liberally to indicate alternative formulations, doubts or disagreements. At the top of the front page of the first draft, and *each* redraft, put the date (and if necessary the time) when it was produced. This avoids much confusion later. Include also the name of the originator (state or international organisation).

Even if you follow all these precepts, the final text will little resemble your first draft. But at least you will have got the process off to good start, and the final text will be the better for your efforts.

[89] 1678 UNTS 222 No. 29004; 27 ILM (1988) 672; UKTS (1995) No. 64; [1993] ATS 10.

Appendix A

Vienna Convention on the Law of Treaties

Vienna Convention on the Law of Treaties

The States Parties to the present Convention,

Considering the fundamental role of treaties in the history of international relations,

Recognizing the ever-increasing importance of treaties as a source of international law and as a means of developing peaceful co-operation among nations, whatever their constitutional and social systems,

Noting that the principles of free consent and of good faith and the *pacta sunt servanda* rule are universally recognized,

Affirming that disputes concerning treaties, like other international disputes, should be settled by peaceful means and in conformity with the principles of justice and international law,

Recalling the determination of the peoples of the United Nations to establish conditions under which justice and respect for the obligations arising from treaties can be maintained,

Having in mind the principles of international law embodied in the Charter of the United Nations, such as the principles of the equal rights and self-determination of peoples, of the sovereign equality and independence of all States, of non-interference in the domestic affairs of States, of the prohibition of the threat or use of force and of universal respect for, and observance of, human rights and fundamental freedoms for all,

Believing that the codification and progressive development of the law of treaties achieved in the present Convention will promote the purposes of the United Nations set forth in the Charter, namely, the maintenance of international peace and security, the development of friendly relations and the achievement of co-operation among nations,

Affirming that the rules of customary international law will continue to govern questions not regulated by the provisions of the present Convention,

Have agreed as follows:

Part I Introduction

Article 1 Scope of the present Convention

The present Convention applies to treaties between States.

Article 2 Use of terms

1. For the purposes of the present Convention:
   (a) 'treaty' means an international agreement concluded between States in written form and governed by international law, whether embodied in a single instrument or in two or more related instruments and whatever its particular designation;
   (b) 'ratification', 'acceptance', 'approval' and 'accession' mean in each case the international act so named whereby a State establishes on the international plane its consent to be bound by a treaty;
   (c) 'full powers' means a document emanating from the competent authority of a State designating a person or persons to represent the State for negotiating, adopting or authenticating the text of a treaty, for expressing the consent of the State to be bound by a treaty, or for accomplishing any other act with respect to a treaty;
   (d) 'reservation' means a unilateral statement, however phrased or named, made by a State, when signing, ratifying, accepting, approving or acceding to a treaty, whereby it purports to exclude or to modify the legal effect of certain provisions of the treaty in their application to that State;
   (e) 'negotiating State' means a State which took part in the drawing up and adoption of the text of the treaty;
   (f) 'contracting State' means a State which has consented to be bound by the treaty, whether or not the treaty has entered into force;
   (g) 'party' means a State which has consented to be bound by the treaty and for which the treaty is in force;
   (h) 'third State' means a State not a party to the treaty;
   (i) 'international organization' means an intergovernmental organization.
2. The provisions of paragraph 1 regarding the use of terms in the present Convention are without prejudice to the use of those terms or to the meanings which may be given to them in the internal law of any State.

Article 3 International agreements not within the scope of the present Convention

The fact that the present Convention does not apply to international agreements concluded between States and other subjects of international law or between such other subjects of international law, or to international agreements not in written form, shall not affect:

(a) the legal force of such agreements;
(b) the application to them of any of the rules set forth in the present Convention to which they would be subject under international law independently of the Convention;

(c) the application of the Convention to the relations of States as between themselves under international agreements to which other subjects of international law are also parties.

Article 4 Non-retroactivity of the present Convention

Without prejudice to the application of any rules set forth in the present Convention to which treaties would be subject under international law independently of the Convention, the Convention applies only to treaties which are concluded by States after the entry into force of the present Convention with regard to such States.

Article 5 Treaties constituting international organizations and treaties adopted within an international organization

The present Convention applies to any treaty which is the constituent instrument of an international organization and to any treaty adopted within an international organization without prejudice to any relevant rules of the organization.

Part II Conclusion and entry into force of treaties

Section 1 Conclusion of treaties

Article 6 Capacity of states to conclude treaties

Every State possesses capacity to conclude treaties.

Article 7 Full powers

1. A person is considered as representing a State for the purpose of adopting or authenticating the text of a treaty or for the purpose of expressing the consent of the State to be bound by a treaty if:
   (a) he produces appropriate full powers; or
   (b) it appears from the practice of the States concerned or from other circumstances that their intention was to consider that person as representing the State for such purposes and to dispense with full powers.
2. In virtue of their functions and without having to produce full powers, the following are considered as representing their State:
   (a) Heads of State, Heads of Government and Ministers for Foreign Affairs, for the purpose of performing all acts relating to the conclusion of a treaty;
   (b) heads of diplomatic missions, for the purpose of adopting the text of a treaty between the accrediting State and the State to which they are accredited;
   (c) representatives accredited by States to an international conference or to an international organization or one of its organs, for the purpose of adopting the text of a treaty in that conference, organization or organ.

Article 8 Subsequent confirmation of an act performed without authorization

An act relating to the conclusion of a treaty performed by a person who cannot be considered under article 7 as authorised to represent a State for that purpose is without legal effect unless afterwards confirmed by that State.

Article 9 Adoption of the text

1. The adoption of the text of a treaty takes place by the consent of all the States participating in its drawing up except as provided in paragraph 2.
2. The adoption of the text of a treaty at an international conference takes place by the vote of two-thirds of the States present and voting, unless by the same majority they shall decide to apply a different rule.

Article 10 Authentication of the text

The text of a treaty is established as authentic and definitive:

(a) by such procedure as may be provided for in the text or agreed upon by the States participating in its drawing up; or
(b) failing such procedure, by the signature, signature *ad referendum* or initialling by the representatives of those States of the text of the treaty or of the Final Act of a conference incorporating the text.

Article 11 Means of expressing consent to be bound by a treaty

The consent of a State to be bound by a treaty may be expressed by signature, exchange of instruments constituting a treaty, ratification, acceptance, approval or accession, or by any other means if so agreed.

Article 12 Consent to be bound by a treaty expressed by signature

1. The consent of a State to be bound by a treaty is expressed by the signature of its representative when:
   (a) the treaty provides that signature shall have that effect;
   (b) it is otherwise established that the negotiating States were agreed that signature should have that effect; or
   (c) the intention of the State to give that effect to the signature appears from the full powers of its representative or was expressed during the negotiation.
2. For the purposes of paragraph 1:
   (a) the initialling of a text constitutes a signature of the treaty when it is established that the negotiating States so agreed;
   (b) the signature *ad referendum* of a treaty by a representative, if confirmed by his State, constitutes a full signature of the treaty.

Article 13 Consent to be bound by a treaty expressed by an exchange of instruments constituting a treaty

The consent of States to be bound by a treaty constituted by instruments exchanged between them is expressed by that exchange when:

(a) the instruments provide that their exchange shall have that effect; or
(b) it is otherwise established that those States were agreed that the exchange of instruments should have that effect.

Article 14 Consent to be bound by a treaty expressed by ratification, acceptance or approval

1. The consent of a State to be bound by a treaty is expressed by ratification when:
   (a) the treaty provides for such consent to be expressed by means of ratification;
   (b) it is otherwise established that the negotiating States were agreed that ratification should be required;
   (c) the representative of the State has signed the treaty subject to ratification; or
   (d) the intention of the State to sign the treaty subject to ratification appears from the full powers of its representative or was expressed during the negotiation.
2. The consent of a State to be bound by a treaty is expressed by acceptance or approval under conditions similar to those which apply to ratification.

Article 15 Consent to be bound by a treaty expressed by accession

The consent of a State to be bound by a treaty is expressed by accession when:

(a) the treaty provides that such consent may be expressed by that State by means of accession;
(b) it is otherwise established that the negotiating States were agreed that such consent may be expressed by that State by means of accession; or
(c) all the parties have subsequently agreed that such consent may be expressed by that State by means of accession.

Article 16 Exchange or deposit of instruments of ratification, acceptance, approval or accession

Unless the treaty otherwise provides, instruments of ratification, acceptance, approval or accession establish the consent of a State to be bound by a treaty upon:

(a) their exchange between the contracting States;
(b) their deposit with the depositary; or
(c) their notification to the contracting States or to the depositary, if so agreed.

Article 17 Consent to be bound by part of a treaty and choice of differing provisions

1. Without prejudice to articles 19 to 23, the consent of a State to be bound by part of a treaty is effective only if the treaty so permits or the other contracting States so agree.
2. The consent of a State to be bound by a treaty which permits a choice between differing provisions is effective only if it is made clear to which of the provisions the consent relates.

Article 18 Obligation not to defeat the object and purpose of a treaty prior to its entry into force

A State is obliged to refrain from acts which would defeat the object and purpose of a treaty when:

(a) it has signed the treaty or has exchanged instruments constituting the treaty subject to ratification, acceptance or approval, until it shall have made its intention clear not to become a party to the treaty; or

(b) it has expressed its consent to be bound by the treaty, pending the entry into force of the treaty and provided that such entry into force is not unduly delayed.

Section 2 Reservations

Article 19 Formulation of reservations

A State may, when signing, ratifying, accepting, approving or acceding to a treaty, formulate a reservation unless:

(a) the reservation is prohibited by the treaty;
(b) the treaty provides that only specified reservations, which do not include the reservation in question, may be made; or
(c) in cases not falling under sub-paragraphs (a) and (b), the reservation is incompatible with the object and purpose of the treaty.

Article 20 Acceptance of and objection to reservations

1. A reservation expressly authorized by a treaty does not require any subsequent acceptance by the other contracting States unless the treaty so provides.
2. When it appears from the limited number of negotiating States and the object and purpose of a treaty that the application of the treaty in its entirety between all the parties is an essential condition of the consent of each one to be bound by the treaty, a reservation requires acceptance by all the parties.
3. When a treaty is a constituent instrument of an international organization and unless it otherwise provides, a reservation requires the acceptance of the competent organ of that organization.
4. In cases not falling under the preceding paragraphs and unless the treaty otherwise provides:
   (a) acceptance by another contracting State of a reservation constitutes the reserving State a party to the treaty in relation to that other State if or when the treaty is in force for those States;
   (b) an objection by another contracting State to a reservation does not preclude the entry into force of the treaty as between the objecting and reserving States unless a contrary intention is definitely expressed by the objecting State;
   (c) an act expressing a State's consent to be bound by the treaty and containing a reservation is effective as soon as at least one other contracting State has accepted the reservation.
5. For the purposes of paragraphs 2 and 4 and unless the treaty otherwise provides, a reservation is considered to have been accepted by a State if it shall have raised no objection to the reservation by the end of a period of twelve months after it was notified of the reservation or by the date on which it expressed its consent to be bound by the treaty, whichever is later.

Article 21 Legal effects of reservations and of objections to reservations

1. A reservation established with regard to another party in accordance with articles 19, 20 and 23:
   (a) modifies for the reserving State in its relations with that other party the provisions of the treaty to which the reservation relates to the extent of the reservation; and

(b) modifies those provisions to the same extent for that other party in its relations with the reserving State.

2. The reservation does not modify the provisions of the treaty for the other parties to the treaty *inter se.*
3. When a State objecting to a reservation has not opposed the entry into force of the treaty between itself and the reserving State, the provisions to which the reservation relates do not apply as between the two States to the extent of the reservation.

Article 22 Withdrawal of reservations and of objections to reservations

1. Unless the treaty otherwise provides, a reservation may be withdrawn at any time and the consent of a State which has accepted the reservation is not required for its withdrawal.
2. Unless the treaty otherwise provides, an objection to a reservation may be withdrawn at any time.
3. Unless the treaty otherwise provides, or it is otherwise agreed:
   (a) the withdrawal of a reservation becomes operative in relation to another contracting State only when notice of it has been received by that State;
   (b) the withdrawal of an objection to a reservation becomes operative only when notice of it has been received by the State which formulated the reservation.

Article 23 Procedure regarding reservations

1. A reservation, an express acceptance of a reservation and an objection to a reservation must be formulated in writing and communicated to the contracting States and other States entitled to become parties to the treaty.
2. If formulated when signing the treaty subject to ratification, acceptance or approval, a reservation must be formally confirmed by the reserving State when expressing its consent to be bound by the treaty. In such a case the reservation shall be considered as having been made on the date of its confirmation.
3. An express acceptance of, or an objection to, a reservation made previously to confirmation of the reservation does not itself require confirmation.
4. The withdrawal of a reservation or of an objection to a reservation must be formulated in writing.

Section 3 Entry into force and provisional application of treaties

Article 24 Entry into force

1. A treaty enters into force in such manner and upon such date as it may provide or as the negotiating States may agree.
2. Failing any such provision or agreement, a treaty enters into force as soon as consent to be bound by the treaty has been established for all the negotiating States.
3. When the consent of a State to be bound by a treaty is established on a date after the treaty has come into force, the treaty enters into force for that State on that date, unless the treaty otherwise provides.
4. The provisions of a treaty regulating the authentication of its text, the establishment of the consent of States to be bound by the treaty, the manner or date of its entry into force,

reservations, the functions of the depositary and other matters arising necessarily before the entry into force of the treaty apply from the time of the adoption of its text.

Article 25 Provisional application

1. A treaty or a part of a treaty is applied provisionally pending its entry into force if:
   (a) the treaty itself so provides; or
   (b) the negotiating States have in some other manner so agreed.
2. Unless the treaty otherwise provides or the negotiating States have otherwise agreed, the provisional application of a treaty or a part of a treaty with respect to a State shall be terminated if that State notifies the other States between which the treaty is being applied provisionally of its intention not to become a party to the treaty.

Part III Observance, application and interpretation of treaties

Section 1 Observance of treaties

Article 26 Pacta sunt servanda

Every treaty in force is binding upon the parties to it and must be performed by them in good faith.

Article 27 Internal law and observance of treaties

A party may not invoke the provisions of its internal law as justification for its failure to perform a treaty. This rule is without prejudice to article 46.

Section 2 Application of treaties

Article 28 Non-retroactivity of treaties

Unless a different intention appears from the treaty or is otherwise established, its provisions do not bind a party in relation to any act or fact which took place or any situation which ceased to exist before the date of the entry into force of the treaty with respect to that party.

Article 29 Territorial scope of treaties

Unless a different intention appears from the treaty or is otherwise established, a treaty is binding upon each party in respect of its entire territory.

Article 30 Application of successive treaties relating to the same subject-matter

1. Subject to article 103 of the Charter of the United Nations, the rights and obligations of States parties to successive treaties relating to the same subject-matter shall be determined in accordance with the following paragraphs.
2. When a treaty specifies that it is subject to, or that it is not to be considered as incompatible with, an earlier or later treaty, the provisions of that other treaty prevail.

3. When all the parties to the earlier treaty are parties also to the later treaty but the earlier treaty is not terminated or suspended in operation under article 59, the earlier treaty applies only to the extent that its provisions are compatible with those of the later treaty.
4. When the parties to the later treaty do not include all the parties to the earlier one:
   (a) as between States parties to both treaties the same rule applies as in paragraph 3;
   (b) as between a State party to both treaties and a State party to only one of the treaties, the treaty to which both States are parties governs their mutual rights and obligations.
5. Paragraph 4 is without prejudice to article 41, or to any question of the termination or suspension of the operation of a treaty under article 60 or to any question of responsibility which may arise for a State from the conclusion or application of a treaty the provisions of which are incompatible with its obligations towards another State under another treaty.

Section 3 Interpretation of treaties

Article 31 General rule of interpretation

1. A treaty shall be interpreted in good faith in accordance with the ordinary meaning to be given to the terms of the treaty in their context and in the light of its object and purpose.
2. The context for the purpose of the interpretation of a treaty shall comprise, in addition to the text, including its preamble and annexes:
   (a) any agreement relating to the treaty which was made between all the parties in connexion with the conclusion of the treaty;
   (b) any instrument which was made by one or more parties in connexion with the conclusion of the treaty and accepted by the other parties as an instrument related to the treaty.
3. There shall be taken into account, together with the context:
   (a) any subsequent agreement between the parties regarding the interpretation of the treaty or the application of its provisions;
   (b) any subsequent practice in the application of the treaty which establishes the agreement of the parties regarding its interpretation;
   (c) any relevant rules of international law applicable in the relations between the parties.
4. A special meaning shall be given to a term if it is established that the parties so intended.

Article 32 Supplementary means of interpretation

Recourse may be had to supplementary means of interpretation, including the preparatory work of the treaty and the circumstances of its conclusion, in order to confirm the meaning resulting from the application of article 31, or to determine the meaning when the interpretation according to article 31:

(a) leaves the meaning ambiguous or obscure; or
(b) leads to a result which is manifestly absurd or unreasonable.

Article 33 Interpretation of treaties authenticated in two or more languages

1. When a treaty has been authenticated in two or more languages, the text is equally authoritative in each language, unless the treaty provides or the parties agree that, in case of divergence, a particular text shall prevail.

2. A version of the treaty in a language other than one of those in which the text was authenticated shall be considered an authentic text only if the treaty so provides or the parties so agree.
3. The terms of the treaty are presumed to have the same meaning in each authentic text.
4. Except where a particular text prevails in accordance with paragraph 1, when a comparison of the authentic texts discloses a difference of meaning which the application of articles 31 and 32 does not remove, the meaning which best reconciles the texts, having regard to the object and purpose of the treaty, shall be adopted.

Section 4 Treaties and third States

Article 34 General rule regarding third States

A treaty does not create either obligations or rights for a third State without its consent.

Article 35 Treaties providing for obligations for third States

An obligation arises for a third State from a provision of a treaty if the parties to the treaty intend the provision to be the means of establishing the obligation and the third State expressly accepts that obligation in writing.

Article 36 Treaties providing for rights for third States

1. A right arises for a third State from a provision of a treaty if the parties to the treaty intend the provision to accord that right either to the third State, or to a group of States to which it belongs, or to all States, and the third State assents thereto. Its assent shall be presumed so long as the contrary is not indicated, unless the treaty otherwise provides.
2. A State exercising a right in accordance with paragraph 1 shall comply with the conditions for its exercise provided for in the treaty or established in conformity with the treaty.

Article 37 Revocation or modification of obligations or rights of third States

1. When an obligation has arisen for a third State in conformity with article 35, the obligation may be revoked or modified only with the consent of the parties to the treaty and of the third State, unless it is established that they had otherwise agreed.
2. When a right has arisen for a third State in conformity with article 36, the right may not be revoked or modified by the parties if it is established that the right was intended not to be revocable or subject to modification without the consent of the third State.

Article 38 Rules in a treaty becoming binding on third States through international custom

Nothing in articles 34 to 37 precludes a rule set forth in a treaty from becoming binding upon a third State as a customary rule of international law, recognized as such.

Part IV Amendment and modification of treaties

Article 39 General rule regarding the amendment of treaties

A treaty may be amended by agreement between the parties. The rules laid down in Part II apply to such an agreement except insofar as the treaty may otherwise provide.

Article 40 Amendment of multilateral treaties

1. Unless the treaty otherwise provides, the amendment of multilateral treaties shall be governed by the following paragraphs.
2. Any proposal to amend a multilateral treaty as between all the parties must be notified to all the contracting States, each one of which shall have the right to take part in:
   (a) the decision as to the action to be taken in regard to such proposal;
   (b) the negotiation and conclusion of any agreement for the amendment of the treaty.
3. Every State entitled to become a party to the treaty shall also be entitled to become a party to the treaty as amended.
4. The amending agreement does not bind any State already a party to the treaty which does not become a party to the amending agreement; article 30, paragraph 4 (b), applies in relation to such State.
5. Any State which becomes a party to the treaty after the entry into force of the amending agreement shall, failing an expression of a different intention by that State:
   (a) be considered as a party to the treaty as amended; and
   (b) be considered as a party to the unamended treaty in relation to any party to the treaty not bound by the amending agreement.

Article 41 Agreements to modify multilateral treaties between certain of the parties only

1. Two or more of the parties to a multilateral treaty may conclude an agreement to modify the treaty as between themselves alone if:
   (1) the possibility of such a modification is provided for by the treaty; or
   (2) the modification in question is not prohibited by the treaty and:
      (i) does not affect the enjoyment by the other parties of their rights under the treaty or the performance of their obligations;
      (ii) does not relate to a provision, derogation from which is incompatible with the effective execution of the object and purpose of the treaty as a whole.
2. Unless in a case falling under paragraph 1(a) the treaty otherwise provides, the parties in question shall notify the other parties of their intention to conclude the agreement and of the modification to the treaty for which it provides.

Part V Invalidity, termination and suspension of the operation of treaties

Section 1 General provisions

Article 42 Validity and continuance in force of treaties

1. The validity of a treaty or of the consent of a State to be bound by a treaty may be impeached only through the application of the present Convention.

2. The termination of a treaty, its denunciation or the withdrawal of a party, may take place only as a result of the application of the provisions of the treaty or of the present Convention. The same rule applies to suspension of the operation of a treaty.

Article 43 Obligations imposed by international law independently of a treaty

The invalidity, termination or denunciation of a treaty, the withdrawal of a party from it, or the suspension of its operation, as a result of the application of the present Convention or of the provisions of the treaty shall not in any way impair the duty of any State to fulfil any obligation embodied in the treaty to which it would be subject under international law independently of the treaty.

Article 44 Separability of treaty provisions

1. A right of a party, provided for in a treaty or arising under article 56, to denounce, withdraw from or suspend the operation of the treaty may be exercised only with respect to the whole treaty unless the treaty otherwise provides or the parties otherwise agree.
2. A ground for invalidating, terminating, withdrawing from or suspending the operation of a treaty recognized in the present Convention may be invoked only with respect to the whole treaty except as provided in the following paragraphs or in article 60.
3. If the ground relates solely to particular clauses, it may be invoked only with respect to those clauses where:
   (a) the said clauses are separable from the remainder of the treaty with regard to their application;
   (b) it appears from the treaty or is otherwise established that acceptance of those clauses was not an essential basis of the consent of the other party or parties to be bound by the treaty as a whole; and
   (c) continued performance of the remainder of the treaty would not be unjust.
4. In cases falling under articles 49 and 50 the State entitled to invoke the fraud or corruption may do so with respect either to the whole treaty or, subject to paragraph 3, to the particular clauses alone.
5. In cases falling under articles 51, 52 and 53, no separation of the provisions of the treaty is permitted.

Article 45 Loss of a right to invoke a ground for invalidating, terminating, withdrawing from or suspending the operation of a treaty

A State may no longer invoke a ground for invalidating, terminating, withdrawing from or suspending the operation of a treaty under articles 46 to 50 or articles 60 and 62 if, after becoming aware of the facts:

(a) it shall have expressly agreed that the treaty is valid or remains in force or continues in operation, as the case may be; or
(b) it must by reason of its conduct be considered as having acquiesced in the validity of the treaty or in its maintenance in force or in operation, as the case may be.

Section 2 Invalidity of treaties

Article 46 Provisions of internal law regarding competence to conclude treaties

1. A State may not invoke the fact that its consent to be bound by a treaty has been expressed in violation of a provision of its internal law regarding competence to conclude treaties as invalidating its consent unless that violation was manifest and concerned a rule of its internal law of fundamental importance.
2. A violation is manifest if it would be objectively evident to any State conducting itself in the matter in accordance with normal practice and in good faith.

Article 47 Specific restrictions on authority to express the consent of a State

If the authority of a representative to express the consent of a State to be bound by a particular treaty has been made subject to a specific restriction, his omission to observe that restriction may not be invoked as invalidating the consent expressed by him unless the restriction was notified to the other negotiating States prior to his expressing such consent.

Article 48 Error

1. A State may invoke an error in a treaty as invalidating its consent to be bound by the treaty if the error relates to a fact or situation which was assumed by that State to exist at the time when the treaty was concluded and formed an essential basis of its consent to be bound by the treaty.
2. Paragraph 1 shall not apply if the State in question contributed by its own conduct to the error or if the circumstances were such as to put that State on notice of a possible error.
3. An error relating only to the wording of the text of a treaty does not affect its validity; article 79 then applies.

Article 49 Fraud

If a State has been induced to conclude a treaty by the fraudulent conduct of another negotiating State, the State may invoke the fraud as invalidating its consent to be bound by the treaty.

Article 50 Corruption of a representative of a state

If the expression of a State's consent to be bound by a treaty has been procured through the corruption of its representative directly or indirectly by another negotiating State, the State may invoke such corruption as invalidating its consent to be bound by the treaty.

Article 51 Coercion of a representative of a state

The expression of a State's consent to be bound by a treaty which has been procured by the coercion of its representative through acts or threats directed against him shall be without any legal effect.

Article 52 Coercion of a state by the threat or use of force

A treaty is void if its conclusion has been procured by the threat or use of force in violation of the principles of international law embodied in the Charter of the United Nations.

Article 53 *Treaties conflicting with a peremptory norm of general international law* (jus cogens)

A treaty is void if, at the time of its conclusion, it conflicts with a peremptory norm of general international law. For the purposes of the present Convention, a peremptory norm of general international law is a norm accepted and recognized by the international community of States as a whole as a norm from which no derogation is permitted and which can be modified only by a subsequent norm of general international law having the same character.

Section 3 Termination and suspension of the operation of treaties

Article 54 Termination of or withdrawal from a treaty under its provisions or by consent of the parties

The termination of a treaty or the withdrawal of a party may take place:

(a) in conformity with the provisions of the treaty; or
(b) at any time by consent of all the parties after consultation with the other contracting States.

Article 55 Reduction of the parties to a multilateral treaty below the number necessary for its entry into force

Unless the treaty otherwise provides, a multilateral treaty does not terminate by reason only of the fact that the number of the parties falls below the number necessary for its entry into force.

Article 56 Denunciation of or withdrawal from a treaty containing no provision regarding termination, denunciation or withdrawal

1. A treaty which contains no provision regarding its termination and which does not provide for denunciation or withdrawal is not subject to denunciation or withdrawal unless:
   (a) it is established that the parties intended to admit the possibility of denunciation or withdrawal; or
   (b) a right of denunciation or withdrawal may be implied by the nature of the treaty.
2. A party shall give not less than twelve months' notice of its intention to denounce or withdraw from a treaty under paragraph 1.

Article 57 Suspension of the operation of a treaty under its provisions or by consent of the parties

The operation of a treaty in regard to all the parties or to a particular party may be suspended:

(a) in conformity with the provisions of the treaty; or
(b) at any time by consent of all the parties after consultation with the other contracting States.

Article 58 Suspension of the operation of a multilateral treaty by agreement between certain of the parties only

1. Two or more parties to a multilateral treaty may conclude an agreement to suspend the operation of provisions of the treaty, temporarily and as between themselves alone, if:
   (a) the possibility of such a suspension is provided for by the treaty; or
   (b) the suspension in question is not prohibited by the treaty and:
      (i) does not affect the enjoyment by the other parties of their rights under the treaty or the performance of their obligations;
      (ii) is not incompatible with the object and purpose of the treaty.
2. Unless in a case falling under paragraph 1(a) the treaty otherwise provides, the parties in question shall notify the other parties of their intention to conclude the agreement and of those provisions of the treaty the operation of which they intend to suspend.

Article 59 Termination or suspension of the operation of a treaty implied by conclusion of a later treaty

1. A treaty shall be considered as terminated if all the parties to it conclude a later treaty relating to the same subject-matter and:
   (a) it appears from the later treaty or is otherwise established that the parties intended that the matter should be governed by that treaty; or
   (b) the provisions of the later treaty are so far incompatible with those of the earlier one that the two treaties are not capable of being applied at the same time.
2. The earlier treaty shall be considered as only suspended in operation if it appears from the later treaty or is otherwise established that such was the intention of the parties.

Article 60 Termination or suspension of the operation of a treaty as a consequence of its breach

1. A material breach of a bilateral treaty by one of the parties entitles the other to invoke the breach as a ground for terminating the treaty or suspending its operation in whole or in part.
2. A material breach of a multilateral treaty by one of the parties entitles:
   (a) the other parties by unanimous agreement to suspend the operation of the treaty in whole or in part or to terminate it either:
      (i) in the relations between themselves and the defaulting State, or
      (ii) as between all the parties;
   (b) a party specially affected by the breach to invoke it as a ground for suspending the operation of the treaty in whole or in part in the relations between itself and the defaulting State;
   (c) any party other than the defaulting State to invoke the breach as a ground for suspending the operation of the treaty in whole or in part with respect to itself if the treaty is of such a character that a material breach of its provisions by one party radically changes the position of every party with respect to the further performance of its obligations under the treaty.

3. A material breach of a treaty, for the purposes of this article, consists in:
   (a) a repudiation of the treaty not sanctioned by the present Convention; or
   (b) the violation of a provision essential to the accomplishment of the object or purpose of the treaty.
4. The foregoing paragraphs are without prejudice to any provision in the treaty applicable in the event of a breach.
5. Paragraphs 1 to 3 do not apply to provisions relating to the protection of the human person contained in treaties of a humanitarian character, in particular to provisions prohibiting any form of reprisals against persons protected by such treaties.

Article 61 Supervening impossibility of performance

1. A party may invoke the impossibility of performing a treaty as a ground for terminating or withdrawing from it if the impossibility results from the permanent disappearance or destruction of an object indispensable for the execution of the treaty. If the impossibility is temporary, it may be invoked only as a ground for suspending the operation of the treaty.
2. Impossibility of performance may not be invoked by a party as a ground for terminating, withdrawing from or suspending the operation of a treaty if the impossibility is the result of a breach by that party either of an obligation under the treaty or of any other international obligation owed to any other party to the treaty.

Article 62 Fundamental changes of circumstances

1. A fundamental change of circumstances which has occurred with regard to those existing at the time of the conclusion of a treaty, and which was not foreseen by the parties, may not be invoked as a ground for terminating or withdrawing from the treaty unless:
   (a) the existence of those circumstances constituted an essential basis of the consent of the parties to be bound by the treaty; and
   (b) the effect of the change is radically to transform the extent of obligations still to be performed under the treaty.
2. A fundamental change of circumstances may not be invoked as a ground for terminating or withdrawing from a treaty:
   (a) if the treaty establishes a boundary; or
   (b) if the fundamental change is the result of a breach by the party invoking it either of an obligation under the treaty or of any other international obligation owed to any other party to the treaty.
3. If, under the foregoing paragraphs, a party may invoke a fundamental change of circumstances as a ground for terminating or withdrawing from a treaty it may also invoke the change as a ground for suspending the operation of the treaty.

Article 63 Severance of diplomatic or consular relations

The severance of diplomatic or consular relations between parties to a treaty does not affect the legal relations established between them by the treaty except insofar as the existence of diplomatic or consular relations is indispensable for the application of the treaty.

Article 64 Emergence of a new peremptory norm of general international law (*jus cogens*)

If a new peremptory norm of general international law emerges, any existing treaty which is in conflict with that norm becomes void and terminates.

Section 4 Procedure

Article 65 Procedure to be followed with respect to invalidity, termination, withdrawal from or suspension of the operation of a treaty

1. A party which, under the provisions of the present Convention, invokes either a defect in its consent to be bound by a treaty or a ground for impeaching the validity of a treaty, terminating it, withdrawing from it or suspending its operation, must notify the other parties of its claim. The notification shall indicate the measure proposed to be taken with respect to the treaty and the reasons therefor.
2. If, after the expiry of a period which, except in cases of special urgency, shall not be less than three months after the receipt of the notification, no party has raised any objection, the party making the notification may carry out in the manner provided in article 67 the measure which it has proposed.
3. If, however, objection has been raised by any other party, the parties shall seek a solution through the means indicated in Article 33 of the Charter of the United Nations.
4. Nothing in the foregoing paragraphs shall affect the rights or obligations of the parties under any provisions in force binding the parties with regard to the settlement of disputes.
5. Without prejudice to article 45, the fact that a State has not previously made the notification prescribed in paragraph 1 shall not prevent it from making such notification in answer to another party claiming performance of the treaty or alleging its violation.

Article 66 Procedures for judicial settlement, arbitration and conciliation

If, under paragraph 3 of article 65, no solution has been reached within a period of 12 months following the date on which the objection was raised, the following procedures shall be followed:

(a) any one of the parties to a dispute concerning the application or the interpretation of articles 53 or 64 may, by a written application, submit it to the International Court of Justice for a decision unless the parties by common consent agree to submit the dispute to arbitration;
(b) any one of the parties to a dispute concerning the application or the interpretation of any of the other articles in Part V of the present Convention may set in motion the procedure specified in the Annex to the Convention by submitting a request to that effect to the Secretary-General of the United Nations.

Article 67 Instruments for declaring invalid, terminating, withdrawing from or suspending the operation of a treaty

1. The notification provided for under article 65, paragraph 1 must be made in writing.
2. Any act declaring invalid, terminating, withdrawing from or suspending the operation of a treaty pursuant to the provisions of the treaty or of paragraphs 2 or 3 of article 65 shall be

carried out through an instrument communicated to the other parties. If the instrument is not signed by the Head of State, Head of Government or Minister for Foreign Affairs, the representative of the State communicating it may be called upon to produce full powers.

Article 68 Revocation of notifications and instruments provided for in articles 65 and 67

A notification or instrument provided for in articles 65 or 67 may be revoked at any time before it takes effect.

Section 5 Consequences of the invalidity, termination or suspension of the operation of a treaty

Article 69 Consequences of the invalidity of a treaty

1. A treaty the invalidity of which is established under the present Convention is void. The provisions of a void treaty have no legal force.
2. If acts have nevertheless been performed in reliance on such a treaty:
   (a) each party may require any other party to establish as far as possible in their mutual relations the position that would have existed if the acts had not been performed;
   (b) acts performed in good faith before the invalidity was invoked are not rendered unlawful by reason only of the invalidity of the treaty.
3. In cases falling under articles 49, 50, 51 or 52, paragraph 2 does not apply with respect to the party to which the fraud, the act of corruption or the coercion is imputable.
4. In the case of the invalidity of a particular State's consent to be bound by a multilateral treaty, the foregoing rules apply in the relations between that State and the parties to the treaty.

Article 70 Consequences of the termination of a treaty

1. Unless the treaty otherwise provides or the parties otherwise agree, the termination of a treaty under its provisions or in accordance with the present Convention:
   (a) releases the parties from any obligation further to perform the treaty;
   (b) does not affect any right, obligation or legal situation of the parties created through the execution of the treaty prior to its termination.
2. If a State denounces or withdraws from a multilateral treaty, paragraph 1 applies in the relations between that State and each of the other parties to the treaty from the date when such denunciation or withdrawal takes effect.

Article 71 Consequences of the invalidity of a treaty which conflicts with a peremptory norm of general international law

1. In the case of a treaty which is void under article 53 the parties shall:
   (a) eliminate as far as possible the consequences of any act performed in reliance on any provision which conflicts with the peremptory norm of general international law; and
   (b) bring their mutual relations into conformity with the peremptory norm of general international law.

2. In the case of a treaty which becomes void and terminates under article 64, the termination of the treaty:
   (a) releases the parties from any obligation further to perform the treaty;
   (b) does not affect any right, obligation or legal situation of the parties created through the execution of the treaty prior to its termination; provided that those rights, obligations or situations may thereafter be maintained only to the extent that their maintenance is not in itself in conflict with the new peremptory norm of general international law.

Article 72 Consequences of the suspension of the operation of a treaty

1. Unless the treaty otherwise provides or the parties otherwise agree, the suspension of the operation of a treaty under its provisions or in accordance with the present Convention:
   (a) releases the parties between which the operation of the treaty is suspended from the obligation to perform the treaty in their mutual relations during the period of the suspension;
   (b) does not otherwise affect the legal relations between the parties established by the treaty.
2. During the period of the suspension the parties shall refrain from acts tending to obstruct the resumption of the operation of the treaty.

Part VI Miscellaneous provisions

Article 73 Cases of state succession, state responsibility and outbreak of hostilities

The provisions of the present Convention shall not prejudge any question that may arise in regard to a treaty from a succession of States or from the international responsibility of a State or from the outbreak of hostilities between States.

Article 74 Diplomatic and consular relations and the conclusion of treaties

The severance or absence of diplomatic or consular relations between two or more States does not prevent the conclusion of treaties between those States. The conclusion of a treaty does not in itself affect the situation in regard to diplomatic or consular relations.

Article 75 Case of an aggressor state

The provisions of the present Convention are without prejudice to any obligation in relation to a treaty which may arise for an aggressor State in consequence of measures taken in conformity with the Charter of the United Nations with reference to that State's aggression.

Part VII Depositaries, notifications, corrections and registration

Article 76 Depositaries of treaties

1. The designation of the depositary of a treaty may be made by the negotiating States, either in the treaty itself or in some other manner. The depositary may be one or more States, an international organization or the chief administrative officer of the organization.
2. The functions of the depositary of a treaty are international in character and the depositary is under an obligation to act impartially in their performance. In particular, the fact that a

treaty has not entered into force between certain of the parties or that a difference has appeared between a State and a depositary with regard to the performance of the latter's functions shall not affect that obligation.

Article 77 Functions of depositaries

1. The functions of a depositary, unless otherwise provided in the treaty or agreed by the contracting States, comprise in particular:
   (a) keeping custody of the original text of the treaty and of any full powers delivered to the depositary;
   (b) preparing certified copies of the original text and preparing any further text of the treaty in such additional languages as may be required by the treaty and transmitting them to the parties and to the States entitled to become parties to the treaty;
   (c) receiving any signatures to the treaty and receiving and keeping custody of any instruments, notifications and communications relating to it;
   (d) examining whether the signature or any instrument, notification or communication relating to the treaty is in due and proper form and, if need be, bringing the matter to the attention of the State in question;
   (e) informing the parties and the States entitled to become parties to the treaty of acts, notifications and communications relating to the treaty;
   (f) informing the States entitled to become parties to the treaty when the number of signatures or of instruments of ratification, acceptance, approval or accession required for the entry into force of the treaty has been received or deposited;
   (g) registering the treaty with the Secretariat of the United Nations;
   (h) performing the functions specified in other provisions of the present Convention.
2. In the event of any difference appearing between a State and the depositary as to the performance of the latter's functions, the depositary shall bring the question to the attention of the signatory States and the contracting States or, where appropriate, of the competent organ of the international organization concerned.

Article 78 Notifications and communications

Except as the treaty or the present Convention otherwise provide, any notification or communication to be made by any State under the present Convention shall:

(a) if there is no depositary, be transmitted direct to the States for which it is intended, or if there is a depositary, to the latter;
(b) be considered as having been made by the State in question only upon its receipt by the State to which it was transmitted or, as the case may be, upon its receipt by the depositary;
(c) if transmitted to a depositary, be considered as received by the State for which it was intended only when the latter State has been informed by the depositary in accordance with article 77, paragraph 1(e).

Article 79 Correction of errors in texts or in certified copies of treaties

1. Where, after the authentication of the text of a treaty, the signatory States and the contracting States are agreed that it contains an error, the error shall, unless they decide upon some other means of correction, be corrected:

(a) by having the appropriate correction made in the text and causing the correction to be initialled by duly authorized representatives;
(b) by executing or exchanging an instrument or instruments setting out the correction which it has been agreed to make; or
(c) by executing a corrected text of the whole treaty by the same procedure as in the case of the original text.

2. Where the treaty is one for which there is a depositary, the latter shall notify the signatory States and the contracting States of the error and of the proposal to correct it and shall specify an appropriate time-limit within which objection to the proposed correction may be raised. If, on the expiry of the time-limit:
   (a) no objection has been raised, the depositary shall make and initial the correction in the text and shall execute a *procès-verbal* of the rectification of the text and communicate a copy of it to the parties and to the States entitled to become parties to the treaty;
   (b) an objection has been raised, the depositary shall communicate the objection to the signatory States and to the contracting States.
3. The rules in paragraphs 1 and 2 apply also where the text has been authenticated in two or more languages and it appears that there is a lack of concordance which the signatory States and the contracting States agree should be corrected.
4. The corrected text replaces the defective text *ab initio,* unless the signatory States and the contracting States otherwise decide.
5. The correction of the text of a treaty that has been registered shall be notified to the Secretariat of the United Nations.
6. Where an error is discovered in a certified copy of a treaty, the depositary shall execute a *procès-verbal* specifying the rectification and communicate a copy of it to the signatory States and to the contracting States.

Article 80 Registration and publication of treaties

1. Treaties shall, after their entry into force, be transmitted to the Secretariat of the United Nations for registration or filing and recording, as the case may be, and for publication.
2. The designation of a depositary shall constitute authorization for it to perform the acts specified in the preceding paragraph.

Part VIII Final provisions

Article 81 Signature

The present Convention shall be open for signature by all States Members of the United Nations or of any of the specialized agencies or of the International Atomic Energy Agency or parties to the Statute of the International Court of Justice, and by any other State invited by the General Assembly of the United Nations to become a party to the Convention, as follows: until 30 November 1969, at the Federal Ministry for Foreign Affairs of the Republic of Austria, and subsequently, until 30 April 1970, at United Nations Headquarters, New York.

Article 82 Ratification

The present Convention is subject to ratification. The instruments of ratification shall be deposited with the Secretary-General of the United Nations.

Article 83 Accession

The present Convention shall remain open for accession by any State belonging to any of the categories mentioned in article 81. The instruments of accession shall be deposited with the Secretary-General of the United Nations.

Article 84 Entry into force

1. The present Convention shall enter into force on the thirtieth day following the date of deposit of the thirty-fifth instrument of ratification or accession.
2. For each State ratifying or acceding to the Convention after the deposit of the thirty-fifth instrument of ratification or accession, the Convention shall enter into force on the thirtieth day after deposit by such State of its instrument of ratification or accession.

Article 85 Authentic texts

The original of the present Convention, of which the Chinese, English, French, Russian and Spanish texts are equally authentic, shall be deposited with the Secretary-General of the United Nations.

In witness whereof the undersigned Plenipotentiaries, being duly authorized thereto by their respective Governments, have signed the present Convention.

Done at Vienna, this twenty-third day of May, one thousand nine hundred and sixty-nine.

Annex

1. A list of conciliators consisting of qualified jurists shall be drawn up and maintained by the Secretary-General of the United Nations. To this end, every State which is a Member of the United Nations or a party to the present Convention shall be invited to nominate two conciliators, and the names of the persons so nominated shall constitute the list. The term of a conciliator, including that of any conciliator nominated to fill a casual vacancy, shall be five years and may be renewed. A conciliator whose term expires shall continue to fulfil any function for which he shall have been chosen under the following paragraph.
2. When a request has been made to the Secretary-General under article 66, the Secretary-General shall bring the dispute before a conciliation commission constituted as follows:

   The State or States constituting one of the parties to the dispute shall appoint:

   (a) one conciliator of the nationality of that State or of one of those States, who may or may not be chosen from the list referred to in paragraph 1; and

   (b) one conciliator not of the nationality of that State or of any of those States, who shall be chosen from the list.

   The State or States constituting the other party to the dispute shall appoint two conciliators in the same way. The four conciliators chosen by the parties shall be appointed within sixty days following the date on which the Secretary-General receives the request.

The four conciliators shall, within sixty days following the date of the last of their own appointments, appoint a fifth conciliator chosen from the list, who shall be chairman.

If the appointment of the chairman or of any of the other conciliators has not been made within the period prescribed above for such appointment, it shall be made by the Secretary-General within sixty days following the expiry of that period. The appointment of the chairman may be made by the Secretary-General either from the list or from the membership of the International Law Commission. Any of the periods within which appointments must be made may be extended by agreement between the parties to the dispute.

Any vacancy shall be filled in the manner prescribed for the initial appointment.

3. The Conciliation Commission shall decide its own procedure. The Commission, with the consent of the parties to the dispute, may invite any party to the treaty to submit to it its view orally or in writing. Decisions and recommendations of the Commission shall be made by a majority vote of the five members.
4. The Commission may draw the attention of the parties to the dispute to any measures which might facilitate an amicable settlement.
5. The Commission shall hear the parties, examine the claims and objections, and make proposals to the parties with a view to reaching an amicable settlement of the dispute.
6. The Commission shall report within twelve months of its constitution. Its report shall be deposited with the Secretary-General and transmitted to the parties to the dispute. The report of the Commission, including any conclusions stated therein regarding the facts or questions of law, shall not be binding upon the parties and it shall have no other character than that of recommendations submitted for the consideration of the parties in order to facilitate an amicable settlement of the dispute.
7. The Secretary-General shall provide the Commission with such assistance and facilities as it may require. The expenses of the Commission shall be borne by the United Nations.

Appendix B

Single Instrument Treaty

AGREEMENT ON CO-OPERATION IN THE FIELD OF TOURISM BETWEEN THE GOVERNMENT OF THE UNITED KINGDOM OF GREAT BRITAIN AND NORTHERN IRELAND AND THE GOVERNMENT OF THE REPUBLIC OF ALBANIA

The Government of the United Kingdom of Great Britain and Northern Ireland and the Government of the Republic of Albania (hereinafter referred to as 'the Contracting Parties');

Desirous to further strengthen co-operation and to consolidate existing relations between the peoples of Albania and the peoples of the United Kingdom, and;

In order to further strengthen the relations that exist between them;

In view of the importance they attach to the exchange of information at the popular level, particularly in the field of tourism, the two sides have agreed as follows:

Article 1

The Contracting Parties undertake to facilitate tourist visits between the two countries.

Article 2

The Contracting Parties undertake to exchange material and publications on tourist information from their respective National Tourist Boards.

Article 3

The Contracting Parties shall allow the importation of such documents and material required for tourist promotion.

Article 4

The Contracting Parties shall encourage and create favourable conditions for nationals of the other side to participate in the construction, management and maintenance of tourist projects and other aspects of the tourism industry.

Article 5

(1) The Agreement shall enter into force upon signature.
(2) It shall remain in force for an indefinite period. Either side may terminate it by giving six months' advance notice in writing through diplomatic channels to the other side.

In witness whereof, the undersigned, being duly authorised thereto by their respective Governments, have signed this Agreement.

Done in duplicate at London this Thirtieth day of March 1994 in the English and Albanian languages, both texts being equally authoritative.

For the Government of the United Kingdom of Great Britain and Northern Ireland:

DOUGLAS HURD

For the Government of the Republic of Albania:

B. KOPLIKU

Appendix C

Single Instrument MOU

MEMORANDUM OF UNDERSTANDING ON DEFENCE CONTACTS AND COOPERATION BETWEEN THE GOVERNMENT OF THE REPUBLIC OF AUSTRIA AND THE GOVERNMENT OF THE UNITED KINGDOM OF GREAT BRITAIN AND NORTHERN IRELAND

The Government of the Republic of Austria and the Government of the United Kingdom of Great Britain and Northern Ireland, being known hereafter as the Participants,

- acting in the spirit of partnership and cooperation,
- acting also in the interests of strengthening security and stability in Europe as a whole and in support of the work plan of the Euro-Atlantic Partnership Council and Partnership for Peace,
- sharing the aim of strengthening the good defence relations and increasing the understanding and confidence already established between their respective countries,
- with the aim of developing jointly programmes of practical cooperation on a wide range of defence related matters,

have identified, to fulfil these purposes, the following activities:

- exchanges between the staffs and students of military colleges and academies with the aim of strengthening confidence and cooperation in defence studies and military education for senior officers,
- consultations and exchanges between experts in the field of management of the armed forces in a democratic society,
- visits to exchange views on military doctrine, concepts of security and restructuring,
- visits to develop friendly relations between the personnel of the armed forces and to share experience of both operational and professional training,
- exchanges to share experience of the work of the Directorates of the Ministries of Defence,
- visits to discuss the current state of, and the future outlook for, UK–Austria relations in the defence field,
- visits to discuss possible future requirements in the defence equipment field,
- cooperation on military geography,
- and visits to establish personal contacts between the leadership and the command of the armed forces of the two countries.

The Participants have decided that, on the basis of this Memorandum of Understanding, the detail of a rolling two-year programme of defence contacts, for use as a flexible management tool, will be presented prior to the Defence Staff Talks, for discussion at the Talks.

They have further decided that each government is to bear its own administrative costs for implementation of the rolling two-year programme of defence contacts, as specified above. Specific financial procedures will be negotiated as part of the Implementing Arrangements, to be jointly determined by the Participants, if further cooperation of the type specified below is to take place.

The Participants have decided that the provisions of this Memorandum do not preclude other contacts and cooperation, including attendance on military training courses, joint exercises, use of military facilities or professional assignment to units, as may be mutually determined between the Participants in an Implementing Arrangement. The visits of Ministers of Defence will be arranged separately.

Information and documentation received by either of the Participants as a result of the programme will not be given to a third party without the prior written consent of the originator. Any classified information and material exchanged or generated in connection with this memorandum will be used, transmitted, stored, handled and safeguarded in accordance with the General Security Arrangement (GSA) between The United Kingdom of Great Britain and Northern Ireland and The Republic of Austria, concerning the Protection of Non-Atomic Classified Information Exchanged for the Purpose of Defence Production, Research and Procurement between the Two Countries dated 25 September 1995. International visits between the Participants will be covered in accordance with paragraphs 7.1–7.5 of the above mentioned GSA.

This Memorandum becomes effective upon the date of last signature, and will remain in operation until terminated by either Participant, giving the other three months' written notice of termination.

The foregoing represents the understandings reached between the Government of the Republic of Austria and the Government of the United Kingdom of Great Britain and Northern Ireland upon the matters referred to herein.

Signed in duplicate in the English language at Vienna on 9 July 1997.

For the Government of the United Kingdom of Great Britain and Northern Ireland

Chief of the Air Staff of the Royal Air Force
Sir Richard Johns
Air Chief Marshal

For the Government of the Republic of Austria

Chief of Defence
Karl Majcen
General

Appendix D

Model Single Instrument MOU

MEMORANDUM OF UNDERSTANDING BETWEEN
THE GOVERNMENT OF [ ]
AND
THE GOVERNMENT OF [ ] CONCERNING [ ]

The Government of [ ] and the Government of [ ] ('the Participants'),

Desiring to [ ];

Have reached the following understanding:

Section 1

Purpose

The Participants will seek to ....

Section 2

[heading]

The Participants will ....

Section [ ]

Amendment

This Memorandum may be amended at any time by the mutual written consent of the Participants.

Section [ ]

Termination

This Memorandum may be terminated by either Participant giving six months' written notice. The Participants will consult to determine how any outstanding matters should be dealt with. Termination will not affect the validity of any contract made under this Memorandum.

Section [ ]

Disputes

Any dispute about the interpretation or application of this Memorandum will be resolved by consultations between the Participants, and will not be referred to any national or international tribunal or third party for settlement.

Section [ ]

Duration and effective date

This Memorandum will come into effect on [the date of signature]. The foregoing represents the understanding reached between the Participants on the matters referred to in this Memorandum.

Signed in duplicate at [place] on [date] in [the language] and [in the language], both texts having equal validity.

For the Government of [ ]   For the Government of [ ]

Appendix E

Treaty Constituted by an Exchange of Notes in First Person

No. 1

Her Majesty's Ambassador at Montevideo to the Secretary General at the Ministry of Foreign Affairs of the Oriental Republic of Uruguay

British Embassy
Montevideo
8 December 1997

Your Excellency,

I have the honour to refer to the hut at Hope Bay (Bahía Esperanza) in the Peninsula in Antarctica which is owned by the Natural Environmental Research Council (NERC), the parent body of the British Antarctic Survey (BAS). The British Government, having consulted both NERC and BAS is pleased to confirm that the hut is not being used, and that if the Uruguayan Government wish to take over the hut, free of charge and indefinitely, NERC would not assert any right or title to the hut, or its facilities, and would relinquish all responsibility for them.

If the Uruguayan Government, acting within the framework of the Antarctic Treaty, in particular Article II, is ready to take over the hut and its facilities on the above-mentioned basis, and accept responsibility for the future use and upkeep of the hut and its facilities, neither NERC nor the British Government would have any objection.

If the Government of Uruguay accepts this proposal, I have the honour to propose that this Note and your reply in the affirmative shall constitute an Agreement between our two Governments, and that the transfer of the hut and its facilities shall take effect on the date of your reply.

I avail myself of this opportunity to renew to Your Excellency the assurances of my highest consideration.

ROBERT HENDRIE

No. 2

The Secretary General at the Ministry of Foreign Affairs of the Oriental Republic of Uruguay to Her Majesty's Ambassador at Montevideo

Montevideo
8 de diciembre 1997

Señor Embajador:

Tengo el honor de dirigirme a Vuestra Excelencia en relación a su Nota del día de la fecha, por la que se propone el establecimiento de un Acuerdo entre la República Oriental del Uruguay y el Reino Unido de Gran Bretaña e Irlanda del Norte sobre la toma de posesión del refugio ubicado en Hope Bay (Bahía Esperanza) en la Península Antártica. El texto de su Nota se transcribe en idioma español como sigue:

'Su Excelencia:

Tengo el honor de hacer referencia al refugio ubicado en Hope Bay (Bahía Esperanza) en la Península Antártica, que es propiedad del Consejo de Investigación del Medio Ambiente Natural (NERC), organismo rector del Instituto de Investigaciones Antárticas (BAS). Habiendo consultado tanto al NERC como al BAS, El Gobierno Británico tiene el placer de confirmar que dicho refugio no está siendo utilizado y que si el Gobierno Uruguayo deseara tomar posesión del mismo, libre de cargo y por tiempo indefinido, el NERC no hará valer sus derechos de propiedad sobre dicho refugio y renunciará a toda responsabilidad por el mismo.

Si el Gobierno Uruguayo, actuando dentro del marco del Tratado Antártico, en particular del Artículo II, está dispuesto a tomar posesión del refugio y sus instalaciones en las condiciones arriba mencionadas y a aceptar toda responsabilidad por el futuro uso y mantenimiento del refugio y de sus instalaciones, ni el NERC ni el Gobierno Británico tendrán objeción alguna.

Si el Gobierno de Uruguay acepta esta propuesta, tengo el honor de proponer que esta Nota y su respuesta afirmativa constituyan un Acuerdo entre nuestros dos gobiernos y que la transferencia del refugio y sus instalaciones entre en vigencia en la fecha de su respuesta.

Me valgo de la oportunidad para reiterar a su Excelencia las seguridades de mi más alta y distinguida consideración.'

Al respecto, cumplo en poner en conocimiento de Vuestra Excelencia la conformidad del Gobierno de la República Oriental del Uruguay con las disposiciones transcriptas, por lo que la presente Nota y la de Vuestra Excelencia constituyen un Acuerdo entre nuestros dos Gobiernos que entrará en vigor en el día de la fecha.

Reitero a Vuestra Excelencia las seguridades de mi más alta consideración.

G. LASARTE

Translation of No. 2

Ambassador:

I have the honour to write to Your Excellency regarding your Note of today's date, by which an Agreement is proposed between the Oriental Republic of Uruguay and the United Kingdom of Great Britain and Northern Ireland on the transfer of the hut located in Hope Bay (Bahía Esperanza) in the Antarctic Peninsula. The text of your Note is transcribed in Spanish as follows:

[As in No. 1]

With regard to the above, I wish to inform Your Excellency of the consent of the Government of the Oriental Republic of Uruguay to the arrangements as set out, and therefore this Note and Your Excellency's Note shall constitute an Agreement between our two Governments which will come into force today.

I renew to Your Excellency the assurances of my highest consideration.

G. LASARTE

Appendix F

Treaty Constituted by an Exchange of Notes in Third Person

No. 1

Her Britannic Majesty's Embassy, Copenhagen to the Royal Danish Ministry of Foreign Affairs

22 October 2009

Her Britannic Majesty's Embassy presents its compliments to the Royal Danish Ministry of Foreign Affairs and, acting upon instructions from the Government of the United Kingdom of Great Britain and Northern Ireland, has the honour to state that, once the Marine and Coastal Access Bill currently before the United Kingdom Parliament becomes law, the United Kingdom is proposing to declare an Exclusive Economic Zone, in accordance with the United Nations Convention on the Law of the Sea. The Government of the United Kingdom wishes to confirm that in the North Sea the limits of the United Kingdom's Exclusive Economic Zone will follow the boundary of the continental shelf between the Kingdom of Denmark and the United Kingdom, as set out in the Agreement dated 25 November 1971.

The Government of the United Kingdom has further the honour to propose that, following discussions between the respective experts of the two States, the boundary set out in the aforesaid Agreement will be expressed on WGS84 Datum and joined by geodesics, as follows:

1. 56°05'09.56"N 03°14'54.85"E
2. 55°55'06.96"N 03°20'54.88"E

The Government of the United Kingdom can confirm that the Norwegian and German authorities are content with this formulation on WGS84 Datum of points 1 and 2, respectively.

If the foregoing proposal is acceptable to the Government of the Kingdom of Denmark, the Government of the United Kingdom has the honour to suggest that the present Note Verbale and the Ministry's reply in the affirmative shall be regarded as constituting an Agreement between the two Governments.

Her Britannic Majesty's Embassy avails itself of this opportunity to renew to the Royal Danish Ministry of Foreign Affairs the assurances of its highest consideration.

BRITISH EMBASSY
Copenhagen

No.2

The Royal Danish Ministry of Foreign Affairs to Her Britannic Majesty's Embassy, Copenhagen

22 October 2009

The Ministry of Foreign Affairs has the honour to acknowledge receipt of the Note Verbale 25 of Her Britannic Majesty's Embassy, dated 22 October 2009, which reads as follows:

[As in No. 1]

In reply, the Royal Danish Ministry of Foreign Affairs has the honour to state that the Government of the Kingdom of Denmark accepts the proposal of the Government of the United Kingdom and agrees that the Note Verbale of Her Britannic Majesty's Embassy and the present reply shall constitute an Agreement between the two Governments.

MINISTRY OF FOREIGN AFFAIRS
Copenhagen

Appendix G

Model Exchange of Notes Recording an Understanding

Initiating note

Your Excellency,

I have the honour to refer to discussions which have taken place between our two Governments concerning [ ]. As a result of those discussions it is the understanding of the Government of [ ] that the following arrangements will apply:

1. The Government of [ ] will . . . .
2. The Government of [ ] will . . . .
3. These arrangements may be terminated if either Government gives three months' written notice.

If the arrangements set out above are acceptable to the Government of [ ], I have the honour to suggest that this Note and your Excellency's reply to that effect will place on record the understanding of our two Governments in this matter, which will come into effect on [the date of your reply].

I avail myself etc.

Reply note

Your Excellency,

I have the honour to acknowledge receipt of your Note No. [ ] dated [ ] concerning [ ] and which reads as follows:

Text of the initiating Note set out in full, if necessary in translation

I have the honour to confirm that the above arrangements are acceptable to the Government of [ ], and that your Note and this reply will place on record the understanding of our two Governments in the matter and which will come into effect [today].

I avail myself etc.

Appendix H

Treaty and Non-Binding Instrument (NBI) Terminology: Comparative Table

Treaty	NBI
Article	paragraph
agree	decide, accept, approve
agreement	arrangement(s), understanding(s)
agreed	decided, accepted, approved
authentic	equally valid
authoritative	equally valid
clause	paragraph
conditions	provisions
continue in force	continue to have effect
Done	Signed
enter into force	come into effect, come into operation
mutually agreed	jointly decided
obligations	commitments
Parties	Participants, Governments
Preamble	Introduction
rights	benefits
shall	will
terms	provisions
undertake	carry out
undertakings	understandings

Note: Treaty terms such as 'party' or 'rights' can, of course, be used in an NBI if the context requires it, e.g., 'third party' and 'intellectual property rights'.

Appendix I

Credentials

March 1997

Mr Daniel Tarschys
Secretary General
Council of Europe

I have the honour to transmit to your Excellency the names of the Representatives who will represent Her Majesty's Government at the Diplomatic conference for the Adoption of the Draft Council of Europe/UNESCO Convention on the Recognition of Qualifications concerning Higher Education in the European Region to be held in Lisbon from 8–11 April 1997.

Miss Caroline Elisabeth Macready,
Divisional Manager
Higher Education Quality Division
Department for Education and Employment

Mr Nigel Acheson Drummond Lambert,
Legal Adviser
Legal Adviser's Office
Department for Education and Employment

I have the honour to convey to you, Sir, the assurances of my highest consideration.

MALCOLM RIFKIND

Appendix J

Full Powers

Sir Michael Hastings Jay, KCMG, Her Majesty's Ambassador at Paris, is hereby granted full powers to sign, on behalf of the Government of the United Kingdom of Great Britain and Northern Ireland, the Agreement between the Government of the United Kingdom of Great Britain and Northern Ireland and the Governments of the French Republic and the Federal Republic of Germany concerning scientific personnel at the Max Von Laue-Paul Langevin Institute.

In witness whereof I, Robin Cook, Her Majesty's Principal Secretary of State for Foreign and Commonwealth Affairs, have signed these presents.

Signed and sealed at the Foreign and Commonwealth Office, London, the Fourth day of September, One thousand Nine hundred and Ninety-seven.

Appendix K

General Full Powers for Permanent Representative to the United Nations

Her Excellency, Ms [full names], is hereby granted full powers to sign on behalf of the Government of [ ], subject if necessary to ratification, any treaty or other instrument deposited with the Secretary-General of the United Nations and any notification related thereto.

In witness whereof, I [full names], [President, Prime Minister or Minister of Foreign Affairs] have signed these presents.

Signed [and sealed] at [ ], this day of 202[ ]

Appendix L

Instrument of Ratification

Whereas a Convention on Prohibitions or Restrictions on the Use of certain Conventional Weapons which may be deemed to be excessively injurious or to have indiscriminate effects was open for signature by all States at the United Nations Headquarters in New York from the Tenth day of April, One thousand Nine hundred and Eighty-one until the Tenth day of April, One thousand Nine hundred and Eighty-two;

And whereas the Convention was signed by the Government of the United Kingdom on the Tenth day of April, One thousand Nine hundred and Eighty-one;

Now therefore the Government of the United Kingdom of Great Britain and Northern Ireland, having considered the Convention aforesaid, hereby confirm and ratify the same and undertake faithfully to perform and carry out all the stipulations therein contained, subject to the terms of the declaration contained in the accompanying Note.

In witness whereof this Instrument of Ratification is signed and sealed by Her Majesty's Principal Secretary of State for Foreign and Commonwealth Affairs.

Done at London the Ninth day of February, One thousand Nine hundred and Ninety-five.

Appendix M

Certificate of exchange of instruments of ratification

The Undersigned having met together for the purpose of exchanging the Instruments of Ratification of a Treaty between the United Kingdom of Great Britain and Northern Ireland and the [name of country] relating to [name of Treaty/Protocol/Convention/Agreement], which was signed at [place] on [date], by representatives of the Government of the United Kingdom of Great Britain and Northern Ireland and the Government of [name of country); and the respective Instruments of Ratification of the said Treaty/Protocol/Convention having been found in good and due form, the said exchange took place this day.

In witness whereof the Undersigned have signed the present Certificate

Done in duplicate in the English and (name of language) languages at .... the .... day of .... 202[ ]

For the United Kingdom of Great Britain and Northern Ireland:	For the [name of country]:

Appendix N

Model Exchange of Notes Correcting an Error in an Exchange of Notes

Initiating Note

Your Excellency,

I have the honour to refer to the Exchange of Notes between our two Governments of [date] concerning [subject]. An examination of the text has revealed a clerical error in both Notes. It is proposed to correct this error before publication, as follows:

[In paragraph 1, replace '1 April 1900' by '1 April 2000']

I have the honour to propose that my Government make the above correction in the original copy of the Note from your Government and that your Government make the correction in the original Note from my Government, and that the Exchange of Notes be published as so corrected.

I avail myself etc.

Reply Note

Your Excellency,

I have the honour to acknowledge receipt of your Note No. [ ] of [date] concerning correction of a clerical error in the Exchange of Notes between our two Governments of [date] concerning [subject]. I have the honour to confirm* that the proposal in your Note is acceptable to my Government and that it will make the correction in the original Note from your Government and publish the Exchange of Notes as so corrected.

I avail myself etc.

(* Note: this exchange of notes does *not* constitute a treaty and is *not* published.)

Appendix O

Procès-verbal of Rectification

***Procès-verbal* of Rectification of the text of the Protocol on Environmental Protection to the Antarctic Treaty, with four annexes, done at Madrid on October 4, 1991**

I CERTIFY

(1) That the Protocol on Environmental Protection to the Antarctic Treaty, with four annexes, was done at Madrid on October 4, 1991, in the English, French, Russian and Spanish languages;

(2) That the Government of the United States of America, as depositary for the aforesaid Protocol, has received from the Government of Japan a communication drawing attention to an error in wording in the second sentence of Article 13, paragraph 1, of Annex 3 of the English language text of that Protocol;

(3) That an examination of the English language text of the aforesaid Protocol reveals that the use of the word 'amendment' in Article 13 of Annex 3 is not consistent with amendment provisions in the French, Russian and Spanish language texts where a word equivalent to 'measure' is used and therefore the Government of the United States of America believes that the use of the word 'amendment' in Annex 3 is a typographical error and that the word 'measure' should be substituted;

(4) That, accordingly, the English language text of the aforesaid Protocol shall be deemed to be corrected as set forth in Article 13, paragraph 1 of Annex 3, which appears below:

   1. This Annex may be amended or modified by a measure adopted in accordance with Article IX (1) of the Antarctic Treaty. Unless the measure specifies otherwise, the amendment or modification shall be deemed to have been approved, and shall become effective, one year after the close of the Antarctic Treaty Consultative Meeting at which it was adopted, unless one or more of the Antarctic Treaty Consultative Parties notifies the Depositary, within that time period, that it wishes an extension of that period or that it is unable to approve the measure.

IN TESTIMONY WHEREOF, I, WARREN CHRISTOPHER, Secretary of State of the United States of America, have hereunto caused the seal of the Department of State to be affixed and my name subscribed by the Authentication Officer of the said Department, at the city of Washington, in the District of Columbia, this twenty-fifth day of January, 1996.

______________________ Secretary of State

By ______________________ Authentication Officer, Department of State

INDEX

For EU product safety concerns, contact us at
Calle de José Abascal, 56–1°, 28003 Madrid, Spain
or eugpsr@cambridge.org.

Batch number: 10726310

Printed by Printforce, the Netherlands